THE UNITY OF THE BOOK
OF GENESIS

THE UNITY OF THE BOOK OF GENESIS

BY

WILLIAM HENRY GREEN, D.D., LL.D.

PROFESSOR OF ORIENTAL AND OLD TESTAMENT LITERATURE IN PRINCETON
THEOLOGICAL SEMINARY

Introduction by
RONALD YOUNGBLOOD

BAKER BOOK HOUSE
Grand Rapids, Michigan

Reprinted from the 1895 edition
published by Charles Scribner's Sons.
Paperback edition issued 1979
by Baker Book House.
ISBN: 0-8010-3738-7

Introduction by Ronald Youngblood
copyrighted 1979 by
Baker Book House Company

PHOTOLITHOPRINTED BY CUSHING - MALLOY, INC.
ANN ARBOR, MICHIGAN, UNITED STATES OF AMERICA
1979

INTRODUCTION

1895 was a banner year in the publishing career of William Henry Green, for nearly a half century the professor of Oriental and Old Testament literature at Princeton Theological Seminary. In addition to his magnum opus, *The Higher Criticism of the Pentateuch*,[1] his comprehensive study of the first book of Moses, entitled *The Unity of the Book of Genesis,* also appeared in that year.

The latter volume, three times as long as the former, is a remarkable achievement indeed. In it Green answers point by point, section by section, and often verse by verse the attacks made against the consistency, harmony, unity, and Mosaic authorship of Genesis by destructive higher criticism. He takes issue with the assertions of a host of liberal scholars, whose works he has obviously read and carefully digested. His responses to them are models of courteous but forthright rebuttal, and his conclusions, based on a thorough understanding of and familiarity with the Hebrew text of the Old Testament, make the volume useful as an introduction and commentary while at the same time fulfilling the goal set forth in its title: a defense of the unity of Genesis.

The mythical redactor so universally posited by proponents of the documentary hypothesis respecting Pentateuchal origins is submitted to unsparing criticism at the hands of Green. In a classic passage he demonstrates how the critics are forced to

---

1. Reissued in 1978 by Baker Book House in a paperback edition, in which cf. my introduction (pp. v–xviii) for additional details of Green's life as well as a brief overview of Pentateuchal criticism from his time to our own.

pit the redactor against himself in order to shore up the major
tenets of the hypothesis (pp. 471–72). The force, the beauty,
the animation, the dramatic power of Genesis are destroyed by
scholars who insist that its narratives have been mechanically
pieced together from "jejune or fragmentary accounts" (p.
330). Subjective methodology results only in "speculative fancy,
without the slightest historical value" (p. 396). On the contrary, says Green, the narrative of the life of Abraham—and,
by implication, the book of Genesis as a whole—can be de-
cisively shown to display "the evidence of inviolable unity, in
which every part fits precisely in its place in the plan of the
whole," which, in turn, "the divine purpose" rivets together
"with hooks of steel which no critical art can sever" (p. 219).

While adhering firmly to the Mosaic authorship of Genesis,
Green admits the possibility of later minor and insignificant
changes in the text, at one point referring to "him to whom
Genesis owes its present form, be he author or compiler" (p.
97). Although he personally feels that the Dan of Genesis
14:14 is not the city known as Laish until the period of the
judges, he is not opposed in principle to later editorial up-
dating of such place-names (pp. 201–2). In short, Green would
experience a sense of collegiality with and cordiality toward
those of his present-day evangelical brethren who solidly affirm
the unity and Mosaic authorship of Genesis while at the same
time detecting in its pages evidence of a minimal number of
post-Mosaica.

Continuing archaeological discovery since Green's time has
served to strengthen the causes he so magnificently championed.[2]

2. This is not the place to review the positive contributions made to our
understanding of Genesis by excavations at Mari, Nuzi, Ugarit, and else-
where. For treatments of such materials cf., e.g., K. A. Kitchen, *Ancient
Orient and Old Testament* (Chicago: Inter-Varsity, 1966), pp. 35–36, 79–
81, 88–90, 112–38, 153–56; James B. Pritchard, ed., *Ancient Near Eastern
Texts Relating to the Old Testament*, 2nd ed. (Princeton, N.J.: Princeton
University, 1955), p. 520; Walter Beyerlin, ed., *Near Eastern Religious
Texts Relating to the Old Testament*, trans. John Bowden (Philadelphia:

Sodom and *Gomorrah,* as well as the royal name *Birsha* (stated to have been the king of Gomorrah in Genesis 14:2), appear in the Ebla tablets unearthed from 1974 to 1977 at Tell Mardikh in northern Syria and dating from perhaps as early as the middle of the third millennium B.C. Attested there also are personal names such as *Abram, Ishmael, Esau,* and *Israel.* The king of Ebla was Ebrium, whose name is cognate to that of Eber (Gen. 10:24-25), the ancestor of the Hebrews. And the name *Mi-ka-ya* ("Who Is Like Yah[weh]?") at Ebla is evidence of the great antiquity of the tetragrammaton, *YHWH.*[3] If that reading and interpretation hold up under further investigation, they will reduce to absurdity, once and for all, the insistence in higher critical circles that the divine name *Yahweh* was unknown to the patriarchs.

On another front the development of new methods of literary analysis, beginning with form criticism[4] and culminating (for the moment, at least) with structuralism, have consistently obliterated the artificial joins posited by the critics. The unity of the Genesis flood story, for example, has recently received formidable support from the detailed investigations of its sur-

---

Westminster, 1978), p. 279; W. G. Lambert and A. R. Millard, *Atra-ḫasīs: The Babylonian Story of the Flood* (Oxford: Clarendon, 1969), pp. 1-25; Jack Finegan, *In the Beginning: A Journey Through Genesis* (New York: Harper, 1962); Howard F. Vos, *Genesis and Archaeology* (Chicago: Moody, 1963); Nahum H. Sarna, *Understanding Genesis* (New York: Schocken, 1966); E. A. Speiser, *Genesis: Introduction, Translation, and Notes* (Garden City, N.Y.: Doubleday, 1964); André Parrot, *Abraham and His Times,* trans. James H. Farley (Philadelphia: Fortress, 1968); idem, *The Tower of Babel,* trans. Edwin Hudson (New York: Philosophical Library, 1955).

3. Giovanni Pettinato, "The Royal Archives of Tell Mardikh—Ebla," *Biblical Archeologist* 39 (1976): 50; for additional possible theophoric names at Ebla containing the divine element -ya, cf. the comments by Dennis J. McCarthy, "Exod 3:14: History, Philology and Theology," *The Catholic Biblical Quarterly* 40 (1978): 315.

4. Cf. especially Hermann Gunkel, *Die Sagen der Genesis (I. Buch Mose),* 2nd ed. (Göttingen: Vandenhoeck und Ruprecht, 1901).

face and deep structures undertaken by Robert E. Longacre.[5]
When these are added to (1) the already well-known fact that
Tablet XI of the Akkadian Gilgamesh epic is a flood narrative
that bears numerous similarities to the Genesis account *in it*
present form but is clearly not an editorial patchwork and (2)
the lexical, linguistic, and literary studies of Green himself (pp.
65–130), it becomes evident to the impartial observer that "the
documents of the critics are a chimera" (p. 472), since what
can be demonstrated for the flood story can be just as conclusively shown to be the case for every other discrete account
in the book of Genesis.[6]

It is regrettable that the brilliant teaching and writing career
of William Henry Green was terminated in 1896, just one
year after his two best-known volumes were published. But we
who are his spiritual heirs and who find his views eminently
compatible with our own can rejoice that his formidable ener-
gies were put to such salutary use. Although *The Unity of the
Book of Genesis* has long been out of print, the results of
Green's researches have served the church well for more than
eighty years. Baker Book House is therefore to be applauded
for its decision to reissue the present volume.

RONALD YOUNGBLOOD
Associate Dean
Professor of Old Testament
Wheaton Graduate School

5. "The Discourse Structure of the Flood Narrative," in *Society of Biblical Literature 1976 Seminar Papers*, ed. George MacRae (Missoula, Mont.:
Scholars, 1976), pp. 235–62.

6. Additional helpful commentaries and other studies of Genesis that stress
its early date and overall unity include Umberto Cassuto, *A Commentary
on the Book of Genesis*, trans. Israel Abrahams, 2 vols. (Jerusalem: Magnes,
1961–1964); John J. Davis, *Paradise to Prison: Studies in Genesis* (Grand
Rapids: Baker, 1975); Derek Kidner, *Genesis: An Introduction and Commentary* (Chicago: Inter-Varsity, 1967); Ronald Youngblood, *Faith of Our
Fathers: A Bible Commentary for Laymen: Genesis 12–50* (Glendale, Calif.:
Gospel Light, 1976).

PREFACE

ALL tradition, from whatever source it is derived, whether inspired or uninspired, unanimously affirms that the first five books of the Bible were written by one man and that man was Moses. There is no counter-testimony in any quarter. From the predominant character of their contents these books are commonly called the Law. All the statutes contained in them are expressly declared to have been written by Moses or to have been given by the LORD to Moses. And if the entire law is his, the history, which is plainly preparatory for, or subsidiary to, the law, must be his likewise.

The Mosaic authorship of the Pentateuch has, however, been challenged in modern times in the name of the higher criticism on two distinct and independent grounds. One is that of the document hypothesis in its various forms and modifications, which occupies itself with the narrative portion of the Pentateuch, and on the ground of literary criteria claims that this is not the product of any one writer, but that it has been compiled from different documents, which are clearly distinguishable in diction, style, conception, plan, and design, and which belong to widely separated ages. The other is that of the development hypothesis, which has attached itself to the preceding, but deals characteristically with a different portion of the Pentateuch and employs a different style of argument. Its field of operation is the laws, which it claims were not and could not have been given by Moses, nor at any one period in the history of Israel.

It professes to trace the growth of this legislation from
simple and primitive forms to those which are more
complex and which imply a later and more developed
civilization. And it confidently affirms that these laws
could not have been committed to writing in their present form for many centuries after the age of Moses.

These hypotheses are discussed in a general way in my
"Higher Criticism of the Pentateuch," where the fallacy
and inconclusiveness of the reasoning by which they are
defended and the falsity of the conclusions deduced from
them are exposed. In order to a complete refutation of
these hypotheses it is necessary to show still further by
a detailed examination their inapplicability to, and incompatibility with, the phenomena of the Pentateuch,
and that, so far from solving the question of its origin,
they are destitute of any real basis; they find no support
in the Pentateuch itself, but are simply the creations of
learned ingenuity and a lively imagination.

The present treatise occupies itself exclusively with
the document hypothesis, and aims to prove that the
book of Genesis is not a compilation from different documents, but is the continuous work of a single writer.
The demonstration that this hypothesis has no foothold
in Genesis effectually overturns it for the rest of the
Pentateuch, or, if the critics please, the Hexateuch. It
took its rise in Genesis; the most plausible arguments
in its favor are drawn from that book; and the verdict
rendered by that book substantially settles the case for
those that follow. It is on the basis of the assumption
that it is firmly established in Genesis that it is carried
through the Hexateuch. If that assumption is proved
to be false, the hypothesis collapses entirely.

What is here proposed is a critical study of Genesis
from beginning to end, chapter by chapter and section
by section. The history of critical opinion is given in

full in the more important passages, and is throughout
traced sufficiently to place before the reader the various
views that have been entertained, together with the
grounds adduced on their behalf. Pains have been taken
to carefully collate and frankly state whatever has been
urged in defence of the hypothesis by its ablest and
most eminent advocates on each successive passage ; and
this is then subjected to a thorough and candid examination. The reader will thus be put in possession of the
reasons for and against it to the best of the writer's abil-
ity, and can form his own conclusion. The writer, while
aiming at entire fairness in presenting both sides of the
argument, does not conceal his own assured conviction
of the overwhelming preponderance in favor of the faith
of ages and against the divisive hypothesis of modern
times.

As the alleged criteria of the different documents are
most fully and clearly stated by Dr. Dillmann, his presentation of them is followed throughout the book, unless
where some other authority is expressly mentioned.

To avoid constant circumlocution P, J, E, and D are
frequently spoken of as though they were the real entities that the critics declare them to be, and passages
are said to belong to one or the other because critics so
affirm. Such language adopted for brevity must not be
understood as an admission that the documents so called
ever existed.

In replying to the objections of Bishop Colenso in
1863 the author ventured the suggestion that he might
at some future time prepare a work on the criticism of
the Pentateuch. Since that time the positions then
taken by leading critics have been abandoned by themselves, and their whole conception of the origin and constitution of the Pentateuch has been revolutionized.

The complex character of the Pentateuchal question

and the tedious minuteness required in its thorough examination doubtless supply the reason why so many
critics are content with repeating or building upon the
conclusions of their predecessors without investigating
for themselves the soundness of the basis on which these
conclusions rest. The author frankly confesses for himself that, while he felt at every point the weakness and
unsatisfactory character of the arguments of the divisive
critics, he was long deterred by the complexity of the
task from undertaking to prepare such a treatise as the
nature of the case required. He might have continued
still to shrink from it but for the proposal, in 1888,
by his friend Dr. W. R. Harper, of an amicable discussion of the subject in the columns of the *Hebraica.*
The kindly proposal was accepted, though with some
hesitation lest the cause whose defence was thus undertaken might suffer from unskilful advocacy. It seemed,
however, to involve less responsibility and to be a less
onerous undertaking to engage in such a discussion,
piecemeal, in the columns of a quarterly journal, at
the solicitation of a friend, than to set myself to the
preparation of a work on the entire subject of my own
motion. The discussion thus begun was continued at
intervals, step by step, through the whole of the narrative
portion of the Pentateuch. Though convinced at the
outset of the unsoundness in the main of the arguments
urged on behalf of the critical partition of the Pentateuch by its principal defenders, I did not know but
there might be some fire where there was so much
smoke, and some possible foundation for the positive
assertions in which the critics are so prone to indulge.
The discussion was accordingly begun with no absolute
prepossession on my part for or against the existence of
Pentateuchal documents. One thing was clear to my
mind from the beginning, that the Pentateuch as inspired

of God was a true and trustworthy record; everything else was left to be determined by the evidence which it should supply. As the discussion proceeded I found myself unable to discover sufficient reason anywhere for the assumption that the Pentateuch was a compilation from pre-existing documents; and by the time that my task was completed I had settled down in the assured belief that the so-called documents were a chimera, and that the much-vaunted discovery of Astruc was no discovery at all, but an *ignis fatuus* which has misled critics ever since into a long and weary and fruitless search through fog and mire, that might better be abandoned for a forward march on *terra firma*.

The discussion in the *Hebraica* prepared the way for the volume now offered to the public, in which the attempt is made to treat the question with more thoroughness than was possible in the limitations necessarily imposed in a crowded quarterly. The ground there traversed has been carefully re-examined and explored afresh in the light shed upon it by the ablest minds on either side of the controversy. The prominence accorded to German scholars is due to the fact that they have been the chief laborers in the field. The various partition hypotheses, after Astruc's conjecture, as he himself termed it, had pointed out the way, have been originated and elaborated by German scholars. And if they have failed to put them upon a solid basis, it is from no lack of learning, ingenuity, or perseverance, but from the inherent weakness of the cause.

It is hoped that this volume may prove a serviceable text-book for the study of criticism; that it may meet the wants of theological students and ministers who desire to acquaint themselves thoroughly with a subject of such prominence and importance; and that it may likewise prove helpful to intelligent laymen who, omitting the discussion of Hebrew words that are necessarily introduced, may be led by it to a better understanding of the book of Genesis in its connection and the mutual relation of its several parts, and be helped in the solution of difficulties and the removal of objections. It stands on the common ground, dear alike to all who regard the Pentateuch as the word of God through Moses, whether Jew or Christian, Catholic or Protestant, clergyman or layman. If by the divine blessing it shall be made to contribute in any measure to the elucidation or defence of this part of Holy Scripture, or to the confirmation of the faith of any, or to the relief of such as may have been perplexed or troubled by anxious doubts or misgivings, the author will be profoundly grateful to Him to whom all praise is due.

PRINCETON, N. J., September 26, 1895.

TABLE OF CONTENTS

IV

V

VI

WORKS REFERRED TO IN THIS VOLUME

*_** *These works are here arranged in the order of their publication. The reader can thus see at a glance where each belongs in the history of critical opinion.*

Matthew Poole, Annotations upon the Holy Bible, First Edition, 1683.

Astruc, Conjectures sur les Mémoires Originaux, dont il paroit, que Moyse s'est servi pour composer le Livre de la Genèse, 1753.

Harmer, Observations on Divers Passages of Scripture, Second Edition, 1776.

Ilgen, Die Urkunden des ersten Buchs von Moses in ihrer Urgestalt, 1798.

Vater, Commentar über den Pentateuch, Theil i., ii., 1802 ; Theil iii., 1805.

Eichhorn, Einleitung in das Alte Testament, Dritte Ausgabe, 1803 ; Vierte Ausgabe, 1823.

DeWette, Beiträge zur Einleitung in das Alte Testament, Erstes Bändchen, 1806 ; Zweiter Band, 1807.

Ewald, Die Komposition der Genesis kritisch untersucht, 1823.

Gramberg, Libri Geneseos Secundum Fontes rite dignoscendos Adumbratio nova, 1828.

F. H. Ranke, Untersuchungen über den Pentateuch aus dem Gebiete der höheren Kritik, Erster Band, 1831 ; Zweiter Band, 1840.

Hengstenberg, Die Authentie des Pentateuches, Erster Band, 1836 ; Zweiter Band, 1839.

Movers, Review of von Bohlen's Genesis in Zeitschrift für Philosophie und Katholische Theologie, 1836.

Hävernick, Handbuch der historisch-kritischen Einleitung in das Alte Testament, Erster Theil, Zweite Abtheilung, 1837.

Tuch, Kommentar über die Genesis, 1838 ; Zweite Auflage, 1871.

Stähelin, Kritische Untersuchungen über den Pentateuch, die Bücher Josua, Richter, Samuels, und der Könige, 1843.

Kurtz, Die Einheit der Genesis, 1846.

Winer, Biblisches Realwörterbuch, Dritte Auflage, 1847.

Ewald, Jahrbücher der Biblischen Wissenchaft for 1851–52.

Knobel, Die Genesis, 1852.

Delitzsch, Die Genesis, 1852, Dritte Ausgabe, 1860 ; Vierte Ausgabe, 1872. Neuer Commentar über die Genesis, 1887.

Kurtz, Geschichte des Alten Bundes, Erster Band, Zweite Auflage, 1853.

Hupfeld, Die Quellen der Genesis und die Art ihrer Zusammensetzung, 1853.

Robinson, Biblical Researches in Palestine and in the Adjacent Regions, 1856.

Böhmer, Das Erste Buch der Thora, Übersetzung seiner drei Quellenschriften und der Redactionszusätze mit kritischen, exegetischen, historischen Erörterungen, 1862.

Nöldeke, Untersuchungen zur Kritik des Alten Testaments, 1869.

Merx, Article on Dinah in Schenkel's Bibel-Lexikon, 1869.

Schrader, Editor of the "eighth thoroughly improved, greatly enlarged and in part wholly transformed edition" of DeWette's Lehrbuch der historisch-kritischen Einleitung in die kanonischen und apokryphischen Bücher des Alten Testaments, 1869.

Kayser, Das vorexilische Buch der Urgeschichte Israels und seine Erweiterungen, ein Beitrag zur Pentateuch-kritik, 1874.

George Smith, Translation of the flood tablets in his Assyrian Discoveries, 1875 ; the Chaldean Account of Genesis, 1876 ; and Records of the Past, vol. vii., 1876.

Wellhausen, Die Composition des Hexateuchs, in the Jahrbücher für Deutsche Theologie, 1876–1877 ; republished in Skizzen und Vorarbeiten, Zweites Heft, 1885 ; and again in Die Composition des Hexateuchs und der historischen Bücher des Alten Testaments, 1889.

Kuenen, The Religion of Israel to the Fall of the Jewish State, translated by A. H. May, vol. i., 1874.

Dillmann, Die Genesis, first edition published as the third edition of Knobel's Commentary, 1875 ; second edition (Knobel's fourth), 1882 ; third edition (Knobel's fifth), 1886.

Wellhausen, Geschichte Israels, 1878, republished as Prolegomena zur Geschichte Israels, 1883. Third edition, 1886.

Oort, The Bible for Learners, English translation, 1878.

Colenso, The Pentateuch and Book of Joshua critically examined, Part vii., 1879.

Reuss, Die Geschichte der Heiligen Schriften Alten Testaments, 1881.

Haupt, Der keilinschriftliche Sintfluthbericht, in Schrader's Die Keilinschriften und das Alte Testament, 1883.

Budde, Die Biblische Urgeschichte (Gen. i—xii. 5), 1883.

Kuenen, An Historico-critical Inquiry into the Origin and Composition of the Hexateuch. Translated by P. H. Wicksteed, 1886.

Vatke, Historisch-kritische Einleitung in das Alte Testament, 1886.

Stade, Geschichte des Volkes Israel, 1887.

Kittel, Geschichte der Hebräer, 1888.

Harper, The Pentateuchal Question, in the Hebraica for 1888-1892.

Kautzsch und Socin, Die Genesis mit äusserer Unterscheidung der Quellenschriften, 1888 ; Zweite Auflage, 1891. Reproduced in English as Genesis Printed in Colors, showing the original sources from which it is supposed to have been compiled, with an introduction by E. C. Bissell.

Cornill, Einleitung in das Alte Testament, 1891.

Driver, An Introduction to the Literature of the Old Testament, 1891.

Strack, Die Genesis, 1892.

Davis, Genesis and Semitic Tradition, 1894.

Kuenen, Gesammelte Abhandlungen zur Biblischen Wissenchaft. Aus dem Hollandischen übersetzt von K. Budde, 1894.

THE UNITY OF THE BOOK OF GENESIS

THE BOOK OF GENESIS

THE history opens with an introductory section (ch. i.–ii. 3), which declares how God in the beginning created the heavens and the earth as the theatre upon which it was to be transacted. This is followed by ten sections of unequal length, which make up the rest of the book of Genesis, and are introduced by titles of a uniform pattern. These titles are as follows:

1. Gen. ii. 4.   These are the generations of the heaven and of the earth.

2. Gen. v. 1.   This is the book of the generations of Adam.

3. Gen. vi. 9.   These are the generations of Noah.

4. Gen. x. 1.   These are the generations of the sons of Noah.

5. Gen. xi. 10.   These are the generations of Shem.

6. Gen. xi. 27.   These are the generations of Terah.

7. Gen. xxv. 12.   These are the generations of Ishmael.

8. Gen. xxv. 19.   These are the generations of Isaac.

9. Gen. xxxvi. 1.   These are the generations of Esau.[1]

10. Gen. xxxvii. 2.   These are the generations of Jacob.

[1] Repeated, ver. 9, for a reason to be explained when that chapter comes under consideration.

These titles are designed to emphasize and render more prominent and palpable an important feature of the book, the genealogical character of its history. This results from its main design, which is to trace the line of descent of the chosen race from the beginning to the point where it was ready to expand to a great nation, whose future organization was already foreshadowed, its tribes being represented in the twelve sons of Jacob, and its tribal divisions in their children. The genealogies contained in the book are not merely incidental or subordinate, but essential, and the real basis of the whole. They are not to be regarded as addenda to the narrative, scraps of information introduced into it ; they constitute the skeleton or framework of the history itself. They are not separate productions culled from different sources, and here inserted by the author as he found them. From whatever quarters the materials may have been obtained they were cast into their present form by the writer himself, as is evident from the uniformity of the construction of those relating to the chosen race on the one hand, and those of alien races on the other, together with the unbroken continuity of the former. These exhibit at once the kinship of Israel to all the nations of the earth, all being of one blood and sprung from one common stock, and their separation from the rest of mankind for a special divine purpose, God's gracious choice of them to be his peculiar people until the· time should arrive for spreading the blessing of Abraham over all the earth.

There is, accordingly, a regular series of genealogies of like structure, or rather one continuous genealogy extending from Adam to the family of Jacob. This is interrupted or suspended from time to time, as occasion requires, for the sake of introducing or incorporating facts of the history at particular points where they belong ;

after which it is resumed again precisely at the same point, and proceeds regularly as before until it reaches its utmost limit, thus embracing the entire history within itself. Thus, for example, the genealogy in ch. v. states in identically recurring formulæ the age of each parent at the birth of his child, the number of years that he lived subsequently, and the length of his entire life. But when the name of Noah is reached, the record is, ver. 32, " And Noah was five hundred years old ; and Noah begat Shem, Ham, and Japheth," three sons being mentioned instead of one, as was uniformly the case before. And here the genealogy abruptly terminates without the further statements that analogy would lead us to expect, how long Noah lived after the birth of his children, and how many years he lived in all. This is not the end of a genealogical fragment, disconnected from all that follows. It is merely interrupted for a time in order to introduce the account of the deluge, which so intimately concerned Noah and his three sons ; after which the missing members are supplied, and the series resumed in substantially the same form as before (ix. 28, 29). Again, the genealogy continued in xi. 10 sqq. breaks off (ver. 26) precisely as it had done before, by stating the age of a father at the birth of his three sons. " And Terah lived seventy years, and begat Abram, Nahor, and Haran ; " the usual statement as to the length of his life and the fact of his death being postponed to ver. 32, in order to introduce some facts respecting Terah and particularly respecting his sons, which had an important bearing on the subsequent history. And the entire life of Abraham is fitted into the next link of the genealogy : his age at the birth of his son Isaac (xxi. 5), whom he begat (xxv. 19), and his full age at the time of his death (xxv. 7, 8).

THE CREATION OF THE HEAVENS AND THE EARTH (CH. I.
1–II. 3).

The critics assign this opening section of Genesis to P,
because of its unvarying use of Elohim, as well as on the
ground of its style and diction. They also include in
this section ii. 4a, which they regard as a summary statement of its contents. This and the alleged difference of
style between this section and the next can best be considered hereafter. For the present it will be sufficient to
give attention to the diction. Dr. Dillmann adduces the
following words and expressions as indicative of P : מִין
kind, species (vs. 11, 12, 21, 24, 25) ; חַיַּת הָאָרֶץ *beast of the
earth* (vs. 24, 25, 30) ; שָׁרַץ *creep, swarm, bring forth abundantly,* and שֶׁרֶץ *moving creature* (vs. 20, 21) ; רָמַשׂ *creep,*
and רֶמֶשׂ *creeping thing* (vs. 21, 24–26, 28, 30) ; כָּבַשׁ *subdue*
(ver. 28) ; אָכְלָה *food* (ver. 30) ; מִקְוֶה *gathering together, collection* (ver. 10) ; פָּרָה וְרָבָה *be fruitful and multiply* (vs. 22,
28) ; זָכָר וּנְקֵבָה *male and female* (ver. 27) ; הִבְדִּיל *divide* (vs.
4, 6, 7, 14, 18) ; דְּמוּת *likeness* (ver. 26).

The distribution of these words in the Hexateuch is
instructive. That which is rendered "likeness" occurs
besides in it only Gen. v. 1, 3, where it is used with express allusion to i. 26. "Subdue" occurs besides in the
Hexateuch only Num. xxxii. 22, 29 (a chapter in which,
according to the critics, the documents P, J, and E are
intermingled, and both of these verses contain what are
reckoned indications of JE), and Josh. xviii. 1, an isolated verse in a JE paragraph. The rest of these words
and phrases occur nowhere else in Genesis, unless it be
in the account of the flood. And the reason why most
of them are to be found there is obvious. The different
classes of land animals brought into being at the creation
perished in the flood, and it is natural that they should
be mentioned in both cases ; like mention is also made

of "food" as necessary to life; the perpetuation of the species leads to the reference to the sexes. The full phrase, as used in Gen. i., "Be fruitful and multiply and fill," or "replenish," only occurs again (ix. 1), in the blessing pronounced upon mankind after the flood, which was as appropriate as after the creation; the phrase "Be fruitful and multiply" occurs besides only in application to Abraham and his descendants, where it is equally in place. Such of these words as occur elsewhere are found only in the ritual law. "Food" and "kind" and different sorts of animals are, as a matter of course, spoken of, where direction is given in respect to what may or may not be eaten; and sex in like manner in prescribing the animals to be offered in sacrifice, or the purifications at the birth of children, or the rite of circumcision. "Divide" does not occur in the narrative of the flood, but is found again in the ritual law with reference to the distinctions there made in regard to clean and unclean, holy and unholy or common, or separating to special functions or purposes, or to cleavage in sacrifice. The word translated "gathering together" is found but twice in the Hexateuch apart from Gen. i., viz., Ex. vii. 19, Lev. xi. 36, where collections of water are referred to, and nowhere else in this sense in the entire Old Testament.

It is manifest from the foregoing that the occurrence of these words is determined, not by the predilection of a particular writer, but by the subject which calls for their employment. They belong not to the characteristics of a document, but are the common property of all who use the language, and may be found whenever there is occasion to describe the object denoted by them. Their absence from all the paragraphs or clauses assigned by the critics to J or E is to be accounted for precisely as their absence from every paragraph of P but those designated above.

For a more detailed account of the usage of the words common to the creation and flood, see under ch. vi.–ix., Marks of P.

Elohim is plainly the appropriate name for God throughout this section, which regards the Most High as working in nature and in the world at large. True, the creative act may be ascribed to Jehovah (Ex. xx. 11), when the thought to be conveyed is that Israel's God, who brought him out of the land of Egypt, was the creator of the world; but when the announcement to be made simply is that the world had a divine creator, Elohim is the proper term, and is hence constantly used in the account of the creation.

I

THE GENERATIONS OF THE HEAVENS AND THE EARTH (CH. II. 4–IV.)

PRIMITIVE STATE AND FALL OF MAN (CH. II. 4–III. 24)

THE question to be considered is, Do these chapters continue the narrative begun in the preceding section, or do they introduce a new and independent narrative from an altogether different source? The critics allege that they stand in no relation to what goes before, that a new beginning is here made, and that this account is taken from another document, that of J. It is said that the second chapter of Genesis cannot have been written by the author of the first chapter; for (1) it is a second account of the creation, and is superfluous for that reason ; (2) it differs from the first account, and is irreconcilable with it ; (3) the diction and style are different.

FALSE CRITICAL METHODS

The critics here bring into operation at the outset two vicious methods, which characterize their whole course of procedure and are the most potent instruments which they employ in effecting the partition of the text.

The first is the arbitrary assumption that two different parts of a narrative, relating to matters which are quite distinct, are variant accounts of the same thing. It is very easy to take two narratives or two parts of the same narrative, which have certain points in common but which really describe different transactions, and lay them alongside of one another and point out the lack of correspondence between them. The artifice of the critics consists in their identifying distinct things, and then every divergence of the one from the other is claimed as evidence that these are variant traditions, and that these discrepant accounts cannot be by the same author; they must have been taken from different documents. Whereas, there is no mystery in the case and no occasion for any such extraordinary conclusion. The simple fact is that the writer has finished one part of his story and has proceeded to another; and, as might be expected, he does not detail over again what he had just detailed before.

The second of the vicious methods, which is continually practised by the divisive critics and is one of their most effective weapons, also finds exemplification in the chapters now under consideration. It is their constant effort to create a discordance where none really exists. Passages are sundered from their context, which elucidate and determine their meaning, and then any form of expression which admits of a signification at variance with what is stated elsewhere is seized upon and pressed to the utmost and urged as a proof of diverse representations, requiring the assumption of different documents; when, if it were only allowed to bear its natural sense in the connection in which it stands, all appearance of discrepancy will disappear. There is nothing for which the critics seem to have such an aversion as a harmonizing interpretation; and very naturally, for it annuls all their work. And yet it is the plain dictate of common sense that the different parts of the same instrument should be interpreted in harmony, provided the language employed will in fairness admit of such an interpretation.

The simple observance of this obvious rule, together
with the principle before referred to, that things which
are really distinct should be treated as distinct, will not
only relieve all the critical doubts and perplexities relative to the chapters now before us, but the great majority of those which are raised in the rest of Genesis and
of the Pentateuch as well.

NO DUPLICATE ACCOUNT OF THE CREATION

That the second chapter does not contain another account of the creation additional to that in the first can
be readily shown.

And in the first place it does not profess to be an account of the creation, but something additional to and
different from it. It is in express terms declared to be a
sequel of the narrative of the creation. The second section is introduced by a special descriptive title (ver. 4a) :
"These are the generations of the heavens and of the
earth when they were created." It is very important to
understand the precise meaning of these words and the
purpose for which they are introduced. There has been
much dispute both as to the proper connection of this
clause and how it is to be understood.

Is it a subscription to the preceding section, setting
forth its contents? Or is it introductory to the following
section and descriptive of its contents? It can be shown
beyond question that it is the heading of the section that
follows, and is here introduced to announce its subject.

The formula "These are the generations," etc., occurs
ten times in the book of Genesis, and in every instance
but the present indisputably as the title of the section to
which it is prefixed. The history is parcelled into "the
generations of Adam" (v. 1), "the generations of Noah"
(vi. 9), "the generations of the sons of Noah" (x. 1),

"the generations of Shem" (xi. 10), "the generations of Terah" (xi. 27), and so on to the end of the book.

Each of these titles introduces a new section of the history, longer or shorter as the case may be, and announces the subject treated in that section. The book of Genesis after the first or preliminary chapter is thus, in the plan of its author, divided into ten distinct sections, to each of which he has given a separate heading of this uniform pattern. They are called "generations" because the framework of the entire history is a genealogy, which is traced in a direct line from Adam to Jacob and his posterity. All the facts that are related and the statements made are introduced between the links of this genealogy. The line of descent is arrested at the proper point, the narratives belonging there are inserted, and then the line of descent is taken up again just where it left off and proceeds as before. Divergent lines are traced, as occasion arises, to a sufficient distance, and are then dropped, the writer uniformly reverting to the main line of descent, that of the chosen race, which is his principal theme. This being the constant plan of the book this formula, which in every other instance is the title of the section to which it is prefixed, must be the same in this case likewise. It is the heading of the second section, and can be nothing else.

This conclusion is not only demanded by the uniform analogy of the entire series of similar titles but by other considerations likewise :

1. It is confirmed by the identical structure of the immediately following clause here and in v. 1, where the connection is unquestioned. "In the day of Jehovah Elohim's making earth and heaven," follows the title "the generations of the heaven and of the earth," in precise conformity with "in the day of Elohim's creating Adam," after the title "the generations of Adam."

2. If ii. 4a is a subscription to the preceding section, then ii. 4b–iv. 26 is the only portion of the book without a title, while i. 1–ii. 3 will have two titles, one which is entirely appropriate at the beginning (i. 1), and one which is altogether unsuitable at the end.

3. On the divisive hypothesis the additional incongruity results, that when the section ascribed to J (ii. 4b–ch. iv.) is excluded, and the connection restored, as it originally existed in P, ii. 4a will be immediately followed by v. 1, and thus two titles will have stood in direct juxtaposition.

Now what does the generations of the heavens and of the earth mean? It has sometimes been interpreted to mean an account of the origin of the heavens and of the earth, such as we find in ch. i., to which it is then claimed that this must be attached as explanatory of the contents of that chapter. But neither the words themselves nor their usage elsewhere will admit of this interpretation.

"The book of the generations of Adam " (v. 1) is a list of the descendants of Adam. " The generations of Noah " (vi. 9) records the history of Noah's family. " The generations of the sons of Noah " (x. 1) and " the generations of Shem" (xi. 10), trace the various lines of their descendants. And so it is uniformly. " The generations of A or B " do not detail his ancestry or his origin, but either give the history of his immediate family or the continuous line of his descendants. And this the proper signification of the Hebrew word so rendered necessarily demands. It denotes " generations " in the sense of that which is generated or begotten, the offspring of a progenitor.

Accordingly this title, " the generations of the heaven and the earth," must announce as the subject of the section which it introduces not an account of the way in which the heaven and the earth were themselves brought

into being, but an account of the offspring of heaven and
earth ; in other words, of man who is the child of both
worlds, his body formed of the dust of the earth, his soul
of heavenly origin, inbreathed by God himself. And so
the sections proceed regularly. First, Gen. i. 1, " In
the beginning God created the heaven and the earth," the
title announcing that the theme of the first chapter is
the creation. Then ii. 4, " The generations of the heavens and the earth," announcing that the theme of what
follows is the offspring of heaven and earth, or the history of Adam and his family. Then v. 1, " The generations of Adam," in which his descendants are traced to
Noah and his sons. Then vi. 4, "The generations of
Noah," or the history of Noah's family, and so on to the
end of the book.

But here we are met by Dr. Dillmann and other leading advocates of the divisive hypothesis, who say, It is
true that " the generations of the heavens and the earth "
denote that which has sprung from the heavens and the
earth ; but this is the title of ch. i. nevertheless, which
records how grass and trees and animals and man came
forth from the earth, and the sun, moon, and stars made
their appearance in the heavens. This must, therefore,
originally have stood at the beginning of ch. i., and it has
been transposed to its present position by the redactor.
This shows what a useful person the redactor is in the
service of the critics. Here is a clause which is seriously
in their way where it stands at present. It rivets the
second chapter to the first in more ways than one. It
declares positively that ch. ii. is not a parallel account of
the creation taken from another source, but is a sequel
to the narrative of the creation already given in ch. i.
Moreover, this formula, which the critics tell us is one of
the marks of the document P, to which the first chapter
is alleged to belong, as distinguished from the document

J, to which the section before us is referred, and whose words are the words of P and not of J, is here found attached to the wrong document, thus annulling in certain marked respects their favorite argument from diction and style. It is an obstacle to be gotten rid of, therefore, at all hazards. The aid of the redactor is accordingly called in, and the disturbing clause is spirited away to a safe distance and located at the beginning of the first chapter, instead of the beginning of the second section, where it actually stands.

Only it is unfortunate that the redactor is of no avail in the present instance. The clause in question never could have been the title of ch. i. It is obvious that the heavens and the earth must first be brought into existence before the generations of the heavens and the earth can be spoken of, just as Adam and Noah must precede the generations of Adam and the generations of Noah. Besides, it would be altogether inappropriate as a title of ch. i. The firmament and the heavenly bodies, the seas and the dry land, the work of the first four days, are identical with the heavens and the earth, not their offspring. The creating and shaping of the material universe cannot with propriety be included under the " generations " of the heavens and the earth, and the writer of the chapter could never have expressed its purport in such terms. And even the vegetable and animal products, which by creative fiat were made to issue from the earth on the third, fifth, and sixth days, were wholly of an earthly, not a heavenly, mould. And the title, if understood of such products, would stand in no relation to the subsequent titles of the book. Grass and trees and animals supply no stepping-stone to the next title, the Generations of Adam. It is only Adam himself that can do this. It is not until ver. 26 that the creation of man is reached. And man in ch. i. is considered simply in his place in the general scheme of created things. He is introduced into the world; but there is no record of what befell him or his family, such as we are authorized to expect, such as is in fact given in ii. 4b–iv. 26. Every similar title in Genesis is followed either by a history of the immediate offspring or by successive generations of descendants.

The clause which we have been considering is an obstacle to the partition of the first two chapters which it has not been possible to remove by any critical device. It plainly declares the subject of the second section to be not the creation of the world, but the formation of man and the first stage of human history.

It remains to be added that an examination of the second section itself will show that it does not in point of fact contain a fresh account of the creation. The opening words, "In the day that Jehovah God made the earth and the heavens," do not introduce an account of making earth and heaven, but presuppose it as having already taken place, and the writer proceeds to indicate the condition of things when it was done and what followed subsequently. No mention is made of the formation of the earth or the production of the dry land; none of the sea and its occupants; none of the firmament or of the sun, moon, and stars; none of covering the earth with its varied vegetation, but only of planting a garden in Eden and making its trees grow from the ground (vs. 8, 9). When banished from Eden, man was to eat "the herb of the field" (iii. 18), whose existence is thus assumed, but whose production is only spoken of in ch. i. These particulars could not be omitted from an account of the creation. To say, as is done by Dr. Dillmann, that they may originally have been contained in ch. ii., but were omitted by R because they were treated sufficiently in ch. i., is to make an assumption without a particle of evidence, which amounts simply to a confession that ch. ii. is not what it would have been if the writer had intended to give a narrative of the creation, and that its omissions are with definite reference to the contents of ch. i. In other words, ch. ii. has no claim to be regarded as a separate and complete account of the creation; and it has not been prepared independently of ch. i., but is designedly supplementary to it.

Chapter ii. has thus far been considered negatively, and it has been shown what it is not. It is not a second account of the creation ; and it has not been prepared independently of ch. i. and without regard to the contents of that first chapter. It is now in order to state positively what ch. ii. actually is. It is evidently throughout preliminary to ch. iii., the narrative of the fall. In order to make this intelligible it was necessary to explain (1), the two constituents of man's nature, his body formed of the dust of the ground, and the breath of life imparted directly by God himself (ver. 7). It was necessary that this should be known, that the reader might comprehend on the one hand the potential immortality set within his reach, and on the other the sentence actually incurred that dust must return to dust (iii. 19). (2) The locality, which was the scene of the temptation and fall, the garden of Eden, with its tree of life and the tree of the knowledge of good and evil (vs. 8–17). (3) The actors, Adam and Eve, in their superiority to the rest of the creation, and their relation to each other (vs. 18–25). These particulars could not have been incorporated in ch. i. without marring its symmetry. That deals with the creation of the world at large. Everything is on a universal scale. And to introduce a detailed description of the garden of Eden, with its arrangements and man's position in it, would have been quite inappropriate. The plan and purpose of ch. i. made it necessary to reserve this for the following section, and it is accordingly given in ch. ii.

It follows from what has been said that all comparisons made, or contrasts drawn, between ch. i. and ch. ii. on the assumption that they are separate and independent accounts of the same transaction are necessarily fallacious. In the one the scene embraces the whole world with all that it contains. In the other it is limited to the garden of Eden, which is fitted up for the habitation of the first human pair. The first advances by a succession of almighty fiats from the initial production of inanimate matter to the culmination of the whole grand process in the creation of man in the image of God. The second deals exclusively with the primitive state of man, which is minutely explained with a special view to the temptation and fall; all is on the plane of individual life and moves steadily forward to that first transgression by which man lost his original holiness and communion with God. The second chapter is thus in no sense parallel to the first, but is its natural sequel. It is the succeeding scene in the sacred history, the next act, so to speak, in the divine drama which is here transacting. It introduces the reader to a new and distinct stage in the unfolding of that plan of God which it is the purpose of the book of Genesis to record.

With such marked differences in the design and the contents of the two chapters, it follows, of course, that each has a character of its own distinct from the other. It is very easy to set one over against the other and to point out their distinctive qualities. But the dissimilar features, which so readily offer themselves to the observer, result directly and necessarily from the diversity of the subjects respectively treated in each, and require no assumption of the idiosyncrasies of different writers or the peculiarities of separate documents to account for them.

Thus, for example, if it be said with Dr. Harper ("Hebraica," vol. i., pp. 25–27) that ch. i. is "generic," dealing with species and classes, and ch. ii. is "individual," how could they be otherwise, considering their respective themes? One records the formation of the world as a whole, and of the various orders of beings that are in it; the other deals specifically with the first human pair.

If it be said that the first chapter is "systematic," "chronological," and "scientific," the reason is that the nature of its subject brings these features into marked prominence. When the work of six successive days is to be stated, each advancing upon the preceding by regular gradations, and together embracing all the various ranks of created things, the subject itself prescribes the mode of treatment adapted to it, which must be systematic, chronological, and scientific, if the theme proposed is to be clearly and satisfactorily presented. But why should a writer who shows his capacity for the classification of genera and species where his subject demands it, lug in his scientific terms or methods where no such classification is called for? If he has pursued a chronological method in ch. i., where the subject divides itself into successive periods, what is to hinder his adoption of a topical method in chs. ii. and iii., where he groups the various incidents and particulars with masterly skill, and all leads as directly up to the catastrophe of the fall as in ch. i. all marches steadily forward to the Sabbath-day of rest? There is as clear evidence of system in the logical order of the narration in chs. ii. and iii. as in the chronological order of ch. i. And there is the same graphic power and masterly presentation in the grand and majestic tableaux of ch. i. as in the simple and touching scenes so delicately depicted in chs. ii. and iii. When it is said that ch. ii. is "picturesque and poet-

ical," it may be said with equal propriety that ch. i. is
sublimely poetical. The scenes are drawn in bold relief,
and stand as vividly before the reader as anything in the
chapters that follow; only the scenes themselves are of
a different description. One gives the impression of im-
mensity and power and vast terrestrial changes; the
other of beauty and pathos and the development of personal character. Cannot the same writer handle diverse
themes? And if he do, must he not be expected to treat
each in the way appropriate to itself?

It is claimed that ch. i. deals in "stereotyped"
phrases and is "verbose and repetitious," while the
style of chs. ii. and iii. is "free and flowing." This
again is due to the nature of the subjects with which
they respectively deal. Ch. i. is monumental, conducted
on a scale of vastness and magnificence, and its characters are massive and unyielding as if carved in granite.
Chs. ii. and iii. deal with plastic forms of quiet beauty,
the charms of paradise, the fateful experiences of Adam
and Eve. In the onward progress of creation all is conducted by the word of omnipotence, to which the result
precisely corresponds. To mark this correspondence in
the most emphatic manner, the command is issued in
explicit terms; and the answering result, which exactly
matches it, is described in identical language. There are,
besides, certain constant and abiding features, which
characterize the creative work from first to last, and
which abide the same in the midst of all the majestic
changes which are going forward. There is the regular recurrence of each creative day, of the daily putting
forth of almighty power, of God's approval of his work
which perfectly represents the divine idea, the name
given to indicate its character, the blessing bestowed to
enable it to accomplish its end. To mark all this in the
most emphatic manner, the identical phrases are re-

peated throughout from first to last. The solemn and impressive monotone, which thus runs through the whole, heightens the grandeur of the description, and is suggestive of that divine serenity which steadily and undeviatingly moves onward in its appointed course, while the ponderous periods aptly befit the massive objects with which they deal. There is no call for such a style in simple narrative like ch. ii., where it would be utterly out of place and stilted in the extreme. That the characteristics which have been referred to are due to the subject of ch. i., and not to some imaginary peculiarity of the writer, is plain, even if the critical partition of Genesis were accepted. For the narratives, which the critics assign to the same document as ch. i., differ as widely from it as ch. ii. does.

In like manner Dr. Dillmann urges, in proof of a diversity of writers, that the author of ch. i. " restricts himself to the great facts without entering in an explanatory way into particular details," and that he uses " a ceremonious, solemn, formal style of writing," as distinguished from the " evenness " of chs. ii. and iii. This is sufficiently answered in what has been already said. The difference arises from the nature of the subject, not from the habit of the writer. As Dr. Dillmann himself justly says : " The author in writing was fully conscious of the unique loftiness of his subject ; there is not a word too much, yet all is clear and well defined ; nowhere is there anything artificial and far-fetched ; only once in an appropriate place he allows himself to rise to elevated poetic speech (ver. 27) ; even the expressions savoring of a remote antiquity, which he here and there employs (vs. 2, 24), have evidently come down to him with the matter from the olden time, and serve admirably to enhance the impression of exalted dignity."

It is said that ch. i. proceeds from the lower to the

higher, ending with man ; while, on the contrary, ch. ii.
begins with the highest, viz., with man, and proceeds to
the lower forms of life.   But as ch. ii. continues the history begun in ch. i., it naturally starts where ch. i. ends,
that is to say, with the creation of man, especially as the
whole object of the chapter is to depict his primitive
condition.

These various contrasts between ch. i. and ii. explain
themselves at once, as has now been shown from the diversity of theme.   They could only be supposed to lend
support to the critical hypothesis of different documents
on the false assumption that the theme of both chapters
was the same.

NO DISCREPANCIES.

While each of these chapters pursues consistently and
steadily its own proper aim, they have certain points of
contact, in which it is to be remarked that the second
chapter supplements the first, but there is no discrepancy between them.   In fact it is as inconsistent with
the document hypothesis as it is with that of unity of
authorship to suppose that we have here two divergent
stories of the creation.   The redactor does not place
them side by side, as two varying accounts, which he
makes no attempt to reconcile, but lays before his readers precisely as he found them.   There is no intimation
that they are alternatives, one or the other of which may
be accepted at pleasure.   On the contrary, chs. i. and ii.
are recorded as equally true and to be credited alike.
The inference cannot reasonably be avoided that the redactor, if there was one, saw no inconsistency in these
narratives.   Elsewhere the critics tell us he has corrected
divergent accounts into harmony.   He could have seen
no need of correction here, for he has made none.   The

case is supposable indeed that some minute and subtle inconsistency may have escaped his notice. But there can be no open or glaring inconsistency, or he would have detected and removed it, or at least remarked upon it. To suppose otherwise is to charge him with deficiency in ordinary intelligence.

The first chapter continues the narrative of the creation until the crowning-piece was put upon the work by making man in the image of God, and giving him, as God's vicegerent, dominion over all in this lower world. To prepare the way for the history of the temptation and fall, which comes next in order, it was needful to give further particulars respecting man's primitive condition, which it would have been incongruous to include in the general account of the creation of the world in ch. i. These are accordingly supplied in ch. ii.

One of these particulars is his location in the garden of Eden. In order to lead up in a simple and natural way to the description of this garden, the writer reminds his readers, in precise conformity with ch. i., that when heaven and earth were first made the latter contained nothing for the subsistence of man. Ch. ii. 4, 5 should be rendered, "In the day that Jehovah God made earth and heaven no bush of the field was yet in the earth, and no herb of the field had yet sprung up." There was neither bush nor herb to serve man for food. The threefold classification of i. 11, 12—grass, herb, and tree—is not repeated here, for grass was the food of beasts, and therefore not to the purpose. "Bush" is used rather than "tree," to make the negative stronger. There was not only no tree, there was not even a bush. Subsequently trees (ii. 9) and herbs (iii. 18) are named, as the plants yielding food for human use, just as in i. 29.

The suggestion that in ch. i. both trees and herbs are assigned to man as his food from the beginning, while in chs. ii., iii. he eats the fruit of trees in Eden, and is condemned to eat herbs after his fall (iii. 18), overlooks the real point of contrast, which is not between trees and herbs, but between the trees of the garden and the herb of the field, between the tillage of paradise and gaining his bread by the sweat of his face from a reluctant soil bringing forth thistles and thorns. Only trees are expressly spoken of in Eden, because one tree was the test of obedience, and another the pledge of immortal life; but there is no more reason for denying the existence of esculent herbs in paradise than for assuming that there were no fruit-trees outside of it.

The form of expression, "In the day that Jehovah God made earth and heaven," has given occasion to cavil, as though that was here assigned to one day, which ch. i. divides between the second and third creative days. It might as well be said that Num. iii. 1, "In the day that Jehovah spake unto Moses in Mount Sinai" implies that all the revelations given to Moses at Sinai were made within the compass of a single day; or that "the day of adversity" means a period of twenty-four hours. The use of "day," in the general sense of "time," is too familiar to require further comment.

The reason given for the absence of food-bearing plants is twofold; there was no rain to moisten the earth, and no man to till the ground.[1] There is no variance here with ch. i. The suggestion that if the land had just emerged from the water, rain would not be

[1] My friend, Dr. C. M. Mead, of Hartford Theological Seminary, in a casual conversation on this subject suggested what, if my memory serves me, was also maintained by Ebrard in a little tract on Natural Science and the Bible, issued several years since, that the last clause of ii. 5 is not connected with that which immediately precedes. "There was no plant (for there had been no rain), and there was no man." Upon this construction there is not even the semblance of an intimation that man existed before plants.

needed, leaves out of view that according to i. 9, 10, the separation of land and water was complete, and the earth was dry land, before any plants appeared upon its surface. A well-watered garden with ever-flowing streams was to be the abode of man; in anticipation of this it was natural to refer to the need of rain. And there is no implication that man was made prior to the existence of vegetation, contrary to i. 12, 27. For

1. Ch. ii. alleges nothing respecting the relative priority of man or plants. It does not deal with the general vegetation of the globe any further than to carry us back to a time when it did not exist. Of its actual production ch. ii. says nothing. Its positive statement is restricted to the trees of the garden of Eden (vs. 8, 9), and we are nowhere informed that these were brought into being at the same time with vegetation elsewhere. Nothing is said of the origin of grass and herbs, or of trees, outside of Eden, except in ch. i. Dr. Dillmann admits this. He says: "One would expect that in what follows, either before or after ver. 7, mention should be made of the production of the vegetable world, and completing the formation of the world itself. But there is nothing of the sort. There can hardly have been such a gap originally; it rather appears that something has been omitted by R, either because it seemed a needless repetition after ch. i., or disagreed with ch. i." The passage does not fulfil the critics' expectation, for the simple reason that the writer had no such intention as they impute to him. He is not giving another account of the creation. He is merely going to speak of the garden of Eden; and that is all he does.

2. The existence of man is stated to be a condition of that of plants designed for human use, not as an antecedent but as a concomitant. His tillage is requisite (ii. 5), not to their production but to their subsequent care

and cultivation. Jehovah planted the garden and made
the trees grow in it, and then set man to till it, ver. 15,
where the same verb is used as in ver. 5.

3. The order of statement is plainly not that of time,
but of association in thought. Ver. 7, man is formed;
ver. 8, the garden is planted and man put in it; ver. 9,
trees are made to spring up there; ver. 15, man is taken
and put in it. We cannot suppose the writer's meaning
to be that man was made before there was any place in
which to put him, and that he was kept in suspense until
the garden was planted; that he was then put there before the trees that were to supply him with food had
sprung up; and that after the trees were in readiness he
was put there a second time. It is easy to deduce the
most preposterous conclusions from a writer's words by
imputing to them a sense which he never intended. In
order to pave the way for an account of the primitive
paradise, he had spoken of the earth as originally destitute of any plants on which man might subsist, the existence of such plants being conditioned on that of man
himself. This naturally leads him to speak, first, of the
formation of man (ver. 7); then of the garden in which
he was put (ver. 8). A more particular description of the
garden is then given (vs. 9–14), and the narrative is again
resumed by repeating that man was placed there (ver. 15).
As there was plainly no intention to note the strict
chronological succession of events, it cannot in fairness
be inferred from the order of the narrative that man was
made prior to the trees and plants of Eden, much less

¹ The critics' assumption that vs. 10–15 is an interpolation, inasmuch
as the description of the garden is a departure from strict narrative
which is afterward resumed, as well as Budde's notion (Biblische Urgeschichte, pp. 48 sqq.) that the tree of life is to be erased from ver. 9
and elsewhere, as not belonging to the narrative originally, deserve
notice only as illustrating the perfectly arbitrary standard of genuineness which is set up.

that he preceded those of the world at large, of which nothing is here said.

But what cannot be accomplished by the order of the narrative some critics propose to effect by means of a grammatical construction. They put vs. 5, 6, in a parenthesis, and link ver. 4 directly to ver. 7, and read thus : Ver. 4, In the day that Jehovah God made the earth and the heavens (ver. 5, Now no bush of the field was yet in the earth, and no herb of the field had yet sprung up; for Jehovah God had not caused it to rain upon the earth, and there was not a man to till the ground. Ver. 6, And there went up vapor from the earth, and watered the whole face of the ground). Ver. 7, Then Jehovah God formed man, etc. The meaning will then be : " In the day that Jehovah God made earth and heaven, Jehovah God formed man of the dust of the ground, while no bush of the field was yet in the earth, and no herb of the field had yet sprung up." But apart from the fact that the assumption of so long a parenthesis is of very doubtful propriety in Hebrew construction generally, it is absolutely impossible here. Ver. 5 states a twofold reason why there were no plants adapted to human use; there had been no rain and there was no man to use them. The first of these conditions is supplied in ver. 6, vapor rises, and falling in rain waters the ground ; the second, in ver. 7, man is made ; vs. 6 and 7 must accordingly stand in like relation to ver. 5, so that ver. 6 cannot be included in the parenthesis and ver. 7 be linked back to ver. 4.

Furthermore, ch. ii. does not contradict ch. i. in respect to the order of the creation of man and of the lower animals. The allegation that it does rests upon the assumption that the Hebrew tense here used necessarily implies a sequence in the order of time, which is not correct. The record is (ver. 19), " And out of the ground

Jehovah God formed all the beasts of the field, and all
the fowls of heaven, and brought them to Adam." According to Hebrew usage this need not mean that the
formation of the birds and the beasts was subsequent to
all that is previously recorded in the chapter, or that they
were then first formed with the view of providing a suitable companion for Adam. And when the scope of the
passage is duly considered it will be seen that this cannot be its meaning.

It is a significant fact that Dr. Delitzsch, who is an
adherent of the document hypothesis, and can be suspected of no bias against it, and who in all the former
editions of his " Commentary on Genesis " found ch. i.
and ch. ii. at variance on this point, in the last edition,
embodying his most matured views, affirms that there is
no discrepancy whatever, that " et formavit . . . et
adduxit = et cum formasset adduxit," and that this is
both possible in point of style and consonant to the
mode of writing in the Bible history.

The English rendering which best suggests the relation of the clauses is, " Jehovah God having formed out
of the ground every beast of the field, and every fowl of
heaven, brought them unto the man." The Hebrew
phrase suggests that forming the animals preceded their
being brought to the man, but need not suggest anything
whatever as to the relation of time between their formation and what had been mentioned just before in the narrative. In numberless passages in the English version
of the Bible similar expressions are paraphrased in order
to express this subordination of the first verb to the
second. Thus in Gen. iii. 6 the Hebrew reads, " And
the woman saw that the tree was good for food, . . .
and she took of the fruit thereof," for which the English
version correctly substitutes, " And when the woman saw
. . . she took." It might with equal propriety be

rendered, "The woman seeing that the tree was good for food . . . took of the fruit thereof."

Dr. Dillmann admits that the tense here used might antedate what immediately precedes, but insists that ver. 18, "I will make him an help meet for him," implies that the animals were now made as well as brought to Adam. But to suppose that the beasts and birds were made in execution of this divine purpose is not only a grotesque conception in itself, but involves the incongruity that the LORD's first attempts were failures. If there are critics who account this "the natural interpretation," it is in the face of the whole Israelitish conception of God as expressed by every writer in the Old Testament. Observe that God's original purpose, as here announced, is not I will make him a companion of some sort, or such a companion as he may be willing to have, but I will make him an help meet for him, or, more exactly rendered, a help corresponding to him, a precise counterpart to himself. The beasts were brought to Adam not as the companion intended for him, but "to see what he would call them," i.e., to let them make their impression on him and thus awaken in his mind a sense both of his need of companionship and of their unfitness for the purpose. When this had been accomplished Eve was made. The animals are here regarded simply with a view to this end. If the writer were describing the creation of the inferior animals as such, he would speak of all the orders of living things, not neglecting reptiles and aquatic animals.

The LORD made the birds and beasts and brought them to Adam. The main point is that they were brought to Adam. It was of no consequence, so far as the immediate purpose of the narrative is concerned, when they were made, whether before Adam or after, and the mere order of statement cannot in fairness be pressed as though it determined the order of time in this particu-

lar. If, however, this is insisted upon, and we are told
that according to the "natural interpretation" of this
passage it teaches that the birds and beasts were not
made until after Adam, then it must be said that the
same sort of "natural interpretation" will create absurdities and contradictions in many other passages beside.
Thus in Gen. xxiv. 64, 65, "Rebekah saw Isaac and lighted off the camel, and she said to the servant, What man
is this, and the servant said, It is my master." Here, if
the order of statement is made the order of time, Rebekah alighted, out of respect to her future husband, before she had inquired and learned who the man was that
she saw. So Ex. iv. 31, "And the people believed and
they heard, . . . and they bowed their heads and worshipped." According to this the people believed the
words of Moses and Aaron before they heard them. It
is said of the men sent by Joshua to spy out Jericho,
(Josh. ii. 22), "They came unto the mountain and abode
there three days until the pursuers were returned; and
the pursuers sought them and found them not." From
which it appears that the pursuers returned from their
unsuccessful search before their search was begun. The
old prophet in Bethel asked his sons about the man of
God who came from Judah (1 Kin. xiii. 12), "What way
went he? And his sons saw what way the man of God
went." Here "saw" is plainly equivalent to "had seen,"
since the man had left some time before. Isa. xxxvii.
2-5, Hezekiah sent Eliakim and others to Isaiah, and
they said unto him, Thus saith Hezekiah so and so:
and the servants of Hezekiah came to Isaiah and Isaiah
said unto them, etc. That is, they told Isaiah what they
had been bidden to say before they came to him. Deut.
xxxi. 9, "And Moses wrote this law and delivered it
unto the priests," i.e., he delivered to them the law
which he had written; the delivery of the law was subse-

quent to the address to Joshua (vers. 7, 8), but not the writing of it.

Now, any candid man may judge whether declining to accept a principle of interpretation which leads to such absurd results can be called wresting Scripture from its natural sense? If not, then no suspicion of wresting Scripture language can possibly attach to the assertion that there is not a shadow of contrariety between ch. i. and ch. ii. in respect to the order of creation.

It is clear that the alleged inconsistencies do not exist in the record but are of the critics' own making. It is surprising that they do not see that in their eagerness to create discrepancies in evidence of a diversity of writers they are cutting away the ground beneath their own feet. Glaring discrepancies might consist with the fragmentary but not with the documentary hypothesis. The manner in which these documents are supposed to be woven together demands a high degree of skill and intelligence in the redactor; and to allege at the same time that "he did not have insight sufficient to enable him to see that he was all the time committing grave blunders" is self-contradictory.

In the diction of these chapters Dillmann notes the following words and phrases as indicative of J:

1. עָשָׂה *make* or יָצַר *form*, instead of בָּרָא *create*, as in ch. i. But "make" is used ten times in the first section, and of the same things as "create," cf. i. 1 with vs. 7, 8; i. 26 with ver. 27; i. 21 with ver. 25, ii. 3. In ch. i. the prominent thought is that of the immediate exercise of divine almighty power, hence, ver. 1, "God created the heaven and the earth;" ver. 21, "created whales and winged fowl;" ver. 27, "created man," so v. i. 2; "all which God created" ii. 3; and these are all the P passages in which the word occurs. Ch. ii. directs attention to the material, of which the bodies were composed; hence, ver. 7, "formed man

of dust;" ver. 19, "formed beasts out of the ground." In
Isa. xliii. 1; xlv. 7, 12, 18, "create," "form," and "make"
are used together, and in the same sentence, of God's
creative agency. "Form" occurs nowhere in the Hexateuch except in this chapter; in the only other instance
in which the creation of man is alluded to in a paragraph
assigned to J, Gen. vi. 7 the word "create" is used; it
likewise occurs in Ex. xxxiv. 10; Num. xvi. 30 J. And if
the absence of "form" from the rest of J has no significance, why is there any in its absence from P?

2. חַיַּת הַשָּׂדֶה *beast of the field* (ii. 19, 20; iii. 1, 14) instead
of חַיַּת הָאָרֶץ *beast of the earth*, as i. 24, 25; also שִׂיחַ הַשָּׂדֶה
bush of the field (ii. 5), עֵשֶׂב הַשָּׂדֶה *herb of the field* (ii. 5; iii.
18). The open field is here in tacit contrast with the enclosed and cultivated garden; cf. iii. 18. "Beast of the
field" is the ordinary phrase throughout the Bible. But
when terrestrial are contrasted with aquatic animals
(i. 21, 22), and especially when the whole broad earth
is spoken of, they are naturally called "beasts of the
earth."

3. הַפַּעַם *this time, now* (ii. 23). See chs. xviii., xix.,
Marks of J, No. 9.

4. בַּעֲבוּר *because* (iii. 17). See chs. vi.–ix., Marks of J,
No. 17.

5. לְבִלְתִּי *not to* (iii. 11). See chs. xviii., xix., Marks of
J, No. 14.

6. מַה זֹּאת *what is this* (iii. 13). See ch. xii. 10–22,
Marks of J, No. 7.

7. עִצָּבוֹן *sorrow, toil* (iii. 16, 17); it occurs but once
besides in the Old Testament (v. 29), and with express
allusion to this passage.

8. גֵּרֵשׁ *drive out* (iii. 24). See ch. xxi. 1–21, Marks of
E, No. 5.

9. שָׁמַע לְקוֹל *hearken unto the voice* (iii. 17). See ch.
xvi., Marks of J, No. 8.

10. הַרְבָּה הַרְבָּה *greatly multiply* (iii. 16). See ch. xvi.,
Marks of J, No. 10.

Jehovah is distinctively the God of revelation and of
redemption; hence in this section, where God's grace to
man is the prominent thought, his care and favor bestowed upon him in his original estate, the primal promise of mercy after the fall, and the goodness mingled with
severity which marked the whole ordering of his condition subsequently, that salutary course of discipline which
was instituted with a view to gracious ends, Jehovah is
appropriately used. At the same time, to make it plain
that Jehovah is not a different or inferior deity, but that
the God of grace is one with God the Creator, Jehovah
Elohim are here combined. In the interview of Eve with
the serpent (iii. 1–5), however, Elohim is used, as is customary when aliens speak or are spoken to. This shows
that these names are used discriminatingly, and that the
employment of one or the other is regulated not by the
mere habit of different writers, but by their suitableness
to the subject-matter.

It is alleged that a different conception of God is presented in this section from that which is found in the
preceding. "Jehovah *forms* men and beasts, *breathes* the
breath of life into man's nostrils, *builds* a rib into a woman,
plants a garden, *takes* a man and *puts* him into it, *brings*
the beasts to the man, *walks* in the cool of the day, speaks
(iii. 22) as though he were *jealous* of the man." But as
Elohim and Jehovah are words of different signification
and represent the Most High under different aspects of
his being, they must when used correctly and with regard
to their proper meaning be associated with different conceptions of God. This does not argue a diversity of
writers, but simply that the divine name has each time
been selected in accordance with the idea to be expressed.

Elohim is the more general designation of God as the

Creator and providential Governor of the world and of all mankind. Jehovah is his personal name, and that by which he has made himself known when entering into close relations with men, and particularly the chosen race, as the God of revelation and grace. The intimacy thus established between the Creator and the creature involves a condescension to man and placing himself in accord with man, which requires anthropomorphisms for its expression and can be made intelligible in no other way. There is not the slightest inconsistency between the anthropomorphisms of chs. ii., iii., and the lofty conceptions of ch. i., and no ground whatever for assuming that they are the ideas of distinct writers. They abound alike in the Prophets and in the Psalms, where they are freely intermingled in their devout utterances. With one breath the Psalmist speaks of God as knowing the secrets of the heart (xliv. 22), and with the next calls upon him, "Awake, why sleepest thou?" (ver. 24). Ps. cxxxix. links with the most exalted description in human language of the omnipresence and omniscience of the infinite God the prayer, (ver. 23), "Search me and know my heart," as though it was necessary for the Most High to make a careful investigation in order to ascertain what is hidden there.

It should be observed further that the preceding section, with all its grandeur and simplicity, has its anthropomorphisms likewise. Each creative fiat is uttered in human language (i. 3, 6 sqq.). God "called the light יוֹם " (i. 5), giving Hebrew names to that and various other objects. He "saw the light that it was good" (i. 4), thus inspecting the work of each day and pronouncing upon its quality. He uttered a formula of blessing upon the various orders of living things (i. 22, 28). He deliberated with himself prior to the creation of man (i. 26). Man was made "in the image of God," an expression which has been wrested to imply a material form. Time was

spent upon the work, and this was divided into six successive days, like so many working periods of men.
When the work was done, God rested on the seventh
day (ii. 2); and thus the week was completed, another
human measure of time. All this is anthropomorphic.
He who would speak intelligibly to finite comprehension
of the infinite God must use anthropomorphisms. The
difference is not of kind, but of degree.

MUTUAL RELATION OF THIS AND THE PRECEDING SECTION.

The inter-relation between these sections is such as to
show that they cannot be, as the critics claim, from separate and independent documents.
1. The distribution of the matter gives evidence of pre-
arrangement and cannot be purely accidental. The creation of the world, heaven, earth, and sea, with all that
they contain, is described in ch. i., and is assumed in ch.
ii. The latter simply gives details, which were necessarily passed over in the plan of the former, respecting the
separate formation of man and woman and fitting up the
garden for their habitation. Ch. ii. 19 is the only apparent exception to the specific and limited character of
this section. But even this is no real exception, since it
is obvious, as has already been shown, that the formation
of the beasts and birds is only incidentally mentioned as
subordinate to the principal statement, and the one of
chief importance in the connection that God brought
them to Adam to receive their names. Again, God gave
names to certain things in ch. i.; Adam gave names to
others in chs. ii., iii.; and these are precisely adjusted to
one another, neither duplicating nor omitting any. God
gave names to day and night, heaven, earth, and seas (i.
5, 8, 10), and to Adam (v. 1). Adam gave names to the
inferior animals (ii. 20), and to Eve (ii. 23; iii. 20).

2. The title ii. 4a has been shown to belong to this
section, and contains explicit reference to the preceding
of which this is declared to be the sequel. And in the
body of the section there are numerous allusions to, or
coincidences with, the preceding or other so-called P sections. If the construction of i. 1 adopted by Dillmann
be correct, there is a striking similarity in structure between i. 1, 2 P, and ii. 4b, 5 J, "in the beginning when
God created, etc., the earth was waste and void," corresponding to " in the day that Jehovah God made, etc., no
bush of the field was yet in the earth."   J ii. 4b strikingly
resembles P v. 1b in the form of expression ; so do i. 4a
P and vi. 2a J ; i. 31a, vi. 12a P and viii. 13b J ; אֶרֶץ *earth*,
without the article, i. 24 P, as ii. 4 J.   The paronomasia
תֹּהוּ וָבֹהוּ (i. 2), פָּרוּ וּרְבוּ (i. 22, 28) P recalls in J אָדָם . . .
עָפָר וָאֵפֶר (iv. 14), נָע וָנָד (ver. 23), אִשָּׁה . . . אִישׁ (ii. 7), אֲדָמָה
(xviii. 27).   The first person plural used of God (i. 26
P), notwithstanding the strictness of Hebrew monotheism
has its counterpart in J, iii. 22 ; xi. 7.   The use of עָשָׂה
made (iii. 1 J) in reference to the beasts, instead of יָצַר
formed, as ii. 19 J, is a reminiscence of i. 25 P.   כְּרוּבִים
cherubim (iii. 24 J) occurs in the Pentateuch besides only
in P.

3. The repeated occurrence of Jehovah Elohim
throughout chs. ii., iii. is with evident reference to ch. i.
This combination of divine names occurs nowhere else
with such regularity and frequency, though it is found
in a few other passages, *e.g.*, Ex. ix. 30 ; 2 Sam. vii. 22,
25 ; 1 Chron. xvii. 16, 17 ; Jon. iv. 6 ; cf. 1 Sam. vi. 20.
This relieves it from Dr. Harper's charge [1] of being " an
un-Hebraic expression," and refutes the notion of Hupfeld [2] that it is adopted here without reference to ch. i.,
because as the full name of God it was appropriate to
the state of paradise, from which there was a descent to

---

[1] Hebraica, vol. i., p. 23.   [2] Quellen der Genesis, p. 124.

Jehovah alone after the fall; that of Reuss[1] that it is
indicative of a special document distinct from both P
and J, and that of Budde[2] that it arose from the combination of two documents, one of which used the name
Jehovah and the other Elohim. In every other passage,
in which it is found, it denotes that Jehovah the God of
Israel is likewise Elohim the God of the universe. It
must have the same meaning here; it can only be intended to suggest that Jehovah, now first introduced, is
identical with Elohim before spoken of in ch. i. This
is admitted by the critics generally, who seek, however, to
evade the natural inference of the common authorship of
both sections by the assumption, which has no other
basis than the hypothesis that it is adduced to support,
that Elohim was inserted by R.

And while it is plain that chs. ii., iii. is thus adjusted to
ch. i., it is no less clear that i. 1–ii. 3 anticipates what is
to follow, and purposely prepares the way for it.

1. The emphasis with which it is repeated at the close
of each creative act, " and God saw that it was good " (i.
4, 10, 12, etc.), and affirmed at the end of the whole, " behold, it was very good " (ver. 31), would be unmeaning
except as a designed preliminary to the reverse which
was shortly to follow in the fall (ch. iii.). And this,
moreover, is necessary to explain the otherwise unaccountable declaration (vi. 11 P), that " the earth was corrupt before God," the mystery of which is unrelieved by
anything that P contains.

2. Ch. ii. 3 is evidently preliminary to the fourth commandment (Ex. xx. 8–11), which again in its terms distinctly refers back to i. 1–ii. 3. The ten commandments
in Ex. xx. are by the critics referred to E, with which,
according to Dillmann, J was acquainted. He must,

---

[1] Geschichte der heiligen Schriften d. A. T., p. 257.
[2] Biblische Urgeschichte, pp. 233, 234.

therefore, have known and believed that the world was
created in six days, and can have written nothing in
Gen. ii., iii., inconsistent with this belief. This can only
be evaded by alleging that the commandments are not
preserved in Ex. xx. in their genuine original form. Dillmann disputes Ex. xx. 11, because a different reason is
given for observing the Sabbath in Deut. v. 15. But Ex.
xx. is the authentic transcript, while Deut. v. is a repro-
duction with hortatory modifications. This Dillmann
admits in other instances; but Delitzsch very properly
contends that this is no exception. The rejection of the
verse is simply the usual device of the critics for disposing of whatever contravenes their hypothesis. Instead
of adapting their hypothesis to the phenomena presented
by the text, they insist upon remodelling the text into
accordance with their hypothesis. The advantage of
this method is that the critic can thus triumphantly establish whatever he sets out to prove.

CAIN AND ABEL—CAIN'S DESCENDANTS (CH. IV.).

It is said that vs. 17–24 is at variance with the rest of
the chapter, and with the J document generally in respect both to the life of Cain and the fact of the deluge.
It is hence claimed that extracts from separate documents
have here been combined.

While Cain is represented in vs. 11, 14, as condemned
for the murder of his brother to be a fugitive and a wanderer in the earth, it is affirmed that, according to ver. 17,
he led a settled life and built a city. But (1) it then remains to be accounted for, if these stories are in such
direct antagonism, that R could have put them together without explanation or remark, as though he perceived no conflict between them and had no idea that his
readers would suspect any. (2) The fact is that Cain was

expelled from the seat of God's presence, the society of
man, and cultivated land, to the wild steppes of the land
of Nod (so called from נָד *wanderer*, in his sentence),
equivalent to the nomad region. The Hebrew word for
city is in usage broad enough to cover a nomadic encampment (Num. xiii. 19; 2 Kin. xvii. 9). The dread lest his
murder might be avenged (ver. 14), betrayed itself afresh
in his constructing such a defence for himself and his
family, which subsequently may have grown from these
small beginnings[1] into much larger proportions. The
builders of the first huts on the site of Chicago may be
said to have laid the foundations of the city. (3) Cain
had previously been a " tiller of the ground." That he
continued to be an agriculturist is certainly not stated in
the text and is in fact inconsistent with it. The arts developed by his descendants are those of nomads, viz.,
pasturage, music, and metallurgy, but not the cultivation
of the soil. Jabal was " the father of such as dwell in
tents and have cattle," in a very different sense from that
in which Abel was a " keeper of sheep " at his paternal
home. (4) The explicit reference in iv. 24, where Lamech
speaks of Cain being avenged sevenfold, to the pledge
which the LORD had given him in ver. 15, shows very
plainly that both belong to the same continuous narrative. Dillmann can find no escape from this but either
by putting the cart before the horse and supposing the
allusion to be the other way, and that ver. 15 was shaped
into conformity with ver. 24, or else by ejecting ver. 15a
from the text as an addition by R. Budde ("Biblische
Urgeschichte," pp. 184, 185) strangely imagines that the
language of Lamech gave rise to the story of Cain's
murder.

---

[1] Observe the form of statement in the Hebrew, which is significant,
וַיְהִי בֹּנֶה " he was building a city," as a work in progress, not "he
built it," as though it were completed by him.

A still more surprising inference from vs. 17–24 is that
the writer knew nothing of the interruption of human
history by the deluge.   This inference hangs by a very
slender thread.   As the invention of various arts is here
traced to the sons of Lamech in the line of Cain, the
conclusion is drawn that as the arts have been perpetuated, so must the race have been that invented them ;
which is an evident *non sequitur*.   As though an art invented by one race of men could not be adopted by another race, and the knowledge of it be kept alive though
the original inventors had passed away.   That the race
of Cain was extinct seems to be implied by the fact that
the genealogy breaks off as it does, without being continued, like every other genealogy in Genesis, to tribes or
persons existing in the writer's own day.   Wellhausen in-
trepidly suggests that Cain is a collective name for the
Kenites, as in Num. xxiv. 22, who are thus traced up to
the origin of mankind ; a piece of historical criticism akin
to that which finds an allusion to South America in " the
gold of Parvaim " (2 Chron. iii. 6), since Parvaim is the
dual of Peru.

Wellhausen maintains that this section, in which the
arts of building cities, care of cattle, music, and metallurgy are traced to the godless descendants of Cain is a
sequel to the narrative of the fall in chs. ii., iii., in which
the tree of knowledge bears forbidden fruit.   The common idea in both, he claims, is that knowledge is peril-
ous, and Jehovah jealously restrains man from its possession ; advancing civilization betokens growing corruption.
These two sections, pervaded by this idea, he sunders
from the J of the rest of Genesis, and supposes that they
belong to some antecedent document, J', which J has here
incorporated in his own production.   Dillmann agrees
with him that the first half of ch. iv., containing the
story of Cain and Abel, is by a different writer from the

second half of the chapter, containing the account of
Cain's descendants ; but insists that it is the former and
not the latter which is by the author of the narrative of
the fall and is its continuation. And he points in evidence of this to ver. 7b, which is repeated from iii. 16b ;
the mention of Eden (ver. 16); the identity of aim, viz., to
trace the growth of sin, the beginning of which is described in ch. iii., and the sameness of the diction as
shown in a number of words and expressions common
to vs. 1–16 and chs. ii., iii., as well as other passages referred to J. On the other hand, Budde ("Biblische
Urgeschichte," pp. 220, 221) points out coincidences
in expression between vs. 17–24 and various J passages.
Whereupon Dillmann concludes that if any significance
is to be attached to these coincidences, the author of chs.
ii., iii. may himself have introduced vs. 17–24 from its
original source into his own document, regardless of the
discrepancy in ver. 17, not so much with a view to the
invention of arts as the development of crime as shown
in Lamech's impious speech. As it has already been
shown that there is no inconsistency between ver. 17 and
the preceding verses, the entire critical structure based on
that assumption collapses. Dillmann is right in linking chs. ii., iii. with iv. 1–16, and Wellhausen in linking
those chapters with vs. 17–24. And there is but one
author for the whole.

MARKS OF J.

Dillmann finds the following points in common between
chs. ii., iii., and the diction of vs. 1–16.

1. אֲדָמָה ground (vs. 2, 3, 10, 12). See ch. xxviii. 10–
22, Marks of J, No. 4.

2. שָׂדֶה field (ver. 8). See chs. ii., iii., Marks of J, No. 2.
This word is by no means peculiar to J. It occurs re-

peatedly also in P, *e.g.,* xxiii. 9, 11, 13, 17, 19, 20, and often elsewhere.

3. עָבַד הָאֲדָמָה *till the ground* (vs. 2, 12, as ii. 5 ; iii. 23). As the phrase occurs nowhere else in the Hexateuch, its absence from P sections is to be explained in the same manner as its absence from all the rest of those that are assigned to J. No argument for a diversity of documents can be derived from it.

4. גֵּרֵשׁ *drive out* (ver. 14, as iii. 24). See ch. xxi. 1–21, Marks of E, No. 5.

5. לְבִלְתִּי *not to* (ver. 15, as iii. 11). See chs. xviii., xix., Marks of J, No. 14.

6. אָרוּר אַתָּה *thou art cursed* (ver. 11, as iii. 14). This verb is always referred either to J, E, or D, there being no occasion for its employment in any of the passages ascribed to P.

7. The questions asked by the LORD (vs. 9, 10) are similar to those in iii. 9, 13. These various points of similarity between vs. 1–16 and chs. ii., iii. create a strong presumption that they are from the same writer, as Dillmann urges, but afford no proof that he is distinct from the author of the passages referred to P.

He also finds the following expressions in vs. 1–16, which recur in J passages elsewhere :

8. הוֹסִיף in the adverbial sense *again* (vs. 2, 12). This is uniformly referred to J or E, except in Lev. xxvi. 18.

9. חָרָה לוֹ *be angry* (vs. 5, 6). See chs. xviii., xix., Marks of J, No. 30.

10. פָּצָה פֶה *open the mouth* (ver. 11). This occurs but twice besides in the Hexateuch (Num. xvi. 30, J ; Deut. xi. 6 D).

Budde finds the following indications of J in vs. 17–24.

11. יָלַד *beget* (ver. 18). See chs. vi.–ix., Marks of P, No. 20 ; also under ch. x.

12. גַּם הִוא (ver. 22), *she also.* See ch. xxii. 20–24, Marks of J, No. 3.

13. וְשֵׁם אָחִיו (ver. 21) *and his brother's name,* as x. 25. These are the only two instances in the Hexateuch in which a second son is introduced by this particular formula.

The divine names are appropriately used. It is to Jehovah, who had given her the promise of offspring, that Eve gratefully ascribes the bestowment of her first child (ver. 1). To Jehovah offerings are brought by Cain and Abel (vs. 3, 4). It is Jehovah, who condescendingly remonstrates with Cain and explains to him the defect in his offering and how it may be remedied (vs. 6, 7). It is Jehovah again, the defender of his own people, who arraigns Cain for his awful crime, and while sparing his guilty life banishes him from his presence (vs. 9–16). It is Jehovah upon whose name the pious race of Seth and Enosh devoutly call, iv. 26.

It might at first sight appear surprising that Eve, who had recognized the grace of Jehovah in the birth of Cain, should speak of Seth as coming to her from Elohim (ver. 25). But there is a reason for this. The good gift of God is set in contrast with the evil deed of man. "Elohim hath appointed me another seed instead of Abel; for Cain slew him." It is to be observed that Elohim here occurs in a J section; so that the critics themselves must admit that it is discriminatingly used, and that there is a special propriety in its employment.

II

THE GENERATIONS OF ADAM (CH. V. 1–VI. 8)

ADAM TO NOAH (CH. V.)

THOSE who insist upon regarding the entire antediluvian history of the Bible as mythical, and on a par with the early myths of heathen nations, labor, though with small success, to find ancient parallels to the genealogy contained in this chapter. The nearest approach to it is the ten antediluvian kings of Chaldean story with reigns on an average of 43,000 years each, as reported by Berosus. Whether Lenormant is correct or not in giving them an astronomical interpretation, their names plainly stand in no relation to the names in this Scriptural list. The sole point of resemblance is in the number ten; and this is vague enough. Others have sought to find meanings in the names mentioned in this chapter, which might suggest the idea which lay at the basis of the genealogy and account for its formation. They are interpreted by Boettcher[1] as indicative of the successive stages by which the human race advanced in civilization; by Ewald[2] as in part at least the names of various deities; and by Knobel as representing the Western Asiatics, while the descendants of Cain denote the Chinese and other populations of Eastern Asia. It is evident, however, that in the intent of the sacred historian it simply traces the line of descent from Adam to Noah in the pious line of Seth.

[1] Exegetisch-kritische Aehrenlese, pp. 4, 5.
[2] Geschichte Israels, 2d edit., i., p. 357.

Budde's[1] inference from the names Jared (descent) and
Methuselah (man of weapon) that while the first five in
the line were good men, the last five, with the exception
of Enoch and Noah, were wicked, rests on purely fanciful interpretations of the names.

The longevity attributed to the antediluvians has been
declared to be inconsistent with physiological laws; but
in our ignorance of the extent to which the conditions
affecting human life may have been modified, such an assertion is unwarranted.

THE CAINITE AND SETHITE GENEALOGIES.

There is a remarkable similarity in the names of the
descendants of Seth in ch. v. and those of Cain, iv. 17,
18, as shown in the following lists:

Adam	**Adam**
Seth	
Enosh	
Kenan	**Cain**
Mahalalel	Enoch
Jared	Irad
Enoch	Mehujael
Methuselah	Methushael
Lamech	Lamech
Noah	

The six names in each column, beginning with Kenan
or Cain, are strikingly alike; and if Mahalalel be transposed with Enoch, they will follow each other in the
same identical order. It is natural to conclude that this
cannot be altogether casual. Buttmann[2] inferred that
these are variants of one and the same genealogy as preserved in two related but hostile tribes. In its original
intent it enumerated the early ancestors of the human

[1] Biblische Urgeschichte, p. 96.   [2] Mythologus, i., pp. 170–172.

race sprung from its first progenitor, who in one form of the myth was called Adam and in the other Enosh, each having the same signification (man). The two were subsequently harmonized by making Enosh the grandson of Adam. The names differed sufficiently for the race of Seth to regard the Cainite tradition as distinct from their own and descriptive of a godless race, and so Cain was held to be the ancestor not of all mankind, but of this hated tribe.

The majority of critics accept this identification of the two genealogies, and have drawn other consequences from it. Dillmann contended that the redactor has transposed the story of Cain and Abel (iv. 1–16) from its true position later in the history. Cain was not the son of Adam, but belongs where Kenan stands in the genealogy (v. 9), with whom he is identical; or, as he has modified his opinion in the latest edition of his " Commentary," Cain and Abel were not the only sons of Adam, but were born subsequent to Seth. He thinks it strange that the distinction between tillers of the ground and keepers of sheep, and between bloody and unbloody offerings, should be found in the first children of primeval man ; and that the advance from the first sin to fratricide should be made so soon. This only shows that his opinion differs from that of the author of the narrative. He appeals also to the words of Cain (iv. 14), " Every one that findeth me shall slay me," which imply a considerable population ; but he forgets how greatly the descendants of Adam may have multiplied by the time that he attained his one hundred and thirtieth year (v. 3, cf. iv. 25). Wellhausen goes so far as to identify Abel with Jabal (iv. 20), " the father of such as have cattle." But—

1. That Wellhausen's wild conjecture expressly contradicts the statements of the history is obvious. And it requires not a little critical manipulation to carry through

the hypothesis of Dillmann. In iv. 25 the word " again,"
in the first clause, and the whole of the last clause after
the word עָרֶז seed, viz., " another instead of Abel, for Cain
slew him," must be thrown out of the text as an interpolation by R. The statement (iv. 1) that Cain was the son
of Adam and Eve must be gotten out of the way, if he is
to be made the same as Kenan the son of Enosh (v. 9).
And R must have reversed the order of the statements
in the chapter for no very intelligible reason.

2. The distinctness of these genealogies is expressly
affirmed. That in iv. 17, 18, J, professes to record the
descendants of Cain after his murder of Abel and his removal to the land of Nod, while that in ch. v., P, records
the descendants of Seth, a different son of Adam. The
critics cannot consistently claim that this is merely a
variant representation by J and P of what is in fact the
same thing, but which R has erroneously set down as
two quite separate lines of descent. For by their own
hypothesis J (iv. 25, 26) traces the line " Adam, Seth,
Enosh " precisely as is done by P (v. 3–6); and v. 29 is
attributed to J as another fragment of the same line.
From this the critics infer that the document J must have
contained a complete genealogy from Adam to Noah parallel to that of P, though the greater portion of it has
been omitted by R as superfluous repetition. Now these
broken and scattered links of J utter the same voice with
the full record of P, that Noah and his father Lamech
were descended not from Cain but from Seth. Both
these genealogies in substantially their present form
were, therefore, according to the critics contained in the
document of J, who in this followed the sources whence
he derived his history. This is a confession that the
same writer can have recorded them both ; consequently
their presence in the existing text of Genesis affords no
argument for critical partition. The unity of Genesis is

not affected by the alleged conversion of one genealogy into two, which on the critics' own theory must have occurred, if at all, in the course of its oral transmission prior to the writing of the book of Genesis, or even of the document J, which is held to be one of its oldest constituents.

And in regard to this it would appear that a sweeping conclusion is drawn from very slender premises. Suppose that we are unable to account for the coincidence of names, does it follow that the persons represented by them never existed? Delitzsch directs attention to the fact that but two names are the same in the entire series, viz., Enoch and Lamech : and in both cases statements are made which show that the persons are quite distinct. The first of these names means *initiation* or *consecration*, and might very well be applied in the former sense to the first son of Cain born in exile, as subsequently to the first-born of Reuben (Gen. xlvi. 9), and in the latter sense to that holy man who walked with God and was not, for God took him. The meaning of the name Lamech is unknown ; but the identification of the persons so called is forbidden by the speeches preserved from them, which reflect totally diverse characters. Cain and Kenan, Irad and Jared are distinct not merely in their form but in their radical letters and probable signification. So is the second and determining member in the compound names Methushael and Methuselah. Mahalalel, *praise of God*, which stands over against Mehujael, *smitten of God*, may suggest that the descendants of Cain have names with a bad meaning and those of Seth have names with a good meaning.

The meaning of most of these ancient names cannot now be ascertained. Several of them do not appear to be Hebrew. And it is doubtful whether even those which simulate Hebrew forms may not be merely modi-

fications of some unknown original to adapt them better
to the Hebrew ear. It is not surprising if these parallel
lists of unintelligible names should undergo changes in
their transmission through long centuries, and if they
should, whether with or without design, be gradually conformed to one another. The disposition to produce like-
sounding contrasts, as in Isa v. 7 מִשְׁפָּט . . . מִשְׂפָּח,
צְדָקָה . . . צְעָקָה, or by slight modifications as of Beel-
zebub into Beelzebul, or Shechem into Sychar, to give a
different turn to the meaning of words, may easily have
been operative. The LXX. has two more names alike in
both lists than the Hebrew, which indicates a tendency
in such cases to come into a closer approximation in the
course of repeated transcription. The Mohammedan
names for Cain and Abel are Kabil and Habil; see Sale's
Koran, note to ch. v. 30.

DUPLICATE STATEMENTS.

Dillmann thinks that the composite character of the
book of Genesis is shown more plainly in the duplicate
mention of the birth of Seth and Enosh (iv. 25, 26 ; v. 3–
6) than anywhere else. Why should the same writer
thus repeat himself? The supplementary critics, as Tuch,
held that J inserted iv. 25, 26, in order to effect the transition from the preceding account of Cain and his descendants to that of the line of Seth. The more recent
critics follow Hupfeld, who regarded these verses, as together with v. 29, the remnants of J's genealogy from
Adam to Noah parallel to that of P in ch. v. R, while
omitting the greater portion as superfluous repetition, saw
fit to retain these three verses because of the additional
information which they convey. He inserted v. 29 in
the body of P's genealogy, but preserved iv. 25, 26 distinct. Now it is difficult to see why the same motive, be

it what it might, which could determine R not to blend
iv. 25, 26 with the corresponding verses of ch. v. as is
done with v. 29, might not be similarly influential with
the original writer. Some reasons for such a separate
statement naturally offer themselves.

1. These closing verses of ch. iv. are necessary to the
proper understanding of ch. v. While the insertion of
those statements in this chapter would have been confusing and would have marred its symmetry, it was important to set v. 3 in its true light in relation to iv. 1, 2.
The critics say that they are contradictory, since they
infer from v. 3 that according to P Seth was the first
child of Adam. But this is not necessarily implied any
more than Ex. ii. 1, 2 implies that Moses was the oldest
child of his parents, though ver. 4 declares the contrary,
not to speak of Ex. vii. 7. To make the matter perfectly
plain to the reader, iv. 25 distinctly states that Seth was
born after the murder of Abel. And then iv. 26 was
added to indicate the character of the godly race of Seth
in contrast with the ungodly race of Cain, and thus prepare the way for the sparing of Noah and his house
when the rest of mankind perished in the flood.

2. Another reason for putting these statements at the
close of ch. iv. grows out of the original plan of the book
of Genesis and its division into successive sections each
in a manner complete in itself and introduced by its own
special title. The section ii. 4–ch. iv. had recorded a
constant descent from bad to worse, the sin of our first
parents, their expulsion from paradise, the murder of
Abel, Cain's descendants reaching in Lamech the climax
of boastful and unrestrained violence. That the section
might not be suffered to end in unrelieved gloom a
brighter outlook is added at the close, precisely as is
done at the end of the next section in vi. 8. Seth is
substituted for Abel, whom Cain slew, and instead of

piety perishing with murdered Abel it reaches a new development in the days of Enosh.

The whole arrangement bears evidence of adaptation and careful thought, and is suggestive of one author, not the combination of separate compositions prepared with no reference to each other.

A further indication of the same sort, implying the original unity of these chapters, is their correspondence with the general plan of Genesis in respect to genealogies. Uniformly the divergent lines are first traced before proceeding with the principal line of descent leading to the chosen people. In ch. x. the various nations of mankind sprung from the three sons of Noah; then (xi. 10 sqq.) the line from Shem to Abram. Nahor's descendants (xxii. 20 sqq.), those of Keturah (xxv. 1 sqq.), and of Ishmael (vs. 13 sqq.), before those of Isaac (vs. 19 sqq.). Those of Esau (xxxvi. 1 sqq.) before those of Jacob (xxxvii. 2 sqq.). In like manner the degenerate and God-forsaken race of Cain is traced (iv. 17 sqq.) before proceeding with that of Seth (ch. v.).

PRIMEVAL CHRONOLOGY.

It should be remarked here that no computation of time is ever built in the Bible upon this or any other genealogy. There is no summation of the years from Adam to Noah, or from Noah to Abraham, as there is of the abode in Egypt (Ex. xii. 40), or of the period from the exodus to the building of the temple (1 Kin. vi. 1). And as the received chronologies and the generally accepted date of the flood and of the creation of the world are derived from computations based on these genealogies, it ought to be remembered that this is a very precarious mode of reckoning. This genealogy could only afford a safe estimate of time on the assumption that no links are missing and that every name in the line of descent has been recorded. But this we have no right to take for granted. The analogy of other biblical genealogies is decidedly against it. Very commonly unimportant names are omitted ; sometimes several consecutive names are dropped together. No one has a right, therefore, to denominate a primeval chronology so constructed the biblical chronology and set it in opposition to the deductions of science, and thence conclude that there is a conflict between the Bible and science. See the article on this subject in the *Bibliotheca Sacra* for April, 1890.

MARKS OF P.

Dillmann finds the following indications of P in this chapter.

1. The back reference from vs. 1–3 to i. 26–28. But it is linked to the same extent and in precisely the same manner with J sections. The genealogy is traced (ver. 32) to Noah and his three sons, all of whom are similarly named in ix. 18 J ; ver. 29 refers back to iii. 17 J. The critics say that ver. 29 is an insertion by R. They say so because their hypothesis requires it and for no other reason. It might just as well be said that R inserted vs. 1, 2, and modified ver. 3. Both passages stand on the same footing, and should be dealt with in the same way.

2. The formality and precision of statement. This is the uniform style of the genealogies leading to the chosen race as distinguished from those belonging to the divergent lines, whether attributed to P or J.

3. תּוֹלְדֹת *generations* (ver. 1). See chs. vi.–ix., Marks of P, No. 1.

4. דְּמוּת *likeness* (vs. 1, 3). See ch. i. 1–ii. 3.

5. צֶלֶם *image* (ver. 3). This word occurs here and

ix. 6, with specific allusion to i. 26, 27; and besides in the Hexateuch only Num. xxxiii. 52 J.

6. זָכָר וּנְקֵבָה *male and female* (ver. 2). See chs. vi.–ix., Marks of P, No. 12.

7. הוֹלִיד *beget* (vs. 3 sqq.). See chs. vi.–ix., Marks of P, No. 20.

8. הִתְהַלֵּךְ אֶת־הָאֱלֹהִים *walk with God* (vs. 22, 24). This phrase occurs besides vi. 9 P, and nowhere else in the Old Testament. The nearest approach to it is *walk before God* (xvii. 1 P; xxiv. 40 J; xlviii. 15 E).

The assertion that according to this writer " this first age of the world was still a time of rest and primitive perfection, into which corruption did not penetrate till toward its close " (vi. 9 sqq.), is gratuitous and unfounded. It has no basis whatever in the sacred text. The universal corruption described in vi. 11, 12, finds its only explanation in the fall of man (ch. iii.), and the subsequent development and spread of evil (ch. iv.; vi. 1–8), and proves conclusively that these passages cannot be separated and assigned to distinct sources.

The names of God are appropriately used in this chapter. Elohim is rendered necessary in ver. 1 by its reference to i. 27, and Jehovah in v. 29 by its reference to iii. 17. Elohim is required in vs. 22, 24, since walking with God is a general designation of piety as contrasted with what is earthly and sensual.

THE SONS OF GOD AND THE DAUGHTERS OF MEN (CH. VI. 1–8)

In regard to the paragraph Gen. vi. 1–8, the most recent critics have fallen back upon the position taken up by fragmentists, such as Vater, who affirmed that it was not only disconnected with the genealogy in ch. v., which precedes, and with the account of the flood which succeeds it (vi. 9 sqq.), but that it falls apart itself into two unrelated paragraphs (vs. 1–4) concerning the primeval giants, J′, and (vs. 5–8) the divine purpose to destroy the world and save Noah, J.

But the fact is that there is the most intimate connection throughout, and this passage can neither itself be split into fragments nor sundered from the context in which it stands. The genealogy in ch. v. conducts the line of descent by regular steps from Adam to Noah, pausing here because there was something to record about Noah before proceeding further, and departing from the analogy of the rest of the chapter by naming three sons of Noah instead of one, as in the case of every preceding patriarch, because they were all concerned in what was to follow. The closing verse of ch. v. is thus directly preparatory for the account of the deluge which comes after. Further, this verse contains the statement of Noah's age at the birth of his children, but the length of his subsequent life and the duration of the whole, which had been regularly given in the case of preceding patriarchs, are here wanting. These are, however, supplied (vii. 6) by the statement of Noah's age at the coming of the flood, and then, after the account of the deluge had been given and all that was to be said further about Noah, there follows in the identical forms of the genealogy (ch. v.) the time that Noah lived after the flood and the total of his years (ix. 28, 29). This is a clear indication that this genealogy, instead of being broken off and terminated at the close of ch. v., is simply enlarged by the insertion of the narrative of the deluge, which is incorporated within it. After this the divergent lines of descent are introduced (ch. x.), and then the main genealogy is resumed, and proceeds (xi. 10–26) until it reaches the name of Abram, when it pauses, or rather is enlarged again, to receive the history of the patriarchs.

Again, vi. 1–8 is formally linked to what precedes in the original Hebrew by Vav Consecutive, and by the statement of men's beginning to multiply on the face of the earth, which sums up the substance of ch. v. in a few words, the expansion of the race being indicated by the statement repeated in the case of each patriarch, "He begat sons and daughters." It is further appropriate to the connection as preparing the way for what follows, by explaining the universality of the corruption which was the moral cause of the flood. This is the subject of vs. 1–4, which is accordingly intimately related to vs. 5–8, and leads directly to it, making that clear which would otherwise be quite unaccountable.

The sons of God (vs. 2, 4) are not angels nor demigods,[1] whose intermarriage with the daughters of men brought forth a race of monsters or superhuman beings.

1. This purely mythological conceit was foisted upon the passage in certain apocryphal books like the book of Enoch; also by Philo and Josephus, who were misled by the analogy of ancient heathen fables. But it was repelled by the great body of Jewish and Christian interpreters from the earliest periods, though it has been taken up again by a number of modern scholars. It is assumed by them that a transgression of angels is here spoken of, though the existence of angels has not been before mentioned nor in any way referred to in the previous part of the book of Genesis. This view has no sanction whatever in Scripture. Jude, vs. 6, 7, and 2

---

[1] The Targums and some other Jewish authorities understand by "sons of God" nobles, men of high rank or official station, who in Ps. lxxxii. 6 are denominated "sons of the Most High"; and by "daughters of men" women of inferior position, as in Ps. xlix. 2; lxii. 9, בני אדם are contrasted with בני איש as men of low degree with men of high degree. But no such contrast is suggested here; and the intermarriage of different classes in society is nowhere represented as displeasing to God or provoking the divine judgment.

Pet. ii. 4 have been tortured into sustaining it ; but they contain no reference to this passage whatever. And there is no analogy anywhere in the Bible for the adoption by the sacred writers of mythological notions in general, or for the idea in particular of the intermarriage of angels and men. Sexual relations are nowhere in Scripture attributed to superior beings. There is no suggestion that angels are married or are given in marriage ; the contrary is expressly declared (Matt. xxii. 30). Male and female deities have no place in the Bible, except as a heathen notion which is uniformly reprobated. The Hebrew language does not even possess a word for " goddess." The whole conception of sexual life, as connected with God or angels, is absolutely foreign to Hebrew thought, and for that reason cannot be supposed to be countenanced here.

2. The sole foundation for this mistaken interpretation is the allegation that "sons of God" must, according to Scriptural usage, mean "angels;" which, however, is not the case. Even if that were the more usual and obvious interpretation of the phrase, which it is not, the connection in which it stands would compel us to seek a different meaning for it here, if that were possible, and one which would be compatible with marriage. "Sons of God" בְּנֵי הָאֱלֹהִים is a poetic designation of angels occurring three times in the book of Job (i. 6 ; ii. 1 ; xxxviii. 7) ; and a like expression בְּנֵי אֵלִים is found twice in the Psalms in the same sense (xxix. 1 ; lxxxix. 6). Daniel iii. 25, בַּר אֱלָהִין " son of the gods," has also been appealed to ; but this has nothing to do with the case, as it is the language of Nebuchadnezzar, and represents a genuine heathen conception. Angels are nowhere so called in the Pentateuch, nor anywhere in the Bible but in the few passages already referred to.

3. On the contrary, " sons of God " is a familiar des-

ignation of the chosen race, the worshippers of the true
God. Moses is instructed to say to Pharaoh (Ex. iv.
22), Thus saith Jehovah, Israel is my son: let my son
go. So Deut. xiv. 1, Ye are the sons of Jehovah your
God. In the Song of Moses (Deut. xxxii.) this idea of
sonship occurs repeatedly. Ver. 5, They have dealt
corruptly with him, they are not his sons. Ver. 6, Is
Jehovah not thy father? Ver. 18, He is called the Rock
that begat thee, the God that gave thee birth : and the
people are called (ver. 19) his sons and his daughters.
Hos. i. 10, Ye are the sons of the living God; xi. 1, Israel is called God's son. Isaiah in repeated passages
speaks of the people as God's sons (Isa. i. 2; xliii. 6 ;
xlv. 11). In Jer. xxxi. 20 the LORD calls Ephraim his
dear son, his favorite child. In Ps. lxxiii. 15 the pious
are called " the generation of God's children." And, on
the other hand, the worshippers of false gods are called
their children. Thus (Num. xxi. 29) the people of Moab
are spoken of as the sons and daughters of Chemosh.
Mal. ii. 11, an Israelite who had taken a foreign wife is
said to have married the daughter of a strange god. It
is in entire accord with this Biblical usage that the pious
race, who adhered to the true worship of God, are called
the sons of God in contrast with the descendants of
Cain, who had gone out from the presence of Jehovah,
and abandoned the seat of his worship entirely.

4. And this brings the verses before us into correspondence with numerous other passages of the Pentateuch in its practical aim. The law of Moses again and
again forbids intermarriage with the Canaanites lest they
should contaminate Israel and seduce them to idolatry.
The book of Genesis inculcates the same lesson when it
depicts Abraham's concern about the marriage of Isaac
(xxiv. 3, 4), and that of Isaac and Rebekah about the
marriage of Jacob (xxvii. 46 ; xxviii. 1, 2), the distress

which Esau's marriage caused his parents (xxvi. 34, 35; xxviii. 6–8), and the trials of Jacob's family at Shechem (ch. xxxiv). If the verses before us point out the ruinous consequences of the intermarriage of the godly race with the ungodly, it furthers an aim which the writer of Genesis and of the Pentateuch evidently had greatly at heart. A warning not to intermarry with angels would be altogether unmeaning.

5. This explanation of how it came to pass that the pious portion of the race were infected with the universal degeneracy is not only appropriate in the connection, but is necessary to account for the universality of the following judgment, which is repeatedly and largely insisted upon. This is an integral and essential part of the narrative, the omission of which would leave an unfilled chasm. The primal source of human corruption had been germinally shown in the fall (ch. iii.); the degeneracy of the Cainites had been traced (ch. iv.). Nothing but good, however, had thus far been said of the race of Seth (iv. 26; v. 22, 24, 29). That this pious race were themselves involved in the degeneracy which had overtaken the rest of mankind, is here stated for the first time. But this is necessary to explain why the whole race of man, with the exception of a single family, should be doomed to destruction.

6. The explanation now given is further confirmed by ver. 3, where sentence is passed for the offence described in the preceding verse. In what the offence consisted, if the sons of God were angels, is not very obvious. It is not illicit intercourse which is described; the terms used denote lawful marriage. But if it was wrong for the angels to marry women, the angels surely were the chief offenders; and yet no penalty is denounced upon angels. The divine sentence falls exclusively upon men. There is such an obvious incongruity in this that

Budde [1] insists that ver. 3 is an interpolation and does not belong in this connection, but has been transferred from the account of the fall of our first parents. The incongruity that is alleged, however, does not show the verse to be an interpolation, but simply that the mythological sense which has been given to the passage is false.

7. The word Nephilim, occurring ver. 4, has given rise to the strange deduction that this passage originally stood in no connection with the account of the flood; that the author of it in fact knew of no such event. The only foundation for this inference is that the same word is found again in Num. xiii. 33, in the evil report of the spies respecting Canaan. If the Nephilim here spoken of were still in existence in the days of Moses, how could there have been a catastrophe in the interval which swept away all mankind except the family of Noah? But this rests upon the unproved assumption that the Nephilim of the book of Numbers were lineal descendants of those of Genesis. And on this uncertain basis the author or compiler of Genesis is charged with the absurdity of introducing a passage as preliminary to the deluge, which by its very terms implies that no deluge had taken place. Could he have so grossly mistaken its meaning? Or is it not possible that modern critics may have put a wrong interpretation on these isolated verses? The mere fact that the same term, "Nephilim," is applied both to antediluvians and to Canaanites is a very slender premise on which to base so extraordinary a conclusion. The word is obscure in its meaning and its derivation. It is more probably an appellative or descriptive term than a gentile noun. The LXX. translates it "giants;" other old Greek versions render it "assailants" or "violent men." It does not occur again in the narrative of the conquest of Canaan, as though it were the proper name of a tribe,

[1] Biblische Urgeschichte, p. 30.

but only in the report of the spies, whose excited imagination could best express the terror inspired by these men of great stature and powerful frame by saying that they were the old giants revived.

It is further to be observed that the Nephilim are not said to have sprung from the union of the sons of God with the daughters of men. The statement is that the Nephilim were in the earth prior to these intermarriages, and also after these intermarriages had taken place. But it is not said that they were in any case the fruit of such marriages. The critics, however, tell us that though this is not expressly stated, it is implied. This is by no means necessarily so. But suppose it to be granted; the mythological interpretation is an impossibility nevertheless. The idea that the Nephilim were a superhuman race sprung from the union of angels with the daughters of men is completely nullified by the explicit declaration that the Nephilim existed before such marriages took place as well as after. No new species of creature can be intended, therefore, whose origin is traced to the intermarriage of different orders of beings.

8. It is objected that "the daughters of men" must have the same universal sense in ver. 2 as in ver. 1; and that the contrast of "the sons of God" with "the daughters of men" shows that different orders of being are here referred to. But this contrast works precisely the other way. It has been already shown that in Scripture language the sons of God are his chosen people—the God-fearing race. In contrast with them "the daughters of men" are necessarily limited to the rest of mankind, the ungodly mass. Abundant illustrations can be given of the restriction put upon universal terms by their context. In Jer. xxxii. 20 God is said to have set signs and wonders in the land of Egypt, in Israel, and among men. It is said of the wicked (Ps. lxxiii. 5), "They are not in

trouble as men; neither are they plagued like men." In Judg. xvi. 17, Samson says: "If I be shaven I shall become weak and be like all men." No one has ever inferred from these passages that Egypt and Israel, the wicked and Samson, belonged to some other race of beings because they are set in contrast with "men." The universal term is restricted by its connection; and hence the English version properly inserts the word "other" and reads "other men." [1] A precisely parallel case may be found in the sentence pronounced upon the serpent (Gen. iii. 15), "I will put enmity between thee and the woman, and between thy seed and her seed." The seed of the woman interpreted by the following verse and taken in its unlimited sense would denote all her descendants. But the contrast with the seed of the serpent necessarily limits it to those of her race who have not fallen under the power of evil, and of whom alone it can be said that they shall bruise the serpent's head.

9. Whatever interpretation be put upon doubtful expressions in ver. 3, it plainly intimates the divine purpose to inflict some penalty affecting the life of the whole human race. "His days shall be an hundred and twenty years," if spoken of the generation then living, would mean that they should not survive that limit; if of successive generations of men, that this should henceforth be the term of human life. The former is demanded by

[1] Professor Strack (Comment. on Genesis, p. 21) refers likewise to several other passages in which general terms are limited by the connection, e.g., Gen. xiv. 16, "the women and the people," i.e., the rest of the people; or in which the same expression is used first in a universal and then in a restricted sense. In Judg. xix. 30 "the children of Israel" means the entire people, but in the immediately following verses (xx. 1–3) all except Benjamin. In 1 Sam. xiii. 6 "the people" first means the whole, then a portion, and in ver. 7, "all the people" means the rest of the people. So Lev. viii. 15, "the blood" and "the" (rest of the) "blood." Compare Ex. xxix. 12; Lev. iv. 7, 18, 25, 30, 34.

the context. The latter is preferred by critics whose uniform usage is to interpret at variance with the context, if possible. It is here absolutely without support. There is no suggestion anywhere that the duration of human life was ever fixed at one hundred and twenty years. It is contradicted by all that is recorded of the ages of subsequent patriarchs from Noah to Jacob. This verse, then, explicitly points to a catastrophe, in which that whole generation should be involved, and which should take place in one hundred and twenty years.

10. Finally, it is to be remarked that the argument for diversity of writers is not here rested in any measure upon differences of diction and style. The attempt which is made in this connection to analyze one of the so-called Pentateuchal documents still further into primitive and secondary portions, and to assign vi. 1–4, with a few other brief passages, to J', in distinction from J'', is stoutly resisted by Dr. Dillmann,[1] who says, " Aim, the writer's style and linguistic peculiarities are alike throughout the alleged older and more recent J passages ; and one cannot see how the later writer could succeed in imitating the primitive document in so deceptive a manner ; moreover, the differences between the passages of the alleged primitive document are actually much greater than between it and that which is alleged to be secondary." Budde,[2] too, has pointed out in detail the exact conformity of vi. 1, 2, in all its clauses and expressions, to the language of other passages, which are ascribed by the critics to the document J.

This passage has been considered thus at length in

---

[1] Die Bücher Numeri, Deuteronomium und Josua, p. 632, so, too, Genesis, p. 89, and yet on p. 117 he not very consistently concludes that vs. 1–4 is a paragraph from a more ancient document which J has incorporated into his work, and has modified the style of vs. 1, 2, into conformity with his own.

[2] Biblische Urgeschichte, p. 6.

order to show how futile is the critical allegation that
the opening verses of ch. vi. are imbued with mythological ideas, and have been inserted here from some unknown document, and made to bear a sense at variance
with their original and proper meaning. We have before
seen how groundless is the assertion that iv. 17–24 implies that there had been no deluge. Neither is there
any such implication in xi. 1–9. The further conclusion
that these passages are isolated extracts from a common
source, which knew nothing of any such catastrophe,
falls of itself.

MARKS OF J.

Dillmann finds the following indications of J in vs. 1,
2, 5–8.

1. Jehovah. The divine names will be considered
separately.

2. הֵחֵל begin, also in P (Num. xvii. 11, 12) (E. V. xvi.
46, 47).

3. עַל־פְּנֵי הָאֲדָמָה on the face of the ground. Though
אֲדָמָה is made a criterion of J, and its presence in a passage is held to warrant its reference to J, it nevertheless
occurs in P (Gen. i. 25 ; vi. 20 ; ix. 2). And it is only by
critical artifice that פְּנֵי אֲדָמָה (viii. 13b) is excluded from
P, though it is enclosed between vs. 13a, 14, which are
both attributed to P, and it is the direct continuation of
13a, and is in structure conformed to vi. 12, P. The
occurrence of אֶרֶץ in 13a and of אֲדָמָה in 13b does not
justify the assumption of different sources any more than
the same change in vii. 3, 4, or in viii. 7, 8 ; see also vs.
9, 11, where no one dreams of a difference of sources.

4. הָאָדָם Though Adam is used as a proper noun in
P, it is also treated as a common noun, and as such has
the article in i. 27 ; vii. 21 ; ix. 5, 6.

5. טוֹב in a physical sense. So in P (Gen. i. 4 ; xxv. 8 ;

Lev. xxvii. 10, 12, 14, 33; Num. xiv. 7; xxxvi. 6). If it is not applied to personal beauty in P, the simple reason is that the critics do not assign to P any passage in which this idea is expressed.

6. יֵצֶר *imagination*. This word occurs but three times in the Hexateuch (Gen. vi. 5; viii. 21; Deut. xxxi. 21), and is uniformly by the critics referred to J.

7. רַק *only*. This word, which occurs repeatedly in J, E, and D, does not chance to be found in the passages attributed to P.

8. הִתְעַצֵּב *to be grieved*. This verb is here found in a J passage (vi. 6). It occurs twice besides in the Hexateuch, once in the same (Hithpael) form (xxxiv. 7), and once in a different species (Niphal) (xlv. 5). The critics claim them all for J, but in so doing have to resort to a somewhat violent procedure. Ch. xxxiv. 7 is in a P connection, the preceding verse and the following verses being given to P; but ver. 7 has this J word, an E phrase, " which ought not to be done " (cf. xx. 9), and a D phrase, " wrought folly in Israel " (Deut. xxii. 21), a combination which is readily explained on the assumption of the unity of the Pentateuch, but on the principles of the divisive critics is sufficiently puzzling. So without more ado the refractory verse is cut out of the connection to which it manifestly belongs, and the entire conglomerate is made over to J. Gen. xlv. 5 is in an E connection, and contains what are regarded as E characteristics, but is split in two in order to give this verb to J.

9. מָחָה *blot out, destroy*. See under chs. vi.–ix., Marks of P, No. 19.

10. מָצָא חֵן *find favor*. It is not surprising that this expression, which naturally has its place chiefly in narrative sections, does not occur in P, to which only occasional scraps of ordinary narrative are assigned. And yet it requires some nice critical surgery to limit it to J.

Gen. xxxiv. 11 is in a P connection. Shechem there continues the entreaty begun by his father (vs. 8–10, P), and the sons of Jacob make reply to Shechem as well as to his father (vs. 13–18, P). Nevertheless this verse is sundered from its connection and given to J on account of this very phrase.

11. "Human feelings attributed to God" (vi. 6, 8). Elohim is the general term for God, and describes him as the creator of the world and its universal governor, while Jehovah is his personal name, and that by which he has made himself known as the God of a gracious revelation. Hence divine acts of condescension to men and of self-manifestation are more naturally associated with the name Jehovah; whence it follows that anthropopathies and anthropomorphisms occur chiefly in Jehovah sections. But there is no inconsistency between the ideas which these are intended to suggest and the most spiritual and exalted notions of the Most High. The loftiest conceptions of God are, throughout the Scriptures, freely combined with anthropomorphic representations. His infinite condescension is no prejudice to his supreme exaltation. These are not different ideas of God separately entertained by different writers, but different aspects of the divine Being which enter alike into every true conception of him. The writer of 1 Sam. xv. 35 does not hesitate to say, "Jehovah repented," though he had said but a few verses before (ver. 29), "he is not a man that he should repent." The prophet Amos describes Jehovah's majestic greatness in lofty terms (v. 8), and yet speaks of his repenting (vii. 3), and of his smelling the odors of Israel's offerings (v. 21). "Jehovah smelled a sweet savour" (Gen. viii. 21, J), is identical in thought and language with the constant phrase of the ritual, "a sweet savour unto Jehovah" (Lev. i. 13, P; cf. Lev. xxvi. 31). There is, accordingly, no incompatibility between

the representations of God as Jehovah and as Elohim. These supplement and complete each other, and there is not the slightest reason for imputing them to the variant conceptions of distinct writers.

Jehovah is used in vs. 3, 5–8 because the reference is to his plan of grace and salvation, which the growing wickedness of men threatened to defeat : in order to prevent this frustration of his purpose he determines to destroy the entire human race with the exception of righteous Noah. Elohim is used in ver. 2, because of the contrast between the human and the divine, those of an earthly and those of a heavenly mind—between the daughters of *men* and the sons of *God*.

III

THE GENERATIONS OF NOAH (CH. VI. 9–IX. 29)

THE FLOOD (CH. VI. 9–IX. 17)

IN the passages hitherto examined the portions referred respectively to P and J have been separate sections ; and an ostensible ground of partition has been found in the alternation of divine names, in difference of subject, or in the varied treatment of the same theme. But now and henceforward P and J are supposed to be blended in what has every appearance of being one consistent and continuous narrative. And great critical tact and skill are needed to separate what has been so intimately joined together. Nevertheless the narrative of the deluge is counted one of the firmest supports of the divisive hypothesis. It is affirmed that—

1. When properly disentangled chs. vi.–ix. will be found to contain two entirely distinct accounts of the deluge, each complete in itself, and that these differ irreconcilably in several respects.

2. There are repetitions which show that two different accounts have been put together.

3. The alternation of divine names in successive paragraphs shows that these have proceeded from different writers.

4. The same thing can be inferred from diversities of language and style.

THE CRITICAL PARTITION OF GEN. VI. 5–IX. 17.

The Prophetic Narrator, J, in Italic.
The Priestly Writer, P, in Roman.
The Redactor in Brackets.

VI. 5. *And the LORD saw that the wickedness of man was great in the earth, and that every imagination of the thoughts of his heart was only evil continually.* 6. *And it repented the LORD that he had made man on the earth, and it grieved him at his heart.* 7. *And the LORD said, I will blot out man whom I have created from the face of the ground* [both man and beast, and creeping thing, and fowl of the heaven] *; for it repenteth me that I have made them.* 8. *But Noah found grace in the eyes of the LORD.*

9. THESE ARE THE GENERATIONS OF NOAH:

Noah was a righteous man, perfect in his generations: Noah walked with God. 10. And Noah begat three sons, Shem, Ham, and Japheth. 11. And the earth was corrupt before God, and the earth was filled with violence. 12. And God saw the earth, and, behold, it was corrupt; for all flesh had corrupted his way upon the earth. 13. And God said unto Noah, The end of all flesh is come before me; for the earth is filled with violence through them; and behold, I will destroy them with the earth. 14. Make thee an ark of gopher wood; rooms shalt thou make in the ark, and shalt pitch it within and without with pitch. 15. And this is how thou shalt make it: the length of the ark three hundred cubits, the breadth of it fifty cubits, and the height of it thirty cubits. 16. A light shalt thou make to the ark, and to a cubit shalt thou finish it upward; and the door of the ark shalt thou set in the side thereof; with lower, second, and third stories shalt thou make it. 17. And I, behold, I do bring the flood of waters upon the earth, to destroy all flesh, wherein is the breath of life, from under heaven; every thing that is in the earth shall die. 18. But I will establish my covenant with thee; and thou shalt come into the ark, thou, and thy sons, and thy wife, and thy son's wives with thee. 19. And of every living thing of all flesh, two of every sort shalt thou bring into the ark, to keep them alive with thee; they shall be male and female. 20. Of the fowl after their kind, and of the cattle after their kind, of every creeping thing of the ground after his kind, two of every sort shall come unto thee, to keep them alive. 21. And take thou unto thee of all food that is eaten, and gather it to thee; and it shall be for food for thee and for them. 22. Thus did Noah; according to all that God commanded him, so did he.

VII. 1. *And the LORD said unto Noah, Come thou and all thy house into the ark; for thee have I seen righteous before me in this generation. 2. Of every clean beast thou shalt take to thee seven and seven, the male and his female: and of the beasts that are not clean two, the male and his female: 3. also of the fowl of the heaven, seven and seven, male and female; to keep seed alive upon the face of all the earth. 4. For yet seven days, and I will cause it to rain upon the earth forty days and forty nights; and every living thing that I have made will I destroy from off the face of the ground. 5. And Noah did according to all that the LORD commanded him.* 6. And Noah was six hundred years old when the flood of waters was upon the earth. 7. *And Noah went in, and his sons, and his wife, and his sons' wives with him, into the ark, because of the waters of the flood.* 8. [*Of clean beasts, and of beasts that are not clean, and of fowls, and of every thing that creepeth upon the ground* 9. *there went in two and two, unto Noah into*

the ark, male and female, as God commanded Noah]. 10.
*And it came to pass after the seven days, that the waters of
the flood were upon the earth.* 11. In the six hundredth
year of Noah's life, in the second month, on the seventeenth day of the month, on the same day were all the
fountains of the great deep broken up, and the windows
of heaven were opened. 12. *And the rain was upon the
earth forty days and forty nights.* 13. In the selfsame day
entered Noah, and Shem, and Ham, and Japheth, the
sons of Noah, and Noah's wife, and the three wives of
his sons with them, into the ark ; 14. they, and every
beast after his kind, and all the cattle after their kind,
and every creeping thing that creepeth upon the earth
after his kind, and every fowl after his kind, every bird
of every sort. 15. And they went in unto Noah into the
ark, two and two of all flesh, wherein is the breath of
life. 16. And they that went in, went in male and female
of all flesh, as God commanded him : *and the LORD shut
him in.* 17. *And the flood was forty days upon the earth ;
and the waters increased, and bare up the ark, and it was
lift up above the earth.* 18. And the waters prevailed,
and increased greatly upon the earth ; and the ark went
upon the face of the waters. 19. And the waters prevailed exceedingly upon the earth ; and all the high
mountains, that were under the whole heaven, were
covered. 20. Fifteen cubits upward did the waters pre-
vail ; and the mountains were covered. 21. And all
flesh died that moved upon the earth, both fowl, and
cattle, and beast, and every creeping thing that creepeth
upon the earth, and every man. 22. *All in whose nostrils
was the breath of the spirit of life, of all that was in the
dry land, died.* 23. *And every living thing was destroyed
which was upon the face of the ground* [*both man, and
cattle, and creeping thing, and fowl of the heaven*] *; and
they were destroyed from the earth: and Noah only was*

left, and they that were with him in the ark. 24. And the waters prevailed upon the earth an hundred and fifty days.

VIII. 1. And God remembered Noah, and every living thing, and all the cattle that were with him in the ark: and God made a wind to pass over the earth, and the waters assuaged; 2. the fountains also of the deep and the windows of heaven were stopped, *and the rain from heaven was restrained;* 3. *and the waters returned from off the earth continually:* and after the end of an hundred and fifty days the waters decreased. 4. And the ark rested in the seventh month, on the seventeenth day of the month, upon the mountains of Ararat. 5. And the waters decreased continually until the tenth month: in the tenth month, on the first day of the month, were the tops of the mountains seen. 6. *And it came to pass at the end of forty days, that Noah opened the window of the ark which he had made:* 7. *and he sent forth the raven, and it went forth to and fro, until the waters were dried up from off the earth.* 8. *And he sent forth the dove from him, to see if the waters were abated from off the face of the ground;* 9. *but the dove found no rest for the sole of her foot, and she returned unto him to the ark, for the waters were on the face of the whole earth: and he put forth his hand, and took her, and brought her in unto him into the ark.* 10. *And he stayed yet other seven days; and again he sent forth the dove out of the ark;* 11. *and the dove came in to him at eventide; and, lo, in her mouth an olive leaf pluckt off: so Noah knew that the waters were abated from off the earth.* 12. *And he stayed yet other seven days; and sent forth the dove; and she returned not again unto him any more.* 13. And it came to pass in the six hundred and first year, in the first month, the first day of the month, the waters were dried up from off the earth; *and Noah removed the covering of the ark, and looked, and, behold, the face of the ground was dried.* 14. And in the second month, on the seven and twentieth day of the month, was the earth dry.

15. And God spake unto Noah, saying, 16. Go forth of the ark, thou, and thy wife, and thy sons, and thy sons' wives with thee. 17. Bring forth with thee every living thing that is with thee of all flesh, both fowl, and cattle, and every creeping thing that creepeth upon the earth ; that they may breed abundantly in the earth, and be fruitful, and multiply upon the earth. 18. And Noah went forth, and his sons, and his wife, and his sons' wives with him : 19. every beast, every creeping thing, and every fowl, whatsoever moveth upon the earth, after their families, went forth out of the ark. 20. *And Noah builded an altar unto the LORD ; and took of every clean beast, and of every clean fowl, and offered burnt- offerings on the altar.* 21. *And the LORD smelled the sweet savour ; and the LORD said in his heart, I will not again curse the ground any more for man's sake, for that the imagination of man's heart is evil from his youth ; neither will I again smite any more every thing living, as I have done.* 22. *While the earth remaineth, seed-time and harvest, and cold and heat, and summer and winter, and day and night shall not cease.*

IX. 1. And God blessed Noah and his sons, and said unto them, Be fruitful, and multiply, and fill the earth. 2. And the fear of you and the dread of you shall be upon every beast of the earth, and upon every fowl of the heaven, even all that moveth upon the ground, and all the fishes of the sea; into your hand are they de- livered. 3. Every moving thing that liveth shall be food for you; as the green herb have I given you all. 4. But flesh with the life thereof, the blood thereof, shall ye not eat. 5. And surely your blood of your lives will I require; at the hand of every beast will I require it, and at the hand of man; at the hand of every man's brother will I require the life of man. 6. Whoso sheddeth man's blood, by man shall his blood be shed: for in the image of God made he man. 7. And you, be ye fruitful, and multiply; bring forth abundantly in the earth, and multiply therein.

8. And God spake unto Noah, and to his sons with him, saying, 9. And I, behold, I establish my covenant with you, and with your seed after you: 10. and with every living creature that is with you, the fowl, the cattle, and every beast of the earth with you; of all that go out of the ark, even every beast of the earth. 11. And I will establish my covenant with you; neither shall all flesh be cut off any more by the waters of the flood; neither shall there any more be a flood to destroy the earth. 12. And God said, This is the token of the covenant which I make between me and you and every living creature that is with you, for perpetual generations: 13. my bow have I set in the cloud, and it shall be for a token of a covenant between me and the earth. 14. And it shall come to pass, when I bring a cloud over the earth, that the bow shall be seen in the cloud, 15. and I will remember my covenant, which is between me and you and every living creature of all flesh; and the waters shall no more become a flood to destroy all flesh. 16. And the bow shall be in the cloud; and I will look upon it, that I may remember the everlasting covenant between God and every living creature of all flesh that is upon the earth. 17. And God said unto Noah, This is the token of the covenant, which I have established between me and all flesh that is upon the earth.

J NOT CONTINUOUS.

Let us now examine the portion of the narrative which is assigned to J, and see whether it gives a complete account of the flood, with no breaks or interruptions. It begins with vi. 5–8. We read in ver. 8, "But Noah found grace in the eyes of the LORD." This implies that the reader had already been made acquainted with Noah. And so he had in the scriptural account, which details his ancestry in ch. v.; but this is given by the critics to P. No previous mention of Noah, or allusion to him is made in the sections attributed to J; yet here he is spoken of as a well-known personage. Evidently something is wanting in J corresponding to what has been abstracted from preceding chapters and assigned to P. The critics endeavor to escape this difficulty by alleging that v. 29, in which Noah is mentioned, belongs to J. But in doing so they violate their own test. It is one of their criteria for distinguishing these documents that in J the mother gives name to the child, but in P the father; see Dillmann on Gen. xvi. 11. Consequently, on their own principles, "And he (Lamech) called his name Noah" must belong to P, and not to J. In ver. 7 we are told that the redactor has inserted the second clause, "both man and beast, and creeping thing, and fowl of the heaven," because such detailed enumerations are foreign to J's supposed style. This is a confession that the text in its present form cannot on critical principles be assigned to J. It does not suit the hypothesis, but must be amended into conformity with the hypothesis. In other words, the hypothesis must here be supported by an inference drawn from the hypothesis. But this clause, though unwelcome to the critics, cannot be omitted from the verse, for the plural pronoun "them" at the end of it refers to these particulars in this second clause, not merely to "man" in the first clause, which would call for a pronoun in the singular; see "his heart," ver. 5.

If, however, we take ver. 7 as the critics have corrected it, leaving out the second clause, then it declares that the

LORD said, not to Noah but to himself, *i.e.*, he resolved,
that he would destroy man, no mention being made of
the way in which this was to be effected, nor whether the
inferior creatures would be involved.   J then springs at
once to vii. 1, where " the LORD said to Noah, Come thou
and all thy house into the ark ; " though there is no
previous allusion in J to the fact that Noah had a family,
or that there was an ark, or any occasion for there being
an ark.   To be sure, all this has been explained before ;
vi. 10 speaks of Noah's three sons, and vs. 13–22 tell
how God told Noah of the coming flood and bid him
build an ark for the safety of his house and the various
species of living things, and that Noah did so.   But all
this is assigned to P; there is not a word of it in J.
Clearly there is something missing in J ; and just that is
missing which has been abstracted from the previous
narrative and given by the critics to P.

In vs. 7–10 we have J's account of Noah's entry into
the ark.   But ver. 9, we are told, has been manipulated
by the redactor.   The words "there went in two and
two," "male and female" and " God " are characteristics
of P.   Here again the text is not in accord with the hypothesis ; a number of P's words and expressions are in
a J paragraph, and it must be the fault of the redactor.
But this is not all.   There is not a verse in the paragraph which is just as it should be, if the critics are
right.   The detailed enumeration, " Noah and his sons,
and his wife, and his sons' wives " (ver. 7), instead of
simply Noah and all his house, as ver. 1, is foreign to J ;
so in ver. 8, " beasts and fowls and every thing that creepeth," instead of " every living thing," as ver. 4 ; and
" waters of the flood "[1] (vs. 7, 10) refer back to P's

---

[1] Nöldeke says that the agreement of J and P is very remarkable in
the words מַבּוּל *flood*, תֵּבָה *ark*, and נֹחַ *Noah*.   Budde and Dillmann
try to escape the admission that ver. 7, J, refers back to ver. 6, P, by
arbitrarily transposing ver. 10 so as to stand before ver. 7.

phrase, vi. 17 ; vii. 6. It is said that the redactor "apparently designed to bring the style a little more closely into harmony with that of P." But why he should be so concerned just here to alter expressions which he leaves unchanged elsewhere, does not appear. And it is particularly surprising that he should of his own motion introduce what the critics consider a discrepancy into J's account. How could he make J appear to say in vs. 8, 9, "of clean beasts and of beasts that are not clean . . . there went in two and two unto Noah into the ark," in open contradiction, as the critics allege, with what he had said just before in ver. 2,[1] that clean beasts were to go in seven and seven, and of beasts not clean two? And yet we are told that the documents "are woven together in a highly artistic manner," and the redactor's work is "admirably" done. If this is so, he must have been an intelligent person and could not have made grossly contradictory statements within the compass of a few lines without perceiving it. He certainly could have seen nothing of the sort here, or he would not gratuitously have inserted a discrepancy in the text of his own accord, which was not there in the document from which he was copying. And if he did not see it, perhaps there is no contradiction after all. It may be that the critics are mistaken in fancying that there is one. And in point of fact there is no discrepancy between the general statement that two of every species, a male and a female, entered the ark and the more particular declaration that there were seven of every species of clean beasts and two of those that were not clean. If, then, the redactor is in harmony with J (vii. 2, 3), there is no discrepancy between J (vii. 2, 3) and P (vi. 19 ; vii. 15).

---

[1] Kayser, p. 8, enlarges the text of vii. 3, to restore it to what he conceives to be its primitive form. So, too, he modifies the text of vii. 7-9 into what he considers its primitive form. The fact that it is not as he would reconstruct it, shows the falsity of his critical presuppositions.

In what follows, the semblance of continuity can only be made out for J by means of scattered sentences and clauses torn from their connection in an arbitrary manner. Thus J proceeds to ver. 12, and then skips to 16b: " And the rain was upon the earth forty days and forty nights . . . and the LORD shut him in." It is natural to ask why the LORD waited forty days before he shut the door of the ark behind Noah. It is obvious that the last clause of ver. 16 has no proper connection with ver. 12, to which the critics attach it. It plainly belongs where it stands in the text. The severance of ver. 16 annuls the significant and evidently intended contrast of the two divine names in this verse, to the significance of which Delitzsch calls attention, thus discrediting the basis of the critical analysis, which he nevertheless accepts. Animals of every species went into the ark, as Elohim, the God of creation and providence directed, mindful of the preservation of what he had made ; Jehovah, the guardian of his people, shut Noah in.

The rise of the waters of the flood is depicted in vs. 17–20 in four successive stages. The critics arbitrarily sunder one of these (ver. 17) from the rest, and assign it to J. The destruction accomplished by the flood is similarly described in three successive statements of growing intensity (vs. 21–23). Two of these are parted from the remaining one and given to J (vs. 22, 23).

The next clause of J is viii. 2b, " and the rain from heaven was restrained." Just before we read in vii. 24, " the waters prevailed upon the earth an hundred and fifty days." The critics find a discrepancy between this and vii. 4, 12, according to which it rained forty days. The intelligent redactor has been at fault here again. He has inserted this clause respecting the stopping of the rain in the wrong place. It should have preceded vii. 24, instead of following it. But we may shelter ourselves behind him once more. If he saw no impropriety in putting this clause where he did, perhaps there was none. He may not thus have brought J into conflict with himself after all. If it had been said that the rain from heaven was not restrained after one hundred and fifty days had passed, there would, indeed, have been a discrepancy. But where is the discrepancy in saying that it had stopped?

The last clause of viii. 2 is separated from the first, one being given to J, and the other to P. But this is severing what of necessity belongs together. We find the same combination here as in vii. 11, 12, where the sources of the flood are described, and the critics split them asunder after the same fashion. These sources were two, viz.: the rushing in of the waters of the ocean upon the land, and the torrents descending from the sky. The tenses of the Hebrew verbs at once indicate to the reader that the bursting forth of the fountains of the great deep and the opening of the windows of heaven are separate items, while the fall of the rain is a sequence of that which just preceded. The opening of the windows of heaven prepares the way for the downpour, but is not the downpour itself. The thought is not complete until the actual fall of rain is added. Comp. Mal. iii. 10. The opening of the windows of heaven cannot, therefore, be attributed to one writer and the rain to another ; both belong indissolubly together. The same is the case with viii. 2 ; the last clause is inseparable from the first. And besides, "the rain *from heaven*" is evidently contrasted with "the fountains of *the deep*," so that the two clauses of the verse are bound together thus again. And ver. 3a cannot be separated from ver. 2. The latter states that the sources of the flood had ceased; but this would not, of itself account for the subsidence of the water. The stopping of the fountains of the deep and of the windows of heaven are purely negative; to this must be added the positive flowing off of the water, if the flood was to be reduced. To sever this clause from P and give it to J, as is done by the critics, leaves P's statement inadequate and incomplete. And the phraseology used shows the same thing; "the waters *returned;*" whither? certainly not to heaven (2b), but to the deep (2a), from which the great body of them had come. So that if the word "returned" is to have anything like its proper force, ver. 3a is tied to 2a, and cannot be severed from it as the critics propose.

Then the sending out of the birds (vs. 6–12) is given to J. In vs. 13, 14, the drying of the earth is stated in two stages; one of these (ver. 13b) is arbitrarily given to J, and the other (ver. 14) to P. J makes no allusion to Noah's leaving the ark, which is another serious break in his narrative. This is spoken of, indeed, in the Scripture account (vs. 15–19); but it is given to P. So that here again we miss in J precisely what has been abstracted by the critics and attributed to the other document. J's account concludes with Noah's sacrifice (vs. 20–22).

Instead, therefore, of a complete account with no interruptions, we find in the portion assigned to J several important gaps created purely by the critical partition; other chasms scantily bridged by scattered clauses torn from their context, in which they are indispensable, or attached to passages where they are inappropriate; expressions which by critical rules cannot belong to J, and require the assumption, which has no other basis than the exigencies of the hypothesis, that the text has been manipulated by the redactor; and discrepancies, so called, which are wholly due to the redactor's gratuitous interference.

P NOT CONTINUOUS

Let us now see how it is with P. The first paragraph assigned to him is vi. 9–22. We here read (vs. 11, 12), " And God saw the earth, and, behold, it was corrupt; " and so corrupt that he was determined to destroy it. The form of expression here is with manifest allusion to i. 31, where P had said, " And God saw every thing that he had made, and, behold, it was very good." The existing state of things is plainly set in designed contrast to the statement made at the creation. But not a word of explanation is offered to account for this dreadful change. It is indeed explained sufficiently in the Scripture narrative. The intervening chapters tell us of the fall, of the growing degeneracy of the ungodly race of Cain, of the infection even of the godly race by intermarriage with the rest. But all this is by the critics attributed to J ; there is nothing of the kind in P. Plainly something is missing here ; and just that is missing which the critics have transferred to another document.

P then proceeds to tell that Noah was instructed to build the ark, which he did, and records his age at the coming of the flood (vii. 6, 11), and his entry with some of all living things into the ark (vs. 13–16).

The sacred writer labors to produce a vivid impression of the enormous rise of the waters of the flood by describing it in four successive stages until it reached the prodigious altitude which it actually attained. First (ver. 17), the water rose sufficiently to float the ark. Then (ver. 18) it rose very much higher still, and the ark mounted aloft upon its surface. Next (ver. 19), it attained such a height as to cover all the high mountains within the entire horizon. Finally (ver. 20), it reached its maximum, fifteen cubits above the mountain-tops.

This regular gradation is broken apart by the critics, who assign the first or lowest stage to J, and the other three stages to P, thus giving to each a truncated description, which when put together match precisely and supply just what before was wanting in each. Is this a lucky accident, or has not this entire description emanated from one mind?

The sacred writer seeks again to give adequate expression to the destruction wrought by the flood by three successive statements of increasing strength. First (ver. 21), he declares with emphatic particularity that all flesh died, fowl and cattle and beast and creeping thing and man. Then (ver. 22), in the most universal terms, "All in whose nostrils was the breath of the spirit of life, of all that was in the dry land, died." Finally (ver. 23), universal and particular terms are combined, and the most forcible expression for complete destruction added in contrast with the sole survivors : "And every living thing was wiped out which was upon the face of the ground, both man and cattle and creeping thing and fowl of the heaven ; and they were wiped out from the earth ; and Noah only was left, and they that were with him in the ark." Disregarding these climactic periods, which are heaped together in order to intensify the contrast of the last clause, the critics give the first of the sentences to P, thus sundering it completely from what follows, the result of which is to make P affirm, in the most absolute manner, the universality of the destruction without so much as a single survivor. The next two verses are given to J in spite of the enumeration of particulars in ver. 23, "both man and cattle and creeping thing and fowl of the heaven," which, according to critical principles, is foreign to his style, and must be thrown out of the text as an insertion by the redactor. The passage does not correspond with the hypothesis, and is hence corrected into conformity with it. And yet this clause, which is objectionable to the critics and which they propose to eliminate, is one of the features of the verse which adapts it to the climactic position that it occupies.

It has before been shown that viii. 2, 3, cannot be partitioned as the critics propose ; and that the severance of vs. 2b, 3, as an insertion from J, would leave P's statement incomplete.

The narrative then proceeds after the same analogy to describe the subsidence of the flood. And it may be proper to note that the seven stages of the decline of the water precisely correspond with the four stages of its rise added to the three statements of its wide-spread desolation. First (viii. 1), a wind passed over the earth, which served to reduce the volume of the water. Secondly (vs. 2–4), the sources of the flood had ceased, and the water flowed off to such an extent that the ark rested on the mountains of Ararat. Thirdly (ver. 5), the water still further decreased and the tops of the mountains appeared. Fourthly (vs. 6–9), as the water continued to sink, a dove was sent forth after forty days, but the flood was still at such a height that no resting-place could be found. Fifthly (vs. 10, 11), after seven days more the water had abated sufficiently for trees to emerge, as was shown by the olive leaf plucked off by the dove. Sixthly (ver. 12), the dove was sent out and returned no more. Seventh, and finally (ver. 13), the day is noted on which Noah discovered that the water was dried up from off the earth. This regular gradation is spoiled by the critics, who assign (vs. 6–12) the mission of the birds, to J ; the consequence of which is that P springs at once from ver. 5, the first appearance of the mountain-tops, to ver. 13, where the waters were dried up from off the earth.

The prominence given to the sending out of the birds

in the Chaldean account of the deluge, which is universally confessed to stand in an intimate relation to that in Genesis, further shows that any narrative of the flood would be incomplete if this were not included. Least of all can this be questioned by those who maintain that the Hebrew narrative was borrowed from the Chaldean.

The paragraph respecting the birds (viii. 6–12) is quite devoid of any critical marks allying it to one or the other of the documents, as is apparent from the history of its treatment. From Astruc and Eichhorn to the supplementary critics Tuch and Knobel, it was almost uniformly assigned to P. Stähelin is uncertain about it. Reuss regards it as the sole surviving remnant of a third account of the flood, distinct from the other two. Hupfeld gives (ver. 7) the raven to J, and (vs. 8–12) the dove to P. Friedrich Delitzsch reverses the matter, and gives the raven to P and the dove to J. Kayser, Wellhausen, Kuenen, Dillmann, and others assign the whole to J, in which they were preceded by the eccentric Ilgen. The motive which at present inclines the majority to J, appears to be twofold. Such a graphic incident is thought to befit the more " picturesque " narrator, and this is the most striking parallel with the cuneiform tablets, with which J is held to stand in the closest relation. Both an argument and an inference are supplied from these two points of view of a somewhat circular character. It is assigned to J because he is picturesque and allied to the tablets ; and being so assigned proves him to be picturesque and allied to the tablets. One cannot but feel that if the critics had anything to gain by so doing, they might with equal ease have imputed to the writer of this paragraph an alleged characteristic of P, and said that his style was " stereotyped," and abounding in " regular formulas " and the " repetition of like phrases," thus : " And he sent forth the raven " (ver. 7) ; cf. " and he sent forth the dove " (ver. 8) ; " and he stayed yet other seven days and sent forth the dove " (twice, vs. 10, 12) ; " waters were abated from off the face of the ground " (twice, vs. 8, 11), cf. also ver. 9 ; " to him into the ark " (twice, ver. 9) ; " going and returning," (twice (in Heb.), vs. 3, 7), cf. ver. 5.

The drying of the ground is likewise stated in two successive stages. First (ver. 13), the surface was so far dried that the water had disappeared. Then (ver. 14), the earth was dry. These are, as before stated, divided by the critics between J and P.

P proceeds to tell of Noah's leaving the ark (vs. 15–19). But he records no act of worship or thanksgiving for this great deliverance. Yet he had spoken of Noah as a righteous man, who walked with God (vi. 9). In fact, throughout the entire patriarchal history P never mentions an altar or sacrifice or any act of worship. These are, indeed, spoken of repeatedly in the sacred history ; but they are invariably referred to other documents, never to P. And yet P, according to the critics, is the priestly writer, who is especially interested in ritual worship and in ceremonial matters. It is he who records the institution of the Sabbath (ii. 3), and of circumcision (xvii. 10), and the prohibition of eating blood (ix. 4) ; and he never relates anything derogatory to the patriarchs, but always exalts them as model men of God. Is it conceivable that he should have omitted to mention that Noah devoutly praised God for his merciful interposition on his behalf ? Surely there has been an omission here ; and the more evidently so, as a sacrifice is so prominent a feature in the Chaldean account of the deluge.

It thus appears also that there are serious chasms in P's account likewise, that the symmetry of the narrative is spoiled in repeated instances by the proposed parti-

tion, and that passages are rent from their connection
and assigned to J, which are indispensable in the context in which they stand.

NO SUPERFLUOUS REPETITIONS.

It is further claimed that there are repetitions which
betray the composite character of the narrative, and show
that it has been made up by combining two separate accounts. But this is a mistake; there are no superfluous
repetitions to warrant such a conclusion. We are pointed
in the first instance to the opening verses. It is said
that vi. 5–7 contains J's account of the wickedness of
man and of the LORD's purpose to destroy the race ; then
follows, in vs. 11–13, P's account of the very same thing ;
but a slight consideration of the circumstances will make
it appear that the critics' conclusion is altogether unwarranted. The title (vi. 9), " These are the generations of
Noah," marks the beginning of a new section of the history, and indicates its subject to be the fortunes of Noah's
family. In entering upon this topic the writer first explains the situation with the view of placing distinctly
before the minds of his readers at the outset the causes
of what was about to take place. He commences by
stating the character of Noah (ver. 9b [1]), which explains
the intimation in ver. 8 of the special favor shown to him.
He then recapitulates some statements previously made,
which are necessary to the understanding of the following narrative. He speaks of Noah's three sons (ver. 10),
though they had been named in identical terms in v. 32,
which the critics likewise refer to P; no one thinks of

---

[1] Kayser (p. 8) says : "Noah was a righteous man and perfect in his
generations," belongs to J (see vii. 1) ; "Noah walked with God," to P,
(v. 21). Other critics quietly ignore this identity of expressions, and
give the entire verse, which manifestly belongs together, to P.

a difference of writers because of this repetition. He
further speaks of the universal corruption (vs. 11, 12);
this had already been mentioned at the close of the preceding section (ver. 5) as a sequence from facts previously
stated.[1] But it lay so at the basis of what was to be recorded in this new section that it is mentioned here again,
And there is no more reason for suspecting a diversity of
writers than there is in ver. 10, which all acknowledge to
be by the same writer as v. 32. It is just such a recapitulation as any writer might be expected to make under
the circumstances. On the other hand, ver. 13 is not a
repetition of the statement made in ver. 7, but is an advance upon it. In ver. 7 mention is made of the LORD's
purpose to destroy man; in ver. 13 this purpose is com-
municated to Noah, which is quite another thing.

In vs. 18–20, while directing Noah to build the ark,
God tells him the purpose for which it was to be made,
and that he was to take with him into it some of every
species of living things in order to keep them alive.
After the ark had been built, and the time for sending
the flood drew nigh, the LORD bade Noah to go into it
with his family and with some of every species of animals (vii. 1–3). But there is no superfluous repetition
here. Two distinct divine communications were made
at different times, and each is reported in its proper
place.

The critics, however, lay great stress upon the fact that
the entry into the ark is twice recorded; vs. 7–9[2], they
tell us, is J's account, and vs. 13–16 that of P. But this,
too, is a mistake; there is nothing here requiring the

---

[1] Nöldeke (p. 16) remarks that other sections (v. 1; x. 1, and xi. 27)
in like manner begin with the repetition of what had been before
stated.

[2] Schrader and Dillmann give vs. 8, 9, to R; Nöldeke gives vs. 7–9
to R as his elaboration of the originally brief words of the Jehovist.

supposition of distinct documents. It has been before shown that vs. 7–9 cannot by critical rules be referred to J, without a reconstruction of the text in each individual verse. But besides this it is to be noted that ver. 6 gives a general statement of Noah's age at the coming of the flood; he was then six hundred years old. In ver. 11 this is stated again with more particularity, in order to indicate the precise day on which the flood began, viz., the six hundredth year of Noah's life, the second month, the seventeenth day of the month. The critics do not find this repetition incompatible with the sameness of the writer; vs. 6 and 11 are both alike referred by them to P. In precisely the same manner, with the view of exhibiting the precision of the divine arrangements, the sacred writer points out .the fact in vs. 13–16 that Noah and all his company entered the ark on the self-same day on which the flood broke forth; and the emphasis which he puts upon this thought appears from the particularity of detail and the iteration in these verses. Now why should this repetition for this evident purpose be any more suggestive of a diversity of writers than the like repetition in regard to Noah's age?

The critics are embarrassed here by their own hypothesis. Different views have been entertained in respect to the relation of J and P. According to some critics J and P each wrote a separate and independent document, and these, after circulating singly for a time, were at length combined by a redactor. These are known as documentary critics. Others have held that J did not write a complete document of his own, but simply edited an enlarged edition of P. The document P was made the basis, to which J simply made additions, supplementing it here and there as he had occasion. These are known as supplementary critics.

In the case before us the documentary make this point

against the supplementary critics, that no editor in supplementing a pre-existing work, would introduce of his own motion what was already in almost identical terms in the work before him. Such a superfluous repetition could only be accounted for by supposing that a redactor was combining two works, for each of which he had a great reverence, so that he was reluctant to omit anything that either of them contained. Thus it came to pass that after copying a statement from one of his sources he finds the same thing stated likewise in the other, and copies it also. This has a plausible sound. It certainly silences the supplementary critics. But there are two insuperable difficulties in the way of accepting the solution which the documentary critics offer. 1. Judged by their own critical rules the compiler has not preserved what was peculiar to J in vs. 7–10, but has conformed it throughout to the style of P. 2. In other cases he has not shown a similar care to preserve all the contents of his sources. Why has he not given a duplicate account of the building of the ark, or of the exit from it, as well as of the entry into it? The obvious reason is that in the former there was no coincidence in time to emphasize, as there was in the latter. Hence the emphatic repetition in the one, whereas there was no occasion for it in the others.

It has before been shown that the statements respecting the rise of the waters, their destructiveness, and their subsequent fall cannot be parcelled between different writers; and that the attempt to find two parallel accounts of these particulars by J and by P is not successful. The verses and clauses which are given to J cannot be sundered from the context in which they stand. Moreover, the description of successive stages is not identical repetition, and as such suggestive of distinct documents. And if it were, four statements of the rise of the waters, three of their destructive effects, and seven of their fall, cannot be distributed between two documents without leaving repetitions in each. More than two documents are necessary, if each repetition is indicative of a separate writer. The critical argument is in this case plainly self-destructive.

It should also be observed that like repetitions are found in other cases which the critics quietly ignore, and never think of tracing to a diversity of documents. Thus the corruption and violence prevailing in the earth is stated four times in as many successive clauses (vi. 11, 12); the entry of all living things into the ark with Noah is repeated three times (vii. 14–16), where Dillmann remarks, "It is as though the author, moved by the momentous character of the day, could not do enough to satisfy himself in the detailed portraiture of the transaction." God's establishment of his covenant with Noah is twice stated, (ix. 9, 11); and the bow in the cloud as the token of the covenant is mentioned again and again (ix. 12–17). In all these cases the critics recognize but one writer. So, too, the triple mention of the names of Noah's sons (v. 32; vi. 10; x. 1) is given to P; the fourth mention of the same (ix. 18) being assigned to J. A rule which plays fast and loose in this manner at the pleasure of the operator, is a very insecure dependence.

It has also been claimed that Noah's sacrifice and the LORD's resolve not to destroy all living things again (viii. 20–22), are parallel to God's blessing Noah, and his covenant not to send another universal flood (ix. 1–17); and that the former is the account of J, and the latter that of P respecting the same thing. But these are not the same; one is the sequel of the other; viii. 21, 22 states the divine purpose, that "the LORD said in his heart;" in ix. 1–17 this purpose is made known to Noah.

The examination of the narrative of the flood thus

shows that so far from everything being duplicated, nothing is duplicated from first to last. except the entry into the ark, and that for a special reason not suggestive of two documents but excluding them.

THE DIVINE NAMES

It is still further urged that the alternation of divine names in successive paragraphs of this narrative gives evidence of its composite character. It is affirmed that this requires the assumption of two different writers, who were in the habit of using different terms in speaking of the Most High. One (P) always spoke of him as "God" (Heb., Elohim); the other (J) as LORD (Heb., Jehovah). The narrative, as we possess it, has been made up from the combination of the accounts in these two documents; and hence the blending of these two names, as they are here found. But this is a superficial and mechanical explanation of what is really due to a different and more satisfactory cause.

There are two aspects, under which the flood can be contemplated, and two points of view from which its place and function in the sacred history can be regarded. It may be looked upon as the act of the Creator, destroying the work of his hands because it had become corrupt and so perverted from its original intent, and at the same time providing for the perpetuation of the several species of living things. Or, on the other hand, it may be considered in its relation to the work of redemption. The wickedness of man threatened to put an end to the scheme of grace and salvation; in order to prevent his merciful designs from being thwarted thus, the Most High resolved to destroy the ungodly race, and rescue the one surviving pious family to be the seed of a new race, among whom true religion might be nurtured until it

should ultimately fill the whole earth. The sacred writer
has both these aspects of this great catastrophe in
mind, and he suggests them to his readers by the alternate use of the divine names. When he has regard to
the divine government and providential care, as manifested in it, he speaks of it as the act of Elohim. When
he has regard to his special guardianship over the pious,
or to aught that concerns divine worship, he uses the
sacred name Jehovah.

Thus it is Elohim who sees with displeasure the dis-
order introduced by the corruption of mankind, and
makes known his purpose to destroy them, but institutes
measures for preserving the various species of animals
by means of an ark to be built for this end (vi. 9–22).
It is Elohim agreeably to whose command creatures of
both sexes went in unto Noah into the ark (vii. 9, 16).
It is Elohim who remembered Noah and every living
thing that was with him in the ark, and who made a wind
pass over the earth to assuage the waters (viii. 1). It is
Elohim who bade Noah go forth of the ark, and bring
forth with him every living thing that they may multiply upon the earth (viii. 15–17). It is Elohim who
blessed Noah and his sons, as he had blessed man at his
creation (i. 28), bidding them Be fruitful, and multiply,
and replenish the earth (ix. 1). It is Elohim who established his covenant with Noah and with every living
creature, pledging that there should be no flood in future
to destroy all flesh (ix. 8–17).

On the other hand, it is Jehovah (E. V., the LORD), in
whose eyes Noah found grace (vi. 8), and who was resolved to put a sudden end to the downward progress of
growing wickedness which infected every imagination of
the thoughts of man's heart and threatened to banish
piety from the earth (vs. 5–7). It is Jehovah who bade
righteous Noah come with all his house into the ark,

and take with him animals fit for sacrifice in larger numbers than the rest (vii. 1–3). It is Jehovah who shut Noah in, after he had entered the ark (ver. 16), though in the very same verse it is Elohim who commanded that the beasts of both sexes should enter in. It is Jehovah to whom Noah builds an altar and offers sacrifice, and who graciously accepts the offering (vs. 20, 21).

It thus appears that the divine names are discriminatingly employed throughout the entire narrative; there are no superfluous repetitions, suggestive of a combination of distinct documents; there are serious gaps and halting-places in each of the accounts, into which the critics propose to divide the history of the deluge; and in numerous instances the partition attempted is impracticable because it would sunder what is plainly indivisible. It is further noteworthy that there is no pretence of basing the critical partition of these chapters on diversity of diction. The scattered clauses assigned to J. which have already been shown to be inseparable from their contexts, have not even this poor pretext in their favor. In fact there is scarcely more than three or four words or phrases in all that is attributed to J in the entire narrative of the deluge which is claimed elsewhere as characteristic of that document; while there are several phrases and forms of speech, as has been already pointed out, that are elsewhere held to be characteristic of P, not to speak of the word " create " (vi. 7), which in ch. i. is made a mark of P in distinction from J.

NO DISCREPANCIES

The attempt is made to create a variance between vi. 5 and ver. 12 by alleging that J attributes the flood to the wickedness of man, but P to the corruption of " all flesh," meaning thereby the entire animal creation as well

as man; and when P speaks of the earth being filled
with violence he refers not merely to human deeds of
violence and crime, but also to the rapacity and ferocity
of beasts which prey upon weaker animals instead of feeding upon the herbage allowed them at their creation (i.
30). But the term "all flesh" has a wider or narrower
meaning as determined by the connection. When it is
said (vii. 21) that "all flesh died" in the flood, men and
animals are both intended. But vii. 15, "two and two of
all flesh went in unto Noah into the ark," has reference
to animals only. And in such phrases as "God of the
spirits of all flesh" (Num. xvi. 22; xxvii. 16; cf. Jer. xxxii.
27); "who is there of all flesh that hath heard the voice
of the living God?" (Deut. v. 23, E. V. 26); "all flesh shall
see the glory of the LORD" (Isa. xl. 5); "I will pour out
my Spirit upon all flesh" (Joel iii. 1, E. V. ii. 28); cf.
also Ps. lvi. 5 (4); lxv. 3 (2); cxlv. 21; Isa. lxvi. 16, 24;
Ezek. xxi. 10 (E. V. 5); Zech. ii. 13, the reference is to all
mankind. This is also evidently the case in Gen. vi. 12,
"all flesh had corrupted his way upon the earth;" for
moral character and responsibility can only be affirmed
of man, not of the inferior animals.

It has before been shown that there is no discrepancy
between the general direction (vi. 19 P), to take a pair of
each kind of animals into the ark in order to preserve
alive the various species, and the more specific requirement, when the time arrived for entering the ark, that
clean beasts should be taken by sevens and the unclean
by twos (vii. 2 J). If it had been said that only two
should be taken of each kind, the case would have been
different. J also relapses into the general form of statement (vii. 9); or if the critics prefer, R does so, which
amounts to the same thing, as by the hypothesis he had
J's previous statement before him. There is no contradiction here any more than there is between the general

and the more exact statement of Noah's age in vii. 6 and 11.

In vii. 10 the flood came seven days, not after Noah entered the ark, but after the announcement, vs. 1–4; so that there is no conflict with vii. 13.

It is alleged that there is a serious variance between J and P in respect to the duration of the flood. According to P (vii. 11) it began on the seventeenth day of the second month, and ended on the twenty-seventh day of the second month of the following year (viii. 13, 14). According to J (vii. 12) it rained forty days, at the end of which (viii. 6–12) Noah sent forth birds at the intervals of three successive periods of seven days, whereupon (ver. 13b) the face of the ground was dried; the flood only lasted, therefore, sixty-one days, or, if the forty days of viii. 6 are additional to the forty of vii. 12, it lasted one hundred and one days, instead of a year and ten days as reckoned by P.

The fallacy of all this is obvious. It is simply parading a part as though it were the whole. "At the end of forty days Noah opened the window of the ark" (viii. 6). Forty days from what? The critics are in doubt whether to reckon from the beginning or the end of the forty days' rain. What, then, is to be thought of the intelligence of R in compiling this narrative? As this verse stands it is not possible to reckon otherwise than from the first day of the tenth month (viii. 5). Adding to this the three periods of seven days, it appears that the dove was sent out for the last time on the first day of the twelfth month. After another month Noah removes the covering of the ark, and in a month and twenty-seven days more he leaves the ark entirely. All is thus in perfect harmony.

The inference of the critics is, besides, quite unfounded upon their own principles. By their own concession J is not complete. His genealogy from Adam to Noah is only preserved in part. His account of building the ark and of Noah's leaving it have been omitted, R not judging it necessary to repeat from J what he had already inserted from P. Whence, then, this sudden confidence that no numbers originally in J have been omitted, notwithstanding the fact that such an assumption gives to his statements a meaning that they cannot now have, sets them in opposition to otherwise uncontradicted statements of P, and convicts R of incapacity or worse?

Just here the perplexity of the critics in respect to vii. 17a is instructive. "The flood was forty days upon the earth," is given entire by Dillmann to J, by Kuenen to R, and with the exception of the words "forty days," by Kautzsch and Socin to P; also by Hupfeld to P without exception, only he insists that the "forty days" must be understood differently from J in vii. 4; Budde gives it to P, but strikes the "forty days" out of the text, and reads "the flood of waters was upon the earth." All is with the design of bringing J and P into conflict regarding the duration of the flood; so that is effected they are not particular about the mode of accomplishing it.

The conjecture that still another estimate of the duration of the flood is intimated in vii. 24, and that the one hundred and fifty days of its increase imply the same length of time for its decrease, so that it must have lasted just three hundred days (see Dillmann, "Genesis," p. 130) is a pure figment with no foundation whatever in the Biblical narrative. The statement is not that the flood continued to increase for one hundred and fifty days, but that having previously reached its full height it continued at its maximum until that time, reckoned from its beginning, and then decreased for seven months and ten days, when the earth was dry.

DIFFERENCE OF DICTION

It is further contended, however, that there are certain characteristics peculiar to each of these so-called documents, which distinguish them from one another in diction, style, mode of conception, and range of ideas; and that these are so marked and constant as to prove diversity of origin. These are most fully and succinctly stated by Dillmann,[1] who has enlarged and corrected the collection diligently gathered by Knobel. He gives the following distinctive marks for the recognition of P in chs. vi.–ix.: (1) The title, vi. 9. (2) Reckoning by the years of Noah's life. (3) The exact statements of time respecting the course of the flood. (4) The measurements of the ark. (5) Weaving in a law, ix. 1–7, and its referring back to i. 27 seq. (6) The covenant and its sign, ix. 8 sqq. (7) Diffuseness and constantly recurring formulæ. (8) The antique description of the sources of the flood, vii. 11; viii. 2; recalling i. 6–8. (9) The image of God, ix. 6. (10) The mode of speaking of Noah's family, vi. 18; vii. 7, 13; viii. 16, 18 (on the contrary, vii. 1). (11) כָּל־בָּשָׂר vi. 12 seq., 17, 19; vii. 15 seq., 21; viii. 17; ix. 11, 15–17. (12) זָכָר וּנְקֵבָה vi. 19; vii. 9, 16. (13) לְמִשְׁפְּחֹתֵיהֶם viii. 19. (14) כֵּן עָשָׂה vi. 22. (15) פָּרָה וְרָבָה viii. 17; ix. 1, 7. (16) הֵקִים בְּרִית or נָתַן vi. 18; ix. 9, 11 seq., 17. (17) You and your seed after you, ix. 9. (18) גָּוַע vi. 17; vii. 21. (19) הִשְׁחִית and שָׁחַת (not מָחָה) vi. 13, 17; ix. 11, 15. (20) הוֹלִיד vi. 10. (21) אָכְלָה vi. 21; ix. 3. (22) חַיָּה wild beast, vii. 14, 21; viii. 1, 17, 19; ix. 2, 5. (23) מִין vi. 20; vii. 14. (24) עֶצֶם self-same, vii. 13. (25) שָׁרַץ and שֶׁרֶץ vii. 21; viii. 17; ix. 7. (26) רָמַשׂ and רֶמֶשׂ vi. 20; vii. 14, 21; viii. 17, 19; ix. 2 seq. (see vi. 7; vii. 8, 23). (27) מְאֹד מְאֹד vii. 19. (28) בְּ used distributively, vii. 21; viii. 17; ix. 10, 15 seq.

[1] Commentary on Genesis.

This certainly has the appearance of a very formidable list. But such lists may prove very delusive. It should be remembered that no piece of composition can be so divided that precisely the same words and phrases and ideas shall occur in each of the parts, and that neither shall contain any that are not to be found in the other. If any such piece should be divided at random, and an elaborate and exhaustive search be instituted to discover what there was in one of the parts that was missing in the other, and *vice versa*, no doubt long lists could be made out of what might be called the characteristic peculiarities of each part. Nevertheless, these would not have the slightest significance, and would have no tendency to prove that these sundered parts ever had a separate and independent existence and were the primal sources from which the composition in question was derived.

More especially is this the case when the partition is made on the basis of certain assumed characteristic differences. It is assumed at the start, we may suppose, that a given production is a composite one, formed by the combination of two pre-existing documents. Two sections respectively assigned to these documents are then compared, and the resulting differences noted as severally characteristic of one or the other. The documents are then made out in detail by the persistent application of the criteria thus furnished. Every paragraph, sentence, or clause, in which any of the one class of characteristics is to be found, is regularly and consistently assigned to the one document, and with like regularity and consistency all, in which any of the other class of characteristics appear, is referred to the other document, the number of the criteria growing as the work proceeds. When now the process is completed, each document will be found to have the assumed series of characteristics for the simple reason that it was throughout constructed by the critic himself upon that pattern. He is arguing in a circle, which of course returns upon itself. He proves the documents by the criteria, and the criteria by the documents; and these match as far as they do because they have been adjusted to one another with the utmost care. But the correspondence may be factitious after all. It may show the ingenuity of the operator, without establishing the objective reality of his conclusions. The documents which he fancies that he has discovered may be purely a creation of his own, and never have had an independent existence.

MARKS OF P

We shall now examine the alleged marks of P *seriatim* with the view of discovering what significance is to be attached to them.

1. The title (vi. 9). (*a*). A like title, " These are the generations," etc., occurs besides in Gen. ii. 4; v. 1; x. 1; xi. 10, 27; xxv. 12, 19; xxxvi. 1, 9; xxxvii. 2; Num. iii. 1, and once out of the Pentateuch in imitation of the phrase as there used.

(*b*). The word " generations " תלדות occurs, apart from the titles just cited, Gen. x. 32; xxv. 13; Ex. vi. 16, 19; xxviii. 10; Num. i. 20–42, and out of the Pentateuch, Ruth iv. 18; 1 Chron. v. 7; vii. 2, 4, 9; viii. 28; ix. 9, 34; xxvi. 31.

These titles are so far from lending any support to the hypothesis that they can only be classed as belonging to P on the prior assumption of the truth of the hypothesis. That in Gen. ii. 4 is assigned to P, not by reason of its environment, but notwithstanding the fact that it is the title of a J section, to which it is assumed that it has been transferred from a former imaginary position at the beginning of ch. i., for which it is not suitable and where

it could never have stood. In xxxvii. 2 it introduces a
section composed of alternate paragraphs of J and E, in
which there is not a single sentence from P until xli. 46,
and then not another till xlvi. 6. In xxv. 19 it is followed
by long passages from J, interspersed with paragraphs
from E, and with scarcely anything from P. Ch. xxxvi.
9 stands at the head of a section about which the critics
are divided ; some refer it to P, others in large part to R
or to JE. The natural inference would seem to be that
these titles, prefixed alike to J and to P sections, were
suggestive of the common authorship of those sections,
or at least that the titles proceeded from him to whom
Genesis owes its present form, be he author or compiler. Hence Kayser [1] says, " The formula ' These are the
generations,' which is commonly regarded as Elohistic,
belongs just as well to the other document." And again,
" This formula, with which the history of Esau or of the
Esauids (xxxvi. 9), as well as the history of Jacob (xxxvii.
2) begins, is not exclusively Elohistic. The Jehovist uses
it here as in xxv. 19, in order to commence a new section
after the death of a patriarch." And the other passages,
in which the word תולדת is found, look in the same direction. Gen. x. 32 occurs at the close of what is considered a J section of a genealogy. Ex. vi. 16, 19 is in a
genealogy which Kayser assigns to R, which in the
judgment of Wellhausen and Kuenen does not belong to
P, but is a later interpolation, and which Dillmann merely
refers to P on the general ground that genealogies as a
rule are to be so referred ; while nevertheless he claims
that the entire context has been seriously manipulated.
Gen. xxv. 13 is in a genealogy which is referred to P on
the same general ground, but is embedded in a J context.
It would seem, consequently, that there is no very solid
ground for the claim that this word is peculiar to P.

[1] Das Vorexilische Buch, pp. 8, 28.

2. " Reckoning by the years of Noah's life."

The arbitrary character of the critical rule that statements of age are to be referred to P appears from the
fact that in repeated instances this is done in defiance of
the context.   Thus Isaac's age at his marriage and at the
birth of his children is cut out of a J context (xxv. 20,
26) ; so that of Joseph when feeding the flock with his
brethren (xxxvii. 2), and when he stood before Pharaoh
(xli. 46), and the length of time that Jacob lived in Egypt
and his age at his death (xlvii. 28) are all severed from a
foreign context, either J or E.   Moreover, the age of Joseph (Gen. l. 26), of Caleb (Josh. xiv. 7, 10), and of
Joshua (Josh. xxiv. 29) is by common critical consent attributed to E.

3. " The exact statements of time respecting the course
of the flood."

(a) P reckons one hundred and fifty days until the
flood began to subside (vii. 24; viii. 3).   But time is
noted with similar exactness in passages referred to the
other documents.   Thus in J seven days until the rain
was to begin, forty days that it was to continue (vii. 4,
10, 12) ; after forty days Noah opened the window of the
ark (viii. 6) ; after seven days he sent forth a dove (vs.
10, 12) ; three months (xxxviii. 24) ; in E twelve years
(Gen. xiv. 4, 5) (so Dillmann) ; seven years (xxix. 20, 27,
30) ; twenty, fourteen, and six years (xxxi. 38, 41) ; two
years (xli. 1) ; seven years (xli. 48, 54) ; two and five
years (xlv. 6).

(b) P notes the month and the day which marked
certain stages of the flood (vii. 11; viii. 4, 5, 13, 14).
But nothing sufficiently momentous to call for such nota-
tion occurs in the rest of Genesis, whether in JE or in
P sections.   And in the remainder of the Hexateuch it is
limited to two things, viz., the annual sacred seasons as
described in detail in the ritual law, and for that reason

assigned to P, and the most signal occurrences in the march of Israel from Egypt to Canaan. Thus the month and day of their leaving Egypt are indicated (Num. xxxiii. 3); of the first gift of manna (Ex. xvi. 1); of the arrival at and departure from Sinai (Ex. xix. 1; Num. x. 11); of setting up the sacred tabernacle (Ex. xl. 2, 17); of numbering the people and organizing the host (Num. i. 1, 18); of the return to Kadesh in the last year of the wandering (Num. xx. 1); of the death of Aaron (Num. xxxiii. 38); of Moses's final exposition of the law (Deut. i. 3); and of the passage of the Jordan just when the predicted term of wandering was complete (Josh. iv. 19). These are all assigned to P in spite of the fact that Ex. xix. 1; Num. xx. 1; Deut. i. 3; Josh. iv. 19 are not in a P context; yet they are severed from their connection and attributed to P because of the prior assumption that "he alone reckons by months and days."

4. " The measurements of the ark."

There is but one other structure of which measures are given in the Pentateuch, viz., the tabernacle and its vessels. And the reason why such detailed statements are made respecting them is not because P had a fancy for recording measures, but because these structures were built by divine direction and on a divine plan which was minutely followed. And this is not the peculiarity of a particular writer, for the author of Kings and the prophet Ezekiel detail in like manner the measures of the temple.

5. " Weaving in a law, ix. 1-7, and its referring back to i. 27 seq."

But the same thing occurs in passages assigned to the other so-called documents; thus in J, the law of marriage is woven into ii. 23, 24; that of levirate marriage, xxxviii. 8; intermarriage with Canaanites disapproved, xxiv. 3, and the institution of sacrifice, ch. iv., viii. 20, 21; in E the payment of tithes, xiv. 20 (referred to E by

Dillmann), xxviii. 22.   And if the reference of ix. 6 to i.
27 links it to P, the reference of xxvii. 45 J to ix. 6 links
it equally to J, and is thus suggestive of the common origin of what the critics consider separate documents.

6. " The covenant and its sign (ix. 8 sqq)."

Three covenants with their appointed signs are spoken
of in the Old Testament, viz.: The covenant with Noah
and the rainbow as its sign, the covenant with Abraham
and his seed and circumcision as its sign (xvii. 10, 11),
and the covenant with Israel and the sabbath as its sign
(Ex. xxxi. 13–17).   These are all referred to P, and no
sections of P but these three make mention of a covenant sign.   If now the absence of this expression from all
the rest of the P sections does not imply difference of
authorship, why should such a significance be attributed
to its absence from the J sections?   But in fact both the
name and the thing are found in sections attributed to J.
Thus Gen. xv. 18, Jehovah made a covenant with Abraham granting him the land of Canaan; and as he asked
for something (ver. 8) whereby he might know that he
should inherit it, a symbol of the divine presence, fire
and smoke, passed between the pieces of the slaughtered
victims, as was customary for contracting parties among
men (Jer. xxxiv. 18, 19).   The word " sign " does not occur in the passage, but Dillmann (" Commentary " in loc.)
correctly calls this " the sign by which the covenant engagement was concluded."   In Ex. iii. 12 E God gives
Moses a sign of his divine commission to deliver Israel.
In Ex. iv. J he gives him a series of signs to confirm the
faith of the people in the same.   The critics assign to P,
with the exception of a few refractory clauses, Ex. xxxi.
12–17, which makes the sabbath the sign of God's covenant with Israel.   And they avow as one of their chief
reasons for doing so (Dillmann in loc.), that P must have
recorded the sign of the Mosaic covenant as he did those

of the covenants with Noah and Abraham. And yet they attribute the entire account of the contracting of the Mosaic covenant (Ex. xxiv. 1–11) to JE, thus separating what manifestly belongs together. How can P report the sign of the Mosaic covenant, if he has said nothing of such a covenant being formed?

7. " Diffuseness and constantly recurring formulæ."

But the emphatic iteration of the historian, who would impress his readers with the magnitude of the world-wide desolation wrought by the flood, is not to be confounded with the aimless diffuseness of a wordy writer. The enlargement upon special features and the repetitions are due to the vastness of the theme, not to needless verbosity. Thus Delitzsch commenting upon vii. 17–20 says : " The description is a model of majestic simplicity, of exalted beauty with no artificial expedients. . . . The tautologies of the account, as it lies before us, picture the frightful monotony of the illimitable watery surface, and the refuge floating securely above it, though encompassed by the terrors of death." And Dillmann says of vii. 16, in which the author repeats for the third time the entry into the ark, " It is as if the author, moved by the momentous character of the day, could not do enough in the way of detailed portraiture of the event." These surely are not unmeaning platitudes.

8. " The antique description of the sources of the flood (vii. 11, viii. 2), reminding one of i. 6–8."

The expression " windows of heaven " occurs twice in the account of the flood, and nowhere else in the Hexateuch. In both passages it is associated with rain, which is only sundered from it by the arbitrary partition of the critics ; and the form of the verb used in both implies that the rain was consequent upon the opening of those windows, and the stoppage of the rain upon closing them. There is not the slightest suggestion of two different conceptions, whether the windows of heaven be interpreted as literal sluices through which the waters of a supernal ocean poured, or as a figurative representation of deluging rains proceeding from the clouds, which are spoken of as waters above the firmament. And that waters from the great deep were united with torrents from the sky in producing the flood can be no ground of literary partition, while it is in exact accord with geologic phenomena.

9. "The image of God (ix. 6)."

This expression is here used with explicit allusion to i. 26, 27, where it occurs in the account of the creation of man; and it is found nowhere else in the Old Testament. This cannot surely be urged as a characteristic of the writer.

10. "The mode of speaking of Noah's family, vi. 18; vii. 7, 13; viii. 16, 18, as opposed to vii. 1."

But why should diversity of authorship be inferred because vi. 18 has "Thou and thy sons, and thy wife, and thy sons' wives with thee," and vii. 1, "Thou and all thy house," any more than from xlv. 10, "Thou and thy children, and thy children's children, and thy flocks, and thy herds, and all that thou hast," while ver. 11 has "Thou and thy house, and all that thou hast," which plainly belong together, and are by the critics commonly assigned to E. Wellhausen, indeed, ascribes xlv. 10, with its detailed enumeration, to J, thus precisely reversing the characteristic brevity imputed to J in vii. 1. Moreover, the detailed statement of Noah's family occurs (vii. 7) in a passage alleged to contain J's account of the entry into the ark, and in connection with expressions claimed to be characteristic of J, "waters of the flood," "clean beasts and beasts that are not clean;" so that the critics find it necessary to resort to the evasion that the text has been manipulated by R, who substituted the present reading for the presumed original, "Noah and his house." And if slight variations in the form of expression are to be made the pretext for assuming a diversity of writers, it is to be observed that vii. 13 is peculiar in giving the names of Noah's sons and the number of their wives, and viii. 16 in mentioning the wife before the sons. Must these verses be referred to a distinct author on this account?

11. כָּל־בָּשָׂר *all flesh* (vi. 12 seq., 17, 19; vii. 15 seq., 21; viii. 17; ix. 11, 15–17).

This expression occurs thirteen times in the passages just recited in the account of the flood, to indicate the universality of corruption and death and the measures for preserving the various species of living things. As there was no occasion to use it elsewhere in Genesis, it occurs besides neither in P nor in J sections. It is found three times in Lev. xvii. 14, "blood the life of all flesh," which Dillmann says ("Commentary," p. 535) is a mixed passage, and he adds that "all flesh" is no sure proof of P. It further occurs in Num. xvi. 22; xxvii. 16, "God of the spirits of all flesh;" and in a law of the consecration of the first-born of all animals (Num. xviii. 15), and nowhere else in the Hexateuch. J passages offer no substitute for it, and do not employ it for the simple reason that they have no occasion to express the same idea. It is further found repeatedly in other books of the Bible, so that it is no peculiar possession of P.

12. זָכָר וּנְקֵבָה *male and female* (vi. 19; vii. 9, 16).

These words can only be expected where there is some reason for referring to the distinction of sex. They are found together (i. 27; v. 2) where the creation of man is spoken of, and (vi. 19; vii. 3, 9, 16) in the measures for the preservation of the various species at the time of the flood, but nowhere else in Genesis. They are also found together in the ritual laws respecting sacrifice (Lev. iii. 1, 6); childbirth (Lev. xii. 7); uncleanness (Lev. xv. 33;

Num. v. 3); vows (Lev. xxvii. 3–7); and nowhere else in the Hexateuch except Deut. iv. 16 referring to objects of idolatrous worship. And it is almost exclusively in ritual connections that the words indicative of sex are used at all, even separately. Thus *male* occurs in Genesis only in relation to circumcision (Gen. xvii. 10, 12, 14, 23; xxxiv. 15, 22, 24, 25); and besides in a like connection in Ex. xii. 48, P; Josh. v. 4, R. It is further found in the Hexateuch in relation to sacrifice (Ex. xii. 5; Lev. i. 3, 10; iv. 23; xxii. 19); hallowing the first-born (Ex. xiii. 12, 15, J; Deut. xv. 19, D); directions concerning the priests (Lev. vi. 11 (E. V., 18), 22 (E. V., 29); vii. 6; Num. xviii. 10); childbirth (Lev. xii. 2); copulation (Lev. xviii. 22; xx. 13, J, so Dillmann; Num. xxxi. 17, 18, 35); the census (Num. i. 2, 20, 22; ch. iii.; xxvi. 62; Josh. xvii. 2, JE, except only the word *males,* so Dillmann); and war (Num. xxxi. 7, 17). *Female* occurs separately in connection with sacrifice (Lev. iv. 28, 32; v. 6); childbirth (Lev. xii. 5); and war (Num. xxxi. 15). As the creation, flood (for the most part), and ritual law are assigned to P, it is not surprising that nearly all the allusions to sex are in the sections and paragraphs attributed to P. And yet in the limited references which J is supposed to make to matters that admit of an allusion to sex, the word *male* finds entrance there also. It is alleged that J uses a different phrase, אִישׁ וְאִשְׁתּוֹ *man and his wife* (vii. 2), instead of *male and female.* Nevertheless, *male and female* likewise occur (vii. 3, 9) in paragraphs assigned to J. The critics say that these words were inserted by R, the only evidence of which is that they are at variance with critical assumptions. And why R should have been concerned to insert them here, and not in vii. 2, does not appear.

13. לְמִשְׁפְּחֹתֵיהֶם *according to their families* (viii. 19.)

This particular form of expression occurs once of the

various species of animals that came forth from the ark.
With that exception it is limited to genealogies, viz., of
the sons of Noah (Gen. x. 5, 20, 31); of Esau (Gen.
xxxvi. 40); and of the Levites (Ex. vi. 17, 25); the census of the tribes (Num. i.–iv., xxvi.); and the division of
Canaan (Num. xxxiii. 54; Josh. xiii., sqq). As these are
for the most part given to P by rule, the word is chiefly
found in P sections as a matter of course. Yet it is
classed as belonging to P in x. 20, 31, though the preceding genealogy to which it relates is given to J. The
word itself is found in J (Gen. xii. 3; xxviii. 14; Josh. vi.
23, JE); and with the same preposition, "according to
your families" (Ex. xii. 21, J); "according to his families" (Num. xi. 10, JE).

14. כֵּן עָשָׂה so did he (vi. 22).

This is part of an emphatic declaration that the divine
directions were punctually obeyed. Such statements are
mostly found in connection with the ritual, and naturally
have their place in P, to which ritual passages are regularly assigned. In Ex. xii. 28 it is preceded and followed
by a J context, with the former of which it is intimately
united, to which it evidently refers, and from which its
meaning is derived. And yet it is torn from this connection and linked with a distant P paragraph solely and
avowedly because it contains the formula in question. It
occurs but once in the book of Genesis, where it describes
the exactness with which Noah heeded the injunctions
given him. The expression in vii. 5 J is less full, but this
is no indication that it is from a different source. The
emphatic formula connected with the general statement
in Ex. xxxix. 32 is preceded, and that in Ex. xl. 16 is
followed, by numerous particular statements with a
briefer formula, but no one suspects a difference of authorship on this account.

15. פָּרָה וְרָבָה be fruitful and multiply (viii. 17; ix. 1, 7).

This phrase occurs ten times in Genesis and once in
Exodus, and in all of them is referred to P. This looks
like a strong case at first sight, but all its seeming
strength is dissipated upon examination. The phrase is
an emphatic combination designed to express exuberant
fertility; and its meaning is repeatedly heightened by the
addition of other synonymous words, or of intensifying
adverbs.[1] It is used in the Pentateuch of three things,
and of these only. 1. The blessing of fruitfulness pronounced upon animals and men at their creation (Gen. i.
22, 28) and after the flood (viii. 17; ix. 1, 7). 2. The promise to the patriarchs of the multiplication of their descendants. 3. The actual multiplication of the children of Israel
in Egypt (Gen. xlvii. 27; Ex. i. 7). Since the entire account
of the creation and almost all of the account of the flood
are given to P, the blessings then pronounced take the
same direction as a matter of course. Of the two statements of the multiplication of the Israelites in Egypt, Gen.
xlvii. 27 stands in a J context, and Ex. i. 7 in an E context; and both are sundered from their proper connection
and referred to P principally on account of the phrase
in question.

In the blessing upon Abraham and his descendants in
Gen. xvii., these two verbs are first used separately—
"multiply," ver. 2, "make fruitful," ver. 6, and then both
are combined in ver. 20. This climactic promise of offspring to Abraham after long years of waiting and when
every natural expectation had vanished, was confirmed
by the announcement that it came from the Almighty
God (ver. 1), who was able to fulfil what nature could

[1] Gen. i. 22, 28; ix. 1.   ·פרו ורבו ומלאו
viii. 17.   ·ושרצו · · · ופרו ורבו
ix. 7.   ·פרו ורבו שרצו · · · ורבו
xlvii. 27.   ·ויפרו וירבו מאד
Ex. i. 7.   ·פרו וישרצו וירבו ויעצמו במאד מאד

not accomplish.[1] This promise was repeated with explicit allusion to this occasion by Isaac to Jacob, xxviii.
3, by God himself to Jacob, xxxv. 11, by Jacob to Joseph, xlviii. 3, 4. In all these cases the emphatic words
of the original promise, "Almighty God," "be fruitful,"
"multiply," are repeated together. These are uniformly
assigned to P, not because of the connection in which
they stand, but because of the critical assumption that
these words are characteristic of P, and must always be
attributed to him. These comprise all the instances in
the Hexateuch, in which "be fruitful" and "multiply"
occur together, except Lev. xxvi. 9, which Driver assigns
to another than P, and Dillmann gives to J.

16. הָקִים בְּרִית or נָתַן, *establish* or *ordain a covenant*
(vi. 18; ix. 9, 11 *seq.*, 17).

These expressions are said to be characteristic of P,
while J habitually uses instead כָּרַת בְּרִית, *conclude a covenant*. The fact is that there is a difference in the signification of these terms, which should be noted, and which
is the true and sufficient explanation of their usage, without the need of having recourse to the proclivities of distinct writers. The first two expressions are used exclusively of God as instituting covenants with men ; *establish*
(lit. "cause to stand") indicates the permanence and sta-
bility of the arrangement divinely made ; *ordain* (lit.
"give"), suggests its divine appointment or bestowment.
These are applied to two covenants granted in perpetuity, that to Noah (*establish*, vi. 8; ix. 9, 11, 17; *ordain*, E.
V. "make," ix. 12) and to Abraham (*establish*, xvii. 7,
19, 21; Ex. vi. 4; *ordain*, E. V. "make," Gen. xvii. 2) ;
and *ordain*, E. V. "give," is once besides applied to the
covenant of a perpetual priesthood granted to Phinehas

[1] Gen. xvii. 1, 2.   אֲנִי אֵל שַׁדַּי. . . . וְאַרְבֶּה אוֹתְךָ בִּמְאֹד מְאֹד.
ver. 6.   וְהִפְרֵתִי אֹתְךָ בִּמְאֹד מְאֹד.
ver. 20.   וְהִפְרֵיתִי אֹתוֹ וְהִרְבֵּיתִי אֹתוֹ בִּמְאֹד מְאֹד.

(Num. xxv. 12). *Conclude* (lit. "cut," E. V. "make")
according to its original signification alludes to the sacrificial rites attending the ratification of a covenant, and
the cutting of the victim asunder for the contracting parties to pass between the separated pieces (Jer. xxxiv. 18,
19). It properly refers, therefore, to the act of concluding a covenant, with predominant allusion, in some instances at least, to the accompanying ceremonies. It is
accordingly used—

a. Of covenants between men; thus between Abraham
and Abimelech (Gen. xxi. 27, 32 E), Isaac and Abimelech (xxvi. 28 J), Laban and Jacob (xxxi. 44 E), Israel and
Canaanites (Ex. xxiii. 32 E; xxxiv. 12, 15 J; Deut. vii. 2 D;
Josh. ix. 6 sqq. E), Joshua and Israel (Josh. xxiv. 25 E).

b. Of the covenants of God with men, when the attention
is directed to the ratification rather than to the perpetuity of the covenant. It occurs once of God's covenant
with Abraham on the occasion of its formal ratification
in condescension to the customs of men, when a symbol
of the Divine Being, by whom the engagement was made,
passed between the parts of the slaughtered victims (Gen.
xv. 18 J). But when the climax was reached and the faith
of childless Abraham had been sufficiently tried, the
covenant conveying the land of Canaan was more explicitly unfolded as a covenant, in which the Almighty God
pledged himself to be a God unto him and to his seed; a
covenant that was not merely entered into, but declared
to be everlasting, and the stronger word *establish* is henceforth used in relation to it (Gen. xvii. 7). *Conclude* (lit.
"cut") is invariably used of God's covenant with Israel,
ratified by sacrifice (Ex. xxiv. 8 J), and solemnly renewed
(Ex. xxxiv. 10, 27 J; Deut. iv. 23; v. 2, 3; ix. 9; xxviii.
69 (E. V. xxix. 1); xxix. 11, 13, 24 (E. V. vs. 12, 14, 25);
xxxi. 16). *Establish* is never used in speaking of this
covenant with Israel, as of that with Abraham, because

the element of perpetuity and inviolability was wanting.
It was liable to be broken. It was once actually ruptured
by the crime of the golden calf and again by their rebellion, when the spies brought an evil report of the promised land and they were in consequence condemned to
die in the wilderness. The people were ever afresh reminded that its persistence was conditioned on their own
fidelity. Only once in the Pentateuch is its perpetuation
set before them as a blessing of the future;[1] if they will
walk in the LORD's statutes, he will establish his covenant
with them (Lev. xxvi. 3, 9 J, Dillm.). It is quite likely,
however, that the phrase is here used in the secondary
sense of performing or fulfilling, as it is in relation to the
covenant with Abraham in Deut. viii. 18. The occurrence
of what is claimed as a P phrase in J and D shows that it
is not the peculiar property of any one of the so-called
Hexateuchal documents. And the superficial exegesis
which finds here only an unmeaning difference of usage
in different writers overlooks the profound significance
which underlies the constant employment of these several terms.

17. "You and your seed after you " (ix. 9).

This or the like phrase, with a simple change of the
pronoun, is uniformly ascribed to P. It occurs in the
promise to Noah (ix. 9) ; Abraham (xvii. 7 bis, 8, 9, 10,
19) ; Jacob (xxxv. 12) ; repeated by Jacob to Joseph (xlviii.
4) ; the injunction to Aaron (Ex. xxviii. 43), and the promise to Phinehas (Num. xxv. 13). But the expression is not
uniform even in passages assigned to P, e.g., " to thee and
to thy seed with thee " (Gen. xxviii. 4 ; Num. xviii. 19) ;
" to him and to his seed throughout their generations " (Ex.
xxx. 21). Why then should a slight additional variation

---

[1] And once besides in the Old Testament (Ezek. xvi, 60, 62), where,
however, it is based not on the fidelity of the people, but on the pre
venient grace of God.

in three additional passages be thought to indicate a different author? viz., "to thee and to thy seed for ever" (Gen. xiii. 15 J) ; "unto thee and unto thy seed" (xxvi. 3 R.; xxviii. 13 J), especially as one author in Deuteronomy uses all these phrases; "unto them and to their seed after them" (i. 8) ; "unto them and to their seed" (xi. 9) ; "thee and thy seed forever" (xxviii. 46).

18. גָּוַע *die, expire*, for which J is said to use מוּת (vi. 17 ; vii. 21).

This word is only found in poetry except in the Hexateuch, where it is an emphatic word, only used of the death of venerated patriarchs or of great catastrophes. It occurs twice in relation to those that perished in the flood (vi. 17 ; vii. 21) ; also of those who were cut off by divine judgment for the rebellion of Korah (Num. xvii. 27, 28, E. V. vs. 12, 13 ; xx. 3 bis), or the trespass of Achan (Josh. xxii. 20). It is used in connection with מוּת *died*, of the death of Abraham (Gen. xxv. 8), Ishmael (ver. 17), Isaac (xxxv. 29), and with the equivalent phrase, " was gathered to his people," of Jacob (xlix. 33) ; also of Aaron (Num. xx. 29), where the preceding verse has מוּת.

The critics improperly sunder Gen. vii. 22, which has מוּת, from its connection with ver. 21, which has גָּוַע, assigning the former for this reason to J and the latter to P ; although ver. 22 directly continues ver. 21, and is a comprehensive restatement in brief, added with the view of giving stronger expression to the thought. Num. xx. 3 b is cut out of an E connection, and referred to P on account of this word גָּוַע, though the similar passage, Num. xiv. 37, shows that it belongs where it stands. This word could not be expected in the passages assigned to J, since they record no death in all the Hexateuch except those of Haran (Gen. xi. 28), the wife of Judah (xxxviii. 12), and a king of Egypt (Ex. ii. 23) ; in all which the word מוּת is appropriately used. The passages

assigned to P in like manner use מוּת of the antediluvians (Gen. v.), Terah (xi. 32), Sarah (xxiii. 2), the kings of
Edom (xxxvi. 33–39 so Dillmann), Nadab and Abihu (Lev.
x. 2), and several times besides as an emphatic addition
to גְּוַע. There is in all this no difference of usage whatever, and certainly nothing to suggest diversity of authorship.

19. הִשְׁחִית and שִׁחֵת destroy, not מָחָה blot out, J (vi.
13, 17 ; ix. 11, 15).

What is here claimed as a P word occurs but once in
P outside of the account of the flood (Gen. xix. 29) ;
while it occurs repeatedly in J (Piel form, Gen. xiii. 10;
xix. 13 ; xxxviii. 9; Ex. xxxii. 7 ; Deut. xxxii. 5) ; and in
E (Piel, Ex. xxi. 26 ; Num. xxxii. 15 ; Josh. xxii. 33), in
J (Hiphil, Gen. xviii. 28, 31, 32 ; xix. 13, 14 ; Ex. xii. 23).
And the alleged J word מָחָה occurs four times in the
narrative of the flood (vi. 7 ; vii. 4, 23 bis) ; and five times
besides in the Hexateuch, twice in J (Ex. xxxii. 32, 33) ;
twice in E (Ex. xvii. 14) ; and once in P (Num. v. 23).
The writer is led to use שָׁחַת in vi. 13, 17 because of the
twofold signification of the word, which may have respect
to character or condition and may mean " to corrupt " or
" to destroy." All flesh had corrupted their way, wherefore God was resolved to destroy them. In vii. 23 מָחָה,
though referred to J, is in connection with the enumeration of " man, beast, creeping thing, and fowl of heaven,"
which is reckoned a characteristic of P, and can only be
accounted for by the assumption that it has been inserted
by R.

20. הוֹלִיד beget (vi. 10), for which J is said to use יָלַד.

As is remarked by Dillmann ("Commentary on Gen.," v.
3), הוֹלִיד, said of the father, belongs to greater precision
of style. Hence this is uniformly used in the direct line
of the genealogies leading to the chosen race, which are
drawn up with special fulness and formality (Gen. v.; vi.

10; xi. 10 sqq.; xxv. 19; Num. xxvi. 29, 58). And ילד is
as uniformly used of the side lines, thus iv. 18 (in the
line of Cain), x. 8, 13, 15, 24, 26 (line of Ham, and that
of Shem outside of the chosen race), xxii. 23 (Bethuel),
xxv. 3 (Keturah). The only apparent exceptions are
not really such; in x. 24 Arpachshad, Shelah, Eber head
a divergent line proceeding with Joktan (cf. xi. 12–17).
In xi. 27 Haran begat (הוליד) Lot, but this is included in
the genealogy with Abraham, just as (xi. 26) Terah begat
(הוליד) three sons, and Noah (v. 32; vi. 10) begat (הוליד)
three sons, these being included in a genealogy of the
direct line. In xvii. 20 the promise that Ishmael shall
beget (יוליד) twelve princes is not in a genealogy, and
besides, it is part of a promise to Abraham. The variation, which the critics attribute to distinct writers, is simply the carrying out of a consistent and uniform plan by
the same writer. Besides, it is only by critical legerdemain that ילד is restricted to J. Gen. xxii. 23 is referred
to J notwithstanding the allusion by P in xxv. 20, which
makes it necessary to assume that P had stated the same
thing in some other passage now lost. This carries with
it xxii. 20, whose allusion to xi. 29 requires the latter to
be torn from its connection and referred to J. And in
xxv. 3 ילד alternates with ובני, which is made a criterion
of P in ch. x.; comp. also xlvi. 9 sqq.; Ex. vi. 15 sqq.

21. אָכְלָה *eating* (E. V. food, vi. 21; ix. 3).

Delitzsch (Commentary on Gen., vi. 21) says, "לֶאֱכֹל *to
eat*, and לְמַאֲכָל *for food*," and quotes with approval from
Driver, "a thing is given לֶאֱכֹל on a particular occasion,
it is given לְאָכְלָה for a continuance." It is said that J
uses מַאֲכָל as its equivalent; but מַאֲכָל and אָכְלָה occur
together in Gen. vi. 21 P, where the difference is plainly
shown; מַאֲכָל denotes that which is eaten, אָכְלָה the act of
eating; אָכְלָה occurs seven times in the Hexateuch. In
each instance some particular article of food is prescribed

for constant eating; and these are the only passages in
which this is done. In Gen. i. 29, 30, to man and beast
at the creation; vi. 21 to Noah and those that were with
him in the ark during the flood; ix. 3 to man after the
flood; Ex. xvi. 15 to Israel manna during their abode in
the wilderness; Lev. xi. 39 to Israel animal food allowed
by the law; xxv. 6 to man and beast during the sabbat-
ical year.

As all these verses are assigned to P, and these comprise all the passages of this description, it is not surprising that אכלה does not occur in J. But some nice
critical work is required to effect this. Ex. xvi. 15 has
to be split in two; its first clause is said to belong to J,
but its last clause is attributed to P because of this very
word (so Dillmann). Kayser (" Das Vorexilische Buch,"
p. 76) refers Lev. xxv. 1–7 to another than P; Kuenen
(" Hexateuch," p. 286) refers it to P′, who is distinguished
from P, or as he prefers to call him, P″, the author of
" the historico-legislative work extending from the creation to the settlement in Canaan " (p. 288).

22. חַיָּה *wild beast* (vii. 14, 21; viii. 1, 17, 19; ix. 2, 5).
There is no difference in this between the passages respectively assigned to the so-called documents. חַיָּה
beast is distinguished from בְּהֵמָה *cattle* in P (i. 24, 25;
vii. 14, 21; viii. 1; ix. 10), but so it is in J (ii. 20). In
i. 30; viii. 19; ix. 2, 5 P, it is used in a more comprehensive sense and includes domestic animals precisely as
it does in ii. 19 J. In vi. 20 P בְּהֵמָה *cattle* is used in
a like comprehensive sense and embraces all quadrupeds
as in vii. 2 J. In the rest of Genesis and of the Hexateuch, while חיה *beast* occurs in the sense of wild beasts
in Gen. xxxvii. 20, 33 JE, Ex. xxiii. 29 E, Deut. vii. 22
D, it is nowhere used in this sense in P, to which it is
conceded that Lev. xvii. 13; xxv. 7; xxvi. 6, 22, do not
properly belong; and in Num. xxxv. 3 P, where beasts

are distinguished from cattle, it is nevertheless plain that domesticated animals are meant.

23. מִין *kind* (vi. 20 ; vii. 14).

This word is only used when there is occasion to refer to various species of living things, as in the account of the creation (Gen. i., ten times), and of the preservation of animals in the ark (vi. 20, four times ; vii. 14, four times), and in the law respecting clean and unclean animals (Lev. xi., nine times ; Deut. xiv., four times). It occurs but once besides in the entire Old Testament (Ezek. xlvii. 10), where reference is made to the various species of fish. As the creation, the flood (in large part), and the ritual law are assigned to P, and there is no occasion to use the word elsewhere, it cannot be expected in passages attributed to J ; not even in vii. 2, 3, 8, where attention is drawn to the distinction maintained between clean and unclean rather than the variety of species preserved, which is sufficiently insisted upon vi. 20 and vii. 14.

24. עֶצֶם *self-same* (vii. 13).

This is an emphatic form of speech, which was but sparingly used, and limited to important epochs whose exact time is thus signalized. It marks two momentous days in the history, that on which Noah entered into the ark (Gen. vii. 13), and that on which Moses the leader and legislator of Israel went up Mount Nebo to die (Deut. xxxii. 48). With these exceptions it occurs mainly in ritual connections. It is used twice in connection with the original institution of circumcision in the family of Abraham (Gen. xvii. 23, 26) ; three times in connection with the institution of the passover on the day that the LORD brought Israel out of Egypt (Ex. xii. 17, 41, 51) ; and five times in Lev. xxiii., the chapter ordaining the sacred festivals, to mark severally the day on which the sheaf of the first-fruits was presented in the passover

week (ver. 14), which is emphasized afresh on the observance of the first passover in Canaan (Josh. v. 11);
also the day on which the two wave loaves were brought
at the feast of weeks (ver. 21); and with triple repetition the great day of atonement (vs. 28–30). Since ritual
passages are regularly assigned to P, and the two emphatic moments in the history calling for the use of this
expression have likewise been given to him, it might not
seem surprising if it had been absolutely limited to P.
And yet it is found once in an admitted JE section
(Josh. x. 27), showing that it can have place in these sections as well as others, if there is occasion for its employment.

25. שָׁרַץ *creep* or *swarm*, and שֶׁרֶץ *creeping* or *swarming
things* (vii. 21; viii. 17; ix. 7).

שֶׁרֶץ *creeping things* occurs among other species of animals at the creation (i. 20), in the flood (vii. 21), and in
the ritual law as a source of defilement (Lev. v. 2; xxii.
5), or prohibited as food (Lev. xi., ten times; Deut. xiv.
19); and it is found nowhere else in the Old Testament.

The verb שָׁרַץ is used with its cognate noun at the
creation (i. 20, 21), and flood (vii. 21), and in the law of
unclean meats (Lev. xi. 29, 41, 42, 43, 46); and in the
sense of swarming or great fertility in the blessings pronounced upon animals and men after the flood (viii. 17;
ix. 7); the immense multiplication of the children of Israel in Egypt (Ex. i. 7); and the production of countless
frogs (Ex. vii. 28, E. V. viii. 3, repeated Ps. cv. 30);
and it is used but once besides in the entire Old Testament. In the creation, flood, and ritual law it is given
to P as a matter of course; but it occurs in J in Ex. vii.
28; and in Ex. i. 7 it is only saved for P by cutting it
out of an E connection.

26. רָמַשׂ *creep* and רֶמֶשׂ *creeping thing.*

These words occur in the account of the creation (i.

21, 24, 25, 26, 28, 30) ; and the flood (vi. 20 ; vii. 14, 21,
23 ; viii. 17, 19 ; ix. 2, 3) P ; also vi. 7 ; vii. 8, 23, in a J
connection ; in the ritual law respecting clean and unclean beasts (Lev. xi. 44, 46 P ; xx. 25 J) (so Dillmann) ;
and in the prohibition of making an image of anything
for worship (Deut. iv. 18) ; and in but three passages besides in the Old Testament (Ps. lxix. 35 ; civ. 20 ; Ezek.
xxxviii. 20). Their signification limits their occurrence
to a class of passages that are mostly assigned to P,
though the noun is likewise found in D, and both noun
and verb are only excluded from J by critical legerdemain.

27. מְאֹד מְאֹד *exceedingly* (vii. 19).

This duplicated intensive adverb is referred to P also
(Ex. i. 7 ; Num. xiv. 7), and with a preposition prefixed
(Gen. xvii. 2, 6, 20). But it is admitted to belong to J
(Gen. xxx. 43).

28. בְּ used distributively (vii. 21 ; viii. 17 ; ix. 10, 15
seq.).

But it occurs in JE likewise (Ex. x. 15).

It appears from the above examination of these words
and phrases that they are for the most part found in the
other so-called documents as well as in P ; when they are
limited to P or preponderate there, it is due not to the
writer's peculiarity, but to the nature of the subject, and
in many cases to critical artifice.

MARKS OF J

The following are alleged to be indications of J :

1. " Distinction of clean and unclean beasts (vii. 2, 8),
mention of altar and sacrifice " (viii. 20, 21 ; comp. iv.
3, 4).

For the reason given under Ch. vi. 1–8, Marks of J, No.
11, it was as Jehovah chiefly that God was worshipped, that

prayer was addressed to him, and offerings made to him. Hence it is almost exclusively in Jehovah sections that mention is made of altars and sacrifices; and the distinction of clean and unclean beasts here made had relation to sacrifice.

The notion of the critics that, according to P, sacrifice was first introduced by Moses at Sinai, is utterly preposterous and altogether unwarranted. It is preposterous to suppose that the pious patriarchs, who were honored with special divine communications and were in favor with God, engaged in no acts of worship. And it is wholly without warrant, for there is no suggestion of any such idea in the paragraphs assigned to P. This is one of those perverse conclusions which are drawn from the absolute severance of what belongs together, and can only be properly understood in combination. The prevalent absence of allusion to sacrifice in passages where God is spoken of as Elohim simply arises from the circumstance that Jehovah is the proper name to use in such a connection.

2. " Prominence given to the inherent sinfulness of men " (viii. 21).

Jehovah's gracious revelation has for its object the recovery of men from sin and their restoration to the divine favor. Now, since the disease and the remedy go together, it is quite appropriate that human sin should be chiefly portrayed in Jehovah sections.

3. אִישׁ וְאִשְׁתּוֹ *a man and his wife*, applied to beasts, " a male and his female " (vii. 2), used instead of " male and female." See above, Marks of P, No. 12.

As these terms are nowhere else applied to the lower animals in J, it is not strange that they are not so applied in P sections. But a fairly parallel case occurs in Ex. xxvi. 3, 5, 6, 17 P, where terms strictly denoting human beings receive a wider application, curtains and

tenons being said to be coupled, "a woman to her sister," *i.e.*, one to another, as it is in Ex. xxxvi. 10, 12, 13,
22. Moreover, in Gen. viii. 19 מִשְׁפָּחָה is used to denote
species in animals, while מִין is always used in this sense
elsewhere. Yet both are alike referred to P by the critics. With what consistency, then, can a difference of
writers be inferred from the fact that אִישׁ וְאִשְׁתּוֹ is used
in one verse (vii. 2) instead of זָכָר וּנְקֵבָה ?

4. לְיָמִים *in days* or *at* the completion of *days* (vii. 4, 10).
This expression occurs nowhere else in the Hexateuch
in this sense ; but the preposition is similarly used (xvii.
21 P ; see Dillmann on Gen. iii. 8, to which he refers
vii. 4 as a parallel).

5. אֶל־לִבּוֹ *at* or *unto his heart* (vi. 6 ; viii. 21).
Nowhere else in the Hexateuch.

6. בַּעֲבוּר *because of* (viii. 21).
This occurs only in narrative passages, viz., 15 times in
Genesis, 7 times in the first twenty chapters of Exodus,
and nowhere else in the Hexateuch. It is 3 times attributed to R (Ex. ix. 14, 16 bis) ; and with this exception the passages in which it is found are divided between J and E, to whom the great bulk of the narrative
in the Hexateuch is ascribed.

7. כָּל־חַי *every living thing* (viii. 21 ; iii. 20), contrary
to vi. 19 P, כָּל־הַחַי *all the living things.*
These words do not occur together again in the Hexateuch, whether with the article or without it. The insertion or omission of the article in such a phrase is a very
slender ground on which to base the assertion of a difference of writers, especially as its insertion in vi. 19 appears to be due to the qualifying expression that follows,
" all the living things of all flesh."

8. נָפֹצָה *was overspread* (ix. 19).
Dillmann says that P writes נִפְרָד (x. 5, 32) ; and then
he annuls the force of his remark by adding, "not quite

in the same sense." If the sense is not the same, why should not the word be different?

Dillmann further calls attention to the fact that different expressions are used for the same thing in different parts of the narrative of the flood. Thus:

9. P, in vi. 16, speaks of צֹהַר *a light*; but J (viii. 6) of חַלּוֹן *a window* in the ark.

There is some obscurity in the description of the former which makes its precise construction doubtful. Dillmann thinks that it was an opening a cubit wide, extending the entire length of all the four sides of the ark just beneath the roof, for the admission of light and air, and only interrupted by the beams which supported the roof. The window was a latticed opening, whose shape and dimensions are not given. There is nothing to forbid its exact correspondence and identity with the opening before mentioned. And there is nothing strange in the use of one term to describe it when considered simply as intended for the admission of light, and another term when reference is made to the lattice which Noah had occasion to unfasten.

10. יְקוּם *living substance* (vii. 4, 23).

This is found but once besides in the Old Testament (Deut. xi. 6). In both the former passages it is given to J, notwithstanding the mixed state of the text, as the critics regard it, in ver. 23. It there stands in combination with "man, cattle, creeping things, and fowl of the heaven," and "who were with him," both which are accounted marks of P.

11. קַל *lightened* or *abated* (viii. 8, 11).

As this word is nowhere else used in a like sense by J it is not strange that it does not occur in P. And as two different words are employed (viii. 1, 3) to express a similar thought, both being referred by the critics to the same writer, why should the use of a third word bearing an analogous sense compel us to think of a different writer altogether?

12. חִיָּה (Piel) *keep alive* (vii. 3) J, while (vi. 19, 20) P has הֶחֱיָה (Hiphil).

But this can be no indication of a diversity of writers, for both forms occur repeatedly in passages assigned to J elsewhere; thus Piel, Gen. xii. 12; xix. 32, 34; Hiphil, xix. 19; xlvii. 25. Both occur in the same connection (Num. xxxi. 15, 18) and are referred to the same writer. The Hiphil is but once again referred to P (Josh. ix. 20), and the Piel, which occurs in the same connection (ver. 15), is only given to another by a critical dissection of the verse. The Piel and Hiphil of this verb are used indiscriminately as those of שָׁחַת are, which are both given to P; see above, Marks of P, No. 19.

13. מֵי הַמַּבּוּל *waters of the flood* (vii. 7, 10; not so vi. 17).

The attempt to create a distinction between the so-called documents in the mode of speaking of the flood is not successful. When the flood is first mentioned the unusual word מַבּוּל is defined by the added phrase " waters upon the earth " (vi. 17; vii. 6 P). We then read (vii. 7, 10 J) of " waters of the flood," and the same in ix. 11 P. Then (vii. 17 J) of "the flood " simply, and so in ix. 15, 28 P.

It thus appears that the so-called characteristics of J are no characteristics at all. They are for the most part words or phrases of rare occurrence, several of them being found nowhere else, and they cannot therefore be adduced as belonging to the writer's ordinary style. And there is not a single instance that is suggestive of a diversity of documents.

The critical arguments for the severance of this narrative thus collapse entirely upon examination. And yet this is accounted one of the most plausible cases of critical partition. As it fails here, so it does everywhere throughout the Pentateuch. The evidences of unity of authorship are everywhere too strong to be overcome by the devices which the critics employ for the purpose.

NUMERICAL CORRESPONDENCE.

The attempt has been made to discover numerical correspondences in the duration of the flood, but without any marked success. The rains began on the 17th day of the 2d month, and on the 27th day of the 2d month in the following year the earth was again dry (viii. 14). If the reckoning was by lunar years of 354 days, this would amount precisely to a solar year of 365 days. But this was plainly not the case, since the 5 months to the resting of the ark (viii. 4; comp. vii. 11) amounted to 150 days (vii. 24). Five lunar months would yield but 147 days. Evidently the reckoning is by months of 30 days. If the year consisted of twelve such months, the flood lasted 371 days; if 5 intercalary days were added, as in the ancient Egyptian year, the flood lasted 376 days. As neither of these sums correspond with any customary division of time, critics have claimed that the text has been remodelled by a later hand, and a conflicting computation inserted, according to which the flood lasted 300 days, rising to its height in 150 days (vii. 24), and subsiding for an equal term. To be sure the period of subsidence is nowhere so reckoned, but the critics suppose that it must have been intended, since 75 days, one-half of this term, elapsed between the resting of the ark on the 17th of the 7th month (viii. 4), and the appearance of the tops of the mountains on the 1st of the 10th month (ver. 5). But it was 4 months and 26 days after this before the earth was sufficiently dry for Noah to leave the ark. There is no conflict of statement, therefore, and no need of remodelling the text. The writer was more concerned for the historical truth of his statement than for a numerical correspondence, such as the critics are so eager to discover, and which the LXX. sought to introduce by changing 17th to 27th in vii. 11, thus making the flood continue exactly a year.

THE ASSYRIAN FLOOD TABLETS.

The Babylonian account of the flood, as reported by Berosus, has long been known to bear a striking similarity to the narrative in Genesis. This has been recently confirmed, and our knowledge of the relation between them materially increased by the discovery of the cuneiform flood tablets belonging to the library of Assurbanipal, and copied from a much older Babylonish original. The coincidences between the Babylonish and the Hebrew account are so pervading and remarkable as clearly to establish a community of origin; while, on the other hand, the divergences are so numerous and so serious as to make it evident that neither has been directly copied from the other. The suggestion of Friedrich Delitzsch and of Haupt, that the story was first adopted by the Jews at the time of the Babylonish captivity, is very justly repelled by Schrader and Dillmann on two distinct grounds. 1. "It is utterly insupposable that the Jews should have appropriated from their foes, the Babylonians, a local tradition altogether foreign to themselves originally, and saturated by the most silly polytheism." 2. Its inseparable connection with portions of the Pentateuch which are demonstrably pre-exilic. The manifest allusions of the earlier prophets to passages in the Pentateuch, which all divisive critics agree to refer to J, make it impossible to assign that so-called document to a later period than the seventh or eighth century before Christ. Beyond all question the story of the flood was known to the Jews at that time, and formed a part of their sacred tradition. The fact that Noah is not explicitly mentioned in the subsequent Scriptures until Isa. liv. 9 (which the critics pronounce exilic) and Ezek. xiv. 14, 20, as a purely negative testimony is of no force against the positive proof above adduced. Dr. Dillmann shows the futility of the argument from that source by adducing the parallel case of the narrative of the fall (Gen. iii.),[1] which is nowhere else alluded to in the Old Testament. Kuenen, Schrader and others maintain that the account of the flood was first brought from Assyria or Babylonia in the seventh or eighth century before Christ. But, as Dillmann urges, why should the Jews have accepted this foreign story, so variant in many particulars from their own style of thought, and enshrined it in the place which it occupies in their sacred traditions and the line of their ancestry, if it was altogether unknown to them before? And why, he asks, should it be imagined that the story of the flood never spread to surrounding nations until so late a period as this? And if to other nations, why not to Israel? The readiness with which high antiquity is conceded to the productions and beliefs of other nations, often on the most slender grounds, while the opposite propensity is manifested in the case of Israel, and everything assigned to the latest possible period, is, to say the least, very singular and is not very creditable to scholarly impartiality and fair dealing.

The well-attested fact of the migration of Abraham, or the ancestors of Israel, from Ur of the Chaldees, gives a point of connection which on any theory of the relation of these narratives satisfactorily explains both their agreement and their divergence. Whether Abraham derived his knowledge of the flood from traditions

[1] The critics themselves refer J to the eighth century B.C.

current in the region of Ur, which were purged of their polytheistic taint by his own purer faith and that of his descendants, or whether, as I believe, a truer account free from mythological conceit was transmitted to him in the line of a pious ancestry, we need not now inquire. But on either view of the case an obvious solution of the whole matter, and one against which no serious objection can be urged, is that Abraham brought with him to Canaan substantially that conception of primeval history which subsequently formed part of the faith of his descendants.   There is not the slightest reason for the assumption that this was a post-Mosaic addition to Israel's creed.

The only further question with which we are at present concerned, is as to the bearing of the flood tablets upon critical partition.   The patent fact is that they stand in equal relation to the entire Hebrew narrative as an undivided whole, with no suggestion of any such line of partition as the critics undertake to draw in it, but both having a like affinity for, and exhibiting a like divergence from, all that lies on either side of the line, or what the critics severally denominate J and P.

The Chaldean account agrees, in the first place, with what is affirmed in P and J paragraphs alike, that there was a great flood, divinely sent, which destroyed all men and animals except those saved in a single vessel with one man, to whom the coming of the catastrophe had been disclosed, and who had gathered into this vessel different species of tame and wild beasts, and the members of his own family.   The Chaldean account adds his relatives, and male and female servants, together with his valuables and a pilot.   Assurance is given in both accounts that mankind should not be again destroyed by a flood ; the Chaldean adds that other forms of judgment might take its place, as wild beasts, famine, and pestilence. There is an intimation near the close of the Chaldean account that the flood was sent because men had offended Bel, one of the gods; but no prominence is given, as in the Hebrew, to the thought that it was a righteous retribution. It is ascribed rather to the hasty temper of Bel, which was censured by the other gods. And the deliverance was not due to the righteousness of any that were saved. Bel was indignant that any escaped the destruction which he had intended for the entire race, and was only calmed by the remonstrance of other deities.

There are special points of agreement between the Chaldean account and the paragraphs assigned to P, viz., that the patriarch was divinely directed to build the vessel, and that of prescribed dimensions, length, breadth, and height (though the measures are not the same), to pitch it within and without with bitumen, and to stock it with provisions; that he entered it on the very day that the flood came, or the day before; that the great deep as well as the heavens supplied the waters of the flood; that the ark rested on a mountain, though the locality is not the same.[1]

There are also special points of agreement between the Chaldean account and the paragraphs assigned to J, viz., the mention of a covering to the ark, of the shutting of the door (by Jehovah in the Hebrew, by the patriarch himself in the Chaldean); of the duration of the storm (though the time stated is different, in the Hebrew forty days and forty nights, in the Chaldean six days and six or perhaps seven nights); of the opening of a window (in the Hebrew after, in the Chaldean before, the resting of the ark); of the sending forth of birds to ascertain

[1] Dr. Haupt at one time understood the tablets to state in addition that a celestial bow was displayed after the occupants of the ark had landed. But he has since abandoned this translation as incorrect.

whether the flood had ceased (in the Chaldean seven days, in the Hebrew forty days after the resting of the ark; in the Chaldean a dove, a swallow, and a raven, each immediately upon the return of its predecessor, the last not returning at all; in the Hebrew a raven, which did not return, then a dove, thrice at intervals of seven days, first returning as it went, the second time with a fresh olive leaf, the third time not returning) ; and after disembarking, of the erection of an altar and offering sacrifice, whose sweet savor was agreeable to the divinity (in the Chaldean the gods gathered like flies about the sweet odor).   The Chaldean makes no mention of the distinction of clean and unclean beasts recognized in the Hebrew.

The Chaldean account departs entirely from the Hebrew in representing the patriarch as apprehending the ridicule of the people if he should build the ship (according to a probable understanding of it), and pleading that such a ship had never before been constructed, and in portraying his distress at beholding the scene of desolation ; also in representing the gods as terrified by the flood and in the whole polytheistic setting of the story, and in the translation of the patriarch and his wife to dwell among the gods.

This common relation of the Chaldean account to the Hebrew narrative as a whole testifies strongly to its unity, and to the arbitrary character of the partition made by the critics.

See the translations of the flood tablets by George Smith, the discoverer of them, in his " Assyrian Discoveries," 1875 ; " Chaldean Account of Genesis," 1876 ; " Records of the Past," vol. vii. ; also by Dr. Paul Haupt in Schrader's " Keilinschriften und das Alte Testament," and by Dr. John D. Davis in the *Presbyterian Review* for July, 1889, and in his Genesis and Semitic Tradition.

NOAH AFTER THE FLOOD (CH. IX. 18-29).

The critics assign the concluding verses of this paragraph (vs. 28, 29) to P. They evidently refer back to the statement of Noah's age at the time of the flood (vii. 6), and complete the record of Noah's life begun in v. 32 in the exact terms of the preceding genealogy. They are thus linked at once with the narrative of the flood and with ch. v., and must be by the same author. We have, however, seen no evidence in these sections of a narrator P as distinguished from J, and none is suggested in the verses before us. It is at any rate a remarkable circumstance, if Genesis is compiled from different documents, all of which must have mentioned the death of each of the patriarchs whose lives they recorded, that the fact of their death is invariably taken from P, and never from J, even when, as in the present instance, a J section immediately precedes.

The opening verses of the paragraph (vs. 18, 19) are assigned to J, who had previously spoken of the sons of Noah (vii. 7) as entering with him into the ark, but had not mentioned their names, while these have been before stated by P (v. 32; vi. 10; vii. 13, and again in x. 1). But if the same writer could repeat their names four times, there is no very evident reason why he might not do so once more, or why the fifth repetition must necessarily imply a different writer. The critics tell us that vs. 18, 19 were in J introductory to the table of nations as given in that document, and were immediately followed by it, though, as they divide ch. x., J only records the descendants of two sons of Noah, Ham and Shem, but none of Japheth; and ver. 18b "Ham is the father of Canaan," plainly shows them to be preparatory to the narrative in vs. 20-27, a conclusion which can only be escaped by rejecting this clause as an interpolation.

Verse 20 is understood to trace the origin of the art of agriculture, and especially the culture of the vine, to Noah. It is hence conjectured that vs. 20–27 is a fragment from an ancient document, to which iv. 17–24 containing a record of the origin of other arts is likewise referred, and from which J is supposed to have again drawn. While in the preceding narrative Noah's sons are spoken of as married, it is alleged that here they are represented as children and occupying the same tent with himself. But this is pure invention ; there is no such declaration or implication in anything that is said. Ham is here called Noah's youngest son (ver. 24); this is held to imply in J a different conception of their relative ages from that of P, who always names them in the order Shem, Ham, and Japheth. But they stand in the same order in ix. 18, which is attributed to J. If it be said that R has in this instance changed J's order to make it conform to that of P, the question arises why he did not likewise correct ver. 24 for the same reason. The fact is that the order of their names is not determined by their respective ages but by an entirely different reason. Shem as the ancestor of the chosen race is placed first, as Abram is for the like cause in xi. 26. Ham, as the ancestor of nations standing in a nearer relation to the Hebrews than the descendants of Japheth, comes next, and Japheth last. In ch. x. the order is precisely reversed. The table of nations begins with those sprung from Japheth as the most remote ; Ham follows, then Shem, the series thus drawing gradually nearer to the chosen race, whose direct genealogy is reserved for xi. 10 sqq.

In ix. 20–27 an ancient prophecy from the mouth of Noah, in which the names of Shem, Japheth, and Canaan appear, is recorded together with the circumstances under which it was delivered.

> Cursed be Canaan ;
> A servant of servants shall he be unto his brethren.
> Blessed be Jehovah the God of Shem ;
> And let Canaan be his servant.
> God enlarge Japheth,
> And let him dwell in the tents of Shem ;
> And let Canaan be his servant.

The critics think the circumstances improbable; therefore they pronounce them untrue. Noah, they say, is here, ver. 20, a " husbandman, a rôle quite distinct from that of a navigator," which he sustains elsewhere ; the remark seems to imply that he should have been cultivating the soil during the flood, or should continue to sail about in the ark after the flood was over. The critics can see no reason why sentence should have been pronounced upon Canaan for the shameful deed of his father ; therefore they conclude that there was no reason, and that it was not done. As though it were not the keenest of inflictions upon a father to be punished in his child ; and as though the law of heredity, the propagation of character, and the perpetuation of the evil consequences of transgression generation after generation, were not among the most patent and familiar facts, of which the beastliness of the Canaanites and their merited doom afford a signal illustration. And now if they may change the text of the narrative on the pretext of conforming it to the prophecy, and so make Shem, Japheth, and Canaan the three sons of Noah, they can bring it into conflict with every other statement on the subject in the history ; whence they infer that this has been extracted from a document J', at variance with both J and P. Or if they may reverse the process and insert Ham instead of Canaan in the prophecy, they can show that it was not

fulfilled. Or if they may put a belittling interpretation
upon the prophecy, and restrict it to tribes inhabiting
Palestine, Shem denoting Israel and Japheth the Philistines in contrast with the Canaanites, as is done by Wellhausen, they can show how the meaning can be perverted
by giving arbitrary senses to words at variance with their
well-known and invariable signification. By this time
they have shown that something is absurd. They think
that it is this venerable prophecy, whose profound and
far-reaching meaning, whose appropriateness in a book
intended for Israel about to enter on the conquest of
Canaan, and whose exact fulfilment have been universally recognized. Most persons will think that the absurdity is in the critical treatment of the passage.

Delitzsch says, in his "Commentary" upon Gen. ix.
18b, "And Ham is the father of Canaan :" "This clause
is now mostly regarded as an addition by the redactor,
since the conclusion is drawn from the curse upon
Canaan that in the original form of the narrative it was
Canaan who sinned against Noah (Dillmann and others).
Some go farther and maintain that in its original shape the
three sons of Noah were not Shem, Ham, and Japheth,
but Shem, Japheth, and Canaan (Wellhausen). From
this Budde, by means of critical operations, which transcend our horizon, obtains the result that the following
narrative originally stood after xi. 9, and began, 'There
went forth also from Babel Noah, the son of Jabal, he
and his wife and his three sons, Shem, Japheth, and
Canaan, and he came to Aram-naharaim and abode there.'
So, as he supposes, wrote J', who, as Wellhausen and
Kuenen also assume, knew nothing of a deluge. We
here see a specimen of what emulation in the art of severing can accomplish."

IV

THE GENERATIONS OF THE SONS OF NOAH (CH. X. 1-XI. 9)

ORIGIN OF NATIONS (CH. X.)

THE generations of the sons of Noah (ch. x. 1-xi. 9) record the dispersion of mankind over the earth ; and the generations of Shem (xi. 10-26) trace the line of descent to Abram. This completes the preliminary portion of the history of Genesis, inasmuch as it fills up the interval between the flood and the birth of Abram, with whom the history of the chosen race properly begins. These sections are intimately related to one another, as well as closely connected both with what precedes and what follows. The genealogical table in ch. x. exhibits the filiation and relationship of the several nations of antiquity, and is intimately united with the antecedent history of Noah's family. Ch. x. 1 contains an explicit reference to the flood, the narrative of which had just been concluded, and proposes to state the descendants of the three sons of Noah, that were born to them after the flood. The way for it had been prepared by God's blessing Noah and his sons (ix. 1, 7), and bidding them multiply and replenish the earth ; as well as by the statement (ix. 19) that of the three sons of Noah was the whole earth overspread. Thus introduced, a detailed account is given of the particular nations sprung from them, which did thus overspread the earth (x. 32). Then follows (xi. 1-9) a narrative of the occurrences at Babel, which led to their being scattered over the earth, of which intimations had already been given (x. 10, 25).

This table of the nations of mankind has its appropriate place in the sacred history. It is inserted just here for a double reason : 1. To make a distinct declaration at the outset of their kinship to the chosen race, with which the history is henceforth more particularly to occupy itself. All are sprung from the same ancestry, and all are ultimately to share in the blessing to come upon all the families of mankind through the seed of Abraham (xii. 3). This conception of the universal brotherhood of man is peculiar to the Hebrew Scriptures, and is as remote as possible from that which was generally entertained by ancient nations, who looked upon foreigners as barbarians and enemies. 2. They are thus in accordance with the uniform plan of the book formally dismissed from the sacred history, which proceeds at once in accordance with the intimation given (ix. 26, 27) to devote itself to the consideration of the chosen seed by tracing the descent of Abram from Shem ; precisely as (iv. 17 sqq.) the descendants of Cain were recorded before leaving them to trace the line of descent through Seth (ch. v.), and as in the various instances that follow the divergent lines are first indicated before proceeding with the direct and principal line.

The speciality with which the Canaanitish tribes are noted and their residences specified (x. 15–19) is also observable, since this is intimately linked with the general purpose of the books of Moses, and with the occasion upon which they were written.

Nöldeke, in common, as he says, with the majority of critics, assigns ch. x. to P, with the exception of a few insertions by R, viz., vs. 8–11, relating to Nimrod and Asshur, ver. 21, and some words in vs. 19 and 25. Kayser gives the entire chapter to J, as is done likewise by

Tuch, Hupfeld, and others, in imitation of Astruc and Eichhorn ; and claims that vs. 8–11 and 21 are properly connected as they stand. Movers [1] divides the chapter, giving vs. 8–19, 21, 24–30, to J, and the rest to P; in this he is followed by Wellhausen (who gives ver. 24 and a clause in ver. 14 to R), Dillmann (who gives R, in addition, ver. 9, and some words in ver. 19), and most recent critics.[2]

This partition is altogether arbitrary. It is principally based upon a variation in the form of expression in different verses of the chapter. Those verses in which the line of descent is traced by the phrase " the sons of," are assigned to P ; the remaining verses, which use the word יָלַד *begat* or יֻלַּד לְ *were born to*, are attributed to J. But—

1. The genealogies assigned by the critics to P are not uniform in this particular; thus while the P sections of this chapter have "the sons of," ch. v. and xi. 10–26 have הוֹלִיד *begat;* nor do the different parts of the same genealogy invariably preserve the same uniform style (Gen. xlvi., see ver. 20 ; Ex. vi. 14 sqq., see vs. 20, 23, 25). There is no propriety, therefore, in making the lack of absolute uniformity here the pretext for critical division.

2. The same diversity of expressions as in ch. x. recurs in other genealogies, which no critic thinks of parcelling between distinct sources on that account. Thus xxv. 1–4 is attributed to J, although ver. 3a has יָלַד *begat*, and vs. 3b, 4, " the sons of." In xlvi. 8–27 " the sons of " and יֻלַּד לְ *were born to*, occur not only in the same indivisible genealogy, but in the same verses (vs. 22, 27). And *were born to* וַיִּוָּלֶד לְ [3] occurs in a P verse

---

[1] Zeitschrift für Philosophie und Katholische Theologie, Heft 18, 1836, p. 102.

[2] Schrader divides it between J and E.

[3] The Niphal future of this verb corresponds to the Pual preterite. Comp. iv. 18, 26 ; xlvi. 20, 27 ; 2 Sam. iii. 2, 5.

in the genealogy before us (x. 1). The attempt has been made to evade this by dividing the verse and assigning ver. 1a to P, and ver. 1b to J. But Dillmann says of this arbitrary sundering of the sentence : "No reason can be seen why ver. 1b should be not from P, but a continuation of ix. 18a J."

3. The proposed partition of this chapter is impracticable for a double reason. (1) The incompleteness of the portion ascribed to J, and (2) the mutual dependence of what is respectively given to J and to P. The critics are compelled to give J a share in this chapter, both in order to justify the intimation given in that document (ix. 18, 19), " of the three sons of Noah was the whole earth overspread," and to find something by which to bridge the chasm from Noah to Abram, who when first introduced in J (xi. 29), is spoken of as though he were already known. And yet the portion attributed to J fails to meet the requirements of the case, since it does not fulfil the expectations legitimately created in either of these respects. As a statement of the descendants of Noah, it begins abruptly, and is fragmentary in its character. Kautzsch imagines that ix. 18, 19 has been transposed by the redactor, and that it originally stood at the head of the genealogical table in J, and was connected with x. 1b. This groundless conjecture is an attempt to supply an appropriate beginning to J which is manifestly lacking. Moreover, it contains no mention of the descendants of Japheth, which must have been included in any conspectus of those who were sprung from the sons of Noah ; see also x. 21 J. And further, there is no introductory statement connecting the descendants of Ham, vs. 8 sqq., with Ham himself. These gaps are all created by the partition, and result from sundering what belongs together. What is thus obviously missing in J lies before us in what the critics have arbitrarily sepa-

rated from it and given to P. And what has been given to J is needed to make up the deficiencies thus created in P. P tells us of Mizraim and Canaan, sons of Ham, but we must look to J for the names of their descendants. Evidently these belong together.

It is claimed that what is missing from J's account may have been contained in that document originally and omitted by R, because already stated with sufficient fulness in the extracts taken from P. It is easy to speculate on what might have been. But the fact is that the gaps in J are adequately supplied in the text as it stands at present. The assumption that another parallel account of the very same things ever existed as a part of the document J is based on the prior assumption of the separate existence of that document as a complete and independent production. An inference from a hypothesis lends no support to that hypothesis, but depends upon it, and is only valid after the hypothesis has first been established.

On the ground of the correspondence between ver. 25 and xi. 16, Wellhausen claims that the former bears witness to the existence of a genealogy in J parallel to xi. 10-26, which traces the descent of Abram from Shem. This is coupled with the assertion that x. 24 is an insertion by R with the view of harmonizing J's account with that of P (xi. 10-14); and that the line from Shem to Abram in J, embraced but seven names (Arpachshad, Shelah, and probably Nahor,[1] the father of Terah, being omitted) as against ten in P (comp. the six names from Adam to Lamech in iv. 17, 18 J, and the nine in ch. v. P, with one to be added to each series for Noah, as Wellhausen conjectures). But this is baseless speculation in all its parts. For x. 24 is indispensable in its place, and cannot have been interpolated by R. In x. 21, Shem is

[1] So Wellhausen, Prolegomena, p. 330.

called "the father of all the children of Eber," *i.e.*, the Hebrews as well as other tribes and nations sprung from the same stock, vs. 26–29. But the links of descent from Shem to Eber are first given in ver. 24. Budde[1] proposes to remove this difficulty by altering the text of x. 21 to "Shem the father of Eber," as the only expedient by which it can be made "a serviceable link in a J genealogy." The need of so violent a remedy exposes the falsity of the assumption which requires it. Ver. 24 is a necessary constituent of the text, and cannot have been a later addition to it. And then the dependence of vs. 24, 25 upon ver. 22, and their substantial identity with xi. 10–16, forbid the notion of their being independent genealogies extracted from distinct sources. The abbreviated form of the former, and the use of יָלַד instead of הוֹלִיד *begat*, are not suggestive of diversity of authorship, but ordinary characteristics of the side lines in distinction from the direct genealogy of the chosen race. Moreover, x. 25 is not a relic of what was originally a complete genealogy from Shem to Abram, the remainder having been omitted by R as a needless parallel to that in ch. xi. It belongs in the line of descent of the tribes named in vs. 26–29, which diverged from that of the chosen race with the birth of Peleg, so named because "in his days was the earth divided." Mention is here made of Peleg with allusion to the narrative of the dispersion of the nations, which is to follow in the next chapter, and as a link of connection binding the two chapters together.

Nor can ver. 21 be sundered from ver. 22 and assigned to a distinct document. The absence of the conjunction וְ *and*, from the beginning of ver. 22 shows that it stands in the same relation to ver. 21 as ver. 2 to ver. 1; while the וְ *and*, of ver. 21 links the paragraph containing the descendants of Shem to the preceding, as in ver. 6 the

[1] Urgeschichte, p. 221, **note.**

descendants of Ham. Driver appeals to גם הוא *to him
also*, as iv. 22, 26 ; xix. 38 ; xxii. 20, 24, and *the father of*,
as characteristics of J. But *the father of* occurs also in
a P genealogy (xxxvi. 9, 43 P, as iv. 20, 21 ; xix. 37, 38 ;
xxii. 21 J) ; and though there does not chance to have
been any occasion for connecting גם with הוא in a P section, it occurs with other pronouns, *e.g.*, Ex. vii. 11 ;
Lev. xxvi. 24 ; Num. xviii. 28.

Nor is there any good reason for regarding vs. 8–12 as
a later addition to this chapter,[1] or as unsuited because
of its individual character to a place in this table of nations. If this were so, it would be a bar to the proposed
critical partition, for it would be as foreign to that portion of the chapter which is imputed to J, as to that of
P. It is introduced in order to connect the Babel to be
spoken of in the next chapter with a descendant of Cush ;
but there is no need on this account of assuming with
Dillmann that it should properly follow xi. 1–9. It is
agreeable to the usage of the author of the Pentateuch
to insert in genealogical tables allusions to persons or
events of note, especially those that have been mentioned
previously or are to figure afterwards, *e.g.*, v. 29 ; x. 25 ;
xxii. 23 ; xxxvi. 6–8, 24 ; xlvi. 12 ; Ex. vi. 20, 23, 25 ;
Num. xxvi. 9–11, 33.

It is further urged in proof of the blending of separate
sources that diverse origins are attributed to the same
people ; thus Havilah and Sheba according to ver. 7 (P)
are descended from Cush the son of Ham, but according
to vs. 28, 29 (J) from Joktan in the line of Shem ; according to ver. 22 (P) Lud sprang from Shem, but according to ver. 13 (J) from Mizraim the son of Ham ;

---

[1] Dillmann urges that Nimrod is not named in ver. 7 among the sons
of Cush ; but they are nations, while he is an individual, and is a son
not in the sense of an immediate descendant, but as Jesus was a son of
David, and David a son of Abraham (Matt. i. 1).

Aram is said to be descended from Shem, and Uz from Aram, vs. 22, 23 (P), but, xxii. 21 (J) Uz and Aram are traced to Nahor, the brother of Abraham, and, xxxvi. 28 (R), Uz is included among the descendants of Seir; Dedan, ver. 7, is included among the descendants of Cush the son of Ham, but, xxv. 3, among those of Abraham by Keturah. It is claimed that these variant representations must have proceeded from different writers. This is, however, by no means a necessary inference. For—

(1) The critics themselves do not adhere to this rule; Sheba (x. 28) was descended from Joktan, but (xxv. 3) from Abraham by Keturah, yet the critics refer both these passages to J.

(2) The apparent difficulty admits of a ready solution in one or other of two ways. The same name may have been borne by distinct peoples. Thus Asshur (x. 22) was descended from Shem; and yet Asshurim are mentioned (xxv. 3) among those that sprang from Abraham by Keturah. Here it is obviously incredible that the author could have meant to identify this obscure tribe with the great Assyrian nation, and to represent the latter as descended from Abraham. Dillmann acknowledges that the Ludim (x. 13), who are not only here but by the prophets (Jer. xlvi. 9; Ezek. xxvii. 10; xxx. 5) associated with the Egyptians and other African peoples, are quite distinct from Lud (x. 22), the Lydians of Asia Minor. These are not to be confounded any more than the Trojans of ancient times with their modern namesakes in the State of New York, or the Indians of America with those of southeastern Asia.

(3) Or tribes may be of mixed origin, and so are properly traceable to different lines of descent. Thus Dillmann [1] says of Sheba: "It is a matter of course that a people with such an extended trade had stations and

---

[1] Genesis, 5th edition, p. 182.

connections everywhere, on the sea and on caravan routes, and came to be mingled with their associates, so that they could be variously connected genealogically." And Delitzsch, commenting on x. 7, says to the same purport of Sheba and Dedan : "Arab tribes of Semitic origin are so called in ver. 28 ; xxv. 3 ; but there is no reason for denying an older Cushite stock in each of these Arab trading peoples." In like manner, in explanation of the double origin of Havilah, he says : "It is an acknowledged fact that migrations of Cushites and Arabs took place to and fro across the Arabian Gulf."

The mention of the same name in different lines of descent accordingly involves no discrepancy in the cases named, and no diversity of writers. If different tribes bearing the same name are of diverse origin, or if the same tribe is partly of one race and partly of another, one writer surely could tell the tale as well as two.

This table of the generations of the sons of Noah contains just 70 names, not reckoning Nimrod (ver. 8), which is the name of a person, viz.: 14 descendants of Japheth + 30 of Ham + 26 of Shem = 70. This was also the number of Jacob's family when they went down into Egypt (Gen. xlvi. 27 ; Ex. i. 5 ; Deut. x. 22), a number perpetuated in the permanent constitution of Israel with its 57 families [1] + 13 tribes, as well as in the representative body of seventy elders (Ex. xxiv. 1, 9 ; Num. xi. 16, 24, 25). The families of Israel are thus set in numerical relation to the families of mankind, which are to be blessed through their instrumentality (Gen. xii. 3). This correspondence seems to be intimated in Deut. xxxii. 8 : "When the Most High gave to the nations their inheritance, when he separated the children of men, he set the bounds of the peoples according to the number of the children of Israel." It is frequently remarked upon by

[1] Num. xxvi., not reckoning the Levitical families.

the rabbins, as in the following passage from the book of Zohar:[1] "Seventy souls went down with Jacob into Egypt, that they might restore the seventy families dispersed by the confusion of tongues." It is scarcely supposable that the seventy names in Gen. x. can be fortuitous.[2] And if it was intentional, the unity of the chapter is a necessary conclusion; for it is only in the chapter as a whole, not in its severed portions, that the number 70 appears. This further excludes the arbitrary conjectures, which have nothing whatever to recommend them, that the clause, "whence went forth the Philistines" (ver. 14), and the names of the Canaanitish tribes (vs. 16–18a, so Wellhausen, Kautzsch), are later additions to the text.

The high antiquity of this table is attested by the fact that several names familiar in later times find no place in it. Thus, while Sidon is mentioned (vs. 15, 19), there is no allusion to Tyre, which by the time of David had already outstripped it; nor do such names occur as Arabians (Isa. xxi. 13), or Minni (Jer. li. 27), or Persians. The tribes of Moab, Ammon, Ishmael, Edom, Amalek, as well as those sprung from Keturah and from Nahor, are

[1] Quoted by Lightfoot, Heb. Exercit. on Luke iii. 36.

[2] Fürst (Geschichte der biblischen Literatur, i., p. 7) and Nöldeke (Untersuchungen zur Kritik des Alten Testaments, p. 17) call attention to the fact that the descendants of Terah's three sons—Abraham, Nahor, and Haran—likewise amount to 70. From Abraham the 12 tribes of Israel; 16 of Edom (Gen. xxxvi.), viz., 5 sons (vs. 4, 5) + 11 grandsons (vs. 15–17); 12 of Ishmael (Gen. xvii. 20; xxv. 13–16); 16 of Keturah (Gen. xxv. 1–4); from Nahor, 12 (Gen. xxii. 20–24); from Haran, the 2 sons of Lot (Gen. xix. 36–38). Total, 12 + 16 + 12 + 16 + 12 + 2 = 70. Such a repetition of this number, which, even where it is not obvious upon the surface, yet underlies the entire scheme of the genealogies of this book, adds its evidence to the significance attached to it by the writer; and it supplies a fresh link to bind together in unity its component parts, and to show that they have all proceeded from the same hand, and that they cannot be distributed between P, J, and R, as is done by the critics.

not included in this table, because their descent is to be stated subsequently. The genealogies of Genesis thus complete one another, and thereby evidence themselves to constitute together one general scheme, and to be from the same hand and not referable to distinct sources, as the critics affirm. Aboriginal races, like the Emim, Anakim, Rephaim, Horim, Zamzummim, and Avim (Deut. ii.), which had almost or quite disappeared in the time of Moses, are of course omitted.

The strange conceit of Wellhausen, and adopted from him by Budde, Stade, and E. Meyer, that the three sons of Noah primarily denoted three different populations which tenanted Palestine—Israel, the Canaanites, and the Philistines—and only at a later time came to be regarded as the progenitors of all mankind, is very justly and emphatically set aside by Dillmann as " so utterly devoid of any foundation in fact that it is not worth while to enter upon it."

MARKS OF P.

The linguistic marks of P in ch. x., according to Dillmann are :

1. The title "these are the generations;" but this is not restricted to P sections.

2. "The concluding formula, vs. 5, 20, 31, 32 ;" but the J genealogy (xxv. 4) has one likewise.

3. "Its verbosity," which simply emphasizes four particulars in order to indicate that this is a genealogy not of individual men, but of *nations*, with their *families* or tribal divisions, speaking various *tongues* and occupying different *countries*, and there are numerous passages attributed to J in which particulars are similarly enumerated in detail, *e.g.*, vii. 7, 23 ; xv. 19–21, where this admission is only escaped by assuming interpolations by

R., xii. 16 ; xxvi. 13, 14 ; xxx. 32–35, 39, 43 ; xxxii. 6, 8 (A. V. vs. 5, 7).

4. "למשפחותם *after their families*," this word occurs eighty times in the Hexateuch, and in a slightly altered orthography למשפחותיהם, twice more ; and it is in every instance referred to P. This sounds like a very significant statement ; but as soon as the facts in the case are examined it appears that it has no bearing whatever upon the question of a diversity of documents. With one single exception it is exclusively found in connection with the genealogies of nations or tribes (Gen. x. 5, 20, 31 ; xxxvi. 40 ; Ex. vi. 17, 25), or the census of the tribes of Israel (Num. i., iii., iv., xxvi.), or the distribution of the promised land among the several tribes (Josh. xiii., xv.–xix., xxi.). And the great body of all such material is given to P. Its occurrence, therefore, is directly traceable to the subject-matter, not to the peculiarity of a particular writer. The one exception is Gen. viii. 18, where the various species of animals that came forth from the ark are figuratively denominated "families." The same form of the word, with the same preposition, in an identical meaning, occurs likewise in J, only with a different suffix ; למשפחתיכם Ex. xii. 21 ; למשפחתיו Num. xi. 10 ; or with the article instead. למשפחות Josh. vii. 14. Apart from genealogies, the census and the apportionment of the land, or laws relating to it, as Num. xxvii. 1–11 ; xxxvi., and Lev. xxv. (the return to family possessions in the jubilee), the word משפחה is exclusively found in J, Gen. xii. 3 ; xxviii. 14 ; xxiv. 38, 40, 41 ; Lev. xx. 5 (J according to Dillmann) ; Josh. vi. 23 ; vii. 14, 17.

5. "The prep. ב in vs. 5, 20, 32," which is certainly a very slender string to hang an argument for diversity of authorship upon. See ch. vi.–ix. Marks of P, No. 28,

MARKS OF J.

The marks of J, besides those already explained, are:
1. " נפצו (ver. 18 as ix. 19) instead of נפרדו P (x. 5,
32) ; " but, as Dillmann on ix. 19 admits, the words are
not used in precisely the same sense. The former means
to be dispersed or spread abroad ; the latter to be divided,
suggesting the idea of distinctness or separation. Moreover, the word, which is here represented to belong to P,
in distinction from J, elsewhere is found almost exclusively in J, viz.: Gen. ii. 10 ; xiii. 9, 14 ; xxv. 23 ; xxx.
40 ; Deut. xxxii. 8 ; and but once in P (Gen. xiii. 11),
where it is cut out of a J connection by a critical ma-
nœuvre.

2. " באכה as *thou comest* (used as an adverb) " (vs. 19
bis, 30) ; this occurs but twice elsewhere (xiii. 10 J, and
xxv. 18, which the critics regard as a gloss). Such criteria are of no account.

TOWER OF BABEL (CH. XI. 1-9).

It is alleged that xi. 1-9 cannot be from the same
author as ch. x., because they represent quite different
conceptions of the cause which led to the dispersion of
mankind over the earth ; one traces it to the simple multiplication of the race, the other to an immediate divine
intervention. Hence Nöldeke assigns ch. x. to P and
xi. 1-9 to J ; Wellhausen, who finds both P and J in ch.
x., attributes xi. 1-9 to J', supposed to be an earlier
stratum in the document J. But the explicit allusions
to Babel and to the dispersion which took place there, in
x. 10, 25, shows that this transaction was before the mind
of the writer of ch. x. And there is not the slightest inconsistency between the two passages. The writer sim-

ply proceeds in ch. xi. to detail in its proper place an additional fact connected with the peopling of the earth.

It is further urged that there is in xi. 1–9 no mention of Noah's three sons and their descendants as in ch. x., but simply of the population of the earth as a unit. To which Dillmann very properly replies : "The sons, grandsons, etc., of Noah can very well be regarded as in the first instance united in one place and forming the entire population of the earth, until God constrained them to disperse." He also enters a caveat against a misconception of the real meaning of what is here narrated : "The author does not say that the manifold languages of men now came into existence ready made on the instant ; he only fixes a point of time at which the divergence of nations and languages began. Still less is he responsible for the conceit of the later Jews and of the church fathers, that Hebrew was the original language from which the others branched off in consequence of this confusion."

Jehovah is the only divine name that occurs in this section, and it is in each instance appropriately used. The builders at Babel are frustrated in their ambitious design by Jehovah (xi. 5, 6, 8, 9), in the interest of his purpose of mercy to the world. The massing of the race together and concentrating them in what must have become one vast ungodly power was thwarted by scattering them over the earth. In x. 9 Nimrod is twice spoken of as " a mighty hunter before Jehovah " (comp. vi. 11). Both the character of the chapter in general, and the connection of this verse with that which precedes and follows, show that Nimrod is here described not as a hunter of wild beasts, but as a conqueror and oppressor of men,[1] and the founder of a great empire. And Jehovah is ob-

---

[1] Dillmann refuses to admit this sense, so obviously demanded by the context, to be the one originally intended, and is obliged in consequence to regard ver. 9 as an interpolation.

servant of all his schemes of conquest, ready to limit and control them in the interest of that divine kingdom which it is his purpose to introduce among men.

MARKS OF J.

1. "שָׂפָה *lip* (vs. 1, 6, 7, 9), instead of לָשׁוֹן *tongue* (x. 5, 20, 31)." But while "lip" may be used for "a language" in the singular, the plural is always expressed by "tongues." Thus Isa. xix. 18, "the lip or language of Canaan," but Isa. lxvi. 18, "all nations and tongues;" Zech. viii. 23, "all tongues of the nations," but Zeph. iii. 9, "a pure lip or language." Moreover, if the same writer can use both "lip" and "tongue" in this sense in the same sentence, as Isa. xxviii. 11; xxxiii. 19; Ezek. iii. 5, 6, why not on successive pages?

2. "Jehovah comes down from heaven" (vs. 5, 7); but in xvii. 22; xxxv. 13, passages attributed to P, it is said that God went up after speaking with Abraham and with Jacob, which implies a previous descent.

3. "The etymology" (ver. 9). But allusions to the significance of names are likewise found in P (Gen. xvii. 5, 17, 19, 20). It should further be observed here that the sacred writer is not to be understood as giving the real derivation of the word Babel, but simply as noting the very significant sense suggested by it to a Hebrew ear. It was an instance of a *nomen et omen*. Cf. John ix. 7, where no one imagines the evangelist's meaning to be that the pool of Siloam derived its name from the circumstance which he relates.

V

THE GENERATIONS OF SHEM (CH. XI. 10–26)

SHEM TO ABRAM (CH. XI. 10–26)

THE table of descent from Shem to Abram is evidently constructed upon a uniform plan with that in ch. v. from Adam to Noah, giving not a bare list of names as in ch. x. and in the side lines generally, but stating the age of the father at the birth of the son through whom the line is continued; then the length of his life after the birth of his son, with the mention of his begetting sons and daughters; and after running through nearly the same number of links (one ten, the other nine), they alike terminate with a father who has three sons, that are all named together without indicating the intervals between their birth. The only difference in their structure is that ch. v. sums up the years of the life of each patriarch, while ch. xi. does not. A close connection is thus established between the genealogy in ch. v. and that in ch. xi., showing that xi. 10–26 could not have constituted a genealogical fragment by itself.

It is manifestly the continuation of the genealogy in ch. v., and yet it could not have been joined directly to it without the sections which now intervene; as though what was once a continuous genealogy had been sundered, and chs. vi.–xi. 9 inserted between the severed parts. The last verse of ch. v. does not complete the statements about Noah in the regular form consistently pursued throughout the genealogy, so that the next term in the genealogy might be expected immediately to follow. It both states more and less than had been regularly stated in each of the preceding terms. More, in that it mentions three sons instead of one, leading us to expect that something is to be said about all three; this is a preparation, therefore, for the narrative of the flood, with which they are concerned, and also for the table of the descendants of each given in ch. x. This verse also states less than was customary in all preceding cases; for while it gives the age of Noah at the birth of his sons, it does not state how long he lived subsequently, nor the entire length of his life. These missing statements are found in what follows by combining vii. 6, 11, with ix. 28, 29. Ch. xi. 10 also implies the preceding narrative of the flood; and vs. 10-26 completes the account of the descendants of Shem, which x. 21-31 (see particularly ver. 25) only gives in part. At xi. 26 the genealogy is again enlarged in the same way to introduce the history that follows.

VI

THE GENERATIONS OF TERAH (CH. XI. 27–XXV. 11)

PRELIMINARY REMARKS

THE sixth section, which extends from the birth to the death of Abraham, is called the Generations of Terah, and begins with a restatement of his three sons, precisely as the fourth section is entitled the "Generations of Noah," and begins with a restatement of his three sons. As this latter section describes the fortunes of Noah, Shem, Ham, and Japheth, so that now before us is occupied with what is to be told respecting Terah, Abram, Nahor, and Haran. The life of Abram, who is the principal figure in this portion of the sacred narrative, was for some time united with that of Lot, the son of Haran, and Abram's son Isaac married Rebekah, the granddaughter of Nahor.

The call of Abraham (xii. 1) is related to the promise to Shem (ix. 26), as its initial fulfilment. In Abraham's life all revolves about the promised land and the promised seed. He is to go to a land that the LORD will show him, and become the father of a great people, and all the families of the earth shall be blessed in him. As soon as he arrives in Canaan, the LORD tells him that this is the land and that his seed shall possess it. Both of these particulars are further defined and confirmed in what follows. He has scarcely arrived in Canaan before he is obliged to leave it in consequence of a famine (xii. 10 sqq.), and go to Egypt. This is a trial of his faith in the future possession of the land. Then follows the risk of losing Sarah, which was a trial of his faith in the promised seed. The peril is averted by divine interference, and enriched he returns with Lot to the land of promise. Lot separates from him (xiii. 5 sqq.), though without leaving Canaan, when a more definite promise is made of giving all the land to Abram and his seed (vs. 14, 15). The land is invaded, and Lot taken captive; Abram pursues and chastises the invaders, rescues his nephew, and is blessed by Melchizedek, king of Salem and priest of the Most High God (ch. xiv.).

Meanwhile Sarah has no son, and the prospect is that Eliezer will be Abram's heir (xv. 2 seq.). But he is assured that it is not merely one born in his house, but a son of his own body who shall be his heir, and whose posterity shall be as numerous as the stars of heaven, (vs. 4–6). A prospect of the future of his seed is shown him. And the LORD by a visible token ratifies a covenant with Abram to give his seed the land, and definitely designates its dimensions (vs. 7–21). The promise of the land has now reached its utmost solemnity and precision. Years pass on, and Sarah abandons all hope of having children, and gives her maid to her husband; she bears him Ishmael (ch. xvi.). At length, twenty-four years after Abram's arrival in Canaan, the LORD appears to him again as the Almighty God, and engages that Sarah, notwithstanding her advanced age, should have a son the very next year, and that her child, and not Ishmael, should be the promised seed. In view of this he was on his part to enter into covenant with God by the rite of circumcision, as God had already formally entered into covenant with him (ch. xvii.). Both the contracting parties having thus sealed the engagement, it is finally concluded by a meal, of which the LORD partakes in human form in the tent of Abraham. And the confidential in-

timacy to which the latter is admitted is further shown
by the communication to him of the divine purpose respecting Sodom (ch. xviii.). Then follows (ch. xix.) the
destruction of Sodom and Lot's deliverance, and the
parentage of Moab and Ammon, tribes related to Israel
and in their vicinity during the forty years' wandering,
respecting which there were special requirements in the
law presupposing this genealogical statement (Deut. ii.
9, 19); so that the history of Lot is preliminary to these
injunctions. At the court of Abimelech Sarah is once
more imperilled, and is divinely delivered (ch. xx.). Isaac
is born; Ishmael must give way to him, and goes with
his mother to the wilderness of Paran (xxi. 1–21). God's
blessing upon Abraham is recognized by Abimelech, who
solicits his friendship (xxi. 22 sqq.).

Then comes Abraham's last and sorest trial in respect
to his son. He is bidden to offer him up to God on the
altar (ch. xxii.). In the act of obedience his hand is
stayed, Isaac is restored to him, and all the promises
previously made to him are repeated in their fullest
form, and confirmed by the new solemnity of an oath.
The period of trial is now over. The successful endur-
ance of this severest test of his faith marks the culmination of Abraham's life, which henceforth flows peacefully
and quietly to its close. The account of Nahor's family
(vs. 20–24) paves the way for the subsequent narrative
of Isaac's marriage. We then read of Sarah's death, and
of the formalities connected with the purchase of a burial-place (ch. xxiii.), the first possession in the promised
land, where Sarah and Abraham were to lie, thus even in
death attesting their faith in this sure inheritance. Then
Rebekah is brought to be the wife of Isaac (ch. xxiv.).
This is followed by the marriage of Keturah, and the
names of her sons; and finally Abraham's death and
burial (xxv. 1–11).

THE DIVINE NAMES.

Throughout this section the divine names are used with evident discrimination. The name Jehovah is used in ch. xii.–xvi.; Elohim does not occur until ch. xvii., where it is found repeatedly, and, with the exception of ver. 1, exclusively. It is Jehovah the God of the chosen race who bids Abram leave his kindred and his father's house (xii. 1–4), with the promise to multiply his seed and to give him Canaan (xii. 2, 7; xiii. 14–17); to whom Abram erected altars in this land and paid his worship (xii. 7, 8; xiii. 4, 18); who guarded Sarah, Abram's wife (xii. 17); who noted and would punish the guilty occupants of the promised land (xiii. 10, 13; xv. 16); to whom Abram appealed as the universal sovereign (xiv. 22), while to Melchizedek he was not Jehovah but El Elyon, God most High (vs. 18–20); who appeared to Abram (xii. 7), spake to him (xii. 1, 4, 7; xiii. 14; ch. xv.), and covenanted with him (xv. 18); whom Sarah recognized as directing all that affected her (xvi. 2, 5); who cared for Hagar as a member of Abram's family (xvi. 7 sqq.), though in the mouth of this Egyptian maid (xvi. 13), as well as in the name of her son (xvi. 11, 15), we find not Jehovah but El.

It may be asked, why is it not still Jehovah, the God of the chosen race, who in ch. xvii. enters into covenant with Abraham and establishes circumcision as the seal of that covenant and the perpetual badge of the covenant people? It is Jehovah who appears to Abram and forms this solemn engagement with him, as is expressly declared, ver. 1. In doing so he announces himself as the Almighty God, and the reason for this is obvious. The promise of a numerous seed made to Abram at the outset had been repeated from time to time for four and

twenty long years, and there had been as yet no indication of its fulfilment. Meanwhile in his advancing age
and that of Sarah all natural hope of offspring had vanished. The time has now come when his persistent faith
shall be rewarded. Nature has failed, but the divine
omnipotence is all-sufficient. Isaac shall be born the
next year. The emphasis here laid on God's almighty
power is indicated by El Shaddai, God Almighty (ver.
1), followed by Elohim, the title of the God of creation,
throughout the interview and to the end of the chapter.

It is Jehovah again in ch. xviii. who in condescending
grace concludes the covenant transaction with Abram by
becoming his guest, and in the familiarity of friendship
admits him to his counsel respecting Sodom and accepts
his intercession on its behalf; and who still further (xix.
1–28) executes the purpose which he had disclosed to
Abraham, of purging his own land of gross offenders
(cf. xiii. 13; xv. 16; xviii. 20, 21). Here the critics claim
that xix. 29 is a fresh account of the destruction of Sodom
and the rescue of Lot, which instead of relating in detail,
as in the previous part of the chapter, despatches all in
a single sentence, using Elohim of the very same matter
in regard to which Jehovah had been before employed
throughout. But—

1. This verse, instead of relating the overthrow of
Sodom, presupposes this event as known and already
narrated, and proceeds to declare what took place when
it occurred. The direct course of the narrative had been
interrupted (vs. 27, 28) to mention Abraham's early
visit to the scene of his former intercession, and what he
there beheld. Then in returning to his narrative the
writer sums up in a single sentence what he had already
related, and proceeds to say what further became of Lot.[1]

---

[1] Thus Gen. ii. 1 recapitulates the work of the six days (ch. i.), in
order to connect with it the rest of the seventh day (ii. 2, 3); xxxix. 1,

2. The reason for the change in the divine name is now apparent. In the paragraph which begins with this verse and extends to the end of the chapter, the writer is speaking of Lot, now and henceforth completely severed from Abraham, and removed beyond the boundaries of the promised land, the ancestor of Moab and Ammon, to whom God is not Jehovah but Elohim, as to all outside of the chosen race.

In like manner in the affair of Abimelech, king of Gerar, a Gentile prince (ch. xx.), Elohim is the proper word, and is accordingly used throughout, both in God's dealings with Abimelech (vs. 3, 6, 17), and in what Abraham says to him (vs. 11, 13). Only in ver. 18, where the writer introduces a statement of his own that the infliction there spoken of was for the protection of Abraham's wife, Jehovah is introduced precisely as in the similar case, xii. 17.

The birth of Isaac recalled alike the pledge of almighty intervention and the gracious promise of Abraham's God; hence the use of Jehovah in xxi. 1, with special reference to xviii. 10, 14, and of Elohim in vs. 2, 4, 6,[1] with reference to xvii. 10, 19, 21. In the narrative of the dismissal of Hagar and Ishmael (vs. 9–21) Elohim is used throughout, because they are now finally severed from the family of Abraham ; whereas in xvi. 7–13, while Hagar still belonged to his family, it is the angel of Jehovah who finds her in the wilderness, and sends her back to her mistress. In Abimelech's visit to Abraham he nat-

after the digression of ch. xxxviii., sums up the narrative of xxxvii. 28–36, on returning to the history of Joseph ; so Ex. vi. 28–30, for a like reason, repeats vs. 10–12 ; Ex. xii. 51 repeats ver. 41 ; Judg. iii. 4, cf. ver. 1 ; xxi. 8, cf. ver. 5 ; 1 Kin. vi. 37, cf. ver. 1.

[1] Cf. with ver. 6 in its allusion to God's almighty intervention in contrast with natural causes, Eve's language at the birth of Seth (iv. 25), with Elohim in what the critics consider a J section because of the implied contrast between God and man.

urally speaks of Elohim (xxi. 22, 23), whereas in Abraham's act of worship he calls on the name of Jehovah (ver. 33).   In ch. xxii. it is Elohim who puts Abraham to trial by the command to offer up Isaac; it is Jehovah who stays his hand.   God the creator has the undoubted right to demand of his creature the dearest and the best; but the God of Abraham, the God of revelation and salvation accepts the spiritual surrender and spares the child.   In ch. xxiii. Elohim occurs but once, and very properly in the mouth of the children of Heth (ver. 6). Jehovah guided Abraham's servant in his search for a wife for Isaac (ch. xxiv.), and this in so conspicuous a manner that even Laban and Bethuel [1] recognize the hand of Jehovah, the God of Abraham in the whole affair (vs. 50, 51), and address the servant as "blessed of Jehovah" (ver. 31).   In xxv. 11, "after the death of Abraham Elohim blessed his son Isaac."   Jehovah, as the guardian and benefactor of the chosen race, would certainly have been appropriate here.   And yet Elohim is appropriate likewise, as suggestive of the general divine beneficence and providential goodness, which bestowed upon Isaac abundant external prosperity.   Such bounty is by no means limited in its exercise to the chosen race.

THE CRITICAL PARTITION.

The constant regard to the distinctive meaning of the divine names, as this has now been exhibited, must be due to the intention of the writer.   It cannot be the accidental result of the combination of separate Elohist and Jehovist documents.   Nevertheless the critics un-

---

[1] So the heathen mariners call upon the name of Jonah's God in the tempest, which they recognize as sent by him.   They cry unto Jehovah and fear Jehovah (Jon. i. 14, 16), though they had previously "cried every man unto his god," ver. 5.

dertake to parcel the contents of this section between P, J, and E ; and in so doing present us with three mutilated and incoherent narratives instead of the one closely connected and continuous narrative which we have already traced in the text as it lies before us.

The only paragraphs of any length ascribed to P are chs. xvii. and xxiii., the former recording the covenant of circumcision, the latter the death of Sarah and the purchase of the cave of Machpelah. But ch. xvii. is closely linked to both the preceding and the following history. Thus it appears from xvii. 8 that Abraham is in Canaan ; and from vs. 18–20 that he has a son Ishmael, who is not the child of Sarah, and that Sarah is shortly to have a son of her own. And the Elohim verse (xix. 29) speaks of Lot, to whom Abraham was attached, and who dwelt in the cities of the plain. The facts thus alluded to are all recorded in full in the accompanying narrative, of which ch. xvii. and xix. 29 are thus shown to form component parts. But the critics seek to detach them from the body of the narrative by singling out scattered verses here and there, rent from their proper connection, sufficient to cover these allusions, and stringing them together so as to create an appearance of continuity for P here, as is done for J in the account of the deluge. It should be borne in mind that there is no evidence whatever that the hypothetical narrative thus produced ever had a separate existence but that which is found in the vague critical criteria, which we shall examine shortly. The skeleton life of Abraham that is ascribed to P is devoid of all real interest or significance. It is stripped of everything indicative of character. There is in it no exercise nor trial of faith ; no act of piety, or generosity, or courage ; no divine purpose ; no providential dealing with him, no divine communication made to him, except on one single occasion four and twenty years after he

had entered Canaan. The life of the father of the faithful, so rich in the most important spiritual lessons, is reduced to a jejune and barren annalistic record. This
the critics not only admit, but insist upon; they tell us
it is the fault of P. He has no taste for narrative; he
has no historic sense, and no interest in history, but
only for legal facts and institutions, dates and figures,
and unmeaning lists of names. It is not disputed that
such a writer is abstractly possible or conceivable;
whether there is proof of his actual existence will be
considered hereafter. All that is proposed at present is
to state the critics' own conception of the matter. The
document of P in the section now before us, apart from
ch. xvii. and xxiii., consists of these few scraps.

xi. 27. Now these are the generations of Terah.
Terah begat Abram, Nahor, and Haran; and Haran
begat Lot. 31. And Terah took Abram his son, and
Lot the son of Haran, his son's son, and Sarai his
daughter-in-law, his son Abram's wife; and they went
forth with them from Ur of the Chaldees, to go into the
land of Canaan; and they came unto Haran and dwelt
there. 32. And the days of Terah were two hundred
and five years: and Terah died in Haran. xii. 4b. And
Abram was seventy and five years old when he departed
out of Haran. 5. And Abram took Sarai his wife, and
Lot his brother's son, and all their substance that they
had gathered, and the souls that they had gotten in
Haran; and they went forth to go into the land of Canaan; and into the land of Canaan they came. xiii. 6.
And the land was not able to bear them, that they might
dwell together: for their substance was great, so that
they could not dwell together. 11b. And they separated
themselves the one from the other. 12a. Abram dwelled
in the land of Canaan, and Lot dwelled in the cities of
the Plain. xvi. 1a. Now Sarai Abram's wife bare him

no children. 3. And Sarai Abram's wife took Hagar the Egyptian, her handmaid, after Abram had dwelt ten years in the land of Canaan, and gave her to Abram her husband to be his wife. 15. And Hagar bare Abram a son : and Abram called the name of his son, whom Hagar bare, Ishmael. 16. And Abram was fourscore and six years old, when Hagar bare Ishmael to Abram. (Here follows ch. xvii. in P.)

xix. 29. And it came to pass, when God destroyed the cities of the plain, that God remembered Abraham, and sent Lot out of the midst of the overthrow, when he overthrew the cities in which Lot dwelt.[1] xxi. 1b. And [the LORD] did unto Sarah as he had spoken 2b. at the set time of which God had spoken to him. 3. And Abraham called the name of his son that was born to him, whom Sarah bare to him, Isaac. 4. And Abraham circumcised his son Isaac when he was eight days old, as God had commanded him. 5. And Abraham was an hundred years old when his son Isaac was born unto him. (Here follows ch. xxiii. in P.)

xxv. 7. And these are the days of the years of Abraham's life which he lived, an hundred threescore and fifteen years. 8. And Abraham gave up the ghost, and died in a good old age, an old man, and full of years ; and was gathered to his people. 9. And Isaac and Ishmael his sons buried him in the cave of Machpelah, in the field of Ephron the son of Zohar the Hittite, which is before Mamre ; 10. the field which Abraham purchased of the children of Heth : there was Abraham buried, and Sarah his wife. 11a. And it came to pass after the death of Abraham that God blessed Isaac his son.

Wellhausen ("Prolegomena," p. 333) thus characterizes

---

[1] In order to find any tolerable connection for this verse it is necessary to suppose that it originally stood immediately after xiii. 12a, and has been transposed by R to its present position.

the document P : "The individuality of the several narratives is not merely modified but absolutely destroyed
by the aim of the whole.   The complex whole leading
up to the law of Moses is everything ; the individual
members signify nothing.   The entire material thus also
itself becomes a perfect vacuity ; apart from covenant-
making it consists only in genealogy and chronology."
This being the sort of material that is attributed to P, in
distinction from J and E, to whom the narrative passages are ascribed, a ready explanation is at once suggested of the difference of style and diction, upon which
such stress is laid as though it indicated diversity of
authorship.

Wellhausen also calls attention to another fact of no
small importance ("Prolegomena," p. 311), that "the historical thread of P runs completely parallel to the history
of JE.   Only thus has it been possible to incorporate
these two writings into one another, as they lie before us
at present in the Pentateuch."   He further shows in detail
(p. 336) that this coincidence in the arrangement of the
materials, which prevails elsewhere, characterizes "also
the patriarchal history ; the outline is the same in P and
JE."   This intimate and pervading relation leads to the
inevitable conclusion that these cannot be altogether independent documents.   Thus he says (p. 356) : "What
is offered us in P is the quintescence of the tradition, not
in an oral but in an already written form.   And the
written shape of the preliminary history which is used
is JE's narrative book.   The arrangement which is there
given to the popular legends [1] is here made the core of

---

[1] In Wellhausen's esteem the sacred history before Abraham is all
myth.   The patriarchal history is legend, containing elements of truth.
"No historical knowledge about the patriarchs is to be gained here,
but only about the time in which the stories about them arose in the
people of Israel ; this later time is here, in its internal and external

the narrative ; the plan, which is there hidden under its detailed treatment, comes out here sharp and distinctly marked, while agreeing throughout, as the main matter of the whole."

A correspondence so remarkable and continuous as to permit the documents to be dovetailed together in the manner alleged by the critics, certainly makes their independent origin quite insupposable. One of two things must be true. Either one of these documents must have taken its shape from the other, or both have alike taken their shape from one common source. Dillmann admits J's dependence upon E, but denies that of P upon JE, alleging that their apparent coincidence in the arrangement of material is due to R, who in combining the documents made P the basis, and transposed the contents of JE to correspond with it. These transpositions are merely conjectural, however, and are of no weight beside the palpable fact of the identical order manifest in these supposed documents, as they lie embedded in the text before us. The majority of the critics accept the former of the alternatives above stated, that of the dependence of one document upon the other. The advocates of the

features, unconsciously projected back into a hoary antiquity, and mirrors itself there as a transfigured fancy picture " (p. 336). While thus converting the lives of the patriarchs into tribal or national occurrences of a later period, he is puzzled what to do with Abraham. " Abraham is certainly not the name of a people like Isaac and Lot ; he is on the whole rather incomprehensible. Naturally we cannot on this account regard him in this connection as a historical person ; he might rather be a free creation involuntarily conceived. He is likely the most recent figure in this company, and probably only prefixed to his son Isaac at a tolerably late period " (p. 337). Unbelieving critics, as a rule, take the same view of the unhistorical character of Genesis, and critics of every shade of belief, who accept the date currently assigned to J and E, in so doing adopt a conclusion based on the assumption that the stories respecting the patriarchs are not records of actual fact, but the inventions of a later period.

old supplementary hypothesis held that J was in possession of P, and made it the basis of his work. Wellhausen and they that follow his lead allege that P was in
possession of JE, and shaped his production by it. The
other alternative, however, affords quite as ready an explanation of the evident relationship. If the Pentateuch
is the original, and the so-called documents are its severed parts, both their agreement in the general, and the
seeming discrepancies which the critics fancy that they
discover, will be fully accounted for. Which of these
alternatives is the true one may be left undecided for the
present.

The narratives ascribed to E in this section are disconnected anecdotes, in which persons figure who do not
belong to the chosen race ; as foreign princes with whom
Abraham is brought into contact (ch. xiv., so Dillmann ;
xx. ; xxi. 22–32), or Hagar and Ishmael in their final departure from his house (xxi. 8–21), and a portion of ch.
xxii. relating to the sacrifice of Isaac. Here it is obvious
that the character of the passages themselves explains
the use of Elohim in them ; so that this does not require
the assumption of a separate writer, who occupied himself exclusively with recording incidents connected with
foreigners, and one solitary demand of the Creator, not
suffered to be carried into execution, but designed to be
a supreme test of Abraham's faith and obedience. All
these incidents have their place and fitness in the life of
the patriarch as a whole, but sundered from the rest and
taken by themselves they lose their chief significance
and value. It is not even pretended that they constitute
a complete life of Abraham, or a connected and continuous
narrative of any sort. They form only a fragmentary
account, with no proper beginning, no mutual connection,
and no governing idea. Only two direct divine communications to Abraham are recorded, one (xxi. 12), direct-

ing him to dismiss Ishmael, and the other (xxii. 1), to sacrifice Isaac. Neither of these can be properly understood
in their isolation ; and the latter especially becomes intelligible only as the crowning act of that long-continued
course of divine discipline and training by which Abraham was fitted for his unique position as the father and
exemplar of the chosen people of God. There is nothing
in these so-called E paragraphs to suggest that they were
ever grouped together in a separate document. And it
is safe to say that such a notion would never have entered the mind of any one, who was not committed to a
hypothesis which required it.

The main body of this section, all of it in fact except
the portions severed from it for P, and for E, for reasons
explained above, is given to J. The predominant use of
Jehovah in this portion of the history is, however, plainly
due to its theme, and creates no presumption that there
was a separate writer whose characteristic habit it was
to employ it.

It is alleged that there are discrepancies in the statements of P, J, and E, and that the same persons and
events are conceived and represented differently. This
charge is based upon the fallacy of making the part
equal to the whole, or of identifying things which are distinct. These alleged discrepancies are used as arguments
for the critical partition, when they are simply the consequences of sundering that which, taken in connection, is
entirely harmonious.

Thus, 1. by splitting the account of Abram's migration
a variant representation is produced of his original home,
which according to P was in Ur of the Chaldees (xi. 31),
while J is said to locate it in Haran (xii. 1 ; xxiv. 4, 7,
10). And yet xv. 7, which is in a J connection, and has

the style and diction of J, expressly declares that Jehovah brought Abram from Ur of the Chaldees.[1] But critics have an easy way of ridding themselves of testimony which is not to their mind. This unwelcome verse, on the sole ground of its annulling a discrepancy which they wish to create, is summarily declared to be an interpolation by R with a view to harmonizing the conflicting sources. The statement of P (xi. 31) clears up the whole matter; Abram went first from Ur to Haran, and thence to Canaan. But this does not satisfy Wellhausen, who suspects that it is only an effort on the part of P to harmonize variant traditions. " If this doubling the point of departure did not originate from the purpose of making a connection with JE, there is no such thing as harmonizing,"[2] or as he puts it in his first edition,[3] " I do not know what harmonizing means." The critics may be allowed to settle between themselves whether it was R or P that did the harmonizing where there was nothing that needed to be harmonized.[4]

2. The charge that in J (xii. 1–4a) Abram went to Canaan by divine direction, but in P (vs. 4b, 5), of his own motion, is made out by rending asunder a statement

[1] See Budde : Urgeschichte, p. 439.

[2] Prolegomena, p. 331.

[3] Geschichte Israels, p. 325, note.

[4] The expression ארץ מולדת (xxiv. 7 ; xxxi. 13) is used interchangeably with ארץ ומולדת (xxiv. 4 ; xxxi. 3). If upon the critics' own hypothesis R saw no difficulty in the latter being used of Haran (xii. 1), just after Abram's migration thither from Ur had been spoken of, why should any difficulty arise from J's employing both these equivalent expressions of Haran likewise ? It is plain from xii. 1 that they cannot be restricted to "land of nativity" in the strict sense, but are properly employed also of Abraham's second home, the land of his kindred. See Delitzsch on Gen. xii. 1. Budde (Urgeschichte, p. 441), who equally with Dillmann and Wellhausen imagines a contradiction in the case, finds it to lie not between P and J, but between the two supposed constituents of the latter document, J" which makes Ur Abram's original home, and J' which makes it Haran.

which is entirely harmonious, and setting its divided parts in opposition.

3. It is said that in J the promise is made to Abram of a land, a numerous seed, and a blessing to all nations of the earth (xii. 1–3 ; xviii. 18 ; xxii. 17, 18) ; but in P (xvii. 4–8), simply of a land and a numerous seed, without any intimation of a blessing to extend beyond his own descendants. But this is simply expecting a complete statement in one which is designedly partial. In the original promise and in the renewal of it upon two occasions of special solemnity, one when the LORD signified his approval of Abraham's unfaltering faith by coming as his guest in human form, and again as a reward of his most signal act of obedience, the blessing is set before him in its most ample sweep. But during all the intervening period of long expectancy of his promised child the divine communications made to him from time to time were designed to keep alive his faith in that particular promise, whose fulfilment was so long delayed ; hence mention is merely made of his numerous seed, and of the land which they were to occupy, alike in xiii. 14–17 ; xv. 5–7, 18, which the critics assign to J, and in xvii. 4–8, which they give to P.

4. It is claimed that according to J (xii. 7, 8 ; xiii. 4, 18), and E (xxii. 13), sacrificial worship existed in the times of the patriarchs ; while P makes no allusion to it until the time of Moses, by whom in his opinion it was first introduced. But this is attributing to distinct documents embodying different conceptions of the patriarchal period that which simply results from the distinction between the divine names Elohim and Jehovah. This distinction is ignored by the critics, and these names treated as though they were practically identical, when in fact they represent the divine being under different aspects. It is not Elohim, God in his general relation to

the world, but Jehovah, as he has made himself known to his own people, who is the object of their worship. Hence Abram built altars to Jehovah (xii. 7 ; xiii. 4, 18), and called on the name of Jehovah (xii. 8 ; xxi. 33) ; and all passages in which the word Jehovah appears are for that reason uniformly ascribed to J.   Their absence from P is due to the principle which governs the partition, not to some peculiar notion as to the origin of sacrifice. In xxii. 1 E it was Elohim, not Jehovah, who bids Abram offer up Isaac, because the Creator might rightfully demand of his creature the surrender of that which he had given him.   But this was only intended as a test of obedience.   Jehovah did not desire the sacrifice of the child.   Accordingly the angel of Jehovah restrained Abram's hand ; and the ram providentially provided was offered up instead of his son (ver. 13).

Wellhausen (" Prolegomena," p. 359) remarks upon the absurdity of the conception which the critics have sought to fasten upon the imaginary author of the document P, that " religion was at first naturalistic, then became somewhat more positive by jumps, and finally altogether positive in the year 1500 B.C.   How is it possible to see historical fidelity in the representation that the patriarchs could slaughter but not sacrifice ; that first the sabbath was introduced, then the rainbow, then circumcision, and finally, under Moses, sacrificial worship ? "   The ridicule here directed against P really falls upon the critics themselves, who are the sole authors of this glaring absurdity.

5. In P (xiii. 6) Abram and Lot separate for want of room simply, while in J (ver. 7a) it is because of the strife of their herdmen.   But this is merely objecting that the part is not equal to the whole.   The story is arbitrarily split in two.   The lack of room which leads to the strife is given to P ; the strife which results from

the lack of room to J. Each part implies the other and is incomplete without it.

6. J (xii. 13, 19) tells of Abram's prevarication about Sarai (so E xx. 2); Sarai's quarrel with Hagar (xvi. 6), (so E xxi. 10); and Lot's incest (xix. 30 sqq.); while P never mentions anything discreditable to the patriarchs. J speaks of angels (xvi. 7–11; xix. 1, 15; xxiv. 7, 40); so E (xxi. 17; xxii. 11); P never does. J tells of a divine communication in a vision (xv. 1), and E in a dream (xx. 3, 6); P mentions neither. According to P Abram dwelt in Mamre or the region of Hebron (xxiii. 2; xxxv. 27); according to E in Gerar (xx. 1), and Beersheba (xxi. 31). P tells of his purchase of the cave of Machpelah as a burial-place and that Sarah was buried there (ch. xxiii.), and Abraham himself (xxv. 9), and subsequently Isaac and Rebekah, and Jacob and Leah (xlix. 31; l. 13); but E and J make no allusion to any such place of common burial. There is no real discrepancy in any of these cases. The apparent variance is created solely by the partition and cannot be adduced in support of that upon which it is itself dependent.

7. It is said that different versions are given of the deliverance of Lot from the overthrow of Sodom. In P (xix. 29) he is saved for Abraham's sake; in J (xviii. 23) because of his own righteous character. In P he was sent out of the midst of the overthrow, implying that time and opportunity were afforded for escape after the destruction had begun; in J the destruction did not come upon the city until after Lot had left it (xix. 22–24). The apparent variance is created by sundering related verses, and then putting an interpretation upon them which their connection forbids. Even on the critical hypothesis of different documents, the true meaning of each must be preserved in their combination, if R is to be trusted. God's remembering Abraham (xix. 29)

and delivering Lot, is a plain allusion to the intercession of the former (xviii. 23), and its meaning is determined by it. God's sending Lot out of the midst of the overthrow, when he overthrew the cities in which Lot dwelt, is a summary statement by way of resumption of what had been narrated (xix. 15–25), and it must be understood accordingly.

8. According to xvii. 24, 25 ; xxi. 5, P, Ishmael was fourteen years old when Isaac was born ; yet it is said that (xxi. 14–20) E represents him after this as a young child needing to be carried by his mother. But the alleged inconsistency is due to misinterpretation. The LXX. has (xxi. 14), " and he put the child on her shoulder ; " and Tuch so interprets the Hebrew. Dillmann, however, admits that this is not the meaning of the existing Hebrew text, in which " putting it on her shoulder " is parenthetic, and refers only to the bread and bottle of water, while " the child " is dependent on the previous clause, " gave unto Hagar." Delitzsch points out a similar construction of the words " and Benjamin," in Gen. xliii. 15. Dillmann's conjecture that the reading of the LXX. is the original one, and that the Hebrew has been altered for the sake of harmonizing, is gratuitous and unfounded. Neither does " she cast the child under one of the shrubs " (ver. 15) imply that he was an infant ; Delitzsch compares Jer. xxxviii. 6, where Jeremiah was cast into a dungeon, and Matt. xv. 30, many were cast at Jesus's feet to be healed. Nor is there any such implication in the direction to Hagar to " lift up the lad " (ver. 18), who was faint and sick, nor in the statement (ver. 20) that he " grew," which simply means that he advanced to manhood.

9. The statement that Sarai was so fair as to attract the attention of Pharaoh, to the peril of her husband's life (xii. 11, 15 J), is said to be incompatible with xii. 4b (cf.

xvii. 17 P), according to which she was at that time up-
wards of sixty-five years of age. And it is said to be still
more incongruous that she should have attracted Abimelech (xx. 2 sqq. E), when (xvii. 17 P) she was more
than ninety years old. The only point of any consequence
in this discussion is not what modern critics may think
of the probability or possibility of what is here narrated,
but whether the sacred historian credited it. On the
hypothesis of the critics, R believed it and recorded it.
What possible ground can they have for assuming that J
and E had less faith than R in what is here told of the
marvellous beauty and attractiveness of the ancestress of
the nation? If the entire narrative could be put together by R, and related by him with no suspicion of
discord, the same thing could just as well have been
done by one original writer. It may be added, if it will
in any measure relieve the minds of doubting critics, that
Abimelech is not said to have been taken with Sarah's
beauty. He may have thought an alliance with " a
mighty prince " (xxiii. 6) like Abraham desirable, even
if Sarah's personal charms were not what they had once
been. And when Abraham lived to the age of one hundred and seventy-five, who can say how well a lady of
ninety may have borne her years?

10. It is said that J and P differ in their conception
of God; J's representation is anthropomorphic, that of
P is more exalted and spiritual. But the two aspects of
God's being, his supreme exaltation and his gracious
condescension, are not mutually exclusive or conflicting,
but mutually supplementary. Both must be combined
in any correct apprehension of his nature and his relation
to man. These are not to be sundered, as though they
were distinct conceptions of separate minds. They are
found together throughout the Bible. Since Elohim is
used of God as the creator and in his relation to the

world at large, while Jehovah is the name by which he
made himself known to his chosen people, his chief acts
of condescending grace naturally appear in connection
with the latter.   It is Jehovah who adopts the forms of
men in covenanting with Abram (xv. 17), and who enters
into familiar intercourse with him (xviii. 1 sqq.).   And
yet the manifestation of Jehovah's presence in smoke
and flame (xv. 17 J) has a precise parallel in P in the
cloud and fire above the tabernacle which guided Israel
through the desert (Ex. xl. 36–38; Num. ix. 15 sqq.).
Jehovah appeared to Abram three times—twice in J (xii.
7; xviii. 1); once in P (xvii. 1), where the critics say
that the text should be Elohim.   Jehovah spake repeatedly to Abram, and on one occasion to Hagar (xvi. 13);
so did God in P to Abram (ch. xvii.), to Noah (vi. 13;
viii. 15), and to the first human pair (i. 28).   If it is
speaking after the manner of men when Jehovah speaks
of going down to Sodom to see how they have done
(xviii. 21), it is no less so when Elohim tests the obedience of Abraham (xxii. 1), a passage which the critics assign to another than P; but in P God went up from
Abraham (xvii. 22), which implies that he had come
down to speak with him.

   We now proceed to consider the critical partition of
this section in detail.

THE FAMILY OF TERAH (CH. XI. 27–32).

   The critics have had no little perplexity in disposing
of this paragraph.   In consequence of its intimate relation to ch. xii., Astruc assigned it to J; Eichhorn, though
with some hesitation, gave it to P.   The majority of
critics thenceforward attributed it to the latter document.
Dillmann did the same in his first edition of Genesis; in
his second edition he followed Wellhausen in referring

ver. 29 to J and the rest to P, ver. 30 being supposed to belong originally at the beginning of ch. xvi., and to have been transferred thence by R; in his third edition he followed Budde and Hupfeld in assigning vs. 27, 31, 32, to P, and vs. 28–30 to J. The critical embarrassment arises from the circumstance that while all parts of the paragraph are knit together in inseparable unity, they are at the same time linked to what precedes and follows with an entire disregard of the critical severance, being bound alike to passages referred to P and to J. Thus, ver. 27 repeats the last words of the preceding genealogy, as is done at the opening of a new section (vi. 10; xxv. 19) ; and ver. 32 sums up the life of Terah in the terms of the genealogy of ch. v., as is done in the case of Noah (ix. 29). It is clear that vs. 27, 32, are from the same hand as the genealogies of chs. v. and xi., which they continue and complete ; they are accordingly held to belong to P. So is ver. 31, whose phraseology is identical with that of xii. 5, which the critics for reasons to be considered hereafter find it convenient to refer to P, though it is cut out of a J connection, to which it manifestly belongs.

On the other hand, according to the latest conclusions of the critics, vs. 28–30 belong to J; ver. 28 since "land of his nativity" is reckoned a J phrase; ver. 29 because it is preliminary to xxii. 20 sqq. J, although xxv. 20 P requires the assumption that P must here or elsewhere have given a similar account of Rebekah's descent from Bethuel and Nahor, which R has not preserved; ver. 30 because it would be premature in P before ch. xvi., whereas it is appropriate in J as preliminary to chs. xii., xiii., and especially xv. 2, 3. And yet this paragraph cannot be torn asunder as the critics propose. For vs. 28, 29 presuppose ver. 27, and are abrupt and unexplained without it; and ver. 31 implies the previous

statement of Abram's marriage (ver. 29), and needs ver.
28 to explain why Lot went with Terah without his
father; and ver. 30 follows naturally and properly after
ver. 29 with the mention of a fact at the outset, upon
which the life of Abraham so largely turned. Moreover,
the portion assigned to J (vs. 28–30) is not only without
any proper beginning, but severed from ver. 31 fails to
explain the fact assumed in ch. xxiv. J, that Abram's
former home was in Mesopotamia and that other descendants of Terah were settled there. How the home
of Abram's ancestors came to be in Ur of the Chaldees
(xi. 31), when the ark landed on the mountains of Ararat (viii. 4 P), and Terah's descendants are subsequently
found in Haran and Canaan, is a puzzle in P. This has
led Dillmann and others to fancy that Ur of the Chaldees
lay in Mesopotamia, in spite of its name and its positive monumental identification, or else that it has been
interpolated in this verse by R. The puzzle is entirely
of the critics' own creation. The missing link, which
explains the course of migration, is found in xi. 1–9,
which is attributed to J ; and the whole trouble arises
from sundering this from P, in which it is indispensable. Dillmann's assertion that if Ur lay in Chaldea, this
must have been inserted in ver. 31 by R in order to connect it with xi. 1–9, simply amounts to a confession of
the real nexus in the case, introduced not by R but by
the original writer.

Still further, the occurrence of " Ur of the Chaldees,"
both in ver. 28 J and in ver. 31 P, annihilates, on the
critics' own showing, the alleged discrepancy between
these imaginary documents as to Abram's original home,
the fallacy of which has been remarked upon before. It
is here bolstered up by assuming that these words do
not properly belong in ver. 28, but have been inserted by
R.

THE CALL OF ABRAM AND HIS JOURNEYS (CH. XII.).

The critics endeavor to make a show of continuity for
P in the history of Abraham, as has before been stated,
by picking out a sentence here and there from chs. xii.-
xvi., sundering it from its connection and transferring it
to P, while the body of these chapters is given to J.
But they have no better reason, and are no more successful in this than in their attempt to establish the continuity of J in the narrative of the flood. In order to
bridge the chasm from ch. xi. to ch. xvii., six verses and
parts of three others, referring to the principal events
that had taken place in the interval, are rent from their
proper context and claimed for P, viz., Abram's removal
from Haran to the land of Canaan (xii. 4b, 5); his separation from Lot (xiii. 6, 11b, 12a); his connection with
Hagar (xvi. 1, 3); and the birth of Ishmael (vs. 15, 16).
These verses and clauses fit perfectly in their context,
and no one would ever dream that they had been inserted from another document, but for the necessity laid
upon the critics to discover something that could be attributed to P, which might explain the situation in ch.
xvii., viz., Abraham's presence in Canaan (ver. 8); his
son Ishmael (vs. 18, 20), born thirteen years before (ver.
25), though Sarah had no child (vs. 17, 19); as well as
Lot's abode in the cities of the Plain (xix. 29). But
notwithstanding this urgent motive, Ilgen (1798) is, so
far as I know, the only critic prior to Hupfeld (1853)
who could find any indication of P in chs. xiii., xv., xvi.
Astruc, Eichhorn, Gramberg, Stähelin, Delitzsch (1st
edition), and even Vater, with his fragmentary proclivities, were equally unable to sunder anything from ch.
xii. Tuch (1838) suggested doubtfully in his exposition,
though with more confidence in the introduction to his

"Commentary," that xii. 5 belonged to P on a ground
which subsequent critics have annulled, viz., its resemblance to xxxvi. 6 and xlvi. 6, which are in a context referred by him to P, but denied by others to be his.[1]

The critics divide this chapter as follows : J, xii. 1–4a,
6–9, 10–20 ; P, vs. 4b, 5. Knobel refers vs. 6, 8a, 9, to
P ; Schrader to E ; Kittel also to E, though ascribing
vs. 6–9 in its present form to J. Wellhausen and Kuenen make ver. 9 an insertion by R. Schrader, Wellhausen, Kuenen regard vs. 10–20 as a later addition to
J ; Dillmann, Kittel, as belonging to J, but transposed
from their original position after ch. xiii.

THE CALL OF ABRAM (CH. XII. 1–9).

P's account of Abram's removal from Haran begins
abruptly (xii. 4b), and in a manner that implies that
something is missing. The statement that "Abram was
seventy and five years old when he departed out of
Haran," presupposes that this departure had been already mentioned. And so in fact it is in what immedi-

[1] An apt illustration is here afforded of the facility with which critics,
by slightly shifting the lines of division, can serve the purpose which
they have in view, or can alter the complexion of the alleged documents with which they are dealing. Tuch (Genesis, p. xliii, note) was
inclined to assign xii. 5, 6, 8 ; xiii. 18 to P. This would account for
the place of Sarah's death and burial (xxiii. 2, 19), which otherwise
there is nothing in P to explain. Knobel reaches a like result by giving P xii. 4b, 5, 6, 8a, 9. The connection in J was thus broken, but
that was no objection on the supplementary hypothesis, of which they
were advocates, that J was not an independent document, but consisted of sections and paragraphs added to P. Schrader gives vs. 6a,
8a, 9, to E, on the ground that one from the northern kingdom, as he is
assumed to be, would feel more interest in associating Abram with Shechem and Bethel, than J from the kingdom of Judah. Dillmann objects that 6b and 8b cannot be separated from 6a and 8a, an objection
equally valid, as is shown in the text, against his own removal of ver.
5, which is a necessary link between ver. 4 and ver. 6.

ately precedes (vs. 1–4a). But this, we are told, belongs to J. So that it is necessary to assume that the preliminary part of P's narrative has been omitted, and these verses from J substituted for it. The attempt has been made to confirm this by alleging that a special title, " These are the generations of Abram," must originally have stood at the beginning of Abram's life [1] in P, as in the case of Isaac (xxv. 19), and Jacob (xxxvii. 2), since a separate section must have been devoted to this greatest of the patriarchs, instead of including him under " the generations of Terah," who is of much less account, and whose life is brought to a formal close in the preceding chapter (xi. 32); but that R, in replacing the opening words of P by those of J, dropped the title of the former as well. Plausible as this may sound, it is clearly a mistake. For—

1. Even if such a substitution had been made, it would not account for the omission of the title, had it been appropriate and originally stood there; for like titles occur at the head of sections which are wholly J's (ii. 4), or in whose opening chapters there is not a single sentence from P (xxxvii. 2).

2. The proper title of this section is " the generations " not of Abram but " of Terah," since it deals not only with Abram but other descendants of Terah as well, who are accordingly for this reason introduced to the reader at the outset (xi. 27, 29), viz., Lot, who journeyed with Abram to Canaan, and Nahor, whose descendants are recited without a separate title (xxii. 20–24), preparatory to the marriage of Isaac into this family of his kindred (ch. xxiv.). Bruston suggests that these last should have had a special title, " the generations of Nahor,"

---

[1] So Knobel, Wellhausen, Dillmann, and others, following a suggestion of Ewald in his review of Delitzsch on Genesis in his Jahrbücher d. Bibl. Wissenschaft for 1851–52, p. 40.

and been inserted at the close of ch. xi. No doubt the author might have disposed his matter differently, and included it under different titles, if he had seen fit to do so. But the question is not what he might have done, nor what in the opinion of the critics he ought to have done, but what he actually did.

3. While it is true that in several instances the sections of Genesis terminate with the death of the person named in the title, this is not necessarily nor invariably the case, *e.g.*, the generations of Adam (ch. v.). " The generations of Terah " are not occupied with the life of Terah, which is only the starting-point. The aim of the section is to trace the fortunes of the three families sprung from him, so far as they came within the proper scope of the sacred history. The limitation of this section to xi. 27–32 makes it altogether unmeaning. It becomes still more glaringly so on the critical hypothesis that vs. 28–30 are from a different document J, and do not belong to the section in its original form in P ; a view of which Dillmann justly said, in his first edition, one can then see no reason for a Terah section at all.

4. The generations of Abram would be an unsuitable designation of a history, the emphasis and interest of which for several successive chapters turns upon the patriarch's childlessness.

5. That this entire section is, in the intention of the author, included under the title " the generations of Terah," not of Abram, further appears from the opening of the next section (xxv. 19), where the genealogy is linked directly with xi. 27, 32, by beginning " Abraham begat Isaac."

No title has been dropped, therefore, from the beginning of ch. xii.; consequently no presumption can be drawn from that source in favor of different narrators. It may be added that as xii. 4b requires 4a to make it in-

telligible, and this is indissolubly bound to vs. 1-3, so
xii. 1 is linked as firmly with the preceding chapter. J's
account cannot have begun with ch. xii. Dillmann (1st ed.),
nor with xi. 29 Dillmann (2nd), nor with xi. 28 Dillmann
(3rd), for in each case Abram is introduced abruptly
and without explanation ; and xi. 27 P is required to
precede them. Thus P is linked with J, and J with P,
each dependent on the other to supply the needed explanation of what it contains, neither complete without
the other, both fitting accurately together and precisely
filling each other's gaps. Is this harmonious production
a piece of patchwork? Can extracts from wholly independent documents be made to match in this manner,
however skilfully arranged ? And how do those repeated
omissions, now from one document, now from the other,
which must of necessity be assumed by the advocates of
the current critical hypothesis, comport with what is alleged of the conduct of R elsewhere, his concern to preserve the briefest and most scanty statements of his
sources, even when they add nothing to fuller narratives
drawn from elsewhere, the insertion being detected by its
being a superfluous and unmeaning duplication? (Cf.
vii. 7-9 with vs. 13-16 ; ix. 18, 19 ; xiii. 6, 11b, 12a ; xix.
29.)

MARKS OF P.

The reference of xii. 4b, 5, to P is argued by Hupfeld
and others on the following grounds :
(1) Because ver. 5 repeats 4a. But—
a. This is no mere identical and superfluous repetition.
A general statement of obedience to the divine command
(ver. 4a) is followed by a more particular account of
what was done in accordance with it (ver. 5). Nothing is
more common in the Hebrew historians than brief sum-
maries of this sort followed by fuller and more specific

details, where no one imagines that there is a diversity
of writers. So Gen. vii. 5, 7 sqq.; xxxvii. 5–8; xli. 45c,
46b; xlii. 19, 20c, 24c, 26 sqq.; Judg. iv. 15c, 17; 1 Sam.
xvii. 49, 50; 2 Sam. xv. 16a, 17; 2 Kin. xi. 16c, 20b.

b. Verse 5 is indispensable to make the connection
between vs. 4a and 6. In 4a Abram goes forth, it is not
said whither. In ver. 6 he is already in Canaan and
passing through it. It is presupposed that he had arrived there, and that the name of the country has been
made known to the reader and need not be repeated.
But the missing statements on these points are only
found in ver. 5.

(2) xii. 5b is parallel to xi. 31b, and evidently its continuation.

This is unhesitatingly admitted, and is quite consistent
with the unity of the book, of which it is a natural sequence.

(3) Verse 5 has words and phrases peculiar to P. The
following instances are adduced, viz.:

1. וַיִּקַּח *took,* as in xi. 31; xxxvi. 6; xlvi. 6. But it is
used in precisely the same manner in J (xxiv. 51; xxxii.
23, 24 (E. V., vs. 22, 23); xliii. 13; xlvii. 2); and in E.
(xx. 14; xxii. 3; xlv. 18, 19).

2. רְכוּשׁ *substance, goods,* and רָכַשׁ *to get, gather,* are
claimed as undoubted characteristics of P, but, as it
would appear, on very slender grounds. The verb and
noun occur together in four passages (Gen. xii. 5; xxxi.
18; xxxvi. 6, 7; xlvi. 6); and the noun alone in six other
places in Genesis, and twice besides in the rest of the
Pentateuch. The critics themselves refer it six times to
another than P (Gen. xiv. 11, 12, 16, 21; xv. 14; Num.
xvi. 32). Once, and once only, it stands in a context by
common consent referred to P (Num. xxxv. 3). In every
other instance the verse or paragraph in which it is
found is cut out of a J or E context, or one of disputed

origin, and is assigned to P mainly because of this very word which is arbitrarily assumed to belong to him.

3. נֶפֶשׁ *person*, is not peculiar to P, as appears from its occurrence in Gen. ii. 7 ; xiv. 21 ; Deut. x. 22; xxiv. 7 ; xxvii. 25; Josh. x. 28–39 ; xi. 11 ; not to speak of Gen. xlvi. 15–27, which several eminent critics ascribe to another than P. Dillmann ("Genesis," p. 230) remarks that "it was scarcely possible to avoid using נֶפֶשׁ for persons of both sexes, free and slave," and ("Exodus, Leviticus," p. 535) that it is not a certain indication of P.

4. אֶרֶץ כְּנַעַן *land of Canaan*, is classed as characteristic of P ; but it occurs repeatedly in both J and E, viz.: xlii. 5, 7, 13, 29, 32; xliv. 8; xlv. 17, 25 ; xlvi. 31; xlvii. 1, 4, 13, 14, 15 ; l. 5, where, as Dillmann remarks, it stands in contrast with the land of Egypt.   In like manner it is used in the passages now in question to designate the land promised to Abram (xvii. 8), in contrast with Haran from which he came (xii. 5 ; xvi. 3), and with the cities of the plain selected by Lot (xiii. 12).

5. It appears, accordingly, that these words, whether regarded singly or collectively, afford no indication of P as distinguished from the other so-called documents. There is, however, a striking resemblance in the phraseology of xii. 5 ; xxxi. 18 ; xxxvi. 6 ; xlvi. 6 ; which creates a strong presumption, if not a certainty, that these verses are all from the same hand.   The critics refer them all alike to P ; but they do so in spite of the fact that xii. 5 is in a J context, xxxi. 18 and xlvi. 6, in an E context, and that of xxxvi. 6 is disputed.   Their assignment to P is altogether arbitrary. They are made to sustain each other in this, while there is no reason for sundering any one of them from the connection in which it stands, and attributing it to a different document, but the mere will of the critics.   Words descriptive of the possessions of the patriarchs are naturally grouped together when

mention is made of their migrations. But the only reason for alleging these words to be characteristic of P is
that these migrations are assigned to him in the arbitrary manner already described. The critics have themselves created the criterion, to which they then confidently point in justification of the partition which they
have made.

(4) This statement could not have been lacking in P.
This is a frank avowal of the motive by which the
critics are actuated in rending ver. 5 from its connection.
It is necessary in order to make out an appearance of
continuity for this supposititious document. Instead of
an argument for the hypothesis it is simply a confession
of the straits to which it is reduced.

(5) The mention of Abram's age in ver. 4b is held to
be a sufficient reason for ascribing it to P.

a. It is a purely arbitrary assumption that dates and
statements of men's ages are to be referred to P, even
when, as in the present instance, the context in which
they are embedded is derived by the critics from some
other document. A particularly glaring case occurs in
xli. 46, where Joseph's age when he stood before Pharaoh
is assigned to P, though there is nothing in that document to which to attach it. It is easy to manufacture a
criterion of this sort, and carry it relentlessly through,
and then point to the fact that all the dates are to be
found in P in evidence of the correctness of the rule.
They are there for the simple reason that this is where
the critics have put them. It has no further significance
if the various statements of the ages of the patriarchs,
when put together, yield a consistent chronology;[1] this is

---

[1] It may be observed here that there is no conflict in the chronology
between xii. 4b and xi. 32 ; though, if there were, this would be no
argument for a diversity of writers, since in the esteem of the critics
both belong to the same document. Abram left Haran many years be-

no excuse for critical surgery, but is only one indication more that the book of Genesis is woven together too firmly to be rent asunder, except by a violence which will destroy the fabric. Inconsistently enough, where a different motive operates, the critics allow that E recorded Joseph's age (Gen. l. 22, 26), and that of Joshua (Josh. xxiv. 29) in which P, as a native of Judah, is presumed to have less interest; and even that of Caleb of the tribe of Judah (Josh. xiv. 7, 10), which occurs in a connection that constrains them to refer it to E.

b. 4b presupposes 4a. It is not a statement that Abram went forth from Haran, but a declaration of his age at the time, implying that the fact of his having done so had been already mentioned; and for this reason it cannot connect with xi. 31, as the critics propose, where no such affirmation is made.

(6) According to vs. 4b, 5, Abram simply continues the migration to Canaan begun by his father (xi. 31), acting from the same impulse, and from natural motives but without any divine call; whereas ver. 1 represents his journey as undertaken at the divine command, Abram not knowing whither he was to go.

But there is no diversity of representation implying that these verses have been drawn from diverse sources. On the contrary they are mutually supplementary. The movement initiated by Terah to find more desirable quarters was carried out by Abram at Jehovah's bidding, who guided him to the land to which his father had originally intended to go. And with this the statement

fore Terah's death. Only the writer, according to his uniform method, completes Terah's life before proceeding to that of Abram (cf. xxv. 7; xxxv. 29). The Samaritan text, in order to relieve this imaginary difficulty, reduces the age of Terah from two hundred and five to one hundred and forty-five years. Acts vii. 4 follows the order of the narrative, not that of time.

of xv. 7 is in full accord. Jehovah providentially led
Abram to accompany Terah to Haran, and then by an
immediate call brought him to Canaan. The divine call
which is expressed in ver. 1 is implied in 4b, according
to which Abram leaves Haran in the lifetime of his
father. Why should he leave Terah behind him if they
were migrating under one common impulse?

Knobel assigns vs. 6, 8a, 9, also to P; to which Dillmann objects that P shows no interest in connecting the
patriarchs with the holy places of later times, though he
excepts xxxv. 9 from this remark. Schrader refers 6a,
8a, 9, to E, who, as a North-Israelite, inclined to link
Abram with Shechem and Bethel. With this Dillmann
and Kittel concur so far as to regard E as the source from
which J, as the author of vs. 6–9, drew the mention of
these localities. This is based upon the notion that the
recorded lives of the patriarchs are not the recital of actual events, but a reflection of the ideas of later times,
and that the places where they are said to have dwelt or
worshipped are so designated because of local sanctuaries established there in subsequent ages, to which credit
was attached by stories that they had been hallowed by
the presence of their ancestors. All speculations about
authorship which spring from this false conception of
the patriarchal history, are, of course, entirely baseless.

Meanwhile the unity of the entire paragraph (vs. 1–9)
is obvious. Verse 8b presupposes 8a, and cannot be separated from it; 8a presupposes ver. 6, and this in its turn
ver. 5, which defines the land referred to and mentions
the arrival there, which is implied, but not stated, in ver.
6. Again, 4b presupposes 4a, and this vs. 1–3. The
grant of the land in ver. 7, notwithstanding its present
occupancy by others (6b), is with express reference to the
promise in ver. 1. And ver. 9 is the natural continuation of the marches in vs. 6, 8. All is thus concatenated

together in a manner to defy critical severance. On the
assumption that vs. 10–20 is an interpolation, it has been
argued that ver. 9 was inserted by R as a connective.
This inference is by no means necessary, even if the assumption were correct ; but it falls as a matter of course
if the latter is shown to be untrue, which will be done
presently.

MARKS OF J.

Dillmann finds the following criteria of the document
J in vs. 1–4a, 6–9, viz. : 1, The divine call ; 2, divine worship ; 3, יהוה *Jehovah ;* 4, כָּל־מִשְׁפְּחֹת הָאֲדָמָה *all the families of the earth ;* 5, נִבְרְכוּ בְ *be blessed in ;* 6, קלֵּל *curse.*
It has been before shown that there is a reason for the
occurrence of the name Jehovah here and elsewhere in
the life of Abram quite independent of the question of
documents ; also that patriarchal worship is as a rule
connected with that name; and there is an equally obvious reason why the call of Abram should likewise be
similarly connected. It will be observed that the linguistic criteria alleged are all limited to one verse (ver.
3). The phrase, " all the families of the earth," occurs
but once besides in the Pentateuch (xxviii. 14), where
the same promise is repeated to Jacob. The other repetitions of this promise are by the critics referred to R
(xviii. 18 ; xxii. 18 ; xxvi. 4), and there the equivalent expression כֹּל גּוֹיֵי הָאָרֶץ *all the nations of the earth,* is used.
The Niphal of בָּרַךְ *to bless,* occurs but three times in the
Old Testament, each time in this same promise (xii. 3 ;
xxviii. 14 J ; and xviii. 18 R). Since these expressions
are limited to this one promise, and occur in J but once
in addition to the verse now before us, they cannot be
classed as indications of the existence of a separate document so called. Moreover, the promise of a blessing
to all nations was given three times to Abram on occa-

sions of special note (xii. 3 ; xviii. 18; xxii. 18), once to
Isaac (xxvi. 4), and once to Jacob (xxviii. 14) ; on all other
occasions in J (xii. 7 ; xiii. 15, 16 ; xv. 5, 7, 18), or P,
(xvii. 4–8; xxviii. 3, 4 ; xxxv. 11, 12) attention is especially
directed to the gift of Canaan and of a numerous posterity without any mention of their relation to the world at
large. And the limitation in these instances is not suggestive of the peculiarity of a particular document, but
grows out of the circumstances of each case. That the
phrases now in question could have no place in these restricted promises is obvious. Neither their occurrence
nor their omission can afford a plea for a diversity of
documents. It remains to be added that while the precise combinations and forms above adduced do not occur
in P, for the reason now given, the words themselves are
found in passages ascribed to P ; thus מִשְׁפָּחָה *family*,
very frequently, and even in application to the nations
of mankind (x. 5, 20, 31, 32); אֲדָמָה *earth* (i. 25 ; vi. 20 ;
ix. 2) ; בֵּרֵךְ *bless* (Gen i. 22, 28 ; ii. 3 ; v. 2 ; ix. 1, etc.).

One word remains of the alleged characteristics of J,
קִלֵּל *curse*, which is as little to the purpose as the preceding. Apart from Gen. xii. 3 it occurs but once in J
(viii. 21) ; four times in P (Lev. xxiv. 11, 14, 15, 23) ;
once in E (Josh. xxiv. 9) ; once in D (Deut. xxiii. 5, E.
V., ver. 4) ; twice in the Book of the Covenant (Ex. xxi.
17; xxii. 27, E. V., ver. 28) ; three times in the Holiness
Laws (Lev. xix. 14; xx. 9 bis).

ABRAM IN EGYPT (VS. 10–20).

Three instances are recorded in which the wives of
the patriarchs attracted the attention of monarchs, and
through the prevarication of their husbands were
brought into peril, from which by God's providence
they were delivered, viz.: Sarai at the court of Pharaoh

in Egypt (xii. 10–20); and again with Abimelech, king
of Gerar (ch. xx.); and Rebekah before another king of
the same name (xxvi. 6–11). These are to the critics variant accounts of the same event, or different forms of
the same legend. Knobel regards ch. xx. as the original
narrative, and chs. xii. and xxvi. as later modifications of
the legend. Kuenen (" Hexateuch," p. 252) says that a
saga, of which Isaac was originally the subject, has here
and in ch. xx. been transferred to Abram. Delitzsch
ventures no positive affirmation, but seems in doubt
whether some duplication or transposition may not have
taken place. " It is enough," he says, " for us to know
that the three histories are three traditions contained in
ancient sources, that the redactor deserves our thanks
for not suppressing one in favor of the others, and that
all these attest God's grace and faithfulness, which render the interference of human weakness and sin with
his plan of grace harmless, and even tributary to its successful issue." But the value of the religious lesson is dependent on the reality of the occurrence. Is this a Jewish notion of God embodied in a fiction, or is it a fact in
which God has himself revealed his character? A distrust of well-accredited facts because of a certain measure of similitude to other facts would throw history into
confusion. Must we regard the battles of Bull Run,
fought in successive years on the same spot, and terminating the same way, but in different periods of the war
and under different commanders, as variant and conflicting accounts of some one transaction that can no longer
be accurately identified? Why might not Abram repeat
in Gerar what he had done in Egypt, when it was understood between him and Sarai that they were to pass for
brother and sister in " every place " to which they
should come (xx. 13)? And why may not Isaac, whose
life was so largely patterned after that of his father, have

been misled into an imitation of his error in this instance?

Wellhausen claims that vs. 10–20 is a later addition to the text of J, because Lot was not with Abram in Egypt, though according to J he was with him both before (ver. 4a) and after (xiii. 5); and Abram was at the very same place in xiii. 4 as in xii. 8, from which it may be inferred that he had not meanwhile changed his position. Dillmann thinks that the true place of this narrative in J was after the separation of Abram and Lot (ch. xiii.), and that it was transposed by R to remove it further from ch. xx. But the visit to Egypt is confirmed by xxvi. 1, 2; the presence of Lot there by the express statement, "Lot with him" (xiii. 1); and Abram is explicitly said to have retraced his steps to the point from which he had started (vs. 3, 4). These positive confirmations are by a stroke of the critics' pen ejected from the text, and attributed to R, for no imaginable reason but that they nullify a baseless critical conjecture. Lot's name does not occur in xii. 10–20, because Abram was the principal party and there was nothing to record respecting Lot. For the same reason he is not mentioned in vs. 6–9, nor Aner, Eshcol, and Mamre, in xiv. 14–23 (cf. vs. 13, 24); nor Nahor in xi. 31, whose migration to Haran can only be inferred from allusions subsequently made (xxiv. 10). It may also be remarked that xvi. 1 lends an incidental confirmation to xii. 16; Pharaoh's gift to Abram explains the presence of an Egyptian maid in his household.

Dillmann notes a few words and phrases in this paragraph as indicative of J. These and others of the same sort noted in other cases are of no account for two reasons. Inasmuch as the bulk of the narrative is given to J or E, and only scattered scraps to P, the great majority of words appropriate to narrative will, of course, be found in J or E, and comparatively few in P. Besides, several of the words adduced occur but rarely even in J, and cannot, therefore, with any propriety be held to be characteristic of his style. If their absence from a large proportion of the paragraphs of J does not prove these to be from a different pen, how can their absence from the paragraphs of P be urged in proof of a diversity of documents, especially if there was no occasion to use them?

MARKS OF J.

1. יהוה *Jehovah,* explained already.

2. הֵיטִיב לְ *treated well,* ver. 16, only once besides in J (Num. x. 32), and twice in E (Ex. i. 20; Josh. xxiv. 20); in the same sense with a different preposition Gen. xxxii. 10, 13, E. V., vs. 9, 12 J; without a preposition Lev. v. 4 P.

3. נָא *I pray thee* (ver. 13), often in J and E, but once at least in P (Gen. xxxiv. 8), perhaps also Num. xx. 10 (so Nöldeke and Schrader).

4. הִנֵּה־נָא *behold now* (ver. 11; xvi. 2; xviii. 27, 31; xix. 2, 8, 19, 20; xxvii. 2 J).

5. בַּעֲבוּר *for the sake of* (vs. 13, 16), always referred to J, E, or R. See ch. vi.–ix., Marks of J, No. 6.

6. בִּגְלַל *because of* (ver. 13), only twice besides in J (xxx. 27; xxxix. 5); in D (Deut. i. 37; xv. 10; xviii. 12); all in the Hexateuch.

7. מַה־זֹּאת עָשִׂיתָ *what is this that thou hast done* (ver. 18; Gen. iii. 13; xxvi. 10; Ex. xiv. 11 J; Gen. xxix. 25; xlii. 28; Ex. xiv. 5 E); once without a verb (Ex. xiii. 14 J).

SEPARATION FROM LOT (CH. XIII.).

The critics divide this chapter thus:
J, vs. 1–5, 7–11a, 12b–18; P, vs. 6, 11b, 12a.

Knobel assigns to P, vs. 3a, 6, 10a,c, 12. 18a.

Schrader parcels the portion of J between J and E thus:

J, vs. 1, 4, 7b, 10b, 13–17, 18b; E, vs. 2, 3, 5, 7a, 8–10a, 11a, 12b, 18a.

Wellhausen gives to R vs. 1, 3, 4, and regards vs. 14–17 as a later addition to J.

Dillmann gives R the words, " and Lot with him," in ver. 1, together with vs. 3, 4.

GROUNDS OF PARTITION.

The manipulation of the text attributed to R by Wellhausen and Dillmann simply means that it is incompatible with their notions respecting xi. 10–20.   Verses 1, 3, 4 describe Abram's return from Egypt with his wife and Lot, and his proceeding by successive stages to the point from which he had set out.   This shows conclusively that he had visited Egypt, and had visited it at that time, as recorded in the preceding chapter.   Wellhausen, to whom the Egyptian episode is a later fabrication, is obliged to rid himself of vs. 1, 3, 4, altogether.   Dillmann, in whose view it occurred after Abram's separation from Lot, is also compelled to reject vs. 3, 4, but he allows ver. 1 to stand as the conclusion of the narrative in its original position, only without the words " and Lot with him," which would wreck his whole assumption.   It is then claimed that vs. 2, 5, connect directly with xii. 8.

That such a factitious connection is possible proves nothing as to the original constitution of the text.   It warrants no suspicion that the omitted portions do not properly belong in their present position.   Paragraphs and sections can be dropped from any narrative or from any piece of composition that ever was written without destroying its apparent continuity.   This is particularly the case with an episode like the present, which, though it has its importance and appropriateness in its place, might be thrown out without disturbing the general current of the history.

The fact is that the connection is perfect as it stands, and there is not the slightest reason for calling in the aid of R except to patch up an unfounded critical conjecture. Abram returns (ver. 1) with his wife and possessions from Egypt to the southern district of Palestine through which he had passed on his way to Egypt (xii. 9). The presence of Lot with him, to which there was no occasion to allude before, is now mentioned as preparatory to the separation which was shortly to take place, and to which the whole narrative is now tending. The riches of Abram (ver. 2), who advances to his former position in the land by stated marches (vs. 3, 4), (the expression is suggestive of the progress of a large company or caravan), and the flocks and herds of Lot (ver. 5), picture the situation. Then follows in ver. 6 precisely what might be expected—the land was incapable of supporting them together. The result was strife between their respective herdmen (ver. 7a), and the difficulty was aggravated (ver. 7b) by the presence of the native inhabitants who tenanted the region.

The exigencies of the divisive hypothesis make it necessary to find material for P as well as J in this chapter. In xix. 29, which is referred to P, it appears that Lot had parted from Abram, and the reader must have been made aware of the fact. In order to find such a statement in P the critics propose to rend ver. 6 from the closely concatenated paragraph just reviewed. In justification of this it is urged—

1. Verse 6 is superfluous beside the detailed account of the separation (vs. 7 sqq.) and is somewhat inconsistent with it in tracing the separation to the general rea-

son of the greatness of their possessions instead of its special occasion the strife of the herdmen ; and its last clause goes beyond what immediately follows and extends to the separation itself (ver. 12). But—

a. This disregards the frequent usage of Hebrew writers to state first in a summary manner what is subsequently unfolded in detail. Thus, Judg. xx. 35, 36a, precedes the more particular recital, vs. 36b–46 ; 1 Kin. v. 9 is expanded in vs. 10–14 (E. V., iv. 29 in vs. 30–34) ; vi. 14 in vs. 15–36 ; xi. 3b in vs. 4–8 ; 2 Kin. xxi. 2 in vs. 3–9. See other examples of a like nature given above under xii. 5.

b. Verse 6 is neither superfluous beside ver. 7, nor inconsistent with it. It explains the occasion of the strife that followed. And it is important as showing that a peaceful separation was the only available remedy. The strife did not spring from petty or accidental causes, which were capable of adjustment. It was inherent in the situation. The land could not furnish pasture and wells enough for their superabundant flocks. Collision was inevitable if they remained together. By erasing ver. 6 this real and pressing necessity disappears. It is to this that the statements respecting the largeness of the possessions of both Abram and Lot were meant to lead up (vs. 2, 5). It is this which is emphasized by the reference to the Canaanite and the Perizzite (ver. 7), which has no meaning otherwise. Ver. 6 is thus essential in the connection, and cannot have belonged to another document.

2. Its close correspondence with xxxvi. 7.

The expressions in the two passages are almost identical, which speaks strongly for their common authorship. And this cannot be too strongly affirmed and insisted upon in the interest of the unity of the book. This is no argument for diversity of documents, and no proof that ver. 6 belongs to any other than its present context. By an arbitrary dictum of the critics the four principal passages recording the migrations of the patriarchs (xii. 5 ; xxxi. 18 ; xxxvi. 6, 7 ; xlvi. 6), which are all of one stamp and evidence themselves to be from the same hand, are referred to a document distinct from the context in which they stand, and their prominent words are classed as criteria of that document. This is then made a base of operations for forcing other passages out of their proper connection, and thus building up this supposititious document. But the argument partakes too much of the character of a vicious circle to be convincing.

The remainder of the chapter is bound as closely together as is that portion already considered. Recognizing the real occasion of the strife, and the only practicable mode of terminating or avoiding it, Abram (vs. 8, 9) proposes a separation and generously offers his younger kinsman his choice of any part of the land. Lot chose in consequence the fertile plain of the Jordan (vs. 10, 11). Thus they separated, Abram dwelling in the land of Canaan, and Lot in the cities of the plain, moving his tent as far as Sodom (ver. 12). The wickedness of this city is then remarked upon (ver. 13), to give an intimation of its approaching doom and of the issue of Lot's unwise choice.

Under the same pressure as before, the critics here propose to sunder vs. 11b, 12a from its context and give it to P. In favor of this it is urged—

1. Verse 11b is unnecessary after 11a ; and 12a represents Lot as having a fixed abode, while according to 11a and 12b he led the wandering life of a nomad in tents. But—*a*. After the mention of Lot's removal eastward it was still important to state distinctly that this effected a separation between him and Abram. This is the very

point of the narrative, as is indicated by the triple repetition of the word ; in ver. 9, " separate thyself," ver. 14,
" after that Lot was separated," ver. 11, " and they separated." This last cannot be severed from the other two.
With all the emphasis thrown upon the fact of separation
the critics would have us suppose that while it was proposed by Abram (ver. 9), and mention is made of what
occurred after it had taken place (ver. 14), the act of separating was not itself noted; and that the record of separation in the text, with its evident allusion to Abram's
proposal, is a fragment from a different document.

b. The structure of the sentences forbids the partition
made by the critics. The repetition of Lot, as the subject of the second verb in ver. 11, can only be explained
by its being contrasted with Abram's remaining behind
in Canaan ; ver. 12a is, therefore, necessary to complete
the construction. Kautzsch and Socin concede as much
when they say that J must have had such a clause but
R omitted it in order to adopt that of P. Still further,
in ver. 14 Jehovah precedes the verb of which it is the
subject. This is also due to contrast with ver. 12, where
the same phenomenon twice appears. What Abram did,
and Lot did, and Jehovah did, stand in manifest relation ; and ver. 12 cannot accordingly be separated from
ver. 14 as an interjected fragment from a different document.

c. As to the alleged diversity in Lot's mode of life, it
is plain that R, or whoever gave the text its present form,
saw none, or he would not have joined mutually inconsistent clauses without explanation. And such diversity,
if it existed, would prove inconvenient to the critics; for
in ch. xix. (J) Lot is not leading a tent life, but dwelling
in one of the cities of the plain, in accordance with what
they here assign to P, but conflicting with what they assign to J. And in ver. 18 the same two verbs are com-

bined in relation to Abram, which are used of Lot in
ver. 12a and b, and are here set in opposition by the
critics. Where is the difficulty in assuming, as both
xiii. 6, 12a (P), and xiii. 12b, ch. xix. (J) require, that Lot
took up his quarters in one of the cities, while those in
charge of his flocks lived in tents on the plain?

2. " Cities of the plain " (xiii. 12) corresponds with
the expression in xix. 29 P, as against xiii. 10, 11, " the
plain of Jordan," and 12b, " Sodom," expressions of J.

But a purely factitious difference is created here by
arbitrarily dividing a sentence, and giving part to one
document and part to another. " The plain of Jordan "
differs from " Sodom " as much as the latter differs from
the " cities of the plain ; " so that if the latter can be
urged in proof of diversity of authorship, the former may
likewise ; and it would follow that what the critics here
assign to J should be partitioned between different writers. " The plain of Jordan " only occurs xiii. 10, 11 ;
elsewhere it is simply " the plain," alike in xix. 17, 25,
28, assigned to J, and in xiii. 12, xix. 29, assigned to P.
Moreover, according to J (xiii. 10; xix. 24, 25, 28; cf. x.
19), there was more than one city in the plain, so that P's
phrase is completely justified.[1]

3. The verses assigned to P (vs. 6, 11b, 12a) have
words and phrases peculiar to that document. But the
futility of this plea is obvious on the slightest examination.

---

[1] " It is alleged that one narrator calls the cities about the Jordan 'the
cities of the plain,' and the other ' all the plain of Jordan.' But the
latter cannot of itself denote those cities, but only the great plain by
the Jordan. Therefore it stands (xiii. 10, 11) quite properly of the land
which Lot chose as well watered, whilst with equal propriety Lot dwells
in the cities of the plain (xiii. 12), and these cities are destroyed by God
(xix. 29)."—Ewald, Komposition d. Genesis, pp. 118, 119.

MARKS OF P

Dillmann specifies the following:

1. רְכוּשׁ *substance.* See word No. 2, under xii. 5.

2. נָשָׂא *to bear* (ver. 6), is claimed for P, by which can only be meant that it occurs once, though only once, in a precisely similar connection—xxxvi. 7—a verse arbitrarily ascribed to P. The verb itself occurs repeatedly in J and E. It is used in the sense of "bearing" in J (Gen. iv. 13; vii. 17; Num. xi. 14; xiv. 33), and in E (Ex. xviii. 22).

3. יָשַׁב *to dwell* (vs. 6, 12), is also claimed for P, whereas it occurs repeatedly in J and E, not only in other applications, but with express reference to the patriarchs in Canaan: J, xiii. 18; xix. 30 (Lot); xxv. 11b; xxvi. 6, 17; E, xx. 1, 15; xxii. 19; xxxv. 1.

4. אֶרֶץ כְּנַעַן *land of Canaan* (ver. 12). See word No. 4, under xii. 5.

5. עָרֵי הַכִּכָּר *cities of the plain* only occurs xiii. 12; xix. 29; cf. ver. 25. See above.

The assertion that xix. 29 has been transposed from its proper position, and that it was originally attached to xiii. 12a, is altogether groundless, and merely betrays the embarrassment created by sundering it from the connection in which it stands, and to which, as we shall see hereafter, it is firmly bound both by its matter and form, the change in the divine name being for a sufficient reason and not suggestive of a different writer.

The significance of Lot's separating from Abram appears from the enlarged promise, of which it furnishes the occasion, of all the land to him and to his seed forever, and the multiplication of his seed as the dust of the earth (vs. 14–17). The thoroughly arbitrary manner in which the critics deal with the text, rejecting from it whatever does not correspond with their preconceived notions, may be illustrated by Wellhausen's treatment of this passage. He says : [1] "Grounds of a general nature, which will convince few, move me to regard xiii. 14–17 as a later addition. It is not the habit of J to let God speak so without ceremony to the patriarchs ; he is always particular to narrate a theophany in a place precisely indicated, which is then hallowed by this appearing for all time." To this Dillmann very properly replies that xii. 1 is of itself sufficient to show that God does not always speak to Abram in theophanies in the passages assigned to J ; besides the place in which the present communication was made is designated (xiii. 3, 4). It may be added further, that the notion of Wellhausen and other critics that the stories of divine manifestations to the patriarchs originated in the local sanctuaries of later times, inverts the order of cause and effect. It was not the sanctity attached to certain spots by the Israelites which gave rise to the stories of the theophanies ; but it was the fact of these theophanies and the sacred associations thence resulting which led to the establishment of illegitimate worship in these places in after-ages.

MARKS OF J

This chapter, exclusive of the verses referred to P and R, is claimed for J on two grounds, viz. :

(1) Its allusions to other J passages, *e.g.*, " garden of the LORD," ver. 10 to chs. ii., iii. ; the wickedness of Sodom, ver. 13 to ch. xix.

But apart from the fact that these J passages did not themselves belong to an independent document, the chapter is likewise linked to so-called P passages ; to xix. 29 P, which implies Lot's separation from Abram and his re-

[1] Composition d. Hexateuchs, p. 23.

moval to the cities of the plain here recorded. The attempt
is indeed made to evade this by slicing vs. 6, 11b, 12a, from
the rest of the narrative; but this has been shown to be
impracticable. Also to xxiii. 2, 19; xxxv. 27 P, which
imply the record in xiii. 18, that Abram made his home
in " Mamre which is in Hebron."

(2) The occurrence in vs. 8, 9, 14–17, of words and expressions which are used in J elsewhere.

1. נָא *I pray thee* (vs. 8, 9, 14). See under ch. xii. 10–
20, Marks of J, No. 3.

2. הֵימִין *go to the right,* הִשְׂמְאִיל *go to the left* (ver. 9);
these verbs occur nowhere else in the Pentateuch; the contrast of right and left occurs Gen. xxiv. 49; Num. xxii.
26 J; Num. xx. 17 E; Ex. xiv. 22, 29 P; and repeatedly in
Deuteronomy; also in Josh. i. 7; xxiii. 6, which Dillmann refers to D.

3. Vs. 14–17 belong to the progressive series of promises given by Jehovah to Abram, and naturally deal in
the same or equivalent phrases. Thus the four points of
the compass, N., S., E., W., as in a like connection, xxviii.
14, where, however, Wellhausen suspects a different
writer because the order is W., E., N., S.; " thy seed
as the dust of the earth," as xxviii. 14; " not to be counted," as xv. 5; xxxii. 13 (E. V., 12); Num. xxiii. 10.

But words and phrases reckoned peculiar to P are also
found in the J portion of this chapter.

לְמַסָּעָיו *on his journeys* (ver. 3); both the word and the
form are said to be characteristic of P; this form of the
word occurs exclusively in P (Ex. xvii. 1; xl. 36, 38;
Num. x. 6, 12; xxxiii. 2); a like use of the same preposition and a suffix with other nouns is held to be a mark
of P in Gen. viii. 19; x. 5, 20, 31, 32; מַסָּע is found besides in P, in other constructions, in Num. x. 2, 28; xxxiii.
1; but nowhere else in the Old Testament except Deut.
x. 11.

נִפְרָד *to be separated* (vs. 9, 14), was claimed as a mark
of P in distinction from J in Gen. x. 5, 32.

"The land is before thee" (ver. 9) has its only parallels in xxxiv. 10; xlvii. 6 (P), and xx. 15 (E).

"The Canaanite was then in the land" (xii. 6), and
"The Canaanite and the Perizzite dwelled then in the
land" (xiii. 7), are not later glosses, since they are closely
connected with the paragraphs in which they stánd, as
has been already shown; nor are they indications of the
post-Mosaic origin of the narrative. They contain no
implication that the Canaanites and Perizzites had passed
away. It is quite as natural to say, "The Canaanites
were then in the land as they still are," as to say, "The
Canaanites were then in the land, but are there no
longer."

The proof already given of the unity and continuity of
this chapter renders it unnecessary to examine in detail
Knobel's enlargement of P or Schrader's subdivision of
J. These are of interest only as showing the facility
with which documents can be subdivided or the lines of
partition changed.

ABRAM'S RESCUE OF LOT (CH. XIV.)

Astruc set the example of referring ch. xiv. to another
source than the principal documents of Genesis, as he
did every passage which concerned foreign tribes or
nations. The critics complain that it is disconnected
and out of harmony with what precedes and follows
in its representation of Abram, but without good reason. The dignity of his position corresponds with the
statements elsewhere made. The greatness of Abram's
retinue is remarked (xii. 5, 16; xiii. 6, 7). The children
of Heth treat him as a mighty prince or a prince of God
(xxiii. 6). The king of the Philistines and the general

of his army court his alliance (xxi. 22 sqq.). It is in perfect accord with this that he is here said to have mus-
tered three hundred and eighteen trained men (ver. 14;
cf. xxxiii. 1); that he was confederate with native princes
(ver. 13); that as the head of a clan, in contrast with
other tribes or nations, he is called Abram the Hebrew
(ver. 13; cf. 1 Sam. xiii. 3, 7; xiv. 21). This appellation
is justified by the situation and does not require Ewald's
assumption that the narrative is from a Canaanitish original. His generous regard for Lot (ver. 14), his magna-
nimity and disinterestedness (vs. 21–24), agree with xiii.
8, 9. His life had been peaceful hitherto, but he adapts
himself to this new emergency. The land had been
given him with new emphasis in all its length and
breadth (xiii. 15, 17), and it is quite in place that he
should act as its champion and defender from invasion
and pillage. The exhortation and the military emblem
(xv. 1) seem to be suggested by his late conflict.

The critics find their chief perplexity, however, in the
fact that this chapter is related to all the documents, and
cannot be brought into harmony with any one. It has
the diffuseness and particularity of P in vs. 8, 9, the P
words רְכֻשׁ *goods* (vs. 11, 12, 16, 21), נֶפֶשׁ *soul* for persons (ver. 21), יְלִידֵי בֵּיתוֹ *born in the house* (ver. 14), as
xvii. 12, 13, 23, 27; Lev. xxii. 11; calls Lot Abram's
brother's son (ver. 12), as xi. 27, 31; xii. 5. At the same
time it has the J words יהוה *Jehovah* (ver 22), לִקְרַאת *to
meet* (ver. 17), בָּרוּךְ *blessed* (vs. 19, 20); brings Abram
into connection with Salem or Jerusalem, the future site
of the temple, to whose priest he pays tithes (vs. 18–20),
(which is held to be indicative of J, who is reputed to belong to Judah); calls Lot Abram's brother (ver. 14),
as xiii. 8; speaks of him as dwelling in Sodom (ver. 12),
as xiii. 12b; and Abram as dwelling by the oaks of
Mamre (ver. 13), as xiii. 18; connects Admah and Zeboiim

with Sodom and Gomorrah (vs. 2, 8), as x. 19, and Zoar,
as xix. 23, while yet Sodom and Gomorrah are accorded
the precedence (vs. 10, 11), and particularly Sodom (vs.
17, 21, 22), as xiii. 10; xviii. 20, 26; ch. xix. With all
this it has several words which occur nowhere else in the
Pentateuch; אֵל עֶלְיוֹן *God Most High* (vs. 18–20, 22); מִגֵּן
to deliver (ver. 20); הֶעֱשִׁיר *to make rich* (ver. 23); or in
the Old Testament קֹנֵה שָׁמַיִם וָאָרֶץ *possessor of heaven
and earth* (vs. 19, 22); בַּעֲלֵי בְרִית *confederate* (ver. 13);
חֲנִיךְ *trained* (ver. 14); הֵרִיק *drew out* said of men (ver. 14);
also several antique or peculiar names of places : Bela
for Zoar (vs. 2, 8), vale of Siddim (vs. 3, 8, 10), Ashte-
roth-karnaim (ver. 5), Zuzim, probably for Zamzummim
(ver. 5), El Paran (ver. 6), En-mishpat for Kadesh (ver.
7), Hazazon-tamar for Engedi (ver. 7), vale of Shaveh for
the King's Vale (ver. 17), Salem for Jerusalem (ver. 18).
Such unusual words and names are thought to point to
E; so the alliance with native princes (ver. 13), as xxi.
32, and the warlike achievement (ver. 15), as xlviii. 22, as
well as the E words בִּלְעָדַי *nothing for me* (ver. 24), the
Amorite instead of Canaanite (vs. 7, 13), as Num. xxi.
21; Josh. xxiv. 8, 12; likewise פָּלִיט *escaped* (ver. 13), and
מָרַד *rebelled* (ver. 4), which Schrader reckons peculiar to
E, but Dillmann does not.

Nöldeke undertakes to prove the narrative to be altogether fictitious, and several of the names to be the invention of the writer. He adopts the Rabbinical conceit
that Bera, king of Sodom, is from רַע *evil ;* and Birsha,
king of Gomorrah, from רֶשַׁע *wickedness ;* and he appears
to approve the Samaritan conversion of Shemeber, king
of Zeboiim, into Shemebed, *whose name has perished,*
though he shrinks from resolving Shinab, king of Admah,
with the Jerusalem Targum into שֹׂנֵא אָב *father-hater*
The object of the story he conceives to be to glorify
Abram as a conqueror. From the allusions to it in Ps.

lxxvi. 3, E. V. 2 (Salem), cx. (Melchizedek), Hos. xi. 8 (מִגֵּן
deliver, Admah, Zeboiim), he infers that it could not have
been written later than 800 B.C.   Kuenen ("Hexateuch,"
p. 324) also makes it absolutely unhistorical, intended in
vs. 18–20 "to glorify the priesthood of Jerusalem and to
justify their claiming tithes," and borrowed by the final
redactor of the Pentateuch from "a postexilian version
of Abram's life, a midrash."   Monumental evidence has,
however, established the historical character of the names
Arioch, Ellasar, Chedorlaomer,[1] and, perhaps, Amraphel,[2]
as well as of invasions and conquests stretching westward
at that early date.   To evade this, E. Meyer propounded
the extraordinary hypothesis that a writer in the exile
became acquainted with the names of these ancient
kings, and invented this story which brought Abram
into contact with them.

It is thus settled beyond reasonable contradiction that
this chapter stands on historic ground.   Its postexilic
origin is accordingly impossible.   This is an effectual
bar to Wellhausen's proposed solution of its eclectic relation to the several documents, and especially its use of
the diction of P, by assuming that it must have been
produced not by J, E, or P, but by a redactor subsequent to them all ; and in his view P is itself postexilic.
The definiteness and precision of its statements, coupled
with the unusual number of ancient names requiring explanation, which are here grouped together, compel to
the assumption that this belongs to a very early date.
Dillmann attributes it to E, the explanatory glosses having been added by a later hand.   This obliges him to
explain away the marks of P and J as interpolations, or
as of no significance, and to reject vs. 17–20 as no part
of the original narrative.   Knobel refers it to an ancient

---

[1] Schrader : Keilinschriften und das Alte Testament.

[2] Hommel, quoted by Delitzsch.

source, of which J availed himself, and to which he added the necessary explanations by introducing modern names where the older ones had become unintelligible. To this Delitzsch gives his assent. This accounts for the archaic names and expressions and for the marks of J, which the chapter contains; but it leaves without explanation the marks of P, which, though emphasized elsewhere, must here be treated as of no account or set aside as later additions to the text. The natural and obvious explanation of the whole matter, to which the critics determinedly shut their eyes, is that these alleged criteria of distinct documents are not such, after all, but are freely used as occasion requires by one and the same writer, and in the same piece of composition.

Dillmann rejects for no other reason than that they contravene his hypothesis vs. 17–20, Jehovah in ver. 22, and "Admah and Zeboiim" in x. 19, as later additions to the text, and claims that the allusions to ch. xiii. imply acquaintance with that chapter,[1] but not that ch. xiv. is by the same author; whereas the use of the phrase "the vale of Siddim" (vs. 3, 8, 10), instead of "the plain of Jordan," as xiii. 10, 11, shows them to be by different writers. But the vale of Siddim is not identical with the plain of the Jordan; it is (ver. 3) expressly declared to be only that part of it which was subsequently covered by the "Salt Sea," that is, the Dead Sea. The expression used is different because the object to be denoted was different. No inference can be drawn from it, consequently, against the presumption of identity of authorship created by the connection of the narrative, the agreement as to the situation and the charac-

---

[1] As he holds that E is older than J, E could not in his opinion have referred to J. He is obliged, therefore, to assume that the allusions to ch. xiii. were no part of ch. xiv. originally, but are later additions to its text.

ter of Abram, the correspondence of diction, and the
direct allusions.

The P words are waived aside in a similar manner.
" Born in his house " (ver. 14) is pronounced a later addition. Such fulness of detail in any but ritual and legal
matters is said not to accord with P's usage elsewhere,
and the style of the chapter is not his ; which simply
means that the critics have arbitrarily partitioned the
text of the Pentateuch between what is ritual and legal
on the one hand and narrative on the other, as though
no writer could produce more than one species of composition, and the diversity of style due to a difference of
matter were· proof of distinct authors.   רְכוּשׁ goods, and
נֶפֶשׁ soul, in the sense of " person," which are elsewhere
declared to be such evident marks of P as to stamp a
verse as his, though in a J connection, are here passed
over lightly, as though they had no such significance.
Thus Delitzsch says that " רְכוּשׁ is no specific criterion ;
it is found in xv. 14, a promise recorded by J or E (Dillmann says R), and at any rate not by P, and it expresses
an idea for which the Biblical language has no other
word."   And Dillmann says : " One could hardly help
using נֶפֶשׁ for persons of both sexes, free and slave."   If,
then, these are the proper words and the only words to
express a given meaning, such as any ordinary speaker
or writer might upon occasion have to employ, how can
they possibly be classed as characteristic of one document rather than another ?   And if not here, neither
can they be elsewhere.   But it is said that ver. 13 says
" the oaks of Mamre," as xiii. 18 ; xviii. 1 ; while P invariably says simply, " Mamre."   So he does (xxiii. 17, 19 ;
xxv. 9 ; xlix. 30 ; l. 13) when speaking, not of the residence
of Abram, but of the location of the cave of Machpelah
" before Mamre," and (xxxv. 27) when speaking of Jacob's
coming " to Mamre, to Kiriath-arba (the same is He-

bron), where Abraham and Isaac sojourned." The exact spot where Abram dwelt was "by the oaks of Mamre;" but when the district so named is referred to in general, as a matter of course the oaks are not spoken of. This surely is no indication of different writers.

In recording this very significant event in the life of the great patriarch the writer has taken pains to preserve the names of localities, and, as it would appear, to some extent, the use of terms as they were at the time referred to, introducing in a supplementary way the more modern names by which they had been superseded, or some explanatory phrase when necessary for the sake of clearness, as vs. 2, 3, 6, 7, 8, 15, 17. In one instance he uses a name current in his own time proleptically, perhaps for the reason that no other expressed his meaning so exactly. Thus he says (vs. 5-7) that the invaders smote the Rephaim, and Zuzim, and Emim, and Horites, and Amorites, and "the country of the Amalekites." His meaning is here carefully guarded by the altered form of expression. They smote not the Amalekites, who derived their name from the grandson of Esau (xxxvi. 12), and accordingly were not in existence in the time of Abram, but the region subsequently occupied by them.

At first sight it might appear as though "Dan" (ver. 14) was to be similarly explained. It is natural to think of the Dan so frequently mentioned in the later Scriptures, which first received this name after the occupation of Canaan (Judg. xviii. 29; Josh. xix. 47), having previously been called Laish. And on this ground it has been urged that this could not have been written by Moses. But—

1. It seems extremely improbable that the analogy of the entire chapter, which on this interpretation would require "Laish, the same is Dan," should be violated in this one instance without any intimation of it, the origi-

nal name being discarded, and the recent one not added to it by way of explanation, but substituted for it. It is more in keeping with the general tenor of the chapter to suppose that it was not the Dan-Laish of later times, which was intended, but a place so called in the time of Abram, perhaps named from this very event, in which God maintained the righteous cause of his servant (Dan = judge; see xv. 14), and possibly perpetuated in the Dan-jaan of 2 Sam. xxiv. 6, cf. also Deut. xxxiv. 1.

2. If the Dan of later times is here meant, the strong probability is that the older name was in the original text, and in the course of transcription one more familiar was substituted for it. The proofs of Mosaic authorship are too numerous and strong to be outweighed by a triviality like this. Critics whose hypothesis requires the assumption of textual changes of the most serious nature cannot consistently deny that there may be occasion for a slight correction here.

PROMISE AND COVENANT OF JEHOVAH (CH. XV.)

Most of the earlier critics refer the whole of this chapter to J. Knobel attributed both ch. xiv. and xv. to what he called the Kriegsbuch, or Book of Wars, one of the sources from which he imagined that J drew his materials. Wellhausen, and others since, undertake the partition of the chapter, and base it on certain alleged incongruities which have no real existence. It is charged that—

1. There is a discrepancy in respect to time. According to ver. 5, it is in the night and the stars are visible; but vs. 7–11 imply that it is in the day; in ver. 12a, the sun is setting, and ver. 17, it has gone down.

But it is not easy to see how any one can imagine a difficulty here. The transaction described required time. The vision (ver. 1) occurred in the night or in the early morning, when the stars still appeared in the sky (ver. 5). A fresh communication was made to Abram (vs. 7 sqq.), which, whether it followed the preceding immediately or after an interval, contained directions that could only be executed in the daytime. Five animals were to be taken and slain, properly prepared and divided, and the parts suitably adjusted. This would occupy a portion of the day, and during the remainder of it he guarded the pieces from the birds of prey. Then came sunset with the prophetic disclosure (vs. 12–16), and finally darkness with the symbolic ratification of the covenant. The narrative is consistent throughout and develops regularly from first to last.

2. A vision is announced in ver. 1, but it cannot possibly be continued through the chapter.

Knobel thinks that the vision does not begin till ver. 12, and ends with ver. 16. This is plainly a mistake; the communication in ver. 1 is expressly said to have been made in a vision. Whether all the communications in the chapter were similarly made, and only vs. 10, 11 belong to Abram's ordinary state, or whether the vision is limited to vs. 1–6, as Wellhausen supposes, it may be difficult to determine, and it is of no account as nothing is dependent on the mode in which the revelation was given.

3. Ver. 8 is inconsistent with ver. 6. In the latter Abram is said to have believed the Lord; and yet he asks in the former for a visible token of the truth of God's word.

But this request does not indicate doubt or distrust, but rather a desire for a more complete assurance and a fresh confirmation of his faith in the fulfilment of promises so far transcending all natural expectation.

On the grounds above stated Wellhausen assigns vs. 1–6 to E; and vs. 7–12, 17, 18, to J, ver. 7 having been

modified, a clause inserted in ver. 12, and vs. 13–16 being no part of the original text, but added in the first instance after vs. 17, 18, and then transposed to its present
position ; vs. 19–21 being also a later addition. He
urges that the clause, "a deep sleep fell upon Abram,"
does not belong to ver. 12, for, though congruous to vs.
13–16, it is not so to vs. 17, 18, a consideration which
might have led him to see that those verses are in their
proper place, and the only incongruity is one of his own
creating.

The revelation by vision (ver. 1) is, on critical principles, referred to E (though מַחֲזֶה vision, occurs besides in
the Pentateuch only in Num. xxiv. 4, 16 J) ; and this is
supposed to be confirmed by the naming of Eliezer (ver.
2), whereas J does not give his name (xxiv. 2 sqq.—the
identity of the persons being commonly assumed) ; also
by the phrase, "after these things" (ver. 1), which occurs
in E, xxii. 1 ; xl. 1 ; xlviii. 1, but also in J, xxii. 20, xxxix.
7, and even in P, Josh. xxiv. 29, unless it is confessed that
P is not alone in stating ages.   The only escape from this
dilemma is by the absurd division of Schrader, who in the
verse last named assigns "and it came to pass after these
things" to E, and all the rest to P.   Jehovah occurs four
times in the first six verses, though by critical rules E
ought always to say Elohim, never Jehovah.   It is necessary, therefore, to assume that R has changed those names.
There are also some of P's expressions אֲנִי (not אָנֹכִי J) ;
אוּר כַּשְׂדִּים Ur of the Chaldees (ver. 7), רְכֻשׁ goods (ver. 14),
בְּשֵׂיבָה טוֹבָה in a good old age (ver. 15 ; see xxv. 8), not to
speak of the chronological statement, ver. 13.   Hence it
is again necessary to assume that the verses that contain
them have been either altered or inserted by R, whose
office it is to rectify whatever is at variance with the hypothesis.   "Come forth out of thy bowels," מֵעִים (ver. 4),
sounds like a variation upon "come forth out of thy

loins," a phrase which P uses in two forms (xxxv. 11, חֲלָצִים; xlvi. 26; Ex. i. 5, יְרֵךְ), and he might easily be supposed to add a third. At any rate no phrase at all approaching it is elsewhere referred to E; xxv. 23 is assigned to J. The animals (ver. 9) are precisely those admissible for sacrifice under the ritual law (P), and not dividing the birds accords with Lev. i. 17. "The word of Jehovah came" (vs. 1, 4) is a phrase familiar in the prophets, but occurring nowhere else in the Pentateuch; it certainly cannot be claimed, therefore, as characteristic of E. The inhabitants of the land are called Amorites (ver. 16), while J calls them Canaanites and Perizzites (xii. 6, xiii. 7); but if this is the mark of a different writer, how could R, who designates them as in ver. 16, have likewise written vs. 19–21?

Dillmann in his 1st edition (Knobel's 3d) ascribed the entire chapter to R, who had introduced expressions of P as well as of J, and based his narrative partly on E, a combination which could not well be disposed of from the critical point of view in any other way. In his 2d edition (Knobel's 4th) he rids himself of most of the P elements by assigning vs. 7, 12–16, to R, and then gives vs. 3, 5, 6, to J, and vs. 1, 2, 4, 8, 9–11, 17, 18, to E, and vs. 19–21 either to E or R. By the portion given to J his partition has an advantage over that of Wellhausen. Abram's childlessness and the promise of offspring without naming the mother (vs. 3, 5) prepares the way for the affair of Hagar (ch. xvi.), in which E is supposed to have no share. And according to Ex. xxxii. 13, J, God had promised Abraham to multiply his seed as the stars of heaven. This emblem occurs three times in Genesis (xv. 5; xxii. 17; xxvi. 4). By common critical consent the last two are by R, who was posterior to J. On critical grounds, therefore, the reference could only be to xv. 5, so that this must have belonged to J and not to E. This

partition is, however, impracticable, for it is at variance
with the divine names ; it assigns vs. 17, 18, to E in spite
of xxiv. 7, J, which directly refers to it ; it sunders ver.
4 from ver. 3, to which it is the immediate response ; it
connects ver. 8 with ver. 4, though they relate to matters as distinct as the birth of his child and the possession of Canaan. In order to link them together he alters the text of ver. 8 without the slightest authority from
אִירָשֶׁנָּה *I shall inherit it,* to יִירָשֶׁ֫נִי *he shall be my heir,* thus
changing its subject entirely. But his own comment on
ver. 18 refutes his emendation and with it his critical
division of the chapter. Ver. 18 remarks expressly that
by the transaction from ver. 9 onward God concluded a
covenant with Abram in relation to the future possession
of the land. This, then, is what the sign for which he
asked in ver. 8 was to certify, and not that Abram's own
child should be his heir. Ver. 8 cannot therefore connect with ver. 4, but relates to a different subject. Accordingly it is not surprising that in his 3d edition
(Knobel's 5th) Dillmann abandons his previous scheme,
and after reviewing what others have attempted in the
same line with no better success, pronounces it impracticable to separate E and J in this chapter. He imagines that J made use of a narrative of E, in drawing
up this account of a covenant with Abram, which was
subsequently modified by R, and enlarged by him or by
others at a still later time. All this rather than confess,
what this confusion of documents really shows, that the
alleged criteria of J, E, and P are not marks of distinct
writers, but are employed by one and the same writer as
he has occasion.

Budde undertook to make a partition in accordance
with the divine names ; and regarding, as his predecessors had done, vs. 12–16, 19–21, as later additions, he
gave to J vs. 1, 2a, 3b, 4, 6–11, 17, 18, and to E vs. 3a, 2b,

5. He thus admits that "after these things" (ver. 1) is not a criterion of E, that Ur of the Chaldees is Abram's original home in J (ver. 7) as well as in P, that there is no contrariety between ver. 6 and ver. 8; but because of the imaginary conflict in time between ver. 17 and ver. 5 he gives the latter to E in spite of Ex. xxxii. 13, and he makes a singular medley of vs. 2, 3. Each verse is split in two, the first clause of ver. 2 is linked with the last of ver. 3, and the intervening clauses are referred in an inverted order to a distinct document.

Kautzsch and Socin follow Budde for the most part, but are not prepared to accept his juggling with vs. 1–3, which they refer to JE without attempting to indicate what belongs to each. Kittel tries to help the matter by giving ver. 2 to E and ver. 3 to J, but it is in defiance of Jehovah in ver. 2. So that there is no resource but to adopt the explanation of Dillmann in his first edition that the author himself interprets in ver. 3 the somewhat antiquated and obscure expressions of ver. 2. The repetition of the thought has not arisen from the blending of two documents, but from the writer's desire to render an ancient and remarkable phrase here employed more intelligible to his readers.

Delitzsch very properly contends that vs. 12–16 cannot be an addition by R, because it is intimately related to vs. 9–11, of which it gives a symbolic explanation; and it is besides preliminary to a proper understanding of the promise in ver. 18. Kittel also asserts the unity and continuity of vs. 7–18, but needlessly assumes that it originally stood in a different connection.

The enumeration of ten nations in Canaan is peculiar to vs. 19–21, other passages naming seven, six, or fewer still. But as Delitzsch rightly maintains, this is no reason for disputing its originality here.

There is, after all, no break in this chapter. Two distinct promises are made in it; but they are closely related, and are in fact interwoven throughout the patriarchal history. And the conspicuous failure of the critics to effect an analysis makes the evidence of its unity more signal and complete. Driver only ventures the vague remark: "Ch. xv. shows signs of composition; but the criteria are indecisive, and no generally accepted analysis has been offered." It is plain enough that no partition of the chapter has been found possible. The signs of its composite character are hard to discover. Its lack of conformity to any one of the so-called documents discredits those documents, not the unity of the chapter.

BIRTH OF ISHMAEL (CH. XVI.)

The motive by which the critics are influenced in giving a fraction of this chapter to P is thus frankly acknowledged by Dillmann, who says: "Inasmuch as the existence of Ishmael is presupposed by P in xvii. 18 sqq., he must previously have mentioned his birth." The consistency of the hypothesis demands it. And yet, though Ilgen (1798) had anticipated the division of the chapter now currently adopted, Tuch (1838) and Stähelin (1843) still gave the whole to J. In P, according to the former (p. lxiv.), "we only learn incidentally in xxi. 9 (which he gave to P, but recent critics to E), that Ishmael was the son of an Egyptian maid." And all that the latter can say [1] is, "It is possible that P may have related something about the barrenness of Sarah, about Hagar, and the birth of Ishmael, which was dropped because J's fuller narrative was put in its place." Hupfeld's analysis, adopted from Ilgen, is now commonly followed, viz.: P xvi. 1 (?), 3, 15, 16; J, vs. 2, 4–14.

The critics are puzzled as to the disposition to be made

[1] Kritische Untersuchungen, p. 46.

of ver. 1. Knobel and Dillmann (3d) give it to P; Kautzsch follows Schrader in giving 1a to P, and 1b to J; Dillmann (1st and 2d) agrees with Wellhausen that the whole verse is J's; Hupfeld seems uncertain. On the one hand it is urged that " Sarai, Abram's wife," " Abram her husband," "Hagar the Egyptian, her hand-maid " (ver. 3), needlessly repeat what is contained in ver. 1; and that these verses must, therefore, be from different sources. But, on the other hand, ver. 3 neces-sarily presupposes a previous mention of Hagar and of Sarai's childlessness, such as is found in ver. 1, and the identity of expressions favors sameness of authorship rather than the reverse, so that they must belong to-gether. Sarai's relation to Abram is not here mentioned for the first time in either document, as the critics divide them (P, xi. 31; xii. 5; J, xi. 29; xii. 11, 17). It is not stated, then, for the sake of acquainting the reader with a fact not before known. But it is reiterated and dwelt upon at this juncture, that it may be kept before the mind in order to a proper understanding of the situation. That Hagar was an handmaid of Sarai and an Egyptian is also important for the correct comprehension of the subsequent history. Hence it is not only repeated here but elsewhere in all the documents, as the critics regard them (J, xvi. 8; E, xxi. 9; P, xxv. 12). There is, accord-ingly, no escape from the admission of repetitions by the same writer but by the indefinite multiplication of doc-uments. The triple statement (xvi. 15, 16) that Hagar bare Ishmael is not due to some supposed diffuseness of style on the part of P, but emphasizes the fact that he was not Sarai's child.

But if ver. 1 is accorded to P, because presupposed in ver. 3, then the narrative in J evidently lacks its begin-ning. It has no suitable introduction, and the references to Sarai's handmaid (ver. 2), and to Hagar (ver. 4), imply

that she had been spoken of before.   Even splitting ver.
1 between the documents will not mend the matter, for,
as Kautzch admits, " By the reception of ver. 1a from P,
the beginning of J's text is cut away."   Wellhausen tries
to evade this difficulty by assuming that xi. 30 originally
stood at the beginning of this chapter, and belonged to
P.   But such a transposition is unwarranted, a statement
of Sarai's childlessness, such as is found in xi. 30, is appropriate at the beginning of Abram's history, is needed
to set the initial promise (xii. 2) in its proper light, is a
necessary antecedent to xv. 2, and would not at any rate
be a sufficient introduction to xvi. 3, where Hagar, her
nationality, and her relation to Sarai are presupposed as
already known.   That xvi. 1a repeats xi. 30 is not suggestive of distinct documents any more than similar repetitions which abound elsewhere.[1]   The trial of Abram's
faith lay largely in this that notwithstanding the repeated
promises of a numerous offspring, Sarai continued childless.   It was this which led to the expedient here detailed.   It was proper, therefore, that this fact, though
mentioned before, should be repeated in this place.

And ver. 3 is not superfluous after ver. 2.   Sarai
first proposed the thing to Abram, and obtained his consent; she then took measures to give effect to her scheme.
By sundering these verses P is made to say that Sarai

---

[1] Compare 1 Sam. i. 3 and iv. 4 ; ii. 11, 18, iii. 1 ; ii. 21b, 26, iii. 19 ;
xiii. 15b, xiv. 2b ; xvi. 6–11, xvii. 13, 14 ; xvii. 2, 19 ; xxv. 1,
xxviii. 3 ; 2 Sam. ii. 11, v. 5 ; iii. 21c, 22c; xiv. 24, 28; 1 Kin. xiv.
21c, 31b ; xv. 16, 32 ; 2 Kin. i. 1, iii. 5 ; viii. 29, ix. 15, 16.   These
examples, as well as many of those previously given are adopted from an
early publication of Ewald, his Komposition der Genesis, 1823, which is
still worthy of attentive perusal, and in which he argues more wisely than
in his later speculations.   There is much truth in his suggestion that
many of the critical objections to the unity of Genesis arise from apply-
ing to it modern and occidental standards, and disregarding the usages
of Hebrew historiography and that of the ancient Orient generally.

imposed her maid upon Abram without having spoken to him on the subject or gained his consent. Neither is verse 3 superfluous before verse 4. Sarai first surrenders her maid to Abram, he then treats her as his wife. All proceeds in regular order as stated in the text. This is not overloaded, and there is nothing to suggest the intrusion of foreign matter in the narrative.

The dates (vs. 3, 16) do not indicate another writer than the author of the rest of the chapter, except on the arbitrary assumption that the latter could not mention dates. Nor is there any significance in the circumstance that in ver. 15 it is the father, whereas in ver. 11 it is the mother, who gives name to the child. It has been alleged that the former is characteristic of P, the latter of J. But this rule does not hold. J makes Seth (iv. 26), Judah (xxxviii. 3), and Moses (Ex. ii. 22), name their children. And of so little account is it to which parent this act is referred, that in iv. 25, 26, J, they alternate in successive verses, and in xxxv. 18, E, both occur in the same verse and in respect to the same child, while in xxv. 25, 26; xxix. 34; xxxviii. 29, 30 (all J), the naming is ascribed to neither, but spoken of indefinitely.

The closing verses are, moreover, essential to the integrity of the chapter. If they be sundered from it and given to P, the result will be that while J records Sarai's anxiety to have children by her maid, Abram's assent to her wishes, Hagar's pregnancy, and the angel's promise of a son, whom he names and characterizes, yet the point of the whole narrative is never reached. J makes no mention of the birth of Hagar's child. So that his story, as the critics furnish it to us, has neither beginning nor end. We are left to presume that it once had these missing parts, corresponding to what the critics have cut away, but that R removed them to make room for statements to the same effect from P. But this presumption is only an inference from the hypothesis, and cannot consequently be adduced in support of the hypothesis, which, if it is to stand, must rest on other ground than conjecture. The natural inference from the facts, as they lie before us, is that the beginning and the ending, which we possess in the text, are the proper complements of the narrative, in which they are found, and are component and inseparable portions of it. There is not the shadow of a proof that other equivalents ever existed, for which those now existing were substituted. And why R should have made such a substitution, as the critics allege, does not appear, especially as at other times he is represented to be so careful to preserve every scrap from his sources, as to insert what is deemed superfluous, interrupts the connection and adds nothing to what had been said before.

Wellhausen, followed by Kautzsch, regards vs. 8–10, and Kuenen and Kittel, vs. 9, 10, as an insertion by R. If these verses were ejected a seeming conflict can be created with P (vs. 15, 16; xvii. 23 sqq.) and E (xxi. 9 sqq.), and it can be made to appear as though Ishmael was born in the desert and not in Abram's house. Wellhausen urges the triple address of the angel to Hagar in proof of the composite character of the passage; but even on his view of the matter R introduces the angel as speaking to her twice with nothing intervening. The formula of address is repeated thrice in order to mark the distinctness of the three communications which he makes to her. Dillmann very appropriately cites as parallels xvii. 3, 9, 15; xxxv. 10, 11; and he argues that it would be a strange hearing of her affliction if the angel had left her helpless in the wilderness; also that the verses assigned to R are identical in style and diction with the context in which they stand. Besides the promise of numberless offspring, ver. 10 is linked with

xv. 5, of which it is a partial fulfilment. And the allegation that J differed from E and P as to the place of
Ishmael's birth would be improbable in itself, even on
the divisive hypothesis, unless sustained by positive
statements, which are not pretended in the present instance. It is, moreover, expressly contradicted by xxv.
6 J (Dillmann, 1st and 2d), though referred to R on
frivolous grounds in Dillmann 3d; if Abram sent Ishmael away, his mother did not finally leave Abram's
house before Ishmael's birth.

The flight of Hagar in this chapter has been said to
be only a variant of her dismissal (ch. xxi.), and both but
legends based on the signification of her name (הָגָר perhaps = *flight;* cf. *hegira*), which are altogether unfounded
assumptions.

MARKS OF P

The following are noted by Dillmann as marks of P :
1. Exact statements of time, viz.: Abram ten years in
Canaan (ver. 3); eighty-six years old (ver. 16). But—
a. Such statements are not confined to P, as the critics themselves divide the documents. Thus J, periods
of seven and forty days in the flood (vii. 4, 10, 12;
viii. 6, 10, 12); four hundred years' affliction (xv. 13;
Del., Kit.); forty years in the wilderness (Num. xiv. 33,
xxxii. 13). E, twelve years' service, thirteenth year rebellion, fourteenth year invasion (xiv. 4, 5, Dill.); Jacob
serving twice seven years (xxix. 20, 30); twenty years of
service, fourteen and six (xxxi. 38, 41); Joseph seventeen years old (xxxvii. 2); at the end of two years (xli. 1)
the same phrase as xvi. 3; seven years of plenty,
seven of famine (xli. 29, 30, 47, 48, 53, 54); two years
and five (xlv. 6, 11); Joseph, one hundred and ten years
old (l. 22, 26); Caleb forty years old at sending of spies,

eighty-five years old forty-five years later (Josh. xiv. 7, 10); Joshua one hundred and ten years old (xxiv. 29).

   b. This repeated mention of ages and of definite periods of time in passages attributed to JE shows that these cannot be made a criterion of P; and that they afford no justification for severing verses in which they occur from their proper connection on the plea that they are thereby proved to be insertions from P. Such passages as xii. 4; xvi. 3, 16; xxv. 20; xli. 46; xlvii. 28, must accordingly be held to belong to the context in which they are found, and from which they are sundered by the arbitrary test which has now been shown to be invalid. It is contended that these verses form part of a chronological scheme traceable throughout the Pentateuch, all the parts of which must of necessity be assigned to the same writer. This is readily admitted; but the conclusion to be drawn from it is the reverse of that deduced by the critics. It is not that these passages are to be rent from the context to which they naturally and properly belong, and attributed to P; but that the sections in which they are found have a common author with all those other sections in which the same scheme appears. And as this scheme runs through P, J, and E sections alike, it binds all indissolubly together as the product of one mind.

   2. לָקַח *took*, 3. יָשַׁב *dwelt*, and 4. אֶרֶץ כְּנַעַן *land of Canaan* (ver. 3) are not peculiar to P, as was shown under ch. xii. 5, Nos. 1 and 4; ch. xiii., Marks of P, No. 3.

   5. אִשָּׁה *wife*, applied to a concubine, is adduced by Dillmann as indicative of P, with a reference in his 1st edition to xxv. 1, in which Keturah is so called, and which is there referred to P, but in both his subsequent editions to E. In xxx. 4a, 9b, the same term is applied to Bilhah and Zilpah; Dillmann says that these clauses " could possibly have been originally derived " from P.

But if so they are entirely isolated in a JE context. On such a showing the proof that this is characteristic of P is rather meagre.

It will be observed that of the words said to be indicative of P in the scraps attributed to him in ch. xii.-xvi. not one occurs in any preceding P section, and but one occurs exclusively in P, viz., " cities of the plain," which is found in but two places and each time in a verse rent from its proper connection.

MARKS OF J

The following are said to be indications of J :

1. The angel (ver. 7 sqq.).

There are two reasons why " angel " does not occur in P. *a.* This is used as a criterion in determining the documents. The presence of this word in an Elohim passage is of itself held to indicate that it belongs not to P but to E. *b.* The bulk of the history is divided between J and E, and only such a residuum assigned to P as affords no occasion for an angel to appear.

2. The notion in ver. 13 that it was dangerous to see God. But—

a. This is based on a wrong interpretation of the verse. Hagar does not speak of her seeing God, but of his seeing her ; not of her continuing to live after this divine vision, but of the ever-living One who had watched over her in her distress. It stands in no relation, therefore, to the truth taught in Ex. xxxiii. 20, " No man shall see me and live."

b. Even if this verse had the meaning attributed to it, the absence of this idea from sections ascribed to P is as readily explained as its absence from other J sections in which God appears to men or speaks with them without allusion being made to danger thus incurred.

3. The unfavorable representation of Hagar and Ishmael. That this is found in J and not in P is simply the
result of the partition. Nothing is conceded to P but
the bare statement of Hagar's union with Abram and
Ishmael's birth. Everything indicative of character is
assigned to J or E. There is no variant representation
in P. Abram's affection for Ishmael (xvii. 18 P) agrees
with xxi. 11 E.

4. The etymologies in vs. 11, 13, 14.

But the like are found in P xvii. 5, 17, 19, 20.

5. The difference between ver. 11 and 15 in respect to
the person naming the child.

It has already been shown (p. 211) that this affords no
criterion for distinguishing different documents.

6. יהוה *Jehovah;* already explained, see page 151.

7. הַגֵּה־נָא *behold now* (ver. 2) ; see ch. xii. 10–20, Marks
of J, No. 4.

8. שָׁמַע לְקוֹל *hearkened to the voice* (ver. 2), occurs in
but two passages besides in J (Gen. iii. 17 ; Ex. iv. 8, 9).
It is found likewise in E (Ex. iii. 18 ; xv. 26 ; xviii. 24).
Commonly this verb has a different construction in J, as
it has in P.

9. עָצַר *restrained* (ver. 2), occurs but once besides in
the Pentateuch in a similar connection (xx. 18), which
the critics refer to R. The word is found three times in
P (Num. xvii. 13, 15, E. V., xvi. 48, 50 ; xxv. 8), but,
nowhere else in J.

10. הַרְבָּה אַרְבֶּה *I will greatly multiply* (ver. 10), and
but twice besides in the Hexateuch (iii. 16 J, and xxii.
17 R, who according to Dillmann has made a free addition of his own). In Ex. xxxii. 13 J, אַרְבֶּה is without the
infinitive, though based upon Gen. xxii. 16, 17. How J
could quote R, who by the hypothesis was subsequent to
his time, it is not easy to say. But if J uses this combination in two places, and failed to employ it when

there was such an obvious reason for his doing so, what
is there surprising in its absence from P, who, moreover,
does use the infinitive absolute with the finite verb in
other cases? *e.g.* Ex. xxxi. 14, 15 ; Lev. vii. 24 ; x. 18 ; xx.
2, 27 ; xxiv. 16, 17 ; xxvii. 29 ; Num. xv. 35 ; xxvi. 65 ;
xxxv. 16–18, 21, 31.

11. לֹא יִסָּפֵר מֵרֹב *shall not be numbered for multitude*
(ver. 10). This phrase occurs but once besides in the
Hexateuch (xxxii. 13, E. V., 12).

12. אוּלַי *it may be* (ver. 2), besides in J (xviii. 24, 28,
29, 32 ; xxiv. 5, 39 ; Ex. xxxii. 30 ; Num. xxii. 33 ; Josh.
ix. 7) ; in E (Gen. xxvii. 12 ; xxxii. 21, E. V. ver. 20 ;
Num. xxii. 6, 11 ; xxiii. 27 ; Josh. xiv. 12). It is not
surprising that this word does not chance to occur in the
very limited amount of narrative accorded to P. Many
other words in ordinary use fail to appear in this document for the same reason.

COVENANT SEALED BY ABRAHAM (CH. XVII.)

This chapter cannot be sundered from what precedes
and follows as an extract from an entirely independent
document, as is done by the critics, who assign it to P.
It is most intimately related to the whole narrative of
which it is a part. Its explicit allusion to antecedent
events obliges the critics to link it with statements of
their occurrence, and thus by means of scattered and
disjointed sentences to make out for P a show of continuity. With how little reason and success this is done, we
have already seen. But even if the analysis which they
propose were better supported, it does not meet the case.
It is not sufficient that there should be a bald mention
of Abram's arrival in Canaan and of the birth of Ishmael.
The significance of these facts in the life of Abram, and
the entire course of training to which he had been sub-

jected, as this is set forth in the whole antecedent narrative, are necessary preliminaries to this chapter. Its form cannot be accounted for nor its contents be understood without it.

The one leading idea in the life of Abram is the trial of his faith, that it might be perfected and exhibited, and that he might become the father of the faithful. Jehovah bade him leave his country and his father's house, promising to give him possession of a land and to make of him a great nation; and this though the land was already occupied by Canaanites and his wife was childless. His faith was soon tried by a grievous famine which obliged him to leave the land and go down to Egypt, where a new trial awaited him in the peril of losing Sarai. She was rescued by divine interference and he was restored to Canaan enriched, but the promised seed was not born. In the long waiting he began to apprehend that his steward, Eliezer, would be his heir. But the promise was made more definite that he should have a child of his own body, not merely a son by adoption, and that his offspring should be as numerous as the stars. And to confirm his faith in his future possession of the land, Jehovah entered into a formal covenant with him, sealing the engagement by a visible symbol of the divine presence. Ten weary years had worn away, and still Sarai had no child. At her suggestion he took Hagar, thinking thus to obtain the promised son. Ishmael was born and had reached his thirteenth year when the promise was made more definite still, and the announcement was given that his long-deferred hope was now to be fulfilled. Not his handmaid but his wife, not Hagar but Sarai, should be the mother of the promised seed. The covenant, which had already been ratified on one side, must now be ratified on the other. Abraham is required to signify his faith in the divine announcement, and to bind himself and his household in covenant with God by the seal of circumcision, and this in anticipation of Isaac's birth. This final ratification of the covenant is followed by Jehovah's condescending to the usages of men, and celebrating the completion of this transaction by coming in human form to feast with Abraham at the door of his tent, where the promise is repeated in the hearing of Sarah. Jehovah also makes a confidential communication of his purpose to Abraham, and admits him on the footing of this newly confirmed friendship to the intimacy of persistent and prevalent intercession.

If ever a narrative bore in itself the evidence of inviolable unity, in which every part fits precisely in its place in the plan of the whole, and is indissolubly linked with every other, all breathing one spirit, contributing to one end, working out one common design, to which each and every item is indispensable, and defying all attempts to rend it asunder, this is the case with the life of Abraham as recorded in the book of Genesis. Though it is told with a charming simplicity and apparent artlessness, the divine purpose rules in the whole, and rivets all together with hooks of steel which no critical art can sever.

We are asked to believe that all this close correspondence and evident adjustment of the several parts is but the result of a lucky accident. Two, or rather three, documents, written quite independently of each other, with entirely distinct aims and frequently at variance in their details, have happened to be so constructed that extracts taken from them could be dovetailed together and yield all the evidence of a consistently constructed, regularly developing scheme, which reaches its most pathetic climax when the faithful patriarch proves his obedience in the last and sharpest trial of all by taking the knife to slay his son, and the approving voice from heaven stays his hand, and confirms the promises previously given by the unheard-of solemnity of the oath of Jehovah swearing by himself.

Is it a supposable thing that ch. xvii. has been extracted from a document, which, as the critics tell us, knows nothing of any previous divine communication made to Abraham? which, on the contrary, represents him as having migrated to Canaan of his own motion, and from no divine impulse, no promises having been made to him, and no measures taken to discipline his faith? So viewed it no longer has the emphasis of being preceded by a series of promises of growing definiteness and clearness, which gradually lead up to it, but is absolutely not only the first, but the only revelation which God makes to Abraham his whole life long. The chapter is then an enigma, and its most significant features lose their point.

Why is it stated (ver. 1) that Abram was ninety-nine years old? In itself that is an altogether unimportant detail. And so are the facts which P is supposed to have registered (xii. 5), that Abram was seventy-five years old when he departed out of Haran, and (xvi. 16) that he was eighty-six years old when Ishmael was born, provided all the intervening years were, as the critics suppose them to have been in this document, absolutely blank, with no promise from God, no expectancy, no event of any kind—mere empty years devoid of all significance. But if these have been years of anxious waiting for the fulfilment of a promise yet unaccomplished, of hope long deferred yet not abandoned, and the affair of Hagar was the rash expedient of despondency from long delay, then we see the significance of these long terms of years. They are no longer barren, but play an important part in the discipline of Abram, and the development of his character. They are full of meaning in the history of his life, which would not stand out before us in the light that it does if they had not been recorded.

And why does Jehovah reveal himself (ver. 1) as God Almighty? The critics rob this of all its significance by making it merely the customary patriarchal denomination of the Most High. But why does this name appear here for the first time? And why in the subsequent employment of it in Genesis is there an almost invariable reference to this occasion and to the promises here made? Why this appeal to the divine omnipotence, enhancing the sense of the magnitude of the promise, and of the might involved in bringing it to pass? Considered as the first utterance of the promise to Abram, the simple word of the Most High should be sufficient to awaken faith in a believing soul, as in xii. 1–4. And it would seem superfluous to precede it by an affirmation of his almighty power. But if the promise had been made long years before, and repeated from time to time, while yet no sign of its accomplishment appeared, and every natural prospect had vanished, and there was danger that faith so long vainly expectant might weaken or utterly die, unless attention was explicitly directed to the limitless strength of him by whom the promise was given, then there was a gracious and most important end to be answered by this form of the divine communication, and we can see why Jehovah's first word to Abram on this occasion should be, " I am God Almighty."

And why is the divine name "Elohim," (God), thenceforward used throughout the chapter? The critics strip this of all its meaning by referring it to the habit of a writer, who with unvarying uniformity made use of Elohim as far as Ex. vi. 2, while chs. xii.–xvi., with their constant use of " Jehovah " (LORD), are traced to a different source. But this brings them into collision

with the first verse of ch. xvii., where it is said that
"Jehovah appeared to Abram." Here they aver that R
has meddled with the text, and substituted "Jehovah"
for "Elohim," which upon their hypothesis this writer
must have said. And this in spite of the identity of the
expression with xii. 7 and xviii. 1, which vouch for its
originality in xvii. 1; and that there is no variant in
MSS. or versions to afford even a seeming pretext for
this purely conjectural change of text. Meanwhile the
real and obvious significance of the name Elohim in this
connection is overlooked, by which the reader is reminded throughout the interview of the character in
which the LORD here announced himself. Nature has
failed and is incompetent. But Jehovah the God of
Abram is also Elohim, the omnipotent Creator, pledging
that which transcends the powers of nature.

And why is there such iteration and reiteration in the
promise of offspring to Abram (vs. 2–8), with such emphatic expressions and such enlargement of its scope beyond any preceding instance? I "will multiply thee
exceedingly" (ver. 2); "thou shalt be a father of many
nations" (ver. 4), (not merely "a great nation," as xii. 2);
and this emphasized (ver. 5) by a change of name from
Abram to Abraham, " for a father of many nations have
I made thee. And I will make thee exceeding fruitful,
and I will make nations of thee, and kings shall come
out of thee" (ver. 6); and "thee and thy seed after thee "
is thrice repeated (vs. 7, 8). Here the critics see nothing
but verbose diffuseness of the writer of this chapter, who
is thus supposed to be distinguished from the author of
ch. xii.–xvi. This is all that can be said, on the critical
hypothesis that this is the first and only occasion on
which this promise is made to Abram. But this is to
miss the very point and meaning of the entire passage.
By this emphatic reiteration God would reassure Abram

after the vain expectation of four and twenty weary years, lift him out of his despondency, and give him to understand that God had by no means forgotten his promise, but it should be most certainly fulfilled and on a most liberal scale.

And why is this subject recurred to again (vs. 15, 16, 19, 21), with explicit and repeated mention of Sarai as the mother of the promised child, and her name, too, changed in pledge of the event to Sarah, indicating that she was to be the mother of nations and that kings should be of her? This is mere superfluous verbiage on the critical hypothesis. But it is full of meaning, if these words are uttered at the end of a long series of disappointments, by which Abram had been tempted to misconstrue the promise which had been made him, and to think first of Eliezer as his heir, and then of Hagar as the mother of his child. Now to put an end to all possible misconception, and to remove all doubts arising from Sarah's advanced age and long-continued barrenness, he is emphatically assured that she and no other shall be the mother of the promised seed.

And why in the midst of these assurances does Abraham interject the petition (ver. 18), "O that Ishmael might live before thee"? The critics see simply an expression of concern for Ishmael. But the connection plainly shows that after the fruitless expectation of years Abraham had at length resigned himself to the belief that Ishmael was the only child that he could ever have, that Sarah's age and his own made any further hope impossible, and all that he could reasonably anticipate was that his race should be perpetuated in Ishmael. Hence the emphasis with which the declaration is made, that not Ishmael, but Sarah's son Isaac, to be born at this set time in the next year, was the child contemplated in the promise.

And why is circumcision introduced just here as the sign of God's covenant with Abraham? The critics say that this covenant is here spoken of as a new thing, with the implication that the writer knew nothing of the previous ratification of the covenant in xv. 17, 18. But this is a wholly unwarranted inference. The covenant was in the first instance ratified by the LORD as one of the contracting parties, a visible symbol of the divine presence passing between the pieces of the slaughtered animals. The time has now arrived for it to be ratified by Abraham as the other party to the covenant. And it is highly significant as a final test of the patriarch's faith, which had been so sorely tried before, that, antecedent to the accomplishment of the promise, he is required by this rite to signify his confidence in that for which he had so long and so vainly waited, and which now seemed to be counter to every natural expectation.

The entire chapter in every part thus presupposes and is shaped by the antecedent experience of Abraham as recorded in chs. xii.–xvi. Severed from that its details have no significance, and merely reflect the extraordinary diffuseness and peculiar verbal preferences of the writer. And by sheer accident his fondness for numerical statements, his employment of an antiquated title for the Supreme Being, his habit of using Elohim, his verbose diffuseness, and his disposition to dwell upon ritual matters yield precisely the emphasis and the form needed to crown the whole series of promises of ever-growing fulness and precision, recorded by another writer, of whom P knew nothing, and whose views he did not share; they are precisely what was needed in a last reassuring utterance to one, whom hope deferred had tempted to misinterpret former declarations, or to grow despondent in respect to their fulfilment. It requires all the credulity of an antisupernatural critic to accept such a conclusion.

And further, ch. xviii. is just as unintelligible without ch. xvii., as the latter is apart from the chapters that precede it. The transaction there recorded is without a parallel in Scripture. It cannot be dismissed as only another instance of J's extraordinary anthropomorphisms, or put on a parallel with heathen myths. There is nothing like it elsewhere in J. Its remarkable and solitary character implies a very unusual occasion. The occasion was in fact absolutely unique. It was the final solemnization of the covenant transacted between God and Abraham as the father of the chosen race, and which had now been separately ratified by each of the parties. It was the starting-point of that scheme of grace by which a people was separated from the rest of the world to be for the time the depositary of God's truth and ordinances with a view to the ultimate salvation of the world. The nearest Scripture parallel is that in which Jehovah, who here covenanted with Abraham, renewed his covenant with his descendants, increased to a nation, at Mount Sinai (Ex. xxiv. 7, 8), which was followed by a sacred meal in which the representatives of the people ate and drank in the immediate presence of the God of Israel visibly manifested before them (vs. 9–11). So here Jehovah in human form, came to the tent of Abraham, and ate of his food in token of the friendly intimacy established, as men who had covenanted were in the habit of eating together in recognition of their oneness and their amicable relations (xxxi. 44, 46). Put this unique act of condescension in connection with the unique relation between God and man just consummated, and all is plain. Sunder it with the critics from the immediately preceding transaction, and the peculiarity of this visit to Abraham has no meaning and is without an object. The section next preceding in J is the story of Hagar, which suggests no explanation of this extraordinary

visit.[1]   This is another instance from the critics' point of
view of the combination of unrelated writings chancing
to impart a profound significance to what in its original
position was unmeaning, not to say grotesque.   The evidently inseparable connection of this whole narrative supplies an argument of unity, which every one who reads it
can appreciate, and which cannot be set aside by any
amount of critical reasoning from microscopic details.

STYLE OF P

It is claimed by the critics that this chapter affords a
striking illustration of the difference between P and J in
the treatment of their respective themes.   Thus Dr.
Harper[2] says that P is "systematic.   Just as the story
of creation led up to the announcement of the Sabbath,
and the story of the deluge culminated in a covenant
with Noah and the law of bloodshed, so this section
brings us to the covenant with Abraham and the institution of circumcision."   On the other hand, he affirms[3]
that J has "no particular system; while the covenant
between Yahweh and Abram is recorded, it is neither
the climax nor the all-important fact of the narrative.
It is connected with no institution; and the promise
made then is only one of many repeatedly made by
Yahweh in his familiar intercourse with the patriarchs."
But in actual fact there is as clear and abundant evi-

---

[1] Nor is it explained by the covenant in ch. xv., which De Wette
(Beiträge, ii. p. 77) affirms to be another form of the "myth" in ch. xvii.
An interval of years is presupposed by ch. xvi., which must necessarily
follow ch. xv. and precede ch. xviii.   In ch. xv. God gives to Abraham
a pledge and assurance of his own engagement.   It is only when, as the
counterpart to this, Abram, in ch. xvii., testifies his faith in God and adds
his seal to the covenant that the way is prepared for the covenant
meal in ch. xviii.

[2] Hebraica, v., 4, p. 244.   [3] Ibid., p. 247.

dence of "system" in that portion of the record which is attributed to J, as in that which is ascribed to P, as the most cursory examination is sufficient to show.

The call of Abraham opens the third period of the world's history, for which, as it appears in J, the way was prepared, and the necessity demonstrated (if God's plan of grace was not to be suffered to fail), by the disastrous issue of both the preceding periods. Mankind descending from Adam became hopelessly corrupt, and was swept away by the deluge, from which righteous Noah was spared to be the head of a new race. Impiety prevailed again after the flood, and mankind were scattered over the face of the earth. But God's purpose of mercy was not abandoned. He selected Abraham to be the head of a chosen nation within which true religion might be perpetuated for the ultimate benefit of the world. We are thus brought by successive steps to the base on which the entire body of Old-Testament institutions repose.

The antecedent history moves on toward this divine scheme of restriction in order to a safe and final diffusion in various distinct though related lines. Thus the successive stages of iniquity depicted by J converge upon this issue. The fall of our first parents; the crime of Cain; the ungodliness of his descendants—reaching its acme in Lamech; the degeneracy of the pious race of Seth, induced by intermarriage with the race of Cain— the sons of God with the daughters of men—thus pointing a lesson of which Genesis and the Pentateuch are full, viz., the criminality and the peril of the chosen seed allying themselves with the ungodly around them, the need and the duty of keeping themselves distinct. And after the world had been purged by the flood, the impious and arrogant combination at Babel, frustrated by immediate divine interference, revealed the continuance of the old leaven, and pointed the argument for some new expedient to prevent the extinction of all goodness.

Add to this the gradual unfolding of the promise in J as set forth in each of these great periods. The seed of the woman shall bruise the serpent's head. Jehovah, the God of Shem, in whose tents Japheth shall dwell. Abraham and his seed a blessing to all the families of the earth.

Also the regular dropping of side lines in J, and following the main line so as to converge upon Abraham, thus indicating the distinctness of the chosen race and at the same time their relationship to the whole body of mankind. Thus the line of descent from Cain is traced and then laid aside in order to pursue that of Seth, which the critics tell us J must have continued down to Noah, though only fragments remain (iv. 25, 26; v. 29). Then the sons of Noah are traced and dropped in J's portion of ch. x., and only that of Shem continued in the direction of Terah. Then in Terah's family Lot's descendants are named (xix. 37, 38), and Nahor's (xxii. 20 sqq.), so in like manner the child of Hagar, and the children of Keturah, and the twin brother of Jacob. These are successively set aside, and Abraham, Isaac, and Jacob left in sole possession of the promise.

Again, the promises to the patriarchs in J are not idle repetitions of the same identical substance. They rise by regular gradations in respect to both the matters to which they relate—the promised land and the promised seed. Jehovah first (xii. 1), bade Abram go to a land that he would show him. After he reached Canaan it was made specific (ver. 7), "Unto thy seed will I give *this* land." After Lot had parted from him the terms are made universal; "*All* the land that thou seest, north, south, east, and west, to thee will I give it and to thy seed *forever*" (xiii. 14, 15). Then in Jehovah's covenant with Abram (ch. xv.), this promise reaches its climax. Its certainty is confirmed by the divine pledge symbolically given. The time of the gift is defined (vs. 13–16), and the limits of the territory are particularly specified (vs. 18–21). The promise has become a formal engagement of the utmost solemnity; what was at first vague and indefinite has attained to the utmost precision, both as to the extent of the grant and the time of its bestowment.

Nevertheless it is true that the covenant transaction in ch. xv. is not in every point of view the climax. It rather marks an important stage in an advancing series traced by J. Jehovah *spake* to Abram before he left his father's house (xii. 1), as he had done to Noah (vii. 1), to Adam (iii. 17), and to Cain (iv. 6). But when Abram entered Canaan an advance was made upon all antecedent revelations. Jehovah *appeared* to him (xii. 7). A step was taken beyond this in ch. xv., when Jehovah ratified a covenant with Abram by a visible token of his presence. Then, when Abram (ch. xvii.),[1] obedient to divine direction, ratified the covenant on his part by the seal of circumcision, the climax was reached (ch. xviii.) in the unequalled condescension of a manifestation unique in the whole Old Testament. Jehovah in human form partakes of a covenant meal as Abraham's guest, acquaints him with the divine counsels, and admits him to the greatest intimacy. And so far from this being " connected with no institution," it is the basis of the whole future constitution of Israel as the people of God (xviii. 19), and the foundation of its national counterpart enacted at Sinai.

The successive trials of Abraham's faith in J again form a graduated series, culminating in the sacrifice of Isaac; see pp. 149, 150.

And the promises to Abraham respecting his offspring

---

[1] This P chapter is thus a necessary link in this J series.

exhibit a corresponding progression. The LORD first engaged (xii. 2) to make of him a great nation, and (xiii. 16) to
make his seed as the dust of the earth. After years of vain
expectation Abraham begins to suspect that he shall have
no offspring of his own, but that an inmate of his house
shall be his heir ; whereupon the LORD assures him he
shall have a child of his own body (xv. 3, 4). But Sarah
was barren ; so at her instance he forms an intimacy with
Hagar, and hopes that Ishmael may prove to be the expected seed (xvi. 2). He is then informed that the child
of the bondwoman is not the promised heir, but that
Sarah his wife shall have a son (xviii. 10). After Isaac is
born he is tried once more by being bidden to offer him
up as a sacrifice ; and when his faith endured this final
test the promise of a numerous and victorious seed that
shall bless the world was renewed in ampler terms than
before and is confirmed by the new sanction of an oath
(xxii. 15–18).[1]

With all this evidence of a developing plan and of
methodical arrangement it surely cannot be said that J
has "no particular system."

The style of P in this chapter and elsewhere is said to
be distinguished from that of J in being " stereotyped,"[2]
and marked by the recurrence of the same unvarying
phrases. The repetition charged is largely for the sake
of emphasis. And it is characteristic of Hebrew writers
generally that they take little pains to vary their expressions. If the same thought is to be conveyed, it is
mostly done in the same or like terms. It is not difficult

---

[1] This is an embarrassing chapter for the critics as we shall see. The
great majority have assumed that an account by J and another by E are
here blended. The present tendency is, with Dillmann, to substitute for
J free additions by R ; in which case an independent production by a
different writer, with an appendix by another still, fits as admirably
into J's scheme as though it had been prepared with special reference
to it.   [2] Ibid., p. 245.

to produce an equal number of identical phrases in J. Thus, "lift up the eyes" (xiii. 10, 14); "unto thy seed will I give this land" (xii. 7; xv. 18); "there he builded an altar unto Jehovah" (xii. 7, 8; xiii. 18); "he called on the name of Jehovah" (xii. 8; xiii. 4); "the Canaanite then in the land" (xii. 6; xiii. 7); "between me and thee" (xiii. 8; xvi. 5).

P is said to be "verbose and repetitious." But the repetitions adduced are all for the sake of emphasizing what was of great consequence in the view of the writer. So "the land of Canaan," twice (xii. 5b), as Abram's objective point, and to mark the contrast with a former unfilled project (xi. 31); Ishmael born of the handmaid not the wife, thrice (xvi. 15, 16); and particularly in ch. xvii. Like repetitions can be pointed out in J, e.g., "Jehovah appeared to him," twice (xii. 7); "Bethel on the west" (ver. 8) repeats what had just been said; "famine in the land," twice (ver. 10); the last clause of ver. 14 adds nothing to that which immediately precedes; xiii. 3b, 4a repeats xii. 8 with great minuteness; "to thee will I give it," twice (xiii. 15, 17); "and the angel of Jehovah said," thrice (xvi. 9, 10, 11).

MARKS OF P

Dillmann finds the following criteria of P in this chapter.

1. Back references to it in later P passages (xxi. 2, 4; xxviii. 4; xxxv. 12; Ex. ii. 24; vi. 3, 4; Lev. xii. 3). But—

a. The most of these occur in brief paragraphs, which are ascribed to P mainly because of these very references, and are enclosed in sections attributed to other documents.

b. Its relation to other P passages and common authorship with them is not only admitted but insisted on as involved in the unity of the entire Pentateuch. It is only denied that these are by a different author from the J passages, of which these references afford no proof.

c. It has already been shown that ch. xvii. is insepar-ably connected with the so-called J section, ch. xii.-xvi.; xviii. 14 J refers back to xvii. 21 (לַמּוֹעֵד *at the set time*); "Abraham" (xviii. 6 J), "Sarah" (ver. 9 J), and so thence-forward regularly, in both J and E passages, is with ex-plicit reference to the change of name (xvii. 5, 15 P). The critics seek to evade this plain indication of unity by gratuitously assuming that R has systematically altered the text throughout to conform to this passage.[1]

2. The promise of nations (vs. 4, 5, 16), of kings (vs. 6, 16), and princes (ver. 20).

a. This is an advance upon the promise (xii. 2) to make of Abram a great nation ; and its form is determined by the new names given to Abraham (father of multitude) and Sarah (princess). Other promises which speak of nations (xxviii. 3 ; xlviii. 4) and kings (xxxv. 11) descended from the patriarchs borrow their expressions from this passage, and are uttered with evident allusion to it. In like manner in xlviii. 19 J, the future superiority of Ephraim over Manasseh is expressed by saying that the latter should become a people and be great, but the former should become nations, what is here said of Abra-ham being applied to one of his descendants.

b. The promise of princes to spring from Ishmael is only found in this one place (ver. 20), and it answers precisely to its fulfilment (xxv. 16).

3. The statements of time (vs. 1, 17, 24, 25).

These are arbitrarily referred to P by rule even in the

[1] Hupfeld (Quellen, p. 198) thinks that R changed the names to con-form with P, not in the following, but in the preceding chapters, the forms " Abram " and " Sarai," which were peculiar to P, being intro-duced by R likewise into J in ch. xi. 29-xvi.

midst of sections or paragraphs ascribed to other documents. Nevertheless in repeated instances the critics find themselves compelled to admit that such statements are not peculiar to P. And this is equivalent to an admission that they cannot be made a criterion of this document. See Chapter xvi., Marks of P, No. 1.

4. The similarity of the covenant with that described in ix. 9 sqq.

The resemblance is in phrases indicating its perpetuity, "establish my covenant," "thee and thy seed after thee;" and in appointing a token of the covenant, the rainbow and circumcision. This identity of terms results from the like nature of the transactions.

5. The great redundancy of the style.

It has already been shown that what the critics consider an idle multiplication of words is in fact such a repeated asseveration as was appropriate in the situation and demanded by it.

6. El Shaddai (ver. 1), Elohim (ver. 3 sqq.).

The significance of these names in the connection has been pointed out. The divine omnipotence is here pledged to accomplish what was beyond the powers of nature. El Shaddai also occurs in E xliii. 14, and Shaddai in J xlix. 25; Num. xxiv. 4, 16.

7. אֲחֻזָּה possession (ver. 8). This is the only word used in this sense in the first four books of the Pentateuch, except מוֹרָשָׁה (Ex. vi. 8, P), and נַחֲלָה inheritance, which is also given to P whenever reference is made to the occupation of Canaan, with the single exception of Ex. xv. 17 in the Song of Moses. Another synonym, יְרֵשָׁה possession, nowhere occurs in the books above named, but is limited to Deut. ii. and iii. and three verses in Joshua. If now אֲחֻזָּה is the proper word to express the idea intended, and all the passages from Genesis to Numbers in which this idea is found, are given to P, never to J or

E, how can it be otherwise than that it should be found
exclusively in P? And yet the critics are not unanimous
in making it altogether peculiar to P; it occurs repeatedly in Lev. xxv. (not P, Well.); also in Num. xxxii. 5,
22 (J, Schrad., Kays.; JE, Well.; ver. 5 J, Dill.); Josh.
xxi. 12 (not P, Dill.); xxii 4 (J, Schrad., Kays.; D, Well.,
Dill.). Dillmann accounts for the presence of this word
in Josh. xxii. 4 by the magisterial assertion, "אֶרֶץ אֲחֻזַּתְכֶם
a phrase of P has been substituted by Rd or some later
hand for אֶרֶץ יְרֻשַּׁתְכֶם."

8. מְגֻרִים *sojournings* (ver. 8). The phrase " land of
sojournings " occurs four times besides with explicit reference to this passage (xxviii. 4; xxxvi. 7; xxxvii. 1; Ex.
vi. 4); and " sojournings " without " land " in Gen. xlvii. 9.
All these passages are referred to P. The corresponding
verb גּוּר is, however, used of the sojournings of the patriarchs alike in each of the so-called documents (P, xxxv.
27; Ex. vi. 4; J, Gen. xxi. 34; xxvi. 3; E, xx. 1; xxi. 23).

9. מִקְנָה *purchase* (vs. 12, 13, 23, 27). The expression
" purchase of silver," or " bought with money," occurs but
once outside of this chapter, viz.: Ex. xii. 44. The word
itself also occurs Gen. xxiii. 18; Lev. xxv. 16, 51; xxvii.
22. These are all referred to P. But as this was the only
word to express the idea, its employment was a matter of
necessity and not peculiar to a particular document.

10. הוֹלִיד *beget* (ver. 20). This is distinguished from
יָלַד. in the same sense, not by the usage of distinct documents, but the employment of the former as the more
dignified and formal in the direct line of descent from
Adam to Israel, and the latter in the divergent line. See
on ch. vi.–ix., Marks of P, No. 20. The present instance
is only a seeming exception; the use of הוֹלִיד is due to the
fact that Ishmael is here contemplated in his relation to
Abraham, and the promise to Ishmael here made is included in the promise to Abraham.

11. נָשִׂיא *prince* (ver. 20). This word is referred by Dillmann to P, except in Ex. xxii. 27 (E. V., 28) E. This is made a criterion of P, and verses and clauses containing it are persistently attributed to this document even at the expense of dividing sentences, as is done Gen. xxxiv. 2a (but Schrad., J; Well., not P, J nor E; Kuen., R), Num. xvi. 2; xxxii. 2b (but Well., JE, Kuen., R); Josh. ix. 15 is split into three parts, and assigned to as many different sources.

12. בֶּן־נֵכָר *stranger* (vs. 12, 27), but twice in the Hexateuch outside of this chapter, viz.: Ex. xii. 43 P; Lev. xxii. 25, not P (Well.); נֵכָר elsewhere in the Hexateuch only in J, Deut. xxxi. 16; xxxii. 12; or E, Gen. xxxv. 2, 4; Josh. xxiv. 20, 23.

13. עֶצֶם *self-same* (vs. 23, 26). See Gen. vi.–ix., Marks of P, No. 24.

14. כָּל־זָכָר *every male* (vs. 10, 12, 23). See Gen. vi.–ix., Marks of P, No. 12.

15. פָּרָה וְרָבָה *be fruitful and multiply* (ver. 20). See Gen. vi.–ix., Marks of P, No. 15.

16. נָתַן בְּרִית and הֵקִים *establish* or *ordain a covenant* (vs. 2, 7, 19, 21), do., No. 16.

17. Expressions compounded with עוֹלָם *eternity, perpetuity*.

Such expressions are found in each of the so-called documents, whenever perpetuity or indefinite duration is to be affirmed of any subject. Thus, " everlasting God " (Gen. xxi. 33 J); " everlasting hills " (Gen. xlix. 26 J; Deut. xxxiii. 15 E); " heap for ever " (Deut. xiii. 16 D; Josh. viii. 28 Rd); " servant for ever " (Deut. xv. 17 D); " days of old " (Deut. xxxii. 7 J); " everlasting arms " (Deut. xxxiii. 27 E). Such combinations are most frequent in the ritual law, all of which is assigned to P; legal phrases are therefore to be expected in this document and in no other. Thus, " statute for ever "

(חֻקַּת עוֹלָם) twenty-one times, (חֹק עוֹלָם) eleven times; "everlasting priesthood" twice; "perpetual covenant" (Ex. xxxi. 16; Lev. xxiv. 8; Num. xviii. 19); "perpetual possession" (Lev. xxv. 34). Exclusive of the ritual law the only expressions of the kind in P are those which declare the perpetuity of God's covenant with Noah (Gen. ix. 12, 16), and Abraham (xvii. 7, 13, 19), and of the possession of Canaan (xvii. 8; xlviii. 4). There is nothing in this surely to indicate diversity of authorship.

18. *Thou and thy seed after thee.* See Gen. vi.-ix., Marks of P, No. 17.

19. לְדֹרֹתָם *throughout their generations* (vs. 7, 9, 12). This phrase, with the pronoun "their" or "your," is used exclusively in ritual connections to denote the perpetuity of the institutions referred to. Since ritual matters are regularly ascribed to P, this phrase is necessarily found only in that document.

20. וְנִכְרְתָה הַנֶּפֶשׁ הַהִוא *That soul shall be cut off* (ver. 14), a technical legal phrase, not to be expected except in legal sections.

21. אֶרֶץ כְּנַעַן *land of Canaan* (ver. 8). See ch. xii., Marks of P, No. 4.

22. מְאֹד מְאֹד *exceedingly* (vs. 2, 6, 20). See ch. vi.-ix., Marks of P, No. 27.

VISIT TO ABRAHAM AND DESTRUCTION OF SODOM (CH. XVIII. 1–XIX. 28).

This narrative of Jehovah's visit to Abraham, and of the subsequent destruction of Sodom, is by the critics referred to J. Wellhausen and Kuenen regard xviii. 17–19, and vs. 22b–33a, as late additions by another hand.

The intimate relation of ch. xviii. to the preceding has already been exhibited. It is the final solemnity connected with the concluding of the covenant to which

Abraham gave his adhesion in ch. xvii., which acceptance by him is accordingly here presupposed. The reason for the change in the divine names has also been stated, the thought of God's Almighty power ruling in ch. xvii., as his gracious condescension does in ch. xviii., see p. 152.

The form of expression in xviii. 1 further shows that it connects with what immediately precedes; "unto him" finds its explanation in "Abraham," who is distinctly mentioned xvii. 26, and who is the prominent subject throughout the whole of ch. xvii. But there is nothing with which to link it in xvi. 7-14, the paragraph which it immediately follows in J, as the text is partitioned by the critics.

The critics allege that xviii. 9-15 is a different account of the promise of Isaac's birth already given (xvii. 15-21). But this is obviously not the case. The latter was made to Abraham, the former was for the benefit of Sarah. That they alike receive the announcement with a measure of incredulity, based on the advanced age of both; that each laughs at what to the natural reason seemed so preposterous, which the writer notes with allusion to the meaning of the name of Isaac; that the interval before the birth is stated in almost identical terms, but little time having elapsed between the two promises, is altogether natural and suggestive of one writer and one continuous narrative, not of two separate stories relative to the same event. The LORD promises to return to Sarah (xviii. 14) not after the birth of her child in a visit which J is imagined to have recorded, and R has not preserved, but he visited her in giving her Isaac (xxi. 1).

Kuenen reaches his conclusion that xviii. 17-19, 22b-33a, are interpolations of a late date in the following manner:[1] "Ch. xii. 3, where 'the families of the land' are mentioned, is certainly more primitive than xviii. 18,

[1] Hexateuch, p. 246.

where 'the peoples of the earth' are substituted. The
latter formula stands (Gen. xviii. 17–19), in a context
that sounds almost Deuteronomic, and may therefore be
brought down with high probability to the seventh century (cf. Jer. iii. 17; iv. 2; xii. 15–17; xxxiii. 9). In the
immediate neighborhood of these verses stands the peri-
cope (vs. 22b–33a), the theme of which, viz., the righteousness of Yahwe in connection with the lot of individuals,
appears again to point to the seventh century, in which,
at all events, it was dealt with by the Deuteronomist (vii.
9, 10; xxiv. 16); Jeremiah (xvii. 14–18; xviii. 19–23; xxxi.
29, 30), and Habakkuk (i. 12 sqq.). While the passage
testifies to continued theological reflection, its soteriology
finds an echo in Gen. xv. 5, 6, which is parallel not with
Isaiah vii. 9b, but with Hab. ii. 4b."

The allegation that these ideas savor of a later age is
pure assumption. Gen. xii. 3 speaks not of " the families
of the land " of Canaan, but of " all the families of the
earth," which is precisely identical with " all the nations
of the earth " in xviii. 18. The doctrine of a world-wide
redemption is rooted in that of the unity of the human
race, and the relationship established between all nations
by their descent from a common stock (ch. x.), and in the
primal promise of a victory by the seed of the woman
over the destroyer (iii. 15). It is a simple unfolding of
what is involved in these earliest disclosures, when the
temporary limitation of God's special blessing to Abraham and his descendants is in the very first announcement made to him declared to be in order to pave the
way for a blessing to all the families of mankind. This
was not a doctrine reserved for the age of Jeremiah.
Moreover, as Dillmann suggests: " Men had reflected on
the righteousness and mercy of God before Jeremiah, e.g.,
Gen. xx. 4, and on the possibility of intercession for the
guilty, e.g., xx. 7, 17; Ex. xxxii. 11 sqq.; besides, God's

disclosure to Abraham (xviii. 20, 21) is altogether aimless and disconnected without vs. 17–19 and 23 sqq." And the supreme importance of faith and obedience was well understood before it was formulated by Habakkuk, *e.g.,* Ex. iv. 5, 31; xiv. 31; Num. xiv. 11.

This is but a specimen of the attempt that is made to impose an arbitrary scheme of the development of religious thought upon the writings of the Old Testament. Such a scheme is devised at the pleasure of the critic. It is then used as a standard for the determination of the age of books or of paragraphs and sections, which are distributed irrespective of their true position according as they correspond with one period or another of this imaginary scheme.

Wellhausen tries to prove the existence of interpolations by a different process. He says that אֲנִי (ver. 17), and יְדַעְתִּיו לְמַעַן אֲשֶׁר *I have known him to the end that* (ver. 19), are suspicious, and vs. 17–19 are allied in contents to xiii. 14–17 and xxii. 15–18, which he likewise pronounces spurious. But אֲנִי occurs, besides, in J xxiv. 45; xxvii. 8, 32; xxviii. 13; xxxiii. 14; xxxiv. 30; xlv. 4; and an unusual construction cannot for that sole reason be summarily ejected from the text, unless no writer can use a phrase which he does not employ more than once. The resemblance of this passage to others, whose genuineness there is no good reason for suspecting, instead of discrediting it, tends rather to their mutual confirmation.

In regard to vs. 22b–33a, there is not even the pretext of a diversity of diction or style. It is claimed that ver. 22a connects well with 33b; "the men went toward Sodom, . . . and Abraham returned unto his place." But the fact that the omission of the intervening verses would create no evident break in the connection is no proof of interpolation, as other critics here confess.

Abraham's awe (vs. 27, 30–32) is not inconsistent with
the attentions shown to his divine guest (vs. 2 sqq.).   It
is true that the men include Jehovah (vs. 2, 16); but
this is not the case (ver. 22) where he is expressly distinguished from them.   The genuineness of the passage is
besides vouched for by vs. 20, 21, which are designed to
prepare the way for the interview that follows; by the
explicit allusion, xix. 27 to xviii. 22b, and the scene that
follows; by the number "two" (xix. 1), which implies
that one had remained behind (xviii. 2); by "angels"
(xix. 1, 15), indicating that they were Jehovah's messengers (see ver. 13), not Jehovah himself; and by the use
of the singular alternating with the plural (xviii. 3, 4, 9,
10), showing that one of the three was the superior, was,
in fact, Jehovah (vs. 13, 17, 20, 22), and this feature does
not reappear after xviii. 22 until xix. 17–22, at which
point it is thus intimated that Jehovah rejoins them.
The assertion that J never uses the plural "angels" is
disproved by this very passage.

MARKS OF J

The following grounds are alleged for assigning this
section to J:

1. "The same beauty and transparency of description,
the same vividness of portraiture, the same depth and
fulness of thought, the same naive and popular anthropomorphism as in ii. 4–iii. 24; xi. 1–9, shows the writer
to be the same."

The correspondence in style and character is freely
admitted, and the identity of authorship affirmed.   Like
qualities are to be expected in compositions by the same
author when the subject admits of similar treatment.
But a different style befits majestic scenes such as the
creation, in ch. i., or those of awful grandeur, as the flood

(ch. vi.–ix.), or the monotonous recital of a genealogy, as ch. v., or the technical enactments of ritual, or when the omnipotence of God is to be emphasized (ch. xvii.) rather than his condescension. Unless it is contended that the author of these chapters could not write upon themes of a different description, his productions may be expected to exhibit a diversity of style corresponding to the variety of matters with which he deals.

2. The back reference, xviii. 18 to xii. 2, 3.

The reference is obvious, but no more so than the use of " Abraham " and " Sarah " throughout ch. xviii. to xvii. 5, 15 ; or xviii. 14 to xvii. 21 ; or xviii. 11, 12, to xvii. 17 ; or the transaction in ch. xviii. to the ratification of the covenant on the part of Abraham in ch. xvii., which it presupposes.

3. Jehovah. See page 152.

4. אֲדֹנָי *my Lord*, xviii. 3, 27, 30–32 ; xix. 18.

Apart from these chapters this word occurs in J, Ex. iv. 10, 13 ; xxxiv. 9 ; Josh. vii. 7, 8 ; E, Gen. xx. 4 ; Ex. xv. 17 ; JE, Gen. xv. 2, 8 ; disputed, Ex. v. 22 J (Well.), E (Dill.) ; R, Num. xiv. 17 ; D, Deut. iii. 24 ; ix. 26. All in Hex.

5. הִבִּיט *look*, xix. 17, 26. Not referred to J in any other place ; JE, Gen. xv. 5 ; E, Ex. iii. 6 ; xxxiii. 8 ; Num. xii. 8 ; xxi. 9 ; xxiii. 21. All in Hex.

6. שָׁקַף *look forth* xviii. 16 ; xix. 28 ; once besides in J, xxvi. 8 ; JE, Ex. xiv. 24 ; doubtful, Num. xxi. 20 ; R, Num. xxiii. 28. All in Hex.

7. צְעָקָה *cry*, xviii. 21 ; xix. 13 ; besides in J, Ex. xi. 6 ; xii. 30 ; E, Gen. xxvii. 34 ; Ex. iii. 7, 9 ; xxii. 23 (Well., R). All in Hex.

8. חָלִלָה *far be it*, xviii. 25 ; besides in J, xliv. 7, 17 ; E, Josh. xxiv. 16 ; R, Josh. xxii. 29. All in Hex.

9. הַפַּעַם *this time*, xviii. 32. This word occurs repeatedly in passages assigned to J. in the singular denoting

this time or this once; in the dual meaning twice; and
in the plural with different numerals, *e.g.*, viz., three times,
Ex. xxxiv. 23, 24; Num. xxiv. 10; seven times, Gen.
xxxiii. 3; Josh. vi. 4, 15. In passages assigned to P
once, twice, and three times do not chance to occur, but
only seven times, Lev. iv. 6, 17, and repeatedly; and ten
times, Num. xiv. 22; the very same word being employed
as in J passages. If, then, this word is to be classed as a
criterion of J, it can only be on the assumption that while
P knew how to say seven times and ten times, he did
not know how to say this time or this once.

10. הִנֵּה־נָא *behold now*, xviii. 27, 31; xix. 2, 8, 19, 20.
See ch. xii. 10–20, Marks of J, No. 4.

11. בַּעֲבוּר *for the sake of*, xviii. 26, 29, 31, 32. See ch.
xii. 10–20, Marks of J, No. 5.

12. פָּצַר *urge, press*, xix. 3, 9; but once besides in Hex.
xxxiii. 11 J.

13. טֶרֶם *before*, xix. 4; besides in J, ii. 5; xxiv. 15, 45;
Ex. ix. 30; x. 7; xii. 34; Josh. ii. 8; JE Josh. iii. 1. With
the prep. בְּ it occurs in J, Gen. xxxvii. 18; xlv. 28; Deut.
xxxi. 21; but also in E, Gen. xxvii. 4, 33; xli. 50; Ex. i.
19; and in P, Lev. xiv. 36.

14. לְבִלְתִּי *not to*, xix. 21; besides in J, iii. 11; iv. 15;
xxxviii. 9; Ex. viii. 18, 25 (E. V., vs. 22, 29); ix. 17;
Lev. xviii. 30; xxvi. 15; Num. xxxii. 9; but also E, Ex.
xx. 20; Josh. xxii. 25; D, Deut. iv. 21; viii. 11; xvii.
12, 20; Josh. xxiii. 6; and P, Lev. xx. 4 (so Nöldeke;
R, Dill.), Num. ix. 7 (Dill. worked over, and this word
alleged in proof).

15. אוּלַי *peradventure*, xviii. 24, 28–32. See ch. xvi.,
Marks of J, No. 12.

16. לִקְרַאת *to meet*, xviii. 2; xix. 1; repeatedly in J, E,
and D; Num. xxxi. 13, according to Dillmann, consists of
"genuine phrases" of P, with the sole exception of this
one word.

17. לָמָּה זֶּה *wherefore*, xviii. 13 ; besides in J, xxv. 22, 82 ; xxxii. 30 (E. V., ver. 29) ; xxxiii. 15 ; Num. xi. 20 ; Josh. vii. 10 ; JE, Num. xiv. 41 ; Ex. v. 22 is referred by Dillmann to E, and by Wellhausen to J. All in Hex.

18. כִּי עַל־כֵּן *for therefore*, xviii. 5 ; xix. 8 ; but four times besides in Hex., all of which are referred to J, viz., xxxiii. 10 ; xxxviii. 26 ; Num. x. 31 ; xiv. 43.

19. אַף *also*, xviii. 13, 23, 24 ; but once besides in J, viz., iii. 1 ; Dillmann also refers to this document, Lev. xxvi., in which this word occurs several times (vs. 16, 24, 28, 39–44), but in this he differs from other critics ; it is besides found in JE, Num. xvi. 14 ; E, Deut. xxxiii. 3, 20 ; and D, Deut. ii. 11 ; xv. 17 ; xxxi. 27.

20. רַק *only*, xix. 8 ; repeatedly in J, E, and D. See ch. vi. 1–8, Marks of J, No. 7.

21. נָא *I pray*, xviii. 3, 4, 21, 30, 32 ; xix. 2, 7, 18, 20, etc. See ch. xii. 10–20, Marks of J, No. 3.

22. Forms in וּן. These occur repeatedly in J, E, and D ; but emphatic forms suited to earnest address or vigorous assertion are scarcely to be expected in the class of passages that are assigned to P. Nevertheless we find רִפְגָּעוּן (Josh. xvii. 10 P) in a simple statement of tribal boundaries. This is in a P context, and the verb is reckoned a P word.

23. אֶל for אֵלֶּה *these*, xix. 8, 25 ; six times besides in Hex. ; Rd, xxvi. 3, 4 ; D, Deut. iv. 42 ; vii. 22 ; xix. 11 ; also in Lev. xviii. 27, which Dillmann supposes to have been extracted from J, but other critics refer it to a different source.

24. *Thy servant* for *I*, xviii. 3, 5 ; xix. 2, 19 ; several times in J, but also in E, xxxii. 21 (E. V., ver. 20) ; xxxiii. 5 ; and D, Deut. iii. 24 ; not in P for the reason that no passages are assigned to this document in which this construction would be possible.

25. כֹּל גּוֹיֵי הָאָרֶץ *all the nations of the earth* (xviii. 18).

This expression is found in but three other passages in the Hexateuch, no one of which is referred to J, viz., in xxii. 18; xxvi. 4 R; and Deut. xxviii. 1 D. The same idea of the universality of the blessing through the patriarchs and their seed occurs xii. 3; xxviii. 14 J, where it is expressed by the phrase כֹּל מִשְׁפְּחֹת הָאֲדָמָה *all the families of the ground.* The promise to Abraham is in three instances extended to three particulars—the land of Canaan, a numerous seed, and a blessing to all nations (xii. 3; xviii. 18; xxii. 18); and in three instances limited to the first two (xiii. 14–17; ch. xv.; ch. xvii.). This promise to Abraham is repeated to his successors, both in its full, xxvi. 4 (to Isaac), xxviii. 13, 14 (to Jacob), and in its restricted form, xxviii. 3, 4 (Isaac to Jacob), xxxv. 11, 12 (God to Jacob), xlviii. 3, 4 (Jacob to Joseph), the language of these last three passages being borrowed from ch. xvii., with explicit reference to the culminating and emphatic utterance there made. There is no suggestion in this of two separate documents or sources, since the promise is uttered in its restricted form alike by Jehovah (J) and by God Almighty (P). And the simple reason why the full form is only found in J is that whenever the name God Almighty is linked with this promise it is with a definite reference to ch. xvii., and it is accordingly shaped into conformity with this model; see No Discrepancies, No. 3, page 163.

26. הִשְׁכִּים בַּבֹּקֶר *rise up early in the morning* (xix. 2, 27). This verb, which is almost always prolonged into the full phrase, occurs eight times in J, and eleven times in E, not reckoning Josh. iii. 1 JE, which it has been found impracticable to separate. It does not occur in P, because the passages assigned to this document offer no occasion for its use.

27. הִשְׁתַּחֲוָה אַרְצָה *bowed himself to the earth* (xviii. 2, xix. 1). The only other passages in the Hexateuch in

which this phrase occurs are xxiv. 52; xxxiii. 3; xlii. 6; xliii. 26 J; xxxvii. 10; xlviii. 12 E; but the verb occurs repeatedly in both J and E without being followed by אַרְצָה *to the earth*. The absence of אַרְצָה in the two instances in which this verb is found in a section assigned to P (xxiii. 7, 12) is therefore not peculiar, and is not suggestive of a different source, especially as its omission is plainly due to the presence of הָאָרֶץ in the same clause. Comp. Ex. xxxiv. 8; Josh. v. 14 J, where it is omitted because of אַרְצָה in the preceding clause.

28. מָצָא חֵן *find favor* (xviii. 3; xix. 19) always in J; not in any paragraph of P. See ch. vi. 1-8, No. 10.

29. עָשָׂה חֶסֶד *show kindness* (xix. 19); besides in the Hex. xxiv. 12, 14, 49; xxxii. 11 (E. V., ver. 10); xlvii. 29; Josh. ii. 12, 14 J; Gen. xx. 13; xxi. 23; xl. 14; Ex. xx. 6 E; Dt. v. 10 D. Not in P.

30. חָרָה *burn*, without אַף *anger*, meaning *to be angry* (xviii. 30, 32); besides in J only, iv. 5, 6; xxxiv. 7; but also in E, xxxi. 35, 36; xxxiv. 7; xlv. 5; Num. xvi. 15. More frequently with אַף both in J and E; thus Gen. xxxix. 19; xliv. 18; Ex. iv. 14; xxxii. 10, 11, 19, 22; Num. xxii. 22, 27; xxiv. 10; xxxii. 10, 13; Dt. xxxi. 17 J; Gen. xxx. 2; Ex. xxii. 23; Num. xi. 1, 10, 33; xii. 9; xxv. 3 E. It can, therefore, be no mark of diversity of authorship that חָרָה in Josh. vii. 1, the single instance in which it occurs in a paragraph assigned to P, is accompanied by אַף.

31. The disjunctive question (xviii. 21); but disjunctive questions are not peculiar to J. They are found in P as well, *e.g.*, xvii. 17.

32. בָּא בַּיָּמִים *advanced in days* (xviii. 11); this expression occurs but once besides in J (xxiv. 1). It is found, also, Josh. xiii. 1 bis; xxiii. 1, 2, where it is referred to D.

33. "The relation of this narrative to P's account in xix. 29."

But xix. 29 is not another account of the overthrow of
the cities of the plain, which is to be referred to another
writer.   It simply reverts to the subject of the overthrow
as previously related, in order to introduce further statements respecting Lot.

34. "The difference between xviii. 12 and xvii. 17."

These are not variant explanations of the origin of the
name of Isaac, as though one writer derived it from the
laughter of Abraham, another from that of Sarah before
Isaac's birth, and still a third from the laughter of Sarah
after his birth (xxi. 6).   These allusions to the significance of the name on different occasions are quite consistent with one another, and with a common authorship.

LOT'S INCEST (CH. XIX. 29-38)

The critics generally attribute vs. 30–38 to J, and ver.
29 to P, alleging that this verse is not connected either
with what precedes or follows, but is a separate and independent account of the destruction of the cities of the
plain.   Kayser, however, substantially concedes the
whole case when he says that ver. 29 " seems like a con-
densation of an account by P of Sodom's overthrow,
which has been omitted by the redactor."   Plainly this
is not a recital, but the summary of a recital elsewhere
given.   And the narrative, which Kayser misses, is just
that which is to be found in the previous part of the
chapter, but which the critics assign to a different document.   Nevertheless this verse is tied to what precedes,
not only by its subject-matter, but by its language.
Dillmann claims that it contains five of P's " characteristic expressions," viz. : *Elohim, remembered* (as viii. 1),
שחת *destroyed* (as vi. 17 ; ix. 11, 15), *cities of the plain* (as
xiii. 12), *in which Lot dwelt* (not " in one of which ; " this
sense is, however, justified by the passage to which he

himself refers, viii. 4, as well as by similar examples,
xxi. 7; Judg. xii. 7; 1 Sam. xvii. 43; 2 Chron. xvi. 14;
Job xxi. 32). But in fact the diction of this verse is too
closely allied to the antecedent narrative to admit of
being sundered from it: שׁחת *destroy*, as xix. 13; xiii. 10;
הפך *overthrow*, as vs. 21, 25; *cities of the plain*, see ver.
25; *in which Lot dwelt* is a plain allusion to xiii. 12,
which the critics for this reason cut out of its connection and assign to P. But, as has been previously shown,
it is indissolubly attached to the context in which it
stands. That Abram continued to dwell in Canaan,
while Lot dwelt elsewhere, is the very point of the whole
narrative, which is further emphasized in the promise
which immediately follows (xiii. 14–17). " *God remembered* " affords a good illustration of critical methods; xxx.
22 is parcelled between P, E, and J, though the words
" and God remembered Rachel " are the only ones in the
entire chapter which are attributed to P. God's remembering Abraham plainly refers back, not to his covenant
with Abraham in ch. xvii. (P), but to Abraham's intercession (xviii. 23–32, J). That no variant representation is
made, whether of the reason of Lot's deliverance or of
the circumstances attending it, was shown, p. 165, No
Discrepancies, No. 7.

Moreover, it is impossible to find a suitable connection
for ver. 29 in P. It is manifestly incongruous to attach
it to the end of ch. xvii., which on the partition hypothesis it immediately follows. It is customary to adopt
Hupfeld's gratuitous assumption that it has been transposed from its original position after xiii. 12. But
apart from the fact that this is building hypothesis upon
hypothesis, this verse could never have stood there. It
is not a declaration that God destroyed the cities of the
plain, but that when he destroyed them he did what is
here stated. This implies a previous account of the de-

struction, or at least a mention of it. But no such
mention is to be found anywhere in P. The verse consequently belongs where it stands.

While ver. 29 is thus a recapitulation of the preceding
narrative, it is not added to it for the sake of rounding it
up to a conclusion, as Delitzsch [1] formerly maintained.
Astruc and Eichhorn correctly regarded it as an introduction to the following paragraph (vs. 30–38), after the
brief digression (vs. 27, 28). And this accounts for the
use of Elohim. Lot had thus far been considered as
under the sheltering protection of Abraham, and so of
the God of Abraham. The last link of connection is
now severed. Lot passes quite beyond the limits of the
holy land, and henceforth stands in no relation whatever
to Abraham or to Abraham's God. He is reduced to the
footing of an alien, and God is Elohim to him as to other
Gentiles. (See pp. 152, 153.)

Nöldeke claims for P, in addition to ver. 29, the
clause in ver. 30, "he dwelt in the mountain," and appeals to xiii. 12 (see Marks of J, No. 3, under ch. xiii.);
xxxvi. 8. Other critics, however, decline in this instance
to abide by a test which they apply elsewhere.

Ilgen referred vs. 30–38 to the Second Elohist, and
Boehmer to the redactor, on the ground that the author
of the preceding narrative, in which Lot is represented
as a righteous person, could not have related this shameful story. But the sacred writers do not conceal the
weaknesses or the sins of even the best of men; not
Abraham's prevarication, nor Jacob's duplicity, nor
Noah's intoxication. The peril in which Lot was involving himself by his inconsiderate choice of a residence is estimated at the outset (xiii. 12, 13); that he
did not wholly escape the infection of Sodom is shown
(xix. 8); preparation is thus made for the infamy here

[1] In the second and third editions of his Genesis.

disclosed. That this paragraph is a continuation of the preceding narrative is further apparent from the points of connection between them. Lot's being in Zoar (ver. 30) corresponds with ver. 23 ; his going to dwell in the mountain with ver. 17; the mention of the two daughters (vs. 15, 16) implies that something further was to be related respecting them ; the absence of his wife is accounted for by her having perished (ver. 26). In fact, the only imaginable reason why Lot is mentioned in the history at all is that he was the ancestor of Moab and Ammon. This concluding paragraph of the chapter is accordingly indispensable to both documents, is equally linked with both, and binds both together in a common unity.

The critical division renders P's mention of Lot altogether nugatory. P particularly records his parentage and his relation to Abram (xi. 27); his accompanying Terah and Abram from Ur of the Chaldees to Haran (ver. 31); his going thence with Abram to Canaan (xii. 5) ; his large property and retinue (xiii. 6) ; his parting from Abram and dwelling in the cities of the plain (vs. 11, 12); the deliverance granted him for Abram's sake when God destroyed these cities (xix. 29). And there he disappears. The very point and purpose of the whole narrative is not reached,[1] viz. : That from Lot sprang the tribes of Moab and Ammon, which are thus, in accordance with the uniform plan of Genesis, removed like Ishmael, the descendants of Keturah, and Esau, beyond the limits of the promised land, that it may remain in the undisturbed possession of the chosen race. The missing paragraph containing the key to the significance of Lot

---

[1] Wellhausen remarks (Composition des Hexateuchs, p. 15) : "Nöldeke calls attention to a break in Q (P) ; he must without doubt have connected the two nations of Moab and Ammon with Lot, who in and of himself has no significance."

(xix. 30–38) is ascribed to J; but his account, too, is mutilated, if not at the end, at the beginning. Lot is suddenly introduced (xii. 4a), with no intimation who he was, and no previous mention of him.

MARKS OF J

The following alleged marks of J evidently afford no indication of the existence of distinct documents.

1. בְּכִירָה *first-born* (vs. 31, 33, 34, 37), occurs but once besides in Hex., viz.: Gen. xxix. 26, which is cut out of an E context and assigned to J purely on account of this and the following word.

2. צְעִירָה *younger* (vs. 31, 34, 35, 38), occurs besides in J, xxv. 23; xliii. 33; in xxix. 26, xlviii. 14, Josh. vi. 26 it occurs in mixed contexts, and is referred to J purely on account of this word.

3. חִיָּה זֶרַע *preserve seed* (vs. 32, 34). See ch. vi.–ix., Marks of J, No. 12.

The charge that this story is a product of national antipathy, and originated in the conflicts of a later period, will only be credited by those who for other reasons distrust the truth of the narratives of Genesis. That a nation sprung from such a source should practise debasing orgies (Num. xxv. 1–3) is not surprising.

ABRAHAM WITH ABIMELECH, KING OF GERAR (CH. XX.)

CRITICAL EMBARRASSMENT

The divisive hypothesis encountered an obstacle in this chapter by which it was seriously embarrassed, and which finally led to the overthrow of its earlier forms. The more minute and thorough the analysis was made, the more apparent it became that neither the document hypothesis, as at first proposed, nor the supplement hypothesis, was capable of being applied to this chapter or to the subsequent portion of Genesis. The alternation of the divine names, Elohim and Jehovah, in successive sections, had been the starting-point of the hypothesis, and was relied upon as the palpable evidence of its reality. Two writers, the Elohist and the Jehovist, were supposed to be thus clearly indicated. The characteristic diction and style of each was made out by a diligent comparison of the sections respectively attributed to them. All went on swimmingly at the beginning, fresh criteria being gathered as the work proceeded.

But unfortunately neither this chapter nor those that follow can be brought into harmony with the conclusions thus far reached. The words associated with Elohim in the account of the creation (Gen. i.) and of the flood (vi.–ix.), have disappeared entirely, or only reappear in Genesis for the most part in Jehovah sections; and Elohim in ch. xx. and henceforth is associated with the diction and the style held to be characteristic of the Jehovist. The natural inference is that the critics have been too hasty in their conclusions. They have made deductions from premises which do not warrant them, and which are nullified by a more extended examination of the facts. They have mistaken the lofty style used in describing grand creative acts or the vocabulary employed in setting forth the universal catastrophe of the deluge for the fixed habit of an Elohist writer, and set it over against the graceful style of ordinary narrative in the early Jehovist sections. But in this chapter and in the rest of Genesis, whenever Elohim occurs in narrative sections, the stately periods of the account of the creation and the vocabulary of the creation and the flood are dropped, and terms appropriate to the common affairs of

life and the ordinary course of human events are employed by the Elohist precisely as they are by the Jehovist.

Elohim occurs throughout this chapter (vs. 3, 6, 11,
13, 17), except in the last verse (ver. 18) where Jehovah
is used. But the words and phrases are those which are
held to be characteristic of the Jehovist.

DICTION OF CHAPTER XX.

1. נָסַע *to journey* (ver. 1), is the standing expression in
J for the journeying of the patriarchs (xii. 9; xiii. 11;
xxxiii. 12, 17).

2. אֶרֶץ הַנֶּגֶב *the land of the south* (ver. 1), occurs three
times in the Hexateuch, and but once besides in the
whole Old Testament, viz.: Gen. xxiv. 62; Josh. xv. 19
J; Num. xiii. 29, in a context where J and E are, in the
opinion of the critics, confusedly mingled, and this verse,
or a part of it, is assigned to E simply and avowedly because of this one expression. הַנֶּגֶב, *the south*, whether as a
part of the country or as a point of the compass, is mentioned nowhere else in Genesis except in J (xii. 9; xiii.
1, 3, 14; xxiv. 62; xxviii. 14).

3. *Kadesh* and *Shur* (ver. 1) are mentioned by J (xvi.
7, 14); so is *Gerar* subsequently as the abode of Isaac
(xxvi. 1), who habitually repeated what his father had
done.

4. אֲדֹנָי *Lord* (ver. 4), as xviii. 3, 27, 30–32 J. See
ch. xviii., xix., Marks of J, No. 4.

5. נָבִיא *prophet* (ver. 7). This term is nowhere else
applied to Abraham in the Hexateuch, but the same
thought is expressed in xviii. 17 sqq. J, where Jehovah
makes him his confidant.

6. מוֹת תָּמוּת *thou shalt surely die* (ver. 7), as ii. 17; iii.
4 J.

7. הִשְׁכִּים בַּבֹּקֶר *rise early in the morning* (ver. 8), as xix. 2, 27; xxvi. 31 J. See ch. xviii., xix., Marks of J, No. 26.

8. מֶה עָשִׂיתָ *what hast thou done* (ver. 9), as iii. 13; iv. 10; xii. 18; xxvi. 10 J. See ch. xii. 10-20, Marks of J, No. 7.

9. לֹא יֵעָשֶׂה *ought not to be done* (ver. 9), as xxxiv. 7 J.

10. רַק *only, surely* (ver. 11), as vi. 5; xix. 8; xxiv. 8, etc., J. See ch. vi. 1-8, Marks of J, No. 7.

11. עַל־דְּבַר *for the sake of* (ver. 11), as xii. 17 J.

12. אָמְנָה *indeed* (ver. 12), only besides in the Old Testament Josh. vii. 20 J.

13. עָשׂה חֶסֶד *show kindness* (ver. 13), as xix. 19; xxiv. 12, 14, 49 J. See ch. xviii., xix., Marks of J, No. 29.

14. שִׁפְחָה *maid-servant* (ver. 14), as xii. 16; xvi. 2; xxiv. 35 J.

15. אַרְצִי לְפָנֶיךָ *my land is before thee* (ver. 15), as xiii. 9; xxxiv. 10; comp. xxiv. 51 J.

16. הוֹכִיחַ *to set right* (ver. 16), as xxiv. 14, 44; Lev. xix. 17 J (so Dillmann). See ch. xxi. 22-34, Marks of E, No. 7.

Knobel sought to adapt the supplement hypothesis to this state of facts by assuming that J, to whom he assigns this chapter, here and in other like passages drew his materials from a written source, which was in the habit of using the divine name Elohim; and that ver. 18 was independently added by J himself. Hupfeld abandoned the supplement hypothesis altogether, and claimed that this and all similar passages belonged to a third document, E, distinct from P and J, but which resembled P in making use of Elohim, and resembled J in style and diction. This is now the popular method among the critics of getting over the difficulty, ver. 18 being commonly attributed to the redactor. It is, how-ever, only an evasion, and an impossible evasion; for this chapter cannot belong to a document distinct from the preceding narrative, to which it is indissolubly linked.

NOT REFERABLE TO A DISTINCT DOCUMENT

Dillmann, indeed, maintains that "it must originally have stood in a different connection, and have been put here by R." And the reason urged is that the narrative is inconsistent with the age ascribed to Sarah. "According to xvii. 17 P, Sarah is ninety years old, according to xviii. 11, 12 J, she is advanced in years and past child-bearing in the course of nature ; so that she cannot possibly have still been attractive to strangers." This has already been fully answered in the preliminary remarks to this general section, under the head of No Discrepancies, No. 9. In the longevity of the patriarchs Sarah may not have been devoid of personal charms even at the age of ninety ; or Abimelech may have been prompted by the desire to form a connection with Abraham, who was the head of a powerful clan. And, at any rate, no argument can thence be drawn for a diversity of documents. Why may not the original writer have believed what, on the critics' own hypothesis, it is manifest that R believed?

He further argues that this chapter can neither be from P nor from J. Not from P, according to whom Abraham dwelt in Hebron (xxiii. 2, 19 ; xxv. 9 ; xxxv. 27), and there is no trace of his dwelling in Gerar or Beersheba ; and not from J, since he has the parallel narrative, xii. 10–20. But there is no inconsistency between this chapter and the passages referred by the critics to P and to J ; and no reason why it could not have been written by the common author of those passages. That Abraham was at Hebron at the time of Sarah's death creates no presumption that he had not been at Gerar at the time of this occurrence thirty-seven years before. And according to the critical partition of the text, Abraham's abode in Hebron is spoken of not by P only, but by J as well (xiii. 18).

The incident related in this chapter bears a striking resemblance to that in xii. 10–20. The critics assume that such an affair could occur but once, and hence conclude that these can only be variant accounts of the same occurrence by two different writers. It is obvious, however, that upon the critical hypothesis R regarded them as distinct events, differing in time, place, and several particulars. And it is difficult to see why the original writer may not have been of the same mind, and inserted both in his narrative. There are numerous indications that this was really the case. It is distinctly declared (ver. 13) that Abraham had concerted with Sarah to have her pass as his sister in more than one place ; and the mention of such an arrangement would be unmeaning if it had not been actually carried into effect. The brevity of the statement in ver. 2 leaves the conduct of both Abraham and Abimelech unexplained, and is an implied reference to a previous narrative of the same sort, in which the motives of the actors are more fully stated. The writer assumes that his readers will understand the situation from the like instance before related, and so thinks it unnecessary to go into particulars. "From thence" (ver. 1) is an explicit reference to a locality mentioned before, which can only be "the oaks of Mamre" (xviii. 1 J), i.e., Hebron (xiii. 18 J, xxiii. 19 P). In xxi. 32, which is universally confessed to be a continuation of the narrative in ch. xx., and by the same hand, Abraham is in Beersheba, just as he is in the following verse (xxi. 33 J), and his presence there is nowhere else explained. And in ver. 34 J speaks of his sojourn in the land of the Philistines, where he was sojourning in ch. xx., for Gerar (vs. 1, 2) was the capital of the Philistine territory; the king of Gerar was the king of the Philistines (xxvi. 1). The nocturnal revelation (vs. 3, 6) has its parallels in J (xxvi. 24; xxviii. 16), and in a section marked by "Jehovah," though its reference to J is arbitrarily disputed (xv. 1, 12, seq.). The language of Abimelech (vs. 9, 10) recalls that of Pharaoh (xii. 18); and Abraham's reply, ver. 11, resembles xii. 12. The representation of the moral character of the people (ver. 11) corresponds with xv. 16. There is no discrepancy between ver. 12 and xi. 29 (J) or 31 (P). As Abraham's wife, Sarah was Terah's daughter-in-law; the mention of the fact that she was also his daughter was purposely reserved for this place, that the difficulty might not be solved before it had arisen. "God caused me to wander" (ver. 13) corresponds precisely with xii. 1, the injunction to go to a land not yet disclosed. Abraham's intercession (ver. 17) for Abimelech is like that for Sodom (xviii. 23 sqq.).

The transaction here recorded also falls precisely into line with both the antecedent and subsequent history of Abraham, which is just a continued succession of trials for testing and enhancing his faith in the promise of God, increasing in intensity until the climax is reached, and a period put to them all in ch. xxii. And it fits exactly into the situation, coming as it does after the definite promise of xvii. 19, 21, and its gracious renewal at that visit of unequalled condescension (xviii. 10), but before the conception and birth of the promised child (xxi. 2). All is now put in peril by the threatened loss of Sarah, which yet was averted by immediate divine interference. This was one more step in that discipline with which the patriarch's life was filled, and that experience of almighty guardianship by which he was trained to implicit confidence in, and obedience to, the word of a covenant-keeping God, and thus fitted for the unique position of the

father of the faithful and the head of the chosen race
(xviii. 18, 19).

The contention that ch. xx. requires more time than
can be allowed in the interval between ch. xviii. and xxi.
rests upon a misinterpretation of vs. 17, 18, as though
the infliction there spoken of was sterility, which could
only become apparent after the lapse of a considerable period. But Abimelech needed to be healed as well as his
wife and maid-servants, and he had thus been hindered
from approaching Sarah (ver. 6). The affection accordingly was one that prevented sexual intercourse, and so
was an obstacle to conception and birth.[1]

---

[1] Ilgen (Urkunden, p. 413) infers that Sarah must have remained in
Abimelech's palace at least two years. And Vater adds that room cannot be found before ch. xxi. for all that took place in ch. xviii.–xx. To
this latter suggestion Ewald very properly replies '' that the author nowhere says that the affair of Lot's daughters (xix. 29–38) took place at
this time ; he merely attaches it to the story of Sodom, as that was a
convenient place." His treatment of the occurrence at Gerar in the
same connection is so admirable that it may be repeated here.   I quote
from his maiden publication (Die Komposition der Genesis kritisch untersucht. 1823, p. 228 sqq).   '' Abraham is still (*i.e.*, in ch. xix.) at the
oaks of Mamre, as the writer had first stated (xiii. 18), and then referred
back to this statement (xiv. 13, and xviii. 1).   Now he removes to Gerar, and although the expression ' from thence ' (xx. 1) does not de-
fine the starting-point of his journey, it refers to what preceded, and the
direction from Mamre to Gerar is so plainly indicated by the added
word ' the south,' that it is an adequate substitute for the name 'oaks
of Mamre.'   Abraham says of his wife at the outset ' she is my sister '
(ver. 2).   In and of itself this is quite unintelligible ; and a Hebrew
narrator would certainly have told this more plainly, if he had not on
a like occasion stated in more detail what moved Abraham to it (xii.
11–13).   Was it necessary now to repeat this here ?   The rapidity with
which he hastens on to the fact itself shows what he presupposes in
the reader.   But while in the first event of the kind (ch. xii.), in Egypt,
the narrator briefly mentions Pharaoh's gifts and plagues, he sets forth
in more detail the cause of Abraham's conduct.   The reader might certainly be surprised that the same thing could happen twice to Abraham.
The narrator is conscious of this ; and in order to remove every doubt
of this sort, which might so easily arise, he lets Abraham clear up the

The identity of language, the intimate connection of
this passage with the context in which it stands, and the
direct allusions to previous portions of the narrative
demonstrate that this chapter cannot belong to a distinct
and independent document, but is a continuation of the
preceding. And the fact that Elohim in an ordinary
historical narrative is associated with precisely the same
style and diction that is found in Jehovah passages annuls the alleged marks of discrimination urged by critics
in previous portions of Genesis, which are thus shown
to be due to a difference, not of writer but of theme.
This chapter not only affords no argument for a third
document E, but renders decisive testimony against it,
and against the hypothesis of documents in general.

Elohim is used throughout this chapter because Abimelech, who is prominent in it is a Gentile. It is no
objection to this that Abimelech uses the name "Jehovah" in speaking to Isaac (xxvi. 28, 29); for he there
means specifically Isaac's God, who had so signally
blessed him ; just as in Ex. xviii., although Elohim is
prevailingly used in describing Jethro's visit to Moses,

puzzle in what he says to Abimelech (vs. 11–13). Thus the narrator
himself meets every objection that could be made, and by the words
'when God caused me to wander from my father's house' (ver. 13),
he looks back so plainly over all thus far related, and at the same time
indicates so exactly the time when he first thought of passing his wife
off as his sister everywhere in foreign lands, that this can only be explained from the previous narrative in ch. xii. Moreover, the circumstances are different in the two narratives. Here Abimelech makes
Abraham a variety of presents after he understood the affair; there
Pharaoh before he understood it. Here God himself appears, there he
simply punishes. Here Abraham is called a prophet (ver. 7), as he
could not have been at once denominated when God had but just called
him. The circumstances, the issue, and the description differ in many
respects, and thus attest that this story is quite distinct from the former
one." In a foot-note Ewald makes light of the objection from Sarah's
age, and appeals to similar instances, which I have no means of verify-
ing.

Jehovah is employed in vs. 9–11, where Jethro refers specifically to the God of Israel in distinction from all other gods. And in the book of Jonah the mariners, who had vainly cried each unto his god to quell the storm (i. 5), turned at length to the God of Jonah and prayed to and worshipped Jehovah (vs. 14, 16). Elohim is construed as a plural in xx. 13, in accommodation to pagan ideas and forms of speech and not as a characteristic of E; cf. Ex. xxxii. 4; 1 Sam. iv. 8; for in passages assigned to E the same construction ordinarily prevails as is usual elsewhere. The plural is used in Gen. xxxv. 7 because a vision of both God and angels is referred to; Ex. xxii. 8 (E. V., ver. 9) is in a code of laws, which in the opinion of the critics was not written by E, but copied by him into his document; Deut. v. 23 (E. V. ver. 26) is referred to D; and in Josh. xxiv. 19 the plural construction of Elohim occurs in conjunction with the name Jehovah. The use of this construction warrants no imputation upon the strictness of the monotheism of E; for like constructions occur in the most rigorously monotheistic contexts, e.g., Deut. v. 23 (26); 2 Sam. vii. 22, 23; Jer. xxiii. 36; cf. in P, Gen. i. 26, and in J, xi. 7.

"Jehovah" in xx. 18 is not traceable to a different writer, whether J (Knobel, Kayser) or R, as Hupfeld and most critics assume. It is Jehovah's interference on behalf of Abraham's wife that is there described. The name is, therefore, strictly appropriate.

MARKS OF E

1. אָמָה maid-servant (ver. 17) occurs besides in passages referred to E (xxi. 10, 12, 13; xxx. 3; xxxi. 33; Ex. ii. 5); in the fourth commandment (Ex. xx. 10) and in the Covenant Code, supposed by the critics not to be the work of E (Ex. xxi. 7, 20, 26, 27, 32; xxiii. 12);

also in P (Lev. xxv. 6, 44 bis); and several times in
Deuteronomy. Notwithstanding the fact that this word
is by no means peculiar to E, it is claimed that E uses it
instead of שִׁפְחָה, which is employed by J and P. But
שִׁפְחָה occurs in E (Gen. xx. 14; xxx. 18), and it is only
by the questionable device of cutting a clause out of an
E context and assigning it to P or J, that the admission
is escaped that E uses it also in xxix. 24, 29; xxx. 4, 7.
Both words occur in this chapter, and are discriminatingly used. אָמָה maid-servant, as a concubine of Abimelech (ver. 17), is clearly distinguished from שִׁפְחָה woman-
servant, given for bond-service to Abraham (ver. 14).
That the former is a less servile term than the latter
plainly appears also from 1 Sam. xxv. 41. This distinction is clearly stated by Ilgen (p. 399), who renders them
respectively "maid" and "slave." The assertion that
שְׁפָחֹת (ver. 14) is a textual error, or that the clause "men-
servants and women-servants" is an addition by R, is
altogether groundless.

2. לֵבָב (for לֵב) heart (vs. 5, 6); besides in E (xxxi. 26;
Ex. xiv. 5; Josh. xiv. 7; xxiv. 23); in J (Lev. xix. 17,
xxvi. 36, 41, so Dill.; Num. xv. 39; Josh. vii. 5); D
(Josh. v. 1; xxii. 5; xxiii. 14); Rd (Josh. ii. 11).

3. הִתְפַּלֵּל to pray (vs. 7, 17); besides in Hexateuch,
only Num. xi. 2; xxi. 7 E; Deut. ix. 20, 26 D.

4. חֲלוֹם dream (vs. 3, 6); besides in E (xxxi. 10, 11,
24; xxxvii. 5, 6, 8, 9 bis, 10, 19, 20; xl. 5 bis, 8, 9 bis,
16; xli. 7, 8, 11 bis, 12, 15 bis, 17, 22, 25, 26, 32; xlii.
9); in J (Num. xii. 6; so Dillmann). The occurrence of
Elohim in connection with the mention of dreams is due
not to the peculiarity of a writer (E), but to the nature
of the case. No dreams are mentioned in the Hexateuch, but those which are prophetic. When God revealed himself to those not of the chosen race, of course
Elohim and not Jehovah would be used, and the method

was uniformly by dreams, as the lowest form of divine communication; thus to Abimelech (xx. 3, 6); Laban (xxxi. 24); the butler and baker of Pharaoh (xl. 5 sqq.); and Pharaoh himself (xli. 1 sqq.). So also to Jacob, when on the point of leaving Canaan for Paddan-aram (xxviii. 12); or for Egypt (xlvi. 2); and in Paddan-aram (xxxi. 11); and to Joseph in his childhood (xxxvii. 5 sqq.). Elohim does not occur in the narrative of Joseph's dreams; nevertheless these are by the critics referred to E under the rule that all dreams must be given to E, a rule which sufficiently explains why no dreams are to be found in J. But J likewise speaks of Jehovah revealing himself to Isaac at night (xxvi. 24); to Jacob in his sleep (xxviii. 16); and similarly to Abram (xv. 1, 12, 13). The futility of the critical attempts to refer these communications made to Abram to E and R, has already been shown. The revelation to Abram (xv. 1) is called a vision, a higher form of divine communication than a dream, just as that to Jacob (xlvi. 2) is called by E. That no divine dreams are granted to Gentiles in J paragraphs is for the sufficient reason that Elohim is necessarily used in such a connection. If God speaks directly to men in J, so he does in E to Abraham (xxi. 12; xxii. 1); and to Jacob (xxxv. 1), without its being said that it was in a dream. In P, according to the division made by the critics, God reveals himself but twice in the entire patriarchal period—once to Abraham (ch. xvii.), and once to Jacob (xxxv. 9), in spite of the explicit mention made (Ex. ii. 24; vi. 3 P) that he had appeared to Isaac and covenanted with him; which is a positive proof that their division is at fault. It has been said that according to E God appears neither formally nor visibly, but only in dreams. And yet, if we may believe Dillmann, it is E who records God's wrestling with Jacob (xxxii. 24–31). And he adds that Wellhausen's " arguments to the contrary prove nothing or rest on mere postulates."

5. אָמַר אֶל (ver. 2), or אָמַר לְ (ver. 13) *say concerning.* No other example is adduced from the Hexateuch. In Num. xxiii. 23, referred to in Ewald's "Hebrew Grammar," § 217, *c,* the expression has not this sense, and is besides attributed by Wellhausen to J.

6. נְקִיוֹן *innocency* (ver. 5); nowhere else in the Hexateuch.

BIRTH OF ISAAC AND DISMISSAL OF ISHMAEL (CH. XXI. 1-21)

CRITICAL PERPLEXITY

The opening verses of this chapter have given some trouble to the critics, and have been very variously apportioned. Astruc and Eichhorn were content to follow the indications of the divine names throughout, and so assigned the first verse and the last two verses of the chapter to J, and all the rest to P. As, however, ver. 1 is intimately related to ver. 2, Gramberg assigned it also to P, assuming that "Jehovah" in each clause had originally been "Elohim," and that the verse was an apt specimen of P's diffuseness. Knobel separated the two clauses of ver. 1, and gave the first to J, being thus able to retain the Jehovah of that clause, while contending that in the second clause it had been substituted for Elohim; P's portion of the chapter was limited by him to vs. 1b-5, all the remainder being transferred to J, who here, as in ch. xx., was supposed to have made use of an earlier source characterized by its employment of Elohim. Hupfeld converted this earlier source into an independent document E, assigning to it vs. 6, 9-32, and giving vs. 7, 8, to J. Nöldeke pointed out that לִזְקֻנָיו *in his old age,* ver. 2 (P) was identical with the expression in ver. 7 (J), and that consequently it must have been

Inserted there by R. But neither is הָרָה *conceived* regarded as a word belonging to P; hence Wellhausen insisted on limiting P's portion of the chapter to vs. 2b–5, and giving ver. 1 to R, who thus effected the transition from the subject of the preceding chapter to the account of the birth of Isaac. The consequence of this is that the paragraph referred to P begins in the middle of a sentence, and that J does not record the birth of Isaac at all. Dillmann, in the last edition of his Genesis, seeks to remedy these incongruities by the artificial process of splitting the first and second verses in two, and uniting their alternate clauses, thus giving to J vs. 1a, 2a, 7; to P 1b, 2b–5; and to E vs. 6, 8–21. Budde[1] carries the splitting process still further by dividing ver. 6 in two, and transposing its second clause to the end of ver. 7. But even thus he lags behind Ilgen in the work of disintegration, who long ago divided ver. 7 as well as ver. 6 between J and E. But in no one of these methods of partition does E make mention of the birth of Isaac. Boehmer endeavors to relieve this difficulty, and to allow each document a share in this announcement[2] by assigning to J vs. 1, 2b, 7; to P vs. 2a, c, 4, 5; and to E vs. 3, 6, 8.

But all this critical toil is as fruitless as it is unnecessary. The whole passage is so closely bound together as neither to require nor to permit partition. "Jehovah" in each clause of ver. 1 forbids the assignment of both or either to an Elohist writer without an arbitrary change of text, which, instead of contributing to the support of the hypothesis, is an inference from the hypothesis. Moreover, this verse is not a doublet, as the critics claim, suggestive of two distinct sources. It is no unmeaning

[1] Urgeschichte, pp. 215, 224.
[2] Ilgen accomplished the same thing after a fashion by giving E ver. 1a, J 1b, and P ver. 2.

repetition, but an emphatic asseveration, in which the second clause is an advance upon the first. It is first stated that Jehovah visited Sarah as he had said (see xviii. 10); then the purpose for which he visited her is added, viz., to fulfil the promise previously given. The mention of a divine visitation is usually followed by an explicit statement of its design; so Gen. l. 24; Ex. iii. 16, 17; xxxii. 34; and in these cases no one suspects different writers. Delitzsch remarks that the structure of ver. 1 is identical with that of ii. 5a.

Wellhausen denies that the author of ch. xviii. could have had any share in this account of Isaac's birth, because according to xviii. 10, 14, Jehovah promised to revisit Sarah in Hebron; but the fact is that no locality is mentioned there. Dillmann insists that according to both J and P Isaac must have been born in Hebron, as they knew nothing of the journey to the south in ch. xx. (E); a discrepancy which, like most of those discovered by the critics, is of their own manufacture, and does not exist in the text as it lies before us.

The critics are here in a dilemma which has perplexed them not a little. If ver. 2a is given to P as by Dillmann (2nd), J makes no mention of Isaac's birth, which is the event to which every promise from ch. xii. onward had pointed, and for which all the history of Abraham up to this time had been preparatory. If it is given to J as by Dillmann (3rd), P goes on to speak of the naming of the child and his circumcision without having told of his birth. And even if "Jehovah" in ver. 1b be changed to "Elohim" to accommodate the critics, and this be given to P, he still merely says that God fulfilled his promise to Sarah without saying what that promise was. It is easy to say that Isaac's birth was mentioned in both documents, but R has only preserved one account of it. But there is no proof that such a duplicate statement ever existed. The critics' assertion that it did brings no support to their hypothesis, for it is itself unsupported, and is a mere inference from the hypothesis which it is adduced to sustain. And it is an inference which imputes the most extraordinary and unaccountable inconsistency to the redactor. In ver. 1 he is supposed to have brought together two clauses identical in signification, one or the other of which is therefore quite superfluous, because he found them in different documents and felt bound to retain them. He retains xix. 29 from P, though in the opinion of the critics it adds nothing to what he had already related in full from J. He records Noah's entry into the ark twice, once from J and then from P, thus overloading his narrative in these and other conspicuous instances with identical repetitions for no other reason than because the same thing was recorded in each of his sources. Why does he not do the same in this matter which is evidently regarded in both documents as of the greatest moment?

"Sarah bore a son at the set time of which God had spoken to him" (ver. 2) is a plain allusion to xvii. 19a, 21; the name Isaac (ver. 3) to xvii. 19; his being circumcised the eighth day (ver. 4) to xvii. 12; the age of Abraham (ver. 5) to xvii. 1, 24. The repetition of "Sarah" four times in vs. 1-3, and the reiteration of the statement that she was the mother of the child are not due to the diffuse style of the writer, but to the emphasis laid upon the fact, as in ch. xvii. The name "Elohim" (vs. 2, 4, 6) is adopted from ch. xvii., which is so prominently referred to. The promise was made and was now fulfilled by Jehovah in the character of God Almighty (xvii. 1); the event was, and was understood by both Abraham and Sarah to be, not the product of natural causes, but of divine omnipotent intervention.

The contention that ver. 6 contains a new explanation

of the name of Isaac, or as Ilgen and Budde will have it, two separate explanations of it, differing from those in xvii. 17 P and xviii. 12 J, and that it must on this account be referred to a third writer, E, is unfounded. These several allusions to the significance of the name are entirely harmonious and are not suggestive of a diversity of writers. Abraham's and Sarah's laugh of incredulity is exchanged for a laugh of joy. Nor does the additional utterance of Sarah (ver. 7), though distinct from the preceding (ver. 6), and separately introduced by the words "And she said," require or justify the assumption that this is from another document any more than the three utterances of the angel of Jehovah to Hagar (xvi. 9–11), which few of the critics think of sundering.

DIVISION IMPOSSIBLE

Hupfeld claims that the narrative of the expulsion of Hagar and Ishmael (vs. 9–21), which is assigned to E, stands in no relation to the account of Isaac's birth, which he divides between J and P. But besides the obvious intimate connection between the two events, the narratives are bound together by ver. 8, which Hupfeld correctly attaches to what precedes as its proper sequence, and other critics with equal propriety attach to what follows as indicating its occasion. It was at the feast to celebrate the weaning of Isaac that Ishmael made himself so obnoxious as to be sent away.

The critics allege that vs. 8–21 is a variant of xvi. 4–14 by a different writer, but without the slightest reason. The two events are quite distinct, and each is appropriate in its place. In ch. xvi. Hagar was treated harshly because of her contemptuous behavior toward her mistress before the birth of Ishmael, and ran away of her own accord, but was sent back by an angel. In this place

Hagar and Ishmael were finally dismissed by Abraham, and an angel appeared to succor them in their distress. That " Jehovah " is used throughout the former passage, and " Elohim " in this, is due not to a difference of writers but of situation. There Hagar was regarded as a member of Abraham's household, and as such still under Jehovah's protection. Here she and Ishmael are finally separated from the patriarch and his family, and are henceforth disconnected from the chosen race. Elohim is, therefore, used with Ishmael as with Lot after he was finally cut off from proximity to, and all connection with, Abraham (xix. 29 sqq.).

The attempt to create a discrepancy in respect to the age of Ishmael is not successful. It is claimed that while Ishmael, according to xvi. 16 ; xxi. 5, was at least sixteen years old, he is in this narrative represented as a young child needing to be carried. Dillmann effects this result by accepting the erroneous rendering of ver. 14 by the LXX. in place of the Hebrew text, as Ilgen had done before him, and reading " put the child on her shoulder," which, according to the text as it stands, was not done. This, as Jerome long since remarked, would bring this verse into variance with ver. 18, where Hagar is bidden to lift up the sick boy and hold him with her hand. Ex quo manifestum est, eum qui tenetur non oneri matri fuisse, sed comitem. To hold him by the hand is a very different thing from carrying him.

It is also inconsistent with ver. 9, where מְצַחֵק cannot denote the innocent laughter of a young child. It is inconceivable that the writer could have intended to charge Sarah with being so seriously provoked by such a cause. It must mean " mocking," and was so understood (Gal. iv. 29) ; but this is the act of a boy of some age. See above, No Discrepancies, No. 8, page 166.

Vater remarks upon this passage, " We have no reason

indeed to presuppose a connection in the accounts of different fragments, but neither have we any reason to seek contradictions where there are none." The fragment hypothesis, in the interest of which Vater wrote, is now universally abandoned in consequence of the abundant proofs of a close connection between all parts of the Pentateuch, which it persistently denied. But the prevalent disposition of the divisive critics "to seek contradictions where there are none," in order to justify their assumption of different documents is really destructive of their own hypothesis; for it imputes an incredible blindness to the redactor who could combine such glaring contradictions in what he offers to his readers as a consistent and credible history.

In ver. 16 Hagar is said to have lifted up her voice and wept. Whereupon it is immediately added (ver. 17), And God heard the voice of the lad. This has been regarded as an incongruity, implying a diversity of writers (Knobel), or an error in the text (LXX., the child lifted up his voice and wept). But every writer can presume upon the intelligence of his readers to supply what is so evident as not to require mention. The cries of the child were natural under the circumstances, and are here implied, though not expressly stated. And as Dillmann suggests, the repetition of the words, "she sat over against him" (ver. 16b), can only be for the purpose of introducing a clause of which Hagar is the subject.

Dillmann observes that the name of the child is not mentioned throughout the paragraph (vs. 9–21), and conjectures that E must have said after vs. 17, 18, that the child was called Ishmael *God hears*, because God had then heard his voice; and that R omitted it. It is remarkable how often the divisive hypothesis leads the critics to the belief that something ought to be in the text which is not there. There has been no omission

here. The name does not occur in vs. 19-21 any more
than in the preceding verses. The naming of the child
and the reason of it had already been stated (xvi. 11, 15);
and the allusion to its signification (xxi. 17), like that in
xvii. 20, is suggestive not of different writers but rather
of all emanating from one common source.

MARKS OF P

Dillmann assigns to P, vs. 1b, 2b-5, "on account of the
back reference of vs. 2b and 4 to ch. xvii.," which is freely
admitted; "the statement of age, ver. 4," but see ch. xii.
1-9, Marks of P No. (5); "the diffuseness, ver. 3," there
is here, however, no needless superfluity of words, but
only emphatic repetition, as above explained, and but
one instance of alleged characteristic diction, viz. :

1. "The form מְאַת ver. 5," the construct state of מֵאָה
a hundred. The fact is that both forms of this numeral
occur repeatedly in passages assigned to P, to which, as
a rule, statements of age and enumerations are attributed.
This number occurs in J but twice, vi. 3 (120 years), xxvi.
12 (100 measures), and in E of but three things, Joseph's
age, l. 22, 26 (110 years), Joshua's age, Josh. xxiv. 29
(110 years), and the price of a field at Shechem, Gen.
xxxiii. 19 ; Josh. xxiv. 32 (100 kesitas); in each of these
cases the absolute form מֵאָה chances to be used. But
the same form is also found in like cases in P, e.g., Gen.
xvii. 17 (100 years); xxiii. 1 (127 years) ; Deut. xxxiv. 7
(120 years), and in a large proportion of those instances
in which the numeral is attached to weights or measures.
There is not the slightest reason, therefore, for assuming
a diversity of usage in respect to this word.

MARKS OF J

Dillmann says, "J, too, as is natural, narrated the birth
of Isaac in what he wrote, but R has adopted nothing

from his account except vs. 1a, 2a, 7 ; at least it is quite
inconceivable that ver. 1a could have been added alongside of 1b by R of his own motion and without finding it
in J ; in vs. 2b and 7 לִזְקֻנָיו *in his old age,* points to J,
and ver. 7 is a doublet of ver. 6." He also urges the
back reference in ver. 1a to xviii. 10 sqq. (which is not
disputed), and that פָּקַד *visited* is decisive against the authorship of P, who says instead זָכַר *remembered.*

But it has been shown above that there is no superfluous repetition in ver. 1 ; and that there is no reason
for assuming that vs. 6 and 7 are by different writers.
And the words here adduced supply no argument for
critical partition.

1. פָּקַד *visited* (ver. 1), occurs in this sense besides in
E (1. 24, 25 ; Ex. iii. 16 ; iv. 31 ; xiii. 19 ; xx. 5 ; Num.
xvi. 29) ; in R (Num. xiv. 18) ; in J (Ex. xxxii. 34 ; xxxiv.
7 ; and, according to Dillmann, Lev. xviii. 25). It is
not easy to see on what grounds this last verse is denied
to P. It stands in what he considers a mixed passage of
J and P, and between two verses which he gives to P,
and why it is separated from them does not appear.
And זָכַר *remembered* (said of God), is not an expression
peculiar to P. It occurs in verses attributed to P (Gen.
viii. 1 ; ix. 15, 16 ; xix. 29 ; xxx. 22; Ex. ii. 24 ; vi. 5) ; but
also in J (Ex. xxxii. 13 ; Lev. xxvi. 42, 45, so Dillmann).
And in Gen. xxx. 22 the clause containing it is cut out of
a J and E connection on account of this word alone.

2. זְקֻנִים *old age* (vs. 2, 7), occurs but twice besides,
viz., xliv. 20 J, and xxxvii. 3, about which critics are divided : Knobel gives it to P ; Kuenen and Wellhausen
to E ; and Dillmann to J.

MARKS OF E

To E is assigned vs. 6, 8–21, and it is contended that
" in spite of Elohim this is not from P, whom the ap-

pearance of the divine angel (ver. 17) does not suit." The reason of the absence of angels from P is that the critical lines of partition exclude this document from the body of the narrative, and the occurrence of the word 'angel' in a paragraph is held to be sufficient to prove that it is not from P. "Nor the explanation of the name of Isaac;" but this has already been shown to be consistent with that of ch. xvii. "Nor the sending away of Hagar and Ishmael;" it is alleged that this is inconsistent with the presence of Ishmael at his father's burial (xxv. 9 P). But it is manifest that he might easily return on such an occasion and for such a purpose. It is besides expressly stated in that immediate connection (xxv. 6) that all the sons of Abraham's concubines were thus dismissed during his lifetime. And whatever disposition the critics may choose to make of this verse, the redactor must have thought it to be in harmony with the statement immediately after, that "his sons Isaac and Ishmael buried him." "Nor the age of Ishmael at the time;" but it has been shown that there is no discrepancy in regard to it. "Expressions like *God was with him* (ver. 20), *hearken unto the voice of* (ver. 12), *rose up early in the morning* (ver. 14), *it was grievous in his eyes* (vs. 11, 12), גֵּרֵשׁ *cast out* (ver. 10), יֶלֶד *child* (vs. 8, 14 sqq.), are foreign to P." The simple explanation of the absence of these and other familiar words and phrases from P is that only the most stinted share in the narrative portion of the Pentateuch is accorded to P, while the great bulk of it is divided between J and E. And these expressions are as freely used in J as in E. They are not the peculiar characteristic of any one writer, but are the common possession of all who use the language.

1. *God was with him* (ver. 20); in J (xxvi. 24, 28; xxviii. 15; xxxix. 2, 21).

2. שְׁמַע בְּקוֹל *hearken unto the voice of* (ver. 12); in J (xxvii. 8, 43; Ex. iv. 1; Num. xxi. 3).

3. הִשְׁכִּים בַּבֹּקֶר *rose up early in the morning* (ver. 14). See ch. xviii. 1—xix. 28, Marks of J, No. 26.

4. רָעַע בְּעֵינַי *to be grievous in the eyes* (vs. 11, 12); in J (xxxviii. 7, 10; xlviii. 17; Num. xxii. 34; xxxii. 13); and once in P (Gen. xxviii. 8).

5. גָּרַשׁ *cast out* (ver. 10); in J (iii. 24; iv. 14; Ex. ii. 17; xii. 39; xxxiv. 11; Lev. xxi. 7, 14 (so Dillmann); Num. xxii. 11).

6. יֶלֶד *child* (vs. 8, 14 sqq.); in J (iv. 23; xxxii. 23, E. V. ver. 22; xxxiii. 1 sqq.; xliv. 20). It is noticeable that יֶלֶד *child*, and נַעַר *lad*, are here used interchangeably of Ishmael; the former, vs. 14, 15, 16; the latter, vs. 12, 17 bis, 18, 19, 20. Knobel regarded the former as the language of J, and the latter as that of the older source from which he supposed him to have drawn this narrative. On the assumption of this double authorship he likewise explained the twofold mention of Ishmael's abode in vs. 20 and 21. Other critics refer the whole of vs. 8-21 to E, and thus admit that the use of two different terms to express the same thing is not necessarily an indication of different writers. The doublet in vs. 20, 21, is also passed over in silence as void of significance.[1]

It is argued that this paragraph must be referred to an author distinct from J on account of " the divine name; " but it has been shown that the employment of Elohim here accords with biblical usage. "The variant explanation of the name of Isaac, ver. 6;" but this has been shown to be in harmony with xviii. 12, 13, as well as xvii. 17, 19. "And above all, that vs. 9-21 is a variant of the story about Hagar and Ishmael told by J in ch.

---

[1] Hupfeld (Quellen, p. 30) doubtfully conjectures that ver. 21 belongs to P, and has been transferred by R from its original position after xxv. 12. I am not aware that any other critic has adopted this view.

xvi.;" but this is not the case; they are distinct occurrences. The additional proofs offered for its reference to a writer E, distinct from J and P, are equally nugatory. These are:

7. "The locality in the Neghebh (South), cf. xx. 1;" but ver. 33 J, Abraham is in that region, of which the paragraphs assigned to E afford the only explanation.

8. חֵמֶת *bottle* vs. 14, 15, 19; nowhere else in the Hexateuch; but once besides in the Old Testament.

9. טָחָה *to shoot* (ver. 16); nowhere else in the Old Testament.

10. רֹבֶה קַשָּׁת *archer* (ver. 20); nowhere else in the Old Testament. This is, moreover, a needless departure both from the Massoretic points and the usual meaning of the words. The text has רֹבֶה קַשָּׁת *as he grew up, an archer*.

11. אָמָה *maid-servant* (vs. 10, 12, 13). See ch. xx., Marks of E, No. 1. Hagar, who had been Sarah's bondmaid, שִׁפְחָה, is now, as Abraham's concubine, regarded as in a less servile position, and is hence called an אָמָה. See Diction of ch. xx., No. 14.

12. שׂוּם לְגוֹי *make a nation* (vs. 13, 18); only besides in the Hexateuch xlvi. 3, referred by Dillmann to E, but by Kautzsch to R; the same construction occurs in J xlvii. 26, שׂוּם לְחֹק *make a statute*.

13. הַרְחֵק *afar off* (ver. 16); also in J (Ex. viii. 24, E. V. ver. 28).

14. עַל אוֹדֹת *on account of* (ver. 11); also in J (xxvi. 32); in Josh. xiv. 6 it occurs in the same clause with an expression of P; apart from Gen. xxi. it occurs in but three passages that are referred to E (Ex. xviii. 8; Num. xii. 1; xiii. 24).

ABRAHAM AT BEERSHEBA (CH. XXI. 22-34)

This paragraph records the covenant between Abimelech and Abraham at Beersheba. Hupfeld here gives vs.

22–32 to E, and vs. 33, 34 to J, because of Elohim in vs. 22, 23, and Jehovah in ver. 33. But ver. 33 cannot be separated from what precedes ; for the subject of the verbs in this verse is not expressed and must be derived from the foregoing verses, and Abraham's presence in Beersheba is not explained by anything that has preceded in J, but only by the antecedent narrative, which is attributed to a different document. Kayser seeks to evade these difficulties by assuming that E's narrative was inserted by J in his document, to which he then attaches vs. 33, 34. But this has found no favor with other critics, because it annuls their chief argument for a writer E in this passage distinct from J, viz., that derived from the alleged J parallel in xxvi. 26–33. Wellhausen tries to compass the same end in a different way, but one equally ineffectual. He gives ver. 33 to E; but this makes it necessary for him to alter the text by expunging the name " Jehovah," and even then the phrase " call on the name " of God remains, which is a stereotype J expression. Hupfeld insists that ver. 34 contradicts ver. 32, and cannot, therefore, be assigned to the same author. In ver. 34 Beersheba was in the land of the Philistines ; in ver. 32 it was not. He struggles to overcome the difficulties of the situation by still another method, that of transposing the text. He transfers xxii. 19b, " And Abraham dwelt," or, as he renders it, " settled in Beersheba," to this place, thus accounting for J's speaking of him as in this locality. He then transposes ver. 33 with ver. 34, and so finds a subject for the verbs in the former. The arbitrary character of these changes of the text, for which no reason can be given except the exigencies of the hypothesis, sufficiently condemns them.

Wellhausen fancies that he discovers a discrepancy between ver. 22 and ver. 32b, in virtue of which he claims that the latter cannot be by the author of the preceding narrative, but must be attributed to R. In ver. 32b Abimelech dwelt at some distance from Abraham; in ver. 22 they lived presumably in the same place, for they held an interview without anything being said of Abimelech's having come away from home for this purpose. As if the reader had not already been informed (xx. 2) that the royal residence was at Gerar, while this transaction is expressly said to have taken place at Beersheba (ver. 31). And in numberless instances facts are implied without being expressly mentioned. God healed Abimelech and his wife and his maid-servants (xx. 17), though it had not been previously stated that they were sick. God heard the voice of Ishmael (xxi. 17), though it had not been before said that he had made a sound. It is implied (ver. 25), though not explicitly declared, that Abimelech restored the well to Abraham which his servants had violently taken away.

Dillmann gives both ver. 32b and ver. 34 to R, thus disregarding Hupfeld's notion that they are mutually inconsistent and must be referred to distinct sources. The occurrence of the expression "land of the Philistines" in these verses, which is not found before in ch. xx. or xxi., is no reason for sundering them from the preceding narrative; for Gerar, where Abimelech resided, and of which he was king (xx. 2), was a Philistine city (xxvi. 1). It was quite natural, therefore, to speak of Abimelech's return to Gerar as a return to the land of the Philistines. And as Beersheba lay in the same region it could also be described as in the land of the Philistines.

Dillmann had a more controlling reason, however, than these superficial trifles, for referring ver. 34 to R. It is evidently preparatory for ch. xxii. Abraham's long sojourn there explains how Isaac, whose birth is recorded xxi. 2, could be spoken of as he is in xxii. 6. But it would conflict with the hypothesis to allow a verse of

J to be introductory to a narrative of E. Hence it is cut out of its connection and attributed to R. But the actual and obvious fact is that this verse is a link of connection, binding together what precedes and what follows as the product of the same pen.

The divine names in this paragraph are in strict accordance with ordinary Bible usage, and supply no reason for suspecting a diversity of documents. Thus we find Elohim in the interview with the Gentile king, Abimelech; but when Abraham offers worship he calls on the name of Jehovah.

MARKS OF E

It is alleged that the diction is not that of P, which, considering the slight amount of narrative given to that document, is not surprising. But the words adduced in proof are all found in J.

1. עָשָׂה חֶסֶד *show kindness* (ver. 23). See ch. xviii., xix., Marks of J, No. 29.

2. כָּרַת בְּרִית *make a covenant* (vs. 27, 32). See ch. vi.–ix., Marks of P, No. 16.

3. בַּעֲבוּר *in order that* (ver. 30); in J (iii. 17; viii. 21; xii. 13, 16; xviii. 26, 29, 31, 32; xxvi. 24; xlvi. 34; Ex. xiii. 8); in E (Ex. xix. 9); JE (Gen. xxvii. 4, 10, 19, 31; Ex. xx. 20 bis); R (Ex. ix. 14, 16 bis). See ch. vi.–ix., Marks of J, No. 6; ch. xii. 10–20, Marks of J, No. 5.

4. בִּלְתִּי *except* (ver. 26). See ch. xviii., xix., Marks of J, No. 14.

5. הֵנָּה *here* (ver. 23); in J (xlv. 5, 13; Josh. viii. 20); in E (Gen. xlii. 15; xlv. 8; Josh. xviii. 6); JE (Josh. ii. 2; iii. 9; R (Gen. xv. 16).

6. Elohim (vs. 22, 23); explained above.

7. הוֹכִיחַ *reproved* (ver. 25); in J (xxiv. 14, 44; Lev. xix. 17, so Dillmann); in E (Gen. xx. 16; xxxi. 37, 42).

8. *God is with thee* (ver. 22).   See ch. xxi. 1-21, Marks of E, No. 1.

9. עַל אֹדֹת *because of* (ver. 25).   See ch. xxi. 1-21, Marks of E, No. 14.

10. נִין וָנֶכֶד *offspring and posterity* (ver. 23); neither word occurs again in the Hexateuch; they are found but twice besides in the Old Testament, viz., Job xviii. 19; Isa. xiv. 22.

"The connection" of this paragraph "with ch. xx. in respect of place and persons" is freely admitted; but there is in this no argument for critical partition.   Nor does the similar occurrence in the life of Isaac (xxvi. 26-33) warrant the inference that these are variant accounts of the same transaction recorded by different writers.

The statement "they made a covenant" (ver. 27b), is repeated (ver. 32a), but no critic suspects a doublet or assigns them to distinct documents.

SACRIFICE OF ISAAC (CH. XXII. 1-19)

The narrative of the offering up of Isaac is closely linked together in every part.   It is identical throughout in style and language; it is an appropriate sequel to all that has gone before.   There is not the slightest reason for partitioning this passage between different writers except the occurrence in it of both Elohim and Jehovah.   This is accordingly made the ground of critical severance; and yet these divine names interpose an obstacle to division which it has been found impossible to remove.   The names, which are the only pretext for division, must first be altered into conformity with the critical scheme before any division is practicable.   The mechanical theory, which undertakes to account for the alternation of these names by the peculiar habit of different writers, and

which loses sight of the distinctive meaning and usage of
the names themselves, is here completely baffled.

THE CRITICAL PARTITION

The first attempt at division was that of Astruc and
Eichhorn, who assigned vs. 1–10 to the Elohist, and vs.
11–19 to the Jehovist; which made it necessary to assume that Elohim (ver. 12) had been altered from Jehovah.[1]

But the Elohist account cannot end with ver. 10,
where Abraham takes the knife to slay his son. The action is thus broken off in the midst, and the verses that
follow are needed to complete it. These following verses
are also linked to what precedes by the expressions used :
"Now I know that thou fearest God " (ver. 12) states
the result of the trial (ver. 1). "Thy son, thine only
son " (ver. 12), repeats the identical language of ver. 2.
And ver. 19, "Abraham returned to his young men," is
an express allusion to his promise made to them (ver. 5).

Accordingly Tuch proposed to give the Elohist vs. 1–
13, 19, and to the Jehovist vs. 14–18. Hupfeld (Quellen, p. 55) adopts the same division ; only he insists that
the Elohist of this chapter, as of ch. xx., xxi., is to be distinguished from the Elohist of the earlier chapters of
Genesis. In this he is followed by subsequent critics
who agree that it is E and not P. Elohim is here found
in connection with the diction and style of J, with the

[1] Ewald, Komposition d. Genesis, pp. 74, 75, shows in detail that the
divine names are in each instance appropriately chosen, and remarks
that the adherents of the divisive hypothesis have a much more difficult task to perform in rending asunder what is so closely knit together.
He then proceeds to say, " Nevertheless two different writers are assumed
for no other reason than the constraint of the divine names. And as even
thus the word Elohim (ver. 12) still makes difficulty, it must fall
under the rigor of consistent criticism to make way for another name."

mention of sacrifice, and with "refined and profound" religious ideas, "like the profound theological passage on the origin of sin and evil ch. ii., iii." Thus it threatened to annihilate every distinction between P and J, which the critics have been at such pains to establish, and to destroy the very foundations of the divisive hypothesis. The suggestion of a second Elohist was, therefore, eagerly welcomed as the only mode of averting so dire a catastrophe.

But whether it be P or E, the divine names still prove refractory, and will not fit into the improved division. Jehovah (ver. 11) must, in spite of the exact parallel in ver. 15, be converted into Elohim. It is also necessary to get rid of "Moriah," *the manifestation* or *appearing of Jehovah* (ver. 2), a proper name, of which Jehovah is one of the constituents. Tuch proposes to substitute for it "the land of Moreh," in the neighborhood of Shechem (xii. 6). Wellhausen objects that "Moreh" was not a land, but a place, and conjectures instead "land of the Hamorites" (a designation of his own manufacture), "where Shechem lay" (see xxxiii. 18, 19), and pleads the Samaritan tradition that Mount Gerizim was the scene of the sacrifice of Isaac.[1] Dillmann shows that Shechem was too remote,[2] and offers another equally unfounded conjectural emendation, "land of the Amorite." But the text is in no need of correction. It is only the perplexity of the critics which demands it, in order to bring it into conformity with their hypothesis.

[1] Stade calls the sacrifice of Isaac "a Shechemite saga," Geschichte Israel, page 583.

[2] According to Robinson's itinerary Shechem was thirty-six hours forty-five minutes distant from Beersheba, and could not have been reached on the third day (ver. 4), as Abraham had all his preparations to make before starting. The distance to Mount Moriah was twenty-two hours fifteen minutes, which corresponds to the requirements of the narrative.

"Moriah" in all probability took its name from this incident in the life of Abraham. In later times David selected it to be the site of the future temple, because of a divine manifestation made to him upon this same spot (2 Chron. iii. 1). There is a congruity in this coincidence that was no doubt in the divine intention when Abraham was directed to this particular summit, which was in after ages to be the appointed place of sacrifice, and which was in close proximity to the place where, in the fulness of time, the one effectual sacrifice here prefigured of God's own and only Son was to be offered. But this chapter gives us no reason to suppose that its author was aware that the mountain thus hallowed by the angelic appearance was to gather additional sacredness whether from the erection of the temple or from the sublime transaction on Calvary. Much less is there the slightest ground for assuming that after the temple had been built the word "Moriah" was inserted into the text of this chapter in order to connect the sacrifice of Isaac with the temple mountain. This is certified to be the true original reading by ver. 8, where "God will provide" is a plain allusion to the name. It is used by prolepsis in ver. 2, as Horeb is called "the mountain of God" (Ex. iii. 1), because of the divine descent upon it at the subsequent giving of the law. If a later writer had meant to identify the scene of Abraham's trial with the location of the temple, he would doubtless have used the word "Zion," in which it was comprehended, and which was its ordinary name. The indefiniteness of the language in ver. 2 is also observable. The mountain was not known to Abraham, but would be pointed out to him. And the name "Moriah" is applied not only to the summit, but to the region in which it stood. There is no subsequent trace of such a usage.

"Moriah" (ver. 2) and "God will provide" (ver. 8) in-

evitably carry with them ver. 14, whose last clause, " in
the mount where Jehovah appears," gives the explanation of the name, and to whose allusive " Jehovah-jireh,"
Jehovah will provide, ver. 8 is preparatory. This verse
must accordingly be attached to the preceding. Dr.
Driver admits this by assigning to E vs. 1–14, 19, in
spite of the twice repeated " Jehovah " in ver. 14. " Jehovah " occurs six times in this chapter, either separately or in composition. If with Dr. Driver's assent four of
these are given to E, how can the other two supply an
argument for separating vs. 15–18 from the rest of the
chapter and giving them to a different document?

Moreover, vs. 15–18 are inseparable from what precedes. " The second time " (ver. 15), which the critics
arbitrarily erase, is an explicit reference to ver. 11. " The
angel of Jehovah " is introduced in both verses in identical terms. " Thou hast not withheld thy son, thine only
son " (ver. 12), recurs again ver. 16 (see also ver. 2).
And these closing verses are essential to the narrative
and an indispensable part of it, since without them it is
not brought to a fitting termination. At every crisis in
his life, and especially after every marked exercise of
faith, a blessing is freshly pronounced upon Abraham.
When in obedience to the divine command he left his
home and kindred and came to Canaan, Jehovah appeared to him and promised him this land (xii. 7). After
he had shown his generosity in parting from Lot, the
same promise was renewed in fuller form (xiii. 14–17).
After his brave rescue of Lot from a pillaging foe, he
was blessed of Melchizedek (xiv. 19, 20). His faith in
Jehovah's promise of seed, made to him in his despondency (xv. 6), is rewarded by a covenant engagement (vs.
18–21). When confiding in God's assurance that the
long-delayed promise should be fulfilled at the set time
in the next year, he accepted the rite of circumcision (ch.

xvii.), Jehovah visited him in his tent on the most confidential terms (ch. xviii.). And it would be most extraordinary if the most conspicuous manifestation of his faith
and obedience, put to the severest test, and this triumphantly borne, were to pass without signal recognition
and reward. The situation calls for just what we actually find in vs. 15–18, a renewal of the promises in their
amplest form, Jehovah by a voice from heaven confirm-
ing them by the added solemnity of an oath.

The question here arises how and by whom the different constituents, which in the opinion of the critics are
here combined, have been put together in their present
form. According to the fundamental assumptions of
the critical hypothesis E could not have used the name
"Jehovah." It is necessary, therefore, to suppose that
the portion assigned to him is not now as he must have
written it, but has been altered by another. Nöldeke
infers that E has both here and elsewhere been worked
over by J. But this would annul one of the chief arguments for the existence of E distinct from J, based upon
alleged discrepancies between their respective narratives;
and Wellhausen interposes an objection on this ground.
Dillmann adds that if J had made these alterations in E,
he would not have suffered Elohim to remain. In the earliest edition of his "Commentary" Dillmann maintained
that there were two independent accounts of this transaction by E and by J, and that R incorporated into E's
account from that of J the mention of Moriah, the name
Jehovah, and the added verses at the end. But the
author of these closing verses must have had those that
precede before him, for there are identical expressions in
both. In subsequent editions Dillmann receded from
this position and insisted that the changes and additions
are to be ascribed to R, and were made by him of his
own motion and not borrowed from an antecedent source.

But then what R has inserted is indistinguishable from J in matter and style; and the same is true of what E has written, with the sole exception of the divine names. So that it might appear as though the agnostic position long ago taken by Gramberg was the safest one for the critics in dealing with this chapter, viz. : that the documents are so blended that it is impossible to effect a partition, and "no one can tell what belongs to the Elohist, what to the Jehovist, and what to the redactor."[1]

In fact some of the critics lean strongly toward the admission of the unity of this narrative. Hupfeld ("Quellen," p. 178) speaks of it as "a complete and articulated whole," that would in every case be the loser by any omission; and he adds, "I cannot conceal the fact that the entire narrative seems to me to bear the stamp of the Jehovist; and certainly one would never think of the Elohist, but for the name Elohim (prop., ha-Elohim), which here (as in part in the history of Joseph) is not supported by the internal phenomena and embarrasses criticism." Knobel gives the entire passage to J, and opens the way to a correct understanding of it by calling attention to the fact, remarked upon before by Hengstenberg and others, that the change of divine names occurs at the crisis of the narrative. It is Elohim who tries the faith of Abraham (vs. 1–10); it is Jehovah who stays the patriarch's hand and blesses him (vs. 11–18). Knobel says, "Apart from Elohim nothing in this narrative reminds us of the Elohist; on the contrary everything speaks for the Jehovist. . . . On account of the divine name Elohim (vs. 1, 3, 8, 9), one might suppose

---

[1] Ilgen splinters this passage in a very remarkable way, splitting verses, duplicating phrases, giving some particulars to E, and others to J, and thus tries to make out two separate narratives of the transaction. No one, even of those who are most prone to adopt similar methods elsewhere, has thought fit to follow him here.

that the author was here giving a story taken from an older source, as in ch. xx., xxi. But the passage contains no other traces of it; and we, therefore, have to assume that the Jehovist here uses Elohim so long as there is reference to a human sacrifice, and only introduces Jehovah (ver. 11) after setting aside such a sacrifice, which was foreign to the religion of Jehovah." And he refers to iii. 1, 3, 5 as an illustrative passage, where in J Elohim is used in the conversation of Eve and the serpent.

The real significance of the divine names as here used is stated in a more satisfactory manner by Delitzsch. He accepts Hupfeld's critical division, but destroys the basis on which it rests by showing that Elohim and Jehovah are here used with a strict regard to their proper meaning, so that they do not afford the slightest ground for assuming a diversity of writers. Delitzsch says, "The God who bids Abraham sacrifice Isaac is called (ha-)Elohim, and the divine manifestation, which prevents the sacrifice, the angel of Jehovah. He who demands from Abraham the surrender of Isaac is God the creator, who has power over life and death, and therefore the power to take back what he has given. But Jehovah in his angel prevents the execution of it at the last extreme; for the son of the promise cannot perish without the promise of God perishing also, and with it his truthfulness and the realization of his purpose of salvation." The Creator is the sovereign Lord of all. He has the right to demand that the dearest and the best shall be surrendered to him. It was not that he from whom nothing can be hid, might ascertain the strength of Abraham's faith, that this test was imposed upon him, but for Abraham's own sake, that his faith might be confirmed and strengthened by this heroic exercise of it, and that the latent power of it might be exhibited to himself and

others. Would Abraham give up his beloved Isaac at
God's bidding, the child for whom he had so long hoped
and waited, the child of promise, and on whom all the
other promises made to him were suspended? Would
he yield him up to God with the same submission with
which the heathen around him sacrificed their children
to their cruel deities? But Abraham's God abhorred
the bloody sacrifice of the first-born. It was the spiritual surrender alone that he required. But that must
be unambiguously expressed in an outward act, that admitted of no pretence and no evasion. It was a terrible
test, safe only in a divine hand, capable of intervening,
as he did intervene, and as it was his purpose from the
first to intervene, as soon as the spiritual end of the trial
was accomplished.

And herein lay, as Delitzsch further observes, "an
eternally valid divine protest against human sacrifice,"
while "the ram in the thorn bush, which Abraham offered
instead of Isaac, is the prototype of the animal sacrifices,
which are here sanctioned on the same mountain, on
which the blood of the typical animal sacrifices was to
flow during the entire period of the Old Testament."
Dillmann's suggestion, that "the reminiscence here still
plainly glimmers through that the Hebrews once stood
in respect to child-sacrifice on a like plane with the other
Shemites and Canaanites," is a gross and utterly unfounded misrepresentation. The lesson of the narrative
is precisely the reverse, that while God put Abraham's
faith and obedience to the severest test, he did not require the sacrifice of his child. It was only in later and
degenerate ages that such sacrifices were known among
the Hebrews, being borrowed from the surrounding
heathen like other idolatrous abominations.

The Elohim of ver. 12 does not invalidate the explanation above given of the divine names occurring in this

passage. As was long since shown by Ewald, Elohim is here the proper word. "Both names of God can be used with the word 'fear,' but with the distinction that 'the fear of Jehovah' respects Jehovah as opposed to strange gods (1 Sam. xii. 24; Ps. cxv. 10, 11; cxxxv. 20); while 'the fear of God' only expresses submission to God or piety in general, as 2 Sam. xxiii. 3; Gen. xx. 11. The latter is evidently demanded here, when the angel says to Abraham that he is God-fearing and submissive to the divine will. The 'fear of Jehovah' would have implied that Abraham had been tempted to idolatry; but it was only his steadfast submission to God that was tested."

MARKS OF E

Dillmann claims that this narrative was not originally drawn up by J, "although in the language there are various things (allerlei) that remind of him," but by E, as shown by—

1. "The prevailing use of Elohim or ha-Elohim"; this is explained above.

2. "The revelation in a vision at night (ver. 1)"; but so also in J. See ch. xx., Marks of E, No. 4.

3. "The call and answer (vs. 1, 7, 11)"; twice besides in E (xxxi. 11; xlvi. 2). In all other passages there is a great diversity of critical opinion; xxvii. 1, 18, is by most critics referred to J, but by Wellhausen and Dillmann to E, simply and solely on account of this very form of speech, while the context is assigned to JE as incapable of separation; xxxvii. 13 stands in a mixed JE context, which Kautzsch cannot unravel, while Wellhausen and Cornill cut out the clause containing this phrase and assign it to E on this account; Ex. iii. 4b is cut out of a J context by Wellhausen on account of this phrase and given to E; it is also assigned to E by Dillmann, who gives ver. 4a to J.

4. "The angel calling out of heaven (ver. 11)." In
one instance and one only "the angel of Elohim" is said
to have called out of heaven (xxi. 17). "The angel of Jehovah" does the same (xxii. 11, 15), which but for critical legerdemain belong to J. Angels come down to earth
in E (xxviii. 12) and meet Jacob on his way (xxxii. 2, E.
V. ver. 1); one spoke to him in a dream (xxxi. 11) without any suggestion of the voice coming out of heaven. It
cannot be reckoned a peculiarity of E, therefore, that
angels call out of heaven.

5. "כֹּה in a local sense (ver. 5)"; so in E (xxxi. 37;
Num. xxiii. 15). It occurs besides in this sense in two
other places in the Hexateuch, one of which (Ex. ii. 12) is
referred to J by Wellhausen, and the other (Num. xi. 31)
by Kuenen. עַד כֹּה the same combination as in Gen. xxii.
5, occurs twice besides in the Hexateuch, in both instances in a temporal sense; of these Ex. vii. 16 is referred to J by Cornill, and Josh. xvii. 14 by Kuenen.

6. "יָחִיד only, vs. 2, 12"; also ver. 16 R (other critics
J); nowhere else in the Hexateuch.

That Isaac is here called Abraham's "only" son implies the previous narrative of the dismissal of Ishmael
(xxi. 14 sqq.); the providential disclosure of the ram to
Abraham (ver. 13) resembles that of the well to Hagar
(xxi. 19); and the return to Beersheba (ver. 19) is based
upon xxi. 31, 32 (but also ver. 33 J). But while this narrative is thus linked with passages ascribed by the critics
to E, it is no less indissolubly tied to those which are
attributed to J. This final trial of Abraham's faith is a
fitting climax to the series of trials previously recorded
by J. And vs. 15–18, whose necessary connection with
the previous part of the chapter, both in matter and in the
form of its expressions, has already been exhibited, repeats with special emphasis promises elsewhere ascribed
to J, preserving both their language and their figurative

form. "I will bless thee," as xii. 2; "multiply thy seed
as the stars of the heaven," as xv. 5; xxvi. 4; "and the
sand which is upon the sea-shore," as xiii. 16; xxxii. 13
(E. V. ver. 12); "thy seed shall possess the gate of his
enemies" as xxiv. 60; "in thy seed shall all the nations
of the earth be blessed," as xii. 3; xviii. 18; xxvi. 4;
"because thou hast obeyed my voice," as xviii. 19;
xxvi. 5.

MARKS OF R

Dillmann repeats Hitzig's objection that vs. 15–18
cannot be by E, the reputed author of the previous part
of the chapter, because this second communication by
the angel instead of being a continuation of ver. 12 is
added afterward in a supplementary manner. But this
carping criticism betrays a lack of appreciation of a feature of the narrative which adds to its beauty and im-
pressiveness regarded merely from a rhetorical point of
view. There is no reason why the angel might not speak
twice, as well as once. It was enough at first to arrest
the patriarch's hand and approve his obedience. The
promise of Jehovah, attested by a solemn oath, most fitly
concludes the scene after Abraham had completed his
act of worship by offering the ram. If this order had
been reversed, and the action continued after the angel
had spoken, attention would have been diverted from
that which now crowns the whole, and upon which chief
stress is laid.

It is further charged that—

1. בִּי נִשְׁבַּעְתִּי *by myself have I sworn* (ver. 16), is a
formula that belongs to a later time, *e.g.*, Isa. xlv. 23;
Jer. xxii. 5; xlix. 13. But that God did thus confirm
his promise to Abraham by an oath is abundantly attested (Gen. xxiv. 7; xxvi. 3; l. 24; Ex. xxxiii. 1; Num.

xxxii. 11; Deut. i. 8, etc.). And that this was an oath
by himself is expressly affirmed (Ex. xxxii. 13). An
equivalent asseveration by his own life is also attributed
to Jehovah in the Pentateuch (Num. xiv. 21, 28 ; Deut.
xxxii. 40).

2. יְהוָה נְאֻם *saith Jehovah* (ver. 16), is also said to be a
prophetic formula of a later period. But the phrase occurs again (Num. xiv. 28). And נְאֻם occurs besides in
the prophecies of Balaam (Num. xxiv. 3, 4, 15, 16), where
its antiquity is vouched for by the obvious imitations in
2 Sam. xxiii. 1 ; Prov. xxx. 1.

3. אֲשֶׁר יַעַן *because* (ver. 16) ; besides in the Hexateuch
Deut. i. 36 ; Josh. xiv. 14. יַעַן occurs also Num. xi. 20 J;
Lev. xxvi. 43 J worked over (so Dillmann); and Num.
xx. 12, which Wellhausen assigns to P, and Dillmann also
to P, except only the clause containing this word, which
he refers to R.

4. אֲשֶׁר עֵקֶב *because* (ver. 18) ; but once besides in the
Hexateuch xxvi. 5. עֵקֶב occurs also Num. xiv. 24 ; Deut.
vii. 12; viii. 20. The employment of these unusual con-
junctions, as of the emphatic absolute infinitives in
ver. 17, is due, as Dillmann correctly observes, to the
solemn and impressive character of this angelic utterance.

5. הִתְבָּרֵךְ *bless one's self*, *i.e.*, seek and obtain a blessing
(ver. 18). This reflexive form of the verb occurs twice
in the promise of a blessing upon all nations through
Abraham and his seed, viz., here and xxvi. 4 ; the passive
form נִבְרַךְ *be blessed*, is used instead three times, viz.,
xii. 3; xviii. 18; xxviii. 14. The sense is substantially
the same. נִבְרַךְ is found nowhere else in the Old Testament. הִתְבָּרֵךְ occurs besides, Deut. xxix. 18 (E. V. ver.
19); Ps. lxxii. 17 ; Isa. lxv. 16 ; Jer. iv. 2. There is nothing to indicate that one form is of later origin than the
other.

NO PROOF OF SEPARATE DOCUMENTS

The diction of these verses cannot prove them to be of later date than the rest of the chapter. There is no occasion, therefore, to call in the aid of R in their production. And neither in this chapter nor in those that precede is there any just ground for assuming the existence of a writer E, distinct from J. Their diction is indistinguishable.[1] The divine names are used discriminatingly throughout, and afford no criterion of diverse authorship.

And the attempt to establish a distinctive diction for P cannot be called successful. Of all the so-called characteristic P words and phrases of the creation and flood Elohim is almost the only one that occurs henceforth in P paragraphs in Genesis. There is not a word in the entire section of the Generations of Terah, which the critics regard as peculiar to P, that is found in antecedent chapters with the exception of a very few expressions in ch. xvii., and these are chiefly due to the fact that God's covenant with Abraham naturally calls for the use of the same terms as his covenant with Noah. And those which are ascribed to P in this section either do not reappear in Genesis, or are found as well in J and E with rare exceptions, which contain their explanation in themselves. It has been previously shown that the differences existing between the Elohist and Jehovist paragraphs in the ante-patriarchal portion of Genesis are not such as to imply distinct authors, but are readily explicable from the

---

[1] In addition to the proofs already given that the alleged diversities are not really such, note the following coincidences between what is ascribed to E in this chapter and what is referred to J elsewhere. נסה (ver. 1) as Ex. xvi. 4; נא (ver. 2) as xii. 13; xviii. 30; לך לך (ver. 2) as xii. 1; אשר אמר אליך (ver. 2) as xxvi. 2, cf. xii. 1; השכים בבקר (ver. 3) as xix. 27.

matter of these paragraphs respectively, and from the special meaning and usage of the divine names Elohim and Jehovah. The same thing is yet more emphatically true of that portion of Genesis which we are now considering. The difference of diction that is here alleged between P and J is wholly factitious, being created by two features of the critical partition, viz. : the scanty fragments of the narrative attributed to P, and the peculiar character of the only two paragraphs of any length (chs. xvii. and xxiii.) which are accorded to him. As only diminutive portions of the narrative are awarded to P, it is not to be expected that these will contain the full vocabulary of the bulk of the narratives, which is shared between the other documents. That numerous words and phrases occur in J and E, which are not to be found in P, thus arises out of the inequality in the apportionment. And when to the difference in quantity is added the difference in the nature of the material assigned to P on the one hand, and to J and E on the other, all the diversity of diction is fully accounted for. And the entire critical superstructure of separate documents which has been built upon it crumbles into nothing.

It may at least be safely affirmed that no evidence of the existence of such documents has been brought to light in that part of Genesis which has thus far been considered. And this is the portion of the book in which the divisive hypothesis has been supposed to be most strongly entrenched. It must find its justification here, if it can do so anywhere.

FAMILY OF NAHOR (CH. XXII. 20-24)

Tuch, Nöldeke, and Knobel refer these verses, which contain a list of the children of Nahor, to P; Wellhausen gives them to E; Hupfeld and Dillmann to J, which last is now the current critical opinion. The determining consideration is that the mention of Rebekah, the only daughter named of any of the twelve sons (ver. 23), is evidently designed to prepare the way for the narrative of Isaac's marriage in ch. xxiv., which is assigned to J. Only those women have a place in the genealogies, of whom there is occasion to speak in the subsequent history. And xxii. 23 is distinctly referred to in xxiv. 15, 24. Accordingly, the E phrase at the beginning, "and it came to pass after these things," as xxii. 1; xl. 1; xlviii. 1, is either quietly ignored, as by Dillmann, or attributed to R, as by Kautzsch. The diffuseness shown in the repetition (ver. 23b) of what had already been stated (ver. 20b), which is elsewhere reckoned a characteristic of P, is also ignored. The assertion that P would have prefixed the title, " These are the generations of Nahor," overlooks the fact that Nahor, like Abraham, belonged to the family of Terah, and all that appertained to both fell properly under the " Generations of Terah." The mention of Milcah (ver. 20), refers back to xi. 29, where her marriage to Nahor is stated in preparation for this very passage. It is this which compelled the critics to claim xi. 29 for J, thus sundering it from xi. 27 P, to which it is indissolubly bound.

MARKS OF J

1. יָלַד *begat* (ver. 23). See ch. vi.–ix., Marks of P, No. 20.

2. פִּילֶגֶשׁ *concubine* (ver. 24); besides in the Hexateuch xxv. 6; xxxv. 22a; xxxvi. 12; and in each instance attributed to R.

3. גַּם הוּא *she also* (vs. 20, 24); in J, besides, iv. 4, 26; x. 21; xxvii. 31; xxxviii. 10, 11; xlviii. 19; in E xxxii. 19 (E. V. ver. 18). גַּם does not chance to occur with this

particular pronoun in the passages assigned to P, but it is used in the same manner with other personal pronouns (Ex. vi. 5; vii. 11; Num. xviii. 3, 28 P). See under ch. x., page 137.

4. וּשְׁמָהּ and *her name, i.e.,* whose name was (ver. 24), claimed by Wellhausen, but not by Dillmann, as a criterion of J; besides, in J, xvi. 1b; xxiv. 29; xxv. 1; xxxviii. 1, 2, 6; in JE, Josh. ii. 1. This is the uniform way throughout the historical books of the Old Testament of introducing the name of a person who has just been mentioned, and cannot be regarded as peculiar to any one writer.

That precisely twelve sons of Nahor are here enumerated, "as of Ishmael, Israel, and Edom," as is correctly explained by Dillmann, "does not rest upon a transfer of Israelitish relations to those of kindred stock (so Knobel), nor upon the mere systematizing of the writer (so Nöldeke), but upon the usages of these peoples," which were in point of fact severally divided into just twelve tribes.

In regard to the alleged variant descent of Aram and Uz (ver. 21, cf. x. 22, 23), see under ch. x. pp. 137–139.

DEATH AND BURIAL OF SARAH (CH. XXIII.)

The land of Canaan had been promised to Abraham and his seed for their permanent possession, xii. 7; xiii. 15; xv. 18; xvii. 8; but he had now for more than sixty years been a wanderer and a sojourner, with no absolute ownership of any portion of the soil. Hence the stress laid in this chapter upon the purchase of the field and cave of Machpelah, the first spot of ground to which he obtained a legal title. The transaction was conducted with punctilious regard to all the necessary formalities, and these are recited in detail; all which evidences not the diffuse style of a particular writer P, but the impor-

2

tance which was attached to the rights thus conveyed. The securing of this burial-place was properly regarded as a first instalment and a pledge of the final fulfilment of the divine promise, and as indicative of Abraham's implicit faith in that promise. The subsequent references to it are also made with a formality and a studied repetition of the language here employed, which show how significant it was held to be, and how it both nurtured and served to give expression to the faith of the patriarchs, and particularly of Jacob, after he had removed to Egypt (xxv. 9, 10; xlix. 29–32; l. 13). For the same reason it is twice emphatically repeated in ch. xxiii. that this was "in the land of Canaan" (vs. 2, 19). And, as Hävernick suggests, the consequence attributed in these various passages to the possession of a burial-place implies that the record was made prior to the actual occupation of Canaan by the Israelites, after which it ceased to be of special interest, and is never again referred to.

Nöldeke imagines a discrepancy with Gen. xxxiii. 19, Josh. xxiv. 32 E, according to which passages "Jacob makes the first acquisition of land at Shechem by purchase." The discrepancy is a sheer creation of the critic. Although Jacob's purchase was sufficiently memorable to be deemed worthy of special record, there is no intimation that it was the first territorial acquisition of the patriarchs.

Eichhorn [1] remarks upon this transaction: "In Mesopotamia, where no Canaanites traded, gold and silver were still rare in Jacob's time; everything was acquired by exchange, and Jacob gives twenty years of service as a herdsman in exchange for two wives, servants, maidservants, and flocks. On the other hand, in Canaan, in the neighborhood of the Phœnicians, who had in their

[1] Einleitung in das Alte Testament, 3d edit., 1803, vol. ii., p. 373.

hands the trade of the world, barter was no longer in
vogue in the time of Abraham, but silver was used as
pretium eminens, not, however, in coins of different de-
nominations, but by weight (ver. 16). Yet in Jacob's
time the Phœnicians probably had rude coins (xxxiii. 19).
. . . . Abraham buys the cave of Machpelah in the
presence of witnesses, and counts upon remaining in undisturbed possession of the field, just as in Homer the
Greeks and Trojans count assuredly upon the fulfilment
of the treaty which has been concluded, because both
armies were present at the oral agreement."

"Abraham *came* to mourn for Sarah" (ver. 2), should
perhaps be rendered "*went in*" to her tent (cf. xviii.
6). Some, however, understand it to mean that he came
from Beersheba, and find here a link of connection with
xxii. 19, and suppose in ver. 4, "a sojourner," an allusion to xxi. 34, "he sojourned in the land of the Philistines."

The single occurrence of Elohim in ch. xxiii. (ver. 6),
in the mouth of the children of Heth is so entirely in
accordance with Hebrew usage that no individual peculiarity of a particular writer can be inferred from it.

Chs. xvii. and xxiii. severally relate to the two chief
promises made to Abraham, and from time to time repeated, viz., his future seed and the land of Canaan. One
records the ordaining of circumcision ; the other the acquisition of the first possession in the land. Both are
thoroughly germane to the entire history, and give no
indication of being interpolated additions. The stress
laid upon each, and the legal precision natural in instituting the rite and in describing the deed of purchase
give to these chapters an appearance of formal repetition,
which does not belong to such portions of ordinary narrative as are ascribed to P. This peculiar material requires, of course, a fitting style and diction, and sufficiently

accounts for any divergence in this respect from other paragraphs.[1]

1. "The chronological statement" (ver. 1). See ch. xvi., Marks of P, No. 1.

2. "The aim of the narrative, the juristic punctilious-ness and formality of the record." It has been shown that the narrative is closely related to the antecedent history, and is precisely in line with the promises to Abraham, which are the burden of the whole; also that the minute exactness of the record corresponds with the character of the transaction. It does not appear why the same historian, who describes other events in the life of Abraham, cannot include this likewise in his narrative, and in doing so cannot adapt his style to the nature of the subject.

3. "Children of Heth" (vs. 3, etc.). This is an obvious reference to x. 15 J, where the tribe or tribal ancestor is called Heth.

4. "Machpelah" (vs. 9, 17, 19), only mentioned elsewhere as the burial-place of patriarchs and with explicit reference to this passage (xxv. 9 ; xlix. 30 ; l. 13). Since all the passages in which this cave is spoken of are referred to P, there is no opportunity for this word to occur in J or E.

5. שְׁנֵי חַיֵּי years of the life of (ver. 1) ; as this phrase is only used when stating the age of a person, and such passages are by rule referred to P, it cannot be expected in J or E.

---

[1] Observe how even Wellhausen (Comp. d. Hex., p. 168), in contending that Lev. xxvi. is by the author of chs. xvii.–xxv., insists that "the differences of language are sufficiently explained by the distinct character of the material ; hitherto laws in dry style suited to the subject, now prophecy in poetic and impassioned discourse."

6. אֲחֻזָּה *possession* (vs. 4, 9, 20). See ch. xvii., Marks of P, No. 7.

7. תּוֹשָׁב *sojourner* (ver. 4); nowhere else in Genesis. Only besides in legal sections (Ex. xii. 45 ; Lev. xxii. 10 ; xxv. 6, 23, 35, 40, 45, 47 ; Num. xxxv. 15), and, therefore, necessarily limited to the document to which such sections are given.

8. נָשִׂיא *prince* (ver. 6). See ch. xvii., Marks of P, No. 11.

9. קוּם *be made sure* (vs. 17, 20); so in P (Lev. xxv. 30 ; xxvii. 14, 17, 19 ; Num. xxx. 5–13, E. V., vs. 4–12). The word is here used in the legal sense of a contract, decision, or vow, *standing, i.e.*, enduring or being valid. This particular application of the word can only be expected where the legal validity of such arrangements is spoken of. It is, however, substantially the same sense as in Josh. ii. 11 JE, *remain;* vii. 12, 13 J, *stand firm;* and in the causative form, *ratify* or *establish* (Gen. xxvi. 3 R (Dillmann) or J (other critics) ; Lev. xxvi. 9 J (so Dillmann) ; Num. xxiii. 19 E).

10. שָׁמַע אֶל *hearken unto* (ver. 16) ; so in J (xvi. 11 ; xxxix. 10 ; xlix. 2) ; in E (xxi. 17 ; xxx. 17).

11. מִקְנָה *possession* (ver. 18). See ch. xvii., Marks of P, No. 9.

12. אֶרֶץ כְּנַעַן *land of Canaan* (vs. 2, 19). See ch. xii. 5, Marks of P, No. 4. Great stress is laid upon the fact that it was in the land of Canaan that Sarah died and was buried, and that the spot purchased by Abraham and formally deeded to him was in that land.

13. " Back references to what is related here in xxv. 9, 10 ; xlix. 29 sqq. ; l. 13." These are freely admitted and are proofs of a close relation between those passages and this chapter, but do not imply that they belong to a different document from other intervening passages.

It will be observed how little there is that is distinctive in the diction of ch. xxiii. to connect it with other P sections in Genesis.

MARRIAGE OF ISAAC (CH. XXIV.)

In xxv. 20 P alludes to Isaac's marriage to Rebekah, daughter of Bethuel and sister of Laban, in a manner implying previous mention of these parties and of this event. Precisely the account thus called for is to be found in ch. xxiv. and the preliminary genealogy (xxii. 20–24), both which, however, the critics assign to J. This makes it necessary for them to assume that a similar narrative was contained in P, but R has thought proper to omit it. It is easy to make conjectural assumptions with the view of evading or explaining away facts at variance with the divisive hypothesis; only it should be borne in mind that these assumptions lend no support to the hypothesis. They are simply inferences based upon the hypothesis. And the necessity of multiplying such assumptions betrays the weakness of the cause that requires them.

J has Aram-naharaim once only (xxiv. 10), while P has Paddan-aram (xxv. 20 and elsewhere); but apart from the fact that these names may not be precise equivalents, as Dillmann admits, this is no more a reason for suspecting diversity of authorship than when J uses two different designations of the same place : [1] xxiv.

[1] It would argue no diversity of writers if, in an account of the landing of the pilgrims, we should read upon one page that they reached the coast of America, and on the next that they disembarked in New England. In the first mention of the region the more general term Aram-naharaim is employed, but ever after Paddan-aram, as indicating more precisely where Haran lay; and Haran occurs in P (xi. 31; xii. 5) as well as in J and E. " Haran is a town situated in Paddan-aram; but a nomad rarely lives shut up in a town. The whole land is his, and he and his flocks traverse it far and wide. The names of the town

10, " city of Nahor," and xxvii. 43, "Haran ; " or uses
שְׁבוּעָה for *oath*, xxiv. 8, but אָלָה, ver. 41. Nor can any
significance be attached to the circumstance that J says
" daughters of the Canaanites " (xxiv. 3, 37), and P,
" daughters of Canaan " (xxviii. 1, 6, 8 ; xxxvi. 2), inasmuch as J himself varies the expression again (xxxiv. 1)
to " daughters of the land." And according to Wellhausen P calls the same persons " daughters of Hittites "
(xxvi. 34), and " daughters of Heth " (xxvii. 46). On the
other hand, it is observable as one of the numberless indications of unity that the same care to avoid intermarriages with the Canaanites is shown in ch. xxiv. as in
xxviii. 1–9, which the critics on this very ground assign
to a different document.

Verse 67 alludes to Sarah's death, recorded in ch. xxiii.
P. But as on critical principles one document cannot
refer to what is contained in another, Dillmann erases
the mention of Sarah here as a later gloss. The allegation that the words "his mother Sarah," in the first
clause of this verse, are inadmissible in Hebrew construction is refuted by numerous examples of the same
sort, *e.g.*, Gen. xxxi. 13 ; Josh. iii. 11; Judg. viii. 11 ; xvi.
14 ; and if they were, this would not affect the reading
in the last clause of the verse. Wellhausen, more bravely
still, proposes to substitute " father " for " mother," as

and of the land can accordingly be interchanged without indicating a
difference of style. But Genesis itself distinguishes yet more narrowly
between these names. When Jacob goes from home, he always goes to
Haran, because he expects to find the family residing in the town
(xxvii. 43 ; xxviii. 10). And when he comes before the gates of the
town (xxix. 4), and asks those who come out, is he not compelled to ask
for Haran ? It is true that the name of the land to which Jacob is going also occurs (xxviii. 2, 5, 6, 7), but only in contrast with the land of
Ishmael (ver. 9). But when Jacob journeys back again to Canaan he
always leaves, not Haran, but Paddan-aram ; for he takes his flight, not
from the town, but from the land, where he was pasturing the flocks
far and wide."—Ewald, Komp. d. Gen., pp. 109, 110.

the last word of ver. 67. He tells us that Abraham must
have died before the servant's return, only R has omitted
the account of his death. And thus by the clever device
of reconstructing the text a twofold advantage is gained.
A troublesome allusion is escaped and a flat contradiction created between J and P, for according to the latter
(xxv. 7, 20) Abraham lived thirty-five years after Isaac's
marriage. Kautzsch is not content with this simple
emendation, but undertakes to correct the narrative
more at large upon the basis suggested by Wellhausen.
He tells us that after ver. 61a there followed the announcement that the servant on his return found Abraham dead ; and consequently, ver. 61b, " the servant took
Rebekah and went his way (ver. 62), in the land of the
South, and came to Isaac ; for he dwelt in the wilderness
of Beer-lahai-roi." There is, he assures us, but one
other possibility, viz., that ver. 62 may have read, " Isaac
was come from the wilderness of Beer-lahai-roi to the
burial of Abraham." One thing is evident, if the critics
are right the text is wrong ; but if the text is right, how
is it with the critics?

In ver. 61 Knobel fancies that the second clause does
not naturally follow the first, and that this indicates two
blended accounts. And as the servant brings Rebekah,
not to Abraham, who had sent him, but to Isaac, and calls
Isaac his master (ver. 65), instead of his master's son, as
vs. 44, 48, 51, the inference is drawn that in the older
narrative, of which there is a fragment in vs. 61–67, it
was Isaac, not Abraham, who deputed the servant upon
his errand. And in his opinion this discovery is corroborated by some " very peculiar expressions " in these
verses, of which other critics who have no end to be
answered by them take no note. It surely is not strange
that a bride should be taken at once to her husband ;
nor that the servant should call Isaac his master, since

he was Abraham's heir, now in mature age, and in charge of all his father's possessions, especially when speaking to Rebekah. It was equally natural, when treating with her father and brother in the name of Isaac's father, that he should speak of Isaac as his master's son.

In his first edition Dillmann accepted Knobel's discovery of a variant account of the mission of the servant, and attributed vs. 62–67 to E. But in subsequent editions he discarded it in favor of Hupfeld's ("Quellen," p. 145) and Wellhausen's version of the story, that Abraham was at the point of death when he sent the servant, and actually died before the servant's return. In conformity with this it is assumed that in J xxv. 1–6, 11b preceded ch. xxiv.; in defence of which it is urged that the statement by the servant (ver. 36), that Abraham had given all that he had unto Isaac is based upon xxv. 5, and Isaac's dwelling at Beer-lahai-roi (xxv. 11b) is presupposed in xxiv. 62. But the servant might state a fact from his own knowledge, which there had been no suitable occasion to mention as yet in the course of the history. And the sacred historian makes no formal mention of the dwelling-place of Isaac until he has recorded the death of Abraham (xxv. 8, 11), precisely as he records the death of Isaac (xxxv. 29) before the like formal mention of the abode of Esau (xxxvi. 6) and of Jacob (xxxvii. 1). The critics say that R transposed xxv. 1–6, 11b, from its original position in order to remove the conflict between J and P as to the time of Abraham's death. The fact is that the critics arbitrarily assume this transposition, and fix the time of Abraham's death at their own liking for the mere purpose of creating a variance between ch. xxiv. and ch. xxv. which does not really exist, and thence deducing an argument for distinct documents. It certainly does not prepossess one in favor of a cause that it should be necessary to resort to such measures in its support.

Knobel imagines that he detects a discrepancy of another sort between J and P, in relation, not to the time of Abraham's death, but that of Sarah. According to J, or the older narrative which he here follows, Isaac was comforted after his mother's death by his marriage with Rebekah (ver. 67). But "according to P he was thirty-six or thirty-seven years old when Sarah died (xvii. 17; xxi. 5; xxiii. 1), and forty when he was married (xxv. 20). He must, therefore, have mourned about four years. But thirty and seventy days were prolonged terms of mourning (l. 3; Num. xx. 29; Deut. xxi. 13; xxxiv. 8). J, therefore, put Sarah's death later, or Isaac's marriage earlier than P." As if the duration of the grief of a loving son for the loss of his mother was to be measured by customary social formalities.

Dillmann scents a doublet in ver. 29b, cf. 30b, but as he can make no use of it, he lets it pass, only insisting that 29b has been transposed from its original position after 30a. But there is no textual error, and there has been no transposition. These verses simply illustrate the inartificial style of Hebrew narrative. The general statement is made first, 29b, that Laban ran out unto the man unto the well; further particulars are added afterward (ver. 30), it was when he saw the ring and bracelets that had been given his sister and heard her words that he came out and found the man standing by the well. Or one aspect of a transaction is stated first, and then followed by another; first (61a) what Rebekah did, she and her damsels followed the man; then (61b) what the servant did, he took Rebekah and went his way. Such seeming repetitions abound in the historical writings of the Old Testament.[1] And they afford an op-

[1] See xxii. 3b, 4; xxvi. 1b 6; xxviii. 5, 10, xxix. 1; Ex. iv. 20, gen'

portunity, of which the critics avail themselves in numerous instances in constructing their imaginary duplicate narratives. The general statement is set over against the detailed particulars, or one partial statement over against the other, as though each had an independent origin. The repetitions of the chapter should also be noted; vs. 37–41 repeat vs. 3–8 almost verbatim; compare also vs. 42–44 with vs. 12–14; vs. 45, 46, with vs. 15–20; vs. 47, 48, with vs. 23–27. J here exceeds the repetitiousness elsewhere reckoned a peculiarity of P. Such repetitions are also seized upon, where they can be made available, as evidences of duplicate narratives. Thus, when Moses reports to the people (Ex. ch. xii., xiii.) the directions given him respecting the passover, the feast of unleavened bread, and the hallowing of the first-born, as the servant here repeats to Bethuel and Laban the charge received from Abraham, and the incidents which had been before related, the critics find material for two documents by giving to one what the LORD says to Moses, and to the other what Moses in consequence says to the people.

As it is the God of Abraham that is throughout spoken of, Jehovah is appropriately used in this chapter. It is by Jehovah that Abraham requires his servant to swear that he will not take a Canaanitish wife for Isaac (ver. 3). It is to the guidance of Jehovah that he commits his servant on his important errand (ver. 7). It is Jehovah, the God of his master Abraham, whom the servant invokes (ver. 12), and whom he recognizes as having made his journey prosperous (vs. 21, 26, 27, etc.), so

eral statement; 21–29, particulars of the journey; 2 Sam. vi. 12b, 13–17; 1 Kin. vi. 14, general statement; vs. 15–36, details of the construction; 2 Chron. xxiv. 10, 11; similar illustrations may be found in the New Testament, e.g., Acts vii. 58a, 59.

that Laban, to whom Rebekah had made report, at once
addressed him as " the blessed of Jehovah; " and when
the servant had given his account of the whole matter,
Laban and Bethuel[1] acknowledged "the thing proceedeth
from Jehovah " (vs. 50, 51).　In recognition of Jehovah's
supreme control Abraham adds the epithet (vs. 3, 7),
"the God of heaven," an expression only found besides
in postexilic writings (2 Chron. xxxvi. 23; Ezr. i. 2; Neh.
i. 4, 5; ii. 4, 20), with the single exception of Jon. i. 9,
which some critics would not count an exception.　If
this had chanced to occur in P, it would have been
urged in proof of the late origin of that document.　But
as it is in J it is quietly ignored, which is an indication
of the little weight that critics themselves attribute to
considerations of this nature, unless they have some end
to answer by them.

MARKS OF J

It is said that J is here distinguished from E by his
not naming Abraham's chief servant, whom E calls Eliezer (xv. 2), nor Rebekah's nurse (ver. 59), whom E calls
Deborah (xxxv. 8), and makes her come to Canaan with
Jacob at a much later time.　But this mark of distinction is precisely reversed in the case of Ishmael, whom J
names (xvi. 11), and E does not (xxi. 9–21).　It is also
nullified by the fact that neither J nor E act uniformly
in this respect in relation to the same persons.　J gives
the names of Moses's wife and son (Ex. ii. 21, 22), but in

---

[1] Kautzsch proposes to expunge "Bethuel" from the text in ver. 50,
because he is not also mentioned in ver. 53.　But upon this Knobel
remarks : " Rebekah's brother Laban takes part in the decision (Dillmann adds, ' and even the first part ').　He was entitled to do so by the
custom of brothers assuming the charge of their sister (xxxiv. 5, 11, 25;
Judg. xxi. 22; 2 Sam. xiii. 22)."

iv. 20 does not. E does not name Moses's sister, ii. 4,
but does, Num. xii. 1; he gives the name of Moses's wife
and sons (xviii. 2-4), but does not name the son (iv. 25),
nor the wife (Num. xii. 1), provided Zipporah is there
meant. And Gen. xxxv. 8 speaks of the death of Deborah, but gives no intimation how or when she came to
Canaan. This cannot, therefore, be accepted as a criterion of distinct documents.

When it is said that the high art shown in the recital
points to the narrator of ch. xviii., xix., and the lofty conception of marriage to the author of ii. 23 sqq., no objection need be made, unless it is implied that this narrator could not adapt his style to subjects requiring legal
precision, nor record genealogies, dates, and the like; or
that lower views of marriage are expressed elsewhere in
this book.

The following words and expressions are adduced as
indicative of J:

1. *The angel of Jehovah* (vs. 7, 40). See ch. xvi.,
Marks of J, No. 1.

2. *The servant of Jehovah* (ver. 14). This expression,
wherever it occurs in the Hexateuch, is by Dillmann referred to J, D, or Rd, even where the verse in which it
occurs is attributed to E, as Num. xii. 7, 8; xiv. 24; Josh.
xiv. 7; xxiv. 29. It occurs in P Lev. xxv. 42, 55.

3. *Aram-naharaim* (ver. 10). Explained above, p. 298.

4. *Daughters of the Canaanites* (ver. 3). Explained
above, p. 299.

5. בָּא בַיָּמִים *advanced in days* (ver. 1). See ch. xviii.,
xix., Marks of J, No. 32.

6. חֶסֶד וֶאֱמֶת *kindness and truth* (vs. 27, 49); occurs besides in the Hexateuch xxxii. 11 (E. V., ver. 10); xlvii.
29; Ex. xxxiv. 6; Josh. ii. 14 J.

7. עָשָׂה חֶסֶד *show kindness* (vs. 12, 14, 49). See ch.
xviii., xix., Marks of J, No. 29.

8. אוּלַי *peradventure* (vs. 5, 39). See ch. xvi., Marks of J, No. 12.

9. רַק *only* (ver. 8). See ch. vi. 1–8, Marks of J, No. 7.

10. נָא *I pray thee* (vs. 2, 12, 14, 17, 23, 42, 43, 45). See ch. xii. 10–20, Marks of J, No. 3.

11. יֵשׁ with a suffix (vs. 42, 49). This particle occurs with a suffix but three times besides in the Hexateuch, viz., xliii. 4 J ; and twice in Deuteronomy, Deut. xiii. 4 ; xxix. 14.

12. רוּץ לִקְרַאת *run to meet* (ver. 17). See ch. xviii., xix., Marks of J, No. 16, ch. xxix., xxx., No. 2.

13. טֹבַת מַרְאֶה *fair to look upon* (ver. 16) ; but once besides in the Hexateuch, xxvi. 7 J. See ch. vi. 1–8, Marks of J, No. 5. In xii. 11 a different phrase יְפַת מַרְאֶה is used to express the same idea ; but no critic thinks of referring it to a different document in consequence.

14. יָדַע *know* (euphemism) (ver. 16). In J iv. 1, 17, 25 ; xix. 8 ; xxxviii. 26 ; in P Num. xxxi. 17, 18, 35 ; all in the Hexateuch.

15. הִקְרָה *send good speed* (ver. 12); only twice besides in the Hexateuch, viz., in J xxvii. 20 ; in P Num. xxxv. 11.

16. הִצְלִיחַ *make prosperous* (vs. 21, 40, 42, 56) ; besides in the Hexateuch xxxix. 2, 3, 23 J (E and R Kautzsch) ; Josh. i. 8 D.

17. דִּבֶּר אֶל־לִבּוֹ *speak in his heart* (ver. 45) ; but once besides in the Hexateuch in this sense, viii. 21 J ; with a different preposition בְּ xxvii. 41, referred to J solely on account of this phrase ; xvii. 17 P ; Deut. vii. 17 ; viii. 17 ; ix. 4 ; xviii. 21 D.

18. שֹׂנֵא *hating* (for אֹיֵב *enemy*) (ver. 60) ; besides in E Ex. i. 10; xxiii. 5 ; several times in D ; but not in J except Lev. xxvi. 17, which Dillmann is alone in referring to that document.

19. יָרַשׁ אֶת־שַׁעַר *possess the gate* (ver. 60) ; but once besides in the Hexateuch xxii. 17 R.

20. קָדַד וְהִשְׁתַּחֲוָה *bow the head and worship* (vs. 26, 48); five times besides in the Hexateuch; all referred to J.

21. הִשְׁתַּחֲוָה אַרְצָה *bow himself to the earth* (ver. 52). See ch. xviii., xix., Marks of J, No. 27.

Here, as elsewhere, such words as occur with any frequency are found in E as well as in J; several of them likewise in P, notwithstanding the small amount of narrative which is assigned to this document.

CONCLUSION OF ABRAHAM'S LIFE (CH. XXV. 1-11)

The divisive critics unanimously refer vs. 7–11a to P, but there is no unanimity among them in regard to the disposition to be made of the other verses of this section. They are not agreed whether vs. 1–4, which record the sons of Keturah, belong to P, J, or E. Astruc was at least consistent in referring all genealogies of nations and tribes outside of the chosen race to a document or documents distinct from P and J. Nöldeke is equally consistent in ascribing all the genealogies in Genesis to P, and finding some remarkable numerical correspondences, which tend to confirm his view. But there is no consistency in referring Keturah's descendants to one document (J or E) and Ishmael's to another (P), though they are combined together and a common disposition made of both in ver. 6. The various genealogies of this book are inserted upon a uniform plan, which binds them all together, and shows that they must all be attributed to the same source. In addition to the direct line which is traced from Adam to the twelve sons of Jacob, the heads respectively of the several tribes of Israel, all the lateral lines of descent are introduced, each in its proper place, and then dropped, thus indicating at once their relation to, and their separateness from, the chosen race.

"And Abraham took another wife" (lit., added and

took a wife, ver. 1) contains an implied reference to
Sarah's death, alluded to in the immediately preceding
verse (xxiv. 67), and recorded in ch. xxiii. P. Dillmann
would be inclined to refer this verse to the author of ch.
xxiii., were it not that P nowhere else uses the word
"added." But as that is the customary way of saying
in Hebrew that a person did again what he had done before, it is difficult to see why any Hebrew writer might
not use the word if he had occasion.

As Abraham reached the age of one hundred and seventy-five (ver. 7), there is no difficulty in his marriage
with Keturah standing where it does, after the death of
Sarah and the marriage of Isaac. The critics, who sunder P from J and E, and insist that the narratives of the
latter have no connection with the chronology of the
former, seek a discrepancy here, and claim that in JE
the marriage with Keturah must have preceded the birth
of Isaac. But the advanced age of Abraham and Sarah,
in consequence of which offspring could not be expected
in the ordinary course of nature, is as plain in P (xvii.
17) as in JE (xviii. 11–14; xxi. 7). But the promise
(xvii. 4–6) that Abraham should be exceedingly fruitful
and the father of many nations, looks beyond the birth
of Isaac, and finds its fulfilment in other descendants as
well. This, like most other alleged discrepancies, is
found not in the text itself, but in arbitrary critical assumptions.

The supplementary critics, who conceived of J as en-
larging P by additions of his own, had no difficulty in
letting P have xxv. 5, though xxiv. 36b was J's. But if
J is an independent document, the identity of the verses
makes it necessary to attribute both to the same source,
and xxv. 5 must belong to J. This statement that
"Abraham gave all that he had unto Isaac," would seem
to carry with it the counter-statement of what became of

his other children. So Dillmann argued in the first and second editions of his "Genesis," and referred ver. 6 to J likewise. And if J spoke in this verse of Abraham's "concubines," he must have given an account of Keturah as well as of Hagar, and accordingly have been the author of vs. 1-4. But on the other hand, ver. 1 calls her a "wife," and ver. 6 a "concubine;" to prevent this imaginary conflict he first assumed that vs. 1-4 was from P, but worked over by R into conformity with J; then that it was impossible to decide from which source vs. 1-4 was taken; and finally, in his third edition, he gives ver. 6 to R, and vs. 1-4 to E, though why E should be so interested in this particular genealogy, when he gives no other, is not clear. This looks like a shift to get rid of a troublesome paragraph, which is assigned to E, not because of any particular affinity with that document, but it must go somewhere, and there seems to be no other place to put it. Keturah is called a wife just as Hagar is (xvi. 3), without at all designing to put either of them on a par with Sarah; so that there is no inconsistency in their being likewise called concubines, and no need of assuming a different writer on this account. Ver. 11 is of necessity assigned to P; but its last clause speaks of Isaac's dwelling by Beer-lahai-roi, which is a plain allusion to xvi. 14; xxiv. 62 J; hence the offending clause must be exscinded or transferred to another context and attached to J. Thus the whole section is chopped into bits, and parcelled among the several documents and the redactor, though it is consistent and continuous throughout and linked to what precedes as a fulfilment of the promise made to Abraham (xvii. 4, 5, P). But if P were allowed to have ver. 6, an opportunity would be missed of creating an apparent divergence by inferring from ver. 9 what is not in it, that Ishmael continued to live with his father to the time of his death, contrary to xxi. 14-21 E.

In ver. 11 it is stated that "after the death of Abraham
Elohim blessed Isaac, his son." Jehovah as the guardian and benefactor of the chosen race would certainly
have been appropriate here. And yet Elohim is appropriate likewise as suggestive of the general divine beneficence, which bestowed upon Isaac abundant external
prosperity. There is no reason accordingly for assuming that the word is suggestive of the peculiarity of a
particular writer.

MARKS OF P (IN VS. 7–11a)

1. Age of Abraham, ver. 7. See ch. vi.–ix., Marks of
P, No. 2, ch. xvi., No. 1.

2. "The statement that Ishmael was still with Abraham (ver. 9)." No such statement is here made or implied. Ishmael's presence at Abraham's burial is not
inconsistent with his residence elsewhere (xxi. 21); so
that this affords no ground for assuming a diversity of
documents.

3. "The cave of Machpelah (ver. 9), the diffuseness of
the style (vs. 9, 10), the children of Heth (ver. 10)."
The expressions in these verses are borrowed from ch.
xxiii., the formality and precision of the language indicating the stress laid upon this first acquisition of property in Canaan.

4. גָּוַע give up the ghost. See ch. vi.–ix., Marks of P,
No. 18.

5. נֶאֱסַף אֶל־עַמָּיו was gathered unto his people, a phrase
used only of the death of the following venerated men,
viz.: Abraham (xxv. 8); Ishmael (ver. 17); Isaac (xxxv.
29); Jacob (xlix. 29, 33); Aaron (Num. xx. 24, 26, ellip-
sis), and Moses (Num. xxvii. 13; xxxi. 2; Deut. xxxii.
50). These are all referred to P for the reason that the
records of the deaths of patriarchs are as a rule referred

to him. The formula henceforth used of the death of patriarchs is in the full form adopted here, " gave up the ghost and died, and was gathered to his people" (xxv. 8, 17 ; xxxv. 29 ; xlix. 33). This formula is not used in the case of any other whose death is recorded by P; yet no critic infers a difference of writers on this account. The same thought is expressed in words spoken by the LORD to Abraham (xv. 15), " go to thy fathers," assigned by the critics to JE, but joined as here with the phrase, " in a good old age," which speaks for the identity of the writers. Dillmann can only account for the coincidence by the interference of R in ch. xv.

6. יְמֵי שְׁנֵי חַיֵּי *days of the years of the life* (ver. 7). See ch. xxiii., Marks of P, No. 5.

7. "The back reference of xlix. 31 P to ver. 10;" this is freely admitted to be from the same writer; but this implies no admission that other parts of Genesis are from a different hand.

The descent attributed to Sheba and Dedan (ver. 3), involves no discrepancy either with x. 7 P, or x. 28 J. See under ch. x., pp. 137-139.

For the use of יָלַד *beget*, in lateral genealogies, see ch. vi.–ix., Marks of P, No. 20. The critics make this a mark of J, yet here it occurs with וּבְנֵי *and the sons of* (vs. 3, 4), which in ch. x. they make a mark of P.

" All these were the children of Keturah " (ver. 4; cf. x. 29b ; ix. 19), has been urged in proof of the authorship of J ; but the same formula occurs in P xlvi. 15, 18, 22, 25.

VII

THE GENERATIONS OF ISHMAEL (CH. XXV. 12–18)

THIS section is related alike to passages assigned by the critics to P, J, and E; hence the diversity of opinion among them as to its origin. It is generally agreed that the title (ver. 12a), ver. 16b "twelve princes" descended from Ishmael in fulfilment of xvii. 20 P, and ver. 17 with the phrases of ver. 8, must be from P. But ver. 12b repeats xxi. 9 E (Dillmann compares xvi. 3, 15 P); the mention of the territory occupied by the tribes descended from Ishmael (ver. 18), is after the analogy of x. 19, 30, J; "he abode in the presence of all his brethren" (ver. 18b), is in fulfilment of xvi. 12 J, and adopts its language. Accordingly Hupfeld gives vs. 13–16a, 18, to J. Kayser gives ver. 16b likewise to J, and seems inclined to follow Boehmer in ascribing ver. 12 to him also, inasmuch as the title, "These are the generations of Ishmael," could hardly have been used to introduce ver. 17, which is all that remains for P. "It is not so well made out," he says, "as is commonly assumed, that this title belongs to P and not to J." Dillmann, on the other hand, feels the difficulty of having a separate P title prefixed to but one or two verses, and claims the entire section for P except ver. 18. The first clause of this verse he attributes to J, and attaches to ver. 6; the last clause he regards as a gloss based upon xvi. 12, because the singular number is used, while the preceding clause has the plural. But no such conclusion is warranted by this change of number, the reason for which is obvious.

To make the reference perfectly distinct, the fulfilment is stated in the very terms of the prediction. The region occupied by Ishmael's descendants is stated in the first clause; thus, as had been foretold, Ishmael abode in the presence of all his brethren. There is no need of assuming a gloss and no need of transposing the verse ; no one would ever have thought of doing either, except in the interest of the divisive hypothesis. All is appropriate and harmonious as it stands.

MARKS OF P

1. The title (ver. 12). See ch. vi.–ix., Marks of P, No. 1, ch. xvi. No. 1.

2. The statement of age (ver. 17). See ch. vi.–ix., Marks of P, No. 2.

3. The formulas of ver. 17. See ch. xxv. 1–11, Marks of P, No. 5.

4. The mention of the first-born (ver. 13, as xxxv. 23 P). This is no discriminating test, for it occurs (x. 15, xxii. 21) in genealogies attributed to J.

5. The "twelve princes" (ver. 16; cf. xvii. 20). This and other correspondences point to the common author-ship of related passages, but afford no ground for the belief that other passages are from a different source.

The territory described in ver. 18 as the home of the Ishmaelites, "from Havilah unto Shur, that is before Egypt," is that in which Saul found the Amalekites (1 Sam. xv. 7). This is a fresh indication of the blending of these roving tribes, of which we have already seen evidence in the occurrence of the same tribal name in different genealogies, e.g., Sheba and Dedan (xxv. 3 and x. 7, 28), and which is further evidenced by the inter-change of different tribal names in application to the same parties (Gen. xxxvii. 28 ; Judg. viii. 1, 12, 24).

VIII

THE GENERATIONS OF ISAAC (CH. XXV. 19-XXXV.)

This section contains the history of Isaac and his family from his marriage until his death.

ESAU AND JACOB (CH. XXV. 19-34)

VATER, though an advocate of the fragment hypothesis, notes ("Pentateuch," i., p. 244) the precise correspondence in the arrangement of ch. xxv. and ch. xxxv.-xxxvii., which is certainly indicative of unity of plan. 1, Abraham's sons by Keturah (xxv. 1-6); 2, his death and burial by his sons Isaac and Ishmael (vs. 7-11); 3, the descendants of Ishmael (vs. 12-18); 4, the history of Isaac's family (vs. 19 sqq.). In like manner : 1, Jacob's sons by his several wives (xxxv. 23-26); 2, Isaac's death and burial by his sons Esau and Jacob (vs. 27-29); 3, the descendants of Esau (ch. xxxvi.); 4, the history of Jacob's family (ch. xxxvii. sqq.).

It should be observed also how closely this portion of the history is knit to what precedes as well as to what follows. The life of Abraham repeats itself in that of Isaac, in the renewal of the same divine promises, in the trial of faith by a long waiting for the expected child on whom the fulfilment of every other promise hinged ; in the divine intervention manifest in the birth ; in the distinction between the child of divine choice and the rejected first-born ; in the care taken that the marriage of the former should be, not with one of the surrounding

Canaanites, but with one of an allied race ; in Isaac's be-
traying the same sinful weakness under temptation as his
father ; and in the divine protection and blessing which
compelled the recognition even of monarchs. The same
ideas are made prominent, the same leading principles
rule throughout the whole.

It was twenty-five years after Abraham entered Canaan before Isaac was born (xii. 4 ; xxi. 5). It was
twenty years after Isaac's marriage before the birth of
Jacob and Esau (xxv. 20, 26). Their birth is traced to
an immediate divine bestowment of what was beyond all
natural expectation. It had been promised to Abraham
that he should be the father of many nations ; two nations were to spring from Rebekah. As Isaac was preferred to Ishmael, so Jacob to Esau. And though these
latter were from the same mother, the divine choice was
made apparent from the first, was independent of personal worth, and was finally ratified, not through the un-
worthy means taken to secure it, but in spite of them.
It was thus plainly shown to be of divine grace, not of
human merit. And at length, by providential discipline,
supplanting Jacob was changed into prevailing Israel.

Tuch, in defending the supplement hypothesis, attributed the whole of this paragraph (vs. 19–34) to P,
save only vs. 21 (except the last clause), 22, 23, where
the repeated occurrence of Jehovah betrayed the hand of
J, who inserted in the work of P, which lay before him
and which he was supplementing, this forecast of the future history of Rebekah's descendants before the children were born. It was inconceivable, he urged, that a
history of the ancestry of Israel should say nothing of
the birth of Jacob, the progenitor of the nation, and of
his twin brother Esau, by whom the course of Jacob's
life was so largely influenced.

This difficulty presses the current divisive hypothesis

in an aggravated form, which attempts to make out three independent documents, without being able to maintain the show of continuity for any one of them. To P are assigned only vs. 19, 20, and the last clause of ver. 26. He accordingly tells how old Isaac was when he was married, though no previous account had been given by P of his marriage; also how old he was when "they were born," presumably his children, though this is not said, and there is no direct mention of their birth such as, it is here implied, had been made. The critics tell us that P must have told about Isaac's marriage and the birth of his sons, but R has not seen fit to preserve that part of his record. P then springs at once to Esau's marriage at forty years of age (xxvi. 34, 35), and Jacob's being sent to Paddan-aram for a wife (xxviii. 1 sqq.), whereupon Esau marries again. Three disconnected clauses follow, relating to persons abruptly introduced with no intimation that they were in any way connected with Jacob: (xxix. 24) "And Laban gave Zilpah his handmaid unto his daughter Leah for her handmaid;" (ver. 29) "And Laban gave to Rachel his daughter Bilhah his handmaid to be her handmaid;" (xxx. 22a) "And God remembered Rachel." Then (xxxi. 18) "He," presumably Jacob, though his name is not mentioned, "carried away all his cattle and all his substance which he had gathered, the cattle of his getting, which he had gathered in Paddan-aram, for to go to Isaac his father unto the land of Canaan." And this is absolutely all that P has to say about Jacob from the time that he left his father's house until his return to Canaan. There is no mention of his arrival in Paddan-aram, or of anything that occurred there, only that he left it possessed of property and cattle with no previous allusion to his having acquired them. He went to Paddan-aram to seek a wife; but there is no intimation whether his search

was successful until several years after he had been again
settled in Canaan, when a bald list is given of his wives
and children in connection with the mention of Isaac's
death (xxxv. 22b-29).

Wellhausen may well call this a " skeleton account."
And it is suitably characterized by Dr. Harper [1] as "cold
and lifeless, nothing but a register of deaths, births, and
marriages ; " and he might have added with the principal births and marriages left out. Is this P's fault or
that of the critics ? Can such scattered snatches be regarded as constituting a separate document, or even accepted as proof that they are the remains of a separate
document, especially when these fragments are essential
in the context in which they are now found, and their
removal leaves unfilled gaps behind them? And is the
title, " The generations of Isaac," intended to introduce
these disconnected fragments, or the body of the narrative to which it is prefixed ? If the latter, we have here
one more proof that these titles to sections of the book
of Genesis do not belong to what the critics are pleased
to call the document P.

But after P's portion of vs. 19-34 is subtracted, the
critics still find the remainder not a unit, and yet very
difficult to disentangle. Wellhausen says that J and E
are here and in ch. xxvii. so involved "that a clear separation is not to be thought of." " Only where the divine names supply a criterion can the double stream be
distinctly recognized." As in vs. 29-34 Esau sells his
birthright of his own accord, while in ch. xxvii. his father's blessing is wrested from him by fraud, it has been
proposed to assign these to separate documents. But,
as Wellhausen contends, it will neither answer to give
the former to E and the latter to J, nor to reverse this
by giving the former to J and the latter to E. For

<hr />

[1] The Hebraica for July, 1889, p. 267.

Esau's voluntary surrender of his birthright would not account for Jacob's flight from home (xxviii. 10 sqq.). Both J and E presuppose a hostility on the part of Esau such as can only be explained by what is related in ch. xxvii. Moreover, xxvii. 36 refers back to the matter of the birthright. Hence, though Wellhausen claims that in the oral tradition the obtaining of the birthright (בכרה) and of the blessing (ברכה) are mere variants, of which he offers no proof, he nevertheless admits that in their written form one is no mere substitute for the other, but the first is a prelude to the second.

Wellhausen proposes to give vs. 29–34 the sale of the birthright to J. The contrast drawn between Esau and Jacob (vs. 27, 28), and the preferences of their parents for them respectively, are preparatory for ch. xxvii., and presupposed in both J and E, and must have been in substance in both documents. Vs. 21–23 is given to J because of " Jehovah ; " vs. 24–26a to E, because the allusion in Hos. xii. 3 to Jacob taking his brother by the heel proves that this tradition was current in the northern kingdom of Israel, to which E is imagined to have belonged, and because ver. 25 suggests a different explanation of Edom from that given in ver. 30, and in ver. 26 Jacob is explained differently from xxvii. 36 J. But thus J records the conception of the children and the prediction respecting them, but does not speak of their birth. It thus becomes necessary to suppose that each document had originally what is contained in the other, only R has not seen fit to preserve it.

A continuous and closely connected paragraph is thus splintered into bits to find material for three documents, each of which proves to be incoherent and fragmentary. The different allusions to the significance of the names Edom and Jacob afford no justification for the partition, since they are not variant etymologies implying different conceptions of the origin of the names and requiring the assumption of distinct writers.

In his second edition Dillmann adopts substantially the partition of Wellhausen, though in his first he had referred the entire paragraph (P excepted) to E, worked over by R, and in his third he refers it to J, only the word " red " (ver. 25), and a few words in ver. 27, having been taken from E. From all this it may be inferred that the critical machinery does not work very smoothly in this instance.

It has been alleged that Rebekah's going to inquire of Jehovah (ver. 22) implies that there were then places where oracular responses were given, or seers through whom the deity could be consulted. Wellhausen proposes to transpose this paragraph after ch. xxvi., where he finds in vs. 23-33 the founding of a sanctuary at Beersheba ; and he jumps to the conclusion that Rebekah went to it to inquire of Jehovah. Stade [1] regards the incident here recorded of Rebekah as " probably a saga respecting the origin of the oracle at Beersheba." But there is no suggestion here or elsewhere in the patriarchal period of an oracle or a seer. And there is not the slightest reason for supposing that either is referred to in the present instance, much less of assuming that this passage lends approval to the separatist sanctuary, which was in later ages established at Beersheba. Hävernick appeals to 1 Sam. xxviii. 6, which shows that those who "inquired of Jehovah " might be answered by dreams as well as by Urim and by prophets. From the frequency with which prophetic dreams are mentioned in Genesis, and from the fact that the answer of Jehovah was given to Rebekah herself, it is natural to infer that the revelation was made to her in a dream. They who dispute the reality of predictive prophecy find here a

[1] Geschichte des Volkes Israel, p. 474, note.

vaticinium post eventum, and an indication of post-Mosaic origin. But those who do not accept the premises will not share the conclusion.

It is argued that Isaac could not have passed Rebekah off as his sister (xxvi. 7) after her children were born and had grown up (xxv. 27). This does not necessarily follow. Still, even if xxvi. 1–33 preceded xxv. 21–34 in point of time, it would not be necessary to suppose that the narratives have been transposed. The historian is not an annalist. He may depart from the chron-.ological arrangement when he has good reasons for grouping events differently. Whatever motive the redactor may be thought to have had for transposing these incidents may equally have influenced the original writer to place them in their present order.

The divine name is properly and discriminatingly employed in vs. 21–23. Jehovah was the God of Isaac no less than of Abraham. It is to Jehovah that he directs his prayer; it is to Jehovah that his wife applies in her perplexity. It is Jehovah who gives to each a gracious answer.

MARKS OF P (VS. 19, 20, 26b)

1. The title (ver. 19). See ch. vi.–ix., Marks of P, No. 1.

2. Age (vs. 20, 26). See ch. vi.–ix., Marks of P, No. 2.

3. הוֹלִיד *beget* (ver. 19). See ch. vi.–ix., Marks of P, No. 20.

4. Paddan-aram (ver. 20); occurs besides in P xxviii. 2, 5–7; xxxv. 9, 26; in xxxi. 18, xxxiii. 18, it is assigned to P in a JE connection; in xlvi. 15 the critics are not agreed whether it belongs to P. See ch. xxiv., Marks of J, No. 3.

5. Bethuel, the Aramæan (ver. 20). Bethuel the father

and Laban the brother of Rebekah are here called Aramæans, in contrast with the Canaanites, with whom Isaac was not to ally himself; so for a like reason in xxviii. 5 P, though not in ver. 2 P, where the same end is accomplished by calling Bethuel the father and Laban the brother of Jacob's mother. Laban is also called the Aramæan in E (xxxi. 20, 24); and he is spoken of without this epithet in P (xlvi. 18, 25). Moreover, Bethuel and Laban were Aramæans according to J, since they lived in Aram-naharaim (xxiv. 10 J). The employment or non-employment of the epithet Aramæan in connection with their names is dependent, therefore, not upon the usage of particular documents, but upon the sense to be conveyed.

MARKS OF J

1. עָתַר *entreat* (ver. 21); nowhere else in Genesis; only besides in the Hexateuch, Ex. viii. 4, 5, 24, 25, 26 (E. V., vs. 8, 9, 28, 29, 30); x. 18, all which are referred to J.

2. צָעִיר *younger* (ver. 23). See ch. xix. 29–38, Marks of J, No. 2.

3. "The similarity of vs. 24–26 to xxxviii. 27 sqq." may be an indication of the common authorship of these passages, but gives no proof that other passages are from a different author.

Dillmann claims that vs. 25 and 27 are "overloaded" by the insertion of words from an assumed parallel account by E. In proof of this he points to "red" (ver. 25), as an explanation of Edom, conflicting with that in ver. 30, and the duplicate characterization of both Edom and Jacob, ver. 27. But this "overloading" never seems to have dawned upon Dillmann himself until he hit upon this expedient for providing at least a semblance of material for E in a paragraph which, as he now confesses, "coheres well together," but the contents of which are presupposed alike in E and in J.

Dillmann remarks upon the indefinite singular, "one called" (ver. 26), contrasted with the plural, "they called" (ver. 25), as suggestive of a different document; but Hupfeld points to the frequent use of the indefinite singular in passages attributed to J, *e.g.*, xi. 9; xvi. 14; xxvii. 36; xxxiii. 17; xxxviii. 29, 30.

ISAAC IN GERAR AND BEERSHEBA (CH. XXVI. 1-33)

This chapter (except vs. 34, 35, P), is in the main assigned to J, but unfilled gaps are thus created in both the other documents. We look in vain in P for a divine grant of the land to Isaac, such as is referred to in xxxv. 12 P, or for a covenant of God with him mentioned Ex. ii. 24 P, or for God appearing to him as he is declared to have done, Ex. vi. 3 [1] P. These are all to be found in the chapter before us, but nowhere else. These passages in P must, therefore, refer to what is contained in J, which is contrary to the hypothesis, or it must be assumed here again that P had just such an account as we find in J, but R has omitted it. So when E (xlvi. 1) speaks of Jacob coming to Beersheba and there offering sacrifices to the God of his father Isaac, there is a plain allusion to the altar which Isaac had built there (xxvi. 25). When Jacob left his father's house for Haran, he went out from Beersheba (xxviii. 10 E), implying Isaac's residence there, as stated xxvi. 23, 25, but nowhere in E. Either E alludes to J, or he must have related the same that is in J, and R has not preserved it.

When we thus find throughout the book of Genesis the

---

[1] Jehovah's revelation of himself (xxvi. 24) as the God of Abraham contains a specific allusion to xvii. 1, and was so understood by Isaac (xxviii. 3, 4).

different documents tied together by cross-references, does not the divisive hypothesis require too many auxiliary hypotheses for its support? It asks us in every instance to assume that the reference is not to the passage which is plainly written before us, and to which it exactly corresponds, but to certain hypothetical passages which may once have existed, but of which there is no other evidence than that the exigencies of the hypothesis demand it.

A doublet is suspected in vs. 1–6. It is said that 2b is incompatible with 1c and 3a. Isaac is already in the land to which the LORD is to tell him to go. Accordingly 1a, 2b, 6, are assigned to E, thus : "And there was a famine in the land; and (God) said to (Isaac), Go not down into Egypt; dwell in the land which I shall tell thee ; and Isaac dwelt in Gerar." Then 1c, 2a, 3a, are given to J, thus : "And Isaac went unto Abimelech, king of the Philistines, unto Gerar. And Jehovah appeared unto him and said, Sojourn in this land, and I will be with thee, and will bless thee." But the fact that by ingenious slicing and piecing two seemingly complete paragraphs can be constructed out of one does not prove that the latter is of duplicate origin. The apparent lack of continuity which gives offence to the critics in these verses is of precisely the same nature as that in xxiv. 29, 30, which has been before explained. In xxvi. 1 the mention of the famine is immediately followed by the statement that Isaac went to Gerar to escape it. It is then added with more particularity how he came to make his abode in Gerar, instead of passing on to Egypt after the example of his father in similar circumstances (xii. 10), and according to his own original intention. Jehovah directed him to dwell in the land that he should tell him of, which was immediately explained to be the land in which he then was. The explicit allusion to the "first famine that was

in the days of Abraham " (1b), is stricken from the text
and referred to R, because E had not spoken of that
famine; whereas it simply proves the falsity of the critical partition which assigns ver. 1a to a different document from xii. 10.

Vs. 3b–5 is also expunged as a later addition to the
text for two reasons :

1st. In order to get rid of its testimony in favor of xxii.
15–18, which the critics attribute to R ; because if here referred to and cited by J it must be genuine and original.

2d. Because the legal phrases in ver. 5 are inappropriate to the times of the patriarchs.

But (1) this verse is in exact accord with others which
show great solicitude to make it clear that Abraham and
his seed were chosen of Jehovah, not to be his favorites
irrespective of character, but to found a pious, God-fearing, obedient race (xvii. 1, 2 ; xviii. 19).

(2) Mention is made of several divine injunctions given
to Abraham.   He was commanded to leave his country,
to perform specified rites in the transaction of the covenant, to institute circumcision, to offer up Isaac.   He
was required to exercise faith in God's promises in spite
of long delays and discouraging circumstances.   He observed sacrificial worship and called on the name of the
LORD.   He recognized the sanctity of an oath (xiv. 22),
and dealt generously with Lot, uprightly with the children of Heth and Abimelech, and in the strictest honesty
with the king of Sodom.   The direction to walk before
God and be perfect (xvii. 1 ; xxiv. 40), and his confidence
that God the judge of all the earth would do right in respect to the righteous and the wicked (xviii. 25), imply
his possession of a standard of rectitude.   So, although
no formal code may have been given to Abraham, it is
not inappropriate to speak of " commandments, statutes,
and laws," which he had obeyed.

(3) The heaping together of these various terms is certainly suggestive of the Mosaic legislation (cf. Ex. xv. 26 ; xvi. 28, etc.). And what is more natural than that the great legislator, who in recording the history of their ancestors had prominent regard to the instruction of his contemporaries, should commend the obedience of Abraham in terms which would make it a fit model for themselves?

Isaac's life was to such an extent an imitation of his father's that no surprise need be felt at his even copying his faults and pretending that his wife was his sister (vs. 7–11). A stratagem that has proved successful once is very likely to be tried again.

Nor does it create any special difficulty in respect to the recorded visit of Abimelech and Phicol to Isaac at Beersheba (vs. 26–31) that a king and general of the same name had covenanted at the same place with Abraham (xxi. 22 – 32). That successive Philistine kings should bear the name Abimelech is no more strange than the Pharaohs of Egypt, or the Cæsars of Rome, or two Napoleons emperors of France, or two presidents of the United States named John Adams. Phicol may for aught that anyone knows have been an official title, or he may have been the namesake of his predecessor. That the name Beersheba should be reimposed on this occasion (ver. 33) is not strange. That the writer regarded it not as a new appellation, but as fresh sanction given to one already in existence, is plain from his use of it (ver. 23), and it is in precise accordance with the general statements (vs. 15, 18) that Isaac had renewed the names previously given to wells by his father. These verses are interpolations by R in the opinion of the critics, for the reason (which others may not deem conclusive) that J cannot be supposed to have referred to what is recorded in E.

The name Jehovah is evidently in place in this chapter.
Jehovah appears to Isaac (vs. 2, 24); and Isaac called on
the name of Jehovah (ver. 25). Jehovah blessed him
(ver. 12) and made room for him (ver. 22); so that even
Abimelech recognized the fact that Isaac's God Jehovah
was with him (ver. 28), and blessed him (ver. 29). In
xxv. 11 it had been said that Elohim blessed him. This
is suggestive of the two aspects under which his outward prosperity could be regarded as the gift of his
covenant God, or of the God of nature and of providence.
This is no more surprising than when the Psalmist makes
his appeal in successive clauses to the God of Israel and
the God of the universe : (Ps. x. 12) " Arise, O Jehovah ;
O Elohim, lift up thine hand." (Ps. xvii. 1, 6) " O Jehovah, attend unto my cry; . . . thou wilt hear me,
O Elohim."

MARKS OF J

1. טוֹבַת מַרְאֶה *fair to look upon* (ver. 7). See ch. xxiv.,
Marks of J, No. 13.

2. הִשְׁקִיף *look out* (ver. 8). See ch. xviii., xix., Marks
of J, No. 6.

3. אָלָה *oath* (ver. 28). Besides in J xxiv. 41 bis ; in P
Lev. v. 1 ; Num. v. 21 bis, 23, 27 ; in D Deut. xxix. 11, 13,
18, 19, 20 (E. V., vs. 12, 14, 19, 20, 21) ; xxx. 7 ; all in
the Hexateuch.

4. בְּרוּךְ יהוה *blessed of Jehovah* (ver. 29) ; in the Hexateuch besides only xxiv. 31 J ; a similar phrase, "blessed
of God Most High" xiv. 19, which is not referred to J.

5. וַיִּקְרָא בְּשֵׁם יהוה *called upon the name of Jehovah* (ver.
25). Prayer and worship were addressed to Jehovah,
the God of revelation and of grace. This divine name
is the appropriate one in such connections, and is not
traceable to the usage of a particular document.

6. " The peril of Rebekah (vs. 7–11), and the origin of

the name Beersheba " (vs. 25–33) are not variant accounts
of the transactions recorded in ch. xx. and xxi. 22–32, but
are distinct events occurring at different times and under
other circumstances. Even on the hypothesis of the
critics they were so regarded by the redactor. If they
either were, or were supposed to be, distinct events, there
is no reason why they may not have been related by the
same writer. They afford no ground, consequently, for
the assumption of separate documents.

Dillmann remarks that in this chapter " much in the
form of expression reminds of E, cf. ver. 10 and xx. 9;
ver. 28 and xxi. 22; ver. 29 and xxi. 23; עַל־אֹדוֹת *concerning* (ver. 32 and xxi. 11, 25); the names (ver. 26)."
He undertakes to account for this by assuming that J had
the document E before him and borrowed expressions
from it. The divisive hypothesis must thus be supported
by a fresh hypothesis, for which there is no foundation
but the very hypothesis which it is adduced to support.
It will be observed that the admitted points of similarity
belong to the narrative of Rebekah's peril and the affair
at Beersheba. If now the author of ch. xxvi. had the corresponding narrative in chs. xx., xxi., before him as he
wrote, he was aware that Abraham had had experiences
similar to those which he was recording of Isaac. And
thus the argument of the critics for a diversity of documents is completely nullified by their own confession.
And the only remaining alternative is to accept the simple and natural inference, from the correspondences between the narratives, that both are from the pen of the
same writer.

It is also worth noting that " digged," in vs. 15, 18,
32, is in Hebrew חָפַר, but in ver. 25 it is כָּרָה, a word
which occurs nowhere else in J, and is only found in the
Hexateuch in E, viz., Gen. l. 5; Ex. xxi. 33; Num. xxi.
18. It thus appears that the same writer can use two

different words to express the same thing with no apparent reason for making the change; and this even though in the opinion of the critics one of the words is nowhere else used by him.

The narrative in ch. xxvii. is indispensable to both J and E, as shown alike by its connection with what precedes and what follows. It has already been seen that the critics find it necessary to assume that xxv. 21–34 belonged alike to both of these documents, and that the portions extracted from one had their equivalents also in the other. But this paragraph was directly preparatory to ch. xxvii. The pre-announcement of the precedence of the younger child (ver. 23), the hairy skin of Esau (ver. 25), Esau's skill in hunting and Jacob's domestic habits (ver. 27), Isaac's partiality for Esau, and relish for his venison, and Rebekah's preference for Jacob (ver. 28), are mentioned with a view to this chapter, and the sale of the birthright (vs. 29–34) is explicitly referred to, xxvii. 36.

In like manner, as is stated by Wellhausen, "we have in xxviii. 10–22 a piece from E almost complete, together with a large fragment from J, which proves that J contained the same narrative and in the same place (cf. ver. 15 and vs. 20, 21). It hence follows by concluding backward that both E and J related the occasion of Jacob's flight, without which it would be without a motive and unintelligible. There must necessarily have been a history like that in ch. xxvii. in both sources, as appears also from ch. xxxii.;" and, as Dillmann adds, xxxv. 3, 7, E.

While, however, it is essential to find both J and E in this chapter, the critics are obliged to acknowledge that they cannot disentangle them so as to separate the two accounts, or even to discover any points of difference between them. The utmost that they can do is to point out several instances of what they consider doublets, and claim on this account that the text is composite, though they are unable to resolve it into its original constituents.

It is claimed that vs. 24-27a repeats vs. 21-23 ; that ver. 24, instead of progressing from ver. 23, goes back to ver. 21, and ver. 23 is as far advanced as ver. 27a, each ending, " and he blessed him." But this is precisely like other alleged doublets before reviewed. The ultimate result is first summarily stated (ver. 23b) ; then further particulars are added (vs. 24-27a), which led up to this result. The paragraphs in question are mutually supplementary ; they are certainly not mutually exclusive. The blind old patriarch, doubtful of his son's identity, first insists upon feeling him (vs. 21-23), and obliges him to say whether he is really Esau (ver. 24). Then, after partaking of what had been brought him, he asks, as a final test, to kiss him, that he may smell the odor of his raiment (ver. 27). There is in all this no repetition, but a steady, onward progress to the final issue.

It is further said that ver. 30b repeats 30a, which it does not ; it more exactly defines the time intended. Isaac had ended his blessing, and Jacob had just gone out when Esau came in. Also that vs. 35-38 repeat vs. 33, 34 ; but the only repetition is that of Esau's importunate entreaty, which is as natural as it is touching. Ver. 44b is repeated in ver. 45a, because this was the thing uppermost in Rebekah's thoughts. She repeats and amplifies what she had said about Esau's fury subsiding, in order to impress upon Jacob her own conviction that his brother's rage was only temporary. If

Jacob would but absent himself for a few days it would be over, and she would send and fetch him home again. She is concerned to present her project to him in the most persuasive way, that he may be induced to do what she feels to be necessary to save his life.

In their eagerness to find material for separate documents, or evidence of duplicate accounts, the critics seem to be ever ready to sacrifice the force and beauty of the narratives with which they deal. They dissect them to the quick, rending them into feeble or incoherent fragments, or they pare them down by the assumption of doublets to the baldest forms of intelligible statement, and thus strip them of those affecting details, which lend them such a charm, because so true to nature. This involves the absurdity of assuming that two jejune or fragmentary accounts, pieced mechanically together, have produced narratives which are not only consistent and complete, but full of animation and dramatic power.

An attempt is made to establish a difference between J and E on the one hand, and P on the other, as to the reason why Jacob went to Paddan-aram. According to the former (ch. xxvii. 1–45), it is to flee from his brother, whom he has enraged by defrauding him of his father's blessing. According to the latter (xxvi. 34, 35 ; xxviii. 1–9), that he may not marry among the Canaanites, as Esau had done, to the great grief of his parents, but obtain a wife from among his kindred. P, we are told, knows of no hostility between the brothers. But all this is spoiled by the statement in xxviii. 7, that " Jacob obeyed his father *and his mother*, and was gone to Paddan-aram." His father sent him to get a wife (xxviii. 1–9) ; but his mother (xxvii. 42–45) to escape Esau's fury ; and there is no incompatibility between these two objects. In order to gain Isaac over to her plan without acquainting him with Esau's murderous designs, Rebekah simply urges her dissatisfaction with the wives of Esau, and her apprehension lest Jacob might contract a similar marriage with some one of the daughters of the land. Isaac had one object in mind, Rebekah another. There is nothing for the critics to do, therefore, but to pronounce the unwelcome words, " and his mother," an interpolation. In order to prove their point they must first adjust the text to suit it.

But tinkering the text in a single passage will not relieve them in the present instance. The hostility of Esau is embedded in the entire narrative, and cannot be sundered from it. Why did Jacob go alone and unattended in quest of a wife, without the retinue or the costly presents for his bride, befitting his rank and wealth ? When Abraham desired a wife for Isaac he sent a princely embassy to woo Rebekah, and conduct her to her future home. Why was Jacob's suit so differently managed, although Isaac imitated Abraham in everything else ? And why did Jacob remain away from his parents and his home, and from the land sacred as the gift of God, for so many long years till his twelve sons were born (xxxv. 26 P) ? This is wholly unaccounted for except by the deadly hostility of Esau. Even the fragmentary notices accorded to P of the sojourn in Paddan-aram thus imply that Jacob had grievously offended Esau ; so that here again P either refers to what J and E alone recorded, or else had given a similar account of the fraud perpetrated by Jacob, which R has not retained.

The name Jehovah occurs appropriately (xxvii. 7, 20) as the God of Isaac, in whose name and by whose authority the blessing was to be pronounced. Only in the blessing itself Jehovah alternates with Elohim in the parallelisms of poetry (vs. 27, 28). On this ground Dillmann assigns vs. 27b, 29b, to J, and vs. 28, 29a, to E.

The consequence of which is that in J a curse is pronounced upon those who curse Jacob, and a blessing upon those who bless him, but not a single blessing bestowed directly upon Jacob himself. Kautzsch tries to mend the matter by a different distribution; but in doing so he separates the last clause of ver. 28 from the sentence to which it belongs, so that " plenty of corn and wine " stands wholly unconnected, and, of course, unmeaning. No critical severance of this closely connected blessing is either admissible or necessary. Elohim, in ver. 28, does not require the assumption of a different document from the Jehovah of ver. 27 any more than such an assumption is demanded by the change of divine names in Ps. xlvii. 2, 3 (E. V., vs. 1, 2). The Jehovah of the blessing is at the same time the God of universal nature, Elohim, who from his general beneficence will bestow "the dew of heaven, and the fatness of the earth, and plenty of corn and wine." In taking leave of Jacob Isaac pronounces upon him the blessing of Abraham (xxviii. 4) ; he is thus led to borrow the language of that signal revelation to Abraham when Jehovah made himself known as God Almighty (xvii. 1), and gave him promises with a special emphasis, which are here repeated. Hence the El Shaddai (ver. 3) and Elohim (ver. 4).

MARKS OF P (XXVI. 34, 35 ; XXVIII. 1-9)

1. "The unadorned character of the narration." But in what respect is the statement of Esau's marriage (xxvi. 34, 35) more " unadorned " than that of Abram and Nahor (xi. 29 J), or Nahor's family table (xxii. 20–24 J) ? or Isaac's charge and commission to Jacob (xxviii. 1–5), than the precisely similar one of Abraham in respect to Isaac (xxiv. 1–10) ?

2. "The chronological statement (xxvi. 34)." See ch. vi.–ix., Marks of P, No. 2; ch. xvi., Marks of P, No. 1.

3. בְּנוֹת כְּנַעַן *daughters of Canaan* (xxviii. 1, 6, 8). See ch. xxiv., Marks of J, No. 4.

4. פַּדַּן אֲרָם *Paddan-aram* (vs. 2, 5–7). See ch. xxv. 19–34, Marks of P, No. 4.

5. אֵל שַׁדַּי *God Almighty* (ver. 3). Explained above; see also ch. xvii., p. 221, and Marks of P, No. 6.

6. קְהַל עַמִּים *company of peoples* (ver. 3). See ch. xvii., Marks of P, No. 2.

7. מְגֻרִים *sojournings* (ver. 4). See ch. xvii., Marks of P, No. 8.

8. הָאֲרַמִּי *the Aramœan* (ver. 5). See ch. xxv. 19–34, Marks of P, No. 5.

MARKS OF J (XXVII. 1–45)

1. הִקְרָה *send good speed* (ver. 20). See ch. xxiv., Marks of J, No. 15.

2. כַּאֲשֶׁר כִּלָּה *when he made an end* (ver. 30); besides in J, xviii. 33; xxiv. 22; xliii. 2; the same construction of כִּלָּה, not introduced by כַּאֲשֶׁר (which is purely incidental), in J, xxiv. 15, 19, 45; Num. xvi. 31; Josh. viii. 24; in E, Josh. x. 20; in P, Gen. xvii. 22; xlix. 33; Ex. xxxi. 18; xxxiv. 33; Lev. xvi. 20; Num. vii. 1; Josh. xix., 49, 51; alleged later stratum of P, Num. iv. 15; in Rd, Deut. xxxi. 24; in D, Deut. xxxii. 45; all in the Hexateuch.

3. אָמַר בְּלִבּוֹ *said in his heart* (ver. 41). See ch. xxiv. Marks of J, No. 17.

4. "The house" (ver. 15). "J speaks of a *house* (not tent) of Isaac, as he also lets Lot live in one in Sodom (xix. 2 sqq.), and Jacob build one at Succoth (xxxiii. 17)." But E also speaks of Jacob coming back to his father's *house* (xxviii. 21).

MARKS OF E

1. אַךְ *only* (vs. 13, 30) as against רַק *only* (xix. 8; xxiv. 8 J). אַךְ occurs besides in Genesis in E, xx. 12; in J, vii.

23; xviii. 32; xxvi. 9; xxix. 14; xliv. 28; in P, ix. 4, 5;
xxiii. 13; xxxiv. 15, 22, 23. רַק occurs repeatedly in J as
well as E. See ch. vi. 1–8, Marks of J, No. 7.

2. בְּטֶרֶם *before* (vs. 4, 33) as against לִפְנֵי (vs. 7, 10).
This particle occurs in J and P as well as E. See chs.
xviii., xix., Marks of J, No. 13.

3. "The form of address (vs. 1b, 18)," as in E, xxii. 1,
7, 11; xxxi. 11; xxxvii. 13; xlvi. 2; Ex. iii. 4. But
xxii. 11 is referred to E in spite of the name Jehovah;
and there is no propriety in sundering xxvii. 1b, 18, from
the connection in which they stand.

4. עַד־מְאֹד *exceedingly* (vs. 33, 34); nowhere else in the
Hexateuch.

It is apparent that the grounds adduced for the partition of ch. xxvii. between J and E are flimsy enough.
The alleged doublets are no doublets at all; the verbal
criteria amount to nothing. But the necessity remains.
Both the preceding and the subsequent history, as assigned respectively to J and E, presuppose what is narrated in this chapter. The only conclusion consistent
with the divisive hypothesis is that it must in substance
have been contained in both these documents. And as
the critics find it impossible to partition the narrative,
they are compelled to content themselves with the attempt to discover traces of both J and E; and these
traces seem to be hard to find. They are repeatedly
pressed by the same difficulty in their endeavor to carry
the hypothesis through the intractable material that yet
remains; and they are obliged to resort to the most
questionable expedients to compass their end.

The last verse of ch. xxvii. links it closely to ch.
xxviii. Rebekah, impressed with Jacob's peril from his
enraged brother, induces Isaac to send him away to obtain a wife. It is necessary, therefore, to get rid of this
verse with its evidence of unity, and it is accordingly at-

tributed to the redactor; and the rather as it tends still farther to combine J and P by explicit reference to P (xxvi. 34, 35), and borrowing its expressions, "daughters of Heth," "daughters of the land," as xxiii. 3, xxxiv. 1, on the one hand, and by similarity to J on the other. Cf. "what good shall my life do me," with xxv. 22, "wherefore do I live?"

JACOB'S DREAM (CH. XXVIII. 10-22)

In xxviii. 5, 7 the general statement is made that Jacob had set out for Paddan-aram; in vs. 10-22 a more particular account is given of what befell him on the way. Jehovah appeared to him as he was leaving the promised land, to assure him of divine protection wherever he should go, and of a safe return and especially to renew to him the promises made to his fathers of the possession of the land in all its length and breadth, and a blessing to all nations through his seed. Like promises were made in similar circumstances to Isaac (xxvi. 2-4), and to Jacob himself, when at a later period he was about to go down into Egypt (xlvi. 3, 4). Cf. a like promise made to Abraham, when the future sojourn of his seed in a foreign land was shown to him (xv. 13-18).

The general statement above mentioned is by the critics given to P, and the particulars included under it to JE. It hence results that though P relates (xxviii. 1-9) that Jacob was sent to Paddan-aram to obtain a wife, and that he actually set out for the purpose, he makes no mention of anything that occurred upon his journey thither, or of his arrival there, or finding his mother's relatives, or his marriage, or anything regarding his long residence there. And yet these things must have been mentioned, for they are presupposed in what is said elsewhere. In xxxv. 9 P, God is said to have appeared to Jacob *again* at Bethel, implying the previous appearance (xxviii. 12 sqq.); xxxi. 18 P, Jacob leaves Paddan-aram with goods and cattle acquired there, implying a previous narrative of how he had obtained them ; and xxxv. 23–26 P gives the names of his wives and the children born to him in Paddan-aram, implying a previous account of his marriage and his family. The matters thus· alluded to are fully recorded in the sacred narrative, but are by the critics assigned to J and E ; not a syllable respecting them is to be found in P, though they are indispensable to the integrity of this document. Just that is missing from P which the critics have sundered from it, and transferred to other supposititious documents. There is here a glaring lack of continuity in P, as well as repeated references in P to the contents of J and E; both of which are inconsistent with the hypothesis of separate and independent documents.

Constrained by the occurrence in this passage of both Elohim (vs. 12, 17 sqq.) and Jehovah (vs. 13–16) the critics undertake to parcel vs. 10–22 between E and J. Wellhausen, followed by Kautzsch (1st edition) and Stade,[1] gives vs. 10–12, 17, 18, 20, 21a, 22, to E, and the rest to J, except 19b, 21b, which are assigned to R. Accordingly E speaks of a dream, in which Jacob saw a ladder and angels, but received no accompanying revelation. J makes no mention of any ladder or angels, but only of the appearance of Jehovah, who stood beside Jacob and gave him promises for the present and the future. Thus divided, the vision which was granted to Jacob, according to E, had no special adaptation to his existing circumstances, but is supposed to be a legend here recorded with the view of enhancing the sacredness of the sanctuary that existed at Bethel in later times. And the point of it is that on that spot communication

[1] Geschichte des Volkes Israel, p. 60.

was opened between earth and heaven by a ladder on which celestial beings ascended and descended. But while in the opinion of the critics the whole intent of E was to glorify the sanctuary at Bethel, he does not once mention Bethel, nor give any intimation where it was that this vision occurred. The name of the place is only to be found in ver. 19a, which is attributed to J.[1]

Moreover, the vision of the ladder and the angels (ver. 12) cannot be separated from the revelation of Jehovah which follows (ver. 13) and interprets it (ver. 15), or rather which is the most essential part of the whole supernatural manifestation. In vs. 11, 12, Jacob goes to sleep and dreams; in ver. 16 he awakes; this is evidently a continuation of the preceding and cannot be referred to a separate document.[2] In its present connection עָלָיו *upon it* or *above it* (ver. 13) plainly refers to the ladder (ver. 12). To sunder it from the preceding and insist that it should be rendered *beside him*, is gratuitously to charge the redactor with having falsified its meaning. A ladder reaching to the skies, on which angels were ascending and descending, might entitle the place to be called "the gate of heaven," but not "the house of God" (ver. 17); nor could it be said that God there appeared unto Jacob (xxxv. 1, 7, E). In his vow (vs. 20, 21a) Jacob adopts the very terms of the promise which Je-

---

[1] Dillmann says, "It may be doubted from which source ver. 19 has been derived; it probably belongs to both, as it cannot be dispensed with in either; E in particular presupposes the name Bethel as already existing" (xxxi. 13; xxxv. 3).

[2] In order to escape this difficulty Stade ventures the suggestion: "It may very well be supposed that in the original connection of J the manifestation did not take place in a dream, so that 'And Jacob awaked out of his sleep,' in ver. 16, has been inserted from E. This is a mode of evasion to which the critics frequently resort with the view of ridding themselves of unwelcome clauses or words. Here it leaves the following verb 'said' without a subject."

hovah had just made (ver. 15) ; so that these cannot be
from distinct documents. And ver. 21b, of which the
critics try to rid themselves because of its "Jehovah," is
most appropriate where it stands, whether it continues
the preamble,[1] or introduces Jacob's own pledge. Jehovah had announced himself as the God of Abraham and
of Isaac (ver. 13), would he likewise be, as was implied
in his promise, Jacob's God ? But if this clause be, as
the critics will have it, an insertion from J or an addition by R, it remains to be explained how either J or
R should have fallen upon a characteristic phrase of P
(xvii. 7 ; Ex. vi. 7 ; xxix. 45).

Verses 10–12 are absolutely necessary to explain the
situation in vs. 13–16 J ; without them there is no suggestion how Jacob came to be at Bethel. But they are
equally necessary to vs. 17, 18, E. If, however, under
the pressure of this latter necessity vs. 10–12 are given
to E, another incongruity will result. The mention of
Beersheba as Jacob's point of departure (ver. 10) implies Isaac's residence there, as recorded by J (xxvi. 33)
but not by E. And Haran, to which he was going, also
points to J (xxvii. 43 ; xxix. 4) ; it does not occur in E.
Hence Hupfeld, Dillmann, and Kautzsch (2d edition)
give ver. 10 to J ; but then E lacks any proper beginning.
Hupfeld made the attempt to split ver. 11 by assigning

---

[1] Hengstenberg (Beiträge, ii., p. 370), followed by Tuch and Baumgar-
ten, extends the preamble to the end of ver. 21, as in the margin of the
Revised Version, " and Jehovah will be my God, then this stone," etc.
This corresponds with the change of tenses from preterite to future at
that point in the sentence, and with the common meaning of the
phrase, "to be the God of anyone," *e.g.*, ver. 13, which is elsewhere
suggestive of the divine regard rather than of the human obligation of
worship. Delitzsch, Knobel, and Dillmann prefer the rendering of the
A. V. and the text of the R. V., which is also that of the LXX. and the
Vulgate. But it is questionable whether they are not influenced in
their decision by the critical partition which sunders vs. 20, 21, from
ver. 13.

"he lighted upon a certain place and took one of the stones of the place and put it under his head," to E, and " he tarried there (where ?) all night because the sun was set, and lay down in that place to sleep," to J ; but he gave it up as impracticable. Any division of the passage creates a gap in both documents, neither of which can be filled but by trenching upon the other. The whole passage is, moreover, closely linked with ch. xxvii., where we have found that a critical division is equally impracticable.

In order to make out the composite character of the passage a doublet is claimed in vs. 16, 17. With the best endeavor to do so I have not been able to comprehend the point of view from which ver. 17 can be considered indicative of a different writer from ver. 16, unless it be on the sole ground of the change of divine names. It is surely the most natural and appropriate exclamation under the circumstances. Ver. 17 does not duplicate ver. 16, but is its suitable sequel. Neither is ver. 22 a duplicate of ver. 19. The relation is not that of equivalence but of dependence. Because God had here manifested his presence Jacob named the place Bethel, "a house of God." And if God would verify the promise there given (ver. 15), Jacob pledges himself to regard this spot as in reality what this name denoted : it should be to him a house of God, and here he would consecrate a tenth of all to him.

Wellhausen finds indications of a diversity of writers in the order in which the points of the compass are named, J (xxviii. 14) W., E., N., S., but R (xiii. 14) N., S., E., W. ; in " all the families of the earth " מִשְׁפְּחֹת הָאֲדָמָה (xii. 3 ; xxviii. 14 J), compared with " all the nations of the earth " גּוֹיֵי הָאָרֶץ (xviii. 18 R) ; and in "thee and thy seed " (xiii. 15 R), and an implied reference to " seed " (xviii. 18 R) compared with " in thee " (xii. 3 J), whence he infers that "in thy seed" (xxviii. 14 J) is an addition by R. But Dillmann and others have no difficulty in attributing all these passages alike to J, and see no occasion for assuming any insertion or manipulation by R. The fact is that where distinct writers are assumed on independent grounds there is no difficulty in gathering up arguments from varying words and phrases to sustain a predetermined conclusion ; but these will be set aside without ceremony by the critics themselves when they have no end to be answered by them.

In Jacob's dream Jehovah, the God of the chosen race, appeared to him (xxviii. 13, 16), in order to assure him that though temporarily exiled from his father's house he would not on that account be severed from the God of his father, as Ishmael had been when sent away from Abraham's household, and Lot when his connection with Abraham was finally cut off by his passing beyond the limit of the promised land. God was thenceforward Elohim to them as to all who were aliens to the chosen race. But Jacob was still under the guardianship of Jehovah, who would continue with him wherever he might go. The angels (ver. 12), however, are not called "angels of Jehovah," which never occurs in the Pentateuch, but "angels of Elohim," as xxxii. 2 (E. V. ver. 1), who are thus distinguished from messengers of men—the Hebrew word for "angel" properly meaning "messenger." This does not mark a distinction between the documents, as though J knew of but one angel, "the angel of Jehovah," the divine angel, while E speaks of "angels ; " for J has "angels" in the plural (xix. 1, 15). The place where Jehovah had thus revealed himself Jacob calls "the house of God" and "the gate of heaven," God in contrast with man, as heaven with earth. It was a spot marked by a divine manifestation. The critical severance will not answer here, for, as already stated, if vs. 13–

16 be exscinded as belonging to J, the vision of angels
(ver. 12) alone would not entitle it to be called the house
of God (ver. 17). The scene of Jehovah's appearing is
called " Beth-El," precisely as Hannah called her child
" Samu-El, because I have asked him of Jehovah" (1
Sam. i. 20). In Jacob's vow (vs. 20, 22) the specifications respect God's general providential care, and hence
he uses Elohim, while nevertheless in a manner perplex-
ing to the critics, who find themselves obliged to erase
the offending clause, he recognizes Jehovah as the God
(ver. 21) to whom he makes his appeal and gives his
pledge.

MARKS OF J (VS. 10, 13-16, 19a)

1. "The contents and form of the promises (vs. 13–
16) "; cf. xiii. 14, 16 ; xii. 3 ; xviii. 18.   See chs. xviii.,
xix., Marks of J, No. 25.

2. עַל נִצָּב stand on or over (ver. 14); elsewhere in J,
xviii. 2 ; xxiv. 13, 43 ; xlv. 1 ; Ex. xxxiii. 21 ; xxxiv. 2 ;
in E, Ex. vii. 15 ; xvii. 9 ; xviii. 14 ; Num. xxiii. 6, 17.

3. פָּרַץ break forth, spread abroad (ver. 14); elsewhere
in J, xxx. 30, 43 ; xxxviii. 29 ; Ex. xix. 22, 24 ; in E, Ex.
i. 12.

4. אֲדָמָה ground, earth, land (vs. 14, 15). This word is
reckoned a criterion of J, and whenever it is practicable,
paragraphs or clauses that contain it are for that reason
referred to J. Nevertheless in repeated instances it cannot be excluded from P and E. It is used to denote (1)
Earth as a material, so in J, Gen. ii. 7, 19 ; iii. 19; in E,
Ex. xx. 24. (2) The soil as tilled and productive, thirty
times, mostly in J ; as no passage relating to tillage is
assigned to P, of course there is no occasion for the use
of the word in this sense; it is found in E, Ex. xxiii.
19. (3) The surface of the earth, the ground, not only in
J, but also in P (Gen. i. 25 ; vi. 20 ; ix. 2) ; and in E, Ex.

iii. 5; Num. xvi. 30, 31 (with אֲדָמָה) is given to J, and
ver. 32a (with אֶרֶץ) to E, though a continuous sentence
is thus cut in two, and ver. 32 corresponds to ver. 30,
and records its fulfilment. (4) The land of Canaan, five
times; four of these are referred to J (Gen. xxviii. 15;
Lev. xx. 24, so Dillmann; Num. xi. 12; xxxii. 11); and
one to E (Ex. xx. 12); אֶרֶץ is mostly used in this sense
by J as well as by P and E. (5) The whole earth, twice;
in J "all the families of the earth" (Gen. xii. 3; xxviii.
14); but the parallel passages have אֶרֶץ (xviii. 18 J, and
xxii. 18; xxvi. 4 referred to R in a J connection). See
ch. vi. 1–8, Marks of J, No. 3.

MARKS OF E (VS. 11, 12, 17, 18, 20, 21a, 22)

1. "These verses have Elohim, but P cannot be regarded as the author on account of xxxv. 9–15." But
that is not a variant account of the same transaction, and
as such implying a different author. It is expressly
stated (xxxv. 9) to be a second divine manifestation in
this place, thus presupposing the narrative in the passage
before us.

2. "The back references (xxxi. 13; xxxv. 3, 7) prove
that it belongs to E." These tend to establish an identity of authorship with those passages, but do not imply
that they belong to a separate document from the rest of
the text in which they are found. The same may be said
of the back reference from xxxii. 13 (E. V., ver. 12) J.

3. פָּגַע בְּ to *light upon* (ver. 11); elsewhere in E, xxxii.
2 (E. V. ver. 1); in JE, Josh. ii. 16; xvii. 10; in P, Gen.
xxiii. 8; Num. xxxv. 19, 21; Josh. xvi. 7; xix. 11, 22, 26,
27, 34.

4. הִשְׁכִּים בַּבֹּקֶר *rose up early in the morning* (ver. 18).
See chs. xviii., xix., Marks of J, No. 26.

5. "The tithe (ver. 22)." Tithes are spoken of besides

in the priest code (Lev. xxvii., Num. xviii.), and the Deuteronomic law, and but once elsewhere in the Pentateuch, viz., Gen. xiv. 20, which Dillmann doubtfully refers to E, while at the same time he holds[1] with other critics that the first certain trace of E is in Gen. xx. The ascription of the passage before us to E on this ground rests thus on a very slender basis. It is far more natural to believe that as the patriarchal institutions supply the germs from which the ritual law was subsequently developed, they are recorded for that reason, and by the same hand as the law itself. The notion, which the critics seek to fasten on P, that the Mosaic ritual had not even a germinal existence in the days of the patriarchs, is without the slightest foundation in the sacred record, or in the nature of things. It is one of the absurdities that grow out of sundering what properly belongs together.

6. "The dream (ver. 12)." See ch. xx., Marks of E, No. 4.

In commenting on xii. 8, Dillmann remarks that there and xiii. 4 the sacredness of Bethel is traced to Abraham, while elsewhere (xxviii. 22; xxxv. 7 sqq.) it is traced to Jacob. In his prefatory remarks upon the section now before us, with the view apparently of removing this fancied divergence, he observes that in xii. 8 it was a place near Bethel, and not Bethel itself, that was consecrated by Abraham. But the sacred writer makes no reference whatever to the idolatrous sanctuary subsequently established at Bethel; least of all is he giving an account of its origin. There is no discrepancy in different patriarchs successively visiting the same place and building altars there. These descriptions of patriarchal worship are not legends to gain credit for the sanctuary; but the superstition of later ages founded sanctuaries in

[1] Die Bücher Num.–Jos., p. 615.

venerated spots, where the patriarchs had worshipped, and where God had revealed himself to them.

JACOB IN HARAN (CHS. XXIX., XXX.)

The critics here find themselves in a serious muddle. According to Hupfeld ("Quellen," p. 65) ch. xxix. bears so evidently the stamp of J that the opposite view, which is perfectly arbitrary, needs no refutation. Wellhausen is just as confident that xxix. 1–30 is, with trifling excep- tions, from E, while Dillmann compromises the matter by making nearly an equal division, and giving vs. 2–15a to J, and the rest almost entirely to E. Hupfeld ("Quel- len," p. 43) maintains that xxx. 1–24 continues J's history without the trace of a seam, with the same basis and presuppositions, the same manner and language; while in the judgment of Wellhausen and Dillmann it is "a very remarkable piece of mosaic from J and E." The trouble in xxix. 1–30 is that there are no divine names; the trouble is increased in xxix. 31–xxx. 24 by the fact that there are divine names.

Dillmann claims that there is a break in the former of these paragraphs at xxix. 15, inasmuch as Laban here asks Jacob what wages he shall pay him, though there had been no previous mention that Jacob had entered Laban's service as a shepherd, or had any thought of doing so. There is, of course, a transition to a new sub- ject, as must be the case whenever a fresh topic is intro- duced; but it is by no means a violent one, since ver. 14 speaks of Jacob's abode with Laban, and it is not a re- mote supposition that he made himself serviceable during his stay (cf. ver. 10). At any rate it fails to justify Dill- mann's own division after ver. 15a, in which the subject of a recompense for service is already broached. Nor is there any implication in vs. 16, 17, that Rachel had not been previously spoken of, from which it might be inferred that vs. 6, 9–12 are from a different document. It had not been before mentioned that Laban had two daughters, that Rachel was the younger, and that she was more attractive than her sister. These facts are introduced here, since they are necessary to explain Jacob's answer (ver. 18) to Laban's proposal.

The arguments urged to establish the duplicate character of the latter paragraph (xxix. 31–xxx. 24) are chiefly—

1. The repeated occurrence of Elohim.

2. The different explanations given of the names Issachar, Zebulun, and Joseph.

To the first of these Hupfeld replies that Elohim in xxx. 2, 8 is no criterion, because the predominant, if not exclusive, biblical usage requires it rather than Jehovah in such expressions as are there employed. And that in the etymologies of the names, *e.g.*, in vs. 6, 8, 18, 20, 23, the general term Elohim, as more poetic, would naturally be preferred, as it is in Proverbs.

Where there are two explanations of the same name he concedes that something has been inserted from another source. But there seems to be little cogency in this consideration. Issachar (*sachar*, hire) is associated with Leah's hiring by mandrakes and hiring by the gift of her maid; Zebulun, with *zabad*, "endow," and *zabal*, "dwell;" Joseph, with *asaph*, "take away," and *yasaph*, "add." These are not to be regarded as discrepant explanations of these names, implying different views of their origin or of the occasion of their being given, but simply different allusions to the meaning or the sound of the names, which by no means exclude each other. Such allusions are multiplied in the case of Isaac. The name means "laughter;" and we are told how Abraham laughed and Sarah laughed incredulously when his birth was pre-

dicted, and how God made her laugh for joy, and all her
friends laugh with her when he was actually born. There
is no inconsistency in these statements, and no need of
parcelling them among different writers. It is the same
writer playfully dwelling upon different aspects of a
theme which interests him.

Dillmann thus apportions the record of the birth of
Jacob's children: J, xxix. 31–35 ; E, xxx. 1–3a (including
bear upon my knees, as l. 23 E); J, 3b (*that I may be builded by her*), as xvi. 2 ; J, or rather P, 4a ; J, 4b, 5 ; E, 6 ;
J, 7 ; E, 8 ; J, 9a ; P, 9b ; J, 10–16 ; E, 17–20a ; J, 20b ;
J or R, 21 ;[1] P, 22a ; E, 22b ; J, 22c ; E, 23 ; J, 24.
And this in a paragraph which bears the most abundant
and positive evidences of unity from first to last in continuity of theme, consistent method of treatment, cross-
references, style, and language.

"Leah was hated" (xxix. 31), see vs. 18, 20, 25, 30.
"Opened her womb" (xxix. 31 ; xxx. 22), opposed to
"shut" (xx. 18 ; xvi. 2) ; cf. xxx. 2. "Rachel was bar-

---

[1] The birth of a daughter is never mentioned unless she is to appear
in the subsequent history (cf. xxii. 23). Dinah (xxix. 21) is preparatory to ch. xxxiv. ; and as no part of that chapter is given to E, xxx.
21 is necessarily referred to either J or R. So the numerous allusions
in xxix. 5, 10, 12, 13, to ch. xxiv. J, make it necessary to refer the paragraph containing those verses to J. The frequent references, both forward and backward, in Genesis and the rest of the Pentateuch, bind the
whole together in inseparable unity, and oppose a formidable obstacle
to any divisive scheme. They put an end to the fragment hypothesis, and they compel the advocates of the document hypothesis to use
great adroitness in so adjusting their lines of partition that it may appear as though each document only presupposed or alluded to what is
contained in itself. By using the utmost ingenuity and making a perfectly arbitrary partition, severing what properly belongs together and
splintering the text *ad infinitum,* if need be, they manage to cover a
considerable number of these cross-references. But in spite of every
effort to prevent it, the matter referred to is often in the wrong document, and the hypothesis can only be saved by assuming that it was
originally in the other document likewise, but R has omitted it.

ren" (xxix. 31); see xxx. 1, 2, 22, 23. "Conceived and
bare a son," "called his name," "and said" (xxix. 32), the
same formulas with very slight variations recurring
throughout. The language of the mothers refers in
every case to the jealousy between the wives on account
of Jacob's preference for Rachel and Leah's fertility.
הַפַּעַם *this time, now* (xxix. 34; xxx. 20). "My husband
will—because I have borne him—sons" (xxix. 34; xxx.
20). "She left bearing" (xxix. 35; xxx. 9). "Again"
(xxix. 33, 34, 35; xxx. 7, 19). Bilhah (xxx. 4), Zilpah (ver.
9), cf. xxix. 24, 29. "Fifth" (xxx. 17), "sixth" (ver.
19) son of Leah, referring to the preceding four (xxix.
32–35). "God hearkened unto" (xxx. 17, 22); with the
whole paragraph cf. xxxii. 22; xxxv. 23–26. In formality of set phrases and in repetitions it is equal to any
paragraph attributed to P.

The critics may well infer that this portion of the story
must have been very strikingly alike in J and in E, if R
could thus pass back and forth from one to the other
with no perceptible effect upon his narrative. The fact
is that the paragraph is without seam, woven from the
top throughout, and the critics have mistaken the figures
deftly wrought into the material for patches slightly
stitched together, and they try to rend it accordingly,
but it will not tear. There is really nothing for them to
do but to cast lots for it, which of the documents shall
have it. If the paragraph had been purposely constructed with this view, it could not more effectively
demonstrate the futility of using the divine names and
alleged doublets for parcelling the text of Genesis.

The critical disposition of xxx. 25–43 J is based on the
unfounded assumption of discrepancies between it and
xxxi. 7 sqq., 41 E, both in respect to the chronology and
the contract between Laban and Jacob.

According to xxxi. 41, Jacob served Laban twenty years,

fourteen for his two daughters and six for his cattle. But (xxx. 25 sqq.) the bargain about the cattle was made after the birth of Joseph, and (xxix. 20–28) Jacob was married to Leah and Rachel after he had already served seven years. Now it is alleged that he could not have had eleven children in the next seven years. The fallacy lies in failing to observe that there were four mothers. The narrative is linked throughout by Vav Consecutive; but this does not prove that each several clause follows its predecessor in regular succession.[1] The children are grouped by their mothers, and thus the order of thought deviates from the order of time. Rachel's jealousy was aroused, and Bilhah introduced to Jacob (xxx. 1 sqq.) before Leah ceased bearing (xxix. 35). Leah's four sons were born in rapid succession, and as soon as she found that she was not at once to have another (xxx. 9) she substituted Zilpah, and before Zilpah had her second son she had herself conceived her fifth (ver. 17). Thus her sixth son could be born within the seven years, and Joseph's birth have taken place about the same time. Dinah (ver. 21) was born afterward, and is not to be included within the period in question. The alleged discrepancy, accordingly, is not proved.

How is it with the bargaining between Laban and Jacob ? The latter charges that Laban had sought to defraud him by changing his wages ten times (xxxi. 7, 41), but by God's interference this had been turned to Jacob's profit. On the other hand, in xxx. 31 sqq., Laban assented to an arrangement which Jacob himself proposed, and which Jacob by a trick turned to his own advantage. The two statements are not in conflict, but

---

[1] Hengstenberg (Authentie des Pentateuchs, ii., p. 351) appeals to Ex. ii. 1, where, though Moses was born after Pharaoh's cruel edict (i. 22), the marriage of his parents and the birth of his brother Aaron (Ex. vii. 7) must have preceded it.

supplemental to each other. Chapter xxx. describes the
original arrangement and Jacob's device. Chapter xxxi.
tells how Laban modified it from time to time with a
view to his own interest, but his selfish plans were divinely thwarted.

The comparison of chs. xxx. and xxxi. accordingly supplies no basis for the assumption of discrepant accounts
from different writers. But Wellhausen fancies a discrepancy in ch. xxx. itself, alleging that vs. 32–34 are inconsistent with their context. He understands these
verses to mean that the spotted and brown cattle at that
time in the flocks were to constitute Jacob's hire ;
whereas (vs. 35, 36) they were separated from the flocks
and given not to Jacob but to Laban's sons. The difficulty is altogether imaginary, and is simply due to a
misinterpretation of the brief and elliptical statement in
ver. 32. The real meaning is, as is plain from Jacob's
opening words in ver. 31, and as it is correctly understood by Dillmann, that the speckled and brown cattle
to be born thereafter were to be Jacob's ; and as a preliminary measure those of this description that were
then in the flocks were set apart as Laban's.

The doublets alleged are quite trivial, and appear at
once upon examination to be unreal. Ver. 26a does not
repeat 25b, but supplements it ; Jacob first asks in general terms to be dismissed that he may return to his home,
and then adds, as included in his request, " Give me my
wives and my children and let me go." Ver. 26b is repeated in ver. 29, but it is for the sake of adding ver. 30,
in which Jacob enlarges upon what he had already said,
in order that he may impress upon Laban the obligation
under which he had already laid him. In ver. 31a Laban repeats the offer made in ver. 28, which Jacob had
declined to answer in the first instance, preferring to
state the service which he had rendered, and thus give

Laban an idea of what he was entitled to, before he made any demand. Dillmann himself sets aside Wellhausen's suggestion that 39a is a doublet of 38b. The central clause of ver. 40 is magisterially declared to be a later insertion, but as no reason is given, and none is apparent, no answer is necessary. These can scarcely be regarded as establishing the existence of a composite text derived from distinct sources.

THE DIVINE NAMES

Two things are here observable in relation to the divine names, and have often been remarked : that in this portion of Genesis, and on to the end of the book, they occur less frequently than before ; and that Elohim largely predominates over Jehovah. Several considerations should be noted as bearing upon the explanation of these facts :

1. Jacob was on a lower plane, religiously, than Abraham and Isaac.

2. His life was henceforth largely spent away from the holy land and among those not of the chosen race.

3. Since the relation of Jehovah to the patriarchs had been sufficiently established by the previous use of that name, it seemed less important to continue to repeat it, and of more consequence to guard against the notion that the God of the patriarchs was a mere tribal deity by recurring to the general term Elohim, suggestive of his relation to the world at large.

4. The fuller revelation of God as Jehovah in the Mosaic age threw that made to the patriarchs comparatively into the shade ; so that while in the beginning, in contrast with the times before Abraham, the patriarchal age was marked by new manifestations of Jehovah, those granted toward its close seemed of inferior grade in comparison with the more resplendent revelations that were

to come after, and so more fitly associated with the general term Elohim than the personal name Jehovah. The solution offered by the critics is that the materials are henceforth largely drawn from the document E. But the hypothesis of different documents will not meet the case. It has already been seen what confusion it introduces in the chapters now before us. It encounters like perplexities in the chapters that follow. If the alternation of Elohim and Jehovah is not in every instance regulated in as marked and conspicuous a manner as heretofore by the meanings of the names, there is, nevertheless, nothing counter to the general usage of the rest of Scripture in their employment, or that suggests the idea that it was mechanically determined by the particular document from which any given extract chanced to be drawn. In many cases either name would be appropriate, and it is at the option of the writer to use one or the other. And it is no valid ground of objection to the unity of Genesis if a like freedom prevails there as in other books of the Bible, where it might often be difficult to assign a definite reason for the occurrence of Elohim rather than Jehovah, or *vice versa.*

The birth of Jacob's children is capable of being viewed in a twofold light, as the gracious gift of Jehovah, the God of the chosen race, who watched over and directed its enlargement, or as blessings bestowed in the ordinary providence of God. Leah's first children, granted to her notwithstanding the disfavor of her husband, are viewed under the former aspect (xxix. 31-35). Those that follow, in ch. xxx., are regarded under the latter aspect, viz., the children of the handmaids, sprung from the jealous strife of Jacob's wives ; those of Leah [1]

---

[1] Note Leah's lingering heathenism in her allusions to "fortune" (Gad) and "good luck" (Asher) (vs. 11-13) ; and Rachel's theft of her father's images (xxxi. 30, 34).

after she had bargained for her husband's presence; and Rachel's son, born after her long envy and impatience. Upon his birth she gives utterance to her hope that her husband's God, Jehovah, would add to her yet another. Thus both Elohim and Jehovah are associated with children of both Leah and Rachel; and Jehovah begins and ends the series, encircling the whole and enclosing the providential favors granted between these limits.

If any object that this appears to be an artificial arrangement it can at least be said that the critics have nothing better to propose. The narrative of these successive births is plainly one and indivisible, and cannot be rent asunder and converted into such a piece of patchwork as they are obliged to make of it. The style and method are the same, the language and phrases are the same, the narrative is continuous, each part being bound to and implying the others. So that even Vater,[1] with all his predilection for the fragment hypothesis, enters his protest against subdivision here, and against the assumption on which it rests, that the same writer could not use both Elohim and Jehovah; an assumption that is falsified by nearly every book in the Bible. Delitzsch holds that "the interchange of divine names is based upon the interchange of sources from which extracts are taken," and then annuls the ground upon which this opinion rests by the admission that "the author of Genesis has intentionally woven both divine names into the origin of Israel, and it is probably also not accidental that the name Jehovah is impressed on the first four births, and the name Elohim on the remaining seven. On the whole, we are to get the impression that in laying the foundation of Israel Jehovah's fidelity to his promises and Elohim's miracle-working power wrought in combination."

[1] Pentateuch, ii., p. 724.

It remains to be added that in xxx. 2, where Jacob
says, "Am I in God's stead," Elohim is evidently in
place from the suggested contrast of God and man. So
ver. 8, where Rachel says, "with wrestlings of God have
I wrestled," whether the genitive is that of the object,
i.e., wrestlings after God, after a token of the divine
favor in giving me a child, or that of the subject, *i.e.*, divine or superhuman wrestlings. In either case Elohim
is the proper word. But in vs. 27, 30, Jehovah is appropriate because Laban, though not of the chosen race,
recognizes that it was Jacob's God who had blessed him
for Jacob's sake.

MARKS OF J

1. אֲשֶׁר לְ *which* belong *to* (xxix. 9); besides repeated in
J, but also in E (xxxi. 21; xxxii. 24 (E. V. ver. 23); xli.
43; xlv. 10, 11); xl. 5b, and xlvi. 1 are cut out of E contexts and assigned to J.

2. רוּץ לִקְרַאת *run to meet* (ver. 13). This particular
expression occurs three times besides in the Hexateuch,
and is each time referred to J, viz., xviii. 2; xxiv. 17;
xxxiii. 4; but both the words occur in E, and there is no
reason why any Hebrew writer might not have used them
if he had occasion to do so. See chs. xviii., xix., Marks
of J, No. 16.

3. עַצְמִי וּבְשָׂרִי *my bone and my flesh* (ver. 14). A like
expression occurs in ii. 23 J, but nowhere else in the
Hexateuch. It is used, however, by other writers also
(Judg. ix. 2; 2 Sam. v. 1; xix. 13, 14, E. V., vs. 12, 13).

4. שִׁפְחָה *bondmaid* (xxix. 24, 29; xxx. 4, 7, 9, 10, 12,
18, 43). This word is said to be characteristic of P and
J, as opposed to E, who uses אָמָה *maid,* as xxx. 3. It occurs, however, several times in these chapters in what
the critics consider wrong connections, and the corrective
is unhesitatingly applied by exscinding the offending

clause. Thus in xxix. 24, 29, it is found in an E connection, and these isolated verses are cut out and given to P,
where they are quite unmeaning, and there is nothing
with which to connect them. They evidently belong
where they stand as preparatory for xxx. 4, 9. It is a
mere evasion to sunder these verses from their proper
context because of the manifest reference to them and
their repetition in identical terms in xlvi. 18, 25 P, which
is at variance with the critics' hypothesis. Wellhausen
erases the word, " Rachel's handmaid " from xxxi. 7, as
an insertion by R, because he gives the verse to E; Dillmann suffers the words to stand because he assigns the
verse to J. But both these critics agree that R must
have substituted שִׁפְחָה for אָמָה in xxxi. 18, which they
refer to E. The occurrence of אָמָה *maid,* in xxx. 3, is not
indicative of a particular document E; Rachel, in offering her bondmaid שִׁפְחָה to Jacob as a concubine, uses
the less servile term. See ch. xx., Marks of E, No. 1;
xxi. 1–21, Marks of E, No. 11.

5. אִם־נָא מָצָאתִי חֵן *if now I have found favor* (xxx. 27).
See ch. xii. 10–20, Marks of J, No. 3; ch. vi. 1–8, No. 10.

6. בִּגְלַל *for the sake of* (ver. 27). See ch. xii. 10–20,
Marks of J, No. 6.

7. פָּרַץ *break forth, increase* (vs. 30, 43). See ch.
xxviii. 10–22, Marks of J, No. 3.

MARKS OF E

1. מַשְׂכֹּרֶת *wages* (xxix. 15). This is reckoned an E
word, though in the Hexateuch it only occurs besides in
xxxi. 7, 41 E. It is here used interchangeably with its
equivalent from the same root, שָׂכָר, which is found alike
in E (xxx. 18; xxxi. 8 bis; Ex. ii. 9; xxii. 14; E. V., 15);
in J (xxx. 28, 32, 33); in JE (xv. 1); in P (Num. xviii.
31); and in D (Deut. xv. 18; xxiv. 15).

2. קְטַנָּה, גְּדֹלָה in respect to age, *elder, younger* (xxix. 16, 18). These words are here attributed to E in contrast with צְעִירָה, בְּכִירָה, which are supposed to belong to J. But as these latter words occur (ver. 26) in an E context, it is necessary to cut this verse out of its connection and give it to J for this reason alone. But these alleged E words are nowhere else regarded as such. גְּדוֹל *elder,* is assigned to J (x. 21; xxvii. 15; xliv. 12) ; to JE (xxvii. 1, 42). קָטֹן *younger,* occurs in J (ix. 24 ; xxvii. 15 ; xliv. 12, 20) ; in JE (xxvii. 42). If, now, upon the critics' own partition of the text, J uses both pairs of words, how can either pair be regarded as an indication of a different document? See ch. xix. 29–38, Marks of J, No. 1, 2.

3. יְפַת תֹּאַר וִיפַת מַרְאֶה *fair of form and fair to look upon* (xxix. 17). The entire expression occurs but once besides, viz., xxxix. 6, which is referred to J ; "fair to look upon " occurs in J (xii. 11); in E (xli. 2, 4, 18) ; "fair of form" occurs but once more in the Hexateuch, viz., Deut. xxi. 11 D. See ch. xxiv., Marks of J, No. 13.

It will be observed that not one of these so-called E words or phrases is peculiar to that document ; and such as they are, they are all taken from xxix. 15–18. The only other words adduced from the entire two chapters as belonging to E, and suggestive of E paragraphs, are *Elohim,* אָמָה *maid* (xxx. 3 ; see above, Marks of J, No. 4), and two expressions in xxix. 1, which occur nowhere else in the Hexateuch, either in J or E, viz., "*lifted up his feet*" (E. V., went on his journey), " *land of the children of the east.*" It is said that this region is called Paddan-aram by P, and Aram-naharaim (xxiv. 10) by J, consequently this third designation must be that of E. But if J can call the same place Haran (xxix. 4) and the city of Nahor (xxiv. 10), why may he not use more than one designation for the region in which it stood ? See under ch. xxiv., p. 298.

Dillmann points out three E words, as he considers them, in the midst of a paragraph assigned to J, viz., רְהָטִים *gutters* (xxx. 38, 41), as Ex. ii. 16 E ; תַּיִשׁ *he-goat* (xxx. 35), as xxxii. 15 (E. V., 14) E ; עָקֹד *ring-streaked* (xxx. 35, 39, 40), as xxxi. 8, 10, 12 E. The adoption of E words and phrases by J here and frequently elsewhere, together with the close correspondence between J and E in matter and form, which must be assumed in this chapter, and in many other passages of like character, makes it necessary, so Dillmann infers, to suppose that J was in possession of the document E, and made use of it in preparing his own work. Knobel and Kayser go farther, and find it unnecessary to assume the existence of a redactor to combine the separate documents of J and E, preferring to regard the combined work JE as the production of J who had E (or a similar source differently named by Knobel) before him, and incorporated such portions of it as he saw fit. Wellhausen objects that J must have been entirely independent of E ; for, if he drew from E, he would not have varied from it and contradicted it in so many instances. There is a measure of truth in the position taken by each of these critics. If such documents as are attributed to J and E ever existed, there are abundant indications that J must have been acquainted with E. And if so, Wellhausen is right in holding that he could not have been guilty of introducing such glaring discrepancies into his own work as the critics profess to find there. Whether the combination was effected by J or by a redactor, neither the one nor the other could have been so senseless as to insert palpable contradictions in what he put forth as credible history. And in fact these alleged discrepancies and contradictions prove upon examination not to be such, but to be capable of ready reconciliation. And as these supply the principal argument for the separate existence of

J and E, the main prop of this portion of the hypothesis collapses with their disappearance ; and it becomes easy to see how J can use E words, and show familiarity with the contents of E sections, if J and E are identical.

JACOB'S RETURN FROM HARAN (CHS. XXXI.-XXXII. 3; E. V., VER. 2)

Chapter xxxi. 1-43 is by the critics mainly assigned to E on account of the repeated occurrence of Elohim, its alleged contrariety to ch. xxx., and the revelations in dreams to Jacob (vs. 11 sqq.) and Laban (ver. 24) ; also the reference in ver. 13 to xxviii. 20 sqq., which we have no disposition to dispute. While this passage is assigned by the critics to E, it has already been shown to be intimately connected with xxx. 31 sqq., with which it is entirely consistent, and from which the attempt is vainly made to sunder it.

It is claimed that while this paragraph is for the most part from E, vs. 1, 3, 21b, 25, 27 are insertions from J. But ver. 2 is not an idle repetition of ver. 1 ; it is additional to it. Laban as well as his sons had become disaffected toward Jacob. In speaking to his wives (ver. 5) he only mentions their father's disfavor, because this was of supreme consequence to himself, and made it plainly undesirable for him to remain longer in his service. Both vs. 1 and 2 prepare the way for Jehovah's direction to Jacob to return to the land of his fathers (ver. 3), which stands in no special relation to ver. 1, as the scheme of the critics implies. Nor does ver. 3 interrupt the connection. It supplies the occasion of Jacob's summoning Rachel and Leah (ver. 4) ; and ver. 5 explicitly refers to and repeats the language of both ver. 2 and ver. 3. It is true that ver. 3 has " Jehovah," which is unwelcome to the critics here, but it cannot be helped. It is

precisely equivalent to "the God of my father" (ver. 5).
The verse is appropriate and required where it stands,
and Jacob adopts its very words (ver. 13) in reciting at
length to his wives what is briefly and summarily stated
in this verse.

The middle clause of ver. 21 is no superfluous repetition. The account of Jacob's leaving (vs. 17, 18) is interrupted by a necessary digression (vs. 19, 20) explaining that it was without Laban's knowledge. Verse 21a
resumes the notice of this departure; 21b repeats the
opening words of ver. 17 to add that he crossed the
Euphrates; 21c states the direction of his flight. All
proceeds regularly and naturally. On the ground that
it would have been impossible to reach Gilead from Haran in seven days [1] (ver. 23), Dillmann infers that Laban's residence must, in E's account, have been much
nearer to Gilead than Haran, and that he must either
have meant some other river than the Euphrates in ver.
21, or else "he rose up and passed over the river" must
have been taken from J. To which Delitzsch replies that
Laban's home was in Haran, according to both J and E;
so that in any event this affords no argument for critical
partition. As to the accuracy of the statement the historian is responsible. It should not, however, be forgotten
that there is some indefiniteness in the localities. Laban
may have been with his sheep at some distance from
Haran (ver. 19); and the limits of Gilead are not clearly
defined.

That Laban's pursuit was successful is summarily
stated (ver. 23b). Then further details are given: Laban's dream before he came up with Jacob (ver. 24); Laban's overtaking Jacob, and the respective location of the
two parties (ver. 25). There is no doublet here any more

[1] In his first edition Dillmann did not seem to think this impossible,
but simply that it would require "very vigorous" marching.

than there is in the various instances of a like nature which have been reviewed before. Nor is ver. 27 a doublet of ver. 26. If the repetition of a thought so prominent in Laban's mind offends the critics, how is it that they can refer ver. 27, with its triple repetition, to a single writer?

According to Wellhausen vs. 10, 12 is an interpolation of uncertain origin. Dillmann, who deals largely in transpositions to accomplish critical ends or to relieve fancied difficulties, thinks that R took them from a narrative of E, which he had omitted in its proper place, and inserted them here rather inappropriately in this address of Jacob to his wives. What motive he could have had for such a piece of stupidity we are not informed. The genuineness of the verses is saved, but it is at the expense of R's good sense. It may be, however, that the writer thought these verses appropriate, whether the critics do or not.

There is no discrepancy between the revelation as recorded in ver. 3 and as subsequently related by Jacob (vs. 11–13). When a writer has occasion to speak of the same matter in different connections three courses are open to him. He may narrate it both times in all its details, he may narrate it fully in the first instance and refer to it more briefly afterward, or he may content himself with a brief statement at first and reserve the details until he recurs to it again. In the directions to build the tabernacle minute specifications are given (Ex. xxv. 10–ch. xxx.) ; in its actual construction all the details are stated afresh (xxxvi. 8–ch. xxxix.), the sacredness of the edifice making it essential to note the exactness with which the divine directions were carried into effect in every particular. Detailed directions are given for building the ark (Gen. vi. 14 sqq.), but in recording its construction the general statement is deemed suffi-

cient that Noah did as he was commanded (ver. 22).
Pharaoh's dreams, because of their importance in the
history, are twice narrated in full and almost identical
language (Gen. xli. 1–7, 17–24).   So the dream of Laban
(xxxi. 24, 29), the story of Abraham's servant (xxiv. 3
sqq., 37 sqq.), the fiats of creation (Gen. ch. i.).   But the
dreams of Joseph (xxxvii. 5 sqq.) and of Pharaoh's servants (xl. 5, 9 sqq.) are simply mentioned as facts and
the details reserved until they come to be narrated by
the dreamers.

In the instance at present before us instead of twice
recording the divine communication made to Jacob in all
its details, the writer simply states at first that Jehovah
directed Jacob to return to the land of his fathers (xxxi.
3), leaving a more minute account of the whole matter
to be introduced subsequently in a recital by Jacob.   It
is entirely appropriate in the connection that the revelation here made to Jacob should concern both his relation to Laban and his return to Canaan.   The only
seeming difficulty is created by the needless assumption
that things are combined in it which belong to different
periods of time; that what is said respecting the cattle
must belong to the early period of Laban's dealings with
Jacob,[1] while it is united in the same dream with the
command to return to Canaan.   The dream is retrospec-
tive and was intended to teach Jacob that while he had
been relying upon his own arts to increase his compensation, the true cause of his prosperity was to be found in
the favor of God.   And this shows why the arts of
Jacob are detailed in ch. xxx. without allusion to the di-

[1] עֵת יַחֵם הַצֹּאן (ver. 10) denotes a season of the year, the time of
copulation of flocks, and should be rendered "the time when flocks
conceive," as a usual thing, rather than "conceived," as though the
reference were to a definite event in the past.   It is as applicable,
therefore, to the last year of Jacob's abode with Laban as to any that
had preceded.

vine agency, the latter being alone insisted on in ch. xxxi.
It is not that these have proceeded from distinct writers
who had different conceptions of the transaction. It is
simply that the writer designed to lead his readers to the
true result by the same route through which Jacob himself passed, without any premature explanation.[1] Wellhausen alleges that the words of the divine angel must
have begun with the words "I am the God," etc. (ver.
13); but this is disposed of by a reference to Ex. iii. 4–
6. Dillmann remarks that E uses בָּרֹד *grisled* (xxxi. 10,
12), where J has טָלוּא *speckled* (xxx. 32, 33), which simply shows, not that there are two writers, in which case
the identical expressions in these verses could be less
easily accounted for, but that the writer was not aiming
at a nice precision in regard to terms so closely akin.
Dillmann also calls attention to the fact that in J (xxx.
35) עָקֹד *ring-streaked*, and נָקֹד *speckled*, are used interchangeably, while in E (xxxi. 8–10, 12) they are distinguished ; but that this is no ground for critical partition
is plain, since they are similarly distinguished in J (xxx.
39).

Verse 18 (except the first clause) is assigned to P. It

---

[1] Kuenen, Hexateuch, p. 235, remarks upon these passages : " Gen.
xxx. 28–43 and xxxi. 4–13 explain Jacob's great wealth by his own
cunning and by the care of Elohim respectively. The former is in perfect harmony with the uniform representation of Jacob's character.
Can the latter be anything but an ethico religious improvement upon
it ? For observe that the mutual agreement of the two passages forbids
us to regard them as independent, so that one must in any case be a
transformation of the other." Kuenen's conclusion that the E passage
is a later improvement upon that of J is in direct conflict with Dillmann's contention that E is the earlier document, from which J repeatedly borrows. The intimate mutual relation of the passages respectively assigned to J and E is confessed by both these critics.
Kuenen has here mistaken a later stage in Jacob's own understanding
of the secret of his success for a second and modified form of the transaction itself.

has the usual phrases of patriarchal removals (cf. xii. 5 ; xiii. 6 ; xxxvi. 6, 7 ; xlvi. 6). The resemblance between these verses is certainly such as to suggest their common origin ; and the critics refer them uniformly to P, but upon what ground it is difficult to see. It is at variance with the connection in every individual case; xii. 5, xiii. 6 are torn from a J context ; xxxi. 18, xlvi. 6 from an E context,[1] and the context of xxxvi. 6, 7, is disputed. The minute specification of particulars, alleged to be characteristic of P, is no greater than in xxxii. 6, 23 (E. V. vs. 5, 22) J, xxxiv. 28, 29 R, taken perhaps from E, xlv. 10 E or J. Of the words and phrases in these verses said to be indicative of P, not one is peculiar to him. "To go to his father" (ver. 18) links it with xxxv. 27 P indeed, but equally with xxviii. 31 E. No good reason can be given why these verses should not be reckoned an integral part of the context in which they are found. This is particularly so in this instance, in which the presence of E words [2] at the beginning makes it necessary to divide the sentence, leaving only an incomplete fragment for P, in which nevertheless one of these very words (מִקְנֶה) recurs, as it does also in a like connection, xxxvi. 6.

HIATUS IN THE DOCUMENT P

But accepting the partition on the sole dictum of the critics, the result is an enormous gap in P. He makes

---

[1] The supplement hypothesis, which identified E and P, had a basis here for the reference of these verses to the "Grundschrift," which the present critical hypothesis has not.

[2] מִקְנֶה cattle, is claimed for J or JE ; נָהַג carried away, which recurs in E, ver. 26, with explicit reference to this passage, and is found besides in the Hexateuch (except twice in Deut.), Ex. iii. 1. ; xiv. 25 E ; Ex. x. 13 J. If to avoid mutilating the sentence the whole verse is given to P, the argument from the JE use of these words elsewhere is confessed to be worthless.

no mention of Jacob's arrival in Paddan-aram, or of his
residence there, or anything that occurred during his stay
in that region, not even of his marriage, the one sole purpose for which he went, as the critics understand P, or
of the birth of his children, or of his accumulation of
property. There are only the disconnected and consequently unmeaning statements (xxix. 24, 29) that Laban
gave maids to his two daughters, and (xxx. 22) that God
remembered Rachel. But what either the daughters or
their maids had to do with the life of Jacob does not
appear. And now Jacob is returning with cattle and
property to which there has been no previous allusion,
and no suggestion of how they were obtained, but no
hint that he had a family.[1]   J and E supply what is lacking, though a marriage was no part of the purpose with
which, according to them, Jacob left his home. And
further, P at a later time (xxxv. 22b-26) recites the names
of Jacob's children in the order of their birth, and refers
them to their different mothers in exact accordance with
the detailed account in JE, which is thus presupposed.
What the critics sunder from P is thus an essential part
of his narrative. And it is necessary for them to resort
again to the assumption that P did write just such an
account as we find in J and E, but R has not preserved
it. Nevertheless R, who has here dropped P's entire
story at a most important epoch, that which laid the
foundation for the tribal division of Israel, and thus reduced his narrative to incoherent fragments, elsewhere
introduces clauses and sentences which in the judgment
of the critics are quite superfluous repetitions of what

---

[1] Nöldeke endeavored to account for this vast chasm in P by the
wholly gratuitous assumption that the narrative of P was inconsistent
with that of J and E, and R omitted it for that reason. The supplement hypothesis, which made E and P one document, here again escaped this incongruity.

had been more fully stated before, for the mere sake of preserving everything contained in his sources.[1]

But the strangest feature of P's account, as conceived by the critics, is thus clearly and succinctly stated by Dr. Harper : " The absence of the theological element is quite conspicuous : (1) The daily life of the patriarchs (with the exception of a few special and formal theophanies) is barren of all religious worship. (2) This is especially noticeable in the case of Jacob; he leaves home to seek for the wife who is to be the mother of Israel; he sojourns many years in the land from which Abram was by special command sent away ; he marries according to the instruction of his parents, and begets the children who are to become the tribes of Israel—still no sacrifice or offering is made to God for his providential care, not even a prayer is addressed to the Deity. (3) Nor does God, on his part, descend to take part or interest in human affairs ; He gives no encouragement to Jacob as he leaves home, nor does he send any word to him to return." [2]

This comes near enough to the " unthinkable " to be a refutation of that critical analysis which is responsible for such a result. P is the priestly narrator, to whom the ordinances of worship are supremely sacred, and they absorb his whole interest ; whose history of the patriarchs is only preliminary and subsidiary to the law regulating the services of the sanctuary. The patriarchs are to him the heroes and the models of Israel, whom, we are told, he is so intent upon glorifying that he reports none of their weaknesses, no strifes, no act of disingenuousness, no strange gods in their households, nothing

---

[1] *E.g.*, vii. 13–15, 17, 22, 23 ; viii. 2b, 3a ; xiii. 6 ; xix. 29, not to speak of the innumerable doublets which the critics fancy that they have discovered.

[2] Hebraica, v. 4, p. 276.

low or degrading. He singles out for prominent mention the sabbath (ii. 2, 3); the prohibition of eating blood (ix. 4); the ordinance of circumcision (xvii. 10 sqq.). God appears to Abraham and establishes his covenant with him and with his seed, with the express condition of his walking before him and being perfect, *i.e.*, whole-hearted in his service (xvii. 1 sqq.). And yet P's account of the patriarchs, as the critics furnish it to us, is almost absolutely denuded of any religious character. Is P really so absurd and self-contradictory, or have the critics made a mistake in their partition?

THE COVENANT OF LABAN AND JACOB

The account of the covenant between Laban and Jacob (vs. 44–54) is, in the opinion of the critics, a mass of doublets and glosses. There are two monuments, a pillar (ver. 45) and a heap of stones (ver. 46); two covenant meals (vs. 46b, 54); two names with their respective etymologies (vs. 48, 49); two (or rather three) appeals to God to watch, witness, and judge between them (vs. 49, 50, 53); and the substance of the contract is stated twice, and in different terms (vs. 50, 52). The symmetry of this statement is somewhat spoiled by the triplicity of one of the items. But the passage would seem to afford ample scope for critical acumen. There has, however, been great divergence in the results that have been reached, and no partition that has been devised has proved generally satisfactory.[1] Dillmann, who in the

[1] Astruc, followed by Schrader, gives vs. 48–50 to the Jehovist, and the remainder to the Elohist. Eichhorn, and after him Tuch, limits the Jehovist to ver. 49. Ilgen gives the whole passage to the second Elohist, except vs. 48, 49, which he throws out of the text as a later gloss, and makes several transpositions in order to obtain what he considers a more suitable arrangement.

Other critics divide as follows : Knobel (Commentary): Ancient

main here adopts the division of Wellhausen, assigns vs.
46, 48–50 to J, who accordingly tells of the heap of
stones in pledge that Jacob would treat his wives as he
should, with some dislocations, to be sure, which Dillmann corrects as usual by the necessary transpositions ;
the covenant meal (ver. 46b), and the naming of the heap
(ver. 48b), ought in his opinion to come after the engagement (ver. 50). Of course R is charged with having removed these clauses from their proper place, and no
very good reason is given for his having done so. E (vs.
45, 47, 51–54) records the erection of a pillar as a boundary between the Hebrews on the one side and the Aramæans on the other.

But Delitzsch mars this arrangement by calling attention to Jehovah in ver. 49, and Elohim in ver. 50, showing that both J and E related Jacob's pledge in relation
to his wives ; also to the triple combination of the heap
and the pillar in vs. 51, 52, showing that J and E also
united in fixing the boundary between Laban and Jacob.
So that it appears after all that there were not two covenants, but two stipulations in the same covenant. Dillmann is further constrained to confess that E speaks of a

Source, vs. 45, 46, 48–50, 53b. J, vs. 47, 51, 52, 53a. (Appendix):
First Source, vs. 44, 48–50, 53, 54. Second Source, vs. 45–47, 51, 52.

Hupfeld : E, vs. 46b, 48a, 50. J, vs. 45, 46a, 47, 51–54, 48b, 49.

Boehmer : E, vs 44, 46, 47, 51, 52 (expunging the '' pillar '' twice),
53b, 54a. J, vs. 45, 48 (And Laban said), 53a, 54b. R, vs. 48 (after
the opening words), 49, 50.

Kittel : E, vs. 45 (substitute '' Laban '' for '' Jacob ''), 46, 48a, 50, 53,
54. J, vs. 51, 52 (expunge the '' pillar '' twice). R, vs. 48b, 49.

Vatke : E, vs. 45, 47, 48a, 50, 54. J, vs. 46, 48b, 49, 51–53.

Delitzsch : E, vs. 45, 47, 50, 53b, 54. J, vs. 46, 48, 49. JE, inex-
tricably combined, vs. 51–53a. R, in ver. 49, the words, '' And Mizpah ; for.''

Kayser gives up the partition as impracticable, and says, '' The separation of the two elements cannot be effected without tearing asunder
the well-ordered connection.''

גַּל "heap" as well as a "pillar" in ver. 52, inasmuch as
ver. 47b is on critical principles a doublet of ver. 48b,
and E as well as J located this scene in Mt. Gilead, and
was concerned to find an allusion to its name in the
transaction. He clogs his admission with the assertion
that E uses גַּל in a different sense from J, meaning a
mountain ridge and not a heap thrown up by hand. But
after all the critical erasures made for the purpose this
is still unproved. He has merely demonstrated his desire to create a variance which does not exist. And ver.
47, which he assigns to E, is indissolubly linked to ver.
48 J.

We thus have good critical authority for saying that
one and the same writer has spoken of both the monuments and of both the contracts, involving, of course, the
double appeal to God to watch over their fulfilment.
And from this there is no escape but by the critical
knife, of which Wellhausen makes free use here, as he
never fails to do in an extremity. Verse 47 [1] is thrown
out of the text as a piece of "superfluous learning;" but
Dillmann replies that E calls Laban "the Aramæan"
(vs. 20, 24), that he likewise speaks of the "heap," in
ver. 52, and may have given an explanation of the name
"Gilead;" [2] and that the location of the place on the

---

[1] Tuch, on the contrary, finds in the Aramæan name in this verse an
apt parallel to the Aramæan פַּדַּן אֲרָם (for which Hosea xii. 13 (E. V.
ver. 12) substitutes the Hebrew equivalent שְׂדֵה אֲרָם), and he refers
both alike to the same writer.

[2] It is alleged that a false explanation is given (ver. 48) of the name
"Gilead," which means hard or rough, not "heap of witness." It is
not necessary, however, to suppose that it was the intention of the sacred writer to affirm that Gilead derived its name from the transaction
here recorded. It bears that name in his narrative before this transaction took place (vs. 21, 23, 25). His meaning rather is that the name
which it had long borne was particularly appropriate by reason of this
new association, which was naturally suggested by its sound to a Hebrew ear (cf. xxvii. 36).

boundary between the Aramæans and the Hebrews may account for the twofold denomination. "Jehovah watch between me and thee when we are absent one from another" (ver. 49), is also expunged; and "Mizpah," at the beginning of the verse, which is a clear voucher for the genuineness of the doomed clause, and a name which the historian was at pains to link with this transaction, as well as Gilead and Mahanaim (xxxii. 3, E. V., ver. 2), is by a stroke of the pen converted into *Mazzebah*, and then ejected from the text. "No man is with us; see, Elohim is witness betwixt me and thee" (ver. 50), is in like manner declared to be an insertion by the redactor, on the ground that it conflicts with ver. 48, which makes the heap the witness; but, as Delitzsch observes, there is obviously no collision between these statements. "This heap" with its adjuncts is twice erased (vs. 51, 52a), and "this pillar" (ver. 52b), so as to read, "Behold, the pillar, which I have set, is a witness betwixt me and thee, that I will not pass over this wall (not a heap newly cast up, but a boundary of long standing) to thee, and that thou shalt not pass over this wall unto me." With the text thus cleared of obstructions, and altered to suit his purpose, he has a comparatively clear course.

It is obvious to observe further that the two covenant meals are a fiction. Upon the erection of the heap preliminary mention is made (ver. 46) of the feast held beside it, which is then recorded more fully, after other details have been given, in ver. 54. We have already met repeated examples of the same kind. Delitzsch refers to such parallels as xxvii. 23; xxviii. 5. Dillmann himself said (in his first edition) of the eating together in ver. 46: "This was the covenant meal, which is related ver. 54. It is here only referred to proleptically (as ii. 8 and 15; xxiv. 29, 30), and it is not necessary, therefore, to assign the verse to a different author from vs. 53, 54, especially as 'his brethren' corresponds with vs. 32, 37."

With the doublets thus disposed of, the analysis, which has no further basis, collapses entirely. The carping objection that acts in which both participated are (vs. 45, 46) attributed to Jacob, and (ver. 51), claimed by Laban, gives no aid nor comfort to the critics, for the discrepancy, such as it is, is between contiguous verses of the same document. Wellhausen on this ground eliminates "Jacob" from the text of vs. 45, 46, and substitutes "Laban." Dillmann (in his first edition) quoted with approval Knobel's statement, "It is self-evident that all this was done in common by both the leaders and their adherents;" and again, on ver. 51, "Laban, as the one who proposed the covenant, rightly prescribes to Jacob the words to be sworn, and attributes to himself, as the originator of it (ver. 44), the erection of the two witnesses." The suspicion cast upon "the God (or gods) of their father" (ver. 53), because the verb is interposed between it and "the God of Nahor," with which it is in apposition, is a pure question of textual criticism without further consequences. Here again Dillmann comes to the rescue in his first edition. "The God of Abraham and the God of Nahor are then both designated by the apposition 'the gods of their father,' as once worshipped by Terah, as if Terah's two sons had divided in the worship of the gods of Terah."

THE DIVINE NAMES

The divine names are used discriminatingly throughout. It was Jehovah (ver. 3) who bade Jacob return to the land of his fathers; but in repeating this to his wives, who were but partially reclaimed from idolatry (xxx. 11; xxxi. 34; xxxv. 2, 4), he constantly uses Elohim (xxxi. 4–

13) (once, more definitely, the God of my father, ver. 5),
as they also do in reply (ver. 16). In like manner it is
Elohim, who speaks to Laban the Aramæan (ver. 24),
and of whom Jacob speaks to Laban (ver. 42), though
both of them recognize his identity with the God of Abraham and of Isaac (vs. 29, 42). When they covenant, appeal is made both to Jehovah and to Elohim (vs. 49, 50)
as the God of Abraham and the God of Nahor (ver. 53).
Jacob swears by the Fear of his father Isaac (ver. 53),
the Being whom his father reverently worshipped, and
whose gracious care he had himself experienced (ver. 42).
In xxxii. 2, 3 (E. V., vs. 1, 2), "angels of Elohim," "the
host of Elohim," are so called in distinction from messengers of men and armies under human command; it
is a detachment divinely sent to welcome and escort
him as he returns to the holy land.

MARKS OF P (VER. 18)

1. רְכֻשׁ substance, and רָכַשׁ to gather. See ch. xii. 5,
Marks of P, No. 2.

2. קִנְיָן getting; besides in the Hexateuch, xxxiv. 23;
Josh. xiv. 4 P; Lev. xxii. 11, which, according to Wellhausen, is not in P; and Gen. xxxvi. 6, which is cut out
of a disputed context and given to P.

3. *Paddan-aram.* See ch. xxv. 19-34, Marks of P,
No. 4.

4. אֶרֶץ כְּנַעַן *land of Canaan.* See ch. xii. 5, Marks of
P, No. 4.

5. The diffuseness; but this is no greater than in vs.
1, 3 J, and vs. 26, 27, 43 E. See ch. xvii., Marks of P,
No. 5.

MARKS OF E

1. The back reference (ver. 13) to xxviii. 20 sqq., which
is readily admitted.

2. The revelations in dreams (vs. 10. 11, 24). See ch. xx., Marks of E, No. 4.

3. *Teraphim* (vs. 19, 34, 35); nowhere else in the Hexateuch.

4. *Laban, the Aramœan.* See ch. xxv. 19–34, Marks of P, No. 5.

5. אָמָה *maid-servant* (ver. 33); here used rather than שִׁפְחָה, because they are spoken of not as bondmaids, but as wives of Jacob. See ch. xx., Marks of E, No. 1.

6. לֵבָב *heart* (ver. 26). See ch. xx., Marks of E, No. 2.

7. כֹּה *here* (ver. 37). See ch. xxii. 1–19, Marks of E, No. 5.

8. פָּגַע *met* (xxxii. 2, E. V., ver. 1). See ch. xxviii. 10–22, Marks of E, No. 3.

9. פַּחַד יִצְחָק *the Fear of Isaac* (xxxi. 42, 53); nowhere else; and even פַּחַד besides, in the Hexateuch, only in Deut. and Ex. xv. 16, a passage supposed to have been borrowed from an older document, but not written by E.

10. מֹנִים *times* (xxxi. 7, 41); nowhere else.

תְּמוֹל שִׁלְשׁוֹם *before time* (xxxi. 2, 5), is reckoned an E phrase; it occurs besides, Ex. v. 7, 8, 14; xxi. 29, 36 E; but also Ex. iv. 10 J; Josh. xx. 5 P. עָשֹׂו (ver. 28), a like form of the infinitive, occurs xlviii. 11; l. 20; Ex. xviii. 18 E; but also Gen. xxvi. 28; Ex. xxxii. 6 J. חִפֵּשׂ *search* (ver. 35); only besides in the Hexateuch xliv. 12 J. יְחַר בְּעֵינֵי *burn in the eyes of, be displeasing to* (ver. 35), besides in xlv. 5, where it is included between two J expressions in the same clause. וַיִּחַר לְ *was wroth* (ver. 36), as iv. 5 J. The use of לָקַח by E (vs. 45, 46) resembles what Dillmann affirms to be characteristic of P, xii. 5, and elsewhere. The various words and phrases alleged as marks of E, in this section as elsewhere, are for the most part either limited to a single passage, or are also found in J. Consequently they do not in fact supply any argument for a document E distinct from J.

It may further be noted that by the confession of the critics the same writer may use different terms to express the same thought. Thus ver. 2 speaks of the countenance of Laban being *with* Jacob, but ver. 5 of its being *toward* him; to "set up" (a pillar) is, in ver. 45, הֵרִים, but in xxviii. 18, 22, שִׂים, and in xxxv. 20, הִצִּיב; and "collecting stones" is expressed differently in successive clauses of ver. 46. Yet all these forms of expression are attributed alike to E.

MEETING OF JACOB AND ESAU (CH. XXXII. 4[1]-XXXIII. 17)

Hupfeld is commonly acute enough in detecting grounds of division, but here for once he is completely at fault. This entire section seemed to him[2] to bear the most conclusive marks of unity in language, in the continuity of the narrative, and in the close connection of the several parts, which mutually presuppose and are indispensable to each other. The interchange of divine names, Jehovah (xxxii. 10) and Elohim, gives him no trouble, since the latter occurs only where, according to general Hebrew usage, "Jehovah would not be appropriate" (xxxii. 29, 31 ; xxxiii. 10), or "Elohim is preferable" (xxxiii. 5, 11). He accordingly attributed the whole of this section to J. Schrader, on the contrary, assigns it all to E, with the exception of vs. 10–13 J, and ver. 33, about which he is in doubt whether it belongs to J or is a later gloss. In his first edition Dillmann re-

---

[1] The last verse of ch. xxxi. in the English version is the first verse of ch. xxxii. in the Hebrew, and the consequent difference in numeration is continued through ch. xxxii. The numbers given in the text are those of the Hebrew, from which one must be deducted for the corresponding verse in the English Bible.

[2] *Quellen*, p. 45.

ferred xxxii. 8–13 to J, and vs. 23–32 to E, while the
remainder (xxxii. 4–7, 14–22 ; xxxiii. 1–16) contained
so many indications of both E and J that he felt obliged
to assume that J had taken the substance of it from E,
and remodelled it after his own fashion. Such mingled
texts, in which are confusedly blended what the critics
regard as the characteristics of different documents,
simply show how mistaken is every attempt to apportion
among distinct writers expressions which are thus seen
to flow freely from the same pen.

Wellhausen admits that this whole section is closely
connected throughout, and that it gives the impression
of having been drawn from but a single source. " One
will surely wonder," he adds, " at the idle acuteness
which nevertheless succeeds here in sundering J and E."
He has discovered a doublet, which had previously escaped all eyes, and by its aid he undertakes to rend the
passage in twain. Verse 14a is repeated ver. 22b. He
infers that vs. 14b–22a only carries the narrative to the
point already reached by vs. 4–13 ; and that consequently these two paragraphs are not consecutive as
they appear to be, and as the nature of their contents
would seem to imply, but are parallel accounts of the
same transaction, drawn respectively from J and E. In
his first edition Dillmann was so far from agreeing with
this position as to maintain that the night spoken of in
ver. 22 is not the same as that in ver. 14, but is the next
ensuing. In subsequent editions, however, he follows,
as he has unfortunately so often done, in the wake of
Wellhausen, as though the latter had made a veritable
discovery. But even though the night is the same, the
paragraphs, which these verses respectively conclude, are
plainly not identical in their contents, nor can they by
possibility be variant accounts of the same transaction.

Jacob had taken the precaution to notify Esau of his

return, and was informed that Esau was on his way to
meet him with four hundred men (vs. 4–7). He was in
consequence greatly alarmed, not, as Tuch imagined, by
the vague apprehension of what a horde of robber Bed-
ouins might possibly do. This notion was advocated
by him in the interest of the supplement hypothesis,
which admitted but one Elohist, and supposed that he
knew nothing of any strife between the brothers. But it
is quite inadmissible in the present form of the divisive
hypothesis, according to which E and J alike record
Jacob's fraud in obtaining his father's blessing, and
Esau's murderous wrath in consequence. Jacob well
knew that he had an enraged brother to deal with, and
he feared the worst. He shaped his measures accordingly. He first divides his flocks and herds, together
with his retinue, into two separate companies, that if one
should be attacked the other might escape (vs. 8, 9).
He then makes his earnest appeal to Jehovah, the God
of his fathers, who had bidden him return, acknowledging his unworthiness of past mercies, pleading the
promises divinely made to him, and praying for deliverance from this impending peril (vs. 10–13). Upon this
he selects a valuable present of goats and sheep and
camels and asses, and sends them forward in successive
droves to placate Esau [1] and announce his own coming
(vs. 14–22). These are evidently distinct measures,
wisely planned to avert the danger which he had so
much reason to apprehend.

The repeated mention of the night, then coming on,
which was the most eventful in Jacob's life, upon which

---

[1] The assertion that there are two variant conceptions of the present
to Esau, that in ver. 14 E it is simply a token of respect, while in ver.
21b (which Dillmann cuts out of its connection and assigns to J) it is designed to appease Esau's anger, is at variance with the uniform tenor of
the entire passage.

so much depended, and in which so much was done, is by no means surprising. Preliminary mention is made (ver. 14) of Jacob's lodging that night himself, while he sent forward the present to his brother, which is then described in detail with the accompanying arrangements (vs. 14b–22a). At the close of this description the narrative, thus interrupted, is once more resumed by repeating the statement that Jacob "lodged that night in the company" (ver. 22b). This clause, as Dillmann correctly remarked in his first edition, is a "connecting link" with the following account of what further took place that same night, which was so momentous a crisis not only in respect to the peril encountered, but as the turning-point in the spiritual history and character of Jacob. The repetition of this clause tends in no way to create the suspicion that the narrative is a composite one; on the contrary, it proceeds by regular and closely related steps, every one of which has a direct and manifest bearing upon the final issue.

An additional evidence of duplication is sought in the double allusion to the name Mahanaim, which, we are told, E and J understand and explain differently. Only it is unfortunate for the effect of this argument that Wellhausen and Dillmann cannot agree how E did understand it. They are clear, however, that J regarded it as a dual, and meant to explain it by the "two companies," or camps, into which Jacob divided his train (vs. 8, 9, 11); whereupon, they tell us, he must have added, "Therefore the place was called Mahanaim." R prudently omitted this statement because of its conflict with ver. 3, where the origin of the name is accounted for in another way. But such a mention of the name of the place by J is thought to be implied in ver. 14a, "he lodged *there*." Undoubtedly "there" refers to a place before spoken of, either one actually found in the text

(xxxii. 3 E, the wrong document for the critics), or one that they tell us ought to be there, though it is not. About E's view of the matter there is not the same agreement. Wellhausen alleges that he took Mahanaim for a singular, and was correct in so doing, *aim* being a modified form of the local ending *am*, and hence in ver. 22 he writes it as a singular, Mahane, the name being suggested by his meeting a host of angels. Dillmann regards it as a dual in E also, suggested by the two companies or camps, that of the angels and that of Jacob. But however this question may be settled, different allusions to the signification of the name Mahanaim in the same connection are not an indication of distinct writers, as we have already seen repeatedly in other instances. It is further said that ver. 22 speaks of Jacob's company as a unit; the writer knows nothing of its division into two companies as in vs. 8, 9. But in precisely the same way Esau speaks (xxxiii. 8) of the five successive droves which he had met, being the present which Jacob designed for him (xxxii. 14–17) as a single company.

Further, according to the division of the critics, E (ver. 18) presupposes the coming of Esau announced in J (ver. 7), and all the arrangements made in E imply apprehensions which are only stated in J (vs. 8, 9). They are in fact so interwoven that they cannot be separated. And Dillmann finds it necessary to assume that vs. 4–7 are preliminary alike to E and J, though his only ground for suspecting their composite character is the twofold designation of the region (ver. 4) as "the land of Seir, the field of Edom." Certainly no one but a critic intent on doublets could have suspected one here. Mount Seir had been spoken of (xiv. 6) as the country of the Horites. Esau had now taken up his quarters, provisionally at least, in what was to be his future abode and that of his descendants. This is here intimated by calling Seir by anticipation " the field of Edom."

But Dillmann has found another doublet, which even Wellhausen had failed to see ; ver. 23 is J's, and ver. 24 E's account of crossing the Jabbok. In the former Jacob crosses with his family ; in the latter he sends his family before him and himself remains behind. And this is paraded as a variance, requiring two distinct writers. Is it not as plain as day that ver. 23 is a general statement of the fact that they all alike crossed the stream, while in ver. 24 it is stated more particularly that he first sent over his family, and then his goods, and that a very remarkable incident occurred to himself after he was thus left alone ? Dillmann himself so explained it in his first edition, his only doubt being whether Jacob crossed with the rest to the south bank of the Jabbok, and was there left behind while they moved on, or whether he continued for a while on the north bank after all had been sent over. The latter is the common opinion, though the former might be consistent with the language used. As Penuel has not been identified, it may be uncertain on which side of the stream the mysterious conflict described in the following verses took place.

JACOB'S WRESTLING WITH THE ANGEL

Here again the critics diverge. Are vs. 24–33 by J, the author of xxxii. 4–14a and xxxiii. 1–17? or by E, the author of xxxii. 14b–22 ? Wellhausen says J most decidedly ; Kuenen and Driver agree with him ; Dillmann says E with equal positiveness. Other critics follow their liking one way or the other. There is a conflict of criteria. The literary tests point one way, the matter of the passage the other. Thus Wellhausen : " The whole character of the narrative points to J. E, who has God appear in dreams, and call from heaven, and then, too, sometimes introduces the angel or angels as a medium, cannot have related such a corporeal theophany; on the other hand we are reminded of xv. 17 seq., and of ch. xviii., xix. J." Kuenen ("Hexateuch," p. 250) claims on the same ground that " it falls in far better with J's than with E's tone of thought." Dillmann points to Elohim (vs. 29, 31) as decisive for E, and claims that " Wellhausen's opposing grounds prove nothing or rest on bare postulates." Delitzsch says, " The name Elohim is by itself alone no decisive criterion against J," thus dislodging the very foundation-stone of the divisive hypothesis, and adds, "The answer to the question whether J or E is the narrator remains uncertain and purely subjective."

The readiness with which the critics can upon occasion set aside their own tests, whether derived from the matter or the literary form, tends to confirm the belief that they are of a precarious nature generally, and that the verdict of Delitzsch as to the subjective character of critical conclusions is applicable to other instances besides the present. Dr. Harper uses the following language in relation to this and the preceding chapters : [1] " The individual variations of critics, touching this section (xxviii. 10–xxxiii. 17), many and arbitrary as they may be, are due to special considerations. They are unanimous as to the existence of an analysis. This section, it is universally admitted, is very unsatisfactory; the duplicates and differences relate wholly to details, not to general narratives, while the omissions are many and important. If it were necessary to rely wholly on this section, no critic would claim an analysis." All critical differences are thus sunk in one grand consensus. "They are unanimous as to the existence of an analysis," whether they can agree upon any particular analysis or

[1] Hebraica, V. iv., p. 284.

not. And we have had abundant exemplification of the fact that where there is a determination to effect the partition of a passage, notwithstanding the clearest evidences of its unity, it can always be done with reason or without it.

In his first edition Dillmann ventured the suggestion that " in E this narrative (of Jacob's wrestling with the angel) did not necessarily stand in any intimate connection with the meeting of the two brothers ; and at all events its peculiar significance as preparatory to the meeting with Esau, and as supplementary to the prayer (vs. 10–13), was first acquired by its being fitted into its present place by R." By thus isolating the passage from the connection, from which its whole significance is derived, in a manner better suited to the fragment than the document hypothesis, it is easy to pervert its whole meaning and character, as though it stood on a level with the stories of heathen mythology, just as the same thing is done with vi. 1–4, by sundering it from all that goes before and that comes after. In subsequent editions Dillmann regards the wrestling with the angel as parallel to the prayer (vs. 10–13), only he apportions them to different documents, and thus impairs the unity of the narrative.

Jacob has hitherto been relying upon his own strength and skill, and has sought success by artifices of his own. He is now taught that his own strength is of no avail in wrestling with God. Disabled by the touch of his divine antagonist he is obliged to resort to importunate petition for the blessing which he craved, and which he could not do without.

The verb "abak," *wrestled* (vs. 25, 26), which occurs nowhere else, is here used with allusion to the name of the stream, Jabbok, on the bank of which it occurred, without, however, implying that it received this name from this occurrence. The double allusion to the significance of the name Penuel (xxxii. 31; xxxiii. 10 [1]) is adduced as evidencing two distinct documents, which it manifestly does not.

NO PROOF OF A PARALLEL NARRATIVE

While xxxiii. 1–17 is referred to J, Dillmann seeks to show that E must have had a similar account by pointing out what he considers indications of fragments from E, which have been inserted by R, viz., Elohim, which occurs inconveniently in a J paragraph (vs. 5, 11) (but not ver. 10, where he says Jehovah could not be used), the repetition (ver. 11) of the request (ver. 10) that Esau would accept the present offered him (which simply indicates Jacob's urgency), and ver. 4, where "fell on his neck" follows "embraced him," whereas the reverse would be the natural order (the same hypercritical argument might be applied to Acts v. 30, "whom ye slew and hanged on a tree"). It can scarcely be said that such proofs are of even the slightest weight.

THE DIVINE NAMES

The divine names are appropriately used. Jacob addresses his prayer to Jehovah (xxxii. 10). Elohim occurs (xxxii. 29, 31; xxxiii. 10) because of the contrast with men, expressed or implied, and xxxiii. 5, 11, because the reference is to the providential benefits of the Most High, as well as for the additional reason that Esau is addressed, who is outside of the line of the covenant.

[1] The absurdities to which critical partition, aided by a lively imagination, can lead is well illustrated by Wellhausen's discovery, based on these verses, that "the God in J, who meets Jacob in Penuel, is Esau in E," an identification which he thinks of some importance in the history of religion, as adding another to the list of deities.

MARKS OF J

1. The back reference in xxxii. 10 to xxviii. 13; xxxi. 3; and in ver. 13 to xxviii. 14, the expressions being in part conformed to xxii. 17 (of which by the hypothesis J could know nothing), xvi. 10. This is not only readily conceded, but affirmed.

2. עָשָׂה חֶסֶד וֶאֱמֶת *show mercy and truth* (xxxii. 11). See ch. xviii., xix., Marks of J, No. 29, ch. xxiv., Marks of J, No. 6.

3. שִׁפְחָה *bondmaid* (xxxii. 6), where this is the only proper word; and xxxiii. 1, 2, 6, where the reference is to Zilpah and Bilhah, and either שִׁפְחָה or אָמָה would be appropriate. See ch. xxi. 1–21, Marks of E, No. 11, ch. xxix., xxx., Marks of J, No. 4.

4. רוּץ לִקְרַאת *run to meet* (xxxiii. 4). See ch. xxix., xxx., Marks of J, No. 2.

5. חָצָה *divided* (xxxiii. 1; xxxii. 8); nowhere else in J; it occurs besides in the Hexateuch only, Ex. xxii. 35 bis E; Num. xxxi. 27, 42 a later stratum of P.

6. אִם־נָא מָצָאתִי חֵן בְּעֵינֶי *if now I have found favor in the sight of* (xxxii. 6; xxxiii. 8, 10). See ch. xii. 10–20, Marks of J, No. 3; ch. vi. 1–8, Marks of J, No. 10.

No words or expressions are claimed for E in this section. Alleged doublets and variant conceptions are the only indications of this document here adduced, and these have all been considered above. יֶלֶד *child,* which is claimed as an E word in xxi. 1–21 (see Marks of E, No. 6) occurs here, xxxii., 23; xxxiii. 1, 2, 5, 6, 7, 13, 14, all which are referred to J. This word is used throughout this narrative because the children were quite young, only from six to thirteen years of age.

THE RAPE OF DINAH (CH. XXXIII. 18–XXXIV.)

This passage is a fresh puzzle for the critics, which they labor to resolve in various ways, and hence there is no little divergence among them. The difficulty here is not the chronic one of disentangling J and E, but of releasing P from the meshes in which it is involved. It is a notable refutation of the common assertion that whatever difficulty may attend the separation of J and E, it is always easy to distinguish P from them both. And it is a clear illustration of the fact that, wherever part of a narrative is conceded to P it is interlocked with the other documents as closely as they are with one another. This passage is so linked with what precedes and follows in the history, there are so many references to other passages in it and from other passages to it, it is so allied by forms of expression and ideas contained in it to passages elsewhere, and all this runs counter in so many ways to the prepossessions and conclusions of the critics, as to form a veritable labyrinth through which it requires all their adroitness to thread their way.

The name of God occurs but once in the entire passage (xxxiii. 20), so that all pretext is cut off for division on that ground. "El-Elohe-Israel," the Mighty God, the God of Israel, to whom Jacob dedicates the altar, is the distinctive name of him whom he adores. The God of Abraham and of Isaac has been with him, and kept him, and provided for him, and brought him back to the land of his fathers in peace, and has thus shown himself to be the God of Jacob (xxviii. 13, 15, 20, 21) ; or adopting the new name, indicative of the changed character of the patriarch (xxxii. 29), he is the God of Israel.

JACOB'S ARRIVAL IN SHECHEM

Ch. xxxiii. 18–20 completes an important stage of Jacob's journey, begun xxxi. 17, and continued ch. xxxv., while it is immediately preliminary to the incident recorded in ch. xxxiv. The simple statements contained in these verses, naturally as they belong together, give no small trouble to the critics, who are obliged to parcel them among the different documents.

"And Jacob came in peace to the city of Shechem, which is in the *land of Canaan*, when he came from *Paddan-aram*" (ver. 18a), is given to P because of the italicized expressions; and yet it explicitly alludes to Jacob's vow (xxviii. 21 E), whose condition is declared to have been fulfilled, and hence (xxxv. 1 E) the performance of what he then stipulated is demanded. There is no escape from this manifest reference in one document to the contents of another but by striking "in peace" out of the text. Again, P here records the termination of an expedition on which he had laid great stress at Jacob's setting out (xxviii. 1–5), but all between these limits is almost an absolute blank. P has not said one word to indicate whether Jacob had accomplished the purpose for which he went to Paddan-aram. Still further, Jacob's route, it is said, is purposely laid through the holy places, Shechem and Bethel (xxxv. 6, 15). The fact is just the reverse of what is alleged. The hallowing of certain localities in later times did not give rise to the stories of their having been visited by patriarchs and being the scene of divine manifestations. But their association with the history of the patriarchs imparted a sacredness, which led to their selection as places of idolatrous worship. Admitting, however, the explanation of the critics, why should P and J (see also

xii. 6, 8), who belonged to Judah, be concerned to put
honor on the schismatical sanctuaries of northern Israel ?

" Shechem, which is in the land of Canaan ; " the relative clause is not a needless expletive, due to P's customary verbosity. It emphasizes the fact that Jacob has
now at length reached the holy land, from which he had
been so long absent. And " Luz, which is in the land of
Canaan " (xxxv. 6), has the same significance ; the implied contrast is not with another Luz, but with another
land in which Jacob had been ever since he was at Luz
before.

Verse 19 is repeated in Josh. xxiv. 32, which records the
burial of the bones of Joseph in the plot of ground here
purchased, and by critical rules is assigned to E, who as
a North-Israelite would be interested in this event as P
and J would not. Jacob's ownership of land near Shechem is confirmed by his flocks subsequently feeding
there (xxxvii. 12 in J, who thus seems to be aware of a
fact only stated in E). This peaceable purchase, however, is alleged by Kuenen and others to be at variance
with the violent seizure related xxxiv. 25–27, as though
this were a conflicting account from another source of the
way in which Jacob came into the possession of property
in that quarter. And yet ver. 19 is plainly preparatory
for ch. xxxiv. Hamor is called " Shechem's father " for
no other reason than to introduce the reader to the prominent actor in the narrative that follows (xxxiv. 2) ; this
can only be evaded by pronouncing " Shechem's father "
a spurious addition by R. E, too (xlviii. 22), refers to a
conquest by force of arms, which must have been additional to the purchase ; a conclusion which Wellhausen
seeks to escape by giving ver. 19 to J (Judæan though he
is), and ascribing xxxiv. 27 not to J, but to some unknown
source. Jacob's purchase recalls that of Abraham (ch.

xxiii. P), and is based on the same principle of acquiring
a permanent and a legal right to a property in the holy
land. There is certainly as good reason to claim that
they are by the same author as the critics are able to
advance in many instances in which they assume identity of authorship as undoubted.

" El - Elohe - Israel " (ver. 20) clearly refers back to
xxxii. 29, the change of the patriarch's name, thus
clinching Dillmann's conclusion that the wrestling on
the banks of the Jabbok must on critical grounds be assigned to E, whose anthropomorphism here equals that
of J. But this name (xxxiii. 20), which points to E, is
linked with the erection of an altar, which is commonly
distinctive of J (xii. 7, 8, etc.). E for the most part sets
up pillars instead (xxviii. 18 ; xxxv. 14, 20). The text
must accordingly be adjusted to the hypothesis. The
only question about which there is a difference of opinion is, shall " altar " be erased and " pillar " substituted ?
Or shall R be supposed to have had two texts before
him, " built an altar " (J), and " set up a pillar " (E),
which he has mixed by taking the verb from E and the
noun from J.

Dillmann suspects that ver. 18b is from J, because of
וַיִּחַן encamped, which occurs but once besides in Genesis
(xxvi. 17 J), though in subsequent books repeatedly
both in P and E, and אֶת־פְּנֵי before (xix. 13, 27 ; Ex.
xxxiv. 23, 24 J ; but also Lev. iv. 6, 17; x. 4 P ; and
Gen. xxvii. 30 ; Ex. x. 11 E). If J relates what occurred at Shechem (ch. xxxiv.), it is certainly to be expected that he would mention Jacob's arrival there ;
hence the eagerness of the critics to find some indications of J in these verses. So that P, J, E, and R are
all represented in fragments of these three verses ; and
one scarcely knows which to admire most, the ingenuity
of a redactor who could construct a continuous narra-

tive in this piecemeal fashion, or that of the modern
critic who can unravel such a tangled web.

The stress laid upon circumcision in ch. xxxiv. by the
sons of Jacob, recalls its institution in the family of
Abraham (ch. xvii.), and the transactions in the public
meeting of citizens resemble those in ch. xxiii., and there
is a striking similarity of expressions in these chapters ;
e.g.: הִמּוֹל לָכֶם כָּל־זָכָר *every male of you be circumcised*
(vs. 15, 22 ; cf. the identical expression, xvii. 10, 12) ;
כָּל־זָכָר *every male* (vs. 24, 25 ; cf. xvii. 23) ; עָרְלָה *foreskin,
uncircumcised* (ver. 14 ; cf. xvii. 11, 14, 23 sqq.) ; נָשִׂיא
prince (ver. 2 ; cf. xvii. 20 ; xxiii. 6) ; הֵאָחֲזוּ *get you possessions* (ver. 10) ; cf. אֲחֻזָּה *possession* (xvii. 8 ; xxiii. 4, 9,
20) ; סָחַר *trade* (vs. 10, 21), cf. סֹחֵר *trader* (xxiii. 16) ;
כָּל־יֹצְאֵי שַׁעַר עִירוֹ *all that went out of the gate of his city*
(ver. 24 bis), cf. כֹּל בָּאֵי שַׁעַר עִירוֹ *all that went in at the
gate of his city* (xxiii. 10, 18) ; טִמֵּא *defile* (vs. 5, 13, 27) is
a technical term of the ritual law, and is found nowhere
else in the Pentateuch. Knobel adds, as characteristic
of P from the critical stand-point : בְּנוֹת הָאָרֶץ *daughters
of the land* (ver. 1) ; שָׁמַע אֶל־ *hearken unto* (vs. 17, 24) ;
קִנְיָן *substance ;* בְּהֵמָה *beast* (ver. 23). Dillmann further
adds אַךְ *only* (vs. 15, 22, 23).

All this points to P as the author of the chapter. But
according to the current critical analysis P knows nothing of the various characters here introduced, nor of the
chain of events with which this narrative is concatenated ; and in fact the narrative itself is altogether out of
harmony with the spirit and tone of this document as
the critics conceive it. It is E (xxx. 21) that records
the birth of Dinah,[1] evidently with a view to what is

---

[1] Von Bohlen imagines a chronological contradiction between xxx. 21
and ch. xxxiv. He calculates that Dinah could be " scarcely six or

here related of her; just as xxix. 24, 29 is preparatory
for xxx. 4, 9; xxii. 23 for xxiv. 15 sqq.; xix. 15 for vs. 30
sqq. Otherwise it would not have been mentioned (cf.
xxxii. 23; xxxvii. 35; xlvi. 7). It is J and E that tell
of the sons of Jacob (xxxiv. 7, 27; cf. xxix. 32 sqq.), and
particularly of Simeon and Levi, own brothers of Dinah
(xxxiv. 25). It is E that tells of the change of Jacob's
name to Israel (xxxiv. 7; cf. xxxii. 29), and introduces
the reader to Shechem and his father Hamor (xxxiv. 2;
cf. xxxiii. 19). It is J and E that detail the various
trials with which the life of Jacob was filled in one continuous series from the time of the fraud which he practised upon his aged father and his brother Esau, viz., his
compulsory flight, Laban's deceiving him in his marriage, attempting to defraud him in his wages and pur-
suing him with hostile intent on his way to Canaan, his
alarm at the approach of Esau, and last and sorest of all,
the loss of his favorite, Joseph. According to the critical partition, P makes no allusion to any of these troub-
les. They are all of one tenor and evidently belong together, and this disgrace of Jacob's daughter fits into its
place among them. And we are told that it is alien to
P to record anything derogatory to any of the patriarchs.

seven years old " at the time referred to in ch. xxxiv., inasmuch as she
was Leah's seventh child, Jacob married Leah after seven years of service, and he remained in all twenty years with Laban. But he overlooks the fact that Jacob had meanwhile resided for a considerable
time both at Succoth (xxxiii. 17), where " he built him a house," and at
Shechem, where (ver. 19) " he bought a parcel of ground." The length
of his stay in these two places is not particularly stated. But as Joseph
was born (xxx. 25) when Jacob had served Laban fourteen years, he was
six years old when they left Paddan-aram. Eleven years consequently
elapsed between the departure from Paddan-aram and what is recorded
in ch. xxxvii. (see ver. 2). We are at entire liberty to assume that ten
of these had passed before ch. xxxiv., in which case Dinah would be
sixteen or seventeen. Her youth is implied ver. 4, where she is called
יַלְדָּה.

There are subsequent allusions also to this history in J (xlix. 5, 6) and in E (xxxv. 5 ; xlviii. 22).

DIVERGENCE OF THE CRITICS

Thus this chapter is strongly bound to P on the one hand, and to J and E on the other, in a manner that is not compatible with the original separateness of these so-called documents. The early critics, Astruc and Eichhorn, accepted the unity of ch. xxxiv. without question. Ilgen did the same, notwithstanding his disposition to splinter whatever seemed capable of separation. Tuch, who recognized no distinction between P and E, unhesitatingly assigned the whole of the chapter to P ; so did Ewald, Gramberg, and Stähelin. Hupfeld, unable to dispute the unity of the chapter, gave it in the first instance to E, in spite of its admitted relationship to P ("Quellen," p. 46) ; but on second thought he assigned it to J (" Quellen," pp. 186 sqq.), in which Kayser and Schrader follow him.[1]

On the ground of language and the comparison of xlix. 5-7, from which the inference was drawn that in the original form of the story Simeon and Levi were the only actors and no plunder was taken, Knobel supposed that the groundwork of the story was by P, but this was

[1] In how serious a quandary Hupfeld found himself in regard to the disposition of this chapter is apparent from the manner of his argument in reversing his former decision. He says that the grounds for referring it to P are " weighty and difficult to be set aside ; " on his original assumption that xxxiii. 19 and xxxv. 5 belong to E, he cannot conclude otherwise in regard to ch. xxxiv. ; nevertheless xlix. 5-7 compels him to assign it to J, while xlviii. 22 makes it necessary to maintain that E had here a similar narrative which R has not preserved. He then frees himself from the embarrassment created by xxxiii. 19 and xxxv. 5 by transferring these verses to J. In a note he offers the conjecture, of which others have since availed themselves, that vs. 27-29 may be an interpolation or inserted from another source.

supplemented and enlarged by J with matter taken from another source.[1] Dillmann made a different partition and maintained that the want of agreement and coherence between the parts is such as to show that two separate narratives have been fused together by a redactor. In his first

[1] The different critical analyses of ch. xxxiv.

Knobel: Grundschrift, vs. 1–4, 6, 15–18, 20–26. Kriegsbuch, vs. 5, 7–14, 19, 27–31.

Dillmann (1st): P, vs. 1, 2a, 4, 6, 8–10, 15–18a, 20–24 (25, 26 in part). J, vs. 2b, 3, 5, 7, 11–14, 18b, 19 (25, 26 in part), 27–31.

Dillmann (3d): P, vs. 1a, 2a, 4, 6, 8–10, 15, (14)–17, 20–24. J, vs. 2b, 3, 5, 7, 11–13 (14), 19, 25*, 26, 30, 31. R, vs. 27–29.

Kittell follows Dillmann (3d).

Wellhausen: J, vs. 3, 7*, 11, 12, 19, 25*, 26, 30, 31. Unknown Source, vs. 1*, 2*, 4–6, 8–10, 13*, 14*, 15–17, 20–24, 25*, 27–29.

Oort: Interpolation, "deceitfully," ver. 13, vs. 27, 28.

Boehmer: J, vs. 1*, 2*, 3, 4, 6, 8–12, 13*, 14–22, 24–26a, 28–30. R, vs. 1b, 2b, 5, 7, 13*, 23, 26b, 27, 31.

Delitzsch: P, vs. 1, 2, 4, 6, 8–10, 14–18, 20–24. J, vs. 3, 5, 7, 11, 12, 19, 25, 26, 30, 31. E, vs. 13, 27–29.

Colenso (Pentateuch, Part VII. Appendix, p. 149): J, vs. 1, 2a, 3a, 4, 6, 7a, 8–13a, 14–24. D, vs. 2b, 3b, 5, 7b, 13b, 25–31.

Driver: J, vs. 2b, 3, 5, 7, 11, 12, 19, 25*, 26, 30, 31. P, vs. 1, 2a, 4, 6, 8–10, 13–18, 20–24, 25*, 27–29.

Dr. Driver, while confessing that "the analysis is not throughout equally certain," adopts substantially Wellhausen's division. Only (1) he attributes to P, on the ground of unmistakable marks of P's style, what Wellhausen and Kuenen positively declare could not be his, thus annulling (as he has frequent occasion besides to do in the middle books of the Pentateuch) his often-repeated statement that P is clearly distinguishable from J, and even his more carefully guarded assertion that "in Genesis as regards the limits of P there is practically no difference of opinion among critics."—Literature of Old Testament. p. 9. And (2) he somewhat inconsistently transfers ver. 5 to J, though he thinks it to be at variance with ver. 30 : "In ver. 30 Jacob expresses dissatisfaction at what his sons have done, while from ver. 5 it would be inferred that they had merely given effect to their father's resentment." If this discrepancy is no bar to the reference of vs. 5 and 30 to the same document. why should the other discrepancies "inferred" by the critics, but which are also purely imaginary, hinder our belief in the common authorship of the entire chapter ?

edition he held that, according to the earlier form of the story given by P, Shechem, a native prince, asks the hand of Dinah in marriage, whereupon Jacob and his sons promise to consent to intermarriages between themselves and the Shechemites on condition of the circumcision of the latter. And the house of Jacob was on the point of affiliating with the citizens of Shechem when Simeon and Levi, whose zeal was aroused for the purity of their race and to prevent its contamination by intermingling with Gentiles, frustrated the plan by assaulting the city and putting Shechem and his father to death. In a later form of the story given by J, Jacob's sons were angered not at the prospect of their sister's marriage with a foreigner, but at her actual dishonor. They propose the circumcision of the Shechemites, not sincerely as in P, but craftily, with the design of avenging their sister's betrayal. And the credit of punishing the crime of Shechem is assigned, not to Simeon and Levi alone, but to all the sons of Jacob.

In later editions Dillmann modifies his view materially by rejecting vs. 27–29 as a later interpolation, and transferring vs. 25, 26 from P to J, thus no longer making P prior to J, and relieving P from recording a variance in the patriarchal family. P's account is then simply concerned with the legal question as to the proper procedure in giving a daughter in marriage to a foreigner. The answer given is, that in order to intermarriage with the Shechemites they must first be circumcised. To this they assent in the persuasion that the advantage will be greatly on their side, and that the house of Jacob, losing its distinctive character, will become a part of themselves (vs. 21–24). Here the narrative breaks off unfinished without disclosing the final issue. If P approved of this arrangement he must, as Kuenen[1] argues, "have been

[1] Gesammelte Abhandlungen, p. 263.

more of a Hamorite than an Israelite, or at least neutral in respect to the two clans." And he positively refuses "to admit the existence of such a species until another specimen of it is discovered." J's account on this scheme is that the most honored man in Shechem (ver. 19) carried off Dinah and dishonored her. But as his love to her grew, he desired her in marriage from Jacob and his sons, and offers any compensation in the way of bridal gift. The brothers, exasperated at the disgrace of their sister, deceitfully make the condition the circumcision of Shechem (whether that of the other citizens of the place also is uncertain), and when he is disabled by the resulting sickness, Simeon and Levi kill him and recover their sister. Jacob blames them severely for having placed him and his family in peril by their rash deed. The redactor is responsible for confusing the accounts to some extent, and especially for inserting the circumcision and massacre of the Shechemites in J's account in ver. 25; and he betrays his later stand-point by the strong expression, "defile their sister" (vs. 27, 13b, 5; see also ver. 14b).

Wellhausen makes a different disposition of several verses and brings out quite a different result. He takes his point of departure from an alleged discrepancy between vs. 26 and 27. In vs. 25, 26, and again ver. 30, the deed is imputed to Simeon and Levi, but in ver. 27 to the sons of Jacob, i.e., the children of Israel. One account, J's, represented in the former of these passages, but only preserved in a fragmentary way, makes of it a family affair. Simeon and Levi avenge the wrong done their sister by entering Hamor's house and killing Shechem, when he was off his guard, to the great offence of Jacob. There was no circumcision in the case. Shechem had offered any dowry, however large, in order to obtain Dinah in marriage. We have no means of knowing how much was demanded ; but, whatever it was, Shechem had promptly paid it. The other, which is the principal account, deals with international relations, out of which perhaps the story grew. It cannot therefore belong to either P or E, but is of unknown origin. It is an affair between the Bne Israel and the Bne Hamor, whose capital was Shechem. The latter submitted to circumcision with a view to a friendly alliance, and when disabled in consequence were treacherously massacred. Though E is excluded from this chapter by Wellhausen, the evident allusions to this history in E oblige him to confess that he must have had a similar narrative in this place as the motive for Jacob's removal from Shechem (see xxxv. 5). It is also unfortunate for his analysis that ver. 25 has to be reconstructed; for in its present form it implies the circumcision and affirms the assault upon the city and the massacre of its citizens, showing that Simeon and Levi had assistance. And this is confirmed by ver. 30, where Jacob apprehends reprisals, not from the Shechemites, but from the inhabitants of the land generally, and also by xlix. 5, 6, which speaks of violence done to oxen as well as men.

Oort [1] held that this chapter (freed from the interpolations vs. 27, 28, and "deceitfully," ver. 13) dates from the period of the judges, and is explanatory of the situation described in Judg. ix. (see ver. 28.)[2] "In the form of

---

[1] Oort's Bible for Learners, English Translation, vol. i., p. 398.

[2] This passage, by which Oort seeks to discredit the narrative in Gen. xxxiv., is, on the contrary, urged by Hävernick in confirmation of its historical accuracy. Gaal's appeal to the Shechemites, to " serve the men of Hamor, the father of Shechem," implies that the descendants of Hamor were the prominent ruling family of the place. The title, " father of the city of Shechem," suggests that Hamor was its founder, naming it after his son. When Abram passed through the place (Gen. xii. 6) there is no intimation that there was as yet any city. This is first mentioned in the time of Jacob ; and its recent

a family history of the patriarchal period the narrator
has here given us a fragment of the history of the Israelite people, or at any rate of some of the tribes. . . .
The legend deals with one of the burning questions of
the period of the Judges—the question whether Israelites
and Canaanites might intermarry. The practice was
very advantageous to both parties, and especially to the
conquered race ; but to the Israelite of pure blood, who
looked down with contempt upon the old inhabitants of
the place, it was an abomination. The Canaanites are
represented in the legend under the person of Shechem,
the son of Hamor, which shows that this question was
debated in the city of Shechem, where the Hamorites, a
Hivite tribe, were settled. This fact enables us to bring
the legend into connection with the history of Abimelech,
and to find the counterparts of the zealots, Simeon and
Levi, in Gaal and his brothers."

Kuenen, in his "Religion of Israel," i., pp. 311, 409,
accepted this view of Oort, though differing from him as
to the date and analysis of the chapter and its specific
reference to the particular occasion spoken of in Judg.
ix. Nevertheless he "fully assented to Oort's main idea,"
that Gen. xxxiv. "gives us historical reminiscences from
the period of the Judges in the form of a narrative about
the patriarchal age." "Shechem and his father Hamor
represent in this narrative the Canaanites, who are inclined to intermarry with Israel, and who submit to the
conditions attached to this step. Simeon and Levi consider such a contract an abomination and feign satisfac-
tion with it only to hinder it the more effectually. This
narrative already discloses the idea that the violent
measures to which the adherents of the strictly national
tendency were obliged to resort in order to attain their
origin and consequent insignificance accounts for the successful attack
upon it by Simeon and Levi and their adherents.

purpose, were looked upon by many as questionable and dangerous " (ver. 30).

In an article [1] published in 1880, Kuenen accepts the analysis of Wellhausen, and agrees with him that in J's account Jacob and his sons impose a heavy money forfeit upon Shechem and assent to his marriage with Dinah, which would have taken place if Simeon and Levi, less yielding than the rest, had not interfered and killed Shechem. He differs from Wellhausen in regard to the rest of the chapter, which in his esteem is not a separate account, that once existed by itself and was subsequently combined with that of J by a redactor. J's account was distasteful to post-exilic readers, and was in consequence remodelled into the form in which we possess it now. The Philistines are the only ones spoken of in pre-exilic writings as uncircumcised,[2] and they did not belong to the original inhabitants of Canaan. The idea that the Bne Hamor, or any other Canaanitish tribe, were distinguished from the family of Jacob by being uncircumcised, and that they must be circumcised prior to intermarriage with them, could not have arisen before the exile. The deed of Shechem is judged with such extreme severity, and no punishment however treacherous and cruel, is esteemed too great because he had "defiled" Dinah (vs. 5, 13, 27), which is much worse than robbing her of her honor. The word conjures up that frightful phantom of post-exilic Judaism, alliance with foreigners (see Ezra ix., x.). Shechem's deed, and no less his effort to make it good, was a crime against the people of God to be prevented by fire and sword. On these grounds he concludes that this chapter has been remodelled, not indeed by P, who could not

[1] Gesammelte Abhandlungen, pp. 255–276.
[2] Judg. xiv. 3; xv. 18; 1 Sam. xiv. 6; xvii. 26, 36; xxxi. 4; 2 Sam. i. 20.

depart so far from his usage as to introduce this tale of
treachery and plunder, but by a post-exilic diaskeuast of
the school of P, who has borrowed his style and his
ideas.
All this reasoning, as Dillmann suggests, is of no force
to those who do not accept Kuenen's assertion that circumcision was regarded with indifference in pre-exilic
times. In fact he overturns it himself in his "Hexateuch,"
p. 326, by leaving it "an open question" whether J's account "had itself represented the circumcision of Shechem (not of all the citizens) as a condition laid down
in good faith by the sons of Jacob."

Merx [1] follows Boehmer in eliminating from the narrative all that relates to the dishonor of Dinah, the deceit
of her brothers, and the plunder of the city as interpolations. What is left is regarded as the original story as
told by a writer in North Israel. It is to the effect that
Shechem asked the hand of Dinah in honorable marriage,
giving the required dowry and submitting likewise to the
condition of being circumcised, together with his people.
But Simeon and Levi treacherously fell upon them in
their sickness and murdered them, to Jacob's great alarm.
The rest of his sons did not participate in the deed. He
thus saves the honor of Dinah, but takes away all motive
for the conduct of Simeon and Levi. The design of the
original narrator was to affix a stigma upon Simeon and
Levi, as these tribes adhered to the southern kingdom
and the worship of Jerusalem. The interpolations of the
Judaic redactor were apologetic. They represent Simeon and Levi as avenging the honor of their house,
while the other tribes are also involved in the transaction
and are solely responsible for the plunder that followed.
In his first edition Delitzsch assigned the entire chap-

[1] Schenkel's Bibel-Lexicon, Art., Dina.

ter to P ; he did the same in the third and fourth editions, only excepting vs. 27–29 as inserted from another
source, the sons of Jacob there spoken of being identical
with Simeon and Levi of ver. 25. In his last edition,
however, he partitions the chapter somewhat differently
from his predecessors, and finds two accounts by P and
by J [1] essentially agreeing. In both Dinah is seduced
by the young prince, who then earnestly desires her in
marriage; the circumcision of the Shechemites is made
the condition in both; in both Dinah is taken off and
brought back again. There is, besides, a brief passage
from E, recording the capture and sack of Shechem simply as an exploit of the sons of Jacob.

The critics have thus demonstrated that it is possible to sunder this chapter into parts, each of which taken
separately shall yield a different narrative ; and that this
can be done very variously, and with the most remarkable divergence in the results. Now which are we to believe, Dillmann, Wellhausen, Oort, Kuenen, Merx, or Delitzsch? They each profess to give us the original form
or forms of the story, and no two agree. Is it not apparent that the critical process of each is purely subjective?
The critic makes out of the narrative just what he pleases,
selecting such portions as suit him and discarding the
rest. The result is a mere speculative fancy, without
the slightest historical value. Delitzsch correctly says,

---

[1] In defending his analysis Delitzsch remarks that נַעֲרָה = נַעַר, in each
of the twenty-one times in which it occurs, belongs to J or D. To note
this as characteristic of a particular writer is to affirm that it belonged
to the text as originally written. This is equivalent, therefore, to a re-
traction of his opinion expressed in Luthardt's Zeitschrift for 1880, Art.
No. 8, that the use of this word as a feminine as well as הִוא = הוּא is
traceable to the manipulation of the text by later diaskeuasts, instead
of being, as it has commonly been regarded, an archaic form properly
belonging to the original text of the passages in which it occurs and
characteristic of the Pentateuch.

"Evidence and agreement are here scarcely attainable." And what is so obvious here in this discord of the critics attaches equally to their methods and results where they follow in each other's tracks. The text is decomposed *ad libitum* into fragments of documents, and emendations or additions by various editors and redactors. The whole thing is regulated by the will or the preconceived ideas of the critic, and is a mere subjective creation, with only basis enough in the literary phenomena to give it a faint savor of plausibility.

The abruptness of this narrative in P, who has made no previous mention of any of the parties concerned, has already been referred to. Its incompleteness, as made out by Dillmann, is suggested by the question to which no answer can be given, what became of Dinah? It is insupposable that negotiations of such a character should be carried on to the extent indicated and no mention made of the issue. It seems that Dinah could not have married Shechem since P speaks of her as a member of Jacob's family, when he went down into Egypt (xlvi. 15). If not, why not, since the condition on which it was dependent was fulfilled? Why is nothing further heard of this circumcised community at Shechem, and of the intercourse and intermarriages here anticipated? Is there any explanation of this silence, except that given in the verses which Dillmann has so carefully exscinded, and of which Kuenen justly says ("Hexateuch," p. 326), "I cannot see any possibility of separating these verses (27–29) and the corresponding expressions in vs. 5, 13 from P's account."

It is said in explanation of the incompleteness of this story in P that it has a legal rather than a historical purpose. But it is surely very inconsistent in P to enact such a law as is here supposed. He informs us that Esau's marriage with Canaanites was a great grief to his

parents (xxvi. 35 ; xxviii. 8), and that they would not
consent to such a marriage on the part of Jacob (xxvii.
46 ; xxviii. 1, 6). And yet here he is supposed by Dillmann to favor a general regulation for intermarriage with
Canaanites on condition of their being circumcised. J's
estimate of the Canaanites and of the peril of contamination from alliances with them agrees with P's (xxiv.
3 ; xiii. 13 ; xv. 16 ; xviii. 20 seq. ; ch. xix. ; cf. ver. 29
P). Even on the principles of the critics themselves it
cannot be imagined that P here sanctions what is in direct antagonism to the positive injunctions of every code
of laws in the Pentateuch, viz. : E, Ex. xxiii. 32, 33 ; J,
Ex. xxxiv. 12, 15, 16 ; Num. xxxiii. 52, 55, 56 ; Holiness
Laws, Lev. xviii. 24, 25 ; xx. 22, 23 ; D, Deut. vii. 3 ; as
well as the unanimous voice of tradition (Josh. xxiii. 12,
13; Judg. iii. 6 ; 1 Kin. xi. 1, 4). And if P be thought
to be post-exilic, it would be more inconceivable still
(Ezra ix., x.; Neh. x. 30). And if he formulated such a
law, what is to be thought of the honesty or the loyalty
of R in perverting it to its opposite, as is done in this
narrative ?

NOT COMPOSITE

But though the critics differ so widely in their partition of this chapter, and though each partition that has
been proposed is unsatisfactory, it may still be said that
there are positive proofs of its composite character, even
though it has not yet been successfully resolved into its
proper component parts. The bare recital of the proofs
offered is, however, sufficient to show how inconclusive
and trivial they are.

Thus it is argued that, according to vs. 4, 6, 8, Hamor
conducted the negotiation on behalf of his son, whereas
in vs. 11, 12, Shechem is represented as himself suing for
the hand of Dinah. Kuenen here admits the possibility

of the very natural explanation that " Shechem, in vs. 11, 12, undertakes to speak after his father; his love for Dinah does not permit him to be silent; he must also on his own part further apply every possible pressure." His objection that we would not infer from vs. 4, 8, that Shechem was present at the interview is of no force; for his request that his father would intercede on his behalf, and the prominent part taken by Hamor in the matter are not inconsistent with Shechem's accompanying him on an errand in which he was so deeply interested. That Hamor and Shechem were together at the interview is distinctly stated (vs. 13, 18), where the critics are obliged to assume that R has mixed the two accounts.

It is said that in ver. 6 P the conference is held with Jacob, but in ver. 11 J with Jacob and his sons; which only shows that the entry of Jacob's sons (ver. 7) cannot be sundered from ver. 6, as is done by the critics. While Hamor was on the way to see Jacob, the sons of the latter came in from the field, so that they were all together at the interview. Accordingly (ver. 8), Hamor communed with *them*, not with *him*, as if he spoke to Jacob alone; and (ver. 14) " they said unto them," not he unto him; and " our sister," instead of " my daughter," as if Jacob was the sole speaker. As this does not correspond with the assumption of the critics, they tell us that R must have altered the text here again.

It is claimed that there is a duplicate account. Hamor makes his application (vs. 8–10), receives his answer (vs. 15 (14)–17), and lays this (vs. 20–24) before a meeting of the citizens ; again (vs. 11, 12), Shechem makes the application, and after receiving the answer at once subjects himself (ver. 19) to the condition imposed. But nothing is duplicated. There is no variant account and no repetition. All proceeds regularly. Shechem (ver. 11) seconds his father's application ; the answer is made to them both (vs. 13–17), and pleases both (ver. 18). Shechem is eager to have the condition fulfilled without delay (ver. 19), and he and his father at once bring it to the attention of their townsmen (vs. 20–23), who consent and comply with the condition (ver. 24).

It is alleged that the answer in vs. 13–17 is made to Hamor's proposal in vs. 8–10 of trade and intermarriage between the two clans, and not to Shechem's offer (vs. 11, 12) of a large dowry in return for the hand of Dinah. But, in fact, one common answer is given to both proposals, each of which is distinctly referred to. And it is perfectly true to nature that Shechem should have but one thought, his love for Dinah, while his father proposes general amicable relations, under which the acceptance of his son's suit would follow by legitimate consequence.

It is charged that vs. 2b, 26b, conflict with ver. 17b. According to the former, Shechem had carried off Dinah to his own house, from whence she was rescued by her brothers ; but, according to the latter, she was in the possession of Jacob's family. This is a mistake. Her brothers declare their intention (ver. 17) to take her away if their demand was not complied with ; to take her, that is, from the place where she then was, wherever that might be. The verb is identical with that in ver. 26, where they took her out of Shechem's house.

"After vs. 2b, 3, one expects the father to be asked to apologize to Jacob for the offence committed ; but instead of this the marriage negotiations are introduced, as though all were still intact and the girl was with her parents ; not a word is said of what had taken place." What reparation could be made but marriage ? and this is the thing proposed.

It is further charged as an inconsistency that the deed of violence is in ver. 30 attributed to Simeon and Levi,

as vs. 25, 26, not to the sons of Jacob generally, as vs.
27–29. Simeon and Levi were the leaders and instiga-
tors, and as such were chiefly responsible. The massacre
is attributed to them; to the others only a participation
in the subsequent plunder of the city. Why Simeon
and Levi in particular were so prominent in the affair
is intimated in ver. 25, where they are spoken of as
" Dinah's brothers." As sons of Leah they were her
own brothers; and next to Reuben, whose weak and vac-
illating character incapacitated him for resolute action,
they were her oldest brothers, to whom the protection of
their sister and the redress of her wrongs naturally de-
volved (cf. xxiv. 50, 55, 59). Hence Jacob, after hearing
of the outrage (ver. 5), waits for the return of his sons
before any steps are taken, and then he leaves the whole
matter in their hands. The treacherous and murderous
scheme concocted and executed by Simeon and Levi,
with the concurrence of the other sons (ver. 13), was
without Jacob's knowledge and privity, and incurred his
severe reprobation (xlix. 5–7).

Knobel remarks that in xxxiv. 30 " Jacob blames not
the immorality of the action, but the inconsiderateness of
his sons, which has plunged him into trouble." But as
Hengstenberg[1] observes, we see from xxxv. 5 why pre-

[1] Authentie des Pentateuches, ii., p. 535. Hengstenberg further
points to the fact that it is the habit of the sacred historian simply to
report the actions of the patriarchs, without commenting upon their
moral quality, leaving this to be suggested by the providential retribution which followed in the results of their misdeeds. No censure is
formally passed upon Abram's connection with Hagar; but the unhap-
piness which sprang from it constrained him to dismiss her. Jacob
deceived his father and defrauded his brother, and was in his turn deceived and defrauded by Laban; twenty years of toil and enforced
absence from home, and his alarm at meeting Esau, were the fruit of
that act of sin. Rebekah's participation in the fraud was punished by
lifelong separation from her favorite son. Reuben's crime is simply
related (xxxv. 22); judgment upon it is reserved until Jacob's dying

cisely these words of Jacob are recorded here. Attention is drawn to the peril of the situation in order to
bring to view the divine protection which warded off all
dangerous consequences.

That there is no inconsistency in the narrative in its
present form is substantially admitted by Kuenen, who
finds no evidence of separate and variant documents, but
only that the chapter has been remodelled so as to give
it a different complexion from that which it originally
had. There may be different opinions as to the remodelling, whether it was the work of ancient diaskeuasts
or of modern critics; but we can at least agree with
Kuenen that the text tells a uniform story as it now
stands.

MARKS OF P

1. Diffuseness, *e.g.*, the daughter of Leah, which she
bore unto Jacob (ver. 1). In what respect is there a
greater redundancy here than in the almost identical
repetition xxii. 20b, 23b J ?

2. נָשִׂיא *prince* (ver. 2). See ch. xvii., Marks of P, No.
11.

3. חָשַׁק *to long for* (ver. 8) ; nowhere else in the Hexateuch, except in Deuteronomy. The occurrence of דָּבַק
to cleave unto (ver. 3), as an equivalent is no proof of a
diversity of writers. See ch. xxxi.–xxxii. 3, Marks of E,
at the end.

4. נאחֲזוּ *to get possessions* (ver. 10) ; besides in P (xlvii.
27 ; Num. xxxii. 30 ; Josh. xxii. 9, 19) ; in E (Gen. xxii.
13) in a different sense.

5. הִמּוֹל לָכֶם כָּל־זָכָר *every male of you be circumcised*
(vs. 15, 22), as xvii. 10, 12.

6. כָּל־זָכָר *every male* (ver. 24). See ch. vi.–ix., Marks
of P, No. 12.

words in respect to it are recorded (xlix. 3, 4). It is precisely the same
with the deed of Simeon and Levi.

7. שָׁמַע אֶל hearken unto (vs. 17, 24). See ch. xxiii., Marks of P, No. 10.

8. קִנְיָן substance (ver. 23). See ch. xxxi.–xxxii. 3, Marks of P, No. 2.

9. בְּהֵמָה beast (ver. 23); often besides in P; but also in J (ii. 20; iii. 14; vii. 2, 8; viii. 20, etc.). It is associated with מִקְנֶה cattle as here, also in P (xxxvi. 6); in a so-called secondary stratum in P (Num. xxxi. 9); in J (Gen. xlvii. 18; Ex. ix. 19; Num. xxxii. 26); nowhere else in the Hexateuch.

10. אַךְ only (vs. 15, 23). See ch. xxvi. 34–xxviii. 9, Marks of E, No. 1.

11. כָּל־יֹצְאֵי שַׁעַר עִיר all that went out of the gate of the city (ver. 24), as xxiii. 10, 18.

MARKS OF J

1. דָּבַק to cleave unto (ver. 3); besides in J (ii. 24; xix. 19); in E (xxxi. 23); in P (Num. xxxvi. 7, 9); in D (Josh. xxii. 5; xxiii. 8, 12) and several times in Deut.

2. נַעַר damsel (vs. 3, 12), young man (ver. 19); the occurrence of יַלְדָּה (ver. 4) as a feminine equivalent is no indication of a difference of writers. See ch. xxi. 1–21, Marks of E, No. 6.

3. הִתְעַצֵּב to be grieved (ver. 7). See ch. vi. 1–8, Marks of J, No. 8.

4. חָרָה לוֹ to be wroth (ver. 7). See ch. xviii., xix., Marks of J, No. 30.

5. כֵּן לֹא יֵעָשֶׂה which ought not to be done (ver. 7); assigned besides to J (xxix. 26), but this is cut out of an E connection; in E (xx. 9); in P (Lev. iv. 2, 13, 22, 27; v. 17).

6. מָצָא חֵן בְּעֵינֵי to find grace in the eyes of (ver. 11). See ch. vi. 1–8, Marks of J, No. 10.

7. לְפִי חָרֶב with the edge of the sword (ver. 26); besides

in J (Josh. viii. 24 bis); in E (Ex. xvii. 13; Num. xxi. 24); in JE (Josh. vi. 21; xix. 47, in a P connection); in D (Josh. x. 28, 30, 32, 35, 37, 39; xi. 11, 12, 14) and several times in Deut.

8. עָכַר *to trouble* (ver. 30); besides in the Hexateuch only Josh. vi. 18 E; vii. 25 bis JE.

'" Wrought folly in Israel" is claimed as a D phrase (Deut. xxii. 21). Knobel says : " The author here naively applies this later expression to patriarchal times, when there was as yet no people of Israel." The patriarch had already received the name of Israel, and he was the leader of a powerful clan, which subsequently developed into the nation. There is no inappropriateness in the great legislator employing here the legal phrase current in his own day.

JACOB AT BETHEL, AND ISAAC'S DEATH (CH. XXXV.)

The divine names afford no ground for the division of this chapter, since El and Elohim alone occur. The reason is evident. The prominence here given to the names Bethel (vs. 1, 3, 6, 7, 8, 15) and Israel (ver. 10), leads to the quadruple repetition of El (vs. 1, 3, 7, 11), with which Elohim is most naturally associated (see particularly vs. 7, 15, also vs. 1, 9, 10, 11, 13). Elohim is appropriately used in ver. 5 to indicate that the terror was divinely inspired, and did not proceed from any human source. Eichhorn had no difficulty in admitting the unity of the chapter. Tuch did the same, only excepting the last clause of both vs. 1 and 7, which speak of the flight from Esau, of which, on his hypothesis, the Elohist knew nothing. Ilgen [1] parcelled it between the two Elohists, and this is at present the prevalent fash-

---

[1] Ilgen's division is almost identical with that of Dillmann ; he gives to E vs. 1–8, 16a, c, 17, 18, 20–22 ; to P vs. 9–15, 16b, 19, 23–29.

ion. Dillmann gives vs. 1–8 to E (except ver. 5 R, ver. 6a P), vs. 9–15 to P, vs. 16–22a to R, and vs. 22b–29 to P.

JACOB AT BETHEL

Vs. 1–15 plainly form one continuous narrative. Jacob goes by divine direction to Bethel and builds an altar there, whereupon God appears to him and blesses him. According to the partition proposed above, however, E (vs. 1, 4, 7) speaks of God having appeared to Jacob in Bethel and answered him in his distress, plainly referring to xxviii. 12 sqq. But as the critics divide that passage, E tells of the vision of a ladder with angels ; it is only J who tells of God appearing to Jacob and speaking with him. Hence Dillmann finds it necessary to assume that R has here meddled with the text and adapted it to J. In ver. 5 the danger of pursuit, from which they were protected by a terror divinely sent upon the cities round about, points to the deed of blood in ch. xxxiv., and to the apprehension which this awakened in Jacob (ver. 30). But as that was recorded by J, not by E, this verse is cut out of its connection and assigned by Hupfeld to J (in spite of Elohim), and by others to R. Ver. 6a is given to P, because E calls the place Bethel (vs. 1, 3). That, however, was the sacred name given to it by Jacob ; its popular name was Luz, and its introduction here is with allusion to xxviii. 19. The added clause, "which is in the land of Canaan," is not a superfluous appendage due to P's diffuseness ; but like the same words in xxxiii. 18, it calls attention to the fact that Jacob, after his long absence, is now again in the land to which the Lord had promised to bring him (xxviii. 15). That promise, on which Jacob's vow to revisit Bethel was conditioned, was now fulfilled. Why R should find it necessary here to insert a clause from P in order to state so simple a fact as Jacob's arrival at the place, to which, according to E, he had been directed to go, is not very obvious. Nevertheless the consequence is that P speaks of Jacob's coming to Bethel, but E does not; and "there" (ver. 7) has nothing to refer to. The burial of Deborah (ver. 8) is said to be abruptly introduced and out of connection with what precedes. But it only interrupts the narrative, as the event itself interrupted the sacred transaction in the midst of which it occurred. Moreover, the mention of Rebekah's nurse in E is once more a reference to J (xxiv. 59), by whom alone she had been spoken of before, and that merely to prepare the way for what is here recorded. The question how she came to be with Jacob at this time cannot be answered for lack of information. The writer is not giving her biography, and we have no right to expect an account of all her movements. After Rebekah's death it was quite natural that she should go to be with Rebekah's favorite son. The "strange gods" in Jacob's family (vs. 2, 4) find their explanation in xxxi. 19, 30 sqq. E. The name El-bethel (ver. 7) is identical with that by which God announced himself to Jacob (xxxi. 13 E).

P (ver. 9) speaks of God appearing to Jacob *again*, when he came out of Paddan-aram, with definite reference to his having appeared to him the first time on his way to Paddan-aram (ver. 1 E), as related neither by P nor by E, but by J (xxviii. 13). The word "again" is therefore unceremoniously stricken from the text to make it correspond with the hypothesis. Reference is made (ver. 12) to God's giving the land to Isaac; no such fact is recorded by P, only by J or R (xxvi. 3, 4). God appears to Jacob (ver. 9), as in xvii. 1 P (cf. xii. 7; xviii. 1; xxvi. 2, 24 J), speaks to him in condescending terms (vs. 10–12) and goes up from him (ver. 13), from which it is plain that a descent of the LORD, as in xi. 5, 7, is not peculiar to J. The reimposition of the names "Israel" (ver. 10) and "Bethel" (ver. 15) is judged to be incredible by the critics, and claimed as evidence of two discrepant accounts. But it gave no trouble to R, and need not to us. There are other like instances in the sacred narrative. It is quite as likely that the original writer thought such repetitions possible and reported them accordingly, as that the redactor could do so. That no explanation of Israel is here given is, as Dillmann confesses, because xxxii. 29 made it unnecessary, and so it is an implied reference to that passage in E Dillm. (or J Well., Kuen.). Only his critical stand-point obliges him to assume that P must have given an explanation, which R has omitted, the only evidence of which is that the hypothesis requires it. In vs. 11, 12, God pronounces upon Jacob the identical blessing granted to Abraham in terms corresponding with ch. xvii., thus fulfilling the desire of Isaac (xxviii. 3, 4) on his behalf. In ver. 14 (P) Jacob sets up a pillar, which is esteemed a characteristic of E, as in ver. 20 E, and pours oil upon it, as xxviii. 18 E, and a drink-offering, in evident contradiction to the critical notion that according to P offerings had no existence prior to the Mosaic period. Hence Kuenen ("Hexateuch," p. 327) thinks it necessary to attribute ver. 14 to R.

The manifold references to P, J, and E, scattered throughout this closely connected paragraph (vs. 1–15), are not accounted for by the division proposed; and it is impossible to make a division that will account for them. The common relation of this paragraph to all the documents cannot be explained by tearing it to shreds to conform with the partition elsewhere made. That partition, which is irreconcilable with this paragraph, must be itself at fault in sundering what, as is here shown, belongs together.

THE DEATH OF RACHEL

The next paragraph (vs. 16–20) is tied to different documents in a like embarrassing manner. Ch. xlviii. 7 (P) speaks of the death and burial of Rachel at Ephrath, in terms nearly identical with vs. 16, 19. Ch. xxix. 32–xxx. 24 (J and E) records the birth of eleven of Jacob's sons, and finds its complement in this account of the birth of Benjamin. This final paragraph, which completes the number of his sons, is preparatory to the recapitulation (vs. 22b–26 P), in which they are arranged according to their respective mothers, and in the order of their birth, in exact correspondence with the detailed narrative previously given. That the child now born is Rachel's, agrees with xxx. 24b J. That she loses her life in giving him birth is an evident reminder of xxx. 1 E. The birth scene recalls xxv. 24–26 ; xxxviii. 27 sqq. J. In ver. 18 the name is given both by the mother as in J and E (see ch. xxx.), and by the father as in P (see xvi. 15 ; xxi. 3). It is alleged that P could not have connected the birth of Benjamin with his mother's death at Ephrath, since this is in conflict with vs. 24, 26, P, where Jacob's twelve sons are said to have been born in Paddan-aram. But in like manner, it is said (xlvi. 15), that Leah bare thirty-three sons and daughters to Jacob in Paddan-aram, and (ver. 18) Zilpah bare unto Jacob sixteen. In Ex. i. 5, seventy souls are said to have come out of the loins of Jacob, including Jacob himself (cf. Gen. xlvi. 26, 27). 1 Cor. xv. 5 speaks of Christ being " seen of the twelve " after his resurrection, although Judas had gone to his own place. R had no difficulty in understanding that Jacob's sons could be spoken of in the general as born in Paddan-aram, though Benjamin's birth in Canaan had just been mentioned. Is R's interpretation less rational than that of the critics? May not the writer have meant it as the redactor understood it? Dillmann further urges that E could not have mentioned Rachel's death at this time, since that is in conflict with xxxvii. 10 E. But instead of contrariety there is perfect accord. As the eleven stars denoted Joseph's brethren, Benjamin must have been one of them. Rachel's death is likewise implied, for had she been living, as well as Leah, there would have been two moons to make obeisance instead of one.

The reference of this paragraph to R, who is supposed to have written it with reference to P, J, and E, is equivalent to a confession that it is an indivisible unit as it now stands, and that it was written by one cognizant of matter to be found in each of the documents; by one, that is, who gave Genesis its present form, of which the so-called documents are component parts, a view which is quite consistent with their never having had a separate existence.

There is a difficulty in respect to the location of Rachel's sepulchre. According to vs. 16, 19; xlviii. 7, it lay upon the road from Bethel, where "there was still some way to come to Ephrath" or Bethlehem; this corresponds with its traditional site, a short distance north of Bethlehem. But according to 1 Sam. x. 2, Saul in returning to Gibeah from Samuel, whose home was in Ramah, passed by Rachel's sepulchre; from which it might be inferred that it lay considerably further north. Thenius, Dillmann, and others cut the knot by rejecting the clause "the same is Bethlehem" (xxxv. 19; xlviii. 7), as an erroneous gloss, and assuming that there was a another Ephrath, not otherwise known, much nearer to Bethel. But the correctness of its identification with Bethlehem is confirmed by Ruth iv. 11; Mic. v. 1 (E. V., ver. 2). Delitzsch, in the fourth edition of his "Gene-

sis," adhered to the traditional site and assumed that
Samuel directed Saul to take " an unreasonably circuitous route " on his way homeward. In his last edition he
conceives that variant traditions as to the place of Rachel's burial are represented in these passages. Kurtz [1]
seeks a solution in the indefiniteness of the term כִּבְרַת
some way, which is of doubtful meaning, and only occurs
once besides (2 Kin. v. 19). He supposes it to mean
quite a long distance, so that the place described might
be remote from Bethlehem, and in the neighborhood of
Ramah.

Possibly, however, Dr. Robinson uncovers the real
source of the difficulty by suggesting that we do not
know where it was that Saul met with Samuel. Ramah,
the home of Samuel, is in his opinion not the Ramah of
Benjamin, north of Jerusalem, and has not yet been certainly identified. And he adds,[2] " After all, there is
perhaps a question lying back of this whole discussion,
viz., whether the city where Saul and the servant came
to Samuel was his own city, Ramah? The name of the
city is nowhere given ; and the answer of the maidens
(1 Sam. ix. 11, 12) would perhaps rather imply that
Samuel had just arrived, possibly on one of his yearly
circuits, in which he judged Israel in various cities (1
Sam. vii. 15–17)." If now, in the absence of definite information on the subject, it is permissible with Keil to
conjecture that Saul found Samuel in some city south-
west of Bethlehem, Rachel's sepulchre might easily be
on his way back to Gibeah. Samuel's statement that he
would " find two men by Rachel's sepulchre, in the border of Benjamin, at Zelzah," need create no embarrassment, for Benjamin's southern boundary ran through the
valley of Hinnom, south of Jerusalem to En-rogel (Josh.

---

[1] Geschichte des Alten Bundes, i., p. 270.
[2] Biblical Researches, ii., p. 10 (Edition of 1856).

xviii. 16), about three miles from Rachel's sepulchre,
which is sufficiently near to justify the form of expression
used.

If, however, Samuel was at Ramah, and this is the
same with the Ramah north of Jerusalem, Rachel's sepulchre of 1 Sam. x. 2 cannot well be that of Genesis.
But as the bones of Joseph were transported to the inheritance of the tribes descended from him (Josh. xxiv.
32), why may not the Benjamites have erected a ceno-
taph in their territory in honor of the mother of their
tribe ?

The repetition of the word וַיִּסַּע *journeyed* (xxxv. 21),
marks this as a continuation of the narrative of vs. 5 and
16 ; but the critics complete the patchwork of the chapter by giving ver. 22a to J, because of the reference to it
in xlix. 4, and ver. 21 must necessarily go with it.   And
this though "Israel" in these verses is a plain allusion
to ver. 10 P, or xxxii. 29 E (so Dillmann) ; and "the
tower of Eder" was at Bethlehem, the objective point of
vs. 16, 19, R or P.

GROUNDS OF PARTITION IRRELEVANT

While the entire chapter is thus closely linked together
in all its parts, it is observable that the critical severance
is based not upon the contents of the chapter, whether
matter or diction, but upon its numerous points of connection with other passages, which the critics have seen
fit to parcel among the so-called documents.   It is an attempt to force the hypothesis through this chapter for
reasons which lie wholly outside of itself.   And it is
still further observable that the critics have not succeeded in adjusting this chapter into conformity with the
partition elsewhere.   In spite of the attempt to prevent
it, its several sections are in repeated instances related

to other documents than those to which the critics assign
them. These intimate bonds of relationship with other
passages accordingly constrain to precisely the opposite
conclusion from that which has been claimed. They do
not justify the reduction of the chapter to a series of
fragments of diverse origin in spite of its manifest unity ;
but this unity shows the falsity of that partition in other
parts of Genesis which is irreconcilable with it.

CONCLUSION OF THE SECTION

Jacob's family is now complete, and he is settled in
Canaan. His subordinate position as a member of the
family of Isaac terminates here, and he is henceforth regarded as the head of the chosen race, which is to bear
his name, Israel. That division of the history entitled
the Generations of Isaac is accordingly concluded at
this point, and is followed, according to the usage of the
book, first, by the divergent line, the Generations of
Esau ; and then by the direct line, the Generations of
Jacob.

Isaac's death is mentioned at the close of this chapter,
not because this is its exact chronological place, but in
order to bring this section of the history to a close before entering upon Jacob's family life in Canaan ; just
as the death of Terah (xi. 32), and that of Abraham (xxv.
8), are recorded in order to prepare the way for the history of their successors. But as Terah survived the call
of Abraham (xii. 1, 4), and even the birth of Isaac (xxi.
5 ; cf. xi. 26), and as Abraham survived the birth of Jacob and Esau (xxv. 26 ; cf. ver. 7), so Isaac continued to
live until Joseph had reached his thirtieth year, and was
advanced to be the second ruler in Egypt. Jacob was
one hundred and thirty years old when presented before
Pharaoh (xlvii. 9), in the second year of the famine (xlv.

11). In the year preceding the first of plenty he was, therefore, one hundred and twenty, and Joseph was thirty (xli. 46); this was the year of Isaac's death (xxxv. 28; xxv. 26). It thus appears that Jacob was ninety years old when Joseph was born; he had then been with Laban fourteen years (xxx. 25 sqq.; xxxi. 41). He was consequently seventy-six when he left home for Paddan-aram. Isaac was at that time one hundred and thirty-six, and was old and blind, and might well say that he "knew not the day of his death" (xxvii. 1, 2); but it is not said, as has sometimes been alleged, that he was on his deathbed and near his end. He lived forty-four years longer; and there is no statement or implication in the text inconsistent with this.

Dillmann infers from xxvi. 34, 35; xxvii. 46; and xxviii. 1–9, that Jacob could only have been between forty and fifty when he went to Paddan-aram. But the facts that Esau married at forty, that his Canaanitish wives gave great offence to Isaac and Rebekah, and that this is made a reason for Jacob's going elsewhere for a wife, do not warrant a conclusion as to Jacob's age at variance with definite data elsewhere supplied. Esau had been married thirty-five years when Jacob left home. Judged by the present standard of human life, Jacob's marriage took place at a very advanced age. But this must be considered in connection with patriarchal longevity. Jacob reached the age of one hundred and forty-seven (xlvii. 28); Isaac, one hundred and eighty (xxxv. 28); Abraham, one hundred and seventy-five (xxv. 7). Abraham was eighty-six years old when his first son Ishmael was born (xvi. 16), and one hundred at the birth of Isaac (xxi. 5).

No argument for critical partition is drawn by Dillmann from the diction of this chapter. The words commonly classed as belonging to P, in vs. 11, 12, are borrowed from ch. xvii., where they have already been considered; and those of vs. 28, 29, are identical with xxv. 7, 8. It should be noted that for הִטָּהֲרוּ וְהַחֲלִיפוּ שִׂמְלֹתֵיכֶם *purify yourselves and change your garments* (ver. 2), Ex. xix. 10 substitutes וְקִדַּשְׁתָּם וְכִבְּסוּ שִׂמְלֹתָם *sanctify them and let them wash their garments*, though both are referred to E. Also in the phrase *come forth from the loins*, ver. 11 has חֲלָצָיִם, while xlvi. 26 ; Ex. i. 5, have יְרֵךְ, though all are referred to P. The same writer may thus, by the confession of the critics, use different expressions for the same idea. Accordingly, such differences are not always nor necessarily an indication of distinct documents.

IX

THE GENERATIONS OF ESAU (CH. XXXVI.; XXXVII. 1)

OPINIONS OF CRITICS

EICHHORN[1] attributed ch. xxxvi. to an independent source, different from both P and J, and sought thus to account for its divergence from other passages in Genesis, particularly in certain proper names; he did not, however, dispute its unity.

Vater[2] considered it a mass of fragments. He says : "No reader of ch. xxxvi. can fail to see that it is made up of many pieces. There are six titles in it, viz., vs. 1, 9, 15, 20, 31, 40. With each of the first three titles there begins a special family-tree of Esau, and the repetition of all the identical names strikes the eye at once. The same concluding words occur in ver. 19 as those with which another fragment closes (ver. 8). The piece that begins with ver. 31, as well as that which begins with ver. 40, is a list of the kings of Edom ; and that from ver. 31 is expressly a list of the kings who reigned in the land of Edom before the Israelites had a king."

After the masterly refutation of Vater by F. H. Ranke,[3] it became customary to refer the entire chapter to P. Thus Knobel : " The Horite-Edomite tribal list, though not preserved altogether unaltered (see ver. 2), is a work of the Elohist, who composed all the regularly

[1] Einleitung in das Alte Testament, 4th Edition, iii., p. 135.
[2] Commentar über den Pentateuch, iii., p. 435.
[3] Untersuchungen über den Pentateuch, i., pp. 243 sqq.

drawn up genealogical tables of Genesis, and could not omit the Edomites, since they stood nearer to the Israelites than the other peoples descended from Terah the father of Abraham."

The assault upon the unity of the chapter was, however, renewed by Hupfeld,[1] who declared that "its heterogeneous genealogical lists were only held together by a geographical conception, their relation to the land of Edom and its inhabitants;" that "the primitive inhabitants of the country, the Horites, and the earliest Edomite kings, do not stand in the remotest relation to the theocratic history of the patriarchs, as traced by P; and that even the lines of descent from Esau cannot be from P in their present form." He ascribed to P only vs. 1–8; and even here he maintained that the last clause in both ver. 1 and ver. 8 is a later gloss, and that the names of Esau's wives (vs. 2, 3) have been corrupted into conformity with the other sources, from which the rest of the chapter was taken by J or R. Kayser assigns vs. 1–8 to P, the rest to J. Wellhausen attributes vs. 6–8, 40–43 to P; vs. 31–39 are preserved unaltered from JE, and the remainder is derived from other sources, principally JE, and remodelled after the style of P. Schrader gives the whole chapter to P, except vs. 40–43. Kuenen[2] adopts the division of Wellhausen, but adds: "The result is not quite satisfactory, for one would have expected more ample information concerning the Edomites than is contained in vs. 40–43. Perhaps a list of Esau's descendants, which was given at this point in P, has been superseded by vs. 1–5, 9–19." So that after removing part of the chapter, the critics feel the need of it or its equivalent. Dillmann, followed by Delitzsch and Vatke, regards the whole chapter as belonging to P, though modified in some particulars by R.

---

[1] Quellen, p. 61.   [2] Hexateuch, p. 68.

It would appear, therefore, that here is another instance in which the critics' affirmation does not hold good, that " whatever difficulty may attend the separation of J and E, the writer P, as opposed to both of them, is always distinct and decisive."

UNITY OF THE CHAPTER

As no name of God occurs in this chapter, no plea for division can arise from this quarter. We have the authority of Dillmann for saying that the style is uniform throughout, and there is nothing in the language that militates against the unity of the chapter. In his second edition he says expressly : " The fine adjustment and arrangement of the piece speaks for the unity of the composition and for P. This piece is rather a model of the way and manner in which he was accustomed to present the material that lay before him." To the objections that the Horites (vs. 20 sqq.), and the kings of Edom (vs. 31 sqq.), do not fall within the author's plan he very properly attributes no weight whatever. The scheme upon which the book of Genesis is constructed made it essential that an account should be given of the descendants of Esau ; and the greater nearness of his relation to Jacob made it natural that a larger space should be given to them than to the descendants of Ishmael and of Keturah (ch. xxv.) : It had been revealed to Rebekah that two nations would spring from her twin children (xxv. 23). This must be verified in the case of Esau as well as of Jacob. If the princes sprung from Ishmael were enumerated, why not the chiefs and kings of the race of Esau? The Horites were the primitive inhabitants of Mount Seir. These were subjugated and in part destroyed by Esau and his descendants (Deut. ii. 12, 22), who amalgamated with the remnant, as appears from the chapter before us (ver. 2 cf. ver. 24, ver. 12 cf. ver. 22). In order to a correct and comprehensive view of the Edomites it was consequently necessary to include the Horites, as is here done.

The materials embraced in the chapter are, therefore, the proper ones to be introduced in this place. They are, in addition, clearly and systematically arranged. There is first a statement of Esau's immediate family (vs. 1–5), which is summed up (ver. 5b) in the words: "These are the sons of Esau, which were born unto him in the land of Canaan," precisely corresponding to the summary of Jacob's family (xxxv. 26b): "These are the sons of Jacob, which were born to him in Paddan-aram." This naturally leads to the mention of Esau's removal from Canaan to Mount Seir (vs. 6–8). The paragraph relating to his immediate family (vs. 1–8) is preliminary to the section which follows concerning the nation descended from him. This is indicated by the title prefixed to them respectively (ver. 1): "These are the generations of Esau; the same is Edom," where, as in ver. 8b, Edom is his personal name (cf. xxv. 30); but in ver. 9: "These are the generations of Esau, the father of Edom, in Mount Seir," as in ver. 43b, Edom is the national name. In tracing the unfolding of Esau's family to a nation precisely the same method is pursued as in the like development of Jacob's family in ch. xlvi., whose sons give name to the tribes, and their sons to the tribal divisions or families (cf. Num. xxvi. 5 sqq.). So here the sons are again named, no longer as individuals as in vs. 4, 5, but as progenitors of the nation, and their sons are given (vs. 10–14), who, it is immediately added, were chieftains of their respective clans (vs. 15–19). The same method is next followed with the Horites by first naming the sons or principal divisions, then their sons or the subdivisions, the national purport of the list being again indicated by enumerating the sons as chieftains of their respective clans (vs. 20–30). Since these various clans were combined into one national organization, with a monarch at its head, a list is next given of the kings who had reigned in the land of Edom (vs. 31–39). And to this is added finally (vs. 40–43) a list of those who presided over the various districts or territorial divisions of the country, " the chiefs of Edom, according to their habitations in the land of their possession," as distinguished from the families or genealogical divisions before given (vs. 15–19). The lack of correspondence between the names in these two divisions, made on an entirely different principle, involves no contradiction, as is assumed by Wellhausen and Schrader, and is the basis of their disintegrating analysis, in which they reach such opposite conclusions.

And the dislocations and erasures proposed by Bruston [1] are not only arbitrary, but mar the symmetry of the chapter as now exhibited. The omission of ver. 1, so as to attach vs. 2–8 to the previous section of the history, the Generations of Isaac, disregards the fact that it had been brought to a formal close by the death and burial of Isaac (xxxv. 29 ; cf. xxv. 8–10, ix. 29), and sunders the record of Esau's family from that of the nation sprung from him, both of which properly belong to the Generations of Esau. And the transfer of xxxvii. 1, so as immediately to follow xxxvi. 8, needlessly interrupts the statements concerning Esau ; the verse is in its proper place after those statements are concluded, and just preceding the next section (xxxvii. 2 sqq.), to which it is preparatory. Nor are vs. 20–28 to be dropped on the plea that vs. 20, 21 are a doublet to vs. 29, 30 ; they sustain precisely the same relation to one another as vs. 15–18 to vs. 10–14, a relation not of mutual exclusion but of co-existence, as indicated in ver. 19. And the correspondence of

[1] As quoted by Dillmann.

vs. 24, 25 to ver. 2, and of ver. 22 to ver. 12, instead of
discrediting the paragraph in which they are found, tends
to confirm its right to a place in this chapter.

The unity and the self-consistency of the chapter have
now been sufficiently vindicated. We are not concerned
to establish its correspondence with P or any one of the
so-called documents, which exist only in the fancy of the
critics. And when Wellhausen objects that a remark interjected in the midst of a genealogy like that in ver. 24,
"this is Anah who found the hot springs in the wilderness, as he fed the asses of Zibeon his father," is without
analogy in P, though frequent in JE, and Dillmann contends, on the other hand, that the peculiar style of P runs
through the entire chapter; or when Wellhausen affirms
that the allusion to kings in Israel (ver. 31) cannot possibly be from P, and Dillmann maintains, *per contra*, that
P and P alone of all the documents makes such allusions,
we must leave the critics to settle these domestic differences between themselves. It only remains for us to
consider the alleged discrepancies between this chapter
and other parts of Genesis, and alleged anachronisms
which are supposed to be inconsistent with the authorship of Moses.

NO DISCREPANCIES

It is claimed that xxxvi. 2, 3 conflicts with xxvi. 34,
xxviii. 9, in respect to the wives of Esau. In the opinion of Wellhausen [1] "this is the most open contradiction
in the whole of Genesis;" and he adds, "either the entire literary criticism of the biblical historical books is
baseless and nugatory, or these passages are from different
sources." We thank him for the word. If the divisive
criticism stakes its all on finding a discrepancy here, its
prospects are not very brilliant.

[1] Composition des Hexateuchs, p. 49.

Esau's wives, according to chs. xxvi., xxviii., were Judith, the daughter of Beeri the Hittite, Basemath, the daughter of Elon the Hittite, and Mahalath, the daughter of Ishmael and the sister of Nebaioth. According to ch. xxxvi., they were Adah, the daughter of Elon the Hittite, Aholibamah, the daughter of Anah, the daughter of Zibeon the Hivite, and Basemath, Ishmael's daughter, sister of Nebaioth.

There is a difference here in the names of the women and of their fathers. Nevertheless, Nöldeke finds no difficulty in referring all to P, and assuming that he derived his materials from discrepant authorities. And it is not easy to see why the original author, be he P or who he may, may not have done this as well as R. But the discrepancy is, after all, imaginary. It is quite insupposable that R or P, or any sensible writer, could have inserted without comment or explanation the bald contradiction here alleged. That the passages in question are not unrelated is plain from the back reference in xxxvi. 2a, "Esau took his wives of the daughters of Canaan," to xxviii. 1, 8 ; and that they are not altogether at variance is apparent from the fact that according to both statements Esau had three wives ; two were Canaanites, one of these being the daughter of Elon the Hittite, and the third was a daughter of Ishmael and sister of Nebaioth. The other Canaanitess is said (xxvi. 34) to have been the daughter of Beeri the Hittite, and (xxxvi. 2) the daughter of Anah, the daughter of Zibeon the Hivite. Ranke understands this to mean that Beeri was her father and Anah her mother, so that there is no variance between the statements, which are mutually supplementary, as when Dinah is called (xxxiv. 1) the daughter of Leah, and (ver. 3) the daughter of Jacob. But this is incorrect, since Anah, the parent of Aholibamah, was the son, and not the daughter, of Zibeon (xxxvi. 24, 25). **Two**

solutions here offer themselves of the apparent discrepancy.   It is exceedingly probable that Beeri was another
name of Anah, given to him, as Hengstenberg suggests,
in consequence of his discovery of warm springs (ver. 24)
(Beer, *spring;* Beeri, *spring-man*).   Or Beeri may have
been the son of Anah; Aholibamah is said (ver. 2) to be
the daughter of Anah and also the daughter of Zibeon,
as Basemath (ver. 3) is the daughter of Ishmael and the
sister of Nebaioth;   here it is plain that " daughter " in
the second clause cannot be taken in the strict sense of
an immediate offspring, but must have the wider meaning of descendant (cf. also ver. 39).   Why not in the
preceding clause likewise?   Why may she not have been
the daughter of Beeri, the granddaughter of Anah, and
the great-granddaughter of Zibeon (cf. Matt. i. 1, and
compare Ezra v. 1 with Zech. i. 1)? the writer preferring
to link her name in this genealogy with her distinguished
ancestors rather than with her own father, who may have
been of less note.   We may not have the data for determining with certainty which is the true solution.   But
so long as any reasonable solution can be shown to exist,
the difficulty cannot be pronounced insoluble.

And as her parentage is thus readily explicable, so are
the seemingly variant statements respecting her nationality.   That she is said (xxvi. 34) to be of Hittite and
(xxxvi. 2) of Hivite descent is not more strange than that
Zibeon is called a Hivite (ver. 2) and a Horite (ver. 20).
The critics commonly insist that the former is a textual
error, and that Hivite should here be changed to Horite,
which involves only a slight alteration in a single letter
(חוי to חרי).   Then if (ver. 2) Esau's wife can be a daughter of Canaan, and at the same time descended from a
Horite, what is there in her being a Hittite to conflict
with her Horite descent?   The fact is that the names of
the Canaanitish tribes are not always used with rigorous

precision. Hittite (Josh. i. 4), like Canaanite and Amorite (Gen. xv. 16), may be used in a narrower or a wider sense, either of the particular tribe so designated or of the population of Palestine generally. And the term Horite is not properly indicative of race or descent, but of a particular style of habitation; it is equivalent to cave-dweller. There is no evidence that the Horites might not be allied in whole or in part to the Hivites; and Hittite might be applied in a general sense to a Hivite.[1]

The only remaining ground of objection is that Esau's wives bear different names in the two passages. If but one was changed, it might be thought an error of transcription. But as all three are altered, it must be due to some common cause. Nothing, however, is more common than this duplication of names (cf. Gen. xvii. 5, 15; xxv. 30; xxxv. 10, 18; xli. 45; Ex. ii. 18, cf. iii. 1; Num. xiii. 16; Judg. vii. 1; 2 Kin. xxiii. 34; xxiv. 17; Dan. i. 7, etc.), especially at some important crisis or change of life. So Tabitha was also called Dorcas (Acts ix. 36), and Peter Cephas, and Thomas Didymus, and Joses Barnabas, and Saul Paul. If a former emperor of the French were called Napoleon on one page and Buonaparte on another, or a late prime minister of England were spoken of at one time as Disraeli and at another as Beaconsfield, it would create no surprise. Harmer[2] observes that " the Eastern people are oftentimes known by several names; this might arise from their having more names than one given them at first; or it might arise from their assuming a new and different name upon particular occurrences in life. This last is most probable, since such a custom continues in the East to this day;

---

[1] In like manner Amorite is used (xlviii. 22) in a general sense of the Hivites (xxxiv. 2).

[2] Observations on Divers Passages of Scripture, vol. ii., p. 501.

and it evidently was sometimes done anciently." And
he cites in the same connection the following from Sir
John Chardin : "The reason why the Israelites and
other Eastern people are called by different names is because they frequently change them, as they change in
point of age, condition, or religion. This custom has continued to our times in the East, and is generally practised upon changing religions ; and it is pretty common
upon changing condition. The Persians have preserved
this custom more than any other nation. I have seen
many governors of provinces among them assume new
names with their new dignity. But the example of the
reigning king of Persia (he began his reign in 1667, and
died in 1694) is more remarkable: the first years of the
reign of this prince having been unhappy, on account of
wars and famine in many provinces, his counsellors persuaded him that the name he had till then borne was
fatal, and that the fortune of the empire would not be
changed till he changed that name. This was done ; the
prince was crowned again under the name of Soliman ;
all the seals, all the coins, that had the name of Sefi were
broken, the same as if the king had been dead, and another had taken possession. *The women more frequently
change their names than the men. . . . Women that
marry again*, or let themselves out anew, and slaves,
commonly alter their names upon these changes." Esau's
wives at their marriage left their own tribes to become
the heads of a new race ; is it strange that they should
adopt new names ?

Another alleged inconsistency relates to the separation
of Esau and Jacob. According to xxxii. 4 (E. V., ver. 3)
Esau was already in Seir before Jacob's return from Paddan-aram. But xxxvi. 6, 7 states that he removed from
Canaan from the face of Jacob, because there was not
room for both of them to dwell together. There is no

real discrepancy here, however. Esau with a band of men had a provisional residence in Mount Seir before Jacob's return home ; but it is nowhere said that he had entirely abandoned Canaan and removed his family and effects from it. Though he had fixed his head-quarters for a season in Seir, he had no disposition to yield Canaan or to surrender his right to the paternal inheritance to Jacob, who had defrauded him of his father's blessing. Hence he came out with an armed force to obstruct his return to the land of his fathers. It was only after Jacob's fervent supplication (xxxii. 10 sqq., E. V., vs. 9 sqq.), and his importunate wrestling for a blessing on the bank of the Jabbok (vs. 25 sqq.), that Esau's deadly hate (xxvii. 41) was by divine influence changed to fraternal love (xxxiii. 4). He thenceforth abandoned his claim to the possession of Canaan, and peaceably withdrew with all that he had from the land. He returned again at the interment of his father (xxxv. 29), as Ishmael had done at the burying of Abraham (xxv. 9); and then the final separation of the brothers took place.

NO ANACHRONISM

An alleged anachronism yet remains to be considered. It is confidently affirmed that Moses could not possibly have written vs. 31–39. Verse 31 reads, " And these are the kings that reigned in the land of Edom, before there reigned any king over the children of Israel."

The first impression upon a cursory reading of this verse might naturally be that it was written after the establishment of the monarchy in Israel. Wellhausen contends that vs. 31–39 could not possibly have been written by P, " since this document keeps much too strictly to its archaistic stand-point for us to attribute to it the unconcealed reference to the period of the Israelitish kings in ver. 31." We so far agree with him as to think it incredible that the writer of the Pentateuch should in this one instance have departed so far from the Mosaic stand-point, which he elsewhere steadfastly maintains throughout, as to have introduced here a passage which must be dated as late as the time of Saul or David. And in fact a careful examination of the passage reveals several particulars calculated to modify the first cursory impression. Eight kings of Edom are named in these verses who are nowhere else mentioned in the history; and we have no data for determining just when they reigned. No king is succeeded by his own son. It would seem, therefore, to have been an elective, not an hereditary, monarchy. The death of the first seven kings is mentioned, but not that of the eighth, whence it is probable that he was still reigning when this passage was written. This probability is enhanced by the consideration that the writer seems to be better acquainted with the domestic relations of this king than of his predecessors; at least he mentions the name and lineage of his wife, which is not done in the case of any other.

There was a kingdom in Edom in the time of David (1 Kin. xi. 14–17), and reference is made to Hadad " of the king's seed in Edom." He cannot be identified with Hadad (ver. 36), or with Hadar (ver. 39) of the passage before us, as he seems never to have reached the throne; or if he did, it must have been after the beginning of Solomon's reign, so that he was not one who reigned before there was any king in Israel. Moreover, the expression used shows that the succession to the throne was then hereditary. The kingdom consequently is not that which is described in the verses now under discussion; it was on a different basis.

There was also a king in Edom in the time of Moses (Num. xx. 14 ; cf. Judg. xi. 17), as well as in the kindred

nations of Moab (Num. xxii. 4), Midian (xxxi. 8), and
Amalek (xxiv. 7; cf. 1 Sam. xv. 20). We read also at
that time of dukes in Edom (Ex. xv. 15), showing that the
kingdom was superinduced upon and coexisted with the
dukedoms that are likewise spoken of in Gen. xxxvi.;
this is a coincidence worth noting. From the death of
Moses to the choice of Saul as king were three hundred
and fifty-seven years (1 Kin. vi. 1; 2 Sam. v. 4; Acts
xiii. 21; Num. xiv. 33). Now, even supposing the king
in the Mosaic age to have been the first that ruled in
Edom, we must assign to each of his successors a reign
of fifty-one years to fill up the interval to the time of
Saul, which is quite insupposable; and the more so as
elective monarchs would in all probability be chosen in
mature age, and their reigns be on the average briefer in
consequence. This list of kings does not, therefore, extend to the reign of Saul. It cannot, consequently, have
been written after the establishment of the kingdom in
Israel, and intended to enumerate all the kings that had
reigned in Edom up to that time.

Furthermore, the fourth of these kings, it is said (ver.
35), "smote Midian in the field of Moab." Midian was
in alliance with Moab in the time of Moses (Num. xxii.
4, 7); we are not informed that they were so subsequently. Israel occupied the plains of Moab before
crossing the Jordan (Num. xxxi. 12), and were thenceforward adjacent to its territory. This event was in all
probability pre-Mosaic.

Edom was so powerful and warlike a people in the
Mosaic age that Israel did not venture to force a passage
through their territory (Num. xx. 20, 21). This seems to
imply that the kingdom had not been recently established. The same thing may be inferred from the mention of "the king's highway" (xx. 17).

These various considerations conspire to make it ex-

tremely probable that several of these kings, at least,
were pre-Mosaic; why not all? Why may not the last
of the series be the one with whom Moses had dealings,
and this be the explanation of the fact that the series is
carried no further? Esau's final settlement in Seir took
place before the death of Isaac. And Isaac died ten
years before Jacob went down to Egypt (Gen. xxxv. 28;
xxv. 26; xlvii. 9), and hence four hundred and forty
years before the exodus of the children of Israel (Ex. xii.
41), or four hundred and eighty before the death of
Moses. This affords ample time for the establishment
of the kingdom in Edom, and the reign of eight kings.
There is absolutely no reason in the nature of the case,
or in any known fact, for affirming that any one of these
kings was post-Mosaic.

But could Moses have used the expressions in ver.
31? [1] Why not? It had been explicitly promised to
Abraham (xvii. 6) and to Jacob (xxxv. 11) that kings
should arise from their seed. Balaam foretells the
exalted dignity of the kingdom in Israel (Num. xxiv. 7).
Moses anticipates that when the people were settled in
Canaan they would wish to set a king over them like all
the nations around them; and though he did not enjoin
the establishment of a kingdom, he gave regulations respecting it (Deut. xvii. 14 sqq.). That was the common
usage of the nations. It was the prevalent conception of
a well-ordered and properly administered government.
Now Jacob inherited the blessing, and Esau did not. It
had been foretold that Esau, the elder, should serve Jacob,

---

[1] Astruc urges substantially the same arguments that are presented
above to prove that the kings of Edom here spoken of were pre-Mosaic,
but he supposes that the king in Israel referred to was God, who became their king by formal covenant with them at Sinai (Ex. xix.), and
is so called Deut. xxxiii. 5 (cf. Judg. viii. 22, 23; 1 Sam. viii. 7, xii.
12); or else Moses or Joshua, who, though they are not called kings,
were yet invested with supreme authority under God himself.

the younger; that the people descended from the latter should be stronger than the people descended from the former (xxv. 23); that Jacob should be lord over Esau (xxvii. 29). Yet Esau had been a compact, thoroughly organized kingdom for eight successive reigns, while Israel had just escaped from bondage, had attained to no such organization, had not yet had a single king. How could Moses fail to note so remarkable an occurrence? And why was it not perfectly natural for him to have made precisely the statement which we here find?

Dillmann says that if the last of these kings was a contemporary of Moses, the writer could not have said, "These are the kings that reigned in the land of Edom, before there reigned any king over the children of Israel;" he could only have said, "before the children of Israel went up out of Egypt," or "before they conquered Canaan." This is of weight only against Dillmann's own position. If this line of kings simply extended to Moses's time, as we have seen that there is every reason to believe, no post-Mosaic writer, and especially no one living in or after the time of Saul, could have made the reign of kings in Israel the *terminus ad quem*. No one but Moses himself, or a writer in the Mosaic age, contrasting the facts thus far developed in the line of Esau and Jacob with what had been predicted respecting them, could have used the language here employed. Instead of indicating an anachronism, the form of expression thus points directly to Moses as its author.

While the critics disagree respecting the authorship of this chapter in general, they are unanimous in assigning vs. 6-8 to P, and in claiming that the characteristic expressions of those verses, which are the ones commonly used of patriarchal migrations, are those of P. How little reason they have for this has already been shown under ch. xii. 4b, 5, Marks of P (3), No. 2 and 5.

X

THE GENERATIONS OF JACOB (XXXVII. 2–L.)

THE first thirty-six chapters of Genesis have now been examined, and no justification has yet been found for the critical hypothesis that the book is compounded from pre-existing documents. We proceed to inquire whether this hypothesis has any better support in the next and only remaining section of this book.

THE UNITY OF PLAN

The divisive hypothesis encounters here in full measure the same insuperable difficulty which meets it throughout the book of Genesis, and particularly in the life of Abraham, and the early history of Jacob. The unity of plan and purpose which pervades the whole, so that every constituent part has its place and its function, and nothing can be severed from it without evident mutilation, positively forbids its being rent asunder in the manner proposed by the critics. If ever a literary product bore upon its face the evidence of its oneness, this is true of the exquisite and touching story of Joseph, which is told with such admirable simplicity and a pathos that is unsurpassed, all the incidents being grouped with the most telling effect, until in the supreme crisis the final disclosure is made. No such high work of art was ever produced by piecing together selected fragments of diverse origin.

The critics tell us that the apparent unity is due to

the skill of the redactor. But the suggestion is altogether impracticable. A writer who gathers his materials from various sources may elaborate them in his own mind, and so give unity to his composition. But a redactor who limits himself to piecing together extracts culled from different works by distinct authors, varying in conceptions, method, and design, can by no possibility produce anything but patchwork, which will betray itself by evident seams, mutilated figures, and want of harmony in the pattern. No such incongruities can be detected in the section before us by the most searching examination. All that the critics affect to discover vanish upon a fair and candid inspection.

Moreover, the story of Joseph, complete as it is in itself, is but one link in a uniform and connected chain, and is of the same general pattern with those that precede it. With striking individual diversities, both of character and experience, the lives of the several patriarchs are, nevertheless, cast in the same general mould. Divine revelations are made to Joseph at the outset, forecasting his future (xxxvii. 5 sqq.), as to Abraham (xii. 1 sqq.), and to Jacob (xxviii. 11 sqq.). Each was sent away from his paternal home and subjected to a series of trials, issuing both in discipline of character and in ultimate prosperity and exaltation. And the story of Joseph fits precisely into its place in the general scheme, which it is the purpose of Genesis to trace, by which God was preparing and training a people for himself. By a series of marvellous providences, as the writer does not fail to point out (xlv. 5, 7 ; l. 20), the chosen seed was preserved from extinction and located within the great empire of Egypt, as had been already foreshown to Abraham (xv. 13 sqq.), that they might unfold into a nation ready, when the proper time should arrive, to be transplanted into Canaan.

These broad and general features, in which the same
constructive mind is discernible throughout, are lost
sight of by critics who occupy themselves with petty details, spying out doublets in every emphatic repetition or
in the similar features of distinct events, finding occasions of offence in every transition or digression, however
natural and appropriate, and creating variance by setting
separate parts of the same transaction in antagonism, as
though each were exclusive of the other, when in fact
they belong together and are perfectly consistent; or by
dislocating phrases and paragraphs from their true connection and imposing upon them senses foreign to their
obvious intent.   These artifices are perpetually resorted
to by the critics, and constitute, in fact, their stock arguments, just because they refuse to apprehend the author's
plan, and to judge of the fitness of every particular from
his point of view, but insist instead upon estimating
everything from some self-devised standard of their own.

Vater, to whom the Pentateuch was a collection of
heterogeneous fragments, and who was ready to go to
any length in the work of disintegration, nevertheless
says [1] that the history of Joseph is " a connected whole, to
rend it asunder would be to do violence to the narrative."
And Tuch, who finds a double narrative throughout the
rest of Genesis, declares that it is impossible to do so
here.   " Several wrong courses have been ventured upon,"
he says,[2] " in respect to the narrator of the life of Joseph.
Some relying upon insecure or misunderstood criteria
have sought to extort two divergent accounts.   Others
have held that the documents have been so worked over
that it is impracticable to separate them with any degree
of certainty.   But we must insist upon the close connection of the whole recital, in which one thing carries an-

[1] Commentar über den Pentateuch, i., p. 290 ; iii., p. 435.
[2] Commentar über die Genesis, 2d edit., p. 417.

other along with it, and recognize in that which is continuously written the work of one author." And he adds [1] respecting ch. xxxvii.: "This section in particular has been remarkably maltreated by the divisive document and redactor hypotheses of Ilgen and Gramberg without bringing forth anything but an arbitrary piece of mosaic work, which is shattered by the inner consistency and connection of the passage itself." The posthumous editor of Tuch's "Commentary" interposes the caveat that "since Hupfeld and Boehmer the unity of the history of Joseph can no longer be maintained." But the fact is that no inconsistencies have since been pretended in this narrative which were not already pointed out by Ilgen and Gramberg. Whether the later attempts to establish duplicate accounts have been more successful than those which Tuch so pointedly condemns, we shall inquire presently.

The urgent motive which impels the most recent critics to split the history of Joseph asunder at all hazards is thus frankly stated by Wellhausen : [2] "The principal source for this last section of Genesis is JE. It is to be presumed that this work is here as elsewhere compounded of J and E. Our previous results urge to this conclusion, and would be seriously shaken if this were not demonstrable. I hold, therefore, that the attempt 'to dismember the flowing narrative of Joseph into sources' is not a failure,[3] but is as necessary as the decomposition of Genesis in general."

[1] Commentar über die Genesis, 2d edit., p. 424.
[2] Composition des Hexateuchs, p. 52.
[3] The allusion is to Nöldeke (Untersuchungen, p. 32), who says "the attempt to dismember this flowing narrative into sources is a veritable failure."

LACK OF CONTINUITY IN THE DOCUMENTS

If distinct documents have been combined in this portion of Genesis, the critical analysis which disentangles them and restores each to its original separateness might be expected to bring forth orderly narratives, purged of interpolations and dislocations, with the true connection restored and a consequent gain to each in significance, harmony, and clearness. Instead of this there is nothing to show for P, J, or E but mutilated fragments, which yield no continuous or intelligible narrative, but require for their explanation and to fill their lacunæ precisely those passages which the critical process has rent from them. We are expected to assume, with no other evidence than that the exigencies of the hypothesis require it, that these P, J, and E fragments represent what were originally three complete documents, but that the missing parts were removed by R.

"We now come," as Nöldeke says, "to the most distressing gap in the whole of P." And he undertakes to account for it by the gratuitous assumption that P's account was so decidedly contradictory to that of the other documents that R was obliged to omit it altogether. In fact P is almost as absolute a blank in what follows as it was in regard to Jacob's abode in Paddan-aram.

THE DIVINE NAMES

The divine names here give no aid in the matter of critical division. Jehovah occurs in but three of these fourteen chapters, and in only eight verses, each time with evident appropriateness. It is found in connection with God's dealings with the chosen race, on the one hand his punitive righteousness toward offenders (xxxviii. 7, 10), and on the other his gracious care of Joseph, assurances of which are heaped together at the beginning of his servitude in Egypt (xxxix. 2, 3, 5, 21, 23); after this it appears but once, viz., in a pious ejaculation of the dying patriarch Jacob (xlix. 18). Elohim occurs repeatedly in these chapters, and in a manner which Hupfeld ("Quellen," p. 178) confesses to be embarrassing to the critics as contravening the requirements of their hypothesis. The predominance of this name in this section cannot be traced to the habit of a particular writer, since it is supposed to be about equally shared between J and E. It is regulated by the proprieties of the situation, with which it is always in accord. There are three considerations which explain the matter. Elohim is used—

1. When Egyptians speak or are spoken to, as xli. 16, 38; and Joseph is classed as an Egyptian while he was unknown to his brethren (xlii. 18; xliv. 16).

2. Where God's general providential orderings are referred to (xli. 51, 52); and especially where they are explicitly or implicitly contrasted with the purposes of men (xlv. 5–9; l. 19, 20).

3. Where there is an appeal to God's almighty power (xlvi. 2–4); in this case El Shaddai may be substituted (xliii. 14; xlviii. 3, 4).

DICTION AND STYLE

Neither is the partition conducted on the basis of such literary criteria as diction and style. Only a few scattered scraps, amounting in all to about twenty-five verses,[1] are assigned to P, such as can be severed from

[1] Viz., xxxvii. 2a; xli. 46a; xlvi. 6, 7; xlvii. 5–11, 27b, 28; xlviii. 3–6 (7?); xlix. 1a, 28b–33; l. 12, 13, with a possible addition of xlvi. 8–27, the enumeration of Jacob's descendants, about which the critics are not agreed.

the main body of the narrative as entering least into its
general flow and texture. The mass of the matter, as
has uniformly been the case since ch. xxiii., is divided
between J and E, which by confession of the critics
can only be distinguished with the greatest difficulty.[1]
Whenever it is impossible to effect a partition it is
claimed that R must have blended the documents inex-
tricably together. In other places a few disconnected
clauses are sundered from a J section and given to E, or
from an E section and given to J; and these are claimed
as evidence of two separate narratives. At other times
arbitrary grounds of distinction are invented, such as
assigning to E all dreams that are mentioned, or different incidents of the narrative are parcelled between
them, as though they were varying accounts of the same
thing, whereas they are distinct items in a complete and
harmonious whole. Genealogical tables, dates, removals,
deaths, and legal transactions or ritual enactments are as
a rule given to P. Historical narratives are attributed
to J and E, and are divided between them not by any
definite criteria of style, but by the artifice of imaginary
doublets or arbitrary distinctions, leaving numerous
breaks and unfilled gaps in their train. And in this
halting manner the attempt is made to establish the

---

[1] Thus Kayser says (Das Vorexilische Buch, p. 28) : "The little fragments of the Elohist (P) inserted in Genesis from ch. xxiii. onward all
refer to keeping the race elected in Abraham pure from admixture
with the Canaanitish tribes, and its exclusive right to the possession of
Canaán, which is confirmed both by narratives of acquisition of the soil
and of the departure of the side lines of Ishmael and Esau. Sparse as
they have thus far been found, they become still more rare in what
follows. The attempt of Tuch and Knobel, based on the supplement
hypothesis, to find in the history of Jacob's descendants, especially of
Joseph, a radical portion of the so-called primary document P, has been
shown to be untenable, since Hupfeld has given the proof that the passages referred to the first Elohist by those scholars belong to the second
Elohist, worked over by, and inseparable from, the Jehovist."

existence of what the critics would have us regard as separate and continuous documents. The method itself is sufficient to condemn the whole process and to show that the results are altogether factitious. It could be applied with equal plausibility to any composition, whatever the evidence of its unity.

JOSEPH SOLD INTO EGYPT—(CH. XXXVII. 2–36)

VARIANCE AMONG CRITICS

No pretext for division is here afforded by Elohim or Jehovah, since no name of God occurs in this chapter. Astruc, Eichhorn, and Tuch regard it as a unit, and refer it without abatement to P. It has, however, been variously divided, and it affords a good illustration of the ease with which a narrative embracing several incidents can be partitioned at the pleasure of the critic.[1] Ilgen

[1] This chapter is partitioned by different critics in the following manner :

Ilgen : P, vs. 2, 14 (omit "and he came to Shechem"), 18b, c, 21–23a, b, 24, 25a, 28a, b, d, 29–31, 32b, c, 34, 36. E, vs. 3–13, 14 (last clause), 15–18a, 19, 20, 25b–27, 23, 28c, 32, 33, 35 ; xxxix. 1.

Gramberg: P, vs. 2, 18, 21 (for "Reuben" read "Judah"), 25–27, 28c, d ; xxxix. 1. J, vs. 5–11, 19, 20, 22, 24, 28a, b, 29, 30, 36. Common to both, vs. 3, 4, 12–17, 23, 31–35.

Knobel : P, vs. 2–4, 23–27, 28c, d, 31, 32a. Rechtsbuch, vs. 5–22a, 28a, b, 32b–36. J, vs. 22b, 29, 30.

Boehmer : J, vs. 2a, 3, 4, 11a, 18c, 25b–27, 28b, 32a, c, d, 33a, d, 34, 35a, b. E, vs. 5–10, 11b, 12 (omit "in Shechem"), 14a, b, 17c, 18a, b, 19–21, 22a, 23–25a, 28a, 29–31, 32b, 33b, c, 35c, 36. R, vs. 2b, 5b, 8b, 12 (in Shechem), 13, 14c, 15–17a, b, d, 22b, 23c, 28c, 36 (Potiphar).

Hupfeld : J, vs. 25b–27, 28c. E, vs. 2–25a, 28a, b, d–36.

Schrader : J, vs. 23–27, 28c, d, 31–35. E, vs. 2b–22, 28a, b, 29, 30, 36.

Wellhausen : J, vs. 12, 13a, b, 14–17, 19–21 (for "Reuben" read "Judah"), 23, 24, 25–27, 28c, 31–36. E, vs. 2b–11, 13c, 18, 22, 28a, b, d–30.

partitions it between the two Elohists with the following result : P uses the name Jacob (vs. 1, 34), represents Joseph as habitually with the flocks (ver. 2), wearing an ordinary coat (vs. 23a, 32b, 33), incurring the hatred of his brothers by bringing an evil report of them to his father (ver. 2). Reuben as the first-born takes a prominent part, counsels not to kill Joseph, and is afterward inconsolable (vs. 21, 22, 29, 30). Midianites take Joseph from the pit without the knowledge of his brothers (ver. 28), and sell him into Egypt to Potiphar, an officer of Pharaoh (ver. 36). E, on the contrary, uses the name Israel (vs. 3, 13), and represents Joseph as the son of his father's old age (ver. 3), unacquainted with the flocks (vs. 15, 16), wearing a coat of many colors (or rather a long garment with sleeves) (vs. 3, 23b, 32a), hated by his brothers because of his distinguished dress and his father's partiality for him (ver. 4), and hated still more for his dreams (vs. 5–11). Judah acts the part of the first-born (ver. 26) ; his brothers on his advice sell Joseph to

Dillmann, 1st edition: J, vs. 3, 4, 23c, 25–27, 28c, some expressions in 32–35. J and E mixed, vs. 23, 32, 34, 35. E, the remainder.

Dillmann, 3d edition : J, vs. 2b, 3, 4, 18b, 21 (for " Reuben " read " Judah "), 23*–27, 28c, 31*–35*. J and E mixed, vs. 23, 31, 32 (" coat " and " long tunic " in combination), vs. 34, 35 (34b and 35b doublets). R, vs. 5b, 8b, Israel, Shechem, and Hebron in 14, slight change in 18. In ver. 9, " and told it to his brethren," is an interpolation. E, rest of the chapter.

Kittell: J, vs. 2b, 3, 4a, 11a, 12, 13a, 14–18, 21 (for " Reuben " read " Judah "), 23c, 25b–27, 28c, 32, 33 (in great part), 35 (except the last part). E, vs. 2a, c, 4b–10, 11b, 13b, 19, 20 (except " and cast him into one of the pits "), 22, 23a, b, 24, 25a, 28a, b, d, 29–31, parts of 32 and 33, 34, the last three words of 35, 36.

Kautzsch : J, vs. 3, 4, 21 (for " Reuben " read " Judah "), 23c, 25b–27, 28c, 32, 33, 35. E, vs. 2c, 5a, 6–11, 19, 20, 22, 28a, b, d–31, 32 (first verb), 34, 36. JE, vs. 2a, 12–18, 23a, b, 24, 25a. R, vs. 2b, 5b, 8b, 10a.

Driver : J, vs. 12–21, 25–27, 28c, 31–35. E, vs. 2b–11, 22–24, 28a, b, d–30, 36.

the Ishmaelites (vs. 27, 28b). His father says that he will go down to Sheol mourning for his son (ver. 35). Joseph is sold to some Egyptian whose name is not given (xxxix. 1 ; " Potiphar, an officer of Pharaoh, captain of the guard," is ejected from this verse as an interpolation). De Wette [1] charges Ilgen with being arbitrary and going too far, but agrees with him to a certain extent. He fancies that there are inconsistencies in the narrative, which can only be relieved by the assumption that two variant accounts have been blended. After the adoption of Reuben's proposal (ver. 23) to cast Joseph into a pit instead of killing him, Judah says (ver. 26), " What profit is it if we slay our brother? " as if they still intended to kill him. Reuben makes no objection to Judah's proposal to sell Joseph ; and yet he is afterward distressed at not finding Joseph in the pit, though there had been no mention of his absence when the sale was effected. This indicates that different stories are here confused together. According to one, Joseph was cast at Reuben's suggestion into a pit, and subsequently drawn out and carried off by Midianite merchants who were passing. According to the other, Joseph's brothers had conspired to kill him, but sold him instead to Ishmaelites.

Gramberg distributes the chapter between P and J, certain paragraphs being common to both. Both tell that Joseph was his father's favorite, and had been presented by him with a long robe, which excited his brothers' hostility. Both tell that Joseph was sent by his father from Hebron to Shechem to find his brothers, who were with the flocks. And both describe the deception practised upon Jacob, and his inconsolable grief at the loss of Joseph. P tells of Judah and the sale to the

[1] Beiträge zur Einleitung in das Alte Testament, ii., pp. 142 sqq.

Ishmaelites, and J of Reuben and Joseph being carried
off by the Midianites ; which is the reverse of Ilgen's assignment, who makes P tell of the latter and E of the
former.

Knobel, the latest and most minutely elaborate of the
supplementary critics, recognizes in Genesis only an
Elohist Primary Document, P, which gives a comparatively trustworthy statement of facts ; and a Jehovist
Reviser, J, who incorporates with the preceding the leg-
endary embellishments of later times. P's account is
that Joseph's reporting his brothers' misdeeds and his
father's partiality for him so exasperated his brothers,
with whom he was feeding the flocks, that they threw
him into a pit, and then at Judah's instance sold him to
Ishmaelites, who took him to Egypt ; after this they dip
Joseph's coat in blood and send it to their father. J
adds from some other authority the prophetic dreams,
Joseph's being sent by his father in quest of his brothers, their conspiring against him as they saw him approaching, Reuben's proposal not to shed his blood but
to put him in a pit (meaning, in the intent of the authority from which this was drawn, to let him perish there ;
but, by inserting ver. 22b, J converts this into a purpose
to restore him to his father ; and he further introduces
in the same vein (vs. 29, 30) Reuben's subsequent distress at not finding Joseph in the pit). J makes no mention of the adoption of Reuben's proposal ; but this is to
be presumed, as Midianites pass, who draw Joseph out
of the pit and sell him to Potiphar. Finally, Jacob's
grief is depicted at the sight of his son's coat, which was
sent to him.

Böhmer divides the chapter between J, E, and R, assigning nothing whatever to P. Even the title of the
section (ver. 2a), "These are the generations of Jacob,"
which the critics commonly claim for P, though most un-

reasonably, is given by him to J. A large share is imputed to R, in order to cover the halting-places of the analysis, or to carry the principle of subdivision consistently through. As three reasons are assigned for the hostility of Joseph's brothers, viz., his evil report of their conduct, his father's partiality, and his dreams, and the last two are divided between J and E, the first (ver. 2b) is given to R. As each document is supposed to speak of but one ground of hostility, this could not be represented as augmenting what had not been before alluded to ; hence, vs. 5b, 8b, must have been introduced by R. As E never speaks of Shechem,[1] and J would not have the sons of Jacob feed their flocks where they had committed such a deed of violence [2] (xxxiv. 25–27) ; moreover, as Hebron was the abode of the patriarchs in P (xxiii. 2, xxxv. 27), but not in J or E, vs. 13, 14c and the words " in Shechem " (ver. 12) must belong to R. For a like reason the designation of Dothan as the scene of the transaction that follows is not referable to J or E, hence vs. 15–17 are given to R, except the single clause in ver. 17c, "and Joseph went after his brethren." R inserted ver. 22b to

---

[1] Böhmer assigns xxxiii. 18 to J, and xxxv. 4 to R.

[2] Matthew Poole remarked upon this : " One may rather wonder that he durst venture his sons and his cattle there, where that barbarous massacre had been committed. But those pastures being his own (xxxiii. 19) and convenient for his use, he did commit himself and them to that same good Providence which watched over him then and ever since, and still kept up that terror which then he sent upon them. Besides, Jacob's sons and servants made a considerable company, and the men of Shechem being universally slain, others were not very forward to revenge their quarrel, where there was any hazard to themselves in such an enterprise." It may be added that in the time which had since elapsed Jacob had had opportunity to acquaint himself with the temper of the surrounding population and to re-establish peaceful relations with them. It is not even necessary to suppose with Astruc (Conjectures, p. 401) that the affair of Dinah took place after Joseph had been sold into Egypt.

make it appear that Reuben intended to restore Joseph
to his father, which was not his intention in the original
story. Ver. 23c must also be referred to him, since E
could not mention " the long robe," of which only J had
spoken (ver. 3) ; also ver. 28c, because it duplicates xxxix.
1. Finally, the name " Potiphar " is struck out of ver. 36
as an insertion by R. This is with the view of creating
a discrepancy between this verse and xxxix. 1. " Potiphar " is erased from the former, and " an officer of Pharaoh, captain of the guard," is erased from the latter, and
then it is claimed that these verses contain variant representations of the person to whom Joseph was sold.
Other critics accomplish the same end by retaining
" Potiphar," in ver. 36, and erasing it in xxxix. 1. All
which shows how easy it is to reverse a writer's positive
statements, and create divergences where there are none
by simply making free with the text.

Hupfeld (" Quellen," pp. 67 sqq.) reproduces the view
of De Wette by giving the entire chapter to E, except vs.
25b–27, 28c. The narrative is thus resolved into two
accounts differing in three points, viz., the name of the
brother who saved Joseph's life, how he came to Egypt,
and the person who bought him. According to E Reuben proposed to put him in a pit, whence he was secretly drawn out by passing Midianites, who sold him to
Potiphar, captain of the guard. According to J, at Judah's suggestion Joseph's brothers sell him to a caravan
of Ishmaelites, of whom he was bought by an unnamed
Egyptian (xxxix. 1). It is claimed that each account is
complete and separable ; only in ver. 28 they are so combined that the verbs are referred to wrong subjects. The
clause, " and sold Joseph to the Ishmaelites for twenty
pieces of silver," is to be sundered from the rest of the
verse and attached to ver. 27. Verse 28 will then read,
" and there passed by Midianites, merchantmen ; and

they (the Midianites) drew and lifted up Joseph out of
the pit. And they brought Joseph into Egypt." This
connects back with ver. 25a; it occurred while Joseph's
brothers were sitting together taking bread. It does not
appear from J that Joseph was put into a pit at all.
Schrader enlarges J's portion by adding to it (vs. 23, 24,
31-35), with the effect of transferring the statement of
Joseph's being put in the pit, and of his father's grief,
from E to J. This still leaves the whole of the narrative prior to ver. 23 with E, and nothing in J respecting
the relation of Joseph to his brothers, until suddenly,
without a word of explanation, they are found deliberat-
ing whether to kill him or to sell him as a slave.

Wellhausen is too acute a critic and too ingenious in
discovering doublets to suffer this state of things to
continue. He remarks:[1] "Verses 12-24 are preparatory
to vs. 25 sqq., and are indispensable for both E and J.
To be sure, no certain conclusion can be drawn from this
alone as to its composite character, but a presumption is
created in its favor which is confirmed by actual traces
of its being double." Acting upon this presumption he
sets himself to discover the traces. It seems to him that
"Here am I," is not the proper answer to what Israel
says to Joseph (ver. 13); and that ver. 18 does not fit in
between vs. 17 and 19. "They saw him afar off" implies that he had not yet "found them;" and "they conspired against him to slay him," is a parallel to ver. 20.
Verses 21 and 22 are also doublets, only instead of "Reuben," in ver. 21 (an old suggestion of Gramberg's) we
should read "Judah," whose proposal is to cast him into
the pit (ver. 20), to perish, without killing him themselves, while Reuben (ver. 22) has the secret purpose of
rescuing him. From these premises he concludes that
while J is the principal narrator in this paragraph, as

[1] Composition des Hexateuchs. p. 53,

shown by Israel (ver. 13), Hebron (ver. 14), and verbal
suffixes *passim*, nevertheless vs. 13c, 14a, 18, 22, and parts
of vs. 23, 24, in which אֹתוֹ repeatedly occurs instead of a
suffix attached to the verb, belong to E and represent his
parallel narrative, which has only been preserved in this
fragmentary way.

In vs. 2b–11 he is less successful in discovering traces
of twofold authorship. These verses are attributed to
E, who deals more largely with dreams than J, and who,
moreover, has בֶּן זְקֻנִים *son of his old age* (ver. 3 as xxi. 2)
against יֶלֶד זְקֻנִים *child of his old age* (xliv. 20 J); כְּתֹנֶת
פַּסִּים *long tunic* (ver. 3 as vs. 23, 32) against כְּתֹנֶת *coat*, J,
and especially has אֹתוֹ constantly (vs. 4, 5, 8, 9), instead
of a verbal suffix, in marked contrast with vs. 12 sqq.
" With the sons of Bilhah," etc. (ver. 2) does not accord
accurately with the preceding clause, and " he told it to
his father and to his brethren " (J ver. 10) deviates from
the statement in ver. 9; but he thinks these to be additions by a later hand and not from J. He has, however,
one resource; vs. 19, 20, J, speak of Joseph's dreams,
consequently J must have given some account of them,
though it has not been preserved.

Dillmann proves in this instance to have had sharper
eyes than Wellhausen, and has found the desired doublets where the latter could discover none. To be sure,
he unceremoniously sets aside Wellhausen's criteria.
He gives vs. 19, 20, to E (not J) in spite of repeated verbal suffixes which he will not recognize here as a discriminating mark, in spite, too, of הַלָּזֶה which occurs
xxiv. 65 J, and nowhere else in the Old Testament; and
accordingly he does not allow the inference that J gave a
parallel account of the dreams. But taking the hint
from Böhmer he finds the coveted parallel by setting
vs. 3, 4, as J's explanation of the hatred of Joseph, over
against that of E in vs. 5–11. According to J, his broth-

ers hated him because he was his father's favorite ; according to E, because of his ambitious dreams.[1] J says "they hated him" (ver. 4) וַיִּשְׂנְאוּ ; E " they envied him " (ver. 11) וַיְקַנְאוּ.[2] To be sure שָׂנֵא hated occurs twice over in the E paragraph (vs. 5, 8), and with explicit reference to ver. 4, clearly indicating the identity of the writer. But if anyone imagines that such a trifle as this can disturb a critic's conclusions he is much mistaken. Dillmann blandly says that the unwelcome clauses were inserted by R, and lo ! they disappear at once. The word of a critic is equal to the wand of a magician. When he says that ver. 5b is inappropriate where it stands because the actual recital of the dream follows (vs. 6, 7), Delitzsch reminds him that such anticipatory announcements are quite usual, and cites ii. 8 ; he might have cited ver. 28d from this very chapter. He says the same of ver. 8b, because only one dream had yet been told, forgetting the numerous examples of the generic use of the plural.[3] בֶּן־זְקֻנִים and כְּתֹנֶת פַּסִּים (ver. 3), which Wellhausen adduces as characteristic of E, become with Dillmann indicative of J. Knobel remarks that ver. 7 and xxvi. 12 are the only two passages in the Pentateuch in which the patriarchs are spoken of as cultivating the soil, or

---

[1] Dillmann explains the allusion to Joseph's mother (xxxvii. 10), whose death is mentioned xxxv. 19, by his favorite method of transposition, assuming that the statement of her death in E really occurred after this time ; but R, for the sake of harmonizing with P, inserted it sooner. But it remains to be shown that Leah could not be referred to in this manner after Rachel's death.

[2] Kittell reverses this by connecting ver. 4b with 2c, and ver. 11a with 4a, and so making E speak of Joseph's brothers *hating* him for his talebearing and his dreams, and J of their *envying* him on account of his father's partiality. This shows how easy it is for a critic by adroitly shifting the lines of partition to alter the connection of clauses and modify their meaning.

[3] Cf. Gen. viii. 4; xiii. 12 ; xxi. 7 ; Num. xxvi. 8; Judg. xii. 7 ; 1 Sam. xvii. 43; Job xvii. 1.

otherwise than nomads ; they should, therefore, be ascribed to the same hand. The critics lay stress upon a
point like this when it suits them ; otherwise they quietly ignore it. Dillmann gives ver. 7 to E ; xxvi. 12
to J.

Dillmann further finds a foothold for J in ver. 2, by
insisting that ver. 2a and 2b are mutually exclusive, and
that the former should be given to P or E, and the latter
to J. Delitzsch cannot see why, in point of matter, they
may not have proceeded from the same pen, while in
grammatical construction i. 2, 3 offers a precise parallel.

Critics are divided in opinion as to the share which is
to be allowed P in xxxvii. 2. By common consent they
assign him the initial words, " These are the generations
of Jacob," *i.e.*, an account of Jacob's family from the time
that he was recognized as the independent head of the
chosen race ; and thus we have a P title to a J and E
section. The majority also refer to him the following
clause, ".Joseph was seventeen years old," with or without the rest of the sentence, which then becomes utterly
unmeaning, and is out of connection with anything whatever. The only reason for thus destroying its sense by
severing it from the narrative to which it belongs is the
critical assumption that all dates must be attributed to P.
But Nöldeke revolts at the rigorous enforcement of this
rule. He says, " The mention of the youthful age of
Joseph suits very well in the whole connection as well as
that of his manly age (xli. 46), and of the advanced age
which he attained (l. 26). These numbers also have no
connection whatever with the chronological system of
the Primary Document (P) any more than the twenty
years' abode in Mesopotamia (xxxi. 38, 41)." Wellhausen gives no positive opinion on the subject. Dillmann assigned this clause to E in his first edition, but
in his second and third hesitates between P and E.

In the first four editions of his Genesis Delitzsch could find no evidence of a duplicate narrative in ch. xxxvii. In his last edition he changed his mind, though he was still unable to accept Dillmann's keen analysis, which seemed to him to go "beyond the limits of the knowable." He ventures no further than to assign vs. 28a, b, 29, 30, to E, and ver. 28c, d to J, and to claim that thenceforward the narrative of E and J are in agreement, while the text has prevailingly the coloring of J, only "the Midianites" in ver. 36 are a sure indication of E.

It will not be necessary to proceed with the recital of other proposed partitions, which are sufficiently indicated in a previous note. The critics have shown how variously the same narrative may be divided. And it must be a very intractable material indeed that can resist the persistent application of such methods as they freely employ. The fact that different versions of a story can be constructed out of a narrative by an ingenious partition of its constituent elements by no means proves its composite character. They may be purely subjective, destitute of any historical basis, and of no more value than any clever trick at cross-reading.

GROUNDS OF PARTITION

Wellhausen admits that "the connection of the matter in ch. xxxvii. is certainly such that it would scarcely give occasion for separating it into two threads, were it not for the conclusion (vs. 25-36)." Here it is alleged that there are certain glaring inconsistencies, which cannot be otherwise accounted for than as the fusing together of discordant narratives. Four discrepancies are charged, which lie at the basis of every attempt to partition the chapter.

1. Verses 21, 22, it was Reuben, but ver. 26 it was Judah, who persuaded the brothers not to put Joseph to death.

2. Verses 25, 27, 28, xxxix. 1, Ishmaelites, but vs. 28, 36, Midianites, took Joseph and brought him to Egypt.

3. According to different clauses of ver. 28, Joseph was carried off secretly without the knowledge of his brothers, or was sold by them.

4. Verse 36, he was sold to Potiphar, but xxxix. 1 (purged of interpolations), to an unnamed Egyptian.

These imaginary difficulties are of easy solution.

As to the first. It surely is not surprising that two of the brothers should have taken an active part in the consultations respecting Joseph, nor that the same two should be prominent in the subsequent course of the transactions. Reuben, as the eldest, had special responsibilities and would naturally be forward to express his mind ; while Judah's superior force of character, like that of Peter among the apostles, made him prompt to take the lead, and there is no inconsistency in what is attributed to them. Reuben persuaded them not to kill Joseph, but to cast him alive into a pit, cherishing the purpose, which he did not divulge to them, to restore him to his father. They accede to his proposal intending to let Joseph die in the pit, or to kill him at some future time. To this state of mind Judah addresses himself (ver. 26). The absence of Reuben, when Joseph was sold, is not expressly stated, but is plainly enough implied in his despair and grief at his brother's disappearance. The reply which his brothers made is not recorded ; but there is no implication that they were as ignorant as he of what had become of Joseph. That they had a guilt in the matter which he did not share is distinctly intimated (xlii. 22) ; he must, therefore, have been fully aware that they did something more than put Joseph in the pit at his suggestion.

As to the second point. Ishmaelites in the strict and proper sense were a distinct tribe from the Midianites, and were of different though related origin. It is, however, a familiar fact, which we have had occasion to observe before, that tribal names are not always used with definite exactness (cf. xxxvi. 2 ; see p. 422). And there is explicit evidence that Ishmaelites was used in a wide sense to include Midianites (Judg. viii. 24 ; cf. vii. 1 sqq. ; viii. 1 sqq.). Dillmann's objection that this belonged to a later period comes with a bad grace from one who places the earliest Pentateuchal documents centuries after Gideon. If the invading army referred to in the passages above cited could be called indifferently Midianites and Ishmaelites, why not this caravan of merchants? The British troops at the battle of Trenton in the American revolution were Hessians, and might be properly spoken of under either designation. If a historian were to use these terms interchangeably in describing the engagement, would it follow that variant accounts had been confusedly mingled? The absence of the article before Midianites (ver. 28) does not imply that they were distinct from the Ishmaelites before perceived (vs. 25, 27). They were recognized in the distance as an Ishmaelite caravan, but it was not till they actually came up to them that the Ishmaelites were perceived to be specifically or largely Midianites.

As to the third point. If the first half of ver. 28 were severed from its connection, the words might mean that Midianites drew Joseph out of the pit. But in the connection in which it stands such a sense is simply impossible. And the suggestion that R had two statements before him : one, that Midianites drew Joseph out of the pit without his brothers' knowledge and carried him off to Egypt; the other, that his brothers drew him from the pit and sold him to the Ishmaelites; and that he combined them as we have them now, is to charge him with inconceivable stupidity or reckless falsification. There can be no manner of doubt how the author of the book in its present form understood the transaction. There is no possible suggestion of more than one meaning in the words before us. The invention of another sense may illustrate the critic's wit, but it has no more merit than any other perversion of an author's obvious meaning. And it derives no warrant from xl. 15; Joseph was "stolen away," even though his captors bought him from those who had no right to dispose of him.

The fourth point can be best considered when we come to ch. xxxix.

MARKS OF 'J

Dillmann does not pretend to base the partition of this chapter upon peculiarities of diction. But in the course of his exposition he notes the following words as though they were confirmatory of it :

1. Israel (ver. 3 J; 13 E, modified by R); Jacob (ver. 34a), referred to E solely on account of this word. Dillmann undertakes to carry consistently through the rule laid down by Wellhausen,[1] but which through the fault of R he admits has not been strictly observed,[2] viz., that after xxxv. 10 J calls the patriarch Israel, E calls him Jacob, but his sons the sons of Israel, while P continues to speak of Jacob and the sons of Jacob. Whence results this curious circumstance : P (xxxv. 10) and E (xxxii. 29; so Dillmann) record the change of name to Israel, but never use it; J alone makes use of it, and, according to Dillmann, he does not record the change at all. There is a singular inconsistency likewise in the conduct of R.

[1] Composition des Hexateuchs, p. 59.   [2] Ibid., p. 60.

P alone mentions the change in the names of Abraham and Sarah (xvii. 5, 15), but R is so concerned to have the documents uniform in this respect that from this point onward he alters these names in J and E to correspond with P ; why does he not here in like manner bring P and E into correspondence with J ? And it is only by palpable forcing that Dillmann succeeds in uniformly assigning "Israel" to J (see *e.g.*, xlv. 27, 28 ; xlvi. 1, 2; xlvii. 27 ; xlviii. 2, 8, 10, 11, 14, 21). Kuenen admits that " numerous exceptions to the rule occur." At this period of transition when the family is branching out into the nation these two names seem to be used interchangeably. If any distinction whatever is intended, it is purely in the writer's point of view, who may have used the personal name Jacob when he regarded the patriarch strictly as an individual, and the name Israel when he thought of him as the head and representative of the chosen race.

2. כְּתֹנֶת פַּסִּים *long tunic* (vs. 3, 23, 32). The expression occurs nowhere in the Hexateuch but in this chapter. It is alleged that, according to J, Joseph wore a "long tunic," the special gift of his father, but according to E only an ordinary "tunic" כְּתֹנֶת. But these expressions are combined or used interchangeably in vs. 23, 31, 32; and they can only be referred to distinct documents by partitioning closely connected clauses in an arbitrary manner.

3. הוֹרִיד *bring down* (into Egypt) (ver. 25); besides in J xxxix. 1; xliii. 11, 22; xliv. 21; for which E has הֵבִיא *bring* (ver. 28); but no difference of conception is implied by this varied phrase, since E has repeatedly יָרַד *go down* (into Egypt) (xlii. 2b, 3; xlv. 9; xlvi. 3, 4), as J (xliii. 15, 20; xliv. 23, 26); xlii. 38 is sundered from its proper connection in E and ascribed to J; J also has בּוֹא *come* (xlvi. 31; xlvii. 1, 4; cf. xliii. 2).

That varied forms of expression are consistent with sameness of authorship by confession of the critics appears from the phrase " rent his clothes," in which ver. 29 has בֶּגֶד and ver. 34a has שִׂמְלָה, yet both are referred to E.

It is also worth noting that דִּבָּה *report* (ver. 2) is referred by Dillmann to J, though it only occurs besides in the Hexateuch in Num. xiii. 32 ; xiv. 36, 37 P ; also דִּבֶּר *speak* (ver. 4), which only occurs besides in the Hexateuch, with the accusative of the person; in Num. xxvi. 3 P ; and הִתְנַכֵּל *conspire against* (ver. 18b). This verb occurs but once besides in the Hexateuch (Num. xxv. 18 P), where it is in the Piel form. And שְׂעִיר עִזִּים *he-goat* (ver. 31) is ascribed to E, though it is only found besides in the Hexateuch in the ritual law, where it occurs repeatedly and is uniformly ascribed to P.

THE NARRATIVE OF JUDAH AND TAMAR (CH. XXXVIII.)

NO LACK OF ORDER

Because the narrative concerning Joseph is interrupted by ch. xxxviii., De Wette [1] inferred that " we have here a compilation, not a continuous history by one narrator." The charge of displacement has been regularly repeated ever since, though obviously unfounded. This chapter is entirely germane to the subject treated, and it belongs precisely where it is in the author's plan. He is professedly giving an account of " the generations of Jacob " (xxxvii. 2), not the life of Joseph simply, but the history of Jacob's family. Joseph is necessarily thrown into prominence, since the events which brought about the removal of the chosen race to Egypt were so largely connected with him. But the incidents of this chapter have their importance in the constitution of Jacob's family at

[1] Beiträge, ii., p. 146.

the time of the migration to Egypt (xlvi. 12), and in the permanent tribal arrangements of Israel (Num. xxvi. 19 sqq.), as explanatory of the origin of the tribal families of Judah. The writer conducts Joseph to Egypt, where he is sold as a slave. There he leaves him for a while until these facts in Judah's family are related, when he resumes the thread of Joseph's narrative precisely where he left off, and proceeds as before. It is just the method that the best writers pursue in similar circumstances. So far from suggesting confusion or disarrangement, it argues an orderly well-considered plan.

Judah is said (ver. 1) to have separated himself from his brethren " at that time," that is to say, shortly after Joseph was sold into Egypt. It is not at all unlikely, as Kurtz[1] suggests, that the connection here is much more intimate than that of a simple conjunction in time. Unable to endure the sight of his father's grief (xxxvii. 35), and goaded by Reuben's reproaches (cf. xxxvii. 29, 30 ; xlii. 22), and the upbraidings of his own conscience, he left his father's house, and was thus led into a marriage with a Canaanitess. And the providential retribution followed of successive afflictions in the loss of his sons, in return for the grievous loss which he had inflicted upon his father, and of the deterioration of his character by contact with impurity, and, as it would also appear, with idolatry. The " kedesha " (vs. 21, 22) was one who surrendered herself in the service of the goddess Astarte.

The chronological objection which has been made to this narrative is as futile as that which is directed against its continuity. If Judah's marriage took place soon after Joseph was sold, as is expressly stated, Judah was then twenty years old, and there is no reason why all that is recorded in this chapter may not have taken place within the twenty-two years which preceded the migration into

[1] Geschichte des Alten Bundes, i., p. 277.

Egypt. It implies early marriages on the part of his sons, but not incredibly early.

NO ANACHRONISM

It has still further been objected that the Deuteronomic law of levirate marriages (Deut. xxv. 5 sqq.) is here represented as in force in the time of the patriarchs. But there is no anachronism in this. Genesis shows that in several respects the laws of Moses embodied, or were based upon, patriarchal usages ; while, nevertheless, the modifications show that there has been no transference to a primitive period of the customs of a later time. Under the Mosaic law one who was disinclined to marry his brother's widow might be formally released from the obligation by certain ceremonies ; this is a relaxation of the imperative requirement set forth in this chapter. And the penalty of being burned, with which Tamar was threatened, was not that of the Mosaic law, which was being put to death by stoning (Deut. xxii. 21–24) ; in this Dillmann admits that there is a reminiscence of antelegal times. The critics claim that the Deuteronomic law belongs to the reign of Josiah, yet the levirate was an established institution in the days of the Judges (Ruth iv. 10). How much the argument from silence, of which the critics make so frequent use, amounts to in this case, may be inferred from the fact that such marriages, though their existence is thus trebly vouched for, are nowhere alluded to in the other Pentateuchal codes nor in the later history, until the times of the New Testament (Mat. xxii. 24).

As Perez (ver. 29) was the ancestor of king David (Ruth iv. 18–22), the late date of this chapter has been argued on the assumption that it was written to indicate the origin of the house of David. But if this were so, the writer must have adopted a very unusual method of flattering the pride of a royal house. Nor can the Judaic writer J, to whom it is attributed, have composed it in honor of his tribe. How displeasing it was to national vanity appears from the fact that the Targum converts Judah's wife from the daughter of a Canaanite into that of a merchant, and later legends make Tamar a daughter of Melchizedek. These serious faults of Judah are doubtless related with the same design as other recorded blemishes of the patriarchs. They show that the distinction granted to him among his brethren by making him the father of the royal tribe (xlix. 8), was due not to his personal merit, but to the gracious choice of God. And that the discipline to which he was subjected corrected and reclaimed him, as the providential dealings with Jacob had a like effect upon him, may be inferred from ver. 26, and from his noble conduct subsequently (xliv. 16 sqq.).

Jehovah occurs three times in this chapter (vs. 7, 10), and it is for this reason ascribed to J. But the name is here used not in compliance with the unmeaning habit of the writer, but the requirements of the passage. Jehovah as the ruler and judge of his people is especially offended by their misdeeds. It is Jehovah accordingly who punished these transgressors.

MARKS OF J

1. Etymologies. See ch. xvi., Marks of J, No. 4.
2. רַע בְּעֵינֵי *evil in the eyes of* (vs. 7, 10).[1] See ch. xxi. 1–21, Marks of E, No. 4.

---

[1] "Evil in the eyes of Jehovah" (vs. 7, 10) is a standing phrase, and is found sixty times besides in the Old Testament. "Evil in the eyes of Elohim" occurs but once (1 Chron. xxi. 7), and there it is ha-Elohim with the article. "The eyes of Jehovah" occurs, in addition, thirty-

3. יָדַע *know* (euphemistic) (ver. 26). See ch. xxiv., Marks of J, No. 14.

4. הִכִּיר *recognize* (vs. 25, 26); besides in J (xxxvii. 32, 33); in E (xxvii. 23; xxxi. 32; Deut. xxxiii. 9. In Gen. xlii. 7, 8 bis—the critics give ver. 7 to J, and ver. 8 to E).

5. רֵעַ *friend* (vs. 12, 20); besides in J (xi. 3, 7; xv. 10; xxxi. 49; xliii. 33); in E (Ex. ii. 13; xi. 2; xviii. 7, 16; xxi. 14, 18, 35; xxii. 6–10, 13, 25, E. V. vs. 7–11, 14, 26; xxxii. 27; xxxiii. 11); in JE (Ex. xx. 16, 17); in Holiness Laws (Lev. xix. 13, 16, 18; xx. 10); in Deuteronomy twenty-one times; Josh. xx. 5 is in a P connection, but attributed to D.

6. הָבָה *come* (particle of incitement) (ver. 16); besides in J (xi. 3, 4, 7; xlvii. 15, 16; Deut. xxxii. 3); in E (Gen. xxix. 21; xxx. 1; Ex. i. 10; Josh. xviii. 4); in Rd (Deut. i. 13).

7. לְבִלְתִּי *not* (ver. 9). See ch. xviii., xix., Marks of J, No. 14.

8. כִּי־עַל־כֵּן *forasmuch as* (ver. 26). See ch. xviii., xix., Marks of J, No. 18.

9. נָא *I pray thee* (vs. 16, 25). See ch. xii. 10–20, Marks of J, No. 3.

It may be noted that בָּזֶה *here* (vs. 21, 22) is referred to J, though everywhere else in the Pentateuch it is ascribed to E (xlviii. 9a; Ex. xxiv. 14; Num. xxii. 19; xxiii. 1); or to R (Num. xxiii. 29); so נְתֹן *to give* (ver. 9) is assigned to J, though this form of the infinitive occurs but once besides (Num. xx. 21 E). In ver. 3 Judah names his child, contrary to the rule of the critics that in J the name is given by the mother, and in P by the father; but see under ch. xvi., p. 211.

---

one times in different connections; "the eyes of Elohim" but twice —Num. xxiii. 27, in the words of the heathen king Balak (who says ha-Elohim, for he means the God of Israel); and Prov. iii. 4, where it is occasioned by the contrast of God and man.

JOSEPH IS CAST INTO PRISON (CH. XXXIX.)

NO DISCREPANCIES

The critical partition is here rested partly on the ground of alleged discrepancies, partly on that of diction. It is said that there are varying representations of the purchaser of Joseph. Was he (xxxvii. 36 E) Potiphar, the eunuch or officer of Pharaoh, captain of the guard? or was he, as in J (ch. xxxix.), simply an Egyptian, whose name and official position, if he had any, are unknown? He is nowhere called Potiphar in this chapter except in ver. 1, but only Joseph's master (ver. 3), his Egyptian master (ver. 2), or the Egyptian (ver. 5). And nothing is said outside of ver. 1 of his standing in any special relation to Pharaoh or holding any office under the king; but mention is made of "all that he had in the house and in the field" (ver. 5), implying that he was the owner of a landed estate. It is hence inferred that the words "Potiphar, the eunuch of Pharaoh, captain of the guard," do not properly belong to ver. 1, but were inserted by R to make it correspond with xxxvii. 36; and that originally it simply read "an Egyptian," words which, it is alleged, would be superfluous if his name and title had previously been given. But the argument for this erasure is destitute of force. The name "Potiphar" does not occur in ch. xl., where the critics admit that he is intended by Joseph's master (ver. 7; see also vs. 3, 4). Royal body-guards are not always composed of native troops, so that it may not have been a matter of course that their captain was an Egyptian, nor superfluous to mention it. Knobel thinks that this statement is made in contrast with the Hyksos origin of the monarch. Or, as Delitzsch suggests, it may emphasize the fact that Joseph was not only a slave, but a slave of a foreigner ; the Hebrew servant (vs. 14, 17) had an Egyptian master. But no special reason is needed to justify the expression. Goliath, " from Gath, from the ranks of the Philistines," is further called " the Philistine " (1 Sam. xvii. 23), and throughout the chapter is always denominated " the Philistine," without repeating his name. That Potiphar had landed possessions is surely not inconsistent with his being the captain of the guard. That he was married creates no real difficulty. It is a disputed point whether סָרִים is invariably to be taken in its strict and primary sense of eunuch ; there are strong reasons for believing with Delitzsch, Kurtz, and others, that it sometimes has simply the general meaning of officer or courtier. However this may be, Winer [1] refers to Chardin, Niebuhr, and Burckhardt in proof of the statement that " even in the modern Orient eunuchs have sometimes kept a harem of their own." There is positively no ground, therefore, for assuming an interpolation in ver. 1. And the explicit statement of that verse annuls the critical allegation of variant stories respecting the person of Joseph's master. Moreover, if he was a private gentleman and not an officer of the king, how came it to pass that his slave was put in the same prison with the king's prisoners, and that for an offence usually punished in slaves with death ?

It is further said that Joseph's master is in xxxix. 20, 21 distinguished from the keeper of the prison into which Joseph was put; whereas in xl. 3, 4, 7 they are identical. But the confusion here charged upon the text lies solely in the mind of the interpreters. The narrative is perfectly clear and consistent. The prison was in the house of Joseph's master (xl. 7), the captain of the guard (ver. 3), who had supreme control over it (ver. 4);

[1] Biblisches Realwörterbuch, Art., Verschittene.

and this corresponds exactly with the representation xxxix. 20. Under him there was a subordinate keeper charged with its immediate oversight (xxxix. 21), who was so favorably disposed toward Joseph that he committed all the prisoners into his hands and let him manage everything in the prison (vs. 22, 23). This is neither identical with, nor contradictory to, the statement (xl. 4) that the captain of the guard (who is uniformly distinguished from his subordinate the keeper of the prison) appointed Joseph to attend upon two prisoners of rank from the royal household. It has been said indeed that he waited upon them simply as Potiphar's servant, and that (ch. xl.) E knows nothing of Joseph's imprisonment related by J (ch. xxxix.); and, moreover, uses the term מִשְׁמָר *ward* (xl. 3, 4, as well as xli. 10, E), instead of בֵּית הַסֹּהַר *prison* (xxxix. 20–23). But this result is only reached by expunging from the text without the slightest warrant every clause which directly declares the opposite (xl. 3b, 5b, 15b; xli. 14; cf. xxxix. 20). Of course, if the critics are allowed to doctor the text to suit themselves, they can make it say whatever they please.

THE DIVINE NAMES

Wellhausen parcels the chapter between J and E, giving vs. 1–5, 20–23 to the former on account of the repeated occurrence of Jehovah, and vs. 6–19 to the latter because of Elohim (ver. 9), and certain other expressions alleged to be characteristic of E. The result is that Joseph is in E falsely accused of a gross crime, but there is no intimation how the matter issues; and in J his master, who had the greatest confidence in him and was richly blessed for his sake, puts him in prison for no cause whatever. And the partition is in disregard of the correspondence and manifest allusion in

וְכֹל אֲשֶׁר־יֶשׁ־לוֹ נָתַן בְּיָדוֹ ver. 8 to vs. 4, 5, also of the like construction of בַּאֲשֶׁר *because,* in vs. 9 and 23. Wellhausen, moreover, finds traces of E in the J sections, and of J in the E section. Dillmann admits the indivisible character of the chapter and refers the whole of it to J; but, as the two following chapters are given to E, the consequence is that, according to J, Joseph is put in prison and no information given how or why he was subsequently released; the next that we hear of him he is viceroy of Egypt, with no explanation how it came to pass. The expressions commonly attributed to E, which are found in this chapter, are accounted for by Dillmann as insertions by R. This repeated occurrence of traces of one document in the limits of the other, and the allegation that the documents have in various particulars been modified by R, are simply confessions that the text is not what by the hypothesis of the critics it ought to be. Words and phrases held to be characteristic of J or E in one place are perversely found in the wrong document in another place. So without revising and correcting their own previous conclusions and adjusting their hypothesis to the phenomena as they find them, the critics insist that the document itself is wrong, and that R is to blame for it, the only proof of which is that it is impossible to carry their hypothesis through otherwise. It is obvious that any hypothesis, however at war with the facts of the case, could be bolstered up by similar expedients.

Jehovah occurs eight times in this chapter (vs. 2, 3, 5, 21, 23), and Elohim once (ver. 9). Ilgen gave the whole chapter to E, and claimed that the original reading was Elohim in every case, and that Jehovah had been introduced by the error of R or of subsequent transcribers. Gramberg maintained that the divine names are here no sure test of the writer, but that the repetitiousness, particularly of vs. 2–6, 12, 13, 20–23, proves the chapter to be the work of P. Kuenen[1] speaks of "the wordy style and constant repetitions by which this chapter is unfavorably distinguished from the other J pericopes." Dillmann gives it all to J in spite of Elohim (ver. 9), which J could use in such a case as this (why not then in ch. xx. and in other similar instances?); in spite also of the repetitiousness, which is held to be a mark of P, but which here, and wherever else it suits the purposes of the critics, is explained by R's insertion of equivalent statements from a supposed parallel account by E; and yet no reason is suggested why R should so overload these passages with what are reckoned unmeaning additions while omitting most important portions of each document in turn. The fact is that the divine names are appropriately used, and the emphatic repetitions are precisely in place. Here at the very outset—first of Joseph's bondage and then of his imprisonment—the writer takes pains to impress upon his readers, by marked iteration, that the presence and favor of Jehovah, the guardian of the chosen race, was with Joseph, and gave him success in his apparently forsaken and helpless condition. The unseen hand, which was guiding all in the interest of his scheme of grace, is thus distinctly disclosed; and this is the key to all that follows. In ver. 9 Elohim is the proper word. Joseph is speaking to a Gentile, to whom the name of Jehovah is unknown; and he refuses to commit a crime, which would be not only an offence against Jehovah considered in the light of his special relation to the chosen race, but against God in that general sense in which he was known to all mankind.

[1] Hexateuch, p. 147.

MARKS OF J

1. הִצְלִיחַ *made to prosper* (vs. 2, 3, 23). See ch. xxiv., Marks of J, No. 16.

2. בִּגְלַל *for the sake of* (ver. 5). See ch. xii. 10–20, Marks of J, No. 6.

3. מֵאָז *from the time that* (ver. 5) ; besides in J Ex. iv. 10; v. 23 (in E connection worked over by R after J); ix. 24 (a verse divided between J and E); also in Josh. xiv. 10 E, worked over by Rd after D ; all in the Hexateuch.

4. הוֹרִיד *bring down* (ver. 1). See ch. xxxvii., Marks of J, No. 3.

5. כַּדְּבָרִים הָאֵלֶּה *according to these words* (vs. 17, 19); in J besides, xxiv. 28, xliv. 7 ; all in the Hexateuch.

The following expressions, regarded as characteristic of E, occur in the J text of this chapter : Ver. 4, וַיְשָׁרֶת אֹתוֹ *he ministered unto him*, as xl. 4 ; Ex. xxiv. 13 ; xxxiii. 11 E ; repeatedly also in P ; ver. 6, יְפֵה־תֹאַר וִיפֵה מַרְאֶה *comely and well favored*, as xxix. 17 E ; ver. 7, וַיְהִי אַחַר הַדְּבָרִים הָאֵלֶּה *and it came to pass after these things*, as xv. 1 ; xxii. 1 ; xl. 1 ; xlviii. 1 ; Josh. xxiv. 29 E (but Gen. xxii. 20 R); ver. 21, וַיִּתֵּן חִנּוֹ בְּעֵינֵי *gave him favor in the eyes of*, as Ex. iii. 21 ; xi. 3 E (but xii. 36 J).

There are also expressions which by critical rules belong to P, *e.g.*, שָׁמַע אֶל *hearken unto* (ver. 10), which is claimed as a P phrase in ch. xxiii. (see ch. xxiii., Marks of P, No. 10) ; and אֵצֶל *by, beside* (vs. 10, 15, 16, 18), which apart from this chapter and xli. 3 E only occurs in the Hexateuch Lev. i. 16 ; vi. 3 (E. V., ver. 10) ; x. 12 P, and twice in Deuteronomy.

Varying constructions, as וַיַּפְקִדֵהוּ עַל־בֵּיתוֹ (ver. 4) and הִפְקִיד אֹתוֹ בְּבֵיתוֹ (ver. 5), and of הצליח intransitive (ver. 2), but transitive (vs. 3, 23) would be held to indicate dif-

ferent writers, if it suited the pleasure of the critics to do
so ; as it is they are quietly ignored.

DREAMS OF THE BUTLER AND BAKER (CH. XL.)

Tuch calls attention to the intimate connection between
this chapter and those that precede and follow. Joseph
is here in prison, to which the foregoing narrative brought
him. And ver. 3, where the officers who had offended
the king were put "into the prison, the place where Joseph was bound," points directly to xxxix. 20, where
Joseph was put "into the prison, the place where the
king's prisoners were bound." The statement that he
" was stolen away out of the land of the Hebrews " (ver.
15) is only explicable from xxxvii. 28 sqq., that he was
carried off by the Midianite-Ishmaelites, to whom his unnatural brothers had sold him. His assertion (ver. 15),
" here also have I done nothing that they should put me
into the dungeon," is only intelligible from the narrative in ch. xxxix. This chapter is not only thus tied
to that which goes before, but also prepares the way for
ch. xli., where (ver. 10) the imprisonment of the chief
butler and baker in the house of the captain of the guard
refers back to xl. 1-3 ; xli. 11-13, Joseph's interpretation of their dreams, and their fulfilment is a brief summary of xl. 4-22 ; xli. 14, bringing Joseph out of the
dungeon, corresponds to his statement (xl. 15) that he was
put into the dungeon. The chief butler's memory of his
fault (xli. 9) recalls the fact that Joseph had asked to be
remembered by him when he was restored to his former
position (xl. 14), but the chief butler had forgotten him
(ver. 23). The significant dreams of the butler and
baker (ch. xl.), and those of Pharaoh (ch. xli.), in connection with which Joseph figures so prominently, recall
those of his own early childhood (xxxvii. 5-10), and

plainly belong to the same gradually unfolding scheme.
And Joseph's modest disclaimer of the power of interpretation, and his ascription of it solely to God (xli. 16),
simply repeats xl. 8.

NO DISCREPANCY

Yet, notwithstanding this close relationship of this
chapter in all its parts with the surrounding narrative,
we are told that the principal ground of the partition
here, by which this chapter is given to E, is a glaring
discrepancy between the account given by J and that by
E. According to J (ch. xxxix. as expurgated) Joseph
was sold to an unnamed Egyptian, and by him put in
prison on a false charge preferred by his wife. How he
came to be released and to reach the high station which
he subsequently occupied in Egypt does not appear.
According to E (ch. xl. as expurgated) Joseph was sold
to Potiphar, captain of the guard; Pharaoh's chief butler and baker were committed to Potiphar's custody, and
kept under arrest, not in prison but in his house. And
Joseph, who was not himself under arrest, but was acting simply in the capacity of Potiphar's servant, was appointed to wait upon them. While doing so he interpreted their dreams, which were fulfilled accordingly.

It is unnecessary to say that these variant accounts
are not in the text, but are purely the product of the
critics themselves. The text must be remodelled in order to produce them. We have already seen how xxxix.
1 has to be transformed in order to make it say that
Joseph was sold, not to Potiphar but to some nameless
Egyptian. It requires even more serious tampering with
ch. xl. to eliminate the repeated references to Joseph's
imprisonment, and the statement that the chief butler
and baker were put in the same prison with him. Vs.

3b, 5b, 15b, and a clause of xxxix. 20 (the place where the king's prisoners were bound), as well as of xli. 14 (and they brought him hastily out of the dungeon), must all be erased by the critics before they can get rid of the explicit statements which directly contradict that view of the affair which they undertake to obtrude upon this chapter. It is not surprising that Gramberg, in proposing these erasures, expected his readers to be surprised by such a free handling of the text and perversion of its meaning.

The charge that the clauses in question were insertions by R has no other foundation than the desire to create a discrepancy, which is impossible without removing them. That the prison was in the house of the captain of the guard (ver. 3) is in accordance with modern oriental usage. Thus Chardin says : " The Eastern prisons are not public buildings erected for that purpose, but a part of the house in which their criminal judges dwell. As the governor and provost of a town, or the captain of the watch, imprison such as are accused in their own houses, they set apart a canton of them for that purpose, when they are put into these offices, and choose for the jailer the most proper person they can find of their domestics." [1] That vs. 1, 5 have " the butler and the baker of the king of Egypt," while the rest of the chapter has " chief butler," "chief baker," and " Pharaoh," is no good reason for attributing the former to R, unless on the assumption that a writer cannot occasionally vary his expressions, especially as ver. 1 is indispensable as supplying the reason for ver. 2, and the chief butler is likewise simply called " butler " (ver. 13), and his office simply " butlership " (ver. 23).

In addition to the alleged variance between this chapter and the preceding, which has already been consid-

[1] Harmer's Observations, ii., p. 273.

ered, the following reasons are adduced for referring it
to E : " The dreams," since it is arbitrarily assumed that
all dreams must belong to E;[1] " I was stolen away " (ver.
15), but this is not inconsistent with his being sold by
his brothers, who had no right to dispose of him ; "the
connection of ch. xli. with xl.," which is freely conceded,
but involves no discrepancy with, or separation from, ch.
xxxix. No argument is offered from language but "the
avoidance of the verbal suffix which distinguishes E
from J " (vs. 3, 4, 6, 8, 11, 15, 17, 19); Dillmann here
quietly ignores the fact that he refused to admit this as a
criterion in ch. xxxvii. " And it came to pass after these
things," which is allowed to remain in ver. 1, after the
rest of the verse is erased as an insertion by R, cannot
be a decisive mark of E in this place after having been
found in a J section (xxxix. 7). It can scarcely be
thought that such arguments are of any weight in favor
of critical partition.

NO ANACHRONISM

Nor is there an anachronism in the phrase " land of
the Hebrews " (ver. 15). " Abram the Hebrew " was the
head of a powerful clan (xiv. 13, 14), recognized as such
by native tribes of Canaan (xxiii. 6), and his friendship
sought by the king of the Philistines (xxi. 22, sqq.).
Isaac's greatness is similarly described (xxvi. 13 seq., 26
sqq.). The prince and people of Shechem were willing to submit to circumcision for the sake of friendly intercourse and trade with Jacob, and Jacob's sons avenged
the wrong done their sister by the destruction of the city
(ch. xxxiv.). The Hebrews had been in Canaan for two
centuries, and their presence was influential and widely
known. There is nothing strange, therefore, in the fact

---

[1] See ch. xx., Marks of E, No. 4.

that Potiphar's wife calls Joseph a Hebrew (xxxix. 14, 17), or that he could speak of the country whence he came as the land of the Hebrews.

DICTION

The one divine name in this chapter, Elohim (ver. 8), is doubly appropriate. It is in an address to Gentiles, and there is an obvious contrast between man and God; interpretations belong to the latter, not to the former. Knobel, who gave chs. xl., xli. to P, notes the following words as characteristic of P : קָצַף *was wroth* (xl. 2 ; xli. 10), besides in the Hexateuch Ex. xvi. 20 ; Lev. x. 6, 16 ; Num. xvi. 22; xxxi. 14 P ; Josh. xxii. 18 R ; also Deut. i. 34 ; ix. 7, 8, 19, 22 ; the corresponding noun, קֶצֶף *wrath*, occurs in the Hexateuch Num. i. 53 ; xvii. 11 (E. V., xvi. 46); xviii. 5 ; Josh. ix. 20 P ; Josh. xxii. 20 R ; Deut. xxix. 27 (E. V., ver. 28). סַל *basket* (xl. 16–18) occurs besides in the Hexateuch Ex. xxix. 3, 23, 32; Lev. viii. 2, 26, 31; Num. vi. 15, 17, 19 P. כֵּן *station* (xl. 13 ; xli. 13) occurs besides in the Hexateuch only in application to the base of the laver (Ex. xxx. 18, and repeatedly, P). Dillmann passes these quietly by without remark.

PHARAOH'S DREAMS (CH. XLI.)

Tuch shows that as ch. xl. was both in general and in particular preparatory for ch. xli., so this latter is indispensable for all that follows. It is here related how Joseph, who was chosen of God for high ends, was raised from the prison to the office of vizier ; and the rest of the book (ch. xlii.–xlvii.) turns upon Joseph's services to the people and the king, and upon the predicted famine which brought about the migration of Jacob and his family to Egypt. All this is quite unintelligible without

the narrative which lies here before us. Add the specific
references to ch. xl. previously pointed out, the etymologies of the names Manasseh and Ephraim (vs. 51, 52), after the manner of ch. xxx., and the birth of these sons of
Joseph to prepare the way for their adoption by Jacob
(ch. xlviii.) where xlviii. 5, "born before I came unto
thee into Egypt," plainly points back to xli. 50.

GROUNDS OF PARTITION

The following reasons are assigned by Dillmann for
assigning this chapter to E: The significant dreams and
the power of interpreting them, which are of no more
weight here than in ch. xl.; that Joseph is called "servant to the captain of the guard" (ver. 12), but he was
also a prisoner (ver. 14), which is evaded after the usual
critical fashion by erasing from the text the words "and
they brought him hastily out of the dungeon," as an insertion from a hypothetical parallel of J; but even then
his shaving himself and changing his raiment are an allusion to his prison attire, or why are not the same things
mentioned when others are presented before the king?
The references to ch. xl. (xli. 10–13, cf. xl. 1 sqq.; xli.
16, cf. xl. 8), and unusual words common to both chap-
ters (פָּתַר *interpret*, פִּתְרוֹן *interpretation*, כֵּן *station*, קָצַף *was
wroth*), point to the same author, but in no way imply
that he was not the author of ch. xxxix. and xliii. as well.
Elohim in vs. 16, 25, 32, 38, 39 is in language addressed
to Pharaoh or used by him; vs. 51, 52 are the only instances in which Jehovah could with any propriety be
substituted for it, and even there Elohim is equally appropriate, for the reference is to God's providential blessings, such as men in general may share, rather than to
specific favor granted to one of the chosen race.   בִּלְעֲדֵי
apart from (vs. 16, 44), but once besides in Genesis (xiv.

24, which is referred by Dillmann to E, but by the majority of critics to an independent source); and occurring twice more in the Hexateuch (Num. v. 20 ; Josh. xxii. 19 P). The arguments for considering this chapter a part of the document E are accordingly lame and impotent enough.

We are further informed that this chapter is not a unit as it stands. It is essential for the critics to establish, if possible, the existence of a parallel narrative by J, which may have filled the gap in that document between Joseph's imprisonment and his elevation. Accordingly stress is laid upon some slight verbal changes in repeating Pharaoh's dreams, especially the words added to the description of the lean kine (ver. 19), "such as I never saw in all the land of Egypt for badness," and (ver. 21), "when they had eaten up the fat kine it could not be known that they had eaten them ; but they were still ill-favored as at the beginning." But if this is to show that J gave a parallel account of the dreams, it annuls the criterion, upon which the critics steadfastly insist, that E alone records dreams. A vigorous search is also made for so-called doublets. Wherever the writer does not content himself with a bald and meagre statement of what he is recording, but feels impelled to enlarge and dwell upon it in order to give his thought more adequate expression, the amplifications or repetitions which he employs are seized upon as though they were extraneous additions imported into E's original narrative by R from an imaginary parallel account by J, just as a like fulness of expression in other passages is at the pleasure of the critics declared to be indicative of the verbose and repetitious style of P.

The dreams (vs. 2–7) are repeated (vs. 18–24) in almost identical terms, only in a very few instances equivalent expressions are employed, viz. : מַרְאֶה *form* (vs. 18,

19), for מַרְאֶה *appearance* (vs. 2, 3), but see xxix. 17 E;
xxxix. 6 J; רַק *lean* (ver. 19), for דַק *thin* (ver. 3); מָלֵא *full*
(ver. 22), for בָּרִיא *fat* (ver. 5), but see ver. 7. The alleged doublets are ver. 31 parallel to ver. 30b; ver. 34
יַעֲשֶׂה *make*, parallel to יַפְקֵד *appoint*; ver. 35b to 35a;
vs. 41, 43b, 44, to ver. 40 (Joseph's rule is stated four
times, so that repetition cannot be escaped by parcelling
it between E and J); ver. 49 to 48; vs. 55, 56a, to 54b
(the universality of the famine is repeated three times, including ver. 57b). It is also affirmed that the following
expressions are indicative of J: רָאָה *see* (ver. 41) as xxvii.
27; xxxi. 50; xxxix. 14; כִּי אֵין מִסְפָּר . . . כְּחוֹל הַיָּם
as the sand of the sea, for it was without number (ver 49),
as xxii. 17 R; xxxii. 13 (E. V. ver. 12) J. While it is
claimed that these indicate two narrators, Dillmann admits that in several instances there are no criteria by
which to distinguish which is E and which J. The further occurrence of words in this chapter, which according
to critical rules should belong to P, *e. g.*, חַרְטֹם *magician*
(vs. 8, 24), in the Pentateuch besides only Ex. vii. 11, 22;
viii. 3, 14, 15 (E. V., vs. 7, 18, 19); ix. 11, all P; פִּקָּדוֹן
store (ver. 36), besides in the Old Testament only Lev.
v. 21, 23 (E. V., vi. 2, 4) P; קֹמֶץ *handful* (ver. 47), besides in the Old Testament only Lev. ii. 2; v. 12; vi. 8
(E. V., ver. 15), and the corresponding verb only Lev. ii.
2; v. 12; Num. v. 26, all P, leads one to distrust criteria in other cases, which the critics can thus disregard
at pleasure.

On the whole, then, the critical partition of chs.
xxxvii.–xli. rests upon alleged inconsistencies in the narrative, which plainly do not exist as the text now stands,
but which the critics themselves create by arbitrary erasures and forced interpretations. The literary proof offered of the existence of different documents is of the
scantiest kind. There are no indications of varying dic-

PHARAOH'S DREAMS (CH. XLI.)

tion of any account. And the attempt to bridge the
chasms in the documents by means of a supposed parallel narrative, from which snatches have been preserved
by R, attributes an unaccountable procedure to him, and
falls to pieces at once upon examination.

There are three staple arguments by which the critics
attempt to show that there was, in the sources from which
R is conjectured to have drawn, a second narrative parallel to that in the existing text. Each of these is built
upon a state of facts antagonistic to the hypothesis,
which they ingeniously seek to wrest in its favor by assuming the truth of the very thing to be proved.

1. Facts which are essential to the narrative could
not, it is said, have failed to appear in either document;
it must be presumed, therefore, that each narrator recorded them.

But the perpetual recurrence of such serious gaps in
the so-called documents, which the critics are by every
device laboring to construct, tends rather to show that no
such documents ever really had any separate existence.
That these gaps are due to omissions by R is pure assumption, with no foundation but the unproved hypothesis
which it is adduced to support ; an assumption, moreover,
at variance with the conduct repeatedly attributed to R in
other places, where to relieve other complications of the
hypothesis he is supposed to have scrupulously preserved
unimportant details from one of his sources, even though
they were superfluous repetitions of what had already
been extracted from another.

2. When words and phrases which the critics regard
as characteristic of one document are found, as they frequently are, in sections which they assign to the other,
it is claimed that R has mixed the texts of the different
documents.

But the obvious and natural conclusion from the fact

referred to is, that what are affirmed to be characteristic words of different documents are freely used by the same writer. The allegation that R had anything to do with the matter is an assumption which has no other basis than the hypothesis which it is brought to support. It is plain that any conceit whatever could be carried through successfully if every deviation from its requirements was sufficiently explained by referring it to R.

3. Whenever a thought is repeated or dwelt upon for the sake of giving it more emphatic expression, the critics scent a doublet, affirming that R has appended to the statement in one document the corresponding statement contained in the other.

But here again the agency of R is pure assumption, based on the hypothesis in whose interest it is alleged. That a writer should use more amplitude and fulness in describing matters of special moment is quite intelligible. But why a compiler like R should encumber the narrative by reduplicating what he has already drawn from one source by the equivalent language of another, or why, if this is his method in the instances adduced, he does not consistently pursue it in others, does not appear. Why should he leave serious gaps in matters of real moment, while so solicitous of preserving petty details, which add nothing to what has been said already?

What are so confidently paraded as traces or indications of some missing portion of a critical document are accordingly rather to be esteemed indications that the documents of the critics are a chimera.

On the assumption that it is peculiar to P to record ages Kautzsch assigns to this document ver. 46a, " And Joseph was thirty years old when he stood before Pharaoh king of Egypt." Dillmann gives it the entire verse, as also, though with some hesitation, the statement of Joseph's age at an earlier period, in xxxvii. 2. Isolated clauses are thus rent from their connection, though there is nothing in P to which to attach them, and though their entire significance lies in the light which they shed upon the intervening narrative from which they are arbitrarily separated, whose duration it is their province to indicate. Dillmann himself in his first edition contended that the numbers in these verses did not belong to P. And the critical assumption on which this assignment rests is set aside by Dillmann as well as others in Gen. l. 26 ; Josh. xiv. 7, 10 ; xxiv. 29, where the record of the ages of Joseph, Caleb, and Joshua is attributed to E. Nöldeke, followed by Schrader, Kayser, Kuenen, and others, denies that either of the verses in question belong to P, and finds in xlvi. 6, 7 the first extract from that document in this section of Genesis. Dillmann's suggestion that the full phrase, " Pharaoh king of Egypt " (ver. 46), occurs again (Ex. vi. 11, 13, 27, 29 ; xiv. 8 P) is of little force, because "Pharaoh " alone is uniformly used in all the passages ascribed to P except the verses just named, where the full phrase is emphatically employed, as is evident from the iteration in Ex. vi.

JOURNEYS OF JACOB'S SONS TO EGYPT (CH. XLII.-XLIV.)

The critics tell us that ch. xlii., which records the first journey of Jacob's sons to Egypt, is by E, and chs. xliii., xliv., their second journey, is by J. Yet the second journey implies the first, and is filled throughout with numerous and explicit allusions to it. It was (xliii. 2) after they had eaten up the corn already brought that their father urged them to go again. All then turns upon Joseph's having required them to bring Benjamin (xliii. 3–11 ; cf. xlii. 15, 16, 20, 34). Jacob's solicitude for Benjamin is the same, xlii. 4 as ver. 38 ; xliv. 29. Repeated reference is made to the money returned in their sacks

(xliii. 12, 15, 18–23 ; xliv. 8 ; cf. xlii. 25, 28, 35), and to
Simeon's detention (xliii. 14, 23 ; cf. xlii. 19, 24). Jacob's sense of bereavement (xliii. 14) corresponds with
previous statements (xlii. 36 ; xxxvii. 34, 35). Joseph
speaks of their father and youngest brother, of whom
they had previously told him (xliii. 27–29 ; cf. xlii. 13,
32). They bow before him in fulfilment of his dreams
(xliii. 26, 28 ; xliv. 14 ; cf. xxxvii. 10, xlii. 6, 9). Joseph
orders their money to be replaced in their sacks (xliv. 1),
as before (xlii. 25). And Judah's touching address to
Joseph (xliv. 18–34) recites anew the circumstances of
their former visit, together with their father's grief at the
loss of Joseph (cf. xliv. 28 with xxxvii. 33). It is difficult
to see how two parts of the same narrative could be more
closely bound together.

Nevertheless it is maintained that all these allusions
to what took place in the former journey are not to the
record given of it in ch. xlii., but to a quite different narrative ; that a careful consideration of chs. xliii., xliv. will
show that they are not the sequel of ch. xlii., but of a
parallel account by J, which no longer exists indeed, inasmuch as R did not think fit to preserve it, but which
can be substantially reconstructed from the hints and intimations in these chapters themselves, and must have
varied from that of E in several particulars. R is here,
as always, the scapegoat on whose head these incongruities are laid, though no very intelligible reason can be
given why he should have constructed this inimitable
history in such a disjointed manner. And it is likewise
strange that the discrepancies between the two narratives,
so strenuously urged by Wellhausen and Dillmann, seem
to have escaped the usually observant eye of Hupfeld,
who makes no mention of them. As Ilgen, DeWette, and
Gramberg had raised the same difficulties before, Hupfeld's silence can only mean that he did not deem them

worth repeating. Knobel, though ready enough to undertake a critical division elsewhere, insists on the unity of chs. xlii.-xlv., and maintains that the charge of inconsistencies is unfounded. The same judgment, one would think, must be formed by any candid person.

NO DISCREPANCY

The alleged inconsistencies are the following:

1. In E Reuben is the speaker (xlii. 22), and it is he who becomes surety for Benjamin's safe return (ver. 37). In J Judah is the surety for Benjamin, and takes the lead throughout (xliii. 3-5, 8-10 ; xliv. 14 sqq.).

But these acts and offices do not exclude one another. Why should not more than one of Jacob's sons have sought to influence him in a case of such extreme importance to them all? If Reuben had pleaded without effect, why should not Judah renew the importunity, as the necessity became more urgent? It is here precisely as with the separate proposals of Reuben and Judah (xxxvii. 22, 26), which, as we have seen, the critics likewise seek without reason to array against each other. Reuben's allusion (xlii. 22) to his interference in that instance implies that his remonstrance was not heeded, and that his brothers were responsible for Joseph's death, which he sought to prevent. As the critics represent the matter, this was not the case. At Reuben's instance they put Joseph in a pit instead of shedding his blood. Now if, as the critics will have it, Midianite merchants found him there and carried him off in the absence of all the brothers, the others had no more to do with his disappearance than Reuben had. Reuben's unresisted charge that the rest were guilty of Joseph's death, in which he himself was not implicated, finds no explanation upon the critics' version of the story. It is only when the

sundered parts of the narrative are brought together, and
it is allowed to stand in its complete and proper form,
that Joseph was sold to the Ishmaelites at the suggestion
of Judah, while Reuben supposed him to be still in the
pit and hoped to return him to his father, that his words
have any meaning. No difficulty is created by Reuben's
speaking of his blood as required. The brothers imagined him to be no longer living. Judah, who coun-
selled the sale, speaks of him as dead (xliv. 20 cf. xlii.
32). By selling him into bondage they had, as they
thought, procured his death.

Judah's prominence in ch. xliv. is due entirely to his
suretyship for Benjamin, solicited and granted in ch.
xliii. As Benjamin was endangered by the discovery of
the cup, it was incumbent upon him to seek to obtain
his release.

Wellhausen contends that xlii. 38 is not the reply to
Reuben's offer to be a surety (ver. 37), inasmuch as this
latter is E's parallel to xliii. 8–10 J, and instead of being
refused it must in E's account have been accepted. He
insists that E's narrative is abruptly broken off at xlii.
37, and left incomplete. The response made to Reuben
is not recorded; it was doubtless the same in substance
that J reports as made to Judah (xliii. 11 sqq.). Instead
of this R introduces an irrelevant verse (xlii. 38), a dis-
located fragment of J, which in its original connection
was a reply to something quite distinct from the words
by which it is here preceded. It must have come after
the equivalent of xliv. 26, and have stood between xliii.
2 and 3. This is simply to manufacture facts in the face
of the plain declarations of the text itself, which leave no
doubt as to the answers respectively given to Reuben
and to Judah. All this confusion, where in reality no
confusion exists, results from the abortive attempt to
create a parallel narrative out of nonentity. The critics

are under the necessity of assigning xlii. 38 to J, since the words " if mischief befall him ye shall bring down my gray hairs with sorrow to the grave " are identical with xliv. 29, 31, and must obviously be from the same writer. This, however, does not demonstrate that the verse is out of place, but simply that chs. xlii. and xliv. are from one pen.

In fact the agency attributed to Reuben and Judah affords a plea, not for the critical partition of these chapters but for their unity. The position accorded to each is consistent throughout, and corresponds with the representation made of them in the blessing of Jacob in ch. xlix. Reuben, as the first-born, was charged with a special responsibility, which led him to come forward at each crisis, while the weakness of his character rendered his interference ineffectual. He did not accomplish his purpose of rescuing Joseph. His father, whom he had grievously wronged, would not trust him with Benjamin. Judah's bold and energetic nature fitted him to grasp the reins which Reuben was incompetent to hold. He led the brothers in their passionate determination to rid themselves of Joseph and nullify his ambitious dreams. Sobered by the discipline of years he rose to the occasion, when a new peril threatened his father in the loss of his favorite Benjamin, and he assumed the leadership with an unselfish courage and a tenderness of heart which marked him out as one fitted to rule, and which deservedly won for him the position among his brothers indicated by his dying father. Plainly we have here not two separate sagas, each glorifying a favorite son of Jacob, but one self-consistent historical account, in which both appear in their proper characters.

It is further claimed that—

2. J knows nothing of Simeon's detention related by E (xlii. 19, 24). Judah nowhere alludes to it in arguing

with his father (xliii. 3–10), when he might have urged the prospect of releasing Simeon as an additional reason for their speedy return ; nor does he refer to it in his address to Joseph (xliv. 18–34).

But the supreme interest on both these occasions centred about Benjamin. Would his father consent to let him go? Would Joseph allow him to return to his father? These were the questions quite apart from the case of Simeon, so that in dealing with them there was no occasion to allude to him. But Simeon is directly spoken of twice in ch. xliii. When Jacob is starting them on their return he prays (ver. 14) " God Almighty give you mercy before the man, that he may release unto you *your other brother* and Benjamin." And (ver. 23) when they reach the house of Joseph the steward " brought Simeon out unto them." These explicit allusions to Simeon's imprisonment are evaded by declaring them to be interpolations from E. The argument for suppressing them may be fairly stated thus : Because Simeon is not referred to where there is no occasion for speaking of him, therefore the mention which is made of him in the proper place cannot be an integral part of the text. In other words, whatever the critics desire to eliminate from a passage is eliminated without further ceremony by declaring it spurious. If it does not accord with their theory, that is enough ; no other proof is necessary.

Dillmann's contention that xlii. 38 is not the direct reply to ver. 37, because Simeon is not spoken of in it, is futile on its face; for as Reuben makes no allusion to him in his proposal there is no reason why Jacob should do so in his answer. Simeon was kept a prisoner to insure the return of the rest, having been selected doubtless because he was second in age. Joseph may naturally have passed over Reuben because of the kindly disposition which he had manifested toward himself.

3. "In ch. xlii. Joseph will, by detaining Simeon, compel the brothers at all events to come back again with or without Benjamin; in chs. xliii., xliv., on the contrary, he forbids them to come back if Benjamin is not with them. In ch. xlii. they are treated as spies; at first they are all put into prison together, and then only set free on bail to bring Benjamin, and thus confirm the truth of their declarations. But in chs. xliii., xliv. they do not go back to Egypt from the moral obligation of clearing themselves and releasing Simeon, but wait till the corn is all gone and the famine constrains them. The charge that they were spies was not brought against the brothers at all according to xliii. 5–7; xliv. 18 sqq.; it was not this which induced them, as in ch. xlii., to explain to Joseph who and whence they really were, and thus involuntarily to make mention of Benjamin, but Joseph directly asked them, Is your father yet alive? have ye another brother? and then commanded them not to come into his presence again without him." [1]

All this is only an attempt to create a conflict where there is none. One part of a transaction is set in opposition to another equally belonging to it. One motive is arrayed against another, as though they were incompatible, when both were alike operative. When Joseph told his brothers that they must verify their words by Benjamin's coming or be considered spies (xlii. 15, 16, 20, 34), he in effect told them that they should not see his face again unless Benjamin was with them. They delay their return until the corn was all used up, because nothing less than imminent starvation will induce Jacob, who has already lost two sons, to risk the loss of his darling. That Joseph directly interrogated them about their father

[1] Wellhausen, Comp. d. Hexateuchs, p. 55.

and brother is not expressly said in ch. xlii. ; but as the
entire interview is not narrated in detail, there is nothing
to forbid it. The critics do not themselves insist on the
absolute conformity of related passages, unless they have
some end to answer by it. The words of Reuben, as reported xlii. 22, are not identical with those ascribed to
him xxxvii. 22; and nothing is said in ch. xxxvii. of
Joseph's beseeching his brothers in the anguish of his
soul, as in xlii. 21. Jacob's sons, in rehearsing their experience to their father (xlii. 29–34) omit his first propo-
sition to keep all of them but one, and their three days'
imprisonment, and add that if they prove true they might
traffic in the land. Judah, in relating the words of his
father (xliv. 27–29), does not limit himself to language
which, according to xliii. 2 sqq., he uttered on the occasion referred to. In these instances the critics find no
discrepancies within the limits of the same document,
but count it sufficient that the general sense is preserved.
If they would interpret with equal candor elsewhere
their imaginary difficulties would all melt away.

4. A discrepancy is alleged regarding the money found
in the sacks. According to xliii. 21 J the discovery was
made at the lodging on their way home, but according
to xlii. 35 E, after their arrival home, and in the presence
of their father.

But there is no necessary variance here. The statement in xlii. 27, 28 is that one of the brothers, on opening his sack at the lodging, found his money, and reported
the fact to the rest, whereat they were greatly alarmed.
Now, the critics argue if one opened his sack to give his
ass provender, must not the rest have done the same,
and made the same discovery ? and especially as .they
were so agitated by the fact that one had found his money
in his sack, would not the rest have made instant search
in theirs ? Dillmann further pleads that הָאֶחָד *the one*, in

ver. 27, properly means *the first* in order, implying that
the others subsequently did the same. And Wellhausen
tells us that R has omitted a clause, which must originally have stood in these verses, "then the others also
opened their sacks, and behold, every man's money was
in his sack, their money in full weight." These verses,
it is claimed, are in exact correspondence with xliii. 21,
and belong not to E's, but to J's, account. This conjectural reasoning and this hypothetical change of text
are of course of no account. But if the critics are correct in the interpretation which they put upon these
verses, as implying, even though they do not expressly
state, that the discovery of his money by one led to its
discovery by all the rest at the inn, there is not the
shadow of a discrepancy in the entire record. This is
in fact the explanation adopted by Matthew Poole in
order to harmonize the whole account. He thus comments upon the words in ver. 27, " one of them opened
his sack : " " And after him the rest, by his example and
information did so, as is affirmed xliii. 21, and not denied here." And then, when they reached home and
emptied their sacks in the presence of their father, and
they and he saw the bundles of money, " their fear returned upon them with more violence."

If, however, xlii. 27 is to be understood as meaning
that only one happened upon the discovery of his money
at the inn, and that the others, having no occasion to
open their sacks, since Joseph had ordered that provision
be given them for the way (ver. 25), did not find that
theirs had been restored till they were at their journey's
end, it will still supply no argument for critical partition.
The discrepancy, such as it is, lies between xlii. 27, 28,
and xliii. 22, both of which are referred to J. It amounts
simply to this : in reporting their discovery of the money
to Joseph's steward the brothers do not detail the suc-

cessive steps by which they came to a full knowledge of
the case. The one important fact was that they all
found their money in their sacks. That part was found
at one time, and part at another, was a subordinate matter on which no stress need be laid. So in speaking of
the first discovery made at the inn they include in it all
that they afterward learned. Their statement, though
not minutely accurate, was yet for their purpose substantially true.

THE DIVINE NAMES

The divine names afford no pretext for the partition of
these chapters. Elohim occurs once in E (xlii. 18), and
three times in J (xlii. 28; xliii. 29; xliv. 16). And El
Shaddai, *God Almighty*, which is regarded as a peculiar
characteristic of P, occurs in xliii. 14 J. R is invoked to
relieve the difficulty in xlii. 28 and xliii. 14; while in
xliii. 29; xliv. 16, the critical principle is abandoned,
which traces the occurrence of Elohim to the usage of
the particular document in which it is found and it is
confessed that its employment is due to the distinctive
usage of the word itself. These names are in every case
appropriately used. Jacob commends his sons to the
omnipotent care of him who alone could effectually aid
in his helpless extremity (xliii. 14). As Joseph was acting the part of an Egyptian, Elohim is the proper word
when he is speaking (xlii. 18; xliii. 29), or is spoken to
(xliv. 16); even when he refers specifically to the God of
the chosen race he uses a periphrasis instead of employing the name Jehovah (xliii. 23). Contrast with this the
critical claim in xxvi. 28, 29, that J uses Jehovah even
when Gentiles are the speakers. In xlii. 28 the brothers,
recognizing in what has taken place the divine ordering
as contrasted with merely human agency, say to one another, What is this that God (Elohim) hath done to us?

MARKS OF J AND E

1. מִסְפּוֹא *fodder*, is attributed to J, though it is the proper word to express this idea, and cannot be regarded as characterizing any particular writer. It is used four times in the Hexateuch, twice in this narrative (xlii. 27, cut out of an E connection and given to J; xliii. 24 J), and twice in the story of Abraham's servant (xxiv. 25, 32, J).

2. מָלוֹן *lodging-place*, is claimed as belonging to J. It occurs twice in this narrative (xlii. 27, cut out of an E context and given to J; xliii. 21 J), and in two passages besides in the Hexateuch (Ex. iv. 24; Josh. iv. 3, 8).

3. אַמְתַּחַת *sack*, a word peculiar to this narrative, is claimed for J, while E's word for the same is said to be שָׂק. The latter properly denotes the coarse material from which sacks and the dress of mourners were made, and is then applied to anything made of this material. אַמְתַּחַת from מָתַח *to expand*, is the specific term for a bag or sack. The grain sacks are first mentioned xlii. 25, where the general term כְּלִי *vessel*, is used together with שָׂק; then in vs. 27, 28, שָׂק together with אַמְתַּחַת; in ver. 35 שַׂק alone, and thenceforward אַמְתַּחַת, as the proper and specific term, is steadfastly adhered to in the rest of the narrative throughout chs. xliii. and xliv. That this affords no argument for sundering vs. 27, 28 from their present connection and assigning them to another writer is obvious, since both שָׂק and אַמְתַּחַת occur there together; moreover, Elohim in the last clause of ver. 28 forbids it being assigned to J. Dillmann evades these difficulties by assuming that these verses have been manipulated by R, who inserted שָׂק and transposed the unwelcome clause from its original position after ver. 35. What cannot a critic prove with the help of R?

4. נַעַר *lad*, as Benjamin is called by J (xliii. 8 ; xliv.
22–34) ; but E uses instead יֶלֶד *child* (xlii. 22 E, said of
Joseph at the time when he was sold). J, however, likewise calls Benjamin יֶלֶד (xliv. 20), and uses the same
word repeatedly elsewhere, *e.g.*, xxxii. 23 ; xxxiii. 1–14
(9 times) ; while E uses נַעַר with equal frequency (xiv. 24 ;
xxi. 12–20 (6 times)) ; ch. xxii. (5 times), etc. See ch. xxi.
1–21, Marks of E, No. 6.

5. *Israel* (xliii. 6, 8, 14 J) ; but *Jacob*, xlii. 1, 4, 29, 36,
E ; also *sons of Israel*, xlii. 5 E. See ch. xxxvii., Marks
of J, No. 1.

6. הָאִישׁ *the man*, said of Joseph (xliii. 3, 5, 6, 7, 13,
14 ; xliv. 26 J), while E says הָאִישׁ אֲדֹנֵי הָאָרֶץ *the man,
the lord of the land* (xlii. 30, 33). The full phrase was
necessary at first in order to indicate the person intended ; its constant repetition afterward would be cum-
brous. In like manner " the man who was over Joseph's
house " (xliii. 16, 19) is simply called " the man " (ver.
17). The plural construct אֲדֹנֵי is used in a singular
sense but once besides in the Pentateuch (xxxix. 20),
where it is attributed to J.

7. בֵּית הַסֹּחַר *prison*, is used by J (xxxix. 20–23), while
E has מִשְׁמָר *ward* (xlii. 17, 19), as xl. 3, 4, 7 ; xli. 10 ; but
the former also occurs in an E context (xl. 3, 5), only the
clause containing it is cut out and assigned to J because
of this very phrase.

8. כֻּלָּנָה *all of them*, the prolonged form of the feminine
plural suffix is used by E (xlii. 36), as xxi. 29 ; xxxi. 6 ; xli.
21 ; but J has the same יָחֵמְנָּה for יָחֵמְן xxx. 41.

9. צֵדָה *provision* (xlii. 25 E), as xlv. 21 ; Josh. ix. 11 ;
but so J xxvii. 3 ; Ex. xii. 39 ; all in Hexateuch except
Josh. i. 11 D.

10. צָרָה *distress* (xlii. 21 bis E) ; but so J Deut. xxxi.
17, 21 ; all in Hexateuch.

11. זָכַר *remember* (xlii. 9 E), as xl. 14 bis, 23 ; xli. 9 ;

Ex. xx. 8 (?), 24; xxiii. 13; but so J Ex. xiii. 3; xxxii. 13; Lev. xxvi. 42 (three times), 45 (?), Num. xi. 5; xv. 39, 40; P, Gen. viii. 1; ix. 15, 16; xix. 29; xxx. 22; Ex. ii. 24; vi. 5; Num. v. 15 (?); x. 9 (?); all in Pentateuch except Deuteronomy.

12. אֹכֶל *food,* is claimed for J (xliii. 2, 4, 20, 22; xliv. 1, 25) in distinction from בַּר *grain* (E xli. 35, 49; xlii. 3, 25; xlv. 23); but the former occurs in E xli. 35 bis, 36, 48 bis; xlii. 7, 10; xlvii. 24, unless the clauses containing it are arbitrarily severed from their context.

13. יָרַד *go down,* and הוֹרִיד *bring down* (into Egypt), are said to be used by J, while E has הֵבִיא *bring.* See ch. xxxvii., Marks of J, No. 3.

14. כָּבֵד *heavy* (xliii. 1); mostly referred by rule to J, even when it has to be cut out of an E connection for the purpose, as Gen. xli. 31; Ex. xix. 16; Num. xx. 20; yet it is given to E Ex. xvii. 12; xviii. 18. So, too, the corresponding verb is mostly assigned to J, and is in Ex. v. 9 cut out of an E connection for the purpose; it is, however, given to E Num. xxii. 15, 17, 37; and to P Ex. xiv. 4, 17, 18; Lev. x. 3.

15. כִּלָּה with לְ and the infinitive *made an end* (xliii. 2 J). See ch. xxvi. 34–xxviii. 9, Marks of J, No. 2.

16. מְעַט *a little* (xliii. 2, 11; xliv. 25 J); besides in J xviii. 4; xxiv. 17, 43; xxvi. 10; xxx. 15, 30; Josh. vii. 3; in JE Num. xvi. 13; in E Ex. xvii. 4; xxiii. 30; Num. xiii. 18; in P Gen. xlvii. 9; Lev. xxv. 52; Num. xvi. 9 (worked over); xxvi. 54, 56; xxxiii. 54; xxxv. 8; in Deut. 5 times; R Josh. xxii. 17; all in Hexateuch.

17. יֵשׁ with suffix and participle (xliii. 4 J). See ch. xxiv., Marks of J, No. 11.

18. הִתְמַהְמַהּ *linger* (xliii. 10 J); besides in J xix. 16; Ex. xii. 39; all in Hexateuch.

19. אוּלַי *peradventure* (ver. 12 J). See ch. xvi., Marks of J, No. 12.

20. פֶּתַח door (ver. 19 J); besides in J iv. 7; xviii. 1, 2, 10 ; xix. 6, 11 ; xxxviii. 14; Ex. xii. 22, 23; Num. xi. 10 ; in E Ex. xxxiii. 8, 9, 10 ; Num. xii. 5; in JE Num. xvi. 27; in P Gen. vi. 16 and fifty-five times besides; twice in Deut., and once referred to Rd, viz., Josh. viii. 29.

21. קָדַד וְהִשְׁתַּחֲוָה bow the head and make obeisance (ver. 28 J). See ch. xxiv., Marks of J, No. 20.

22. בִּי particle of entreaty (xliii. 20 ; xliv. 18 J); besides in J Ex. iv. 10, 13 ; Num. xii. 11 ; Josh. vii. 8; all in Hexateuch.

23. כַּדְּבָרִים הָאֵלֶּה according to these words (xliv. 7 J). See ch. xxxix., Marks of J, No. 5.

24. חָלִילָה לְ far be it, followed by מִן with the infinitive (xliv. 7, 17). See ch. xviii., xix., Marks of J, No. 8.

25. The ending וּן (xliv. 1, 23 J). See ch. xviii., xix., Marks of J, No. 22.

The attempt to establish a parallel narrative to ch. xlii. for J, and to chs. xliii., xliv. for E, rests on very slender grounds. Snatches of the former are suspected in xlii. 2a, 4b, 6, 7, 10, 27, 28, 38, and of the latter in xliii. 14, 23b. It is alleged that xlii. 2a is superfluous beside ver. 1a, which it is not ; ver. 4b is sundered from its connection and given to J because of the phrase יִקְרָאֶנּוּ אָסוֹן mischief befall him, though these words are found as well in E, and their recurrence (ver. 38 ; xliv. 29), instead of being a reason for partition, is indicative rather of the unity of the entire narrative ; ver. 6 because of שַׁלִּיט governor, which occurs nowhere else in the Hexateuch, and is here used instead of אֲדֹנִים lord, as vs. 30, 33, E, or מֹשֵׁל ruler, as xlv. 8, 26, E ; but if the same writer can speak of Joseph as אֲדֹנִים and מֹשֵׁל, why not also as שַׁלִּיט, especially as שַׁלִּיט in the opinion of Dillmann " may here be a technical word traditionally preserved, since it agrees remarkably with Salitis or Silitis, the name of the first ruler of the Hyksos in Egypt;" moreover, it is very inconsistent for the critics to refer ver. 6 to another than E, notwithstanding the plain allusion to Joseph's dreams in the last clause where his brothers bow themselves to the ground before him (cf. xxxvii. 10). "He knew them, but made himself strange unto them," in ver. 7, is said to be an insertion from J because of the repetition in ver. 8, which, however, is for the sake of adding a contrasted thought, and the removal of this clause leaves the following words, "spake roughly with them," unexplained, so that Dillmann finds it necessary to transpose them after ver. 9a. So ver. 10 because of אֹכֶל food, though this is equally found in E. And vs. 27, 28, 38, for reasons already sufficiently discussed. Furthermore, xliii. 14, 23b, are cut out of their connection and given to E, because they flatly contradict the critical allegation that J knows nothing of Simeon's imprisonment and that he never says El Shaddai.

It will be observed that the phrase "land of Canaan," previously claimed as characteristic of P, here appears repeatedly in E (xlii. 5, 7, 13, 29, 32) and J (xliv. 8). See ch. xii. 5, Marks of P, No. 4.

JOSEPH MAKES HIMSELF KNOWN (CH. XLV.)

THE complications of the immediately preceding chapters, as is correctly observed by Tuch, simply serve to prepare the way for the surprising *dénouement* in ch. xlv., which is a sufficient proof that this chapter must be from the narrator of the foregoing circumstances; and in like manner ch. xlv. leads directly to ch. xlvi. Nevertheless the critics assign this chapter in the main to E, on the ground of alleged discrepancies with what precedes and follows. How, it is said, could Joseph ask (ver. 3) whether his father was yet living after his own previous inquiry (xliii. 27, 28), and Judah's speech (xliv. 18–34), as reported by J? The suggestion only shows how utterly this cold and captious criticism is out of sympathy with the writer, and with the whole situation. Joseph's heart is bursting with long-suppressed emotion. He had asked about the old man of whom they spake. He can maintain this distance and reserve no longer. With the disclosure "I am Joseph," his first utterance follows the bent of his affections, " How is my father?"

Again, it is objected that Pharaoh had bidden Joseph bring his father with his household to Egypt, promising him the good of the land (vs. 17, 18), yet (xlvii. 1) Joseph announces their coming to Pharaoh, as though he had never heard of it before ; they petition (ver. 4) to be allowed to dwell in Goshen, and Pharaoh grants it (ver. 6), without any allusion to his previous invitation and promise.

But there is no implication in this last act that the first had not preceded it. All proceeds quite naturally in the narrative. At the first intimation of the presence of Joseph's brethren Pharaoh asks them to Egypt to share the good of the land, assigning them no residence, and only offering them subsistence in this time of scarcity. Upon their actual arrival with their father and all their possessions Joseph notifies Pharaoh of the fact, and presents his brethren to him with the request that they may dwell in Goshen as best suited to their occupation. And when this is granted he presents his aged father to the king. All is as consistent and natural as possible.

It is further urged that there are back references to this chapter and coincidences with it in other E passages which are indicative of their common origin. Thus, xlvi. 5 makes mention of the wagons sent by Pharaoh to bring the wives of Joseph's brethren, and their little ones, and their father, agreeably to xlv. 19, 21. Chs. xlvii.

12, l. 21 allude to Joseph's promise (xlv. 11) to nourish his father and his household. The reference of all that had befallen Joseph to the providence of God (xlv. 7, 8) is as l. 20; and the exalted position assigned to Joseph in Egypt (xlv. 8) is as xli. 40–43. The common authorship of these so-called E passages is freely admitted. But this is no concession to critical partition. Precisely the same line of proof from allusions and coincidences links this chapter indissolubly to J passages likewise. The constitution of the chapter is clearly at variance with the hypothesis of the critics, since what they allege to be criteria of distinct documents, whether in language or in the contents of the narrative, are here inseparably blended. Their only resource here, as elsewhere, is to interpret these damaging clauses as insertions by R, which they accordingly cut out of their proper connection and assign to J as though they were scraps taken from a supposed parallel narrative of his.

Verse 1a is given to J because of הִתְאַפֵּק *refrain himself;* only besides in the Hexateuch xliii. 31 J; but 1b, closely connected with it, is assigned to E because of הִתְוַדַּע *made himself known;* only besides in the Old Testament Num. xii. 6 E.

Verse 2 is declared superfluous in its connection beside ver. 16. But it is not. The action progresses regularly. Joseph's weeping was heard by those outside (ver. 2), but the occasion of it became known subsequently (ver. 16).

Verse 4b, the sale of Joseph into Egypt is in the wrong document; of course excision is necessary.

Verse 5 is a singular medley; no two successive clauses can be assigned to the same document. The first clause has תֵּעָצְבוּ *be grieved,* J, as vi. 6; xxxiv. 7; the second יִחַר בְּעֵינֵיכֶם (anger) *burn in your eyes,* only besides in the

Old Testament xxxi. 35 E; the third, the sale of Joseph,
J; the fourth, *Elohim*, E.

Verse 7a repeats 5b, but Elohim occurs in both, com-
pelling the critics to give both to E, and so confess that
repetition is not proof of a doublet, or else, as Kautzsch
proposes, to change one Elohim to Jehovah, and throw
the blame on R. Dillmann remarks upon the construction as unusual and difficult, which affords him a pretext for the conjecture that it is a mutilated insertion
from J. It is of little consequence how it is accomplished, so that a foothold is found in the verse for J.

Verse 10, Joseph's naming Goshen as their place of
abode is implied in xlvi. 28 J, where Jacob goes directly
thither. It is hence severed from its connection and
given to J, in whole or in part, while its minute enumeration of particulars is such as is elsewhere held to characterize P in distinction from both J and E.

Verse 13 is assigned to J because of הוֹרִיד *bring down*,
as xxxix. 1, and because it repeats ver. 9; so ver. 14, because of נָפַל עַל צַוְּאָרֵי *fell upon the neck*, as xxxiii. 4, xlvi.
29; while ver. 15, a part of the same scene, is given to E.
Wellhausen by comparison with xxxiii. 4 tries to establish a diversity between J and E in the construction of
נָשַׁק *kissed*, a conclusion which Dillmann thinks " weak in
its feet."

Verse 19. לְטַפְּכֶם וְלִנְשֵׁיכֶם *for your little ones and for your
wives*, is a J phrase.

Verse 20. עֵינְכֶם אַל־תָּחֹס *let not your eye spare* (E. V.,
regard not), is peculiar to D; "the good of all the land
of Egypt is yours" duplicates ver. 18.

Verse 21. "And the children of Israel did so," is
such a preliminary statement of what is more fully detailed afterward as the critics are in the habit of reckoning a duplicate account.

Verse 28 is the response to ver. 27; but one verse has

" Jacob," and must be assigned to E, while the other has "Israel," and is given to J.

It is apparent here, as in many other cases, that the assignment of verses and clauses is simply the enforcement, *nolens volens*, of an arbitrary determination of the critics. No one would dream of sundering these mutually unrelated scraps from the rest of the chapter, with which they are closely connected, but for the application of alleged criteria which the critics have devised in other places in framing their hypothesis. These are carried rigorously through at whatever disturbance of the connection or havoc of the sense, because to abandon them would be to give up the hypothesis. The very least that can be said is that this mincing work, to which the critics find themselves compelled to resort to so great an extent in Genesis, and increasingly so in the books that follow, lends no support to the hypothesis, but is simply a dead weight upon it. The hypothesis is plainly not an outgrowth of this and similar chapters, but is obtruded upon them ; and the only question is how much lumber of this sort it can carry without signally breaking down.

Elohim occurs four times in this chapter (vs. 5, 7, 8, 9), in the address of Joseph to his brothers. As he is no longer acting the part of an Egyptian, he might have spoken of Jehovah as consulting for the welfare of the chosen race. But Elohim is equally appropriate, since the prominent thought here and throughout the history of Joseph is that it is God, and not man, who guided the course of events (ver. 8 ; l. 20).

MARKS OF E

1. יַעֲקֹב *Jacob* (ver. 25). See ch. xxxvii., Marks of J, No. 1 ; ch. xlii.–xliv., Marks of E, No. 5.

2. חָרָה בְּעֵינָיו (anger) *burn in one's eyes.* Only besides xxxi. 35 E.

3. מָעֵן *lade* (ver. 17); nowhere else in the Old Testament.

4. צֵדָה *provision* (ver. 21). See ch. xlii.–xliv., Marks of E, No. 9.

5. בַּר *grain* (ver. 23). See ch. xlii.–xliv., Marks of E, No. 12.

REMOVAL TO EGYPT (CH. XLVI. 1–27)

Verses 1–5 are assigned to E on account of the back reference in ver. 5b to xlv. 19, 21 (but if these verses belong to R, as Dillmann affirms, ver. 5b must be given to R likewise), and other criteria; only ver. 1a is given to J or R because of "Israel" and "took his journey" וַיִּסַּע. This affords an opportunity for creating a discrepancy. Jacob starts in E (ver. 5) from Beersheba, in J from some other place, presumably from Hebron (xxxvii. 14), and takes Beersheba on his way. It scarcely need be stated that the discrepancy is purely the result of the critical partition, and has no existence in the text itself. In ver. 2 "Elohim" and "visions of the night," which are held to be characteristics of E,[1] conflict with "Israel," a mark of J. The difficulty is adjusted by erasing the unwelcome name and tracing its insertion to R.

Verses 6, 7 are attributed to P on account of words and phrases which are claimed as peculiar to P, but on very slight grounds as has been previously shown. P's last generally acknowledged statement[2] is that, in contrast to Esau's removal to Mount Seir (xxxvi. 6–8), Jacob dwelt in the land of Canaan (xxxvii. 1). And yet here follows, without a word of explanation, the removal of

---

[1] The repetition of the name, and the answer "Here I am," as Gen. xxii. 11, Ex. iii. 4, is also claimed for E; but Gen. xxii. 11 can only be assigned to E by manipulating the text and expunging "Jehovah."

[2] Two isolated and unexplained statements of Joseph's age, when tending flocks (xxxvii. 2), and when standing before Pharaoh (xli. 46), are given to P by some critics, and denied to him by others.

Jacob and his family to Egypt; and it comes out in subsequent allusions that Joseph was already settled there
and married into a priestly family (xlvi. 20, 27), that he
was in high favor with Pharaoh, and it was he who gave
his father and brethren a possession in the land of Egypt
(xlvii. 7, 11). But how all this came about P does not
inform us. The critics are greatly exercised to account
for so egregious a gap as this. Kayser suggests that P
was theoretical rather than historical; Nöldeke that R
omitted P's account because it was contradictory to E
and J ; others, because it agreed with theirs. And yet
elsewhere R is careful to preserve even the smallest
scraps of P, though they are quite superfluous beside the
more extended narratives of E or J, e.g., xix. 29, and if
we may believe the critics he is not deterred by inconsistencies.

The list of Jacob's family (vs. 8–27) is a critical puzzle.
It is in the style of other genealogies attributed to P,
and has expressions claimed as his, viz., "Paddan-aram "
(ver. 15), "souls " (vs. 15, 18, 22, 25–27), "came out of
his loins " (ver. 26). And yet there are duplicates of it
in P (Ex. i. 1–5; vi. 14–25; Num. xxvi. 5 sqq.) ; Israel
(ver. 8) is a mark of J, and, as Kayser affirms, it has
too many allusions to J and E to admit of their being
explained as interpolations. Thus (ver. 12), "Er and
Onan died in the land of Canaan," refers to xxxviii. 7–10
J ; ver. 18, " Zilpah, whom Laban gave to Leah," and
ver. 25, " Bilhah, whom Laban gave unto Rachel,"to xxix.
24, 29 [1] E ; vs. 20, 27, Joseph's marriage and sons to xli.
50–52 E.[2] So Hupfeld attributes this list to J, Well-

[1] It is with the view of quietly evading this difficulty that Wellhausen
and Dillmann absurdly sunder these verses from the rest of ch. xxix.,
and give them to P.

[2] Also (ver. 15) " Dinah " refers to xxx. 21, if Kayser and Schrader
are correct in ascribing ch. xxxiv. entire to J.

hausen to a later writer who derived his materials from
P, or according to Kayser, from P and J, or in the opinion of Kuenen one who was acquainted with Genesis in
its present form, and with Num. xxvi. ("Hexateuch," p. 68),
while Dillmann follows Nöldeke in imputing it to P, but
worked over by R, who supplied the additions from J
and E. But such a linking together of J, E, and P as
we find in this passage, and repeatedly in others, occurs
too frequently to be set aside by any critical device.
These cannot be separate and independent documents,
since their alleged criteria are indiscriminately mingled
in the same continuous paragraphs, and are to all appearance freely used by the same writer.

As (ver. 8) this list professes to give "the names of the
children of Israel who came into Egypt," Dillmann affirms that the mention of Er and Onan (ver. 12) implies
that they were living at that time (the clause which
speaks of their death in Canaan being, as he contends, an
interpolation from ch. xxxviii.), and that they are in fact
counted in making up the number thirty-three in ver. 15.
He hence concludes that the author of this list is here at
variance with ch. xxxviii. This is a most extraordinary
attempt to create a discrepancy in defiance of the plain
language of the verse, by throwing out of the text its explicit statement on the subject. It only shows what ex-
travagances can be made to result from critical partition.
Er and Onan are not included in the summation (ver. 15).
The number is completed by adding Jacob, who in ver.
8 is reckoned one of "the children of Israel" (in its national sense), and Dinah, the total embracing, as is distinctly declared in ver. 15, "daughters" as well as "sons."
To make out his case Dillmann is obliged here again to
expunge "daughters" from the text.

A further discrepancy is alleged in the chronology. It
is said that the antecedent narratives of J and E do not

allow time enough for the birth of all the children named in this list of P. This is based on the assumption, which even Wellhausen [1] repels, that every individual person named in the list was born before the migration into Egypt. Such an inference might indeed be drawn from vs. 8, 26, strictly taken., But to press the letter of such general statements into contradiction with the particulars embraced under them is in violation of the evident meaning of the writer. So ver. 15 rigorously interpreted would make Leah to have borne thirty-three children to Jacob in Paddanaram, one of whom was Jacob himself. Zilpah (ver. 18) and Bilhah (ver. 25) bare their grandsons as well as their sons. Benjamin is included (xxxv. 24, 26) among Jacob's sons born in Paddan-aram, though his birth near Ephrath is recorded but a few verses before. The numerical correspondences of the table, a total of seventy, the descendants of each maid precisely half those of her mistress (Leah 32, Zilpah 16, Rachel 14, Bilhah 7), suggest design and can scarcely be altogether accidental. And a comparison of Num. xxvi. leads to the belief that regard was had to the subsequent national organization in constructing this table, and that its design was to include those descendants of Jacob from whom permanent families or tribal divisions sprang, even if in a few instances they did not chance to have been born before the descent into Egypt. As a rule Jacob's sons gave names to the tribes, and his grandsons to the tribal divisions. To this, however, there were some exceptions. Joseph's sons, Manasseh and Ephraim, were adopted by Jacob as his own (xlviii. 5), and tribes were called after them. In like manner (ver. 12), Hezron and Hamul,

---

[1] Composition d. Hexateuchs, p. 51 : "This list once and again bursts through the historic bounds of Genesis." Critical consistency requires this admission from those who assign the numbers in xxxvii. 2 and xli. 46 to P, or this document will be in conflict with itself.

grandsons of Judah, are included in this list as substitutes for his two deceased sons ; and (ver. 21) ten sons of Benjamin [1] are enumerated, though some of those who are here spoken of as sons were really grandsons (Num. xxvi. 40 ; 1 Chron. viii. 3, 4). And so no difficulty is created by the circumstance that four sons are ascribed to Reuben, ver. 9, but only two, xlii. 37. A few names are here recorded of those who were still in the loins of their fathers (Heb. vii. 9, 10) at the time of the migration. It is no departure from the usages of Hebrew thought to conceive of unborn children as included in the persons of their parents (ver. 4b). The Septuagint goes farther in this direction than the Hebrew text by inserting in ver. 20 five sons and grandsons of Ephraim and Manasseh, thus making the total in ver. 27 seventy-five instead of seventy ; and so in the speech of Stephen, Acts vii. 14.

The statement in ver. 27, that seventy of Jacob's family came into Egypt, is repeated Deut. x. 22, which can only be accounted for on the Wellhausen hypothesis, which makes this list postexilic and Deuteronomy a product of the age of Josiah, by assuming that these two identical statements were made independently of each other.

The divine names in this chapter are grouped together in the opening verses (vs. 1-3). These verses, though

---

[1] It has been paraded as an absolute inconsistency that Benjamin is in this list spoken of as the father of ten sons, whereas in the narrative (xliii. 8 ; xliv. 22 sqq.) he is called נַעַר lad ; but Rehoboam is called נַעַר young (2 Chron. xiii. 7) when he was upward of forty years of age (xii. 13). The epithet הַקָּטֹן the youngest, which is applied to Benjamin (xlii. 13, 15, 20 sqq.), denotes relative, not absolute age, and has no reference to size. Though Benjamin was tenderly treated as the youngest of the family, and Jacob's darling, the sole remaining son of his favorite wife, it must not be inferred that he was still in his boyhood. Of the ten named in this list as sprung from him, five at least were grandsons, and some of the remainder may have been born in Egypt.

attributed to E, are filled with references to former J
passages, which is at variance with every form of the divisive hypothesis. The name "Israel," not only in ver.
1a, which is given to J, but in ver. 2, is a mark of J.
Jacob's coming to Beersheba, and offering sacrifices there
to the God of his father Isaac, is in evident allusion to
the altar built there by Isaac and the divine manifestation and promise there made to him (xxvi. 23–25 J).
And the language which God here addresses to Jacob in
the night, " I am the God of thy father; fear not.   . . .
I will go down with thee," is a repetition of what he said
to Isaac likewise in the night, "I am the God of Abraham
thy father; fear not, for I am with thee." " I will make
of thee a great nation " (ver. 3) is a repetition of the
promise made to Abraham (xii. 2 J).   "I will go down
with thee into Egypt; and I will also surely bring thee
up again " (ver. 4), is the renewal of the promise made
to Jacob himself on a like occasion before, when he was
on the point of leaving the land of Canaan : "I am with
thee, and will keep thee whithersoever thou goest, and
will bring thee again into this land " (xxviii. 15 J).   This
obvious dependence upon J passages throughout is sufficient to assure us that there can be no variance in the
use of the divine names.   And in point of fact there is
none.   " The God of Isaac " is a designation equivalent
to Jehovah (xxviii. 13 ; xxxii. 10, E. V., ver. 9 J).   And
there are special reasons for joining with this name the
term הָאֵל ha-El (ver. 3), from its association with the name
" Israel," here significantly employed, from its allusion
to xxxv. 11, where the promises of a multiplied offspring
and of the gift of Canaan were made to him on his return
to this land, which are now emphatically repeated as he
is again about to leave it, and from its meaning *the
Mighty One*, with its assurance, just then especially
needed, of omnipotent protection and blessing ; and a

like assurance is involved in Elohim (ver. 2), the God of creation and of universal providence.

MARKS OF J (VER. 1a)

1. נָסַע *journeyed.* See Diction of ch. xx., No. 1.
2. *Israel.* See ch. xxxvii., Marks of J, No. 1; ch. xlii.–xliv., No. 5.

MARKS OF E (vs. 1b–5a)

1. Night Vision. See ch. xx., Marks of E, No. 4.
2. שִׂים לְגוֹי *make a nation.* See ch. xxi. 1–21, Marks of E, No. 12.
3. רְדָה *to go down;* this form of the infinitive occurs but once besides in the Hexateuch, viz., דֵעָה *to know* (Ex. ii. 4 E). A form of so rare occurrence in this document cannot be regarded as characteristic of it.

MARKS OF P

1. רְכוּשׁ *goods,* רָכַשׁ *had gotten* (ver. 6). See ch. xii. 5, Marks of P, No. 2.
2. זַרְעוֹ אִתּוֹ *his seed with him* (vs. 6, 7); while equivalent phrases occur repeatedly in all the documents, this precise form of speech is found but twice besides in the Hexateuch (Gen. xxviii. 4; Num. xviii. 19 P).
3. יַעֲקֹב *Jacob.* See ch. xlii.–xliv., Marks of E, No. 5.
4. בְּכוֹר *first-born* (ver. 8). See ch. xxv. 12–18, Marks of P, No. 4.
5. *Paddan-aram* (ver. 15). See ch. xxv. 19–34, Marks of P, No. 4.
6. נֶפֶשׁ *souls* (vs. 15, 18, 22, 25–27). See ch. xii. 5, Marks of P, No. 3.
7. יֹצְאֵי יְרֵכוֹ *came out of his thigh* (ver. 26); this precise form of expression occurs in the Hexateuch but

once besides (Ex. i. 5 P), where it is borrowed from the present passage; an equivalent expression is found in xxxv. 11 P, יָצָא מֵחֲלָצֶיךָ *come out of thy loins*, and one closely related in xv. 4 J, יָצָא מִמֵּעֶיךָ *come out of thy bowels.* The same conception is involved when an oath relating to posterity (xxiv. 2 J), or to be fulfilled after the death of him who has imposed it (xlvii. 29 J), is taken with the hand under the thigh.

SETTLEMENT IN GOSHEN (CH. XLVI. 28–XLVII. 11)

Dillmann assigns xlvi. 28–xlvii. 5a, 6b, to J ; and xlvii. 5b, 6a, 7–11, to P.

It is argued that xlvi. 28 sqq. belongs to a different document from the preceding, because in ver. 6 (P) Jacob and his family had already come into Egypt, whereas in ver. 28 he is still on the way thither, and sends Judah before him to Joseph to obtain the necessary directions about admission to Goshen. This, it is said, is J's account; and according to Wellhausen it connects directly with ver. 5. But that belongs to E. According to the usual method of Hebrew writing, a summary statement of the journey is made at the outset (vs. 5, 6), and the details are introduced afterward (vs. 28 sqq.). These the critics erect into two separate accounts, as they are accustomed to do elsewhere and with just as little reason.

Wellhausen finds a discrepancy between the modest request (ver. 34 J) for the land of Goshen and the grand offer previously made by Pharaoh (xlv. 18 E) of the best portion of the land of Egypt. But, as Dillmann explains, this is not the meaning of Pharaoh's offer. He has no thought of their taking up their abode in Egypt. His proposal is not to present them with a choice part of the country as their residence, but to supply their necessities during the prevalence of the famine. "The good of the land," which he says that he will give them, denotes, as is plain from vs. 20, 23 ; xxiv. 10 ; 2 Kin. viii. 9, the good things, the best and choicest products of the land. The sons of Jacob make an advance upon the promise given them by the king, when instructed by Joseph they ask that Goshen may be assigned to them to dwell in. And when in response to this request the king assures them that they may dwell in Goshen, " in the best of the land " (xlvii. 6), he uses a different term from that contained in his original offer (not טוּב, but מֵיטַב).

The critics allege that Pharaoh's invitation to Joseph's father and brethren in ch. xlv. E is here entirely ignored, and their coming is announced to the king (xlvi. 31 ; xlvii. 1), as something altogether new and unexpected ; this must, therefore, be a variant account of the matter as given by J. But this is by no means the case. Pharaoh had invited them to come, and now Joseph goes to tell him that they have arrived. The invitation is accepted ; what occasion was there to say more ?

The attempt is also made to produce two divergent accounts of the reception by Pharaoh. The critics employ for this purpose their customary method of making the part stand for the whole, and arraying successive incidents against each other as though they were variant reports of the same transaction. Joseph first presents five of his brethren to the king that they may tell him their occupation and have an appropriate residence assigned them. He then presents his father, *causa honoris*, for a formal interview. This is all natural enough. The complaint is made that the father, as the head of the clan, ought to be have been presented first. The objector may settle that matter with the historian, or, if he pleases, with R. The sons were the active members of the family, and the reason given in the narrative itself

for the order of procedure is sufficient. How the sons
were deferred to in matters of importance affecting the
family is plain from other narratives likewise (cf. xxiv.
50, 53, 55, 59 ; xxxiv. 5, 11, 13). Moreover, the critics will
have it that there was but one presentation ; according
to J (vs. 2 sqq.) Joseph presented his brothers unto
Pharaoh ; on the contrary, P states (vs. 7–11) that it was
his father that Joseph presented. The simple fact is
that he presented both at different times, as the narrative declares; so there is no discrepancy whatever.
Hupfeld evidently saw none, as he does not separate vs.
7–11 from the preceding verses ; neither did Delitzsch in
the first four editions of his " Commentary."

Kayser gives ver. 11 to E, on account of its manifest
connection with vs. 5, 6. Wellhausen, Dillmann, and
others reverse the argument, and give vs. 5b, 6a, to P on
account of their correspondence in thought and expression with ver. 11. This gives an opportunity to claim
that J and P use different designations for the territory
assigned to Israel ; what the former calls Goshen (vs. 4,
6b), the latter denominates the land of Rameses (ver. 11).
Yet " the land of Rameses " is found only in this single
passage ; it is called " Goshen " in ver. 27 P, where a
critical process is necessary to eliminate it, and, as Kayser observes, Rameses occurs in Ex. i. 11 E ; xii. 37 J, as
the name of a city, from which the surrounding region
might readily derive its appellation ; and it is admitted
that the land of Rameses and Goshen have precisely the
same signification.

The authority of the LXX. is here adduced to justify
the critical severance of vs. 5, 6. The LXX. have here,
as so frequently elsewhere, rearranged the text for reasons of their own, which in this instance are quite apparent. In order to bring Pharaoh's answer into more exact correspondence with the request of Joseph's brothers,

they limit it to ver. 6b, which they attach to the opening words of ver. 5; and then to prepare the way for the clauses which have been passed over, vs. 5b, 6a are introduced by the following insertion, " And Jacob and his sons came into Egypt to Joseph, and Pharaoh the king of Egypt heard it; and Pharaoh spake to Joseph, saying." The critics eagerly catch at this, and claim that it supplies a missing portion of the original text of P. But surely no unbiassed person would think of substituting this for the Masoretic text of these verses.

MARKS OF P

1. The statement of age (ver. 9). See ch. vi.–ix., Marks of P, No. 2; ch. xvi., No. 1.

2. יְמֵי חַיֵּי שְׁנֵי *the days of the years of the life of* (vs. 8, 9). See ch. xxiii., Marks of P, No. 5. The same phrase also 2 Sam. xix. 35 (E. V., ver. 34).

3. מְגֻרִים *pilgrimage* (ver. 9). See ch. xvii., Marks of P, No. 8.

4. אֲחֻזָּה *possession* (ver. 11). See ch. xvii., Marks of P, No. 7.

MARKS OF J

1. נָפַל עַל־צַוָּארָיו *fell on his neck* (xlvi. 29); only besides in J xxxiii. 4; in xlv. 14 it is cut out of an E connection on account of this very phrase.

2. *Israel* (xlvi. 29, 30). See ch. xxxvii., Marks of J, No. 1; ch. xlii.–xliv., No. 5.

3. הַפַּעַם *this time*, E. V., now (ver. 30). See ch. xviii., xix., Marks of J, No. 9.

4. עוֹדְךָ חַי *thou art yet alive* (ver. 30). The repetition of this and equivalent expressions in this narrative is due on the one hand to Joseph's solicitude about his father, and on the other his father's long-continued ap-

prehension that Joseph was dead. It is the natural way of expressing the thought, and cannot with any propriety be classed as the characteristic of any particular document. It is found besides in J (xliii. 7, 27, 28), in E (xlv. 3, 26), and in ver. 28, which is cut out of an E connection and given to J; also in E (Ex. iv. 18); in D or Rd. (Deut. xxxi. 27); in other books, 1 Sam. xx. 14; 2 Sam. xii. 22; xviii. 14; 1 Kin. xx. 32.

5. מִנְּעוּרִים *from youth* (ver. 34). The word "youth" occurs but once besides in the Hexateuch with this preposition (Gen. viii. 21 J), and but twice without it (Lev. xxii. 13 P; Num. xxx. 4 (E. V., ver. 3)) commonly referred to P, though Dillmann is disposed to assign it to a code of laws which he denominates S. In other books of the Bible "from youth" occurs repeatedly; and it is plainly not the peculiar property of any one writer.

6. תּוֹעֵבָה *abomination* (ver. 34); in the Hexateuch besides, xliii. 32; Ex. viii. 22 (E. V., ver. 26) J; Lev. xviii. 22, 26, 27, 29, 30; xx. 13, and repeatedly in Deuteronomy.

7. הִצִּיג *presented* (xlvii. 2); besides in Hexateuch, xxx. 38; xxxiii. 15; xliii. 9 J; Ex. x. 24 E; Deut. xxviii. 56 D. That הֶעֱמִיד is used in ver. 7 P in the same sense is no indication of a different document, since it is used likewise in J (Num. xi. 24).

8. כָּבֵד *heavy, sore* (ver. 4). See ch. xlii.–xliv., Marks of J, No. 14.

9. בַּעֲבוּר *in order that* (xlvi. 34). See xxi. 22–34, Marks of E, No. 3.

10. גַּם . . . גַּם *both* . . . *and* (ver. 34); besides in J (xxiv. 25, 44; xliii. 8; xliv. 16; xlvii. 3; l. 9); in J, based on E and worked over by R (xlvii. 19); an ancient writing inserted in J (Deut. xxxii. 25); in E (Gen. xxxii. 20, E. V., ver. 19; Ex. xii. 32; xviii. 18); in P (Num. xviii. 3).

Jacob commissions Judah (xlvi. 28) rather than Reuben, because of the confidence inspired by his character, which made him an acknowledged leader among his brethren (xlix. 8), as Peter among the apostles. This is not the invention of a writer partial to Judah, and so a criterion of one document in distinction from another.

JOSEPH'S ARRANGEMENTS IN EGYPT (CH. XLVII. 12–27)

An account is here given of the measures adopted by Joseph during the famine. The only source of supply was the stores of grain, which as the chief officer of the government he had amassed from the over-production of the seven years of plenty (xli. 34–36, 47–49). In purchasing their necessary food during the years of scarcity that followed, the people parted first with all their money, then with all their cattle and beasts of burden, and finally with their lands.[1] Thus the land became the property of the king ; and it became the established rule in Egypt that the people should pay to him, as the owner of the land, a rental of one-fifth of its produce.

Wellhausen says that this peculiar passage (vs. 13–26) has no proper connection either in E or J ; he assumes that it originally had its place in a parallel by J to ch. xli. Dillmann thinks that it was written as the continuation of ch. xli., since ver. 13 connects with xli. 55, 56.

The intimate connection between this passage and ch.

---

[1] The LXX., followed by the Samaritan and the Vulgate, read (ver. 21): "He enslaved them as servants to him," i.e., Pharaoh הֶעֱבִיד אֹתוֹ לַעֲבָדִים, as though after disposing of their lands the people sold themselves. This variant text implies that Joseph took the people at their word when they offered (ver. 19) to become bond-servants to Pharaoh for the sake of bread. It agrees also with vs. 23, 25. The Hebrew reads, "He removed them to cities" הֶעֱבִיר אֹתוֹ לֶעָרִים, that they might be nearer the storehouses, and their wants more easily supplied.

xli. is obvious, and it may be said to continue the narrative of that chapter. Chapter xli. records how Joseph stored up the grain during the years of plenty ; and when the years of dearth began to come, the people went to him to buy their food. Then the passage before us tells how the people were impoverished, as the famine continued from year to year, by the purchases that they were obliged to make. But it does not follow from this that it originally formed a part of that chapter, and is now out of its proper place. The narrative of Joseph's dealings with the Egyptians was interrupted in order to tell of the coming of his brothers, and to explain how this resulted in the removal of Jacob and his family to Egypt and their settlement there. This, in fact, is the principal reason why the famine was spoken of at all. When this recital is ended, the unfinished subject of Joseph's dealings with the Egyptians is resumed and completed.

And the details here given upon this subject are not so much designed to impart information about Egypt as to exhibit by contrast the providential care extended over the chosen race in this period of sore distress. While the Egyptians were reduced to the greatest straits, " Joseph nourished his father, and his brethren, and all his father's household with bread " (ver. 12). " And Israel dwelt in the land of Egypt, in the land of Goshen ; and they gat them possessions therein, and were fruitful and multiplied exceedingly " (ver. 27). Verses 12 and 27, from which the critics propose to sunder this paragraph, are thus essential to a proper understanding of it ; and its proper place is where it now stands between them.

This paragraph likewise prepares the way for Ex. i. 8. The oppression of Israel by a king " who knew not Joseph," is a manifest allusion to the service which he had rendered to the nation, and to the advantage which he had secured for the king, as here detailed.

Kayser refers vs. 12–26 to J, Schrader to E; Dillmann thinks that the original account was by E, this was re-written by J, and then worked over by R. Verse 27 he gives to P, except the words "the land of Goshen;" Kayser gives ver. 27a to J on account of this phrase, and 27b to P. Knobel contends that ver. 27 must belong to the preceding paragraph, to which it is attached with the view of contrasting the condition of Israel with the Egyptians, and that it cannot, therefore, be assigned to P, notwithstanding its use of P expressions; especially as it also has the J phrase, "land of Goshen," and it duplicates the P verse (Ex. i. 7). This blending of the alleged characteristics of different documents simply shows that what the critics regard as criteria of distinct writers are freely used by the same writer.

MARKS OF E

1. The accurate account of Egyptian matters, and the analogy between vs. 25, 26, and xli. 34. But these afford no indication of the existence of distinct documents.

2. כִּלְכֵּל *nourished* (ver. 12). This verb is here used with evident reference to its occurrence in Joseph's promise (xlv. 11), which he now fulfils. That these passages are to be attributed to the same writer is readily admitted, but not to a writer E, distinct from the author of xlvi. 6–xlvii. 11, which the critics divide between P and J. According to this partition, E here records Joseph's fulfilment of his promise to nourish his father and his family in Egypt, without having mentioned the fact that they had arrived in Egypt, or even that they had accepted the invitation to come thither.

3. חָזַק *prevailed* (ver. 20), as over against כָּבֵד *sore, severe* (ver. 13 J). See ch. xlii.–xliv., No. 14. That two different words are used in different passages to describe

the intensity of the famine is no indication of a diversity of writers, unless a writer can never vary his expressions.

MARKS OF J

1. כָּבֵד *sore* (ver. 13). See ch. xlii.–xliv., No. 14.

2. הַנִּמְצָא *found* (ver. 14). The participle chances to occur but twice besides in the Hexateuch (Gen. xix. 15 J ; Deut. xx. 11 D), but the verb is of frequent occurrence, and is found in all the so-called documents.

3. תַּם *fail, be spent* (vs. 15, 18) ; besides in J Lev. xxvi. 20 (so Dillm.) ; Num. xxxii. 13 ; Josh. iv. 10, 11 ; E, Num. xiv. 33 ; Josh. iv. 1 ; v. 8 ; x. 20 ; JE, Josh. iii. 16, 17 ; viii. 24 ; P, Lev. xxv. 29 ; Num. xiv. 35 ; xvii. 28 (E. V., ver. 13) ; Deut. xxxiv. 8 ; D, Deut. ii. 14, 15, 16 ; Rd, Deut. xxxi. 24, 30 ; Josh. v. 6.

4. *Horses* (ver. 17). It is alleged that J speaks of horses and horsemen in Egypt, but E does not. This is said to indicate that E was better acquainted with Egyptian affairs, as the monuments give no evidence of the existence of horses there until after the Hyksos period ; and although Diodorus Siculus speaks of horsemen in the army of Sesostris, horses would seem to have been used only for chariots in the first instance, and cavalry to belong to a later period (Isa. xxxi. 1 ; xxxvi. 9). That they have not yet been found upon the monuments of so early a date is a negative testimony which is liable at any time to be set aside by some fresh discovery, and is of no force against the positive statements of the passage under consideration and others like it. Moreover, there is no variance between the passages attributed to J and to E. It is observable that in the presents made by Pharaoh to Abram (xii. 16 J) mention is made of sheep and oxen and asses and camels, but not of horses. J, however, speaks (xlvi. 29) of Joseph making ready his chariot,

which implies horses; and more explicitly (l. 9), of his going with chariots and horsemen to bury his father. Dillmann remarks that while according to E wagons were sent for Jacob by Pharaoh's direction (xlv. 19, 21, 27; xlvi. 5), they may have been drawn by other animals than horses; and at any rate he is disposed to think that these verses though in an E context may have been inserted by R. E, however, speaks of Joseph's chariot (xli. 43). And Ex. xiv. is divided on the assumption that vs. 6, 7, which speak of Pharaoh's chariots, are from E, but vs. 9, 17, 18, 23, 26, 28, which mention horsemen as well as chariots, are from J. The latter is supposed to have put a wrong interpretation upon the words "the horse and his rider," in the Song of Moses (Ex. xv. 1), which is alleged to refer to charioteers, not to horsemen. This whole theory is spoiled, however, by Josh. xxiv. 6 E, which expressly says that the horsemen as well as the chariots of the Egyptians pursued Israel into the Red Sea. Dr. Dillmann tries to evade this result by saying that "chariots and horsemen" cannot be from E, and must therefore have been inserted by R.

The case then stands thus: In vs. 6, 7, of Ex. xiv., chariots are spoken of without separate mention of horsemen, though both are joined together throughout the rest of the chapter. This is made a pretext for assigning those verses to E in distinction from J, and inferring that E never speaks of horsemen. But horsemen are spoken of along with chariots in the E verse Josh. xxiv. 6; this being contrary to the critic's assumption the words are stricken out and declared to be an interpolation by R. And this is all the ground there is for the alleged variance between J and E in this particular.

5. קָצֶה *end* (ver. 21); besides in J, Gen. xix. 4; xlvii. 2; Josh. ix. 16; in E, Ex. xix. 12; Num. xx. 16; xxii. 36, 41; xxiii. 13; in JE, Josh. iii. 2, 8, 15; iv. 19; in D, Deut.

xiii. 8 (E. V., ver. 7); xiv. 28 ; xxviii. 49, 64 ; xxx. 4; in
Rd, Deut. iv. 32 ; Josh. xiii. 27 ; in P, Gen. viii. 3b ; xxiii.
9 ; Ex. xiii. 20 ; xvi. 35 ; xxvi. 5, 28 ; Num. xi. 1 ; xxxiii.
6, 37 ; xxxiv. 3 ; Josh. xv. 1, 2, 5, 8, 21 ; xviii. 15, 16, 19;
later addition to P, Ex. xxxvi. 12, 33.

6. רַק *only* (vs. 22, 26). See ch. vi. 1–8, Marks of J,
No. 7.

7. מָצָא חֵן בְּעֵינֵי *find favor in the eyes of.* See ch. vi.
1–8, Marks of J, No. 10 ; ch. xviii., xix., No. 28.

8. מִקְנֵה הַצֹּאן *possession of flocks,* מִקְנֵה הַבָּקָר *possession
of herds* (ver. 17), מִקְנֵה הַבְּהֵמָה *possession of cattle* (ver.
18) ; only once besides in the Pentateuch (xxvi. 14 J).

9. יָדֹת *parts* (ver. 24) ; only once besides in the Pentateuch in this sense (xliii. 34 J).

The occurrence of a few unusual words in this paragraph need create no difficulty as to its authorship, unless upon the assumption that no writer can use a word
in one place which he has not used elsewhere. The following are noted by Dillmann : לָהַהּ *fainted* (ver. 13), but
once besides in the Old Testament (Prov. xxvi. 18) ; אָפֵס
fail (vs. 15, 16), only besides, Ps. lxxvii. 9 ; Isa. xvi. 4 ;
xxix. 20 ; נַהֵל *fed* (ver. 17), nowhere else in the Old Testament in precisely the same sense ; it is found twice besides
in the Hexateuch, where it means "to lead ; " שָׁמֵם *be deso-
late* (ver. 19), in the Kal form but once besides in the
Hexateuch (Lev. xxvi. 32); הֵא *lo !* (ver. 23), nowhere else
in the Hexateuch, and but once besides in the Old Testament.

MARKS OF P (VER. 27)

1. "Land of Egypt" with "land of Goshen ;" but
this is no mere superfluous repetition, and as such indicative of the blending of two separate accounts. Israel
was settled in the country of Egypt and the province of
Goshen.

2. נֶאֱחַז *had possessions.* See ch. xxxiv., Marks of P, No. 4.

3. פָּרָה וְרָבָה *were fruitful and multiplied.* See ch. vi.–ix., Marks of P, No. 15.

JACOB CHARGES JOSEPH AND ADOPTS HIS SONS (CH. XLVII. 28–XLVIII. 22)

The critics generally agree in giving xlvii. 28; xlviii. 3–6, to P, and xlvii. 29–31 to J. There is less agreement in the partition of the remainder of ch. xlviii., viz., whether vs. 1, 2 belong to J (Schrader), E (Wellhausen), or 2b to J and 1, 2a to E (Dillmann); ver. 7 to P (Hupfeld, Wellhausen, Dillmann), or a gloss (Schrader, Kayser); vs. 8–22 to E (Hupfeld, Schrader, Wellhausen); or vs. 9a, 10b, 11, 12, 15, 16, 20 (in part), 21, 22, to E, and vs. 9b, 10a, 13, 14, 17–19, 20b, to J (Dillmann); Kuenen [1] regards vs. 13, 14, 17–19 as a later interpolation, and gives the rest to E.

Hupfeld claims that there are most evident signs of the diversity of the accounts at the close of Jacob's history in respect to his final charges to his sons and his burial. And Wellhausen adds that there is scarcely a passage in Genesis where the strata of the sources are so palpable as in the latter part of ch. xlvii. and the first of ch. xlviii. In xlvii. 28, he says, there is a beginning by P, in ver. 29 another by J, and in xlviii. 1 a third beginning of the very same history by E. But the fact is that there is no diversity of sources here whatever; all is linked together as one regularly unfolding and continuous narrative. The statement of the full age of a patriarch always immediately precedes the account of his death; so of Noah, ix. 29, Abraham, xxv. 7, and Isaac xxxv. 28. In conformity with this usage the statement

[1] Hexateuch, p. 146.

of Jacob's age (xlvii. 28) is followed by the mention of
his approaching death, in view of which he sends for
Joseph and gives him direction respecting his burial, just
as the mention of Joseph's age (l. 22, 23) is followed by
a similar charge to his brethren respecting the disposition
of his body (vs. 24, 25). Ch. xlvii. 28 is thus plainly preliminary to vs. 29-31, which latter is not a variant account of the same transaction as xlix. 29-32; this belongs to a subsequent occasion, and to an interview of
Jacob with all his sons and not with Joseph only. And
the visit of Joseph to his father in xlviii. 1 is not identical with that described in the preceding verses, but, as is
expressly declared, occurred later; Joseph came, not as
before, on his father's invitation, but of his own motion
on hearing of his father's increased illness; and the subject of the interview is altogether different, concerning
not Jacob's burial but the adoption and blessing of Joseph's sons.

Moreover, xlvii. 29-31 cannot be sundered from ch.
xlviii. The opening words of xlviii. 1, "And it came to
pass after these things," is an explicit reference to what
immediately precedes. The critics tell us that this is a
formula belonging to E; but there is nothing in E with
which to connect it. Dillmann finds traces of E in xlvii.
12-27, but derives this paragraph in its present form
from J, and besides, he holds that it has been transposed
from its original position at the end of ch. xli. Accordingly the last statement in E is xlvi. 5a, " and Jacob rose
up from Beersheba" to go to Egypt.

And in addition to this formal reason there is a material one, which is still more decisive. The effect of
separating ch. xlviii. from the verses that immediately
precede is that while P and E record Jacob's adoption
of Manasseh and Ephraim, J makes no mention of it,
and so does not explain how they came to be included

in the number of the tribes, as they are ever after in J as well as E and P. Wellhausen recognizes this, and admits that the interview of Jacob with Joseph in xlvii. 29–31 is incomplete ; and that J must likewise have contained a parallel to ch. xlviii., only R has not seen fit to preserve it. Dillmann seeks to escape the same difficulty by an elaborate dissection of ch. xlviii., in order to obtain for J a share of its contents. These expedients for relieving a difficulty of their own creation simply show that these chapters cannot be separated. The separation is no sooner effected than they must be brought together again.

The necessity of finding P, J, and E in ch. xlviii. creates a fresh difficulty in regard to the disposal of vs. 1, 2. These verses are essential to the following narrative ; hence they are variously assigned by different critics, with the effect of leaving the account in some of the documents without any proper introduction.

Vs. 3–6 are assigned to P because of the evident allusion to xxxv. 10–12, and are regarded as his account of Jacob's adoption of the two sons of Joseph. But the inverted order, "Ephraim and Manasseh" (ver. 5 ; see xli. 50–52 ; xlvi. 20) requires for its explanation vs. 17–19, showing that these cannot be attributed to different documents. Dillmann has no resource but to assume that R has altered the text. The adoption and the subsequent blessing are consequently successive parts of the transaction, and cannot be set over against each other as though each was a complete and variant account of the whole affair.

Ver. 7 is a fresh source of perplexity to the critics. They cannot imagine why Jacob should have spoken just here of Rachel's death and burial. Some consider it a later gloss; but it is more unaccountable as an interpolation than as an original constituent of the text. For what conceivable motive could any one have for inserting what has no apparent connection with the subject of the chapter? An additional perplexity arises from the fact that "Paddan" (abridged from Paddan-aram) is a P word, while the body of the verse is evidently based upon xxxv. 16, 19, E. This might be avoided by referring the latter passage to P; but then the opportunity of creating an apparent discrepancy between it and xxxv. 22b–26 P would be lost. If P had just before said that Benjamin was born at Ephrath, he could not have intended to include him in the general statement that Jacob's sons were born in Paddan-aram. In spite, however, of its manifest dependence upon an E passage, Wellhausen and Dillmann follow Nöldeke in ascribing ver. 7 to P, as well as in assuming that in the document P it was directly connected with xlix. 29 sqq., and was suggested by the thought that Rachel alone was buried elsewhere than in the family burying-ground which Abraham had purchased. R is credited with having transposed vs. 3–7 to its present position, and thus converted what was said by Jacob in the presence of all his sons into an address to Joseph. Kuenen,[1] with more critical consistency, alleges that the acquaintance with both P and E, which is presupposed in ver. 7, makes it necessary to attribute it to R; still, as he confesses, the question remains "how R could have inserted it in so inapposite a place." From this he seeks relief in the attempted solution of Budde, who never hesitates at any extravagance of conjecture to accomplish his purpose. According to Budde, in P's narrative, xlviii. 3–6 was immediately followed by xlix. 29–33, and the last clause of ver. 31 read, "and there I buried Leah and Rachel." As this flatly contradicted xxxv. 16 sqq., R struck out the words "and Rachel," inserting instead the statement respecting her death and burial,

[1] Hexateuch, p. 327.

which is now found in xlviii. 7, and placed this whole
paragraph thus modified directly after xlviii. 1, 2. At a
later time another redactor rearranged the text by transferring xlix. 29–32 from the place where his predecessor
had put it to its present position after the blessing of
Jacob (xlix. 1–28) ; but "xlviii. 7 was left where it was,
and thus came to occupy its present very singular position." All this wonderful amount of conjectural erasure,
interpolation, transposition, and rearrangement[1] is sum-
moned to remove a difficulty which is no difficulty at
all, except as it is created by the critical partition. What
was more natural than that Jacob, in speaking to the son
of his beloved Rachel, and recalling the divine manifestation granted to him at Luz (xxxv. 9–15), should be led
to speak of the sorrow that befell him immediately after
in the death of Joseph's mother (vs. 16 sqq.) ?

By giving vs. 3–7 to P, on account of El Shaddai and
other alleged criteria, the critics make of it a disconnected fragment, severed from its appropriate introduction and from the rest of the scene in which it has its
proper place. After this has been separated from the
remainder of the chapter, a further difficulty arises from
the intermingling of heterogeneous criteria ; Elohim, a
mark of E, runs through the chapter (vs. 9, 11, 15, 20, 21) ;
but so does Israel, a mark of J (vs. 2b, 8, 10, 11, 13, 14,
(20), 21), these diverse criteria meeting at times in the
same sentence. Wellhausen makes no attempt to divide
them, but gives the whole to E, affirming that it everywhere shows his peculiarities, and that henceforward R
no longer preserves the distinction between J and E in

---

[1] Dillmann's comment upon this proposal of Budde is, "How superfluous, since the alleged contradiction was already removed by erasing
'and Rachel'! and what an injustice to P to introduce into it by an
emendation a contradiction to universal tradition, in order then to let it
be harmonized by R! Such criticism would scarcely be admissible even
in the case of profane writers."

their respective use of Israel and Jacob. But as there is no reason why he should discontinue it here, if he had observed it at all, the admission that it is inadmissible as a criterion in this and the following chapters, discredits its legitimacy in those that have gone before. Dillmann, with sturdy consistency, makes a bold attempt to preserve both these criteria, and to partition the chapter on this basis. As the natural result J and E receive separate portions of the narrative, which when sundered can be made to appear to give variant representations of the affair. Thus in E nothing is said of Jacob's blindness; he embraces and kisses Joseph's sons, but blesses Joseph, placing Ephraim before Manasseh, and giving Shechem to Joseph. In J the preference of Ephraim is the central point of the representation, and the blessing is bestowed upon Joseph's sons. Jacob, who is blind, crosses his hands in order to place his right hand on the head of Ephraim, to which Joseph objects, but Jacob insists.

Notwithstanding its ingenuity, however, this partition is not successful. Dillmann admits that in vs. 8, 11, 21 Israel occurs where he would have expected Jacob. In ver. 8 "Israel *beheld* Joseph's sons," showing that the blindness of ver. 10 J was not total, and hence not inconsistent with ver. 11 E; in vs. 11, 21, "Israel said unto Joseph" is given to J, but as Elohim occurs in what he says, this is given to E. Kautzsch seeks to remedy the matter by assuming that R has in these instances substituted "Israel" for "Jacob;" but why he should do so it is hard to see. In his last edition Dillmann, while retaining his partition, admits that Israel cannot here be made a criterion, since it is carried through the entire narrative. He attempts to explain it by saying that in this instance "R made J the basis and only worked in E." A much simpler account of the matter is that Jacob is used (vs. 2a, 3) as the personal name ; but as the prominent thought throughout the chapter is the elevation of Ephraim and Manasseh to be the heads of separate tribes in the national organization, the name Israel was especially appropriate.

And the attempt to create a distinction between vs. 15, 16, 20, E, and ver. 19 J, as though the blessing was given to Joseph in the former, but to his sons in the latter, is altogether futile ; for Joseph is blessed by invoking a blessing upon " the lads ; " and the allegation that R has substituted " blessed them " for " blessed him " in ver. 20 is at variance with the contents of the verse. In fact, by this partition the whole of the blessing proper is given to E, and only the preliminary arrangements, putting the boys in position and placing the hands on their heads with Joseph's disapproval and Jacob's insistence, are reserved for J ; but these manifestly belong together, and cannot form two separate narratives of the transaction.

A duplicate narrative is inferred from the circumstance that Joseph is twice said to have brought his sons to his father (vs. 10b, 13b). But this is not a twofold mention of the same act. They were first led to Jacob, who affectionately embraced them ; they were then placed in the proper position before him to receive his formal blessing.

It is further claimed that vs. 15, 16 interrupt the account of Jacob's crossing his hands, and that vs. 17–19 interrupt the continuity of the blessing ; hence it is inferred that something has in each case been intruded from another narrative. This simply means that the critic differs from the writer in regard to the proper arrangement of the material which he has introduced into his narrative. He saw fit to continue Jacob's action as far as vs. 15, 16 before proceeding to say in vs. 17–19 how Joseph interrupted it. On the critics' hypothesis R thought this to be the best disposition of the matter; why may not the original writer have been of this opinion?

There is no implication in ver. 11 that this was the first time that Jacob had seen Joseph's sons, any more than that it was the first time that he had seen Joseph himself since his arrival in Egypt. There is no ground, therefore, for assuming a discrepancy with xlvii. 28, and hence a diversity of writers.

Nor does ver. 22 conflict with statements elsewhere. The portion or ridge (Heb., shechem), which Jacob gives to Joseph, and "which," he says, "I took out of the hand of the Amorite with my sword and with my bow," refers to the capture and sack of Shechem by the sons of Jacob (xxxiv. 27–29), which Jacob deprecated (ver. 30), and strongly condemned (xlix. 5–7), but which, nevertheless, was the act of his house, or of the clan of which he was the responsible head ; and the property acquired in a manner which he so sharply censures he bestows not upon those who participated in the deed, but upon Joseph, as a mark of special favor, and an earnest of his future inheritance in the land of promise. Dillmann admits the reference to, and correspondence with, the passage named above, but claims that a diverse representation of the transaction is given in other parts of ch. xxxiv., which was shown to be unfounded when that chapter was under discussion. There is no need, therefore, of supposing that "took" is a prophetic preterite (Tuch), or that Shechem is not referred to, but some other district whose capture is not recorded (Kurtz), or that the allusion is to the land purchased at Shechem by Jacob (xxxiii. 19 ; Josh. xxiv. 32), which he may subsequently have had to defend by force of arms, or of altering the text, with Kuenen, into " not with my sword and with my bow," or imagining that " sword " and " bow " are figuratively used to denote purchase-money as the efficient instrument of gaining possession.

The following divine names occur in this section: El Shaddai (ver. 3), with allusion to xxxv. 11, and to the almighty power which pledged the fulfilment of the promise; Elohim (vs. 9, 11, 20), with reference to general providential blessings; ha-Elohim (ver. 15), "the God before whom my fathers Abraham and Isaac did walk, the God, who fed me all my life long," is but a paraphrase of Jehovah; Elohim (ver. 21) is demanded by the contrast of the human with the divine; Jacob dies, but God the creator and governor of all will be with his descendants.

MARKS OF P

1. Statement of age (xlvii. 28). See ch. vi.–ix., Marks of P, No. 2, ch. xvi., No. 1.

2. *The days of the years of the life of* (ver 28). See ch. xxiii., Marks of P, No. 5.

3. The back reference to xxxv. 6, 9, 11; the common authorship of these passages is not at variance with, but involved in, the unity of Genesis, which we maintain.

4. אֵל שַׁדַּי *God Almighty* (xlviii. 3). See ch. xxvi. 34–xxviii. 9, Marks of P, No. 5.

5. אֲחֻזַּת עוֹלָם *everlasting possession* (ver. 4). See ch. xvii., Marks of P, No. 7 and 17.

6. זַרְעֲךָ אַחֲרֶיךָ *thy seed after thee* (ver. 4). See ch. vi.–ix., Marks of P, No, 17.

7. הוֹלִיד *beget* (ver. 6). See ch. vi.–ix., Marks of P, No. 20, ch. xvii., No. 10.

8. *Paddan* (ver. 7). See ch. xxv. 19–34, Marks of P, No. 4.

MARKS OF E

1. The unusual form of the infinitive רְאֹה (xlviii. 11), as עֲשׂוֹ (xxxi. 28), עֲשֹׂה (l. 20), with suf. עֲשׂהוּ (Ex. xviii.

18) E; there are but two examples besides in the Old Testament, קֹוה (Prov. xvi. 16), and שָׁחוֹ (Prov. xxxi. 4).

2. הַמַּלְאָךְ *the angel* (ver. 16). See ch. xvi., Marks of J, No. 1.

3. יִקָּרֵא בָהֶם שְׁמִי *my name shall be called on them* (ver. 16); this is compared to xxi. 12 E, "in Isaac shall thy seed be called."

4. פַּלֵל *thought* (ver. 11); nowhere else in this sense.

5. דָּגָה *grow*, as fishes increase (ver. 16), occurs nowhere else.

Such rare forms and expressions are no indication of a writer's habitual style.

MARKS OF J

1. צָעִיר *younger* (ver. 14). See xix. 29–38, Marks of J, No. 2.

2. מֵאֵן *refused* (ver. 19); besides in J (xxxvii. 35; xxxix. 8; Ex. iv. 23; vii. 14; x. 3; xvi. 28); in E (Ex. xxii. 16 (E. V., ver. 17); Num. xx. 21; xxii. 13, 14); in D (Deut. xxv. 7).

The majority of critics refer the verses containing these words to E.

JACOB'S BLESSING AND DEATH (CH. XLIX.)

Dillmann and Schrader follow Knobel in assigning to P vs. 1a, 28b–33. But that Jacob's address to his sons (vs. 1b–28a) cannot belong to P, notwithstanding "Shaddai," *Almighty* (ver. 25), is argued from Jehovah (ver. 18), from the depreciation of Levi (ver. 7), from the usage of this document, which nowhere else contains a poetical passage, and from the lack of correspondence between this address and ver. 28b, "he blessed them, every one according to his blessing he blessed them;"

this, it is alleged, is quite inapplicable to what is said to
Reuben, Simeon, and Levi (vs. 3–7), which is the reverse
of a blessing. Nor can it belong to E, since vs. 5–7 are
inconsistent with xlviii. 22, and ver. 4 with the preference shown to Reuben in xxxvii. 21, 22, 29, 30; xlii. 22,
37; and in xlviii. 8 sqq. Jacob blesses Joseph, but not
his other sons. It is accordingly referred to J not as
composed by him, and consequently not on grounds of
diction and style, but as a pre-existing writing incorporated in his work, which is thought to be corroborated by
previous allusions to what is here said of Reuben (ver. 4,
cf. xxxv. 22), and of Simeon and Levi (vs. 5–7, cf. xxxiv.
25, 26, 30), as well as by the prominence given to Judah
(vs. 8–12).

Arguments which are merely inferences from the unproved partition hypothesis amount to nothing, and
may be dismissed without further remark. The fact is
that there is no warrant for attaching this address of the
dying Jacob to any one of the so-called documents in
distinction from the others. It has been inserted in its
place by the author of Genesis as a whole, and contains
nothing inconsistent with any part of the book. That
the reproofs administered to Reuben, Simeon, and Levi
are intimately related to the passages which record the
facts here referred to is obvious and is freely admitted;
and there is not a single passage which they antagonize.
The general tenor of this final address of Jacob to his
sons is that of blessing, and amply justifies the language
used respecting it in ver. 28b. It should also be observed that while Reuben is degraded from the dignity
of the firstborn in consequence of his shameful conduct,
and Simeon and Levi are severely censured for their
deed of cruelty and violence, and a penalty affixed, they
are not utterly disowned or prohibited from sharing in
the blessings and privileges of the covenant people. It

has before been shown that there is no variance between vs. 5–7 and xlviii. 22 (see p. 517); and that the passages in which Reuben is prominent do not clash with those which give the preference to Judah (see pp. 448, 475–477); there is no inconsistency in the representations anywhere made respecting them. The weakness and inefficiency of Reuben appear in perpetual contrast with Judah's manly vigor and strength of character; and the confidence which Jacob reposes in the latter, together with his distrust of the former, corresponds with his attitude toward them in this address.

NO VATICINIUM POST EVENTUM.

The critics try to fix the age of this blessing of Jacob on the assumption that it is a *vaticinium post eventum.* Tuch refers it to the time of Samuel when the tribe of Levi was in ill-repute from the gross misconduct of the sons of Eli and the capture of the ark; Ewald refers it to the time of Samson, the famous judge from the tribe of Dan; Knobel to the reign of David; Reuss to the time of David and Solomon; Wellhausen to the period of the schism and the rival kingdoms of Judah and Joseph; Stade to the time of Ahab; Dillmann seeks to make it all square with the time of the Judges. But the fact is that it is impracticable to find any one period when this blessing could have been composed with the view of setting forth the existing state of things. The sceptre in Judah found no adequate fulfilment until the reign of David; and from that time forth the consideration enjoyed by the tribe of Levi was such that it could not possibly have been spoken of in the terms here employed. So that Kuenen, in despair of finding any one date for the entire blessing, supposes it to be made up of brief sayings which circulated separately in the tribes to

which they severally related. But even this will not solve
the problem. For the censures passed upon the first
three cannot be separated from the blessing of Judah,
for which they evidently prepare the way, as he succeeds
to the right of primogeniture vacated by his predecessors.
The prominence given to Judah and Joseph above their
brethren is clearly intentional, not accidental; and several of the blessings would be insignificant or unmeaning, if taken by themselves and disconnected from the
rest.

The structure and contents of this blessing make it impossible to explain it as a *vaticinium post eventum*. What
is said respecting Levi compels to the conclusion that it
is pre-Mosaic. A dispersion resulting from their priestly
rank could not after the time of Moses be spoken of as a
sentence for the misdeed of their ancestor. The sentence
was fulfilled in that the Levites had no inheritance in
Canaan, but special habitations were assigned to them in
the territory of the other tribes, not, however, as a degra-
dation but a distinction. They were the ministers of the
sanctuary, and the LORD was their inheritance. The
curse was turned into a blessing. The language in
which Moses speaks of Levi in his farewell utterance
(Deut. xxxiii. 8–11) is as different as possible from that
before us. The whole blessing of Jacob is only compre-
hensible as utterances of the dying patriarch, modified
by personal reminiscences, by insight into the characters
of his sons, and by their very names, with its ejaculation
of pious faith, which looked forward to the fulfilment of
the promises so long delayed (ver. 18); and as a forecasting of the future which met its accomplishment at separate epochs and in unexpected ways, and which, while
clear and sharp in a few strongly drawn outlines, is vague
in others, and has no such exactness in minute details as
suggests actual historical experience. The only instance,

in which the specific location of a tribe in the land of promise is hinted at, is in apparent disagreement with the subsequent allotment under Joshua. "Zebulun shall dwell at the haven of the sea ; and he shall be for an haven of ships ; and his border shall be unto Zidon" (ver. 13). And yet Zebulun was separated from the Sea of Galilee by Naphtali, and Asher lay between Zebulun and the Mediterranean. Fortunately the critics are here precluded by their own hypothesis from discrediting the truth of the prophecy. Dillmann explains that "the boundary between Asher and Zebulun is not strictly defined (Josh. xix. 14, 15), and therefore the possibility that Zebulun bordered on the Mediterranean with a strip of land is not excluded ;" and he appeals in confirmation to Josephus ("Antiquities," 5, 8, 22, "Jewish Wars," 3, 3, 1). It is observable, however, that the Song of Deborah (Judg. v. 17), after the settlement in Canaan, in adopting expressions from the verse which we are considering, applies them to other tribes, whose territory lay more entirely upon the coast and thus speaks of *Dan* as abiding in ships and *Asher* as continuing on the seashore. This suggests what might have been expected in Gen. xlix., if it had been composed after Israel's occupation of Canaan.

The same thing appears from the language of ver. 1, which announces as the theme of the prophecy what shall take place "in the last days." As this expression is found repeatedly in the prophets, it has been urged as an indication that this blessing was composed or ver. 1 prefixed to it in the prophetic period. But "the last days" always denotes the ultimate future. Jacob could look forward to the time when the promises made to himself and his fathers would be fulfilled as the ultimate bound of his hopes and expectations. But no one living at any time that the critics may fix upon as the date of

this chapter could have imagined that the ultimate future
was already reached, or could describe the state of things
then existing as what was to befall Israel in "the last
days."

All this points to the genuineness of this blessing as
really the utterance of Jacob, which it claims to be and
is declared to be. Its antiquity is further evidenced, as
is remarked by Dillmann, by the peculiar figures employed in vs. 4, 8, 10, 11, 12, 14, 17, 19, 21–26, and its
many rare expressions that were disused in later times,
פַּחַז *bubbling over,* הוֹתִיר *excel* (ver. 4), מְכֵרָה *sword* (ver 5),
מְחֹקֵק *ruler's staff* (ver. 10), סוּת *clothes* (ver. 11), חַכְלִילִי
red (ver. 12), מִשְׁפְּתַיִם *sheepfolds* (ver. 14), שְׁפִיפוֹן *adder*
(ver. 17), שָׁלֻחָה *slender* (ver. 21), and much besides in vs.
22–26. To which add the citations from it or allusions
to it in the Mosaic period; comp. ver. 9 and Num. xxiv.
9, xxiii. 24 ; vs. 13, 14, Zebulun before Issachar and sub-
sisting by the sea, cf. Deut. xxxiii. 18, 19 ; vs. 25, 26, cf.
Deut. xxxiii. 13–16.

The words, "And Jacob called unto his sons " (ver. 1a),
are sundered from their connection, and linked with vs.
28b–33 P, because the name " Jacob " is regarded as a
mark of P. But as this deprives the blessing of its introduction, which is here indispensable, it is necessary to assume that it was originally prefaced by a like
statement from the pen of J ; though no reason can be
given why R should have removed it in order to substitute words identical in signification, but belonging to a
different place. Wellhausen avoids this senseless transposition by disregarding here, as in the preceding chapter, the alleged criterion from the name of the patriarch.

Jacob's charge to his sons to bury him with his fathers
in the cave of Machpelah (vs. 29, sqq.), is held to be a
variant account by P of the transaction recorded by J in

xlvii. 29–31, P representing that to be enjoined upon all his sons, which according to J was addressed to Joseph alone. Identifying distinct events, as we have seen from the beginning of Genesis to the end, is a favorite artifice of the critics, of which they make abundant use in effecting the partition of the text. It was natural and appropriate that Jacob should in the first instance make his appeal in this matter to Joseph, who was invested with supreme authority, and without whose permission it could not be done ; and when his concurrence had been secured, that he should further make his wish known to all his sons, by whom it was to be carried into effect. The emphatic iteration in vs. 29–32, as in the original account of the transaction referred to (ch. xxiii.), and the repetition of the identical terms of the original purchase, shows the stress laid by the writer on this initial acquisition of a permanent possession in the land of Canaan.

The middle clause of ver. 33, " he gathered up his feet into his bed," contains a plain allusion to the previous mention of his bed in xlvii. 31 ; xlviii. 2. In consequence, Dillmann is constrained to cut out this clause and assign it to J, though there is nothing in J with which to connect it. Budde proposes to find a connection for it by attributing the first clause of the verse likewise to J ; but in doing so it is necessary for him to change " commanding" into " blessing," so as to link it with vs. 1–27, instead of the immediately preceding verses. All this only shows the embarrassment which the critics create for themselves by partitioning among different documents what is one indivisible narrative.

The divine names, El, *God*, and Shaddai, *Almighty*, both suggestive of omnipotence, occur in ver. 25, and Jehovah in ver. 18, where Jacob gives expression to his own pious trust.

MARKS OF P (VS. 29-33)

1. The back reference to ch. xxiii. This is readily admitted, but no argument can be derived from it in favor of critical partition.

2. גְּוַע *expired* (ver. 33). See ch. vi.-ix., Marks of P, No. 18.

3. אֲחֻזָּה *possession* (ver. 30). See ch. xvii., Marks of P, No. 7.

4. נֶאֱסַף אֶל־עַמָּיו *was gathered unto his people* (ver. 33). See ch. xxv. 1-11, Marks of P, No. 5.

5. אֶרֶץ כְּנַעַן *land of Canaan* (ver. 30). See ch. xii. 5, Marks of P, No. 4.

6. The connection with l. 12, 13. The connection is obvious, but yields no proof of critical partition.

THE BURIAL OF JACOB AND DEATH OF JOSEPH (CH. L.)

The critics are unanimous in referring vs. 12, 13 to P; Kayser and Schrader agree with Knobel in assigning the remainder of the chapter to J on the basis of an earlier source ; Wellhausen, followed by Dillmann, attributes vs. 4-11, 14 to J ; vs. 15-26 to E ; Wellhausen does not venture to determine the source of vs. 1-3, together with the first words of ver. 4 ; Dillmann thinks that they are probably to be attributed to J, who may have written on the basis of a previous account by E. The reason of the hesitation about these opening verses is that the reference to embalming is indicative of the same author as in ver. 26 E, while "Israel" (ver. 2) and "fell upon his father's face" are esteemed marks of J. Moreover, J here describes the preparations for the burial of Jacob without having mentioned the fact of his death ; this is found only in P (xlix. 33).

We are told that there are two distinct and varying accounts of Jacob's interment. That, in vs. 4-11, 14, is

assigned to J, because of the explicit reference in ver. 5
to Joseph's solemn promise to bury his father in Canaan (xlvii. 29–31); accordingly in this account Joseph
conducts the funeral with great pomp and an immense
retinue. The other account by P (vs. 12, 13) is conformed to the charge given by Jacob to all his sons
(xlix. 29–32); in it no prominence is given to Joseph,
who is not even separately mentioned; Jacob is carried
to Canaan by his sons, and there buried in the spot
which he had indicated to them. But it has already
been shown that the direction respecting his burial given
by Jacob to Joseph, and that to all his sons, are not variant reports of the same transaction in different documents. Hence the reference to them both in this chapter affords no argument for a diversity of sources here.
And besides, the proposed partition is impracticable; it
simply creates two fragments, neither of which is complete without the other. In J Joseph goes with a great
company to bury his father; he comes back after burying his father; but of the actual burial nothing is said.
The only account of that is in the verses which are cut
out and assigned to P. Again, in P the sons of Jacob
carry him to Canaan and bury him, but nothing is said
of their return to Egypt; that is only to be found in
ver. 14, which is given to J.

It is claimed, however, that there is a discrepancy as
to the place of interment; but the critics are not agreed
as to what or where this discrepancy is. Kayser, to
whom Wellhausen gives his adherence, finds it in ver. 5,
which he translates, "in my grave which I have bought
for me in the land of Canaan, there shalt thou bury me."
From this he infers that the place intended can be no
other than the piece of ground at Shechem purchased
from the sons of Hamor, as related by J (xxxiii. 18–20),
(other critics refer these verses to E). And he goes on

to say that this half-concealed contradiction in respect to the grave of Jacob at Shechem, or at Hebron, is the token of a profound difference between J and P. J, a native of the northern kingdom of Israel,[1] is interested for Shechem in Ephraim; P, who belonged to the southern kingdom, is strongly attached to Hebron in Judah. As this interpretation of Kayser is inconsistent with xlvii. 29, 30, to which ver. 5 expressly refers, he is obliged to assume that these verses have been altered by R into conformity with xlix. 29, 30; though why he should have altered them and allowed ver. 5 to remain without change does not appear. Nöldeke and others find the discrepancy in ver. 10; the burial, he says, must have taken place where the lamentation was made. Kautzsch finds a doublet in ver. 10b, and insists that three distinct places of interment are spoken of, representing as many variant narratives, the threshing-floor of Atad, Abel-mizraim, and the cave of Machpelah. But the difficulty with these attempts to discover a discrepancy is that the cave of Machpelah is the only place at which the burial is said to have been; and with this xlvii. 30 agrees.

A difficulty has been found in the words " beyond Jordan " (ver. 11), as though they implied a very circuitous route for the funeral procession, and were contradicted by " Canaanites " in the same verse, who dwelt west of the Jordan. Jerome, however, identifies Abel-mizraim with Beth-hoglah, in the border of Judah, and Benjamin (Josh., xv. 6; xviii. 19). May not "beyond Jordan" mean beyond Jordan, westward, as in Deut. xi. 30, and be an incidental confirmation of Mosaic authorship?

Verses 15–26 are assigned to E on account of the repeated occurrence of Elohim, notwithstanding the twofold statement of age (vs. 22, 26), such as is regularly else-

[1] Other critics make him a citizen of Judah.

where given to P,[1] and two phrases which are regarded as characteristic of J, "spake to their heart" (ver. 21 as xxxiv. 3), and "the land which he sware to Abraham, to Isaac, and to Jacob" (ver. 24); in the passages assigned to E no promise is given of the land of Canaan to any one of the patriarchs. The proof of unity arising from these frequent cross-references from one document to the other can only be evaded by using the critical knife and invoking the agency of R.

P records the death and the interment; J the embalming, the funeral procession, and the return from the grave; E the subsequent apprehensions of Joseph's brothers and his generous treatment of them. And yet these extracts from separate works, as they are said to be, match as perfectly as though they had come from the same pen, and the continuity of the narrative is as accurately preserved.

Dillmann imagines that ver. 21 implies the continuance of the famine, and hence infers a discrepancy between E and P (xlvii. 28) with respect to the time of Jacob's death. This is built on the groundless assumption that Joseph could not continue to support his brethren after the years of dearth were ended.

The divine names are "the God of thy father" (ver. 17), which is a paraphrase of Jehovah, and Elohim (vs. 19, 20, 24, 25), which is appropriate where the divine is contrasted with the human.

MARKS OF J

1. אִם נָא מָצָאתִי חֵן בְּעֵינֵיכֶם *if now I have found favor in your eyes* (ver. 4). See ch. xii. 10–20, Marks of J, No. 3; ch. vi. 1–8, No. 10; ch. xviii., xix., No. 28.

2. דִּבֶּר בְּאָזְנֵי *speak in the ears of* (ver. 4); besides in J, xliv. 18; Deut. xxxii. 44; in J or R, Num. xiv. 28; in E,

---

[1] Kayser and Schrader cut out ver. 22 and give it to P.

Gen. xx. 8 ; Ex. xi. 2; in P, Gen. xxiii. 13, 16; in D, Deut.
v. 1 ; Josh. xx. 4 ; in Rd, Deut. xxxi. 28, 30.

3. רַק *only* (ver. 8). See ch. vi. 1–8, Marks of J, No. 7.

4. רֶכֶב *chariots*, פָּרָשִׁים *horsemen* (ver. 9). See ch. xlvii.
12–27, Marks of J, No. 4.

5. כָּבֵד *great, grievous* (vs. 9–11). See ch. xlii.–xliv.
Marks of J, No. 14.

6. עַל־כֵּן קָרָא *therefore was called* (ver. 11) ; besides in
J, xi. 9 ; xvi. 14; xix. 22; xxv. 30; xxix. 34; xxxi. 48
(doublet in E connection); xxxiii. 17 ; Josh. vii. 26 (JE);
but also in E, Gen. xxi. 31; Ex. xv. 23. This phrase is
contrasted with *and he called the name*, Gen. xxxii. 3, 31
(E. V., vs. 2, 30), as though the latter was indicative of a
different document ; yet it occurs repeatedly in J, *e.g.*,
Gen. iii. 20 ; iv. 17, 26 ; xix. 37, 38 ; xxvi. 20, 21, 22, 33 ;
xxxviii. 3, 29, 30, Num. xi. 3.

MARKS OF E

1. The connection of vs. 24–26 with Ex. xiii. 19 ; Josh.
xxiv. 32, which is entirely consistent with the unity of
the Pentateuch.

2. כִּלְכֵּל *nourish* (ver. 21) ; only twice besides in the
Pentateuch (xlv. 11; xlvii. 12 E). It occurs exclusively
with reference to Joseph's promise to nourish his father
and brethren in Egypt. Ch. xlvii. 12 is in a context
which is assigned to other documents ; but this solitary
verse is cut out of its connection and given to E because
of this word and its manifest relation to xlv. 11. See
ch. xlvii. 12–27, Marks of E, No. 2.

3. עֲשֹׂה unusual form of the construct infinitive. See
ch. xlvii. 28–xlviii. 22, Marks of E, No. 1.

4. הֲתַחַת אֱלֹהִים אָנִי *am I in the place of God* (ver. 19) ;
but once besides in the Pentateuch (xxx. 2 E).

5. עַל־בִּרְכֵּי *upon the knees of* (ver. 23) ; besides in the
Pentateuch only (xxx. 3 E).

CONCLUSION

WE have now completed the critical study of the Book of Genesis, and it only remains to sum up the result of our investigations. The question before us is whether Genesis is, as tradition unanimously affirms, a continuous production by a single writer, or, as the divisive critics declare, a compilation from different documents by different authors and belonging to different ages.

It is to be noted at the outset that there is no proof whatever, outside of the book itself, that such documents ever existed. And there is no suggestion anywhere that the existence of such documents was ever suspected until recent times. The whole case, then, lies before us. Genesis is its own witness. What testimony does it give?

GROUNDS OF PARTITION

Kittel presents the argument for partition in the following brief but comprehensive manner:[1] "The entire Hexateuchal narrative falls apart in a series of strata, whose individual constituents are closely connected in language, style, and characteristic forms of speech, while they stand in the most decided contrast with other narratives, which are possibly homogeneous with them or related to them in their contents.

---

[1] Geschichte der Hebräer, pp. 30, 31. This passage is abridged by the omission of illustrative examples, since a much more exhaustive statement of them will be given from another source.

"In connection with this phenomenon the further fact appears that many diversities and contradictions are likewise observable in the narrative material. Of a great number of the Hexateuchal narratives we have two or more accounts. Some of these repetitions, the number of which could easily be swelled *ad infinitum*, might possibly be explained as intentional on the part of the writer. At least such an explanation might answer, did not the above-mentioned diversity of language almost always go hand in hand with the repetition of the matter. It is thus already made quite improbable that the repetition is an addition by the writer himself, or is a resumption of the thread of the narrative previously dropped by him. But it becomes positively impossible by perceiving, what is almost always connected with it, that the two or more accounts of the same thing also diverge in their substantive matter in a number of features that are sometimes quite important, sometimes rather subordinate."

REPETITIONS AND DISCREPANCIES

Numberless repetitions with more or less serious discrepancies and a varied diction would seem indeed to be inconsistent with unity of authorship. And when these alleged repetitions and discrepancies are massed together in a formidable list, as they are by Dillmann,[1] it naturally makes the impression that such an accumulation of arguments must be strong indeed; and however weak and inconclusive particular examples may be when viewed singly, the combined force of the whole must be irresistible. But arguments must be weighed and not merely counted. It only requires a patient examination of these cases in detail to show how illusive they are. The entire

[1] Die Genesis, Vorbemerkungen, pp. ix., x.

vast array melts into nothingness as soon as their reality
is tested.

In Dillmann's classification he adduces what he calls
1. "Idle repetitions." These are either not repetitions at all, as Gen. xxi. 1a and 1b, where the first clause
states the fact and the second the purpose of Jehovah's
visit to Sarah; xlvii. 29 sqq. and xlix. 29 sqq., first Jacob's request of Joseph that he might be buried in Canaan, then his charge to all his sons to bury him there;
or the repetition is for a sufficient reason (iv. 25, 26, and
v. 1–6), where the birth of Seth and Enosh are included
in the genealogy from Adam to Noah, and are likewise
mentioned separately in order to introduce some facts
concerning them which could not be inserted in the
genealogy without marring its symmetry and the regularity of its structure.

2. "Two or more accounts of the same thing, which
might possibly be explained by the writer's assuming
that they were different events or wishing to note the
variation in the traditions." These are in every instance
distinct events, which critics assume without reason to
be identical, in spite of the fact that they are recorded as
distinct, and are further shown to be distinct by differences of time, place, and circumstances, which critics
arbitrarily convert into the discrepancies of variant traditions. It is not different versions of the same story
when a like peril befalls Sarah in Egypt (xii. 10 sqq.),
and in Gerar (xx. 1 sqq.), and at a still later time Rebekah
(xxvi. 7 sqq.); or when Hagar flees from her mistress
before the birth of Ishmael (xvi. 6 sqq.), and she is subsequently sent away with Ishmael (xxi. 12 sqq.); or when
God ratifies his covenant with Abraham by a visible
symbol (ch. xv.), and it is afterward ratified by Abraham
by the seal of circumcision (ch. xvii.); or when the promise
of a son by Sarah is first made to Abraham (xvii. 15–17),

and then in the hearing of Sarah (xviii. 9–12); or when Jacob obtains the blessing which his father intended for Esau (ch. xxvii.), and again receives a parting blessing from his father as he was leaving home for Paddan-aram (xxviii. 1–5).

3. "Variant explanations of the same name." These are simply allusive references to the signification of the name made on different occasions, which of course involve no discrepancy; or in some cases they are different suggestions awakened by the sound of the name, where there is no pretence of giving its actual derivation, and, of course, no ground for the charge that different conceptions of its etymology are involved. Thus, with allusion to the name Isaac, which means *laughter*, it is related that when his birth was predicted Abraham (xvii. 17) and Sarah also laughed incredulously (xviii. 12), and when he was born Sarah said that God had made her to laugh for joy, and all that hear would laugh with her (xxi. 6). So Edom, *red*, is associated with the red color of Esau at his birth (xxv. 25), and the red pottage for which he sold his birthright (ver. 30). So the twofold hire linked with the name Issachar (xxx. 16, 18), and the double suggestion of Zebulun (ver. 20) and of Joseph (vs. 23, 24); Mahanaim connected with the host of angels xxxii. 3 (E. V., ver. 2), and with Jacob's two bands, ver. 8 (E. V., 7); Ishmael with God's hearing Hagar in her affliction (xvi. 11), and hearing the voice of the lad in his distress (xxi. 17); and Peniel, where Jacob saw the face of God (xxxii. 31 (E. V., ver. 30)) and the face of Esau (xxxiii. 10) as one seeth the face of God.

4. "Repetitions which are mutually exclusive, since the thing can only have happened once or in one way." Thus the creation (ch. i. and ii.); but, as has been abundantly shown (pp. 9 sqq., 20 sqq.), there is here no duplicate account and no discrepancy. The number of the

animals in the ark and the duration of the flood (ch. vi., vii.) ; but there is no inconsistency between the general statement that two of every species should be taken and the more particular direction to take seven of the clean animals ; and the alleged diversity in reckoning the duration of the flood is a pure figment of the critics with no foundation in the narrative itself. See p. 92. The dispersion of the nations is not differently explained, as though that was traced in ch. x. to the multiplication of Noah's descendants, which in xi. 1-9 (to which x. 25 alludes) is ascribed to immediate divine intervention, since neither of these excludes the other. There is no discrepancy in regard to the origin of the name Beersheba, which was first given by Abraham (xxi. 31), and afterward renewed by Isaac (xxvi. 33), who is expressly said to have digged again the wells of his father, and called them by the names which his father had called them (ver. 18). There was a like renewal of the name Israel divinely given to Jacob (xxxii. 29 E. V., ver. 28 and xxxv. 10), and of Bethel (xxviii. 19 ; xxxv. 15), which Jacob reconsecrated by a solemn rite upon his second visit (xxxv. 1, 14), as he had engaged to do in memory of God's fulfilment of the promise there graciously made (xxviii. 18-22). The reference to the conflict with the Shechemites (xlviii. 22) differs from the account in ch. xxxiv. simply in this, that Jacob as the head of the clan assumes the responsibility of the deed of his sons. The alleged discrepancy in regard to the treatment of Joseph by his brothers and the traders who brought him to Egypt (xxxvii. 19-36) is a sheer invention of the critics, who have themselves created it by an unwarranted partition of the passage.

5. "Other incompatible statements." The allegation that the reduction of human life to one hundred and twenty years (vi. 3) is inconsistent with chs. v.,[1] xi., etc.,

---

[1] The reference to ch. v. is a slip on the part of Dillmann, as the lives

rests upon a misinterpretation of the former passage, which states the limit allowed to the existing generation before it should be swept away by the flood, not that of human life in general. See pp. 59, 60. Abraham's many sons after Sarah's death (xxv. 1, 2) are said to be in conflict with xviii. 11, 12; xvii. 17, but his previous childlessness is uniformly attributed to the barrenness of Sarah (xi. 30; xvi. 1, 2); and Dillmann himself admits (" Genesis," p. 303) that if Abraham lived to be one hundred and seventy-five years old (xxv. 7), it would not be surprising if he had children after he was one hundred and thirty-seven (xxiii. 1; cf. xvii. 17). Esau settled in Seir when Jacob returned from Paddan-aram (xxxii. 4 sqq., E. V., vs. 3 sqq.) is represented to be at variance with xxxvi. 6. But Esau's presence in Seir at that time does not imply that he had already removed his family and his possessions from Canaan, and had abandoned his claim upon it in favor of Jacob. That he had no such intention then is plain from the manner in which he came to meet Jacob (xxxiii. 1), implying a hostile purpose, and at the very least a determination to prevent, or forcibly intercept, his return to Canaan. Jacob so understood it (xxxii. 12, E. V., ver. 11); and the whole narrative shows that Esau's change of mind was due to Jacob's earnest wrestling for the divine blessing in his alarming situation (xxxii. 28). That Rebekah's nurse first came with Jacob from Mesopotamia cannot be inferred from xxxv. 8, which therefore does not contradict xxiv. 59. The general statement that Jacob's sons were born in Paddan-aram (xxxv. 26) is true of all but Benjamin, whose birth near Ephrath had just been recorded (vs. 16–18); to insist upon this as a discrepancy is,

there recorded preceded the sentence in vi. 3, and consequently would not have been inconsistent with it, even if it had had the meaning which he wrongly attributes to it.

on the critics' own theory, to charge the redactor with a negligence as great as would be attributable to the original writer on the theory of the unity of the book. If the latter is not conceivable, neither is the former. The apparent discrepancy between xxvi. 34; xxviii. 9; and xxxvi. 2, 3, as to the names of Esau's wives, is capable of ready reconciliation, as was shown in the discussion of ch. xxxvi. (pp. 420 sqq.). The alleged discrepancy, in regard to Joseph's Egyptian master, between xxxvii. 36 and xxxix. 1; xl. 4, does not exist (pp. 457 sqq.). In reporting to the steward their discovery of the money in their sacks (xliii. 21), Joseph's brethren may perhaps combine with their partial discovery at the inn what they learned more fully on reaching home (xlii. 27, 35); but even this is not certain (pp. 479, 480). Cain's apprehension that he might be slain for the murder of his brother (iv. 14, 15) is not "enigmatical," if the possible increase of Adam's family in one hundred and thirty years (v. 3) be considered; nor his building a "city" (iv. 17), if it be remembered that a fortified nomadic encampment would be so called in Hebrew (pp. 36, 37).

6. "The chronology does not agree with the narratives." It is thought incredible that Sarah should have attracted Pharaoh (xii. 11 sqq.) when sixty-five years of age (xii. 4; xvii. 17), or Abimelech when she was ninety (xx. 2); but this overlooks patriarchal longevity. Ishmael is not represented in xxi. 14 sqq. to be younger than xvii. 24, 25; xxi. 5, 8 would make him. There is no inconsistency between Isaac's apprehending that his end was near (xxvii. 1, 2, 7, 10, 41), and his actually living many years longer (xxxv. 28). It is not Rachel but Leah that is meant in xxxvii. 10, so that there is no conflict with xxxv. 19, which records Rachel's death. The time allowed for the birth of Jacob's children (xxx. 25 sqq.; xxxi. 38, 41) is short, but not too short. See p. 348. If

the list of Jacob's descendants in xlvi. 8–27 contains, as is probable, a few names of those born after the descent into Egypt, it is not inconsistent with the preceding history. There is no implication in l. 21 that the years of famine were still continuing, and accordingly no discrepancy with the previous account of their duration.

7. "Narratives in which certain parts do not accord with the rest, e.g., xxxi. 48–50," where there is no discord but that created by critical manipulation ; "or the end does not accord with the beginning, e.g., xxiv. 62–67," where the discord is purely imaginary.

The contrarieties and discrepancies, of which such account is made as indicative of a diversity of sources, thus disappear upon inspection, being mostly due to the improper identification of distinct events, or to a critical partition by which passages are severed from their connection and interpreted at variance with it.[1]

THE DIVINE NAMES

It is claimed, however, that the narratives of Genesis and of the Pentateuch arrange themselves into continuous strata, each of which consistently preserves the same style and diction and general character, while differing in a marked degree from the others in these respects ; and that the discrepancies which are alleged correspond with, and are corroborated by, these diversities of lan-

[1] The ease with which narratives of unquestioned unity can be sundered by the same methods that are employed in the partition of Genesis and the Pentateuch, and with the same result of apparent discrepancies between the sundered parts, is illustrated in my Higher Criticism of the Pentateuch, pp. 119–125. The same thing is shown in a very effective manner, in application to an entire book, in Romans Dissected, by E. D. McRealsham, the pseudonym of Dr. C. M. Mead, of Hartford Theological Seminary.

guage and ideas. It is hence inferred that Genesis must be a compilation from distinct documents, which can be separated from one another by appropriate tests, and restored in a good measure to their original form. A prominent place is here given to the criterion afforded by the divine names. Certain paragraphs and sections make exclusive use of Elohim, while others characteristically employ Jehovah, when speaking of the Supreme Being. These are called respectively Elohist and Jehovist sections, and are attributed to writers having different proclivities in this respect. But it has been found impossible to divide these sections so that they shall correspond with the alternation of the divine names.

Thus, Elohim occurs in Jehovist sections, viz.: iii. 1, 3, 5, in the conversation of Eve with the serpent; iv. 25, where Seth is substituted for murdered Abel; vii. 9, in the Jehovist's account of Noah's entry into the ark; ix. 27, in the blessing upon Japheth in distinction from Shem (ver. 26); xxxi. 50, in Laban's covenanting with Jacob; xxxii. 29, 31 (E. V. vs. 28, 30), Jacob's wrestling with the angel (so Wellhausen, Kuenen, Kautzsch); xxxiii. 5, 10, 11, in Jacob's interview with Esau; xxxix. 9, Joseph's reply to the solicitations of Potiphar's wife; xliii. 29, Joseph greeting Benjamin; xliv. 16, Judah's confession. El Shaddai also occurs in a Jehovist section (xliii. 14), and Shaddai (xlix. 25), which are reckoned characteristics of the Elohist.

Jehovah also occurs in paragraphs attributed to the Elohist, where it is necessary to assume that it, or the clause containing it, has been inserted by the redactor. Thus four times in xv. 1, 2, 7, 8, the vision granted to Abraham; once in xvii. 1, where Jehovah appears to him; again, xx. 18, where he interferes for the protection of Sarah: xxi. 1b. where he fulfils his promise to Sarah:

xxii. 2, Moriah, which is compounded with an abbreviated form of Jehovah, and ver. 11, the angel of Jehovah; also xxviii. 21, in Jacob's vow.

In other cases the admission that the divine names
occur in the wrong document is only escaped by cutting
the clauses that contain them out of their connection as
insertions from another source, or by sundering passages
that manifestly belong together. Thus the last clause of
vii. 16 is sundered from the rest of the verse notwithstanding the manifest contrast between Jehovah, who
shut Noah in the ark, and Elohim, who gave command
for the preservation of the inferior creatures. In xiv.
22, Jehovah is held to be an insertion by the redactor,
though it represents God as known to Abraham in distinction from what he was to Melchizedek. Abimelech
covenants with Abraham at Beersheba, and speaks of
God as Elohim (xxi. 22–32); Abraham worshipping there
calls upon Jehovah (ver. 33); but the critics ignoring
the real reason of the change of names, regard the latter
as an insertion from J in a narrative of the Elohist. In
ch. xxii. Elohim demands the sacrifice, Jehovah stays the
patriarch's hand (pp. 284, 285); the critics attribute the
latter to a different writer, though it is an essential part of
the narrative. Isaac's blessing pronounced upon Jacob
(xxvii. 27, 28) is rent asunder because Jehovah and Elohim occur in successive clauses, as often elsewhere in the
parallelisms of poetry. Jacob's dream (xxviii. 12–17) is
partitioned because Elohim alternates with Jehovah, so
that he falls asleep in one document and wakes up in the
other. The continuous narrative of the birth of Jacob's
children (ch. xxix., xxx.) is parcelled between the Jehovist and the Elohist in a very remarkable manner. Ch.
xxxv. 5 is cut out of an Elohist connection solely and
avowedly because it alludes to a preceding Jehovist narrative. In xlviii. 8–11 Israel points to the Jehovist and

Elohim to the Elohist, so that a partition can only
be made by confusing the entire passage. Wellhausen gives it up; but Dillmann carries it unflinchingly
through.

In fact the partition hypothesis is based upon a persistent disregard of the real reason which governs the
employment of the divine names, that being attributed
to the mechanical explanation of a diversity of writers
which results from the difference of meaning and usage
of these names themselves. The critics themselves are
obliged to admit that the Jehovist uses both names as he
has occasion. This confession completely undermines
the hypothesis; for it is placing the use of these names
upon another footing than the mere habit of different
writers, and acknowledging that there is an appropriateness in employing one rather than the other in certain
connections.

The distinction between these names is universally
admitted, as certified by the usage of the entire Hebrew
Bible. It is stated by Kuenen in a manner which requires but slight correction in order to solve the whole
mystery, and to show that they afford no ground whatever for assuming the existence of an Elohist and a
Jehovist. He says (" Hexateuch," p. 56), " The original
distinction between Yahwe and Elohim very often accounts for the use of one of these appellations in preference to the other." Again (p. 58, note 19), 1. " When
the God of Israel is placed over-against the gods of the
Gentiles, the former is naturally described by the proper name Yahwe. 2. When Gentiles are introduced as
speaking, they use the word Elohim [unless they specifically mean the God of the chosen race, when they call
him by his proper name, Jehovah]. So, too, the Israelites, when speaking to Gentiles. 3. Where a contrast
between the divine and the human is in the mind of the

author, Elohim is, at any rate, the more suitable word."
[4. When God is spoken of in those general aspects of
his being in which he is related alike to the whole world
and to all mankind, *e.g.*, in creation and providence, Elohim is the proper word ; but when he is spoken of in his
special relation to the chosen race as the God of revelation and of redemption, and the object of their worship,
Jehovah is the appropriate term.] [1]

It has already been shown that the critical partition of
Genesis, though shaped with a view to adapt it to the
occurrence of the divine names, does not in fact correspond with them, and consequently cannot afford an
adequate explanation of them. And in the other books
of the Pentateuch the discrepancy is greater still.[2] On
the other hand, the simple principles above stated meet
the case precisely. It has been shown in detail in the
former part of this volume that every instance in which
Elohim or Jehovah is found in Genesis is capable of
ready explanation. It will not be necessary here to repeat at length what was there said. It will be sufficient
to indicate briefly a few leading facts, which conclusively
demonstrate that the partition hypothesis has no support
from the divine names.

One thing which arrests attention at the outset is the
great predominance of the name Jehovah in three clearly

---

[1] In the above quotation from Kuenen "Gentiles" has been substituted for "heathen" as better conformed to English usage. Correc-
tions and additions are in brackets. Kuenen says that the second
"rule is often violated by an oversight, and the Gentiles are made to
speak of Yahwe (Gen. xxvi. 28, 29 ; 1 Sam. xxix. 6 ; 1 Kin. v. 21, E.
V., ver. 7)." This is corrected in the text. There is no "oversight"
in the passages referred to, which simply suggest the proper limitation
of the rule. Abimelech says "Jehovah" because he means the God of
Isaac ; Achish does the same because he makes appeal to the God of
David, and Hiram because he refers to the God of whom Solomon had
spoken in the verses immediately preceding as "Jehovah my God."

[2] See my Higher Criticism of the Pentateuch, pp. 91–99.

marked sections of the Pentateuch, viz., Gen. ii. 4–iv.; xii.–xxvi.; Ex. iii.–Deut. xxxiv. The explanation of this singular fact lies upon the surface. These sections record three successive stages in the self-revelation of the Most High to our first parents, to the patriarchs, to Moses and the children of Israel. They relate to the three great epochs in the development of God's earthly kingdom and the unfolding of his scheme of grace. There is first God's manifestation of himself to man in his primitive estate, and again after his guilty trespass in the primal promise of mercy, the acceptance of Abel's worship, the ineffectual remonstrance with Cain, who is finally banished from the divine presence, while God is acceptably invoked in the family of Seth.

The next important step in the establishment of God's kingdom among men was his special manifestation of himself to Abraham, who was called from the mass of mankind to be the head of a chosen race, among whom true religion might be nurtured with a view to the ultimate blessing of all the nations of the earth.

The third step in this divine plan of salvation was God's manifestation of himself to Moses, and through him to Israel, in delivering them from the bondage of Egypt and organizing them as the people of God.

As Jehovah is the name appropriate to the Most High as the God of revelation and of redemption, there is a manifest propriety in its employment, as in actual fact it is predominantly employed, at just these signal epochs in which this aspect of his being is most conspicuously exhibited. It requires no assumption of a Jehovist writer to account for what thus follows from the nature of the case. That Jehovah should fall more into the background in the intervals between these signal periods of self-revelation is also what might be expected. Yet it **does not disappear entirely. It recurs with sufficient** frequency to remind the reader of the continuity of that divine purpose of salvation, which is never abandoned, and is never entirely merged in mere general providential control.

As Elohim is the term by which God is denoted in his relation to the world at large, in distinction from his special relation to his own people, it is a matter of course that the creation of heaven and earth and all that they contain is ascribed to him as Elohim (Gen. i.). It is equally natural that when the world, which he had made very good, had become so corrupt as to frustrate the end of its creation, the Creator, Elohim, should interfere to arrest this degeneracy by a flood, and should at the same time devise measures to preserve the various species of living things in order to replenish the earth once more (vi. 11–ix. 17). Here, too, was a case for Jehovah's interference likewise to preserve his plan of grace and salvation from utter failure by sweeping away the corrupt mass and preserving pious Noah and his family from its contamination and its ruin. Hence, while in the description of this catastrophe Elohim predominates, Jehovah is introduced whenever this special feature is particularly alluded to (vi. 1–8; vii. 1–5, 16b; viii. 20–22). And Jehovah interferes again to avert the new peril involved in the impious attempt at Babel (xi. 1–9); and he is not unobservant of the ambitious designs of the kingdom erected there (x. 8–10).

The constancy with which the name Jehovah appears in the life of Abraham, from ch. xii. onward, is first interrupted in ch. xvii., where Jehovah appears in the opening verse as God Almighty, and throughout the chapter is spoken of as Elohim, to indicate that the God of Abraham is likewise the God of the universe. The reason is apparent. God had promised to make of him a great nation, to give his posterity the land of Canaan,

and through them to bless all the nations of the earth.
These promises had been repeated from time to time.
Four and twenty years had now passed of anxious waiting. But the child, upon whom the fulfilment of all
these promises was conditioned, was not yet born.
Meanwhile in Sarah's advancing age, and his own, all
natural hope of offspring had vanished. Hence this appeal
to the divine omnipotence, which was able to accomplish
what was above and beyond the powers of nature, in order to confirm the patriarch's faith in the promise, now
renewed and made more specific than ever before, that
Isaac should be born the next year. There is no need
of an Elohist writer to account for the unvarying repetition of Elohim in this chapter, nor for its recurrence in
xxi. 2, 4, 6, where ch. xvii. is plainly referred to.

The next occurrence of Elohim is in xix. 29, and the
reason is again apparent. Lot is now finally severed
from all further connection with Abraham, and God is
henceforth Elohim to him as to all aliens. Elohim is
also used in dealing with Abimelech (ch. xx. ; xxi. 22, 23),
though it is still Jehovah who interferes for the protection of Sarah in Gerar (xx. 18), as he had previously done
in Egypt (xii. 17), and Abraham continues to call on the
name of Jehovah (xxi. 33), as in xii. 8. So when Hagar
and Ishmael are finally sent away from Abraham (xxi.
9–21), and Hagar is no longer counted a member of his
household, as she was in xvi. 7–14, God is Elohim also to
the children of Heth (xxiii. 6). Elohim the Creator might
rightfully demand that the child which he had given
should be sacrificed to him (xxii. 1–10) ; but Jehovah
stayed the patriarch's hand (vs. 11 sqq.) ; the spiritual
surrender was all that he required. Every instance in
which Elohim is used in the life of Abraham thus explains
itself; and there is no need of having recourse to an Elohist writer to account for its appearance.

The God of Abraham was also the God of Isaac. Hence the constant recurrence of Jehovah in xxv. 19–xxvii., with the single exception of Elohim as a poetic parallel in Isaac's blessing (xxvii. 28). For Elohim, in xxv. 11, xxviii. 4, see pp. 310, 332.

The name Jehovah is less prominent in the chapters that follow for two reasons chiefly : 1. The manifestations of Jehovah and the gradual unfolding of his gracious purposes, which marked the early portion of the patriarchal period, were sufficient for that stage in the development of the divine plan. It was enough to repeat the promises already made to Abraham and Isaac. Revelations surpassing these were reserved for a later stage, when the time arrived to fulfil the promises now made and for Jehovah to make himself known to Israel by manifestations of his power and grace such as their fathers had never witnessed (Ex. vi. 3). 2. The lives of Jacob and Joseph, which occupy nearly all the rest of Genesis, were spent for the most part away from the holy land, amid Gentile surroundings, which made it appropriate to use the name Elohim.

And yet Jehovah recurs often enough to show that his special relation to the chosen race is steadfastly maintained. Jehovah reveals himself to Jacob on his flight from home (xxviii. 13 sqq.) ; is recognized in the first children born to Leah (xxix. 31–35), and in the promise of yet another son to Rachel (xxx. 24), to complete the patriarch's family ; is acknowledged as the source of blessing even to Laban for Jacob's sake (xxx. 27, 30) ; and at length bids Jacob return to the land of his fathers (xxxi. 3). It is Jehovah who punishes the wicked sons of Judah (xxxviii. 7, 10) ; and who protects and blesses Joseph in servitude (xxxix. 2–5), and in prison (vs. 21, 23). It is Jehovah for whose salvation Jacob waits to the last moment of his life (xlix. 18). The appropriateness of Elohim throughout these chapters has been already shown in the discussion of each passage in which it occurs. The divisive hypothesis was invented to account for the alternation of Elohim and Jehovah. We have seen that notwithstanding all the ingenuity expended upon it it still fails to accord with the actual occurrence of these names. It further appears that it is not needed to explain the alternation of these names, the real reason of which lies in the significance of these names themselves. It remains to be added that it cannot render, and does not even pretend to render, a rational account of the employment of these names and their remarkable distribution as this has now been exhibited. It has nothing to suggest but the proclivities of different writers. The Elohist is supposed to be governed by the theory that the name Jehovah was unknown until the time of Moses; he therefore makes no previous use of it. The Jehovist held that it was in use from the earliest ages and employs it accordingly. Each is supposed to use that name to which he is addicted habitually, and without reference to its peculiar signification ; and yet we find these names to be discriminatingly used throughout. How is this to be accounted for? How has it come to pass that each writer has happened to limit himself to recording just those matters, which call for the use of that particular divine name which he is in the habit of employing, and this, though there is no sort of connection between the theories which govern their use of the divine names and these particular portions of the primeval or patriarchal history? The divisive hypothesis can give no reason why the Elohist rather than the Jehovist should have given an account of the creation of the world and all that it contains ; nor why the Jehovist rather than the Elohist should have described the beginnings of God's earthly kingdom in man's primeval condition and the mercy shown him after his fall; nor why the Elohist never speaks of an altar or sacrifice or invocation or any act of patriarchal worship;[1] nor why Jehovah occurs without interruption in the life of Abraham until in ch. xvii. the divine omnipotence is pledged to fulfil the oft-repeated but long-delayed promise; nor why Elohim regularly occurs when Gentiles are concerned, unless specific reference is made to the God of the patriarchs. All this is purely accidental on the divisive hypothesis. But such evident adaptation is not the work of chance. It can only result from the intelligent employment of the divine names in accordance with their proper meaning and recognized usage.

DICTION, STYLE, AND CONCEPTION

Kuenen[2] tells us that "the history of critical investigation has shown that far too much weight has often been laid on agreement in the use of the divine names. It is well, therefore, to utter a warning against laying an exaggerated stress on this one phenomenon." "It is but one of the many marks which must be duly observed in tracing the origin and the mutual relations of the passages." It is claimed that each of these divine names is regularly associated with a characteristic diction, mode of conception, and style of expression, which are clearly

---

[1] The suggestion that in the opinion of the Elohist worship was first introduced by Moses is absurd upon its face, see pp. 163 seq., 364; and it is without the slightest warrant in any Scriptural statement. Besides it leaves the difficulty unsolved. There is no natural connection between his idea that God was exclusively called Elohim in the patriarchal age, and the notion that he was never worshipped then. How did he happen to be possessed of just such a notion as kept him from an inappropriate use of Elohim?

[2] Hexateuch, p. 61, note 29, and p. 58.

indicative of distinct writers. But upon examination this proves to be altogether fallacious.

There is evidently no significance in the fact that a given series of sections or paragraphs contains words and phrases that are not found in another series in which there was no occasion to employ them. And that the same thought is differently expressed in two different passages does not necessarily prove that they are by distinct writers. Long lists of words of this description are paraded by critics as evidence of diversity of authorship, which are of no force whatever; and which could be paralleled with perfect ease from the acknowledged works of well-known authors in ancient or in modern times. Critics are never at a loss for arguments from diction to sustain even the most extravagant positions. The plausible use that can be made of it where it is plainly of no account, and the frequency with which it is disregarded by critics themselves when it does not serve their purpose, shows how precarious this style of argument is, and how important it is to guard against being misled by deceptive appearances.

The earlier forms of the divisive hypothesis were wrecked by their inability to establish a diversity of diction between the Elohist and the Jehovist. All sorts of subterfuges were resorted to in the endeavor to account for the fact that in a multitude of passages they were quite indistinguishable. At length Hupfeld came to the rescue with his suggestion, since accepted as a veritable discovery, that there were two Elohists, P and E, who were alike in their use of Elohim, but differed greatly in every other respect. P is supposed to contrast strongly with J (the Jehovist), while it is exceeding difficult, if not impossible, to discriminate between E and J, except in their use of the divine names.

There are some things about this discovery of Hup-

feld which have a very suspicious look. In the first
place, so large a share of the Elohist passages is surrendered to E as to destroy all semblance of continuity
in P. It was claimed by the advocates of the supplement hypothesis that the Elohist, though he had little
to say of Abraham and Isaac, nevertheless gave a full
account of the patriarch Jacob, the real founder of the
nation of Israel. But with the exception of two events
in the life of Abraham, recorded in chs. xvii. and xxiii.,
nothing is assigned to P in the entire patriarchal period
but a few disconnected sentences, scattered here and
there, which are detached from the narrative to which
they belong.

Another suspicious circumstance is that P breaks off
so near the point where E begins. While sundry attempts have been made to discover fragments of E in
earlier chapters of Genesis, it is generally confessed that
ch. xx. is the first passage that can be confidently attributed to this document. All Elohist passages prior to ch.
xx. are said to belong to P; ch. xx. and all subsequent
Elohist passages belong to E, with the sole exception of
ch. xxiii. and a few meagre snatches found elsewhere.
This certainly looks like rending asunder what belongs
together. And the natural conclusion would seem to be
that the difference of diction and style between the Elohist and the Jehovist, supposed to be made out from a
comparison of the early chapters of Genesis, is nullified
by the later chapters in which no such difference is perceptible. The critics have hastily drawn an inference
from incomplete data, which a wider induction shows to
be unfounded (p. 251).

Moreover, the alleged diversity of diction and style
between P and the other so-called documents is adequately explained by the character of the critical partition without having recourse to the assumption of dis-

tinct writers. The quantity and the quality of what is severally attributed to the different documents solve the whole mystery. As a necessary sequence from the scanty portion allotted to P compared with the amount assigned to J and E, and especially the peculiar character of the matter given to P in distinction from the others, P has the fewest words, and a different class of words, and a style adapted to the nature of its contents. The entire body of ordinary narrative is shared between J and E, while P has only extraordinary events like the creation and deluge, and certain incidents which do not enter into the texture of the history, but constitute rather the framework within which it is adjusted, such as genealogies, dates, births, deaths, and migrations. This being the case, the peculiarities of diction and style follow as a matter of course. The words and phrases and mode of expression appropriate to one have no natural connection with the other. When the matter is similar, as in J and E, the diction and style are alike. When the matter is different, as in P compared with JE, the diction and style are altered. This is just what is to be expected under the circumstances, and requires no diversity of writers to explain it, unless it be seriously contended that a historian cannot describe great catastrophes, nor incorporate in his work genealogies, dates, births, deaths, migrations, and legal enactments.

That the diversity of diction and style observable in P, as compared· with JE, is due to the difference in matter, both in amount and in character, and not to a diversity of writers, further appears from an inspection of the criteria by which they are professedly discriminated. These are specified in detail in the former part of this volume under the head of Marks of P, J, and E. The words and phrases represented to be characteristic of J and E belong to the common stock of the language, such as any writer or speaker might employ upon occasion, and which are not found in P for the simple reason that no passage is assigned to P that calls for their employment. On the other hand, technical legal phrases and such special terms as are suitable for the particular matters attributed to P form the main stock of that document. The formality, verboseness, and repetition imputed to P, as contrasted with the easy and flowing style of J and E, find their explanation in the precision due to legal transactions (pp. 293 seq.), the emphasis laid upon matters of intrinsic importance (pp. 222, 230), or which the writer would impress upon the mind of his readers (pp. 18, 101, 209), or the inevitable sameness of genealogies (p. 50), compared with the varied scenes, the changing incidents and the portraiture of life and character belonging to historical descriptions (pp. 240 seq.). And yet like repetitions, detailed enumerations, stereotyped formulæ, and genealogical tables are found upon occasion in J and E (pp. 81, 141, 231, 292 ; ch. x. 8–19, 21, 24–30, and xxii. 20–24 J ; xxv. 1–4 E).

It is further to be observed that when for any reason P is allowed a share in ordinary narrative, it becomes as difficult to discriminate between P and J as it is elsewhere between J and E ; and the separation has to be made on other grounds than diction and style. A notable instance is afforded in ch. xxxiv. (pp. 388 sqq.), where the wide divergence of the critics shows how baseless the partition is.

The total absence of any reason for regarding P as a separate document is yet more strikingly apparent from the shifting character of the criteria upon which its recognition is made to rest. Each separate portion of the document stands in this respect by itself, and out of relation to the rest. The marks insisted upon in any one portion are, with few exceptions, absent from every other throughout the Book of Genesis, so that different parts of the document are claimed for it on wholly dissimilar grounds. The narratives of the creation and of the flood have much in common, since what was made in the former perished in the latter, after which the earth was again re-peopled as at the beginning. But only two words or phrases noted as characteristic of P in ch. i. recur again in Genesis after ch. ix. viz., זָכָר male, in connection with circumcision (chs. xvii., xxxiv.), and פָּרָה וְרָבָה be fruitful and multiply in the promises made to Abraham and his descendants (pp. 4, 5). After the covenant with Abraham (ch. xvii.), which recalls that with Noah (ch. ix.), almost every mark of P in the preceding part of Genesis disappears entirely (pp. 96 sqq., 141 seq.). Scarcely a word or phrase that is reckoned characteristic of P in ch. xvii. or xxiii. is found in later chapters of Genesis, except where the transaction of the latter is explicitly referred to, or the promises of the former are repeated (pp. 231 sqq., 296 seq.). The migrations of the patriarchs (xii. 5 ; xxxi. 18 ; xxxvi. 6 ; xlvi. 6) are evidently recorded by the same hand ; but these are only arbitrarily referred to P in spite of their context (pp. 177 seq., 188 seq.). So with other snatches, by which the attempt is made to preserve the continuity of P and cover references made elsewhere in this document (pp. 175 seq., 180, 187 seq., 211 seq.).

J and E are confessedly indistinguishable in diction and style (pp. 252 seq., 271 sqq., 276, etc.) apart from the use of Jehovah by the former and Elohim by the latter. But it has already been shown that the divine names are regulated by their appropriateness in the connection, not by the mere habit of different writers. The only remaining ground for assuming that these were distinct documents is alleged contrarieties and contradictions and so-called doublets ; and these have been proved to be imaginary in every individual instance.

Attempts have been made, but without success, to discover a diversity of conception between the documents. It has been affirmed that the anthropomorphisms of J imply a less exalted notion of the Supreme Being than that of P (pp. 31 sqq., 63, 145, 225); that according to P sacrificial worship was first introduced by Moses while J speaks of offerings made by Cain and Abel (pp. 116 seq., 163 seq.); that in J, but not in P, the blessing through Abraham was to extend to all the nations of the earth (pp. 163, 244); that it is peculiar to E to record revelations in dreams (pp. 260 seq.) and the ministry of angels (pp. 271, 340). The falsity of these positions has been shown in the passages referred to.

It should be remembered in this discussion that the so-called Pentateuchal documents do not exist in their separate state. We are not comparing fixed and definite entities, which have come down to us in their proper form. They have been fashioned and their limits determined by the critics on the basis of certain alleged criteria. Their correspondence with these criteria simply results from the mode of their formation, and is no evidence of their reality. The argument moves in a circle and returns upon itself. The documents depend upon the criteria, and the criteria upon the documents; and there is no independent proof of either.

CONTINUITY OF GENESIS

The positive and irrefragable argument for the unity of Genesis is that it is a continuous and connected whole, written with a definite design and upon an evident plan which is steadfastly maintained throughout. The critics attribute this to the skill of the redactor. But they impose upon him an impossible task. An author may draw his materials from a great variety of sources, form his own conception of his subject, elaborate it after a method of his own, and thus give unity to his production. But a compiler, who simply weaves together extracts selected from separate authorities, has not the freedom of the author, and cannot do the same kind of work. He is trammelled by the nature of his undertaking. He cannot reconstruct his materials and adapt them to one another; he must accept them as he finds them. And now, if these authorities, as is alleged, were prepared with different aims and from diverse points of view, if they are unlike in style and diction and discordant in their statements, he never could produce the semblance of unity in his work. The difference of texture would show itself at the points of junction. There would inevitably be chasms, and abrupt transitions, and a want of harmony between the parts. Such a work as Genesis could not have been produced in this way.

It is besides very plain from a comparison of the documents, as the critics profess to reproduce them, that they must have been parallel throughout. The same events are treated in each, and in the same order, and in a manner so nearly resembling one another that they cannot have been altogether independent in their origin, as the critics themselves admit (pp. 158 sqq.).[1]

The text, as we possess it, is harmonious. It is only

---

[1] Dillmann says (Genesis, Vorbemerkungen, p. xiii.) : " In the primeval history there is both in plan and material an unmistakable relationship between J and P (creation, primitive state, Noah's genealogical tree, the flood, table of nations) ; also in the Abraham section and onward they have some narratives in common (separation from Lot, destruction of Sodom and Gomorrah, the history of Dinah, also xlvii. 1–11 ; xlviii. 29 sqq., cf. xlix. 29 sqq). But elsewhere in the patriarchal history, especially that of Jacob and Joseph, J is most closely related to E, so much so that from ch. xxvii. onward the most of J's narratives have their complete parallels in E, and we must necessarily assume the dependence of one upon the other."

when it is resolved into the so-called documents that inconsistencies appear. This makes it evident that these
documents are not the originals and Genesis a compilation from them; but Genesis is the original, and the
documents have been deduced from it. The combination of two or three mutually inconsistent accounts will
not produce a harmonious and symmetrical narrative.
But severing paragraphs and clauses from their proper
connection, and interpreting them at variance with it
will produce the appearance of discord and disagreement.[1]

CHASMS IN THE DOCUMENTS

The real existence of documents in Genesis is still
further discredited by the numerous and serious gaps
that occur in each of them. P records that in the creation all was made very good, and that at the flood the
earth was so corrupt that God resolved to destroy it, but
says nothing to account for the dreadful change; the
missing explanation is only to be found in J (pp. 35, 78).
There is a chasm in P, in the life of Abraham, between
chs. xi. and xvii., which the critics vainly seek to bridge by
scattered clauses torn from the connection to which they
evidently belong (pp. 155, 171, 180, 189 seq., 209 sqq.,
217 sqq.), as they do with regard to J in the flood (pp.
75 sqq.). P's life of Isaac consists of the merest scraps.
Jacob goes to Paddan-aram to get a wife, but his entire
abode there is a blank (pp. 316 seq., 362 sqq.) that can
only be filled up from J and E. Joseph is named by P
among the children of Jacob born in Paddan-aram (xxxv.
24), but not another word is said about him[2] until we
are suddenly informed (xli. 46) that he was thirty years

---

[1] See my Higher Criticism of the Pentateuch, pp. 119 sqq.
[2] The critics are divided about an isolated clause in xxxvii. 2, p.446.

old when he stood before Pharaoh. How he came to be in Egypt, and what led to his elevation there can only be learned from other documents. The next thing that we are told is that Jacob was removing to Egypt with his entire family (xlvi. 6, 7); here again we must look elsewhere for the circumstances by which this was brought about.

J is supposed to have traced the line of descent from Adam to Noah, and from Noah to Abraham, but only disconnected fragments remain (pp. 47, 135 seq.); also to have given an account of the descendants of Noah's sons, which is likewise in a fragmentary state (pp. 134 seq.). His account of Abraham begins abruptly (pp. 169 seq., 175), and is without any fitting termination; in fact he does not record the death of any of the patriarchs (p. 310). E's account of Abraham consists merely of a few disconnected incidents (pp. 160 seq.). J and E are inseparably blended in ch. xxvii. The narrative is incapable of division, and yet is indispensable in each document, so that it cannot be given to one without creating a chasm in the other (pp. 328 sqq.). The partition of chs. xxix. and xxx. between J and E leaves both very incomplete (pp. 344 sqq., 352). And in the life of Joseph every passage assigned to one of these documents creates a break in the other.

There are also numerous cross-references from one document to the contents of another, showing that they have been improperly sundered (pp. 33 sqq., 72 seq., 175, 322, 331, etc.). In other cases these are only evaded by splintering closely connected passages into bits because of the references made to them from different documents (pp. 169, 309, 405 sqq.).

In all these instances of a lack of continuity in the documents and references in one to the contents of another, the critics assume that R is at fault. The missing

matter must have been in the document originally, but
was omitted by R because he had given an equivalent
account from another source, which he thought it unnecessary to duplicate. This assumption, it is to be observed, is simply an inference from the hypothesis which
it is adduced to support. There is nothing to confirm it
apart from the prior assumption of the truth of that
hypothesis, which is the very thing to be proved. The
hypothesis requires it; that is all.

These numerous breaks in the documents are created
by the critical partition. Just what is needed to fill the
gap is in the text as it now stands. But the critics insist
that the lack must be supplied, not by these passages
which are here before us, and which precisely answer
every requirement, but by some hypothetical passage
which may once have existed, but of which there is no
proof whatever except that the hypothesis cannot be
maintained without it. These auxiliary assumptions
have to be made so frequently that nothing but the clearest independent proof of the truth of the hypothesis
could enable it to carry them. And this is utterly wanting. As it is, these unfilled chasms are just so many
proofs that the hypothesis is untenable.

This conclusion is yet more firmly riveted by the inconsistent conduct which the divisive critics are obliged
to impute to the redactor. While omitting in turn matters of the greatest consequence from each of the documents, he is supposed at other times scrupulously to retain even the minutest portion of the sources which he is
using, though it leads to superfluous repetitions in trivial
things. This is not to be evaded by assuming different
redactors, who adopt different methods in their compilation. The redactor who combined J and E, at the very
time that he was sacrificing large and important portions
of each document alternately, is supposed to have in-

corporated clauses or sentences from the omitted sections in the text of the other document, which are betrayed as such by the redundancy thus occasioned.[1] And the redactor who combined P with JE, and at times was particular to preserve all that he found in P, even when it added nothing to what had already been extracted from J[2] (pp. 83 sqq., 175, 265), at other times did not hesitate to throw away the bulk of his narrative and reduce the document to incoherent fragments. And each of these redactors is supposed in a great number of cases to have carefully preserved the contents of his sources, notwithstanding their discrepancies and contradictions, while at other times, without any reason to account for this difference of treatment, he freely modified them in order to bring them into harmony with each other.[3] The redactor is made the scapegoat of the hypothesis. Every thing that does not square with the hypothesis is attributed to him. And this lays upon him incompatible demands, and imputes to him a degree of inconsistency insupposable in any rational man.

[1] Kuenen (Hexateuch, p. 164, note 28) says: "The scrupulous conservatism of the redaction is proclaimed loudly enough by the presence of so many doublets. . . . The little additions to E and J in Gen. xl. sqq. are evidently intended to smooth down the inequalities that must necessarily arise when fragments now of one, now of the other narrative, are successively taken up."

[2] Kuenen (Ibid., p. 320): "R scrupulously inserts even the minor fragments of P in the places that seem best to fit them when the more detailed notices of the older documents might have seemed to a less zealous disciple to have rendered them superfluous."

[3] Hence Kuenen (Hexateuch, p. 255) speaks of "the mingled reverence and freedom, so strange sometimes to our ideas, with which he treats his documents."

WHEN AND WHERE PRODUCED

In undertaking to determine the date and origin of the supposititious Pentateuchal documents, the critics begin by denying the truth of the patriarchal history. Kuenen tells us:[1] "The narratives of Genesis are founded upon a theory of the origin of nations, which the historical science of the present day rejects without the slightest hesitation. The Israelites looked upon nations or tribes as families or large households. The further they carried their thoughts back, the smaller to their ideas became the family, until at last they came upon the father of the tribe or of the whole nation, to whom very naturally they ascribed the same qualities as they had observed in the descendants. This theory of the origin of nations is not the true one. Families become tribes, and eventually nations, not only, nor even chiefly, by multiplying, but also, nay, principally, by combining with the inhabitants of some district, by the subjection of the weaker to the stronger, by the gradual blending together of sometimes very heterogeneous elements." So, too, Dillmann :[2] "It is well understood nowadays that all these narratives respecting the patriarchs belong not to strict history but to saga. That the proper ancestor of no one people on earth can be historically pointed out; that nations are not formed after the manner of a family, but grow together from all sorts of materials; that the division into twelve tribes of all the Hebraic peoples rests not on natural generation and blood relationship, but that art and design, geographical and political or even religious reasons, were controlling

[1] Religion of Israel, vol. i., p. 110. The paragraph cited above is slightly abridged.
[2] Genesis, p. 215.

in it; that the personifications of peoples, tribes, regions, and periods, which are universally recognized in the representations of Genesis as far as ch. xi., do not cease at once with ch. xii., but continue further, and that not merely in the genealogies of peoples which still follow, is to be unconditionally admitted."

To all this Delitzsch,[1] while admitting what is said of the growth of other nations, very properly replies : " The people destined to be the bearer and mediator of revealed religion is, as is emphasized throughout the Scriptures of the Old Testament (e.g., Deut. xxxii. 6), no mere formation of nature ; and we can conceive that there was something unique in the very origination of this people, provided of course that we acknowledge a realm of grace above that of nature, and consequently a realm of the supernatural control of God above that of natural law. Besides, the migration of the Terahids is in itself more than simply a fact of family history. And a shepherd prince like Abraham, who could put. in the field hundreds of servants, that must be regarded as incorporated with his family, is already developing into a tribe ; at least several prominent tribes among the South African Bantu people have arisen in this way from a chief and his adherents. And the family of Jacob, which emigrated to Egypt, and only numbered seventy souls as blood-related kinsmen, grew into a nation, not merely of itself, but by the reception of all sorts of foreign materials."

To one who believes that God designed to form a people for himself and for his own gracious purposes, there is little difficulty in believing that he selected Abraham to be the head of a chosen race, among whom true religion should be preserved and perpetuated until the time should arrive for its diffusion among all the nations of

[1] Genesis, p. 248.

the earth. Such an one can easily credit the fact that
the people of Israel was brought into being in a manner
different from other nations, and better suited to fit them
for the peculiar task that was to be committed to them.
Accordingly he will see no reason to discredit the historical character of the lives of the patriarchs as recorded
in Genesis. The fact that the filiation of nations is exhibited in ch. x. under the form of a genealogy does not
justify the suspicion that Abraham, Isaac, and Jacob,
whose histories are related in detail, are the names not
of individual men, but of tribal communities. That they
were the heads of considerable clans appears from the
narrative itself, p. 466. The immediate object to which
attention is directed at present, however, is not the truth
of the Scriptural declarations on this subject, but the
position of the divisive critics and the process by which
they undertake to determine the time and place in which
the Pentateuchal documents were produced.

Apart from the wild conceits, which have actually
found advocates, that the patriarchs are nature myths,
or that they represent tribal deities, the common conception of those by whom the divisive hypothesis has been
shaped is that they are personifications of the people of
Israel in the earliest periods of their history, or of separate clans or tribes supposed to have been combined in
the formation of that people. Thus Kuenen[1] says : "Jacob-Israel, who appears in Genesis as the ancestor of
the whole people, was originally the personification of
the tribes which ranged themselves round Ephraim. In
the stories about him in Gen. xxvii.–l., Joseph, the father
of Manasseh and Ephraim, is the chief personage."
"The several sagas were probably of local origin. For
example, Isaac belongs originally to Beersheba, and
Jacob to Bethel." "Hebron was Abraham's territorial

[1] Hexateuch, pp. 229, 227, 231, 235.

cradle." Both he and Wellhausen insist that "Isaac, not Abraham, was the protagonist." Abraham was the latest creation of the saga, and the resemblance of his life to that of Isaac is accounted for by "the transference to Abraham of sagas concerning Isaac." Dillmann [1] holds that "if Jacob can be understood as the personal concentration of the twelve-tribe people of Israel, so also Isaac and Abraham as designations of historical antecedent stages of the twelve-tribe people or its related circle. . . . According to Genesis they are at the least concentrations of certain fragments of the Hebrew people out of which Israel was gradually formed." " In the remainder of the Abrahamic immigration after the sundering of the Lot-people, the Ishmaelites, and the Keturah- ites, later generations recognized that portion of the Hebrews which preserved the Abrahamic character in the greatest purity and were their proper ancestors. . . . Jacob-Israel is along with Abraham the proper father of the people of Israel, the representative of a new Hebrew immigration from Mesopotamia, out of which, together with the Isaac-people, Israel was formed. Quite a different part of Canaan is the scene of his actions, viz., the middle (Bethel, Shechem) and eastern portion of the land (Mahanaim, Peniel, Succoth)."

According to Stade [2] there is no basis of truth whatever in the narratives of Genesis. He says : " We maintain that the people of Israel possess no sort of certain and intelligible historical recollections about the events prior to the time of their settlement in the land west of the Jordan. All that subsequently existed of recollections about that earlier time is concentrated in the two names, Moses and Sinai. But what is narrated of these names is simply concluded back from the relations of the

[1] Genesis, pp. 215, 216, 311.
[2] Geschichte des Volkes Israel, pp. 55, 128, 129, 130.

present; it is nothing but saga which takes its bearings from and is reconstructed by these latter." "A pre-Egyptian abode of Israelitish families in the land west of the Jordan is not to be spoken of. . . . This conception cannot be honestly held in view of discovered facts," as he conceives them. "The people of Israel never resided in Egypt. . . . If any Hebraic clan ever resided there, no one knows its name. . . . The investigations respecting the Pharaohs, under whom Israel migrated into and out of Egypt, are useless trifling with numbers and names." "We have not the least knowledge of the pre-Mosaic worship of God in Israel; not a single tradition concerning it is in existence."

Kuenen [1] is not so utterly destructive. He finds the following basis of fact in Genesis: "There occurred a Semitic migration, which issued from Arrapachitis (Arpachshad, Ur Casdim), and moved on in a southwesterly direction. The countries to the south and east of Canaan were gradually occupied by these intruders, the former inhabitants being either expelled or subjugated; Ammon, Moab, Ishmael, and Edom became the ruling nations in those districts. In Canaan the situation was different. The tribes which—at first closely connected with the Edomites, but afterward separated from them—had turned their steps toward Canaan, did not find themselves strong enough either to drive out, or to exact tribute from, the original inhabitants; they continued their wandering life among them, and lived upon the whole at peace with them. But a real settlement was still their aim. When, therefore, they had become more numerous and powerful through the arrival of a number of kindred settlers from Mesopotamia—represented in tradition by the army with which Jacob returns to Canaan—they resumed their march in the same south-

[1] Religion of Israel, vol. i., pp. 114, 115.

westerly direction, until at length they took possession
of fixed habitations in the land of Goshen on the borders
of Egypt. It is not impossible that a single tribe had
preceded them thither and that they undertook the journey to Goshen at the solicitation of that forerunner ;
this would then be the kernel of the narratives relating
to Joseph and his exertions in favor of his brethren." [1]
Dillmann [2] contends for a still larger basis of truth.
In fact he goes so far that it is surprising that he does
not go farther, and admit with Delitzsch that the history
is at least substantially reliable throughout. He says:
" Is there any reason to refuse to these patriarchal sagas
of Israel all historical content, so much so that it has
even been doubted or denied that their ancestors ever
were in Canaan, and they have even been declared to be

---

[1] This mode of manufacturing history by substituting fanciful conjectures for facts, in which the critics so freely indulge in the patriarchal, Mosaic, and even later periods, is well characterized in the following passage from an unpublished lecture of my distinguished predecessor, Dr. Addison Alexander :

" Let us suppose that a future critic of our revolutionary history—
and if a German so much the better—should insist upon the improba-
bility that such a revolution could have been occasioned by causes so
trifling as the Stamp Act or the tax on tea, and should therefore represent them as symbolical myths occasioned by the rivalry of England
and America at a late period in the tea trade with China and by the
disputes respecting an international copyright. Such a writer would,
of course, find no difficulty in going further and regarding Washington
as an unnatural and impossible character, yet highly striking and appropriate as a genuine type of patriotic and republican virtues. It is
plain that this ingenious child's play could be carried on *ad infinitum ;*
and this very facility deprives it of all force as proof that the imaginary process was a real one, or that the stream of history flows backward
from its estuary to its source. In spite of all sophistical refinements
the common sense of mankind will still cleave to the lesson taught by
all analogy, that primitive history must deal with individualities, and
that philosophical myths can only be obtained from them by general-
izing combination."

[2] Genesis, pp. 215, 216.

'tendency' fictions of the period of the kings? . . .
Doubtless the reflection of later persons, times, and relations is thrown back on the saga forms of antiquity, and
the latter become involuntarily types of the former, but
there must first be a background for that which is more
recent to mirror itself upon. . . . It is not impossible even that obscure reminiscences of actual historical
persons may have attached themselves to them, though
naturally no proof of it can be adduced, for extra-
biblical testimonies are wanting. . . . A main consideration here is that the religion founded by Moses
cannot be historically explained without the previous
stage of a purer faith respecting God (at least as compared with ordinary heathenism), such as according to
Genesis was possessed by the patriarchs. . . . And
such a higher religious culture almost necessarily presupposes personal mediators or bearers. As the formation of states only takes place through leading spirits or
heroes, so too the stadia of the development of religion
are linked to prominent persons. The patriarchal sagas
in Genesis represent Abraham as the head of a purer
faith respecting God in the midst of heathen darkness,
as a man of a mind eminently disposed toward God and
faith, who was accustomed to hear and obey the voice
and instruction of God in all the junctures and events of
his life, who made advances in the knowledge of the
being and will of God, and who grounded his family and
his neighborhood in this higher knowledge. We must
almost presuppose the existence of one or more such
men, whether they were called Abraham or something
else, if it be correct that Moses could link on to the God
of his fathers. To be sure, if one denies, as many now
do, the work of Moses likewise, and makes the herdsman Amos or Elijah the opponent of Baal the founder
of the higher God-consciousness of Israel, that linking is

no longer needed. The whole patriarchal saga must dissolve in fog and mist on this way of regarding things."

Stade and Kuenen fix the age of the patriarchal saga on the basis of their revolutionary conception of the history of Israel. Thus Stade [1] says: "Abraham as the father of Isaac and grandfather of Jacob presupposes the government of Judah over all Israel, and the complete amalgamation of the Edomite clan Caleb with Judah; the Jacob-Joseph saga presupposes the divided kingdom." And Kuenen: [2] "The sagas about the patriarchs . . . presuppose the unity of the people (which only came into existence with and by means of the monarchy) as a long-accomplished fact which had come to dominate the whole conception of the past completely." "The welding process (i.e., of the sagas relating to Abraham, Isaac, and Jacob) cannot have begun till the national unity was established; and it must have reached its ultimate completeness when the stories out of which Gen. xii. sqq. is worked up and compiled were written." The conclusion is hence drawn that the Pentateuchal documents must be considerably later than the time of David, or even of Rehoboam. But it rests upon a theory of the history of Israel, which is in the face of the clearest Scriptural statements, and has no real basis in the few passages which have been wrested to its support.

A more common argument of date is drawn from the localities mentioned in the lives of the patriarchs, as Bethel, Shechem, Beersheba, Hebron, etc. Later superstition consecrated these places, where divine communications were made to the patriarchs, or where they erected altars and worshipped God; and idolatrous sanctuaries were established there. By a complete inversion of the real facts of the case it is alleged that the narratives of reve-

[1] Geschichte, p, 128.   [2] Hexateuch, pp. 226, 227.

lations granted to the patriarchs and of worship offered by them are not records of real facts, but are stories which grew up at these sanctuaries to enhance their credit. The authors of these narratives as they appear in Genesis, it is claimed, intended thereby to give sanction to these sanctuaries and express their approval of them. The stern condemnation of the worship at these sanctuaries by the prophets Hosea and Amos indicates, it is said, a change of mind toward them on the part of the best people of that period. This is thought to fix the limit, below which narratives commendatory of these sanctuaries could not have been written. It is hence inferred that J and E, to which the great body of the patriarchal narratives are referred, must have been written shortly before the time of Hosea and Amos.

Two questions still remain to divide the critics in respect to these documents. One is as to their relative age; the other, the part of the country in which they were produced. On the one hand it is argued by Wellhausen and Kuenen that J must be older than E, since it adheres more closely to primitive popular beliefs, as shown in its crude anthropomorphic representations of the Deity. To which Dillmann replies that like anthropomorphisms are found in the prophets and in other writings of the Old Testament along with the most exalted ideas of God, and he adduces what he considers abundant proofs that the author of J was in possession of E, and made use of it in preparing his own history.

Wellhausen and Kuenen maintain that both J and E belonged to the northern kingdom of Israel because of the prominence given to Joseph, the connection of Jacob with Bethel and Shechem, Mahanaim and Penuel, as well as Beersheba, which was a sanctuary reverenced in northern Israel, as appears from Amos v. 5; viii. 14. Dillmann concedes that E was a North-Israelite, but claims that J belonged to the kingdom of Judah, inasmuch as he speaks of Hebron as the abode of Abraham (xiii. 18; xviii. 1) and of Jacob (xxxvii. 14), and gives prominence to Judah in the history of Joseph (xxxvii. 26 sqq.; xliii. 3 sqq.; xliv. 16 sqq.; xlvi. 28), as well as in ch. xxxviii. But J also links Abraham with Bethel and Shechem (xii. 6, 8; xiii. 3, 4), and dwells as largely as E upon the life and dignity of Joseph; and his account of Judah in chs. xxxvii., xxxviii. is not of the most creditable sort. The divergence of the critics as well as the incompatibility of the facts of the narratives with either theory show that these narratives have not been warped by tribal partialities or jealousies; so that the argument for the residence of their authors in either one of the kingdoms is abortive. And even the attempt of Wellhausen and Kuenen to patch up their theory by the assumption of a Judæan edition of both J and E only complicates their scheme without improving it.

One more alleged evidence of the date of the documents is sought in allusions to late historical events which, it is claimed, are found in them, and in the style of religious thought and teaching by which they are characterized. Thus in Noah's prediction (ix. 25–27) of the subjugation of Canaan by Shem, it is said that the reign of Solomon is presupposed; in Isaac's blessing (xxvii. 29, 39 seq.), David's victories over the Edomites, their rebellion under Solomon, and revolt against Jehoram the son of Jehoshaphat; in the covenant of Jacob and Laban (xxxi. 44 sqq.), the wars of the Aramæans and Israelites for the possession of the trans-Jordanic district; in the promise of kings to spring from Abraham (xvii. 16) and Jacob (xxxv. 11), and the blessing upon Judah (xlix. 8–10), the reign of David is presupposed; and in xxxvi. 31 the establishment of the kingdom in Israel. The falsity of the inference deduced from this last passage is shown at length in the discussion of it in the former part of this volume, pp. 425 sqq. The covenant of Jacob and Laban is sufficiently explained by the circumstances of the time. The fulfilment of the predictions in Genesis does not warrant the assumption that they were written after the event, except to him who has no belief in the foreknowledge of God or in the possibility of his making disclosures of the future.

The correspondence between the religious ideas which find expression in various passages of Genesis and the teachings of the prophets is urged in proof that the documents J and E must belong to the period of the prophets. The true course of religious development in Israel must, however, be gathered from a full and careful induction of all the facts bearing upon the subject. The critics reverse the proper order of scientific investigation when they frame their own theory in advance on naturalistic presuppositions, and then attempt to force the facts into agreement with it. They determine what degree of enlightenment can upon their theory be attributed to a given period, and then systematically exclude from that period everything that does not fit into their theory. The amount and character of the religious teaching to be found in the writings of Moses is the only reliable source from which it can be ascertained what his teachings really were. The genuineness of his writings must be independently investigated in the first instance ; and then we shall be in a position to inquire with some confidence into the religion of Moses. But to determine magisterially the limits of his teaching, and then to declare that the writings attributed to him cannot be genuine, and must be referred to an age long posterior to that in which he lived, because they transcend these arbitrarily assumed limitations, is not a legitimate method of procedure.

SUMMARY OF THE ARGUMENT

The argument is now finished. May it not be truly said that the demonstration is complete? The grounds, upon which the existence of documents in Genesis is rested, have been severally examined and shown to be invalid. The alleged repetitions and discrepancies vanish upon examination, being created by the critics themselves, and due either to misinterpretation or the identification of distinct events. The divine names in repeated instances fail to correspond with the requirements of the divisive hypothesis, which is not needed to explain their alternation, since this is most satisfactorily accounted for from their own proper signification and general biblical usage ; moreover, it does not render, and does not even pretend to render, a rational account of their employment and distribution. The alleged diversity of diction, style, and conception is either altogether factitious or is due to differences in the subject matter and not to a diversity of writers. The continuity and self-consistency of Genesis, contrasted with the fragmentary character and mutual inconsistencies of the documents, prove that Genesis is the original, of which the so-called documents are but severed parts. The rôle attributed to the redactor is an impossible one, and proves him to be an unreal personage. And the arguments for the late date of the documents and for their origin in one or other of the divided kingdoms are built upon perversions of the history or upon unproved assumptions. What more is needed to demonstrate the utter futility of the claim that such documents ever existed?

In the legislative portion of the Pentateuch the question turns no longer upon literary criteria, but upon an entirely different principle : Are the institutions and enactments of the Pentateuch the growth of ages or the product of one age and of a single mind? It is here that the battle of the Mosaic authorship must be fought. Meanwhile, the investigations thus far conducted justify at least a negative conclusion. The so-called anachronisms of the Book of Genesis have been examined, and nothing has been found to militate against its being the work of Moses. It is plainly designed to be introductory to the law. And if that law was given by Moses, as has always been believed, and as the Scriptures abundantly declare, then Genesis, too, was his work.

INDEX

OF THE CRITERIA OF THE DIFFERENT DOCUMENTS

III. CHARACTERISTIC WORDS AND PHRASES

(Niphal, Hiphil, Hithpael, and future forms of verbs are arranged under their first
radical letter. Nouns preceded by the article or an inseparable preposition are
arranged in accordance with the initial letter of the noun.)

IV. The English Equivalents

twin brooks series BOOKS IN THE SERIES